Graduate Scholarship Directory

Third Edition

The Complete Guide to Scholarships, Fellowships, Grants and Loans for Graduate and Professional Study

By
Daniel J. Cassidy
National Scholarship Research Service (NSRS)

Graduate Scholarship Directory

Third Edition

The Complete Guide to Scholarships, Fellowships, Grants and Loans for Graduate and Professional Study

By
Daniel J. Cassidy
National Scholarship Research Service (NSRS)

CAREER PRESS
180 Fifth Avenue
P.O. Box 34
Hawthorne, NJ 07507
1-800-CAREER-1
201-427-0229 (outside U.S.)
FAX: 201-427-2037

GRADUATE SCHOLARSHIP DIRECTORY (THIRD EDITION)
THE COMPLETE GUIDE TO SCHOLARSHIPS, FELLOWSHIPS, GRANTS AND
LOANS FOR GRADUATE AND PROFESSIONAL STUDY
ISBN 1-56414-113-6, $24.95
Cover design by Digital Perspectives
Printed in the U.S.A. by Book-mart Press

To order this title by mail, please include price as noted above, $2.50 handling per order, and $1.00 for each book ordered. Send to: Career Press, Inc., 180 Fifth Ave., P.O. Box 34, Hawthorne, NJ 07507

Or call toll-free 1-800-CAREER-1 (Canada: 201-427-0229) to order using VISA or MasterCard, or for further information on books from Career Press.

Library of Congress Cataloging-in-Publication Data

Cassidy, Daniel J., 1956-
    Graduate scholarship directory : the complete guide to
scholarships, fellowships, grants and loans for graduate and
professional study / by Daniel J. Cassidy. --3rd ed.
        p. cm.
    Rev. ed. of: Graduate scholarship book. c1990.
    ISBN 1-56414-113-6 : $24.95
    1. Graduate students--Scholarships, fellowships, etc.--United
States--Directories. 2. Student loan funds--United States-
-Directories. 3. Student aid--United States--Directories.
[1. Cassidy, Daniel J., 1956- Graduate scholarship book.]
I. Title.
LB2337.2.C36   1993
378.2'025'73--dc20   --dc20
[378.3'025'73]
                                                                    93-8799
                                                                    CIP

I want to thank all of those who have made this third edition of THE GRADUATE SCHOLARSHIP DIRECTORY a reality. My sincere thanks and gratitude to:

The staff at NSRS

especially:

My wife, Deirdre Carlin Cassidy, Vice President/Controller

Research & Computer Engineering

William L. Sheppard, Director of Research
Richard Merwin, Computer Systems

Administration & Public Relations

Joe Gargiulo, Public Relations Director
Christina D. Kaufman, Executive Secretary
Julanne C. Lorimor, Secretary

Typesetting

Darcy Mortensen
Advanced Visual Concepts
Rohnert Park, California

A Very Special Thank You to
Jim Eason
KGO Radio, San Francisco
The man who made NSRS possible

And, at Career Press

Thank you to

Ron Fry
President

Betsy Sheldon
Editor

Preface

INTRODUCTION

The information in The Graduate Scholarship Directory was compiled from the data base of the largest Private Sector financial aid research service in the world. Located in Santa Rosa, California, NATIONAL SCHOLARSHIP RESEARCH SERVICE (NSRS) began tracking Private Sector scholarships in the late 1970s, using a specialized computer system. Prospective college students and present under graduates will find the information in this book valuable in directing their applications and broadening their prospects for scholarship selection.

MONEY FOR GRADUATE SCHOOL

Your decision to attend graduate school is a commitment of time — at least one year and usually more — dedication and major expense. If you are like most postgraduates, acceptance to the school of your choice means that you are confronted with the problem to get the money to pay for it. Tuition for the graduate student is generally higher than for the undergraduate and at this point in your life, you may find financial survival more difficult than ever before.

This volume has been compiled to help you seek out and realize possibilities that you may not otherwise have considered. You will be happy to know that there is a broad range of financial assistance sources available at the graduate level, including the federal government, some state governments, the school which you are or will be attending, and the private sector.

THE FACTS

According to the Association of Fund Raising Counsel, more than 80% of the grant applications that went to the 23,000 foundations in the United States were either misdirected or filled out improperly. The National Commission on Student Financial Assistance, a U.S. Congressional Subcommittee, found that while there was more than $7 billion available to students from corporations, only $400 million was used! Some $6.6 billion went unclaimed, not because people were unqualified but because they didn't know where to look. To put that figure in a more understandable perspective, the unused portion of available funds would amount to $600 for each of the 15 million college-bound students in the United States alone. There is a great need to organize this "paper-chase" of information into a workable source for today's student. Utilizing the data collected here students will have a broad base of information to convert to their advantage. The monies are there. Apply for them!

PRIVATE SECTOR FUNDS

Philanthropy in the United States is alive and well. More than 65% of the available scholarships, fellowships, grants and loans are from the Private Sector. These funds, which totaled $56 billion in 1987 increased to a whopping $151 billion in 1992. Of that amount 15%, or $20 billion, goes into the United States educational system. An additional $20 billion is dispersed worldwide.

And that amount increases daily. The interest alone on a properly invested $2 million is easily $200,000 annually. Private Sector resources for higher education are as varied as the awards themselves.

Many scholarships are renewable. You simply sign for them year after year. Others allow you to "piggy-back" several individual scholarships. The average undergraduate scholarship is $4,000, per year, ranging from a low of $100 to a high of $20,000. Graduate level fellowships range from $10,000 to $60,000. Some research projects can yield a quarter of a million dollars or more. As inflation spirals, so do the costs of education and the need for financial assistance.

INVESTIGATE THE POSSIBILITIES

Don't think you can't apply because you earn too much money; 80% of the Private Sector does not require a financial statement or proof of need. Don't think that application deadlines occur only in the fall; Private Sector deadlines are passing daily because often they are set to coincide with the tax year or organizational meeting dates. Don't believe that grades are the only consideration for an award; many application questions deal with personal, occupational, and educational background, organizational affiliation, talent, or ethnic origins; 90% are not concerned with grades. Don't be concerned with a many organizations are interested in the re-entry student and the mid-career development student. The Business and Professional Woman's Foundation awards hundreds of scholarships to applicants who must be older than 25 or even 35. There is a scholarship at the California State Colleges for students over the age of 60.

PREFACE

PLAN TO COMPETE AND QUALIFY

The plan is simple: use this book and every other resource you can find. Inquire at your institution's financial aid office about government assistance and private endowments. If you are a high school sophomore, write to ten or more schools. Choose a good range of institutions that interest you, both large and small; public and private. Request the application materials and catalogs: many private endowments are available in the form of scholarships and fellowships bequeathed by alumni. A significant number of these go unclaimed because qualified students do not know they exist! The information is available but the commitment belongs to the individual.

The Private Sector is easily accessed with this book. The student can use its tables to cross reference the scholarships applicable to his or her personal background and educational goals. Choose twenty or more sources and request application forms and any pertinent materials. Some have specific requirements for applicants such as a personal interview, the submission of an essay or related work, or a promise to work for the company on completion of study and/or the earning of a degree. Others may have paid internships or work advancement programs. Still others may simply require that you fill out of an application form.

The money is there. Billions go unclaimed. The student who does not take the time to inquire loses every advantage. The opportunity to advance to a graduate degree will widen many avenues for your future and the rewards are incalculable. Information is merely a passage waiting to be used. The resources to achieve your goals are available to you; you need only pursue them.

'The resources of the scholar are proportioned to his confidence in the attributes of the intellect"

—Emerson

JUST FOR FUN:
TEN OF THE MOST LUCRATIVE SCHOLARSHIPS

1. Come up smelling like a rose with a **Fragrance Research Fund** grant of up to $50,000.00. This posy is available to clinical psychologists doing post graduate research in aroma-chology. (K97/R17)

2. Reach out, reach out and grab that dough! **AT&T Bell Laboratories** offers full tuition plus fees and a yearly stipend of $13,200 to minority students enrolled in an accredited engi-neering, math, or computer science program at the doctoral level. (K24/R53)

3. Post graduate students could suck up $12,500.00 for research in vacuum science with the **International Union for Vacuum Science's** "Welch Foundation Research Scholarship. (K66/R8)

4. Hey rocket man! The **American Historical Association** offers fellowships in aerospace history to spaced out Ph.D. candidates. Ph.D's can get up to $25,000.00 and Ph.D. candidates up to $16,000.00 — just for spending six months to a year doing research in the NASA historical offices. (K94/R48)

5. Would you like to teach someone a thing or two? The **National Academy of Educators'** "Spencer Fellowship Program" offers post doctorate researchers in education, the humanities, or the social and behavioral sciences $35,000 for research that is relevant to education. (K60/R57)

6. What do you get when you add citizenship in a North American country to a desire to do post doctoral research in mathematics? If you're calculating it right, you could come to the sum of $41,500 from the **American Mathematics Foundation**. (K85/R2)

7. There's a science to getting scholarship money! Post doctoral researchers having the right mixture of achievement and potential could compound that concoction into congressional fellowships from the **Office of Technology Assessment** worth $35,000.00 to $75,000.00. (K26/R64)

8. **Queen Sonja** of Norway extends a royal invitation to vocalists aged 18 to 30 who would like to participate in her **International Music Competition** in 1995. Four finalists will share $40,000.00 in prize money. (K74/R85)

9. Do you wonder why people act the way they do? The **Harry Frank Guggenheim Foundation** wants to help you find out by offering up to $35,000 for post graduate research in the behavioral or social sciences or the humanities. (K26/R53)

10. Feeling financially skinned? Don't flake off. Ph.D. or M.D. holders committed to an academic career in dermatology who want research training may qualify for $25,000.00 from the **Dermatology Foundation**. Now there's an ointment that soothes. (K88/R22)

RECOMMENDATIONS

By using this book to track down your potential sources of funding, you may need additional help. Following are some excellent sources that NSRS recommends:

HOW TO PREPARE A RESEARCH PROPOSAL by David R. Krathwohl, $14.95 plus $2.50 shipping. This 305 page book offers guidelines for funding research projects and writing dissertations.

Order from:

Syracuse University Press
1600 Jamesville Ave.
New York, NY 13244

HAPPIER BY DEGREES by Pam Mendelsohn, $8.95 plus $1.25 shipping and handling. Excellent book for women just starting out or returning to college. This is a comprehensive guide to the entire process of entering into a new academic field, including finan-cial aid, child care, etc.

"I have never seen a more useful guide to the puzzling world of academia."
—Carolyn See, Professor, Loyola Marymount University

Order from:

Ten Speed Press
PO Box 7123
Berkeley, CA 94707

ANNUAL REGISTER OF GRANT SUPPORT, $165 plus $11.55 shipping and handling. Comprehensive annual reference book available in most major libraries. Details thousands of research grants that are open both to individuals and organizations.

Order from:

National Reference Publishing Company
121 Chanlon Rd.
New Providence, NJ 07974

GOVERNMENT ASSISTANCE ALMANAC by J. Robert Dumouchel, $84.00. This 768 page guide details programs of benefit to students, educators, researchers and consumers. It covers more than $600 billion worth of federal programs available to the American public.

Order from:

Omnigraphics, Inc.
2500 Penobscot Building
Detroit, MI 48226

INTERNSHIPS, $28.95 plus $5.75 shipping and handling. This guide lists job training opportunities available in today's job market, arranged by career field and indexed geographically.

"If you are somewhat undecided on the question of a career,
simply browsing through the myriad possibilities may spark an unexpected interest."
—Business Week

Order from:

Peterson's Guides
202 Carnegie Center,
PO Box 2123 Princeton, NJ 08543

COLLEGE DEGREES BY MAIL by John Bear, Ph.D., $12.95 plus $2.50 shipping and handling. This 214 page book tells how you can earn a bachelor's, master's or doctor's degree from accredited colleg-es and universities through home study. The book also lists colleges reputed to be diploma mills and cautions against them.

Order from:

Ten Speed
Press Box 7123
Berkeley, CA 94707

PREFACE

Dr. Bear also represents Heriot-Watt University from which an MBA degree can be earned through home study in as little as one year. The Heriot-Watt tuition is just $5,400. You can get additional information by writing to Dr. Bear at 1780 Shattuck Ave., Berke-ley, CA 94709, telephone 510/204-9995.

THE INTERNATIONAL SCHOLARSHIP DIRECTORY, THIRD EDITION, $24.95. Excellent source for students wishing to study abroad or in their own country. The book will help you tap into billions of dollars available for financing your education anywhere in the world.

Order from:

> National Scholarship Research Service
> PO Box 6609
> Santa Rosa, California 95406-0609

HOW TO FIND OUT ABOUT FINANCIAL AID by Gail Ann Schlachter, $35 plus $4 shipping. This is a comprehensive guide to more than 700 print and on-line directories that identify over $21 billion in financial aid available to both undergraduate and graduate students and researchers.

Order from:

> Reference Service Press
> 1100 Industrial Rd., Suite 9
> San Carlos, CA 94070

THE FOUNDATION DIRECTORY, $150.00 soft cover, $175.00 hard cover. An authoritative annual reference book found in most major libraries. Contains detailed information on more than 8,700 of America's largest foundations. Indexes allow grantseekers, researchers, etc. to quickly located foundations of interest.

Order from:

> The Foundation Center
> 79 Fifth Ave.
> New York, NY 10003

WHERE THE INFORMATION IN THIS BOOK CAME FROM

The information for this book was compiled from the data base of the largest Private Sector college financial aid research service in the world: National Scholarship Research Service (NSRS) located in Santa Rosa, California.

Since the late 1970s, NSRS has been using computers to research and update information on potential sources of financial assistance for college students. Many thousands of students have used NSRS's services to locate sources offering financial aid.

NATIONAL SCHOLARSHIP RESEARCH SERVICE

NSRS's computer stores information on thousands of Private Sector aid programs for all levels of college study: from high school seniors just entering college to post doctoral researchers.

Applicants for NSRS's services first complete a biographical questionnaire, indicating their particular area(s) of interest. This information is entered into the computer which searches NSRS's files for the scholarships the applicant may qualify for. Since each applicant has a different background and each of the thousands of aid programs have different requirements, this computer search can save valuable time and often provides students with potential sources of aid that they might never have considered applying for.

If you consider that all the financial aid programs listed in this book are constantly changing, with new application dates, qualifying requirements, etc., you may want to utilize this company's services.

Since NSRS is a privately owned company, there is a modest fee for its service. For a product list, write or call:

> NATIONAL SCHOLARSHIP RESEARCH SERVICE (NSRS)
> Box 6609
> Santa Rosa, California 95406-0609

> Phone: (707) 546-6777

IMPORTANT NOTE: This book is an abridged version of the National Scholarship Research Service data base. For a more comprehensive search for sources of educational financing, write to NSRS at the address above.

Every effort has been made to supply you with the most accurate and up to date information possible but even as this book goes to print awards are being added and application requirements are being changed by sponsoring organizations. Such circumstances are beyond our control.

Since the information we have supplied may not reflect the current status of any particular award program you are interested in, you should use this book only as a guide. Contact the source of the award for current application information.

If questions arise during your search for education funding, you are welcome to call an NSRS counselor at 707/546-6781.

SAMPLE FORM LETTER
REQUESTING APPLICATION INFORMATION

Use this sample letter as a guide to create a general letter requesting information. Photocopy your letter and address the envelopes for mailing. Remember to apply well in advance of the deadlines. You should keep a calendar to keep track of them.

Scholarship Program Office
ABC Foundation
100 Street Name
Any City, Any State 00000

I am a student at_____ and expect to apply for admission to the Yale University School of Medicine next year.

Please send me application forms for any scholarships or fellow-ships you might offer. I am enclosing a stamped, self addressed envelope for your convenience in replying.

Sincerely,

James Maurice Cassidy
2280 Airport Boulevard
Santa Rosa, California 95403

(707) 546-6777

HOW TO USE THIS BOOK

Each award, book and resource listed has a record number preceding it. All of our indexes are based on these record numbers. Here is a short guide to finding the information you need:

"QUICK FIND" INDEX

Most private sector awards have certain eligibility qualifications. We have selected several of the most common requirements for this "Quick Find" index.

Here you can find awards targeted for people of a particular race, religion, or family ancestry, for people who will be studying in a particular state or community, for the physically handicapped, and much more. Simply go through each of the tables and write down the reference numbers that apply to you. Then proceed to those sources and read each one carefully to see if you qualify.

FIELD OF STUDY INDEX

Since the awards listed in this book also are based on your intended field of study, we have structured this index along the lines of a college catalog.

First, look under your particular field of study. (School of Business, for instance.) Then look under your area of interest (Accounting) and finally, under your specific subject (Banking). In this section you will find record numbers that reference both financial aid awards and other resources that can help you in your career. Again, since there might be several eligibility requirements you must meet in order to be able to qualify for any listed award. Be sure you read each listing carefully and meet the requirements of the award before requesting an application.

SCHOLARSHIP AND AWARD LISTINGS

Each listing contains a very condensed description of the award, its eligibility requirements, deadline dates and where to get more information or an application.

You will notice a large "general" section. These are awards that do not usually specify a particular field of study in their eligibility requirements. You need to use the indexes provided and read each listing carefully to see if you might qualify for one of these awards.

Use the information we have provided only as a guide. Write to the source for a complete description of qualifications.

HELPFUL PUBLICATIONS

This section contains a selection books and pamphlets that we consider helpful to the student. These publications are excellent sources of information on a wide variety of college and financial aid subjects.

If you discover a publication you find particularly helpful, let us know so we can share the information with others.

Record numbers preceded by a "B" are booklets.

CAREER INFORMATION

This is a list of organizations that can help you decide to study, give you information on job opportunities available in your field of study and much more. We encourage you to write to these organizations for information.

Record numbers preceded by a "C" are career sources.

ALPHABETICAL INDEX

A to Z, this index lists the reference number of every award, book and career organization that is included in this book.

Quick Find Index

ARMED FORCES

A Current or Former Member, 1427, 1538, 1552, 1556, 1563, 1591, 1598, 1660, B1707

A Dependent-Current/Former Mbr., 1427, 1429, 1470, 1497, 1501, 1537, 1538, 1564, 1597, 1650, 1659, B1692, B1698, B1707

A Spouse/Widow-Current/Fmr.Mbr., 1430, 1470, 1538, 1564, 1659, B1698, B1707

Current Member, 1349, 1360

Officer, 1349, 1360

State National Guard, 1538

US Air Force (any branch), 1427

US Air Force ROTC, 111, 735, 821

US Air Force-Air Natl Guard Res, 1427

US Army-1st Cavalry Div Assn, 1497

US Army-ROTC, B1761

US Coast Guard (any branch), 1564, B1692

US Marines (any branch), 1564, B1692

US Navy (any branch), 1564, B1692

Vet-Blind, 1470

Vet-Deceased, 1429, 1430, 1497, 1501, 1537, 1538, 1552, 1597, 1650, 1659

Vet-Disabled, 1429, 1430, 1501, 1538, 1552, 1597, 1650

Vet-MIA, 1429, 1430, 1501, 1537, 1538, 1552, 1650

Vet-POW, 1429, 1430, 1501, 1537, 1538, 1552, 1650

Vet-Retired, 1563, 1598, 1660, B1698

Vet-Vietnam, 1501, 1537, 1552, 1556, 1591, 1598

Vet-WWII or Korea, 1501, 1598

CITY/COUNTY INTENDED STUDY

Houston TX/USA, 9, 384, 1215

New York City NY/USA, 39, 89, 188, 405, 543, 557, 974, 1104, 1239, 1324, 1358, 1390, 1417

COMPANIES

H & R Block-D, 1508

Washington Post Carrier, 1654

CONTINENT OF INTENDED STUDY

North America, 258, 383, 882, 1047

COUNTRY OF INTENDED STUDY

Canada, 47, 131, 162, 186, 232, 235, 238, 249, 255, 415, 554, 614, 625, 627, 653, 655, 719, 744, 758, 772, 796, 805, 854, 863, 888, 935, 972, 1038, 1039, 1050, 1102, 1116, 1136, 1176, 1228, 1245, 1307, 1388, 1485, 1520, 1574, 1642, 1644, B1667, B1674, B1684, B1688, B1735, B1737, B1764

United States, 1, 2, 3, 4, 7, 9, 18, 19, 20, 23, 24, 34, 38, 41, 44, 46, 47, 48, 51, 54, 57, 58, 61, 65, 66, 68, 74, 75, 76, 77, 78, 93, 98, 104, 108, 109, 113, 119, 121, 122, 124, 138, 142, 157, 162, 164, 167, 174, 185, 186, 192, 199, 200, 202, 203, 205, 211, 216, 219, 225, 232, 235, 238, 240, 241, 245, 247, 248, 249, 251, 255, 259, 261, 265, 268, 275, 285, 290, 291, 292, 296, 297, 300, 302, 305, 306, 308, 310, 314, 316, 317, 326, 331, 338, 341, 345, 346, 351, 358, 363, 365, 376, 377, 382, 384, 387, 388, 390, 399, 400, 403, 407, 410, 414, 416, 417, 420, 422, 435, 458, 474, 478, 481, 482, 483, 486, 487, 513, 518, 525, 545, 546, 548, 549, 553, 554, 560, 584, 595, 597, 598, 605, 607, 609, 610, 621, 625, 627, 631, 636, 638, 639, 644, 650, 653, 655, 659, 660, 662, 667, 668, 673, 674, 675, 680, 682, 686, 690, 693, 707, 708, 709, 710, 719, 730, 741, 747, 758, 762, 764, 767, 769, 772, 780, 792, 794, 795, 796, 799, 803, 805, 807, 808, 811, 818, 823, 832, 834, 838, 841, 842, 847, 851, 852, 854, 859, 862, 863, 865, 866, 867, 870, 871, 876, 878, 881, 888, 891, 897, 901, 902, 906, 911, 912, 913, 924, 925, 932, 935, 941, 953, 972, 979, 980, 981, 983, 985, 986, 987, 988, 989, 990, 991, 995, 996, 1002, 1005, 1008, 1009, 1013, 1017, 1018, 1019, 1029, 1030, 1032, 1038, 1039, 1040, 1041, 1042, 1043, 1046, 1052, 1058, 1060, 1069, 1072, 1074, 1075, 1078, 1087, 1095, 1102, 1106, 1107, 1111, 1112, 1114, 1116, 1117, 1119, 1122, 1129, 1131, 1136, 1140, 1142, 1144, 1147, 1148, 1154, 1158, 1163, 1174, 1175, 1176, 1185, 1191, 1194, 1201, 1210, 1211, 1212, 1213, 1214, 1215, 1216, 1218, 1223, 1225, 1226, 1228, 1232, 1233, 1238, 1239, 1245, 1249, 1251, 1262, 1263, 1268, 1269, 1270, 1271, 1274, 1275, 1276, 1280, 1281, 1283, 1286, 1289, 1290, 1294, 1295, 1301, 1302, 1307, 1310, 1311, 1314, 1317, 1324, 1330, 1332, 1333, 1335, 1337, 1341, 1345, 1346, 1348, 1355, 1356, 1365, 1366, 1367, 1379, 1380, 1387, 1388, 1389, 1398, 1401, 1403, 1410, 1418, 1428, 1444, 1445, 1447, 1448, 1449, 1458, 1459, 1460, 1471, 1479, 1484, 1487, 1489, 1498, 1511, 1513, 1526, 1538, 1541, 1546, 1547, 1550, 1566, 1574, 1575, 1581, 1586, 1587, 1594, 1596, 1600, 1607, 1612, 1615, 1617, 1622, 1625, 1630, 1631, 1632, 1644, 1648, 1649, 1661, 1662, B1681, B1682, B1683, B1684, B1688, B1693, B1713, B1723, B1724, B1735, B1736, B1737, B1741, B1756, C1892

QUICK FIND INDEX

COUNTRY OF RESIDENCE

CURRENT GRADE POINT AVERAGE

CURRENT SCHOOL PROGRAM

DEGREES RECEIVED

ETHNIC BACKGROUND

EXTRACURRICULAR ACTIVITIES

FAMILY ANCESTRIES

FOREIGN LANGUAGES SPOKEN

LEGAL CITY OF RESIDENCE

QUICK FIND INDEX

LEGAL CONTINENT OF CITIZENSHIP

LEGAL COUNTRY OF CITIZENSHIP

LEGAL COUNTY OF RESIDENCE

LEGAL STATE/PROV OF RESIDENCE

MARITAL STATUS

PHYSICAL HANDICAPS

PRE/CUR/FUT SCHOOLS

RELIGIOUS AFFILIATION

SEX

SORORITY/FRATERNAL

STATE/PROVINCE INTENDED STUDY

UNIONS

UNUSUAL CHARACTERISTICS

Field of Study Index

SCHOOL OF BUSINESS

BUSINESS ADMINISTRATION

General, 6, 15, 16, 18, 21, 24, 25, 32, 35, 37, 41, 43, 47, 52, 55, 57, 60, 87, 99, 102, 124, 133, 142, 208, 263, 280, 297, 307, 356, 375, 610, 615, 621, 695, 767, 773, 777, 799, 806, 813, 838, 848, 984, 1109, 1124, 1131, 1155, 1174, 1181, 1204, 1221, 1226, 1235, 1246, 1269, 1286, 1313, 1339, 1348, 1364, 1369, 1380, 1410, 1414, B1701, C1800, C1801

Accounting, 1, 2, 12, 23, 28, C1770, C1771, C1772

Actuarial Science, 48, 51, C1773, C1861

Advertising, 9, 17, 58, 384, 1215, 1219, 1222, 1249, C1774

Auditing-G, 30

Banking, 18, C1795

Economics, 3, 5, 14, 16, 18, 19, 20, 22, 26, 27, 33, 47, 50, 53, 59, 81, 82, 101, 121, 139, 311, 341, 373, 609, 680, 694, 722, 751, 764, 794, 834, 1194, 1205, 1221, 1266, 1277, 1291, 1313, 1314, 1319, 1329, 1338, 1339, 1341, 1343, 1352, 1353, 1362, 1399, 1407, 1412, 1422, 1424

Finance, 18

Hotel Administration, 54, 1185, C1859

Industrial & Labor Relations, 29

Insurance, 48, C1861, C1862

Labor Studies, 31

Management, 6, 38, C1870, C1871

Marketing, 9, 384, 1215

Public Administration, 7, 16, 20, 38, 39, 44, 45, 60, 121, 188, 199, 609, 680, 764, 794, 834, 1194, 1221, 1313, 1314, 1327, 1339, 1341, 1358, 1361, 1369, 1417, 1418, 1420, 1459

Public Relations, 4, 17, 40, 58, 1213, 1219, 1222, 1240, 1249, 1359, C1916

Purchasing-G, 34

Real Estate, 5, 10, 11, 42, 46, C1786, C1919

Traffic Management, 56

Transportation, 56, C1781

Travel & Tourism, 8, 110

Youth/Human Svc Agcy Adm, 13, 67

SCHOOL OF EDUCATION

EDUCATION

General, 26, 27, 32, 43, 50, 55, 68, 69, 70, 75, 76, 77, 78, 81, 82, 83, 84, 87, 91, 92, 93, 97, 98, 99, 100, 101, 102, 104, 105, 108, 109, 119, 133, 141, 216, 268, 307, 317, 356, 373, 375, 615, 695, 696, 762, 777, 781, 792, 813, 819, 832, 848, 984, 1109, 1155, 1181, 1186, 1204, 1211, 1246, 1277, 1291, 1319, 1352, 1353, 1362, 1364, 1399, 1412, 1414, 1422, 1459, B1702, C1823, C1824, C1924

Administration, 61, 66, 94, 107, B1723, C1923

Blind/Visually Impaired Education, 62, 63, 64, 85, 1084, 1085, 1370, 1371, 1372, 1463

Christian Leadership Education, 79, 80, 588, 590

Deaf/Hearing Impaired Education, 74, 85

Health Education-G, 357

Learning Disabled Education, 71

Physical Education, 13, 67, 72, 89, 95, 96, 110, 357, 543, 974, 982, 1104, 1108, 1390

Reading Education-G, 86

Secondary Education, 103

Special Education, 71, 73, 74, 83, 85, 88, 106, 1097, 1378, 1409, 1463, B1688, C1930, C1931

Student Counseling-G, 65, 90

Youth Leadership, 13, 67, 1653, C1941, C1942

SCHOOL OF ENGINEERING

General, 20, 24, 43, 53, 57, 68, 99, 105, 111, 112, 113, 114, 115, 116, 117, 118, 119, 120, 121, 122, 123, 124, 125, 126, 127, 128, 129, 130, 131, 132, 133, 134, 135, 136, 137, 138, 139, 140, 141, 142, 153, 154, 164, 190, 211, 213, 216, 218, 220, 221, 223, 297, 307, 311, 337, 602, 609, 610, 613, 614, 615, 618, 621, 629, 649, 661, 663, 664, 665, 677, 680, 685, 694, 696, 711, 713, 721, 729, 735, 742, 744, 745, 748, 750, 751, 753, 760, 762, 763, 764, 767, 768, 775, 776, 777, 779, 781, 785, 788, 792, 794, 798, 799, 800, 802, 809, 810, 812, 813, 814, 817, 819, 821, 822, 823, 827, 828, 832, 833, 834, 837, 838, 839, 843, 844, 845, 848, 879, 883, 909, 916, 967, 984, 992, 1068, 1109, 1131, 1155, 1174, 1181, 1186, 1190, 1194, 1202, 1204, 1226, 1264, 1269, 1284, 1314, 1318, 1329, 1340, 1341, 1348, 1357, 1375, 1377, 1380, 1392, 1393, 1394, 1410, 1424, B1703, C1777, C1827, C1828, C1829, C1922

AERONAUTICS

General, 143, 145, 146, 148, 150, 151, 153, 155, 157, 158, 159, 160, 168, 207, 210, 212, 217, 222, 230, 236, 237, 243, 246, 256, 257, 267, 271, 278, 281, 283, 336, 628, 652, 654, 672, 673, 679, 691, 701, 704, 705, 757, 765, 766, 778, 787, 797, 815, 818, 826, 835, 836, 850, 851, 1023, 1031, 1290, C1775, C1781

Aviation, 143, 149, 152, 156, 244, B1746, C1781

Aviation Electronics, 149, 156, 244, C1781

Space Science, 130, 144, 147, 149, 153, 154, 221, 270, 643, 665, 700, 776, 812, 845, 909, 1068, C1776

ART

ENGLISH LANG / LIT

FOREIGN LANGUAGE

Marine Technology, 706, 712, B1743, B1762, C1872, C1894

Oceanography, 146, 336, 628, 652, 659, 660, 679, 703, 704, 706, 709, 710, 712, 761, 791, 807, 808, 831, 1028, 1031, B1743, B1762, C1894

NATURAL HISTORY

General, 129, 664, 681, 713, 717, 724, 729, 775, 810, 844, 1205, 1284, 1357, 1393

Anthropology, 22, 120, 298, 337, 348, 395, 468, 593, 629, 721, 722, 725, 728, 733, 763, 833, 1195, 1264, 1266, 1273, 1340, 1343, 1377, 1407, C1785

Archaeology, 169, 286, 320, 324, 328, 330, 381, 385, 439, 441, 442, 507, 571, 716, 718, 719, 720, 726, 727, 733, 1252, 1261, C1788, C1789

Genealogy, 343, 459, 723

Museum Studies, 192, 422, 423, 730, 731

Paleontology, 269, 641, 715, 727, 732, C1900

SCHOOL OF SCIENCE

General, 53, 111, 127, 131, 132, 136, 137, 139, 153, 223, 254, 299, 311, 612, 614, 618, 642, 661, 685, 694, 698, 711, 734, 735, 736, 739, 740, 741, 742, 743, 744, 745, 748, 749, 750, 751, 779, 793, 817, 820, 821, 1223, 1326, 1329, 1394, 1424, B1703, B1751, C1924

BIOLOGY

General, 20, 24, 35, 43, 68, 99, 105, 112, 117, 119, 120, 121, 124, 125, 129, 130, 133, 136, 141, 145, 151, 154, 155, 168, 207, 208, 210, 212, 216, 218, 221, 222, 223, 230, 237, 243, 257, 259, 263, 267, 271, 278, 280, 281, 297, 307, 337, 609, 610, 615, 618, 629, 654, 664, 665, 672, 680, 691, 696, 701, 703, 705, 713, 721, 729, 748, 753, 757, 760, 761, 762, 763, 764, 766, 767, 768, 769, 771, 773, 774, 775, 776, 777, 778, 779, 781, 782, 783, 785, 787, 788, 791, 792, 794, 797, 799, 800, 803, 806, 810, 812, 813, 815, 817, 819, 822, 826, 828, 831, 832, 833, 834, 836, 838, 839, 841, 844, 845, 848, 850, 879, 903, 909, 984, 1023, 1028, 1052, 1063, 1068, 1080, 1081, 1109, 1131, 1155, 1174, 1181, 1186, 1190, 1194, 1204, 1226, 1264, 1269, 1284, 1314, 1340, 1341, 1348, 1357, 1375, 1377, 1380, 1393, 1410, C1796, C1797, C1924

Botany-G, 623, 632, 756, 770

Enology/Viticulture, 758

Entomology, 632, 770, C1830

Microbiology, 150, 217, 236, 256, 765, 835, C1881

Mycology-G, 772

Ornithology, 754, 755, 784, C1898

Teratology, 780

Zoology, 759, C1782

CHEMISTRY

General, 20, 24, 35, 43, 68, 99, 105, 112, 117, 119, 121, 123, 124, 125, 126, 128, 129, 130, 133, 134, 136, 141, 145, 151, 154, 155, 168, 190, 207, 208, 210, 212, 214, 215, 216, 218, 220, 221, 222, 223, 230, 233, 234, 235, 237, 243, 252, 253, 254, 255, 257, 259, 263, 267, 271, 276, 277, 278, 279, 280, 281, 297, 307, 602, 609, 610, 613, 615, 618, 645, 653, 654, 663, 664, 665, 672, 680, 684, 691, 696, 701, 703, 705, 713, 729, 739, 748, 753, 757, 760, 761, 762, 764, 766, 767, 768, 769, 773, 775, 776, 777, 778, 779, 781, 785, 786, 787, 788, 789, 790, 791, 792, 793, 794, 796, 797, 798, 799, 800, 801, 802, 803, 804, 805, 806, 809, 810, 811, 812, 813, 814, 815, 816, 817, 819, 822, 825, 826, 828, 829, 830, 831, 832, 834, 836, 837, 838, 839, 841, 843, 844, 845, 848, 850, 879, 883, 888, 909, 916, 967, 972, 984, 992, 1023, 1028, 1052, 1068, 1102, 1109, 1131, 1136, 1155, 1174, 1181, 1186, 1190, 1194, 1202, 1204, 1226, 1259, 1269, 1284, 1314, 1318, 1341, 1348, 1357, 1375, 1380, 1392, 1393, 1410, 1582, C1807, C1924

Atmosphere Chemistry, 157, 659, 660, 673, 709, 710, 795, 807, 808, 818, 851, 1290

MATHEMATICS

General, 20, 24, 43, 68, 99, 111, 112, 113, 117, 119, 120, 121, 123, 124, 125, 128, 129, 130, 133, 145, 150, 151, 154, 155, 164, 168, 207, 210, 211, 212, 214, 215, 216, 217, 218, 220, 221, 222, 230, 233, 234, 236, 237, 243, 252, 253, 256, 257, 259, 267, 271, 276, 277, 278, 281, 297, 307, 337, 609, 610, 611, 613, 615, 629, 654, 663, 664, 665, 672, 680, 691, 701, 705, 713, 721, 729, 734, 735, 753, 757, 760, 762, 763, 764, 765, 766, 767, 768, 769, 775, 776, 777, 778, 785, 787, 788, 789, 790, 792, 794, 797, 798, 799, 800, 803, 809, 810, 812, 813, 815, 820, 821, 822, 823, 824, 826, 828, 829, 830, 832, 833, 834, 835, 836, 837, 838, 839, 840, 841, 843, 844, 845, 848, 850, 879, 909, 984, 1023, 1068, 1109, 1131, 1155, 1174, 1181, 1190, 1194, 1198, 1202, 1204, 1226, 1264, 1269, 1279, 1284, 1314, 1340, 1341, 1348, 1357, 1375, 1377, 1380, 1392, 1393, 1410, 1582, B1672, B1748, C1873, C1874

Physics, 111, 113, 116, 120, 123, 145, 153, 157, 164, 168, 211, 212, 213, 214, 219, 230, 233, 240, 241, 252, 259, 266, 271, 276, 337, 629, 645, 649, 662, 673, 677, 701, 703, 721, 735, 757, 761, 763, 769, 786, 787, 789, 791, 798, 803, 818, 821, 823, 825, 826, 827, 829, 831, 833, 837, 841, 842, 846, 847, 851, 1023, 1028, 1259, 1264, 1290, 1340, 1377, C1910

Statistics, 113, 130, 153, 154, 164, 211, 221, 369, 665, 776, 812, 823, 845, 849, 909, 1068, 1243, 1397, 1421, 1582

MEDICAL DOCTOR

General, 125, 126, 130, 134, 154, 190, 218, 221, 331, 585, 602, 603, 665, 738, 746, 747, 752, 768, 771, 776, 800, 802, 805, 812, 814, 839, 845, 854, 856, 857, 858, 859, 862, 863, 865, 866, 868, 869, 870, 871, 872, 873, 874, 875, 876, 877, 878, 879, 880,

MEDICAL RELATED DISCIPLINES

MEDICAL RESEARCH

SCHOOL OF SOCIAL SCIENCE

COMMUNICATIONS

HISTORY

LAW

POLITICAL SCIENCE

PSYCHOLOGY

SOCIOLOGY

SCHOOL OF VOCATIONAL ED

Scholarships and Awards Listings

BUSINESS ADMINISTRATION

1

AMERICAN ACCOUNTING ASSOCIATION
(ARTHUR H CARTER SCHOLARSHIPS)

5717 BESSIE DR
SARASOTA FL 34233
813/921-7747; FAX 813/923-4093

AMOUNT: $2500

DEADLINE(S): APR 1

FIELD(S): ACCOUNTING

OPEN TO UNDERGRADUATE AND MASTER'S
DEGREE CANDIDATES FOR STUDY AT
ACCREDITED USA INSTITUTIONS OFFERING
ACCOUNTING DEGREES. MUST HAVE
COMPLETED AT LEAST 2 YEARS OF
UNDERGRAD STUDY AND HAVE AT LEAST 1
FULL YEAR OF STUDY REMAINING.

SELECTIONS BASED ON MERIT NOT NEED. 50
AWARDS PER YEAR. APPLICATIONS SHOULD
BE OBTAINED FROM DEAN OF ACCOUNTING
AT INDIVIDUAL COLLEGES.

2

AMERICAN ACCOUNTING ASSOCIATION
(FELLOWSHIP PROGRAM IN ACCOUNTING)

5717 BESSIE DRIVE
SARASOTA FL 34233
813/921-7747; FAX 813/923-4093

AMOUNT: $1000

DEADLINE(S): FEB 1

FIELD(S): ACCOUNTING

OPEN TO STUDENTS WHO HAVE BEEN ACCEPTED
TO DOCTORAL PROGRAM ACCREDITED BY
THE AACSB & PLAN TO PURSUE A CAREER
TEACHING IN THE USA OR CANADA. OPEN TO
RESIDENTS OF THE USA OR CANADA.
AWARDS BASED ON MERIT NOT NEED.

5 TO 6 FELLOWSHIPS PER YEAR. WRITE FOR
COMPLETE INFORMATION.

3

AMERICAN INSTITUTE FOR ECONOMIC
RESEARCH (SUMMER FELLOWSHIPS; IN-
ABSENTIA AWARDS)

DIVISION ST
GREAT BARRINGTON MA 01230
413/528-1217

AMOUNT: TUITION; ROOM & BOARD; $125 PER
WEEK STIPEND

DEADLINE(S): MAR 31

FIELD(S): ECONOMICS

SUMMER FELLOWSHIPS IN ECONOMIC SCIENCE
AT THE INSTITUTE OPEN TO
UNDERGRADUATES WHO HAVE COMPLETED
THEIR JUNIOR YEAR & GRADUATE
STUDENTS. PREFERENCE TO GRADUATE
STUDENTS & USA CITIZENS. FOREIGN
STUDENTS MUST BE FLUENT IN ENGLISH.

SUCCESSFUL SUMMER FELLOWS ARE ELIGIBLE
FOR IN-ABSENTIA AWARDS WHICH WILL PAY
TOTAL OR PARTIAL TUITION OR MONTHLY
STIPEND FOR ALL OR PART OF THE
FOLLOWING ACADEMIC YEAR; OR BOTH.
WRITE FOR COMPLETE INFORMATION.

4

AMERICAN INSTITUTE OF POLISH CULTURE
INC. (SCHOLARSHIPS)

1440 79TH STREET CAUSEWAY SUITE 117
MIAMI FL 33141
305/864-2349

AMOUNT: $2500

DEADLINE(S): JAN 15

FIELD(S): JOURNALISM/PUBLIC RELATIONS

SCHOLARSHIPS TO ENCOURAGE YOUNG
AMERICANS OF POLISH DESCENT TO PURSUE
THE ABOVE PROFESSIONS. AWARD CAN BE
USED AT ANY ACCREDITED AMERICAN
COLLEGE. THE RULING CRITERIA FOR
SELECTION ARE ACHIEVEMENT/TALENT &
INVOLVEMENT IN PUBLIC LIFE.

AWARDS RENEWABLE. FOR FULL-TIME STUDY
ONLY. CONTACT PROF. ZDZISLAW
WESOLOWSKI AT ADDRESS ABOVE FOR
COMPLETE INFORMATION.

5

AMERICAN INSTITUTE OF REAL ESTATE
APPRAISERS (THE APPRAISAL INSTITUTE
SCHOLARSHIPS)

875 N MICHIGAN AVE SUITE 2400
CHICAGO IL 60611
312/335-4100

AMOUNT: $2000 FOR UNDERGRADS; $3000 FOR
GRADS

DEADLINE(S): MAR 15

FIELD(S): REAL ESTATE; ECONOMICS;
APPRAISING

BUSINESS ADMINISTRATION

SCHOLARSHIPS OPEN TO UNDERGRADUATE AND GRADUATE STUDENTS WHO ARE ENROLLED IN A COLLEGE OR UNIVERSITY ACCREDITED BY THE AMERICAN ASSEMBLY OF COLLEGIATE SCHOOLS OF BUSINESS. USA CITIZEN.

APPROXIMATELY 50 AWARDS PER YEAR. WRITE FOR COMPLETE INFORMATION.

6

AMERICAN PRODUCTION AND INVENTORY CONTROL SOCIETY INC. (INTERNATIONAL STUDENT PAPER COMPETITION)

500 W. ANNANDALE RD
FALLS CHURCH VA 22046
703/237-8344

AMOUNT: $150 $100 $50 REGION LEVEL; $500 $300 $200 SOCIETY LEVEL

DEADLINE(S): MAY 15 (APPLY THROUGH LOCAL CHAPTER)

FIELD(S): BUSINESS ADMINISTRATION; MANAGEMENT; RESOURCE MANAGEMENT

PRIZE FOR BEST PAPER DEALING WITH OPERATIONS MANAGEMENT; PRODUCTION MANAGEMENT; INDUSTRIAL MANAGEMENT OR BUSINESS ADMINISTRATION. OPEN TO FULL OR PART TIME UNDERGRADUATE OR GRADUATE STUDENTS.

WRITE FOR COMPLETE INFORMATION.

7

AMERICAN PUBLIC WORKS ASSOC EDUCATION FOUNDATION (APWA MATCHING SCHOLARSHIP PROGRAM)

1313 EAST 60TH ST
CHICAGO IL 60637
312/667-2200

AMOUNT: $2500

DEADLINE(S): VARIES

FIELD(S): PUBLIC WORKS ADMIN; CIVIL ENGINEERING

MATCHING SCHOLARSHIP PROGRAM FOR GRADUATE STUDY IN PUBLIC WORKS MANAGEMENT WITHIN MASTERS OF PUBLIC ADMIN OR MASTERS OF CIVIL ENGINEERING DEGREES FROM INSTITUTIONS OFFICIALLY RECOGNIZED BY APWA.

WRITE FOR COMPLETE INFORMATION AND A LIST OF RECOGNIZED SCHOOLS.

8

AMERICAN SOCIETY OF TRAVEL AGENTS (ASTA SCHOLARSHIP FOUNDATION SCHOLARSHIP FUNDS)

1101 KING ST
ALEXANDRIA VA 22314
703/739-2782

AMOUNT: $250 - $3000

DEADLINE(S): JUN 11

FIELD(S): TRAVEL & TOURISM

FOUNDATION ADMINISTERS VARIOUS SCHOLARSHIP FUNDS WHICH ARE OPEN TO STUDENTS ENROLLED IN ACCREDITED PROPRIETARY SCHOOLS; 2-YEAR OR 4-YEAR UNDERGRADUATE SCHOOLS OR GRADUATE SCHOOLS. AT LEAST 3.0 GPA (4.0 SCALE). USA OR CANADIAN CITIZEN.

EACH FUND HAS SPECIFIC ELIGIBILITY REQUIREMENTS & SOME AWARDS ARE RENEWABLE. WRITE FOR COMPLETE INFORMATION.

9

AMERICAN WOMEN IN RADIO & TELEVISION (HOUSTON INTERNSHIP PROGRAM)

APRILLE MEEK; AWRT-HOUSTON; PO BOX 980908
HOUSTON TX 77098
WRITTEN INQUIRY

AMOUNT: $500 PER YEAR

DEADLINE(S): MAR 1

FIELD(S): RADIO; TELEVISION; FILM & VIDEO; ADVERTISING; MARKETING

INTERNSHIPS OPEN TO STUDENTS WHO ARE JUNIORS; SENIORS OR GRADUATE STUDENTS AT GREATER HOUSTON AREA COLLEGES & UNIVERSITIES.

WRITE FOR COMPLETE INFORMATION.

10

APPRAISAL INSTITUTE (EDUCATION TRUST SCHOLARSHIPS)

875 N MICHIGAN AVE - STE 2400
CHICAGO IL 60611
312/335-4136; FAX 312/335-4000

AMOUNT: $3000 GRADUATES; $2000 UNDERGRADS

DEADLINE(S): MAR 15

FIELD(S): REAL ESTATE APPRAISAL; LAND ECONOMICS; REAL ESTATE OR ALLIED FIELDS

OPEN TO USA CITIZENS FOR GRADUATE OR UNDERGRADUATE STUDY IN THE ABOVE FIELDS. AWARDS ARE MADE ON THE BASIS OF ACADEMIC EXCELLENCE. APPLICATIONS WILL BE DISTRIBUTED STARTING SEP 1.

APPROX 50 SCHOLARSHIPS PER YEAR. WRITE FOR COMPLETE INFORMATION.

11

APPRAISAL INSTITUTE EDUCATION TRUST (SCHOLARSHIP PROGRAM)

875 N MICHIGAN AVE.; SUITE 2400
CHICAGO IL 60611
312/335-4100

AMOUNT: $2000 AND $3000

DEADLINE(S): MAR 15

FIELD(S): REAL ESTATE

OPEN TO UNDERGRADUATE & GRADUATE STUDENTS MAJORING IN REAL ESTATE APPRAISAL; LAND ECONOMICS; REAL ESTATE OR ALLIED FIELDS. AWARDS ARE BASED ON ACADEMIC EXCELLENCE.

50 AWARDS PER YEAR. WRITE FOR COMPLETE INFORMATION.

12 ――――――――――――――

ARTHUR ANDERSEN & CO FOUNDATION (FELLOWSHIPS FOR DOCTORAL CANDIDATES AT THE DISSERTATION STAGE)

69 WEST WASHINGTON ST.
CHICAGO IL 60602
312-580-0069

AMOUNT: $18000 STIPEND + TUITION

DEADLINE(S): MAR 1 & OCT 1

FIELD(S): ACCOUNTING; TAXES; RELATED AREAS

DOCTORAL DISSERTATION FELLOWSHIPS TO SUPPORT THE DEVELOPMENT OF UNIVERSITY PROFESSORS IN THE AREAS SHOWN ABOVE. OPEN TO PH.D CANDIDATES WHO AGREE TO TEACH AT THE UNIVERSITY LEVEL FOR 3 YEARS.

WRITE FOR COMPLETE INFORMATION.

13 ――――――――――――――

BOYS & GIRLS CLUBS OF AMERICA (ROBERT W. WOODRUFF FELLOWSHIP)

771 FIRST AVE; HUMAN RESOURCE GROUP
NEW YORK NY 10017
212/351-5962

AMOUNT: UP TO $15000

DEADLINE(S): JUN 15 (APPLICATIONS AVAILABLE MAR 1)

FIELD(S): YOUTH WORKER

OPEN TO BOYS/GIRLS CLUBS OF AMERICA PROFESSIONALS WHO ARE ENROLLED IN AN ACCREDITED GRADUATE DEGREE PROGRAM. RECIPIENTS AGREE TO COMMIT TO 2 YEARS OF FULL-TIME EMPLOYMENT WITH BOYS/ GIRLS CLUBS OF AMERICA FOLLOWING COMPLETION OF STUDIES.

WRITE FOR COMPLETE INFORMATION.

14 ――――――――――――――

BROOKING INSTITUTION (RESEARCH FELLOWSHIPS)

1775 MASSACHUSETTS AVE NW
WASHINGTON DC 20036
202/797-6000

AMOUNT: $13500

DEADLINE(S): DEC 15

FIELD(S): FOREIGN POLICY; GOVERNMENT; ECONOMICS

OPEN TO PH.D CANDIDATES NOMINATED BY THEIR GRADUATE DEPARTMENTS. APPLICATIONS FROM INDIVIDUALS NOT SO NOMINATED CANNOT BE ACCEPTED. AWARDS SUPPORT RESEARCH BY PH.D CANDIDATES WHO HAVE COMPLETED ALL COURSEWORK EXCEPT FOR THE DISSERTATION.

APPROX 10 AWARDS PER YEAR. NOMINATION FORMS MAY BE OBTAINED BY YOUR DEPARTMENT HEAD FROM THE ADDRESS ABOVE.

15 ――――――――――――――

BUSINESS AND PROFESSIONAL WOMEN'S FOUNDATION (BPW/SEARS-ROEBUCK LOAN FUND FOR WOMEN IN GRADUATE BUSINESS STUDIES)

2012 MASSACHUSETTS AVE NW
WASHINGTON DC 20036
202/293-1200

AMOUNT: UP TO $2500

DEADLINE(S): APR 15 POSTMARK (APPS. AVAILABLE -ONLY- OCT 1 - APR 1)

FIELD(S): BUSINESS ADMINISTRATION

OPEN TO WOMEN ACCEPTED FOR ENROLLMENT IN A MASTERS DEGREE PROGRAM AT A COLLEGE OR UNIVERSITY ACCREDITED BY THE AMERICAN ASSEMBLY OF COLLEGIATE SCHOOLS OF BUSINESS. BPW FOUNDATION & SEARS FOUNDATION EMPLOYES -NOT- ELIGIBLE. USA CITIZEN.

MUST DEMONSTRATE FINANCIAL NEED. APPLICATIONS AVAILABLE -ONLY- BETWEEN OCT 1 AND APR 1. SEND SELF-ADDRESSED STAMPED ($.52) #10 ENVELOPE FOR COMPLETE INFORMATION.

16 ――――――――――――――

CDS INTERNATIONAL INC (ROBERT BOSCH FOUNDATION FELLOWSHIPS)

330 SEVENTH AVE
NEW YORK NY 10001
212/760-1400

AMOUNT: 3500 DEUTSCH MARKS PER MONTH + TRAVEL EXPENSES

DEADLINE(S): OCT 15

FIELD(S): BUSINESS ADMIN; ECONOMICS; JOURNALISM; MASS COMMUNICATIONS; LAW; POLITICAL SCIENCE; PUBLIC AFFAIRS

BUSINESS ADMINISTRATION

9-MONTH FELLOWSHIP PROGRAM IN GERMANY INVOLVING WORK INTERNSHIPS IN FEDERAL GOVERNMENT & THEN IN REGIONAL GOVERNMENT OR PRIVATE INDUSTRY; SUPPLEMENTED BY SPECIAL SEMINARS IN BERLIN; PARIS & BRUSSELS. USA CITIZEN.

OPEN TO YOUNG PROFESSIONALS & STUDENTS WHO HOLD A GRADUATE DEGREE IN ANY OF THE ABOVE AREAS OR HAVE EQUIVALENT PROFESSIONAL EXPERIENCE. 15 AWARDS PER YEAR. WRITE FOR COMPLETE INFORMATION.

17 —————————————————

CHARLES PRICE SCHOOL OF ADVERTISING AND JOURNALISM INC. (SCHOLARSHIP PROGRAM)

1700 WALNUT ST
PHILADELPHIA PA 19103
215/546-2747

AMOUNT: $500 - $1000

DEADLINE(S): VARIES

FIELD(S): ADVERTISING/JOURNALISM/PUBLIC RELATIONS

SCHOLARSHIPS FOR STUDY IN ABOVE FIELDS - AT- CHARLES PRICE SCHOOL OF ADVERTISING & JOURNALISM. UNDERGRADUATE JUNIORS AND SENIORS AND GRADUATE STUDENTS MAY APPLY. USA CITIZEN.

6 SCHOLARSHIPS PER YEAR. WRITE FOR COMPLETE INFORMATION.

18 —————————————————

COLUMBIA UNIVERSITY (KNIGHT-BAGEHOT FELLOWSHIP PROGRAM IN ECONOMICS AND BUSINESS JOURNALISM)

GRADUATE SCHOOL OF JOURNALISM
NEW YORK NY 10027
212/854-2711

AMOUNT: TUITION + STIPEND TO OFFSET LIVING EXPENSES

DEADLINE(S): MAR 1

FIELD(S): BUSINESS ADMINISTRATION; ECONOMICS; FINANCE & RELATED FIELDS

GRADUATE FELLOWSHIPS AT COLUMBIA UNIV OPEN TO QUALIFIED JOURNALISTS WITH AT LEAST 4 YEARS EXPERIENCE WHO WISH TO ENHANCE THEIR UNDERSTANDING & KNOWLEDGE IN THE ABOVE FIELDS. FOR USA OR CANADIAN PRINT OR BROADCAST JOURNALISTS.

UP TO 10 FELLOWSHIPS PER YEAR. WRITE FOR COMPLETE INFORMATION.

19 —————————————————

COMMITTEE ON THE STUDY OF THE JAPANESE ECONOMY (DOCTORAL & POSTDOCTORAL FELLOWSHIPS)

PROF. GARY SAXZENHOUSE; DEPT OF ECONOMICS; UNIV. OF MICHIGAN
ANN ARBOR MI 48109
313/764-3296

AMOUNT: VARIES

DEADLINE(S): NONE

FIELD(S): JAPANESE STUDIES - ECONOMICS

DOCTORAL AND SOME POST-DOCTORAL FELLOWSHIPS FOR ADVANCED STUDY OF THE JAPANESE ECONOMY. US CITIZEN OR LEGAL RESIDENT STUDYING IN USA.

FELLOWSHIPS ARE MADE AVAILABLE BY THE JAPAN-US FRIENDSHIP COMMISSION. WRITE FOR COMPLETE INFORMATION.

20 —————————————————

CONGRESSIONAL FELLOWSHIP PROGRAM (MORRIS K. UDALL FELLOWSHIPS)

CONGRESS OF THE UNITED STATES; OFFICE OF TECHNOLOGY ASSESSMENT
WASHINGTON DC 20510
202/224-8713

AMOUNT: $35000 - $70000

DEADLINE(S): JAN 31

FIELD(S): PHYSICAL OR BIOLOGICAL SCIENCES; ENGINEERING; LAW; ECONOMICS; ENVIRONMENTAL OR SOCIAL SCIENCES; PUBLIC POLICY

ONE YEAR FELLOWSHIP PROGRAM HELD -ONLY- IN WASHINGTO DC. CANDIDATES MUST HAVE EXTENSIVE EXPERIENCE IN SCIENCE OR TECHNOLOGY ISSUES OR HAVE COMPLETED DOCTORAL LEVEL RESEARCH. EXCEPTIONAL COMPETENCY IN ABOVE AREAS REQUIRED.

CONSIDERATIONS INCLUDE ACHIEVEMENT RECORDS AND CANDIDATE'S POTENTIAL IN ONE OR MORE OF OTA'S ASSESSMENT STUDIES. WRITE FOR COMPLETE INFORMATION.

21 —————————————————

CONSORTIUM FOR GRADUATE STUDY IN MANAGEMENT (FELLOWSHIPS FOR MINORITIES)

200 S. HANLEY RD. SUITE 616
ST LOUIS MO 63105
314/935-6364; FAX 314/935-5014

AMOUNT: FULL TUITION + $2500 STIPEND PER YEAR

DEADLINE(S): FEB 1

FIELD(S): BUSINESS ADMINISTRATION

FELLOWSHIPS FOR GRADUATE STUDY AT ANY OF 10 SPECIFIED UNIVERSITIES OPEN TO AFRICAN AMERICANS; NATIVE AMERICANS & HISPANIC AMERICANS WHO HAVE RECEIVED BA DEGREE FROM ACCREDITED INSTITUTION. USA CITIZEN.

APPROX 150 AWARDS PER YEAR. WRITE FOR COMPLETE INFORMATION.

22

COUNCIL FOR EUROPEAN STUDIES (PRE-DISSERTATION FELLOWSHIP PROGRAM)

C/O COLUMBIA UNIV; BOX 44 SCHERMERHORN HALL
NEW YORK NY 10027
212/854-4172

AMOUNT: $3000

DEADLINE(S): FEB 1

FIELD(S): EUROPEAN HISTORY; SOCIOLOGY; POLITICAL SCIENCE; ANTHROPOLOGY; ECONOMICS

GRANTS FOR EXPLORATORY RESEARCH IN EUROPE FOR GRAD STUDENTS WHO HAVE COMPLETED AT LEAST TWO YEARS GRADUATE STUDY AND INTEND TO PURSUE A PH.D. USA OR CANADIAN CITIZEN OR LEGAL RESIDENT.

APPLICANTS SHOULD HAVE AT LEAST ONE YEAR OF STUDY IN AN APPROPRIATE FOREIGN LANGUAGE OR MUST SHOW WHY THE REQUIREMENT IS INAPPROPRIATE. WRITE FOR COMPLETE INFORMATION.

23

DELOITTE & TOUCHE FOUNDATION (DOCTORAL FELLOWSHIP PROGRAM)

10 WESTPORT ROAD
WILTON CT 06897
203/761-3339

AMOUNT: $20000

DEADLINE(S): OCT 15

FIELD(S): ACCOUNTING

ANY DOCTORAL STUDENT ENROLLED IN AND SUCCESSFULLY PURSUING A DOCTORAL PROGRAM IN ACCOUNTING IS ELIGIBLE TO APPLY FOR THE FELLOWSHIP PROGRAM AFTER COMPLETING TWO SEMESTERS OR THE EQUIVALENT OF THE DOCTORAL PROGRAM.

10 GRANTS PER YEAR. CONTACT ADDRESS ABOVE FOR COMPLETE INFORMATION.

24

FLORIDA ENDOWMENT FUND FOR HIGHER EDUCATION (MCKNIGHT DOCTORAL FELLOWSHIP PROGRAM)

201 E.KENNEDY BLVD; SUITE 1525
TAMPA FL 33602
813/272-2772

AMOUNT: $11000 STIPEND + $5000 TUITION & FEES (PER YEAR)

DEADLINE(S): JAN 15

FIELD(S): ALL FIELDS (EXCEPT LAW; MEDICINE & EDUCATION)

OPEN TO ALL AFRICAN-AMERICANS WITH AT LEAST A BACHELOR'S DEGREE FROM AN ACCREDITED INSTITUTION WHO WISH TO PURSUE A DOCTORAL DEGREE. PROGRAM RECRUITS NATIONWIDE; HOWEVER FELLOWS MUST ENROLL IN A FLORIDA INSTITUTION. USA CITIZEN.

25 AWARDS PER YEAR. RENEWABLE FOR UP TO 5 YEARS. WRITE FOR COMPLETE INFORMATION.

25

GOLDEN STATE MINORITY FOUNDATION (MINORITY FOUNDATION SCHOLARSHIP)

1999 W. ADAMS BLVD
LOS ANGELES CA 90018
213/731-7771

AMOUNT: UP TO $2000

DEADLINE(S): QUARTERLY

FIELD(S): BUSINESS ADMINISTRATION

OPEN TO MINORITY CALIFORNIA RESIDENTS WHO ATTEND CALIFORNIA COLLEGES & UNIVERSITIES. AWARDS SUPPORT STUDY AT THE UNDERGRADUATE JUNIOR/SENIOR OR GRADUATE LEVELS. MAINTAIN GPA OF 3.0 OR BETTER. USA CITIZEN OR LEGAL RESIDENT.

MAY NOT WORK MORE THAN 25 HOURS A WEEK. INCOME MUST BE INSUFFICIENT TO COVER EXPENSES. APPROX 75 AWARDS PER YEAR. WRITE FOR COMPLETE INFORMATION.

26

HOOVER INSTITUTION ON WAR; REVOLUTION AND PEACE (NATIONAL FELLOWS PROGRAM)

STANFORD UNIVERSITY
STANFORD CA 94305
415/723-0163

AMOUNT: $32000

DEADLINE(S): JAN 13

FIELD(S): SOCIOLOGY; MODERN HISTORY; POLITICAL SCIENCE; ECONOMICS; INT'L RELATIONS; EDUCATION; LAW

BUSINESS ADMINISTRATION

POST-DOCTORAL FELLOWSHIPS THAT PROVIDE PARTICULARLY GIFTED JUNIOR SCHOLARS THE OPPORTUNITY TO SPEND ONE FULL YEAR ON UNRESTRICTED CREATIVE RESEARCH AND WRITING AT THE HOOVER INSTITUTION. USA OR CANADIAN CITIZEN.

12 TO 14 FELLOWSHIPS PER YEAR. RECIPIENTS ARE EXPECTED TO STAY IN RESIDENCY AT THE HOOVER INSTITUTION. WRITE FOR COMPLETE INFORMATION.

27 ──────────────────────

HUDSON INSTITUTE (HERMAN KAHN FELLOWSHIP)

PO BOX 26919; 5395 EMERSON WAY
INDIANAPOLIS IN 46226
317/545-1000

AMOUNT: $18000

DEADLINE(S): APR 15

FIELD(S): EDUCATION; ECONOMICS; NATIONAL SECURITY STUDIES

FELLOWSHIPS FOR PH.D CANDIDATES WHO HAVE COMPLETED ALL COURSEWORK & ARE DOING THEIR DISSERTATION ON A POLICY-RELEVANT ISSUE. DEMONSTRATE HIGH LEVEL OF ACADEMIC ACHIEVEMENT. US CITIZEN.

WRITE FOR COMPLETE INFORMATION.

28 ──────────────────────

INDEPENDENT ACCOUNTANTS INTERNATIONAL EDUCATIONAL FOUNDATION INC (ROBERT KAUFMAN MEMORIAL SCHOLARSHIP AWARD)

9200 S. DADELAND BLVD. SUITE 510
MIAMI FL 33156
305/661-3580

AMOUNT: $250 - $5000

DEADLINE(S): FEB 28

FIELD(S): ACCOUNTING

OPEN TO STUDENTS WHO ARE PURSUING OR PLANNING TO PURSUE AN EDUCATION IN ACCOUNTING AT RECOGNIZED ACADEMIC INSTITUTIONS THROUGHOUT THE WORLD. MUST DEMONSTRATE FINANCIAL NEED FOR LARGER SUMS; NOT REQUIRED FOR $250 HONORARY TEXTBOOK AWARD.

UP TO 20 SCHOLARSHIPS PER YEAR. WRITE FOR COMPLETE INFORMATION.

29 ──────────────────────

INDUSTRIAL RELATIONS COUNCIL ON GRADUATE OPPORTUNITIES ADVANCED LEVEL STUDIES (GOALS MINORITY FELLOWSHIP FOR GRADUATE SCHOOL)

PO BOX 4363
EAST LANSING MI 48826
517/351-6122

AMOUNT: UP TO FULL TUITION + STIPEND

DEADLINE(S): APR 1

FIELD(S): LABOR/INDUSTRIAL RELATIONS; HUMAN RESOURCES

OPEN TO AFRICAN AMERICANS; HISPANICS; NATIVE AMERICANS; NATIVE ALASKANS AND NATIVE HAWAIIANS FOR GRADUATE STUDY IN THE ABOVE AREAS AT A MEMBER UNIVERSITY OF THE GOALS CONSORTIUM. USA CITIZEN.

WRITE FOR COMPLETE INFORMATION.

30 ──────────────────────

INSTITUTE OF INTERNAL AUDITORS RESEARCH FOUNDATION (DISSERTATION GRANT)

249 MAITLAND AVE
ALTAMONTE SPRINGS FL 32701
407/830-7600 EXT 276

AMOUNT: $1000 - $10000

DEADLINE(S): MAY 15; OCT 31

FIELD(S): INTERNAL AUDITING

OPEN TO APPLICANTS WHO ARE ENROLLED IN A SCHOOL WHICH OFFERS A RECOGNIZED DOCTORAL DEGREE IN BUSINESS; HAVE COMPLETED ALL COURSE REQUIREMENTS EXCEPT FOR THE DISSERTATION & INTEND TO TEACH INTERNAL AUDITING FOR AT LEAST 2 YEARS.

GRANTS SUPPORT FULL-TIME DISSERTATION RESEARCH. FUNDING ALSO IS AVAILABLE FOR RESEARCH PROJECTS RELATED TO INTERNAL AUDITING. WRITE FOR COMPLETE INFORMATION.

31 ──────────────────────

INTERNATIONAL FOUNDATION OF EMPLOYEE BENEFIT PLANS (POST-DOCTORAL GRANTS FOR RESEARCH)

18700 WEST BLUEMOUND RD; PO BOX 69
BROOKFIELD WI 53008
414/786-6700

AMOUNT: UP TO $10000

DEADLINE(S): NONE SPECIFIED

FIELD(S): LABOR STUDIES-EMPLOYEE BENEFIT ISSUES

OPEN TO POST-DOCTORAL STUDENTS WHO ARE USA CITIZENS & WORK FOR A NONPROFIT EDUCATIONAL OR RESEARCH INSTITUTION. GRANTS TO SUPPORT ORIGINAL RESEARCH ON SUCH EMPLOYEE BENEFIT ISSUES AS HEALTH CARE; RETIREMENT; INCOME SECURITY.

APPROPRIATE ACADEMIC DISCIPLINES FOR APPLICANTS INCLUDE BUSINESS/FINANCE; LABOR/INDUSTRIAL RELATIONS; ECONOMICS; LAW; SOCIAL/HEALTH SCIENCES. WRITE FOR COMPLETE INFORMATION.

32

**JEWISH COMMUNITY CENTERS ASSOCIATION
(JCCA SCHOLARSHIP PROGRAM)**

SCHOLARSHIP COORDINATOR;
15 E. 26TH ST.
NEW YORK NY 10010
212/532-4949

AMOUNT: $7500

DEADLINE(S): FEB 1

FIELD(S): ADULT EDUCATION; EARLY
CHILDHOOD EDUCATION; PHYSICAL
EDUCATION; SOCIAL WORK; JEWISH
STUDIES; BUSINESS ADMINISTRATION

OPEN TO INDIVIDUALS OF THE JEWISH FAITH
WHO ARE ENROLLED IN A MASTERS DEGREE
PROGRAM AND HAVE A STRONG DESIRE TO
WORK IN THE JEWISH COMMUNITY CENTER
FIELD. USA OR CANADIAN CITIZEN.

10 AWARDS PER YEAR. WRITE FOR COMPLETE
INFORMATION.

33

**JOINT COUNCIL ON ECONOMIC EDUCATION
(INTERNATIONAL PAPER COMPANY
FOUNDATION AWARDS FOR THE
TEACHING OF ECONOMICS)**

432 PARK AVE SOUTH
NEW YORK NY 10016
212/685-5499

AMOUNT: $100 - $1000

DEADLINE(S): JUL 15

FIELD(S): TEACHING - ECONOMICS

ELEMENTARY AND SECONDARY TEACHERS MAY
APPLY FOR AN AWARDS PROGRAM
DESIGNED TO IDENTIFY AND COMMUNICATE
EFFECTIVE TEACHING EXPERIENCES
THROUGH WRITTEN DESCRIPTIONS OF
INDIVIDUAL EXPERIENCES IN THE TEACHING
OF ECONOMICS.

72 AWARDS PER YEAR. WRITE FOR COMPLETE
INFORMATION.

34

**NATIONAL ASSOCIATION OF PURCHASING
MANAGEMENT (NAPM DOCTORAL
RESEARCH FELLOWSHIPS)**

2055 E. CENTENNIAL CIR. POB 22160
TEMPE AZ 85285
201/967-8585

AMOUNT: UP TO $10000

DEADLINE(S): JAN 31

FIELD(S): PURCHASING/MATERIALS
MANAGEMENT

DOCTORAL DISSERTATION FELLOWSHIPS FOR
DOCTORAL CANDIDATES AT AACSB-
ACCREDITED U.S. INSTITUTIONS. U.S.
CITIZEN OR LEGAL RESIDENT.

WRITE FOR COMPLETE INFORMATION.

35

**NATIONAL ASSOCIATION OF WATER
COMPANIES - NEW JERSEY CHAPTER
(SCHOLARSHIP)**

C/O NJ-AMERICAN WATER CO -
EASTERN DIV 661 SHREWSBURY AVE
SHREWSBURY NJ 07702
908/842-6900; FAX 908/842-7541

AMOUNT: $2500

DEADLINE(S): APR 1 (POSTMARK)

FIELD(S): BUSINESS ADMINISTRATION;
BIOLOGY; CHEMISTRY; ENGINEERING

OPEN TO USA CITIZENS WHO HAVE LIVED IN NJ
AT LEAST 5 YEARS AND PLAN A CAREER IN
THE INVESTOR-OWNED WATER UTILITY
INDUSTRY IN DISCIPLINES SUCH AS THOSE
ABOVE. MUST BE UNDERGRAD OR
GRADUATE STUDENT IN A 2 OR 4 YEAR NJ
COLLEGE OR UNIVERSITY.

GPA OF 3.0 OR BETTER REQUIRED. WRITE FOR
COMPLETE INFORMATION.

36

**NATIONAL BLACK MBA ASSOCIATION INC
(ANNUAL SCHOLARSHIP PROGRAM)**

180 N MICHIGAN AVE SUITE 1820
CHICAGO IL 60601
312/236-2622

AMOUNT: VARIES

DEADLINE(S): MAY 1

FIELD(S): BUSINESS OR MANAGEMENT

OPEN TO ETHNIC MINORITIES ENROLLING IN A
GRADUATE BUSINESS ADMINISTRATION OR
MANAGEMENT PROGRAM WHO ARE USA
CITIZENS AND MAINTAIN A 3.0 OR HIGHER
GPA.

RENEWABLE. WRITE FOR COMPLETE
INFORMATION.

37

**NATIONAL BROADCASTING COMPANY INC
(MINORITY FELLOWSHIPS PROGRAM)**

30 ROCKEFELLER PLAZA
NEW YORK NY 10112
212/664-5016

AMOUNT: VARIES

DEADLINE(S): VARIES

FIELD(S): BROADCASTING; JOURNALISM;
BUSINESS ADMINISTRATION

BUSINESS ADMINISTRATION

OPEN TO MINORITY GRADUATE STUDENTS WHO ATTEND DESIGNATED COLLEGES OR UNIVERSITIES. THE SCHOOLS ARE CHANGED EACH YEAR. APPLICANTS MUST BE USA CITIZENS OR LEGAL RESIDENTS.

APPLICATION MUST BE MADE THROUGH STUDENT'S COLLEGE. INQUIRE AT FINANCIAL AID OFFICE OR WRITE FOR COMPLETE INFORMATION.

38

NATIONAL SOCIETY OF PROFESSIONAL ENGINEERS EDUCATIONAL FOUNDATION (MANAGEMENT STUDY FELLOWSHIPS FOR GRADUATE STUDENTS)

1420 KING STREET
ALEXANDRIA VA 22314
703/684-2830

AMOUNT: $2000 - $3000

DEADLINE(S): DEC 3

FIELD(S): MANAGEMENT; PUBLIC ADMINISTRATION

OPEN TO PROFESSIONAL ENGINEERS WHO HAVE BEEN ACCEPTED TO OR ARE ENROLLED IN AN ACCREDITED USA MASTERS DEGREE PROGRAM IN MANAGEMENT OR ADMINISTRATION. MINIMUM GPA OF 3.0 AS AN UNDERGRADUATE.

WRITE FOR COMPLETE INFORMATION.

39

NEW YORK CITY DEPT. OF PERSONNEL (URBAN FELLOWS PROGRAM)

2 WASHINGTON ST.; 15TH FLOOR
NEW YORK NY 10004
212/487-5698

AMOUNT: $17000 STIPEND

DEADLINE(S): JAN 26

FIELD(S): PUBLIC ADMINISTRATION; URBAN PLANNING; GOVERNMENT; PUBLIC SERVICE; URBAN AFFAIRS

FELLOWSHIP PROGRAM PROVIDES ONE ACADEMIC YEAR (9 MONTHS) OF FULL-TIME WORK EXPERIENCE IN URBAN GOVERNMENT. OPEN TO GRADUATING COLLEGE SENIORS AND RECENT COLLEGE GRADUATES. USA CITIZEN.

WRITE FOR COMPLETE INFORMATION.

40

NEW YORK STATE SENATE (LEGISLATIVE FELLOWS PROGRAM; R.J.ROTH JOURNALISM FELLOWSHIP; R.A.WIEBE PUBLIC SERVICE FELLOWSHIP)

STATE CAPITOL ROOM 500A
ALBANY NY 12247
518/455-2611

AMOUNT: $22575

DEADLINE(S): SPRING

FIELD(S): POLITICAL SCIENCE; GOVERNMENT; PUBLIC SERVICE; JOURNALISM; PUBLIC RELATIONS

NY STATE RESIDENT. OPEN TO GRADUATE STUDENTS ENROLLED IN ACCREDITED PROGRAMS IN THE ABOVE AREAS. FELLOWS WORK AS REGULAR LEGISLATIVE STAFF MEMBERS OF THE OFFICES TO WHICH THEY ARE ASSIGNED. USA CITIZEN.

14 FELLOWSHIPS PER YEAR. WRITE FOR COMPLETE INFORMATION.

41

NEWCOMEN SOCIETY OF THE UNITED STATES (NEWCOMEN-HARVARD ANNUAL POST-DOCTORAL FELLOWSHIP IN BUSINESS HISTORY)

412 NEWCOMEN ROAD
EXTON PA 19341
215/363-6600

AMOUNT: $40000

DEADLINE(S): MAR 15

FIELD(S): HISTORY - BUSINESS

INDIVIDUALS HAVING A DOCTORATE IN HISTORY WHO ARE ACTIVE IN EDUCATION MAY APPLY FOR FELLOWSHIPS IN BUSINESS HISTORY AT HARVARD GRADUATE SCHOOL OF BUSINESS ADMINISTRATION.

FOR COMPLETE INFORMATION WRITE TO PROF. THOMAS K. MCCRAW; GRADUATE SCHOOL OF BUSINESS ADMINISTRATION; HARVARD UNIVERSITY; SOLDIERS FIELD ROAD; BOSTON MA 02163.

42

NORTHERN VIRGINIA BOARD OF REALTORS INC (EBNER R.DUNCUN SCHOLARSHIP PROGRAM)

8411 ARLINGTON BLVD
FAIRFAX VA 22116
703/207-3200

AMOUNT: $500 - $1000

DEADLINE(S): APR 30

FIELD(S): REAL ESTATE

FOR NORTHERN VIRGINIA RESIDENTS ONLY. PURPOSE OF THIS PROGRAM IS TO RECOGNIZE & ENCOURAGE THOSE SERIOUS STUDENTS WITH POTENTIAL FOR PROFESSIONAL DEVELOPMENT & CONTRIBUTIONS TO THE REAL ESTATE COMMUNITY TO CONTINUE THEIR COLLEGE EDUCATION.

AWARDS SUPPORT UNDERGRADUATE OR GRADUATE STUDY AT RECOGNIZED COLLEGES & UNIVERSITIES IN NORTHERN VIRGINIA. WRITE FOR COMPLETE INFORMATION.

43

ORGANIZATION OF AMERICAN STATES DEPT OF FELLOWSHIPS & TRAINING (OAS PRA-FELLOWSHIPS)

TRAINEE SELECTION DIVISION
WASHINGTON DC 20006
202/789-3902

AMOUNT: TUITION + FEES; TRAVEL EXP & STIPEND

DEADLINE(S): APR 30; AUG 31

FIELD(S): ALL FIELDS EXCEPT MEDICINE & FOREIGN LANGUAGES

GRADUATE FELLOWSHIPS FOR USA CITIZENS OR PERMANENT RESIDENTS TO STUDY IN AN OAS MEMBER COUNTRY. MUST HAVE UNDERGRADUATE DEGREE AND HAVE DEMONSTRATED ABILITY TO PURSUE ADVANCED STUDIES IN CHOSEN FIELD.

APPLICANTS SHOULD BE FLUENT IN LANGUAGE OF COUNTRY OF INTENDED STUDY. PRIORITY IS GIVEN TO RESEARCH PROJECTS. WRITE FOR COMPLETE INFORMATION.

44

PHOENIX BUDGET & RESEARCH DEPT (MANAGEMENT INTERN PROGRAM)

251 WEST WASHINGTON ST
PHOENIX AZ 85003
602/262-4800

AMOUNT: $1960 PER MONTH

DEADLINE(S): JAN 10

FIELD(S): PUBLIC ADMINISTRATION; URBAN STUDIES & RELATED FIELDS

ANNUAL MANAGEMENT INTERNSHIP PROGRAM OPEN TO CANDIDATES WHO HOLD A MASTER'S DEGREE OR HAVE COMPLETED ALL MASTER'S DEGREE COURSEWORK IN THE ABOVE FIELDS. THIS IS AN INTERNSHIP - NOT- A SCHOLARSHIP OR GRANT.

WRITE FOR COMPLETE INFORMATION.

45

PRESIDENT'S COMMISSION ON WHITE HOUSE FELLOWSHIPS (FELLOWSHIP PROGRAM)

712 JACKSON PLACE NW
WASHINGTON DC 20503
202/395-4522

AMOUNT: WAGE (UP TO GS-15 STEP 3)

DEADLINE(S): DEC 1

FIELD(S): PUBLIC SERVICE; GOVERNMENT; COMMUNITY INVOLVEMENT; LEADERSHIP

OPEN TO COLLEGE GRADUATES BETWEEN THE AGES OF 30 AND 39 WHO DESIRE ONE YEAR OF FIRST HAND EXPERIENCE IN GOVERNMENT. FELLOWSHIPS OPEN TO A WIDE VARIETY OF EDUCATIONAL BACKGROUNDS AND CAREER INTERESTS.

WRITE FOR COMPLETE INFORMATION.

46

REAL ESTATE EDUCATORS ASSN (REEA - HARWOOD SCHOLARSHIP PROGRAM)

111 E WACKER DR #200
CHICAGO IL 60601
313/616-0800

AMOUNT: $250

DEADLINE(S): DEC 6

FIELD(S): REAL ESTATE

OPEN TO UNDERGRADUATE STUDENTS (WHO HAVE COMPLETED AT LEAST 2 SEMESTERS) & GRADUATE STUDENTS. CRITERIA ARE FULL-TIME STUDY AT ACCREDITED USA SCHOOL; AT LEAST 3.2 GPA & INTENT TO PURSUE CAREER IN REAL ESTATE.

10 SCHOLARSHIPS PER YEAR. WRITE FOR COMPLETE INFORMATION.

47

RICHARD D. IRWIN FOUNDATION (DOCTORAL FELLOWSHIPS)

1818 RIDGE ROAD
HOMEWOOD IL 60430
708/798-6000

AMOUNT: $2000 - $2500

DEADLINE(S): FEB 15

FIELD(S): BUSINESS ADMINISTRATION; ECONOMICS

FELLOWSHIPS OPEN TO PH.D CANDIDATES WHO HAVE COMPLETED ALL COURSE WORK EXCEPT FOR THE DISSERTATION. AWARDS TENABLE AT ACCREDITED USA & CANADIAN INSTITUTIONS. PREFERENCE TO APPLICANTS WHO PLAN TO TEACH IN THE USA OR CANADA.

20 AWARDS PER YEAR. WRITE FOR COMPLETE INFORMATION.

48

S.S.HUEBNER FOUNDATION FOR INSURANCE EDUCATION (FELLOWSHIPS)

UNIV OF PENN; 3641 LOCUST WALK;
302 CPC
PHILADELPHIA PA 19104
215/898-7620

AMOUNT: TUITION & FEES + $13000 STIPEND

BUSINESS ADMINISTRATION

DEADLINE(S): FEB 1

FIELD(S): INSURANCE; RISK; ACTUARIAL SCIENCE

DOCTORAL & POST-DOCTORAL FELLOWSHIPS IN THE ABOVE AREAS. AWARDS ARE TENABLE AT THE UNIVERSITY OF PENNSYLVANIA'S WHARTON SCHOOL OF BUSINESS. USA OR CANADIAN CITIZEN.

3 NEW AWARDS PER YEAR. WRITE FOR COMPLETE INFORMATION.

49

SISTERS OF SALISAW FOUNDATION (SCHOLARSHIP)

911 BARTLETT PL
WINDSOR CA 95492
WRITTEN INQUIRY

AMOUNT: $500

DEADLINE(S): AUG 1

FIELD(S): BUSINESS

OPEN TO CHILDREN OF MIGRANT FARM LABORERS RESIDING IN WINDSOR CA WHOSE FAMILY MIGRATED TO CALIFORNIA FROM SALISAW OK DURING THE DUST BOWL ERA OF THE 1930'S. FAMILY MUST HAVE WORKED AT LEAST SIX MONTHS IN THE HERNESTO ONEXIOCA VINEYARDS.

FOR UNDERGRADUATE OR GRADUATE STUDY LEADING TO A DEGREE IN BUSINESS. WRITE FOR COMPLETE INFORMATION.

50

SOCIAL SCIENCE RESEARCH COUNCIL (INTERNATIONAL PREDISSERTATION FELLOWSHIP PROGRAM)

ELLEN PERECMAN; 605 THIRD AVE.
NEW YORK NY 10158
212-661-0280

AMOUNT: VARIES

DEADLINE(S): TO BE ANNOUNCED BY PARTICIPATING UNIVERSITIES

FIELD(S): ECONOMICS; POLITICAL SCIENCE; PSYCHOLOGY SOCIOLOGY; OTHER SOCIAL SCIENCE DISCIPLINES

OPEN TO PH.D CANDIDATES ENROLLED IN SOCIAL SCIENCES PROGRAMS AT SELECTED UNIVERSITIES. STUDENTS SHOULD BE INTERESTED IN SUPPLEMENTING THEIR DISCIPLINARY SKILLS WITH AREA AND LANGUAGE STUDIES.

FELLOWS UNDERTAKE A PROGRAM OF STUDY IN OR ON AFRICA; CHINA; LATIN AMERICA; THE CARIBBEAN; THE NEAR & MIDDLE EAST; SOUTH ASIA OR SOUTHEAST ASIA. WRITE FOR COMPLETE INFORMATION.

51

SOCIETY OF ACTUARIES (ACTUARIAL SCHOLARSHIPS FOR MINORITY STUDENTS)

475 N. MARTINGALE RD. SUITE 800
SCHAUMBURG IL 60173
708/706-3500

AMOUNT: VARIES

DEADLINE(S): MAY 1

FIELD(S): ACTUARIAL SCIENCE

OPEN TO STUDENTS WHO ARE MEMBERS OF ETHNIC MINORITIES AND ARE ENROLLED OR ACCEPTED IN AN ACTUARIAL SCIENCE PROGRAM AT AN ACCREDITED COLLEGE OR UNIVERSITY. MUST DEMONSTRATE FINANCIAL NEED AND BE A USA CITIZEN OR LEGAL RESIDENT.

AMOUNT VARIES ACCORDING TO STUDENT'S NEED AND CREDENTIALS. APPROXIMATELY 40 AWARDS PER YEAR. WRITE FOR COMPLETE INFORMATION.

52

SOIL AND WATER CONSERVATION SOCIETY OF AMERICA (DONALD A WILLIAMS SCHOLARSHIP)

7515 NORTHEAST ANKENY ROAD
ANKENY IA 50021
515/289-2331; FAX 515/289-1227

AMOUNT: $1200

DEADLINE(S): APR 1

FIELD(S): BUSINESS ADMINISTRATION; CONSERVATION

SCHOLARSHIP OPEN TO SOCIETY MEMBERS WHO ARE CURRENTLY EMPLOYED IN NATURAL RESOURCE RELATED FIELD AND WISH TO RETURN TO SCHOOL TO IMPROVE THEIR TECHNICAL OR ADMINISTRATIVE SKILLS. ATTAINMENT OF DEGREE NOT REQUIRED.

APPLICANTS WHO HAVE NOT RECEIVED A BACHELOR'S DEGREE WILL BE GIVEN PREFERENCE. MUST SHOW REASONABLE FINANCIAL NEED. WRITE FOR COMPLETE INFORMATION.

53

SPACE FOUNDATION (SPACE INDUSTRIALIZATION FELLOWSHIP)

4800 RESEARCH FOREST DR
THE WOODLANDS TX 77381
713/363-7944; FAX 713/363-7914

AMOUNT: $4000

DEADLINE(S): OCT 1

FIELD(S): SCIENCES & ENGINEERING; BUSINESS; LAW; ECONOMICS; SOCIAL SCIENCES; ENVIRONMENTAL STUDIES; HUMANITIES

OPEN TO SUPERIOR GRADUATE STUDENTS IN THE ABOVE DISCIPLINES WHO INTEND TO DEVOTE THEIR CAREERS TO THE FURTHERANCE OF PRACTICAL SPACE RESEARCH; ENGINEERING; BUSINESS OR OTHER APPLICATION VENTURES.

CONTACT DR. DAVID J. NORTON; EDUCATIONAL GRANT PROGRAM CHAIRMAN; ADDRESS ABOVE; FOR COMPLETE INFORMATION.

54 ─────────────────

STATLER FOUNDATION (SCHOLARSHIPS)

107 DELAWARE AVE; SUITE 508
BUFFALO NY 14202
716/852-1104

AMOUNT: $500 PER YEAR

DEADLINE(S): APR 15

FIELD(S): FOOD MANAGEMENT; CULINARY ARTS; HOTEL-MOTEL MANAGEMENT

OPEN TO UNDERGRADUATE OR GRADUATE STUDENTS WHO ARE ACCEPTED TO OR ENROLLED FULL TIME AT A USA INSTITUTION IN AN ACCREDITED PROGRAM OF STUDY IN ANY OF THE ABOVE AREAS.

APPROX 900 AWARDS PER YEAR. RENEWABLE. WRITE FOR COMPLETE INFORMATION.

55 ─────────────────

SWEDISH INFORMATION SERVICE (BICENTENNIAL FUND GRANTS)

ONE DAG HAMMARSKJOLD PLAZA;
45TH FLOOR
NEW YORK NY 10017
212/751-5900

AMOUNT: 20000 SWEDISH KRONA

DEADLINE(S): FEB 1

FIELD(S): POLITICAL SCIENCE; BUSINESS ADMIN; EDUCATION; COMMUNICATION; CULTURE; ENVIRONMENTAL STUDIES

GRANTS TO PROVIDE THE OPPORTUNITY FOR THOSE IN A POSITION TO INFLUENCE PUBLIC OPINION AND CONTRIBUTE TO THE DEVELOPMENT OF THEIR SOCIETY. 3-6 WEEK INTENSIVE STUDY VISITS IN SWEDEN IN ANY OF THE ABOVE AREAS OR THEIR RELATED FIELDS.

US CITIZEN OR LEGAL RESIDENT. APPROXIMATELY 10 GRANTS PER YEAR. WRITE FOR COMPLETE INFORMATION.

56 ─────────────────

TRANSPORTATION CLUBS INTERNATIONAL (MEXICO TRAFFIC & TRANSPORTATION SCHOLARSHIPS)

1275 KAMUS DR. SUITE 101
FOX ISLAND WA 98333
206/549-2251

AMOUNT: $500

DEADLINE(S): APR 15

FIELD(S): TRANSPORTATION; TRAFFIC MANAGEMENT

OPEN TO STUDENTS OF MEXICAN NATIONALITY WHO ARE ENROLLED IN A MEXICAN INSTITUTION OF HIGHER LEARNING IN A DEGREE OR VOCATIONAL PROGRAM IN THE ABOVE OR RELATED AREAS.

WRITE FOR COMPLETE INFORMATION.

57 ─────────────────

U.S. DEPT. OF EDUCATION (INDIAN FELLOWSHIP PROGRAM)

400 MARYLAND AVENUE SW; RM 2177; MAIL STOP 6335
WASHINGTON DC 20202
202/401-1902

AMOUNT: $1000 - $34000 (AVERAGE $13000)

DEADLINE(S): FEB 7

FIELD(S): BUSINESS ADMIN; ENGINEERING; NATURAL RESOURCES & RELATED AREAS

FELLOWSHIPS FOR AMERICAN INDIANS OR ALASKAN NATIVES WHO ARE US CITIZENS AND SEEKING UNDERGRADUATE OR GRADUATE DEGREES IN THE ABOVE FIELDS AT ACCREDITED INSTITUTIONS IN USA.

APPROXIMATELY 90 CONTINUATION AND 35 NEW AWARDS PER YEAR. WRITE FOR COMPLETE INFORMATION.

58 ─────────────────

UNIVERSITY OF MARYLAND (FELLOWSHIPS AND ASSISTANTSHIPS)

COLLEGE OF JOURNALISM -
GRADUATE OFFICE
COLLEGE PARK MD 20742
301/405-2380

AMOUNT: $10000 + REMISSION OF 10 CREDITS OF TUITION

DEADLINE(S): FEB 1

FIELD(S): ADVERTISING; PUBLIC RELATIONS; PUBLIC AFFAIRS REPORTING; BROADCAST JOURNALISM

OPEN TO GRADUATE STUDENTS FOR STUDY AT THE UNIVERSITY OF MARYLAND'S COLLEGE OF JOURNALISM. ELIGIBILITY IS BASED ON MERIT.

WRITE FOR COMPLETE INFORMATION.

59 ─────────────────

W.E. UPJOHN INSTITUTE FOR EMPLOYMENT RESEARCH (GRANT PROGRAM)

INSTITUTE GRANT COMMITTEE;
300 S. WESTNEDGE AVE.
KALAMAZOO MI 49007
616/343-5541

EDUCATION

AMOUNT: $45000 MAXIMUM

DEADLINE(S): MAR 23; SEP 21

FIELD(S): ECONOMICS (POLICY ORIENTED)

POST-DOCTORAL GRANTS FOR POLICY-RELEVANT RESEARCH ON EMPLOYMENT AND UNEMPLOYMENT AT THE NATIONAL; STATE AND LOCAL LEVELS. UP TO $25000 ADDITIONAL MAY BE AWARDED TO CONDUCT SURVEYS OR ASSEMBLE NEW ANALYTIC DATA FROM ADMINISTRATIVE SOURCES.

SOME INTERNATIONAL TRAVEL MAY BE FUNDED FOR STUDIES OF THE IMPLICATIONS OF FOREIGN LABOR MARKET POLICIES ON USA ECONOMICS. WRITE FOR COMPLETE INFORMATION.

60

WOLCOTT FOUNDATION (FELLOWSHIP AWARD)

402 BEASLEY ST
MONROE LA 71203
318/343-1602

AMOUNT: TUITION + BOOKS; FEES & UP TO $150 PER MONTH STIPEND

DEADLINE(S): FEB 1

FIELD(S): BUSINESS ADMINISTRATION; PUBLIC SERVICE; INTERNATIONAL RELATIONS; GOVERNMENT; PUBLIC ADMINSTRATION

OPEN TO STUDENTS ENROLLED IN ACCREDITED PROGRAM LEADING TO MASTER'S DEGREE WITH GPA OF AT LEAST 3.0 ON 4.0 SCALE. PREFERENCE TO (BUT NOT LIMITED TO) APPLICANTS WITH MASONIC BACKGROUND. USA CITIZEN.

FELLOWSHIPS ARE FOR 36 SEMESTER HOURS AND TENABLE AT GEORGE WASHINGTON UNIVERSITY. WRITE FOR COMPLETE INFORMATION.

EDUCATION

61

AMERICAN ASSOCIATION OF SCHOOL ADMINISTRATORS (GRADUATE SCHOLARSHIPS IN SCHOOL ADMINISTRATION)

1801 NORTH MOORE STREET
ARLINGTON VA 22209
703/528-0700; FAX 703/841-1543

AMOUNT: $2000

DEADLINE(S): JUN 1

FIELD(S): SCHOOL ADMINISTRATION

OPEN TO GRADUATE STUDENTS CURRENTLY ENROLLED IN A SCHOOL ADMINISTRATION PROGRAM WHO INTEND TO MAKE THE PUBLIC SCHOOL SUPERINTENDENCY A LIFE CAREER. CANDIDATES MUST BE NOMINATED BY THEIR INSTITUTION.

CANDIDATES SHOULD CONTACT COLLEGE DEAN'S OFFICE FOR APPLICATIONS; NOT AASA. FIVE AWARDS ARE GIVEN EACH YEAR.

62

AMERICAN FOUNDATION FOR THE BLIND (DELTA GAMMA FOUNDATION FLORENCE HARVEY MEMORIAL SCHOLARSHIP)

15 WEST 16TH ST
NEW YORK NY 10011
212/620-2000; TDD 212/620-2158

AMOUNT: $1000

DEADLINE(S): APR 1

FIELD(S): REHABILITATION AND/OR EDUCATION OF THE VISUALLY IMPAIRED AND BLIND

OPEN TO LEGALLY BLIND UNDERGRADUATE AND GRADUATE COLLEGE STUDENTS OF GOOD CHARACTER WHO HAVE EXHIBITED ACADEMIC EXCELLENCE AND ARE STUDYING IN THE FIELD OF EDUCATION AND/OR REHABILITATION OF THE VISUALLY IMPAIRED AND BLIND.

MUST BE USA CITIZEN. WRITE FOR COMPLETE INFORMATION.

63

AMERICAN FOUNDATION FOR THE BLIND (RUDOLPH DILLMAN MEMORIAL SCHOLARSHIP)

15 WEST 16TH ST
NEW YORK NY 10011
212/620-2000; TDD 212/620-2158

AMOUNT: $2500

DEADLINE(S): APR 1

FIELD(S): REHABILITATION; EDUCATION OF BLIND & VISUALLY IMPAIRED

OPEN TO LEGALLY BLIND UNDERGRADUATE OR GRADUATE STUDENTS ACCEPTED TO OR ENROLLED IN AN ACCREDITED PROGRAM WITHIN THE BROAD AREAS OF REHABILITATION AND/OR EDUCATION OF THE BLIND AND VISUALLY IMPAIRED. USA CITIZEN.

THREE AWARDS PER YEAR. WRITE FOR COMPLETE INFORMATION.

64

AMERICAN FOUNDATION FOR THE BLIND (TELESENSORY SCHOLARSHIP)

15 WEST 16TH ST
NEW YORK NY 10011
212/620-2000; TDD 212/620-2158

AMOUNT: $1000

DEADLINE(S): APR 1

FIELD(S): REHABILITATION; EDUCATION OF BLIND & VISUALLY IMPAIRED

OPEN TO LEGALLY BLIND UNDERGRADUATE & GRADUATE STUDENTS ACCEPTED TO OR ENROLLED IN AN ACCREDITED PROGRAM WITHIN THE BROAD AREAS OF REHABILITATION AND/OR EDUCATION OF THE BLIND AND VISUALLY IMPAIRED. USA CITIZEN.

WRITE FOR COMPLETE INFORMATION.

65

ARKANSAS SCHOOL COUNSELOR ASSOCIATION (HUGH LOVETT MEMORIAL SCHOLARSHIP)

MIKE CAIN; TREASURER -
BEARDEN ELEMENTARY SCHOOL
BEARDEN AR 71720
WRITTEN INQUIRY

AMOUNT: $1000

DEADLINE(S): MAR 1

FIELD(S): STUDENT COUNSELING

OPEN TO GRADUATE STUDENTS IN STUDENT COUNSELING WHO ARE ENROLLED IN AN APPROVED ARKANSAS INSTITUTION. RECIPIENTS AGREE TO WORK IN EDUCATION IN ARKANSAS FOR THREE YEARS AFTER COMPLETION OF THE PROGRAM.

WRITE FOR COMPLETE INFORMATION.

66

ASSOCIATION OF SCHOOL BUSINESS OFFICIALS INTERNATIONAL (EXHIBITORS SCHOLARSHIPS)

11401 NORTH SHORE DRIVE
RESTON VA 22090
703/478-0405

AMOUNT: $1200

DEADLINE(S): AUG 31

FIELD(S): SCHOOL BUSINESS MANAGEMENT; EDUCATIONAL ADMINISTRATION

OPEN TO CANDIDATES FOR GRADUATE DEGREE WHO HAVE BEEN AN ASBO MEMBER FOR AT LEAST THREE YEARS AND HAVE BEEN EMPLOYED FULL TIME IN A SCHOOL BUSINESS MANAGEMENT POSITION FOR A MINIMUM OF THREE YEARS.

WRITE FOR COMPLETE INFORMATION.

67

BOYS & GIRLS CLUBS OF AMERICA (ROBERT W. WOODRUFF FELLOWSHIP)

771 FIRST AVE;
HUMAN RESOURCE GROUP
NEW YORK NY 10017
212/351-5962

AMOUNT: UP TO $15000

DEADLINE(S): JUN 15 (APPLICATIONS AVAILABLE MAR 1)

FIELD(S): YOUTH WORKER

OPEN TO BOYS/GIRLS CLUBS OF AMERICA PROFESSIONALS WHO ARE ENROLLED IN AN ACCREDITED GRADUATE DEGREE PROGRAM. RECIPIENTS AGREE TO COMMIT TO 2 YEARS OF FULL-TIME EMPLOYMENT WITH BOYS/ GIRLS CLUBS OF AMERICA FOLLOWING COMPLETION OF STUDIES.

WRITE FOR COMPLETE INFORMATION.

68

BUSINESS AND PROFESSIONAL WOMEN'S FOUNDATION (CAREER ADVANCEMENT SCHOLARSHIPS)

2012 MASSACHUSETTS AVE NW
WASHINGTON DC 20036
202/293-1200

AMOUNT: $500 - $1000

DEADLINE(S): APR 15 POSTMARK (APPS AVAILABLE -ONLY- OCT 1 - APR 1)

FIELD(S): COMPUTER SCIENCE; EDUCATION; PARALEGAL; ENGINEERING; SCIENCE (EXCEPT HEALTH CARE)

OPEN TO WOMEN (30 OR OLDER) WITHIN 12-24 MONTHS OF COMPLETING UNDERGRAD OR GRAD STUDY IN USA (INCLUDING PUERTO RICO & THE VIRGIN ISLANDS). SHOULD LEAD TO ENTRY OR REENTRY INTO THE WORK FORCE OR IMPROVE CAREER ADVANCEMENT CHANCES.

MUST SHOW FINANCIAL NEED. SEND SELF-ADDRESSED STAMPED ($.52) #10 ENVELOPE FOR APPLICATION & COMPLETE INFORMATION. NOT FOR STUDY AT DOCTORAL LEVEL.

69

CALIFORNIA STUDENT AID COMMISSION (PAUL DOUGLAS TEACHER SCHOLARSHIP PROGRAM)

PO BOX 510624
SACRAMENTO CA 94245
916/322-2294

AMOUNT: UP TO $5000 PER YEAR FOR UP TO 4 YEARS

DEADLINE(S): JUL 1

FIELD(S): EDUCATION

EDUCATION

CALIFORNIA RESIDENT. FEDERALLY FUNDED PROGRAM OPEN TO TOP HIGH SCHOOL SENIORS & COLLEGE STUDENTS WHO DEMONSTRATE COMMITMENT TO PURSUING TEACHING CAREERS. FOR UNDERGRADUATE & TEACHER PREPARATION STUDY AT ELIGIBLE CALIF SCHOOLS.

USA CITIZEN OR ELIGIBLE NON CITIZEN. RECIPIENTS AGREE TO TEACH 2 YEARS FULL TIME (ANYWHERE IN USA) FOR EACH YEAR THE SCHOLARSHIP IS RECEIVED. RENEWABLE. CONTACT COLLEGE COUNSELOR; FINANCIAL AID OFFICE OR ADDRESS ABOVE.

70

CALIFORNIA TEACHERS ASSN (MARTIN LUTHER KING JR MEMORIAL SCHOLARSHIP FUND)

PO BOX 921; 1705 MURCHISON DR
BURLINGAME CA 94010
415/697-1400

AMOUNT: $250-2000

DEADLINE(S): MAR 15

FIELD(S): EDUCATION

OPEN TO ACTIVE MEMBERS OF CTA OR STUDENT CTA (SCTA) WHO ARE CALIF RESIDENTS; USA CITIZENS AND MEMBERS OF SPECIFIED MINORITIES OR ETHNIC GROUPS. AWARDS TO BE USED IN PURSUIT OF TEACHING CREDENTIAL OR GRADUATE DEGREE IN EDUCATION.

WRITE FOR COMPLETE INFORMATION.

71

CIVITAN INTERNATIONAL FOUNDATION (DR. COURTNEY W. SHROPSHIRE GRANT)

PO BOX 130744
BIRMINGHAM AL 35213
205/591-8910

AMOUNT: $1000 - $1500

DEADLINE(S): FEB 20

FIELD(S): FIELDS RELATING TO MENTAL RETARDATION OR OTHER DEVELOPMENTAL DISABILITIES

OPEN TO UNDERGRADUATE JUNIORS & SENIORS & MASTER'S CANDIDATES ENROLLED IN AN ACCREDITED COLLEGE OR UNIVERSITY WHO PLAN A CAREER IN THE DISTINCTIVE AREA ABOVE. MUST AGREE TO UPHOLD CIVITAN IDEALS. INTERVIEW BY CIVITAN MEMBER REQUIRED.

20-40 AWARDS PER YEAR. WRITE FOR COMPLETE INFORMATION. INCLUDE A SELF ADDRESSED BUSINESS SIZE ENVELOPE WITH POSTAGE SUFFICIENT FOR A 2-OUNCE FIRST CLASS MAILING.

72

DELTA PSI KAPPA (RESEARCH AWARDS)

PO BOX 90264
INDIANAPOLIS IN 46290
317/274-4344

AMOUNT: $500 (BIENNIALLY)

DEADLINE(S): NOV 15

FIELD(S): PHYSICAL EDUCATION

OPEN TO DELTA PSI KAPPA MEMBERS. AWARDS ARE TO SUPPORT GRADUATE RESEARCH IN THE FIELDS OF HEALTH; PHYSICAL EDUCATION & RECREATION.

WRITE FOR COMPLETE INFORMATION.

73

EASTER SEAL SOCIETY OF IOWA (SCHOLARSHIPS & AWARDS)

PO BOX 4002
DES MOINES IA 50333
515/289-1933

AMOUNT: $400 - $600

DEADLINE(S): APR 15

FIELD(S): PHYSICAL REHABILITATION; MENTAL REHABILITATION; & RELATED AREAS

OPEN TO IOWA RESIDENTS WHO ARE FULL-TIME UNDERGRADUATE SOPHOMORES; JUNIORS; SENIORS OR GRADUATE STUDENTS AT ACCREDITED INSTITUTIONS; PLANNING A CAREER IN THE BROAD FIELD OF REHABILITATION; FINANCIALLY NEEDY & IN TOP 40% OF THEIR CLASS.

6 SCHOLARSHIPS PER YEAR. RENEWABLE. WRITE FOR COMPLETE INFORMATION.

74

EMBLEM CLUB SCHOLARSHIP FOUNDATION (SCHOLARSHIP GRANTS)

PO BOX 712
SAN LUIS REY CA 92068
619/757-0619

AMOUNT: UP TO $4000

DEADLINE(S): JUN 1; SEP 1; DEC 1; MAR 1

FIELD(S): SPECIAL EDUCATION; EDUCATION OF THE DEAF & HEARING IMPAIRED

FOR GRADUATE STUDENTS (UNDER AGE 50) WHO ARE ENROLLED IN OR ACCEPTED TO AN ACCREDITED MASTERS PROGRAM IN THE USA THAT PROVIDES TRAINING IN THE ABOVE AREAS. USA CITIZEN OR LEGAL RESIDENT WHO PLANS TO TEACH IN THE USA.

40 AWARDS PER YEAR. WRITE FOR COMPLETE INFORMATION.

75

FLORIDA DEPT. OF EDUCATION (CRITICAL TEACHER SHORTAGE SCHOLARSHIP LOAN PROGRAM)

OFFICE OF STUDENT FINANCIAL ASSISTANCE;
1344 FLORIDA EDUCATION CENTER
TALLAHASSEE FL 32399
904/487-0049

AMOUNT: $4000 PER YEAR FOR A MAXIMUM OF TWO YEARS

DEADLINE(S): MAR 15 POSTMARK

FIELD(S): TEACHER EDUCATION

FOR FULL-TIME UNDERGRAD JUNIOR OR SENIOR OR GRADUATE STUDENT ENROLLED IN A STATE APPROVED TEACHER EDUCATION PROGRAM IN A FLORIDA INSTITUTION. CANDIDATES SHOULD BE PURSUING A DEGREE IN A DESIGNATED CRITICAL TEACHER SHORTAGE FIELD.

LOAN IS REPAID BY TEACHING IN FLORIDA OR IN CASH. 376 AWARDS PER YEAR. WRITE FOR COMPLETE INFORMATION.

76

FLORIDA DEPT. OF EDUCATION (FLORIDA TEACHER TUITION REIMBURSEMENT PROGRAM)

OFFICE OF STUDENT FINANCIAL ASSISTANCE;
1344 FLORIDA EDUCATION CENTER
TALLAHASSEE FL 32399
904/487-0049

AMOUNT: TUITION REIMBURSEMENT PAYMENTS

DEADLINE(S): SPECIFIED ON APPLICATION

FIELD(S): EDUCATION

INCENTIVE PROGRAM TO ENCOURAGE FLORIDA PUBLIC SCHOOL TEACHERS TO BECOME CERTIFIED TO TEACH/OR TO GAIN A GRADUATE DEGREE IN A DEPT OF ED CRITICAL TEACHER SHORTAGE AREA & THEN TEACH IN THAT AREA IN FLORIDA. MUST MAINTAIN 3.0 OR BETTER GPA.

WILL REIMBURSE UP TO $78 PER CREDIT HOUR FOR UP TO 9 HOURS PER ACADEMIC YEAR; FOR UP TO A TOTAL OF 36 CREDIT HOURS. WRITE FOR COMPLETE INFORMATION.

77

FLORIDA DEPT. OF EDUCATION (FLORIDA TEACHER-STUDENT LOAN FORGIVENESS PROGRAM)

OFFICE OF STUDENT FINANCIAL ASSISTANCE;
1344 FLORIDA EDUCATION CENTER
TALLAHASSEE FL 32399
904/487-0049

AMOUNT: SEE BELOW

DEADLINE(S): MAR 1

FIELD(S): TEACHER-FLORIDA CRITICAL SHORTAGE AREA

OPEN TO CERTIFIED FLORIDA PUBLIC SCHOOL TEACHERS. PROGRAM PROVIDES REPAYMENT OF EDUCATION LOANS IN RETURN FOR TEACHING IN DEPT OF ED DESIGNATED CRITICAL TEACHER SHORTAGE AREAS IN FLORIDA PUBLIC SCHOOLS.

UP TO $2500 PER YEAR FOR 4 YEARS FOR TEACHERS WITH UNDERGRADUATE DEGREES; UP TO $5000 PER YEAR FOR UP TO 2 YEARS FOR TEACHERS WITH GRADUATE DEGREES. APPLICATIONS MUST BE SUBMITTED BY JULY 15 AFTER FIRST ACADEMIC YEAR OF TEACHING.

78

FLORIDA DEPT. OF EDUCATION (MASTERS TEACHER SCHOLARSHIP LOAN PROGRAM)

OFFICE OF STUDENT FINANCIAL ASSISTANCE;
1344 FLORIDA EDUCATION CENTER
TALLAHASSEE FL 32399
904/487-0049

AMOUNT: TUITION & FEES PLUS $6000 FOR UP TO 2 SEMESTERS OR 3 QUARTERS & 1 SUMMER TERM

DEADLINE(S): JUN 30

FIELD(S): TEACHING

FELLOWSHIP LOAN PROGRAM CREATED TO ATTRACT LIBERAL ARTS/SCIENCE/& MID-CAREER RETURNING STUDENTS TO TEACHING IN FLORIDA PUBLIC SCHOOLS. MUST BE ADMITTED TO APPROVED MASTERS' PROGRAM FOR TEACHERS AT PARTICIPATING FLORIDA INSTITUTION.

MUST AGREE TO IN A STATE-DESIGNATED HIGH PRIORITY LOCATION SCHOOL. LOAN IS REPAID BY TEACHING SERVICE OR CASH. WRITE FOR COMPLETE INFORMATION.

79

FUND FOR THEOLOGICAL EDUCATION (DISSERTATION YEAR SCHOLARSHIPS FOR AFRO-AMERICANS)

475 RIVERSIDE DR #832
NEW YORK NY 10115
212/870-2058

AMOUNT: VARIES

DEADLINE(S): FEB 10

FIELD(S): THEOLOGY; CHRISTIAN EDUCATION

OPEN TO AFRO-AMERICANS WHO ARE USA OR CANADIAN CITIZENS COMPLETING THEIR PH.D ED.D OR TH.D DISSERTATIONS IN RELIGIOUS STUDIES. MUST BE MEMBERS OF A CHRISTIAN CHURCH AND NOMINATED BY THE COLLEGE.

EDUCATION

RECIPIENTS ARE EXPECTED TO COMPLETE DISSERTATIONS BY THE END OF THE SCHOLARSHIP YEAR. WRITE FOR COMPLETE INFORMATION.

80 ─────────────────────

FUND FOR THEOLOGICAL EDUCATION (MINORITY DOCTORAL SCHOLARSHIPS)

475 RIVERSIDE DR #832
NEW YORK NY 10115
212/870-2058

AMOUNT: VARIES

DEADLINE(S): FEB 10

FIELD(S): THEOLOGY; CHRISTIAN EDUCATION

OPEN TO AFRO-AMERICANS & HISPANIC AMERICANS WHO ARE USA OR CANADIAN CITIZENS AND ARE ENROLLED IN OR APPLYING TO A PH.D TH.D OR ED.D PROGRAM IN A FIELD OF RELIGIOUS STUDY. APPLICANTS SHOULD HAVE COMPLETED NO MORE THAN 1 YEAR OF COURSEWORK.

MUST BE MEMBERS OF A CHRISTIAN CHURCH AND NOMINATED BY THE COLLEGE. WRITE FOR COMPLETE INFORMATION.

81 ─────────────────────

HOOVER INSTITUTION ON WAR; REVOLUTION AND PEACE (NATIONAL FELLOWS PROGRAM)

STANFORD UNIVERSITY
STANFORD CA 94305
415/723-0163

AMOUNT: $32000

DEADLINE(S): JAN 13

FIELD(S): SOCIOLOGY; MODERN HISTORY; POLITICAL SCIENCE; ECONOMICS; INT'L RELATIONS; EDUCATION; LAW

POST-DOCTORAL FELLOWSHIPS THAT PROVIDE PARTICULARLY GIFTED JUNIOR SCHOLARS THE OPPORTUNITY TO SPEND ONE FULL YEAR ON UNRESTRICTED CREATIVE RESEARCH AND WRITING AT THE HOOVER INSTITUTION. USA OR CANADIAN CITIZEN.

12 TO 14 FELLOWSHIPS PER YEAR. RECIPIENTS ARE EXPECTED TO STAY IN RESIDENCY AT THE HOOVER INSTITUTION. WRITE FOR COMPLETE INFORMATION.

82 ─────────────────────

HUDSON INSTITUTE (HERMAN KAHN FELLOWSHIP)

PO BOX 26919; 5395 EMERSON WAY
INDIANAPOLIS IN 46226
317/545-1000

AMOUNT: $18000

DEADLINE(S): APR 15

FIELD(S): EDUCATION; ECONOMICS; NATIONAL SECURITY STUDIES

FELLOWSHIPS FOR PH.D CANDIDATES WHO HAVE COMPLETED ALL COURSEWORK & ARE DOING THEIR DISSERTATION ON A POLICY-RELEVANT ISSUE. DEMONSTRATE HIGH LEVEL OF ACADEMIC ACHIEVEMENT. US CITIZEN.

WRITE FOR COMPLETE INFORMATION.

83 ─────────────────────

INDIANA STATE STUDENT ASSISTANCE COMMISSION (MINORITY TEACHER & SPECIAL EDUCATION TEACHER SCHOLARSHIP PROGRAM)

150 W. MARKET ST - 5TH FLOOR
INDIANAPOLIS IN 46204
317/232-2350

AMOUNT: $1000 - $4000

DEADLINE(S): VARIES WITH COLLEGE

FIELD(S): EDUCATION

OPEN TO BLACK OR HISPANIC RESIDENTS OF INDIANA OR INDIANA RESIDENTS WORKING TOWARD A CERTIFICATE IN SPECIAL EDUCATION. FOR FULL TIME UNDERGRADUATE OR GRADUATE STUDY AT AN INDIANA COLLEGE. GPA OF 2.0 OR BETTER (4.0 SCALE) IS REQUIRED.

MUST DEMONSTRATE FINANCIAL NEED (FAF). WRITE FOR COMPLETE INFORMATION.

84 ─────────────────────

INDIANA STATE STUDENT ASSISTANCE COMMISSION (PAUL DOUGLAS TEACHER SCHOLARSHIP PROGRAM)

150 W. MARKET ST - 5TH FLOOR
INDIANAPOLIS IN 46204
317/232-2350

AMOUNT: $5000

DEADLINE(S): MAR 1

FIELD(S): EDUCATION

OPEN TO INDIANA RESIDENTS FOR UNDERGRADUATE OR GRADUATE STUDY LEADING TO A TEACHING CREDENTIAL. MUST BE IN TOP 10% OF HIGH SCHOOL GRADUATING CLASS OR (IF IN COLLEGE) HAVE 3.0 OR BETTER GPA (4.0 SCALE).

USA CITIZEN. WRITE FOR COMPLETE INFORMATION.

85 ─────────────────────

INTERNATIONAL ORDER OF THE ALHAMBRA (SCHOLARSHIP FUND AND ENDOWMENT FUND)

4200 LEEDS AVE
BALTIMORE MD 21229
301/242-0660

AMOUNT: VARIES

DEADLINE(S): JAN; APR; JUL; OCT

FIELD(S): SPECIAL EDUCATION

OPEN TO UNDERGRADUATE STUDENTS WHO WILL BE ENTERING THEIR JUNIOR OR SENIOR YEAR IN AN ACCREDITED PROGRAM FOR TEACHING THE MENTALLY RETARDED & THE HANDICAPPED. AVAILABLE TO GRADUATE STUDENTS IN CANADA & THE STATES OF CALIFORNIA & VIRGINIA.

USA CITIZENSHIP REQUIRED. WRITE FOR COMPLETE INFORMATION.

86

INTERNATIONAL READING ASSOCIATION (OUTSTANDING DISSERTATION OF THE YEAR AWARD)

PO BOX 8139; 800 BARKSDALE ROAD
NEWARK DE 19714
302/731-1600 EXT 226

AMOUNT: $1000

DEADLINE(S): OCT 1

FIELD(S): READING RESEARCH & DISABILITIES

OPEN TO IRA MEMBERS WHO COMPLETED DISSERTATION IN THE FIELD OF READING BETWEEN SEP 1 1991 AND AUG 31 1992.

WRITE FOR COMPLETE INFORMATION.

87

JEWISH COMMUNITY CENTERS ASSOCIATION (JCCA SCHOLARSHIP PROGRAM)

SCHOLARSHIP COORDINATOR;
15 E. 26TH ST.
NEW YORK NY 10010
212/532-4949

AMOUNT: $7500

DEADLINE(S): FEB 1

FIELD(S): ADULT EDUCATION; EARLY CHILDHOOD EDUCATION; PHYSICAL EDUCATION; SOCIAL WORK; JEWISH STUDIES; BUSINESS ADMINISTRATION

OPEN TO INDIVIDUALS OF THE JEWISH FAITH WHO ARE ENROLLED IN A MASTERS DEGREE PROGRAM AND HAVE A STRONG DESIRE TO WORK IN THE JEWISH COMMUNITY CENTER FIELD. USA OR CANADIAN CITIZEN.

10 AWARDS PER YEAR. WRITE FOR COMPLETE INFORMATION.

88

KNIGHTS OF COLUMBUS (BISHOP GRECO GRADUATE FELLOWSHIP PROGRAM)

P.O. DRAWER 1670
NEW HAVEN CT 06507
203/772-2130

AMOUNT: $500 PER SEMESTER

DEADLINE(S): MAY 1

FIELD(S): EDUCATION OF MENTALLY RETARDED

OPEN TO GRADUATE STUDENTS WHO ARE K OF C MEMBERS IN GOOD STANDING OR ARE DEPENDENTS OF SUCH MEMBER. APPLICANTS MUST HAVE SATISFACTORY ACADEMIC RECORD AND BE INTERESTED IN WORKING WITH THE MENTALLY RETARDED.

WRITE FOR COMPLETE INFORMATION.

89

LABAN/BARTENIEFF INSTITUTE OF MOVEMENT STUDIES (WORKSTUDY PROGRAMS)

11 E. 4TH ST.; 3RD FLOOR
NEW YORK NY 10003
212/477-4299

AMOUNT: $500 - $2500

DEADLINE(S): MAY 1

FIELD(S): HUMAN MOVEMENT STUDIES

OPEN TO GRADUATE STUDENTS & PROFESSIONALS IN DANCE; EDUCATION; HEALTH FIELDS; BEHAVIORAL SCIENCES; FITNESS; ATHLETIC TRAINING; ETC. FOR WORK STUDY -ONLY- AT THE LABAN/ BARTENIEFF INSTITUTE IN THE LABAN MOVEMENT STUDIES CERTIFICATE PROGRAM.

WRITE FOR COMPLETE INFORMATION.

90

MARYLAND ASSOCIATION FOR MULTICULTURAL COUNSELING & DEVELOPMENT (CLEMMIE SOLOMAN SCHOLARSHIP)

RHONDA C. GILL; 1009 FENTON PLACE
UPPER MARLBORO MD 20772
301/742-7780

AMOUNT: $500; $300

DEADLINE(S): MAR 1

FIELD(S): GUIDANCE & COUNSELING/MINORITY STUDENT

GRADUATE SCHOLARSHIP FOR MINORITY STUDENT WHO IS ENROLLED IN A MARYLAND COLLEGE OR UNIVERSITY AND WHO HAS THE POTENTIAL TO MAKE SIGNIFICANT CONTRIBUTIONS TO THE FIELD OF GUIDANCE & COUNSELING FOR THE BENEFIT OF MINORITY POPULATIONS.

USA CITIZEN. WRITE FOR COMPLETE INFORMATION.

91

MARYLAND HIGHER EDUCATION COMMISSION (SHARON CHRISTA MCAULIFFE CRITICAL SHORTAGE TEACHER PROGRAM)

STATE SCHOLARSHIP ADMINISTRATION;
16 FRANCIS ST.
ANNAPOLIS MD 21401
410/974-5370

AMOUNT: UP TO $8000 FOR TUITION; FEES & ROOM & BOARD

DEADLINE(S): DEC 31

FIELD(S): EDUCATION (CRITICAN SHORTAGES DETERMINED ANNUALLY)

MARYLAND RESIDENT. PROGRAM FOR PERSONS WHO AGREE TO TEACH IN CRITICAL SHORTAGE AREA IN MARYLAND FOR UP TO 1 YEAR FOR EACH YEAR OF FUNDING. FOR FULL OR PART TIME UNDERGRAD OR GRAD STUDY AT MARYLAND DEGREE GRANTING INSTITUTION.

RENEWABLE IF 3.0 GPA IS MAINTAINED. WRITE FOR COMPLETE INFORMATION.

92

NATIONAL ACADEMY OF EDUCATION (SPENCER POSTDOCTORAL FELLOWSHIP PROGRAM)

STANFORD UNIV SCHOOL OF EDUCATION - CERAS - 507G
STANFORD CA 94305
415/725-1003

AMOUNT: $35000

DEADLINE(S): JAN 2

FIELD(S): EDUCATION; HUMANITIES; SOCIAL SCIENCES

POSTDOCTORAL FELLOWSHIPS OPEN TO INDIVIDUAL RESEARCHERS IN EDUCATION; HUMANITIES OR SOCIAL & BEHAVIORAL SCIENCES. RESEARCH MUST HAVE APPARENT RELEVANCE TO EDUCATION. DOCTORAL DEGREE MUST HAVE BEEN RECEIVED WITHIN THE LAST 6 YEARS.

30 FELLOWSHIPS PER YEAR. NONRENEWABLE. MANDATORY APPLICATION FORM AVAILABLE THROUGH DEC 15 FROM ADDRESS ABOVE. WRITE FOR COMPLETE INFORMATION.

93

NATIONAL ASSOCIATION FOR CORE CURRICULUM (BOSSING-EDWARDS RESEARCH SCHOLARSHIP)

C/O KENT STATE UNIV; 404E WHITE HALL
KENT OH 44242
216/672-2792

AMOUNT: VARIES

DEADLINE(S): VARIES

FIELD(S): CORE CURRICULUM RESEARCH

OPEN TO GRADUATE STUDENTS WITH AT LEAST ONE YEAR OF EXPERIENCE AS A CORE TEACHER. AWARD IS INTENDED TO SUPPORT RESEARCH THAT PROMOTES DEVELOPMENT OF CORE CURRICULUM.

WRITE FOR COMPLETE INFORMATION.

94

NATIONAL ASSOCIATION FOR WOMEN DEANS ADMINISTRATORS AND COUNSELORS (RUTH STRANG RESEARCH AWARD)

1325 18TH ST NW SUITE 210
WASHINGTON DC 20036
202/659-9330

AMOUNT: $500

DEADLINE(S): NOV 1

FIELD(S): EDUCATION ADMINISTRATION

WOMEN. RESEARCH MANUSCRIPT AWARDS COMPETITION OPEN TO BEGINNING PROFESSIONALS. THE NATURE OF THE PAPER MAY BE HISTORICAL; PHILOSOPHICAL; EXPERIMENTAL; EVALUATIVE; OR DESCRIPTIVE. MUST BE UNPUBLISHED.

WRITE FOR COMPLETE INFORMATION.

95

NATIONAL COLLEGIATE ATHLETIC ASSOCIATION (NCAA ETHNIC MINORITY INTERNSHIP PROGRAM)

6201 COLLEGE BLVD
OVERLAND PARK KS 66211
913/339-1906

AMOUNT: $1300 PER MONTH (INCLUDES $200 HOUSING ALLOWANCE)

DEADLINE(S): FEB 15

FIELD(S): SPORTS ADMINISTRATION; COACHING; OFFICIATING

INTERNSHIPS OF APPROXIMATELY ONE YEAR AT THE NCAA NATIONAL OFFICE OPEN TO MEMBERS OF ETHNIC MINORITIES WHO HAVE COMPLETED THE REQUIREMENTS FOR AN UNDERGRADUATE DEGREE AND HAVE DEMONSTRATED AN IN A CAREER IN THE ADMINISTRATION OF ATHLETICS.

WRITE FOR COMPLETE INFORMATION.

96

NATIONAL STRENGTH & CONDITIONING ASSN (CHALLENGE SCHOLARSHIPS)

PO BOX 81410
LINCOLN NE 68501
402/472-3000

AMOUNT: $1000

DEADLINE(S): APR 17

FIELD(S): FIELDS RELATED TO STRENGTH & CONDITIONING

OPEN TO NATIONAL STRENGTH & CONDITIONING ASSN MEMBERS. AWARDS ARE FOR UNDERGRADUATE OR GRADUATE STUDY.

WRITE FOR COMPLETE INFORMATION.

97 ─────────────────────────

NORTH CAROLINA DEPARTMENT OF PUBLIC INSTRUCTION (SCHOLARSHIP LOAN PROGRAM FOR PROSPECTIVE TEACHERS)

116 W EDENTON ST;
OFFICE OF TEACHER EDUCATION
RALEIGH NC 27603
919/733-0701

AMOUNT: UP TO $2000 PER YEAR

DEADLINE(S): FEB 10

FIELD(S): EDUCATION - TEACHING

OPEN TO NC STUDENTS INTERESTED IN TEACHING IN NC PUBLIC SCHOOLS. AWARDS ARE BASED ON ACADEMIC PERFORMANCE; SCORES ON STANDARDIZED TESTS; CLASS RANK; CONGRESSIONAL DISTRICT; AND RECOMMENDATIONS. USA CITIZENSHIP REQUIRED.

200 AWARDS PER YEAR. WRITE FOR COMPLETE INFORMATION.

98 ─────────────────────────

OREGON PTA (TEACHER EDUCATION SCHOLARSHIPS)

531 S.E. 14TH
PORTLAND OR 97214
503/234-3928

AMOUNT: $250

DEADLINE(S): MAR 1

FIELD(S): EDUCATION

OPEN TO OUTSTANDING STUDENTS WHO ARE OREGON RESIDENTS AND ARE PREPARING TO TEACH IN OREGON AT THE ELEMENTARY OR SECONDARY SCHOOL LEVEL. THE SCHOLARSHIPS MAY BE USED TO ATTEND ANY OREGON PUBLIC COLLEGE.

WRITE FOR COMPLETE INFORMATION.

99 ─────────────────────────

ORGANIZATION OF AMERICAN STATES DEPT OF FELLOWSHIPS & TRAINING (OAS PRA-FELLOWSHIPS)

TRAINEE SELECTION DIVISION
WASHINGTON DC 20006
202/789-3902

AMOUNT: TUITION + FEES; TRAVEL EXP & STIPEND

DEADLINE(S): APR 30; AUG 31

FIELD(S): ALL FIELDS EXCEPT MEDICINE & FOREIGN LANGUAGES

GRADUATE FELLOWSHIPS FOR USA CITIZENS OR PERMANENT RESIDENTS TO STUDY IN AN OAS MEMBER COUNTRY. MUST HAVE UNDERGRADUATE DEGREE AND HAVE DEMONSTRATED ABILITY TO PURSUE ADVANCED STUDIES IN CHOSEN FIELD.

APPLICANTS SHOULD BE FLUENT IN LANGUAGE OF COUNTRY OF INTENDED STUDY. PRIORITY IS GIVEN TO RESEARCH PROJECTS. WRITE FOR COMPLETE INFORMATION.

100 ─────────────────────────

PHI DELTA KAPPA (HOWARD M. SOULE GRADUATE FELLOWSHIPS IN EDUCATIONAL LEADERSHIP)

DIRECTOR OF CHAPTER PROGRAMS; PO BOX 789
BLOOMINGTON IN 47402
WRITTEN INQUIRY

AMOUNT: $1500 (2); $750 (1); $500 (2)

DEADLINE(S): MAY 1

FIELD(S): EDUCATION

OPEN TO PHI DELTA KAPPA MEMBERS IN GOOD STANDING FOR COMPLETION OF MASTER'S; SPECIALIST OR DOCTORAL DEGREES WHICH WILL ENHANCE THE MEMBER'S LEADERSHIP SKILLS IN THE EDUCATION PROFESSION.

WRITE FOR COMPLETE INFORMATION.

101 ─────────────────────────

SOCIAL SCIENCE RESEARCH COUNCIL (INTERNATIONAL PREDISSERTATION FELLOWSHIP PROGRAM)

ELLEN PERECMAN; 605 THIRD AVE.
NEW YORK NY 10158
212-661-0280

AMOUNT: VARIES

DEADLINE(S): TO BE ANNOUNCED BY PARTICIPATING UNIVERSITIES

FIELD(S): ECONOMICS; POLITICAL SCIENCE; PSYCHOLOGY SOCIOLOGY; OTHER SOCIAL SCIENCE DISCIPLINES

OPEN TO PH.D CANDIDATES ENROLLED IN SOCIAL SCIENCES PROGRAMS AT SELECTED UNIVERSITIES. STUDENTS SHOULD BE INTERESTED IN SUPPLEMENTING THEIR DISCIPLINARY SKILLS WITH AREA AND LANGUAGE STUDIES.

FELLOWS UNDERTAKE A PROGRAM OF STUDY IN OR ON AFRICA; CHINA; LATIN AMERICA; THE CARIBBEAN; THE NEAR & MIDDLE EAST; SOUTH ASIA OR SOUTHEAST ASIA. WRITE FOR COMPLETE INFORMATION.

EDUCATION

102

SWEDISH INFORMATION SERVICE (BICENTENNIAL FUND GRANTS)

ONE DAG HAMMARSKJOLD PLAZA;
45TH FLOOR
NEW YORK NY 10017
212/751-5900

AMOUNT: 20000 SWEDISH KRONA

DEADLINE(S): FEB 1

FIELD(S): POLITICAL SCIENCE; BUSINESS ADMIN; EDUCATION; COMMUNICATION; CULTURE; ENVIRONMENTAL STUDIES

GRANTS TO PROVIDE THE OPPORTUNITY FOR THOSE IN A POSITION TO INFLUENCE PUBLIC OPINION AND CONTRIBUTE TO THE DEVELOPMENT OF THEIR SOCIETY. 3-6 WEEK INTENSIVE STUDY VISITS IN SWEDEN IN ANY OF THE ABOVE AREAS OR THEIR RELATED FIELDS.

US CITIZEN OR LEGAL RESIDENT. APPROXIMATELY 10 GRANTS PER YEAR. WRITE FOR COMPLETE INFORMATION.

103

TEACHERS COLLEGE AT COLUMBIA UNIVERSITY (JOSEPH KLINGENSTEIN FELLOWSHIP PROGRAM)

BOX 125
NEW YORK NY 10027
212/678-3156

AMOUNT: $11000 TUITION ALLOWANCE; $22000 STIPEND

DEADLINE(S): JAN 15

FIELD(S): EDUCATION-INDEPENDENT SECONDARY

GRADUATE FELLOWSHIPS AT THE UNIVERSITY OPEN TO TEACHERS CURRENTLY WORKING IN INDEPENDENT SECONDARY SCHOOLS WHO HAVE MORE THAN FIVE YEARS OF TEACHING EXPERIENCE.

12 1-YEAR FELLOWSHIPS PER YEAR. WRITE FOR COMPLETE INFORMATION.

104

TECHNOLOGY STUDENT ASSOCIATION (SCHOLARSHIPS)

1914 ASSOCIATION DR
RESTON VA 22091
703/860-9000

AMOUNT: $250 - $500

DEADLINE(S): MAY 1

FIELD(S): TECHNOLOGY EDUCATION

OPEN TO STUDENT MEMBERS OF THE TECHNOLOGY STUDENT ASSOCIATION WHO CAN DEMONSTRATE FINANCIAL NEED. GRADE POINT AVERAGE IS -NOT- A CONSIDERATION BUT APPLICANTS MUST BE ACCEPTED TO A 4-YEAR COLLEGE OR UNIVERSITY.

FUNDS ARE SENT TO AND ADMINISTERED BY THE RECIPIENT'S COLLEGE OR UNIVERSITY. WRITE FOR COMPLETE INFORMATION.

105

TUSKEGEE INSTITUTE (GRADUATE RESEARCH FELLOWSHIPS AND ASSISTANTSHIPS)

ADMISSIONS OFFICE
TUSKEGEE INSTITUTE AL 36088
205/727-8500

AMOUNT: TUITION

DEADLINE(S): MAR 15

FIELD(S): CHEMISTRY; ENGINEERING; ENVIRONMENTAL SCIENCE; LIFE SCIENCES; NUTRITION; EDUCATION

GRADUATE RESEARCH FELLOWSHIPS AND GRADUATE ASSISTANTSHIPS ARE AVAILABLE TO QUALIFIED INDIVIDUALS WHO WISH TO ENTER TUSKEGEE INSTITUTE'S GRADUATE PROGRAM IN PURSUIT OF A MASTER'S DEGREE.

WRITE FOR COMPLETE INFORMATION.

106

UNITED COMMERCIAL TRAVELERS OF AMERICA (GRADUATE SCHOLARSHIP PROGRAM)

632 NORTH PARK STREET
COLUMBUS OH 43215
614/228-3276

AMOUNT: $750 PER YEAR

DEADLINE(S): NONE

FIELD(S): SPECIAL EDUCATION

OPEN TO UNDERGRADUATE JUNIORS & SENIORS; GRADUATE STUDENTS; TEACHERS & PERSONS WHO PLAN TO TEACH THE MENTALLY RETARDED. AWARDS TENABLE AT ACCREDITED INSTITUTIONS. USA OR CANADIAN CITIZEN.

APPROX 500 AWARDS PER YEAR. PREFERENCE TO (BUT NOT LIMITED TO) UCT MEMBERS. WRITE FOR COMPLETE INFORMATION.

107

UNITED METHODIST CHURCH (ESTHER EDWARDS GRADUATE SCHOLARSHIPS)

PO BOX 871;
OFFICE OF LOANS & SCHOLARSHIPS
NASHVILLE TN 37202
615/340-7344

AMOUNT: $5000

DEADLINE(S): MAR 1

FIELD(S): EDUCATION ADMINISTRATION

OPEN TO WOMEN MEMBERS OF UNITED
METHODIST CHURCH WHO ARE ENROLLED
IN A FULL TIME GRADUATE PROGRAM IN
PREPARATION FOR A CAREER IN HIGHER
EDUCATION ADMINISTRATION WITH A
UNITED METHODIST COLLEGE OR
UNIVERSITY. USA CITIZEN OR LEGAL
RESIDENT.

WRITE OR TELEPHONE FOR COMPLETE
INFORMATION.

108 ───────────────────────

**WOODROW WILSON NATIONAL FELLOWSHIP
FOUNDATION (NEWCOMBE DISSERTATION
FELLOWSHIPS)**

BOX 642
PRINCETON NJ 08542
609/924-4666

AMOUNT: $12000 STIPEND

DEADLINE(S): DEC 13

FIELD(S): SOCIAL SCIENCES; HUMANITIES;
EDUCATION

OPEN TO PH.D; TH.D & ED.D CANDIDATES IN THE
USA WHO WILL COMPLETE ALL DOCTORAL
REQUIREMENTS EXCEPT THE DISSERTATION
BY NOV 29. THESE AWARDS ARE NOT
DESIGNED TO FINANCE FIELD WORK BUT
RATHER THE COMPLETION OF DISSERTATION
WRITING.

ELIGIBLE PROPOSALS WILL HAVE ETHICAL OR
RELIGIOUS VALUES AS A CENTRAL
CONCERN. REQUEST APPLICATION BY NOV.
29. WRITE FOR COMPLETE INFORMATION.

109 ───────────────────────

**WOODROW WILSON NATIONAL FELLOWSHIP
FOUNDATION (SPENCER DISSERTATION
YEAR FELLOWSHIPS)**

BOX 410
PRINCETON NJ 08542
609/924-4666

AMOUNT: $15000 STIPEND

DEADLINE(S): NOV 15

FIELD(S): EDUCATION

OPEN TO PH.D OR ED.D CANDIDATES WHO WILL
SOON COMPLETE ALL DOCTORAL
REQUIREMENTS EXCEPT DISSERTATION.
AWARDS ARE NOT DESIGNED TO FINANCE
DATA COLLECTION BUT RATHER LAST FULL
YEAR OF RESEARCH/WRITING LEADING TO
DISSERTATION COMPLETION.

FOR USA OR CANADIAN CITIZENS ENROLLED IN
AN ACCREDITED DOCTORAL PROGRAM IN
USA. APPROX 30 FELLOWSHIPS PER YEAR.
WRITE FOR COMPLETE INFORMATION.

110 ───────────────────────

**WORLD LEISURE & RECREATION ASSN (TOM &
RUTH RIVERS SCHOLARSHIP PROGRAM)**

PO BOX 309
SHARBOT LAKE ONTARIO K0H 2P0 CANADA
613/279-3173

AMOUNT: VARIES

DEADLINE(S): JAN 1

FIELD(S): RECREATION; LEISURE STUDIES;
RESOURCES EDUCATION

SCHOLARSHIPS INTENDED TO ALLOW COLLEGE
SENIORS OR GRADUATE STUDENTS IN
RECREATION OR LEISURE SERVICES
PROGRAMS TO ATTEND INTERNATIONAL
MEETINGS/CONFERENCES OR CONVENTIONS
THEREBY GAINING A BROADER
PERSPECTIVE OF WORLD LEISURE &
RECREATION.

WRITE FOR COMPLETE INFORMATION.

SCHOOL OF ENGINEERING

111 ───────────────────────

**AEROSPACE EDUCATION FOUNDATION
(THEODORE VON KARMAN GRADUATE
SCHOLARSHIP PROGRAM)**

1501 LEE HIGHWAY
ARLINGTON VA 22209
703/247-5839

AMOUNT: $5000

DEADLINE(S): MAR 1

FIELD(S): SCIENCE; MATHEMATICS;
ENGINEERING

OPEN TO AIR FORCE ROTC GRADUATE STUDENTS
WHO WILL PURSUE ADVANCED DEGREES IN
THE FIELDS OF SCIENCE; MATHEMATICS;
PHYSICS; OR ENGINEERING. USA CITIZEN OR
LEGAL RESIDENT.

10 AWARDS PER YEAR BASED ON APTITUDE;
ATTITUDE AND CAREER PLANS. WRITE FOR
COMPLETE INFORMATION.

112 ───────────────────────

**AMERICAN ASSOCIATION FOR THE
ADVANCEMENT OF SCIENCE (SCIENCE &
ENGINEERING FELLOWSHIPS)**

1333 'H' STREET NW
WASHINGTON DC 20005
202/326-6600

AMOUNT: UP TO $38500

DEADLINE(S): JAN 15

SCHOOL OF ENGINEERING

FIELD(S): SCIENCE; ENGINEERING

POST-DOCTORAL FELLOWSHIPS OPEN TO AAAS MEMBERS OR APPLICANTS CONCURRENTLY APPLYING FOR MEMBERSHIP. PROSPECTIVE FELLOWS MUST DEMONSTRATE EXCEPTIONAL COMPETENCE IN AN AREA OF SCIENCE OR HAVE A BROAD SCIENTIFIC OR TECHNICAL BACKGROUND.

ONE-YEAR FELLOWSHIPS. SEND INQUIRIES TO PROGRAM DIRECTOR; CONGRESSIONAL SCIENCE FELLOWS PROGRAM; ADDRESS ABOVE.

113

AMERICAN ASSOCIATION OF UNIVERSITY WOMEN (SCIENCE & TECHNOLOGY GROUP - SELECTED PROFESSIONS FELLOWSHIPS)

1111 16TH STREET NW
WASHINGTON DC 20036
202/728-7603; FAX 202/872-1430

AMOUNT: $5000 - $9500

DEADLINE(S): DEC 15 (POSTMARK)

FIELD(S): ARCHITECTURE; COMPUTER/ INFORMATION SCIENCE; ENGINEERING; MATHEMATICS/STATISTICS

OPEN TO WOMEN WHO ARE USA CITIZENS OR PERMANENT RESIDENTS WHO ARE IN THEIR FINAL YEAR OF A MASTER'S DEGREE IN THE ABOVE AREAS. APPLICATIONS AVAILABLE AUG 1 - DEC 1.

WRITE FOR COMPLETE INFORMATION.

114

AMERICAN WATER WORKS ASSOCIATION (ABEL WOLMAN FELLOWSHIP)

6666 W. QUINCY
DENVER CO 80235
303/794-7711

AMOUNT: $10000

DEADLINE(S): JAN 15

FIELD(S): ENGINEERING

OPEN TO ENGINEERING STUDENTS WHO SHOW POTENTIAL FOR LEADERSHIP AND ANTICIPATE COMPLETION OF THE REQUIREMENTS FOR A MASTER'S OR PH.D DEGREE WITHIN TWO YEARS OF THE AWARD. MUST BE CITIZEN OR PERMANENT RESIDENT OF THE USA; CANADA OR MEXICO.

WRITE FOR COMPLETE INFORMATION.

115

AMERICAN WATER WORKS ASSOCIATION (HOLLY A. CORNELL SCHOLARSHIP)

6666 W. QUINCY
DENVER CO 80235
303/794-7711

AMOUNT: $5000

DEADLINE(S): JAN 15

FIELD(S): ENGINEERING

OPEN TO FEMALES AND MINORITIES (AS DEFINED BY THE U.S. EQUAL OPPORTUNITY COMMISSION) WHO ANTICIPATE COMPLETION OF A MASTER'S DEGREE IN ENGINEERING NO SOONER THAN DECEMBER OF THE FOLLOWING YEAR.

WRITE FOR COMPLETE INFORMATION.

116

ARGONNE NATIONAL LABORATORY (STUDENT RESEARCH PARTICIPATION PROGRAM; THESIS RESEARCH)

DIV OF EDUCATIONAL PROGRAMS;
9700 SOUTH CASS AVE
ARGONNE IL 60439
312/972-3366

AMOUNT: $200 PER WEEK STIPEND

DEADLINE(S): FEB 1; MAY 15; OCT 15

FIELD(S): PHYSICAL SCIENCES; LIFE SCIENCES; EARTH SCIENCES; MATHEMATICS; COMPUTER SCIENCES; ENGINEERING; FUSION & FISSION ENERGY

1-SEMESTER ACCREDITED INTERNSHIP PROGRAM TO PERMIT STUDENTS TO WORK IN ABOVE AREAS IN RELATION TO ENERGY DEVELOPMENT. OPEN TO FULL-TIME UNDERGRAD JUNIORS; SENIORS & 1ST YEAR GRAD STUDENTS. USA CITIZEN OR LEGAL RESIDENT.

THESIS RESEARCH AWARDS OPEN TO DOCTORAL CANDIDATES WORKING ON THEIR DISSERTATION. WRITE FOR COMPLETE INFORMATION.

117

ASSOCIATION FOR WOMEN IN SCIENCE EDUCATIONAL FOUNDATION (AWIS PRE-DOCTORAL AWARDS)

1522 K STREET NW SUITE 820
WASHINGTON DC 20005
202/408-0742

AMOUNT: $500

DEADLINE(S): JAN 15

FIELD(S): ENGINEERING; LIFE SCIENCES; MATHEMATICS; PHYSICAL SCIENCES; BEHAVIORAL SCIENCES; SOCIAL SCIENCES

SCHOLARSHIP AID & INCENTIVE AWARDS OPEN TO WOMEN WHO ARE WORKING ACTIVELY TOWARDS A DOCTORAL DEGREE IN THE ABOVE AREAS. USA CITIZENS MAY STUDY IN USA OR ABROAD; NON-CITIZENS MUST BE ENROLLED IN USA INSTITUTION.

APPLICATIONS ARE AVAILABLE OCT 1 - DEC 15. WRITE FOR COMPLETE INFORMATION.

118

BUSINESS AND PROFESSIONAL WOMEN'S FOUNDATION (BPW LOANS FOR WOMEN IN ENGINEERING STUDIES)

2012 MASSACHUSETTS AVE NW
WASHINGTON DC 20036
202/293-1200

AMOUNT: UP TO $5000 PER YEAR

DEADLINE(S): APR 15 POSTMARK (APPLICATIONS AVAILABLE -ONLY- OCT 1 - APR 1)

FIELD(S): ENGINEERING

OPEN TO WOMEN WHO ARE ACCEPTED FOR UNDERGRADUATE OR GRADUATE LEVEL STUDY IN A PROGRAM ACCREDITED BY THE ACCREDITATION BOARD FOR ENGINEERING AND TECHNOLOGY. FOR LAST 2 YEARS OF STUDY. USA CITIZEN.

MUST DEMONSTRATE FINANCIAL NEED. APPLICATRIONS AVAILABLE -ONLY- BETWEEN OCT 1 AND APR 1. SEND SELF-ADDRESSED STAMPED ($.52) #10 ENVELOPE FOR APPLICATION & COMPLETE INFORMATION.

119

BUSINESS AND PROFESSIONAL WOMEN'S FOUNDATION (CAREER ADVANCEMENT SCHOLARSHIPS)

2012 MASSACHUSETTS AVE NW
WASHINGTON DC 20036
202/293-1200

AMOUNT: $500 - $1000

DEADLINE(S): APR 15 POSTMARK (APPS AVAILABLE -ONLY- OCT 1 - APR 1)

FIELD(S): COMPUTER SCIENCE; EDUCATION; PARALEGAL; ENGINEERING; SCIENCE (EXCEPT HEALTH CARE)

OPEN TO WOMEN (30 OR OLDER) WITHIN 12-24 MONTHS OF COMPLETING UNDERGRAD OR GRAD STUDY IN USA (INCLUDING PUERTO RICO & THE VIRGIN ISLANDS). SHOULD LEAD TO ENTRY OR REENTRY INTO THE WORK FORCE OR IMPROVE CAREER ADVANCEMENT CHANCES.

MUST SHOW FINANCIAL NEED. SEND SELF-ADDRESSED STAMPED ($.52) #10 ENVELOPE FOR APPLICATION & COMPLETE INFORMATION. NOT FOR STUDY AT DOCTORAL LEVEL.

120

COMMITTEE ON INSTITUTIONAL COOPERATION (CIC PREDOCTORAL FELLOWSHIPS)

KIRKWOOD HALL RM 111; INDIANA UNIV.
BLOOMINGTON IN 47405
812/855-0822

AMOUNT: $9500 + TUITION (5 YEARS)

DEADLINE(S): JAN 2

FIELD(S): HUMANITIES; SOCIAL SCIENCES; NATURAL SCIENCES; MATHEMATICS; ENGINEERING

PREDOCTORAL FELLOWSHIPS FOR USA CITIZENS OF AFRICAN AMERICAN; AMERICAN INDIAN; MEXICAN AMERICAN OR PUERTO RICAN HERITAGE. MUST HOLD OR EXPECT TO RECEIVE BACHELOR'S DEGREE BY LATE SUMMER FROM A REGIONALLY ACCREDITED COLLEGE OR UNIVERSITY.

AWARDS FOR SPECIFIED UNIVERSITIES IN IL; IN; IA; MI; MN; OH; WI; PA. WRITE FOR DETAILS.

121

CONGRESSIONAL FELLOWSHIP PROGRAM (MORRIS K. UDALL FELLOWSHIPS)

CONGRESS OF THE UNITED STATES; OFFICE OF TECHNOLOGY ASSESSMENT
WASHINGTON DC 20510
202/224-8713

AMOUNT: $35000 - $70000

DEADLINE(S): JAN 31

FIELD(S): PHYSICAL OR BIOLOGICAL SCIENCES; ENGINEERING; LAW; ECONOMICS; ENVIRONMENTAL OR SOCIAL SCIENCES; PUBLIC POLICY

ONE YEAR FELLOWSHIP PROGRAM HELD -ONLY- IN WASHINGTO DC. CANDIDATES MUST HAVE EXTENSIVE EXPERIENCE IN SCIENCE OR TECHNOLOGY ISSUES OR HAVE COMPLETED DOCTORAL LEVEL RESEARCH. EXCEPTIONAL COMPETENCY IN ABOVE AREAS REQUIRED.

CONSIDERATIONS INCLUDE ACHIEVEMENT RECORDS AND CANDIDATE'S POTENTIAL IN ONE OR MORE OF OTA'S ASSESSMENT STUDIES. WRITE FOR COMPLETE INFORMATION.

122

ENGINEERING FOUNDATION (ENGINEERING RESEARCH INITIATION GRANTS)

345 E. 47TH ST
NEW YORK NY 10017
212/705-7835

AMOUNT: $23000

DEADLINE(S): NOV 15

FIELD(S): ENGINEERING

GRADUATE & POST-GRADUATE GRANTS FOR RESEARCH PROJECTS IN THE GENERAL FIELD OF ENGINEERING OPEN TO NEW ENGINEERING FACULTY MEMBERS HAVING PROJECTS IN AREAS OF INTEREST TO ASCE; AIME; ASME; IEEE OR AICHE.

QUALIFIED INDIVIDUALS; ORGANIZATIONS AND TECHNICAL SOCIETIES ALSO MAY APPLY. WRITE FOR COMPLETE INFORMATION.

123

FANNIE AND JOHN HERTZ FOUNDATION (DOCTORAL FELLOWSHIP PROGRAM)

BOX 5032
LIVERMORE CA 94551
510/373-1642

AMOUNT: UP TO $10000 FOR TUITION + $16000 STIPEND

DEADLINE(S): NOV 1

FIELD(S): ENGINEERING; APPLIED PHYSICS; MATHEMATICS; CHEMISTRY

FELLOWSHIPS OPEN TO STUDENTS PURSUING A PH.D OR A PROFESSIONAL DEGREE IN THE ABOVE AREAS WITH A 3.75 OR BETTER GPA. STUDENTS PURSUING A JOINT DEGREE SUCH AS PH.D/MD ARE NOT ELIGIBLE TO APPLY. USA CITIZEN.

25 FELLOWSHIPS PER YEAR RENEWABLE UP TO FIVE YEARS. WRITE FOR COMPLETE INFORMATION.

124

FLORIDA ENDOWMENT FUND FOR HIGHER EDUCATION (MCKNIGHT DOCTORAL FELLOWSHIP PROGRAM)

201 E.KENNEDY BLVD; SUITE 1525
TAMPA FL 33602
813/272-2772

AMOUNT: $11000 STIPEND + $5000 TUITION & FEES (PER YEAR)

DEADLINE(S): JAN 15

FIELD(S): ALL FIELDS (EXCEPT LAW; MEDICINE & EDUCATION)

OPEN TO ALL AFRICAN-AMERICANS WITH AT LEAST A BACHELOR'S DEGREE FROM AN ACCREDITED INSTITUTION WHO WISH TO PURSUE A DOCTORAL DEGREE. PROGRAM RECRUITS NATIONWIDE; HOWEVER FELLOWS MUST ENROLL IN A FLORIDA INSTITUTION. USA CITIZEN.

25 AWARDS PER YEAR. RENEWABLE FOR UP TO 5 YEARS. WRITE FOR COMPLETE INFORMATION.

125

FOUNDATION FOR SCIENCE & THE HANDICAPPED (GRANTS PROGRAM)

C/O REBECCA F. SMITH;
115 S. BRAINARD AVE.
LA GRANGE IL 60525
708/352-1091

AMOUNT: $1000

DEADLINE(S): DEC 1

FIELD(S): SCIENCE; MATHEMATICS; MEDICINE; COMPUTER SCIENCE; ENGINEERING

OPEN TO GRADUATE STUDENTS IN THE ABOVE AREAS WHO HAVE SOME PHYSICAL OR SENSORY DISABILITY. APPLICATIONS WILL ALSO BE ACCEPTED FROM UNDERGRADUATE SENIORS WHO HAVE BEEN ACCEPTED TO GRADUATE SCHOOL. USA CITIZEN OR LEGAL RESIDENT.

WRITE FOR COMPLETE INFORMATION.

126

H. FLETCHER BROWN FUND (SCHOLARSHIPS)

C/O BANK OF DELAWARE; TRUST DEPT; PO BOX 791
WILMINGTON DE 19899
302/429-2827

AMOUNT: VARIES

DEADLINE(S): APR 15

FIELD(S): MEDICINE; DENTISTRY; LAW; ENGINEERING; CHEMISTRY

OPEN TO STUDENTS BORN IN DELAWARE; GRADUATED FROM A DELAWARE HIGH SCHOOL & STILL RESIDING IN DELAWARE. FOR FOUR YEARS OF STUDY (UNDERGRAD OR GRAD) LEADING TO A DEGREE THAT ENABLES APPLICANT TO PRACTICE IN CHOSEN FIELD.

SCHOLARSHIPS ARE BASED ON NEED; SCHOLASTIC ACHIEVEMENT; GOOD MORAL CHARACTER. RENEWABLE. WRITE FOR COMPLETE INFORMATION.

127

NATIONAL CONSORTIUM FOR GRADUATE DEGREES FOR MINORITIES IN ENGINEERING & SCIENCE INC. (FELLOWSHIPS)

PO BOX 537
NOTRE DAME IN 46556
219/287-1097; FAX 219/287-1486

AMOUNT: FULL TUITION & FEES + ANNUAL STIPEND

DEADLINE(S): DEC 1

FIELD(S): ENGINEERING; NATURAL SCIENCES

MASTERS & DOCTORATE FELLOWSHIPS FOR ETHNIC/RACIAL MINORITIES (BLACK AMERICAN; MEXICAN AMERICAN; PUERTO RICAN; AMERICAN INDIAN). MUST BE USA CITIZEN AT TIME OF APPLICATION.

250 FELLOWSHIPS PER YEAR. ADDRESS INQUIRIES TO HOWARD G. ADAMS; EXECUTIVE DIRECTOR.

128

NATIONAL RESEARCH COUNCIL (NATIONAL SCIENCE FOUNDATION MINORITY GRADUATE FELLOWSHIPS)

2101 CONSTITUTION AVE.
WASHINGTON DC 20418
202/334-2872

AMOUNT: $14000 STIPEND (12 MONTHS) + UP TO $7500 FOR TUITION AND FEES

DEADLINE(S): NOV 6

FIELD(S): ENGINEERING; MATHEMATICS; COMPUTER SCIENCE; CHEMISTRY; EARTH SCIENCES; LIFE SCIENCES; PSYCHOLOGY; SOCIAL SCIENCES

OPEN MINORITY GRADUATE STUDENTS (MASTERS OR PH.D) WHO ARE USA CITIZENS OR LEGAL RESIDENTS & ARE AT OR NEAR THE BEGINNING OF THEIR GRADUATE STUDY. FELLOWSHIPS TENABLE AT ACCREDITED INSTITUTION OFFERING ADVANCED DEGREES IN THE FIELDS ABOVE.

APPROX 150 NEW 3-YEAR FELLOWSHIPS AWARDED EACH YEAR. WRITE FOR COMPLETE INFORMATION.

129

NATIONAL RESEARCH COUNCIL (NATIONAL SCIENCE FOUNDATION GRADUATE FELLOWSHIPS)

2101 CONSTITUTION AVE
WASHINGTON DC 20418
202/334-2872

AMOUNT: $14000 STIPEND + $7000 TUITION ALLOWANCE

DEADLINE(S): NOV 10

FIELD(S): SOCIAL SCIENCES; PHYSICAL SCIENCES; MATHEMATICS; BIOLOGY; ENGINEERING

DOCTORAL) WHO HAVE NOT COMPLETED MORE THAN 1 YEAR OF GRAD STUDY. FELLOWSHIPS TENABLE AT ANY ACCREDITED INSTITUTION OFFERING ADVANCED DEGREES IN THE AREAS ABOVE. USA CITIZEN OR PERMANENT RESIDENT.

OPEN TO HISTORY & PHILOSOPHY OF SCIENCE STUDENTS ALSO. 950 NEW 3-YEAR FELLOWSHIPS AWARDED EACH YEAR. WRITE FOR COMPLETE INFORMATION.

130

NATIONAL RESEARCH COUNCIL (NRC POSTDOCTORAL & SENIOR RESEARCH ASSOCIATESHIP AWARDS)

ASSOCIATESHIP PROGRAMS GR430/D3; 2101 CONSTITUTION AVE. NW
WASHINGTON DC 20418
202/334-2760

AMOUNT: ANNUAL STIPEND FROM 27750 TO 44000 + BENEFITS

DEADLINE(S): JAN 15; APR 15; AUG 15

FIELD(S): CHEMISTRY; EARTH & ATMOSPHERIC SCIENCES; ENGINEERING & APPLIED SCIENCES; COMPUTER SCIENCE; MATHEMATICS; BIOLOGICAL & MEDICAL SCIENCES SPACE & PLANETARY SCIENCES; PHYSICS

POSTDOCTORAL & SENIOR ASSOCIATESHIP AWARDS FOR RESEARCH AT ONE OF 38 PARTICIPATING SPONSOR FEDERAL LABORATORIES. USA CITIZENSHIP REQUIRED FOR SOME OF THE SPONSOR LABORATORIES; MANY ARE OPEN TO FOREIGN NATIONALS.

WRITE FOR COMPLETE INFORMATION AND APPLICATION MATERIALS.

131

NORTH ATLANTIC TREATY ORGANIZATION (NATO SCIENCE FELLOWSHIPS FOR USA CITIZENS)

B-1110; SCIENCE AFFAIRS DIV
BRUSSELS BELGIUM
2 728-41-11

AMOUNT: VARIES WITH COUNTRY

DEADLINE(S): NOV 1

FIELD(S): SCIENCES

GRADUATE & POST-DOCTORAL FELLOWSHIPS IN ALMOST ALL SCIENTIFIC AREAS; INCLUDING INTERDISCIPLINARY AREAS. OPEN TO USA CITIZENS WHO WISH TO STUDY AND/OR DO RESEARCH IN ANOTHER NATO MEMBER COUNTRY.

THE PROGRAM IS ADMINISTERED IN EACH NATO COUNTRY BY A NATIONAL ADMINISTRATOR. WRITE FOR COMPLETE INFORMATION.

132

NORTH CAROLINA STUDENT LOAN PROGRAM FOR HEALTH; SCIENCE; & MATHEMATICS (LOANS)

3824 BARRETT DR.; SUITE 304
RALEIGH NC 27619
919/733-2164

AMOUNT: $2500 - $7500 PER YEAR

DEADLINE(S): JAN 8 - MAY 5

FIELD(S): HEALTH PROFESSIONS; SCIENCES; ENGINEERING

LOW-INTEREST SCHOLARSHIP LOANS OPEN TO NORTH CAROLINA RESIDENTS OF AT LEAST 1 YEAR WHO ARE PURSUING AN ASSOCIATES; UNDERGRADUATE OR GRADUATE DEGREE IN THE ABOVE FIELDS AT AN ACCREDITED INSTITUTION IN THE USA.

LOANS MAY BE RETIRED AFTER GRADUATION BY WORKING (1 YEAR FOR EACH YEAR FUNDED) AT DESIGNATED INSTITUTIONS. WRITE FOR COMPLETE DETAILS.

133 ORGANIZATION OF AMERICAN STATES DEPT OF FELLOWSHIPS & TRAINING (OAS PRA-FELLOWSHIPS)

TRAINEE SELECTION DIVISION
WASHINGTON DC 20006
202/789-3902

AMOUNT: TUITION + FEES; TRAVEL EXP & STIPEND

DEADLINE(S): APR 30; AUG 31

FIELD(S): ALL FIELDS EXCEPT MEDICINE & FOREIGN LANGUAGES

GRADUATE FELLOWSHIPS FOR USA CITIZENS OR PERMANENT RESIDENTS TO STUDY IN AN OAS MEMBER COUNTRY. MUST HAVE UNDERGRADUATE DEGREE AND HAVE DEMONSTRATED ABILITY TO PURSUE ADVANCED STUDIES IN CHOSEN FIELD.

APPLICANTS SHOULD BE FLUENT IN LANGUAGE OF COUNTRY OF INTENDED STUDY. PRIORITY IS GIVEN TO RESEARCH PROJECTS. WRITE FOR COMPLETE INFORMATION.

134 ROBERT SCHRECK MEMORIAL FUND (GRANTS)

C/O TEXAS COMMERCE BANK-TRUST DEPT; PO DRAWER 140
EL PASO TX 79980
915/546-6515

AMOUNT: $500 - $1500

DEADLINE(S): JUL 15; NOV 15

FIELD(S): MEDICINE; VETERINARY MEDICINE; PHYSICS; CHEMISTRY; ARCHITECTURE; ENGINEERING; EPISCOPAL CLERGY

GRANTS TO UNDERGRADUATE JUNIORS OR SENIORS OR GRADUATE STUDENTS WHO HAVE BEEN RESIDENTS OF EL PASO COUNTY FOR AT LEAST TWO YEARS. MUST BE USA CITIZEN OR LEGAL RESIDENT AND HAVE A HIGH GRADE POINT AVERAGE. FINANCIAL NEED IS A CONSIDERATION.

WRITE FOR COMPLETE INFORMATION.

135 SAE EDUCATIONAL RELATIONS (FORGIVABLE LOANS FOR ENGINEERING STUDENTS)

400 COMMONWEALTH DRIVE
WARRENDALE PA 15096
412/776-4841

AMOUNT: UP TO $5000

DEADLINE(S): APR 1

FIELD(S): ENGINEERING

THE PROGRAM PROVIDES FUNDING TO ASSIST AND ENCOURAGE PROMISING ENGINEERING GRADUATE STUDENTS TO PURSUE TEACHING CAREERS AT THE COLLEGE LEVEL. FOR CITIZENS OF USA; CANADA AND MEXICO WHO ARE ENROLLED IN DOCTORAL PROGRAM. LOANS ARE RENEWABLE.

MUST BE U.S. CANADIAN OR MEXICIAN CITIZEN. MUST BE ENROLLED IN DOCTORAL PROGRAM. LOANS CAN BE RENEWED.

136 SIGMA DELTA EPSILON-GRADUATE WOMEN IN SCIENCE (SDE FELLOWSHIPS; ELOISE GERRY FELLOWSHIPS)

ONE ILLINOIS CENTER;
111 E. WACKER DR.
CHICAGO IL 60601
312/616-0800

AMOUNT: $2600 - $4000 (SDE); $2300 - $2700 (ELOISE GERRY)

DEADLINE(S): DEC 1 (POSTMARK)

FIELD(S): BIOLOGY; CHEMISTRY; NATURAL SCIENCES; PHYSICAL SCIENCES; BIOLOGICAL SCIENCES; COMPUTER SCIENCES

WOMEN ONLY. OPEN TO GRADUATE STUDENTS AND POST-DOCTORAL RESEARCHERS IN THE ABOVE AREAS. FELLOWSHIPS MAY ONLY BE USED TO SUPPORT SCIENTIFIC RESEARCH AND/OR PROJECTS. FINANCIAL NEED IS A MAJOR CONSIDERATION.

ELOISE GERRY FELLOWSHIPS ARE LIMITED TO THE CHEMICAL AND BIOLOGICAL SCIENCES. WRITE FOR COMPLETE INFORMATION.

137 SOCIETY OF HISPANIC PROFESSIONAL ENGINEERS FOUNDATION (SHPE SCHOLARSHIPS)

5400 E. OLYMPIC BLVD. SUITE 306
LOS ANGELES CA 90022
213/888-2080

AMOUNT: $500 - $3000

DEADLINE(S): APR 15

FIELD(S): ENGINEERING & SCIENCE

OPEN TO DESERVING STUDENTS OF HISPANIC DESCENT WHO ARE SEEKING CAREERS IN ENGINEERING AND SCIENCE. FOR FULL TIME UNDERGRADUATE OR GRADUATE STUDY AT A COLLEGE OR UNIVERSITY. ACADEMIC ACHIEVEMENT AND FINANCIAL NEED ARE CONSIDERATIONS.

WRITE FOR COMPLETE INFORMATION.

138

SOCIETY OF WOMEN ENGINEERS (OLIVE LYNN SALEMBIER REENTRY SCHOLARSHIPS)

345 EAST 47TH STREET
NEW YORK NY 10017
212/705-7855

AMOUNT: $2000

DEADLINE(S): MAY 15

FIELD(S): ENGINEERING

OPEN TO WOMEN WHO HAVE BEEN OUT OF THE ENGINEERING JOB MARKET FOR A MINIMUM OF TWO YEARS. AWARD IS TO ENABLE RECIPIENT TO OBTAIN THE CREDENTIALS NECESSARY TO REENTER THE JOB MARKET AS AN ENGINEER. FOR ANY YEAR OF UNDERGRAD OR GRAD STUDY.

APPLICATIONS AVAILABLE MAR THROUGH APR ONLY WITH COMPLETED APPLICATION TO BE POSTMARKED BY MAY 15. SEND SELF ADDRESSED -STAMPED- ENVELOPE FOR COMPLETE INFORMATION.

139

SPACE FOUNDATION (SPACE INDUSTRIALIZATION FELLOWSHIP)

4800 RESEARCH FOREST DR
THE WOODLANDS TX 77381
713/363-7944; FAX 713/363-7914

AMOUNT: $4000

DEADLINE(S): OCT 1

FIELD(S): SCIENCES & ENGINEERING; BUSINESS; LAW; ECONOMICS; SOCIAL SCIENCES; ENVIRONMENTAL STUDIES; HUMANITIES

OPEN TO SUPERIOR GRADUATE STUDENTS IN THE ABOVE DISCIPLINES WHO INTEND TO DEVOTE THEIR CAREERS TO THE FURTHERANCE OF PRACTICAL SPACE RESEARCH; ENGINEERING; BUSINESS OR OTHER APPLICATION VENTURES.

CONTACT DR. DAVID J. NORTON; EDUCATIONAL GRANT PROGRAM CHAIRMAN; ADDRESS ABOVE; FOR COMPLETE INFORMATION.

140

TAU BETA PI ASSOCIATION INC (GRADUATE FELLOWSHIPS)

BOX 8840-UNIVERSITY STATION
KNOXVILLE TN 37996
615-546-4578

AMOUNT: $7500

DEADLINE(S): JAN 19

FIELD(S): ENGINEERING

GRADUATE AWARDS FOR MEMBERS OF TAU BETA PI WHO HOLD A BACHELOR'S DEGREE.

22 FELLOWSHIPS PER YEAR. WRITE FOR COMPLETE INFORMATION.

141

TUSKEGEE INSTITUTE (GRADUATE RESEARCH FELLOWSHIPS AND ASSISTANTSHIPS)

ADMISSIONS OFFICE
TUSKEGEE INSTITUTE AL 36088
205/727-8500

AMOUNT: TUITION

DEADLINE(S): MAR 15

FIELD(S): CHEMISTRY; ENGINEERING; ENVIRONMENTAL SCIENCE; LIFE SCIENCES; NUTRITION; EDUCATION

GRADUATE RESEARCH FELLOWSHIPS AND GRADUATE ASSISTANTSHIPS ARE AVAILABLE TO QUALIFIED INDIVIDUALS WHO WISH TO ENTER TUSKEGEE INSTITUTE'S GRADUATE PROGRAM IN PURSUIT OF A MASTER'S DEGREE.

WRITE FOR COMPLETE INFORMATION.

142

U.S. DEPT. OF EDUCATION (INDIAN FELLOWSHIP PROGRAM)

400 MARYLAND AVENUE SW; RM 2177; MAIL STOP 6335
WASHINGTON DC 20202
202/401-1902

AMOUNT: $1000 - $34000 (AVERAGE $13000)

DEADLINE(S): FEB 7

FIELD(S): BUSINESS ADMIN; ENGINEERING; NATURAL RESOURCES & RELATED AREAS

FELLOWSHIPS FOR AMERICAN INDIANS OR ALASKAN NATIVES WHO ARE US CITIZENS AND SEEKING UNDERGRADUATE OR GRADUATE DEGREES IN THE ABOVE FIELDS AT ACCREDITED INSTITUTIONS IN USA.

APPROXIMATELY 90 CONTINUATION AND 35 NEW AWARDS PER YEAR. WRITE FOR COMPLETE INFORMATION.

AERONAUTICS

143

AIR TRAFFIC CONTROL ASSOCIATION INC (SCHOLARSHIP AWARDS PROGRAM)

2300 CLARENDON BLVD #711
ARLINGTON VA 22201
703/522-5717

AMOUNT: $1500 - $2500

DEADLINE(S): AUG 1

FIELD(S): AERONAUTICS; AVIATION; RELATED AREAS

SCHOLARSHIPS OPEN TO PROMISING MEN & WOMEN WHO ARE FULL-TIME UNDERGRADUATE OR GRADUATE STUDENTS IN THE ABOVE AREAS. SCHOLARSHIPS OF UP TO $600 ALSO AVAILABLE FOR PART-TIME STUDENTS. USA CITIZEN.

FINANCIAL NEED IS A CONSIDERATION BUT NOT DETERMINATIVE. WRITE FOR COMPLETE INFORMATION.

144

AMERICAN GEOLOGICAL INSTITUTE (MINORITY PARTICIPATION PROGRAM SCHOLARSHIPS)

4220 KING ST
ALEXANDRIA VA 22302
703/379-2480

AMOUNT: UP TO $10000 PER YEAR UNDERGRAD; $4000 PER YEAR GRAD

DEADLINE(S): FEB 1

FIELD(S): EARTH SCIENCES; SPACE SCIENCES; MARINE SCIENCES

FOR FULL TIME UNDERGRADUATE OR GRADUATE STUDY IN THE ABOVE FIELDS. OPEN TO AMERICAN BLACKS; NATIVE AMERICANS & HISPANIC AMERICANS. MUST BE USA CITIZEN AND DEMONSTRATE FINANCIAL NEED.

APPROX 80 AWARDS PER YEAR. RENEWALS POSSIBLE WITH REAPPLICATION. WRITE FOR COMPLETE INFORMATION.

145

AMERICAN SOCIETY FOR ENGINEERING EDUCATION (OFFICE OF NAVAL RESEARCH GRADUATE FELLOWSHIP PROGRAM)

ELEVEN DUPONT CIRCLE #200
WASHINGTON DC 20036
202/745-3616

AMOUNT: $15000

DEADLINE(S): JAN 31

FIELD(S): ELEC ENG; MECH ENG; AEROSPACE ENG; MATHEMATICS; PHYSICS; COMPUTER SCIENCE; MATERIALS SCIENCE; BIOLOGICAL-BIOMEDICAL SCIENCE; NAVAL ARCHITECTURE & OCEAN ENG; RELATED FIELDS

LIMITED TO INDIVIDUALS WHO HAVE 'NOT' BEGUN GRADUATE PROGRAMS. FOR STUDY AND RESEARCH LEADING TO DOCTORAL DEGREE. FELLOWSHIPS ARE AWARDED ON THE BASIS OF ABILITY. USA CITIZEN.

50 THREE-YEAR FELLOWSHIPS ARE OFFERED. WRITE FOR COMPLETE INFORMATION.

146

CHARLES A. LINDBERGH FUND INC. (GRANTS FOR RESEARCH PROJECTS)

708 S. THIRD ST.- SUITE 110
MINNEAPOLIS MN 55415
612/338-1703

AMOUNT: UP TO $10580

DEADLINE(S): JUN 15

FIELD(S): AVIATION/AEROSPACE; AGRICULTURE; ARTS & HUMANITIES; BIOMEDICAL RESEARCH; CONSERVATION; EXPLORATION; HEALTH & POPULATION SCIENCES; INTERCULTURAL COMMUNICATION; OCEANOGRAPHY; WASTE DISPOSAL MGMT; WATER RESOURCE MGMT; WILDLIFE PRESERVATION.

RESEARCH GRANTS ARE AWARDED ANNUALLY TO INDIVIDUALS WHOSE PROPOSED PROJECTS REPRESENT A SIGNIFICANT CONTRIBUTION TOWARD THE ACHIEVEMENT OF A BALANCE BETWEEN THE ADVANCE OF TECHNOLOGY & PRESERVATION OF THE NATURAL ENVIRONMENT.

WRITE FOR APPLICATION AND COMPLETE INFORMATION.

147

CIVIL AIR PATROL (CAP GRADUATE SCHOLARSHIPS)

NATIONAL HEADQUARTERS/TT
MAXWELL AFB AL 36112
205/293-5332

AMOUNT: $750

DEADLINE(S): MAR 15

FIELD(S): AEROSPACE EDUCATION; AEROSPACE SCIENCE

OPEN TO CAP MEMBERS FOR GRADUATE WORK IN AEROSPACE EDUCATION OR SCIENCE. APPLICATIONS MUST BE RECEIVED BY CAP NATIONAL HEADQUARTERS BETWEEN JAN 15 AND APR 1.

WRITE FOR COMPLETE INFORMATION.

148

DANIEL AND FLORENCE GUGGENHEIM FOUNDATION (FLIGHT STRUCTURE FELLOWSHIPS)

COLUMBIA UNIV DEPT OF CIVIL ENGINEERING
NEW YORK NY 10027
212/854-2396

AMOUNT: TUITION PLUS STIPEND

DEADLINE(S): FEB 1

FIELD(S): AERONAUTICS

GRADUATE FELLOWSHIPS TO STUDY AERONAUTICS AT COLUMBIA UNIVERSITY OPEN TO STUDENTS WITH B.S. DEGREE IN ENGINEERING. USA CITIZEN.

WRITE FOR COMPLETE INFORMATION.

149 ————————————————————

EASTERN NEW ENGLAND NINETY-NINES INC. (MARJOURIE VAN VLIET AVIATION MEMORIAL SCHOLARSHIP)

207 SANDY POND RD
LINCOLN MA 01773
617/259-0222

AMOUNT: $2000

DEADLINE(S): JAN 31

FIELD(S): AERONAUTICS; AVIATION MAINTENANCE; FLIGHT TRAINING

OPEN TO HIGH SCHOOL SENIORS OR BEYOND WHO LIVE IN ONE OF THE NEW ENGLAND STATES; PLAN A CAREER IN AVIATION AND HAVE APPLIED TO AN AVIATION RELATED EDUCATION OR TRAINING PROGRAM. SHOW FINANCIAL NEED.

CAN USE FOR TUITION AND/OR FLIGHT TRAINING. WRITE FOR COMPLETE INFORMATION.

150 ————————————————————

ELECTRONIC INDUSTRIES FOUNDATION (SCHOLARSHIP FUND)

919 18TH ST.; SUITE 900
WASHINGTON DC 20006
202/955-5814

AMOUNT: $2000

DEADLINE(S): FEB 1

FIELD(S): AERONAUTICS; COMPUTER SCIENCE; ELECTRICAL ENGINEERING; ENGINEERING TECHNOLOGY; APPLIED MATHEMATICS; MICROBIOLOGY

OPEN TO DISABLED STUDENTS WHO ARE PURSUING CAREERS IN HIGH-TECH AREAS THROUGH ACADEMIC OR TECHNICAL TRAINING. AWARDS TENABLE AT RECOGNIZED UNDERGRADUATE & GRADUATE COLLEGES & UNIVERSITIES. USA CITIZEN. FINANCIAL NEED IS A CONSIDERATION.

6 AWARDS PER YEAR. RENEWABLE. WRITE FOR COMPLETE INFORMATION.

151 ————————————————————

EPPLEY FOUNDATION FOR RESEARCH (POST-DOCTORAL RESEARCH GRANTS)

575 LEXINGTON AVE
NEW YORK NY 10022
WRITTEN INQUIRY

AMOUNT: UP TO $25000

DEADLINE(S): FEB 1; MAY 1; AUG 1; NOV 1

FIELD(S): PHYSICAL SCIENCES; BIOLOGICAL SCIENCES

POST-DOCTORAL GRANTS FOR ORIGINAL ADVANCED RESEARCH IN ANY OF THE PHYSICAL OR BIOLOGICAL SCIENCES. OPEN TO ESTABLISHED RESEARCH SCIENTISTS WHO ARE ATTACHED TO A RECOGNIZED INSTITUTION.

WRITE FOR COMPLETE INFORMATION.

152 ————————————————————

INTERNATIONAL SOCIETY OF WOMEN AIRLINE PILOTS (ISA INTERNATIONAL CAREER SCHOLARSHIP/FIORENZA DE BERNARDI MERIT AWARD)

PO BOX 66268
CHICAGO IL 60666
WRITTEN INQUIRY

AMOUNT: $500 - $1500

DEADLINE(S): APR 1

FIELD(S): PURSUIT OF AIRLINE PILOT CAREER

OPEN TO WOMEN THROUGHOUT THE WORLD WHO ARE PURSUING A CAREER AS AN AIRLINE PILOT AND HAVE AT LEAST 350 HRS OF FLIGHT EXPERIENCE. SELECTION BASED ON NEED; DEMONSTRATED DEDICATION TO CAREER GOAL; WORK EXPERIENCE AND HISTORY; RECOMMENDATIONS.

PERSONAL INTERVIEW IS REQUIRED. WRITE FOR COMPLETE INFORMATION.

153 ————————————————————

NATIONAL AERONAUTICS AND SPACE ADMINISTRATION (GRADUATE STUDENT RESEARCHERS PROGRAM)

HIGHER EDUCATION BRANCH -
CODE FEH
WASHINGTON DC 20546
202/453-8344

AMOUNT: $22000 STIPEND

DEADLINE(S): FEB 1

FIELD(S): SCIENCE; MATHEMATICS; ENGINEERING

OPEN TO GRADUATE STUDENTS ENROLLED IN OR ACCEPTED BY AN ACCREDITED USA INSTITUTION. BASED ON ACADEMIC QUALIFICATIONS; QUALITY OF PROPOSED RESEARCH PROGRAM; ITS RELEVANCE TO NASA INTERESTS & UTILIZATION OF RESEARCH FACILITIES. US CITIZEN.

AWARDS ARE FOR ONE-YEAR PERIOD & MAY BE RENEWED ANNUALLY UP TO THREE YEARS BASED ON A PERFORMANCE EVALUATION. WRITE FOR COMPLETE INFORMATION.

154

NATIONAL RESEARCH COUNCIL (NRC POSTDOCTORAL & SENIOR RESEARCH ASSOCIATESHIP AWARDS)

ASSOCIATESHIP PROGRAMS GR430/D3; 2101
CONSTITUTION AVE. NW
WASHINGTON DC 20418
202/334-2760

AMOUNT: ANNUAL STIPEND FROM 27750 TO 44000 + BENEFITS

DEADLINE(S): JAN 15; APR 15; AUG 15

FIELD(S): CHEMISTRY; EARTH & ATMOSPHERIC SCIENCES; ENGINEERING & APPLIED SCIENCES; COMPUTER SCIENCE; MATHEMATICS; BIOLOGICAL & MEDICAL SCIENCES SPACE & PLANETARY SCIENCES; PHYSICS

POSTDOCTORAL & SENIOR ASSOCIATESHIP AWARDS FOR RESEARCH AT ONE OF 38 PARTICIPATING SPONSOR FEDERAL LABORATORIES. USA CITIZENSHIP REQUIRED FOR SOME OF THE SPONSOR LABORATORIES; MANY ARE OPEN TO FOREIGN NATIONALS.

WRITE FOR COMPLETE INFORMATION AND APPLICATION MATERIALS.

155

ROYAL NORWEGIAN COUNCIL FOR SCIENTIFIC & INDUSTRIAL RESEARCH (POST-DOCTORAL RESEARCH FELLOWSHIPS)

PO BOX 70 TAASEN
N-0801 OSLO NORWAY
+4722 23 76 85

AMOUNT: NOK 132000 SINGLE; NOK 156000 MARRIED + EXPENSES

DEADLINE(S): MAR 1; SEP 1

FIELD(S): NATURAL SCIENCES; ENGINEERING

POST-DOCTORAL FELLOWSHIPS OPEN TO YOUNG FOREIGN SCIENTISTS (UNDER AGE 40) WHO WISH TO DO RESEARCH WORK IN NORWAY. THEIR QUALIFICATIONS MUST CORRESPOND AT LEAST TO A BRITISH OR AMERICAN PH.D IN NATURAL SCIENCE OR ENGINEERING.

AWARDS ARE FOR ONE YEAR. 20 AWARDS PER YEAR. RENEWALS CONSIDERED. WRITE FOR COMPLETE INFORMATION.

156

RTCA INC - RADIO TECHNICAL COMMISSION FOR AERONAUTICS (WILLIAM JACKSON AWARD)

1140 CONNECTICUT AVE NW #1020
WASHINGTON DC 20036
202/833-9339; FAX 202/833-9434

AMOUNT: $2000

DEADLINE(S): JUN 30

FIELD(S): AVIATION ELECTRONICS; AVIATION; TELECOMMUNICATIONS

OPEN TO GRADUATE STUDENTS STUDYING IN THE ABOVE FIELDS AND TO POSTGRADUATES WHO SUBMIT A THESIS; PROJECT REPORT OR TECHNICAL JOURNAL PAPER COMPLETED WITHIN THREE YEARS OF THE CLOSING DATE.

WRITE FOR COMPLETE INFORMATION.

157

SMITHSONIAN INSTITUTION (NATIONAL AIR & SPACE MUSEUM GUGGENHEIM FELLOWSHIPS)

INTERPRETIVE PROGRAMS; ROOM 3341; MRC-313;
6TH & INDEPENDENCE AVE SW
WASHINGTON DC 20560
WRITTEN INQUIRY

AMOUNT: $13000 - $21000 STIPEND + TRAVEL ALLOWANCE

DEADLINE(S): JAN 15

FIELD(S): AVIATION; AERONAUTICS; SPACE SCIENCE & EXPLORATION; EARTH & PLANETARY SCIENCES; LIFE SCIENCES

PRE-DOCTORAL APPLICANTS SHOULD HAVE COMPLETED PRELIMINARY COURSE WORK & EXAMS AND BE ENGAGED IN DISSERTATION RESEARCH. POST-DOCTORAL APPLICANTS SHOULD HAVE RECEIVED THEIR PH.D WITHIN THE PAST SEVEN YEARS.

OPEN TO ALL NATIONALITIES. FLUENCY IN ENGLISH REQUIRED. DURATION IS 6-12 MONTHS. WRITE FOR COMPLETE INFORMATION.

158

VERTICAL FLIGHT FOUNDATION (UNDERGRADUATE/GRADUATE SCHOLARSHIPS)

217 N.WASHINGTON ST
ALEXANDRIA VA 22314
703/684-6777

AMOUNT: UP TO $2000

DEADLINE(S): FEB 1

FIELD(S): MECHANICAL ENGINEERING; ELECTRICAL ENGINEERING; AEROSPACE ENGINEERING

ANNUAL SCHOLARSHIPS OPEN TO UNDERGRADUATE & GRADUATE STUDENTS IN THE ABOVE AREAS WHO ARE INTERESTED IN PURSUING CAREERS IN SOME ASPECT OF HELICOPTER OR VERTICAL FLIGHT. FOR FULL TIME STUDY AT ACCREDITED SCHOOL OF ENGINEERING.

WRITE FOR COMPLETE INFORMATION.

159

VON KARMAN INSTITUTE FOR FLUID DYNAMICS (DIPLOMA COURSE SCHOLARSHIP)

72 CHAUSSEE DE WATERLOO
1640 RHODE-ST-GENESE BELGIUM
02/358-19 01

AMOUNT: US$800 PER MONTH

DEADLINE(S): MAR 1

FIELD(S): AERONAUTICS/FLUID DYNAMICS

SCHOLARSHIPS FOR AERONAUTICS; AREOSPACE; TURBOMACHINERY OR INDUSTRIAL FLUID DYNAMICS. MUST BE CITIZEN OF NATO COUNTRY. FOR POST-GRADUATE STUDY AT THE VON KARMAN INSTITUTE.

25 SCHOLARSHIPS PER YEAR. CONTACT J.F.WENDT; DIRECTOR; ADDRESS ABOVE FOR COMPLETE INFORMATION.

160

ZONTA INTERNATIONAL FOUNDATION(AMELIA EARHART FELLOWSHIP AWARDS)

557 W RANDOLPH ST
CHICAGO IL 60661
312/930-5848; FAX 312/930-0951

AMOUNT: $6000

DEADLINE(S): DEC 1

FIELD(S): AEROSPACE SCIENCES AND ENGINEERING

OPEN TO WOMEN WHO HOLD A BACHELOR'S DEGREE IN SCIENCE AND ARE SEEKING A GRADUATE DEGREE IN AEROSPACE SCIENCES. MAY STUDY IN ANY ACCREDITED UNIVERSITY IN THE WORLD. MUST BE OF EXCEPTIONAL ABILITY AND CHARACTER.

40 FELLOWSHIPS PER YEAR. MAY REAPPLY AND COMPETE FOR A SECOND YEAR AWARD. WRITE; CALL OR FAX FOR COMPLETE INFORMATION.

ARCHITECTURE

161

AMERICAN ACADEMY IN ROME (ROME PRIZE FELLOWSHIPS)

41 EAST 65TH STREET
NEW YORK NY 10021
212/535-4250

AMOUNT: $8300 (INCLUDES ROUND TRIP TRAVEL TO ROME AND EUROPEAN TRAVEL ALLOWANCE)

DEADLINE(S): NOV 15

FIELD(S): ARCHITECTURE; LANDSCAPE ARCHITECTURE; MUSICAL COMPOSITION; CLASSICS; ART HISTORY; PAINTING; SCULPTURE AND THE VISUAL ARTS; POST CLASSICAL HUMANISTIC STUDIES.

THE ACADEMY INVITES ARTISTS AND SCHOLARS WHO ARE USA CITIZENS TO APPLY FOR A LIMITED NUMBER OF ROME PRIZE FELLOWSHIPS IN THE ARTS AND HUMANITIES.

16 ROME PRIZE FELLOWSHIPS ANNUALLY. WRITE FOR COMPLETE INFORMATION.

162

AMERICAN ARCHITECTURAL FOUNDATION (AIA/AIAF SCHOLARSHIP PROGRAM)

1735 NEW YORK AVENUE NW
WASHINGTON DC 20006
202/626-7511

AMOUNT: $500 - $2500

DEADLINE(S): FEB 3

FIELD(S): ARCHITECTURE

OPEN TO UNDERGRADUATE STUDENTS IN THEIR FINAL 2 YEARS & GRADUATE STUDENTS PURSUING THEIR MASTER'S DEGREE. AWARDS TENABLE AT ACCREDITED INSTITUTIONS IN THE USA & CANADA.

APPLICATIONS AVAILABLE -ONLY- THROUGH THE OFFICE OF THE DEAN OR DEPARTMENT HEAD AT AN NAAB OR RAIC SCHOOL OF ARCHITECTURE.

163

AMERICAN ARCHITECTURAL FOUNDATION (MINORITY/DISADVANTAGED SCHOLARSHIP PROGRAM)

1735 NEW YORK AVENUE NW
WASHINGTON DC 20006
202/626-7511

AMOUNT: VARIES

DEADLINE(S): DEC 4 FOR NOMINATION; JAN 15 FOR APPLICATION

FIELD(S): ARCHITECTURE

OPEN TO MINORITY &/OR DISADVANTAGED STUDENTS WHO ARE TRANSFERRING TO AN NAAB SCHOOL OF ARCHITECTURE OR COLLEGE FRESHMEN ENTERING A PROGRAM LEADING TO A PROFESSIONAL DEGREE (BACHELOR OR MASTER OF ARCHITECTURE.)

NOMINATION BY AN INDIVIDUAL FAMILIAR WITH STUDENT'S INTEREST AND POTENTIAL TO BE AN ARCHITECT IS REQUIRED. 20 SCHOLARSHIPS PER YEAR. WRITE FOR COMPLETE INFORMATION.

164

AMERICAN ASSOCIATION OF UNIVERSITY WOMEN (SCIENCE & TECHNOLOGY GROUP - SELECTED PROFESSIONS FELLOWSHIPS)

1111 16TH STREET NW
WASHINGTON DC 20036
202/728-7603; FAX 202/872-1430

AMOUNT: $5000 - $9500

DEADLINE(S): DEC 15 (POSTMARK)

FIELD(S): ARCHITECTURE; COMPUTER/ INFORMATION SCIENCE; ENGINEERING; MATHEMATICS/STATISTICS

OPEN TO WOMEN WHO ARE USA CITIZENS OR PERMANENT RESIDENTS WHO ARE IN THEIR FINAL YEAR OF A MASTER'S DEGREE IN THE ABOVE AREAS. APPLICATIONS AVAILABLE AUG 1 - DEC 1.

WRITE FOR COMPLETE INFORMATION.

165

AMERICAN INSTITUTE OF ARCHITECTS; NEW YORK CHAPTER (ARNOLD W. BRUNNER GRANT)

457 MADISON AVE - 3RD FLOOR
NEW YORK NY 10022
212/838-9670

AMOUNT: $15000

DEADLINE(S): MAY 1

FIELD(S): ARCHITECTURE RESEARCH

RESEARCH GRANTS FOR ADVANCED PROJECTS WHICH WILL CONTRIBUTE TO THE PRACTICE; TEACHING OR KNOWLEDGE OF THE ART & SCIENCE OF ARCHITECTURE. OPEN TO PROFESSIONAL ARCHITECTS AND THOSE IN RELATED FIELDS WHO ARE USA CITIZENS.

-NOT- FOR UNDERGRADUATE STUDY. TRAVELING FELLOWSHIPS FOR RESEARCH ALSO AVAILABLE. WRITE FOR COMPLETE INFORMATION.

166

AMERICAN PLANNING ASSOCIATION (CHARLES ABRAMS SCHOLARSHIP PROGRAM)

1776 MASSACHUSETTS AVE NW
WASHINGTON DC 20036
202/872-0611

AMOUNT: $2000

DEADLINE(S): APR 30

FIELD(S): URBAN PLANNING

FOR GRADUATE PLANNING STUDENTS AT COLUMBIA; HARVARD; NEW SCHOOL FOR SOCIAL RESEARCH IN NYC; UNIV OF PENN & MASS INSTITUTE OF TECHNOLOGY WHO ARE NOMINATED BY THEIR SCHOOLS & CAN DEMONSTRATE FINANCIAL NEED.

CONTACT YOUR DEPARTMENT HEAD OR ADDRESS ABOVE FOR COMPLETE INFORMATION.

167

AMERICAN PLANNING ASSOCIATION (MINORITY FELLOWSHIP PROGRAM)

1776 MASSACHUSETTS AVE NW
WASHINGTON DC 20036
202/872-0611

AMOUNT: $2000 - $5000

DEADLINE(S): MAY 15

FIELD(S): URBAN PLANNING

AWARDS FOR FIRST & SECOND YEAR OF GRADUATE STUDY AT A PAB-ACCREDITED PLANNING PROGRAM IN USA OR CANADA. OPEN TO USA OR CANADIAN CITIZENS WHO ARE BLACK; HISPANIC OR NATIVE AMERICAN AND CAN DEMONSTRATE FINANCIAL NEED.

WRITE FOR COMPLETE INFORMATION.

168

AMERICAN SOCIETY FOR ENGINEERING EDUCATION (OFFICE OF NAVAL RESEARCH GRADUATE FELLOWSHIP PROGRAM)

ELEVEN DUPONT CIRCLE #200
WASHINGTON DC 20036
202/745-3616

AMOUNT: $15000

DEADLINE(S): JAN 31

FIELD(S): ELEC ENG; MECH ENG; AEROSPACE ENG; MATHEMATICS; PHYSICS; COMPUTER SCIENCE; MATERIALS SCIENCE; BIOLOGICAL-BIOMEDICAL SCIENCE; NAVAL ARCHITECTURE & OCEAN ENG; RELATED FIELDS

LIMITED TO INDIVIDUALS WHO HAVE 'NOT' BEGUN GRADUATE PROGRAMS. FOR STUDY AND RESEARCH LEADING TO DOCTORAL DEGREE. FELLOWSHIPS ARE AWARDED ON THE BASIS OF ABILITY. USA CITIZEN.

50 THREE-YEAR FELLOWSHIPS ARE OFFERED. WRITE FOR COMPLETE INFORMATION.

169

ARCHAEOLOGICAL INSTITUTE OF AMERICA (OLIVIA JAMES TRAVELING FELLOWSHIP)

675 COMMONWEALTH AVE
BOSTON MA 02215
617/353-9361; DZ 617/353-6550

AMOUNT: $11500 STIPEND

DEADLINE(S): NOV 15

FIELD(S): ARCHAEOLOGY; CLASSICS; SCULPTURE; HISTORY; ARCHITECTURE

FOR GRADUATE OR POST-GRADUATE STUDY IN GREECE; AEGEAN ISLANDS; SICILY; SOUTHERN ITALY; ASIA MINOR OR MESOPOTAMIA. PREFERENCE IS FOR DISSERTATION OR RECENT PH.D RESEARCH. WILL NOT SUPPORT FIELD EXCAVATION. USA CITIZEN OR LEGAL RESIDENT.

WRITE FOR COMPLETE INFORMATION.

170

ARTS INTERNATIONAL; INSTITUTE OF INTERNATIONAL EDUCATION (CINTAS FELLOWSHIP PROGRAM)

809 UNITED NATIONS PLAZA
NEW YORK NY 10017
212/984-5370

AMOUNT: $10000

DEADLINE(S): MAR 1

FIELD(S): ARCHITECTURE; PAINTING; PHOTOGRAPHY; SCULPTURE; PRINTMAKING; MUSIC COMPOSITION; CREATIVE WRITING

FELLOWSHIPS OPEN TO ARTISTS WHO ARE OF CUBAN ANCESTRY OR CUBAN CITIZENS LIVING OUTSIDE OF CUBA. THEY ARE INTENDED TO FOSTER & ENCOURAGE THE PROFESSIONAL DEVELOPMENT & RECOGNITION OF TALENTED CREATIVE ARTISTS IN THE ABOVE AREA.

FELLOWSHIPS ARE NOT AWARDED FOR FUTHERANCE OF ACADEMIC STUDY. 5-10 AWARDS PER YEAR. WRITE FOR COMPLETE INFORMATION.

171

BOSTON SOCIETY OF ARCHITECTS (ROTCH TRAVELING SCHOLARSHIP

52 BROAD ST. 4TH FLOOR
BOSTON MA 02109
617/951-1433 EXT 227

AMOUNT: $30000 STIPEND

DEADLINE(S): JAN 2

FIELD(S): ARCHITECTURE

MUST HOLD DEGREE IN ARCHITECTURE PLUS ONE FULL YEAR OF PROFESSIONAL EXPERIENCE IN A MASS. ARCHITECTURAL OFFICE OR HOLD A DEGREE FROM A MASS. SCHOOL OF ARCHITECTURE AND HAVE ONE FULL YEAR OR EXPERIENCE IN ANY USA ARCHITECTURE FIRM.

FOR FOREIGN TRAVEL. WRITE FOR COMPLETE INFORMATION.

172

DUMBARTON OAKS (AWARDS IN BYZANTINE STUDIES; PRECOLUMBIAN STUDIES; AND THE HISTORY OF LANDSCAPE ARCHITECTURE)

1703 32ND ST NW
WASHINGTON DC 20007
202/342-3232

AMOUNT: UP TO $31700 PER ACADEMIC YEAR

DEADLINE(S): NOV 1

FIELD(S): BYZANTINE STUDIES; PRECOLUMBIAN STUDIES; HISTORY OF LANDSCAPE ARCHITECTURE

DOCTORAL & POST-DOCTORAL FELLOWSHIPS; JUNIOR FELLOWSHIPS & SUMMER FELLOWSHIPS TO SUPPORT STUDY AND/OR RESEARCH IN THE ABOVE AREAS. ALL FELLOWS ARE EXPECTED TO BE ABLE TO COMMUNICATE SATISFACTORILY IN ENGLISH.

WRITE FOR COMPLETE INFORMATION.

173

GRAHAM FOUNDATION FOR ADVANCED STUDIES IN THE FINE ARTS (RESEARCH GRANTS)

FOUR WEST BURTON PLACE
CHICAGO IL 60610
312/787-4071

AMOUNT: UP TO $10000

DEADLINE(S): JUN 1; DEC 1

FIELD(S): ARCHITECTURE

RESEARCH GRANTS OPEN TO INDIVIDUALS & INSTITUTIONS FOR SPECIFIC PROJECTS RELATING TO CONTEMPORARY ARCHITECTURE PLANNING. GRANTS DO NOT SUPPORT STUDY OR RESEARCH IN PURSUIT OF AN ACADEMIC DEGREE.

95-100 AWARDS PER YEAR. WRITE FOR COMPLETE INFORMATION.

174

LANDSCAPE ARCHITECTURE FOUNDATION (CLASS FUND SCHOLARSHIPS)

4401 CONNECTICUT AVE NW; SUITE 500
WASHINGTON DC 20008
202/686-0068

AMOUNT: $500 - $2000

DEADLINE(S): APR 3

FIELD(S): LANDSCAPE ARCHITECTURE

OPEN TO SOUTHERN CALIFORNIA STUDENTS ENROLLED AT CALIFORNIA POLYTECHNIC INSTITUTE (POMONA OR SAN LUIS OBISPO); USC; UCLA & UC-IRVINE WHO SHOW PROMISE & A COMMITMENT TO LANDSCAPE ARCHITECTURE AS A PROFESSION.

ARCHITECTURE

WRITE FOR COMPLETE INFORMATION.

175

LANDSCAPE ARCHITECTURE FOUNDATION (GRACE & ROBERT FRASER LANDSCAPE AWARD)

4401 CONNECTICUT AVE NW; SUITE 500
WASHINGTON DC 20008
202/686-0068

AMOUNT: $500

DEADLINE(S): MAY 4

FIELD(S): LANDSCAPE ARCHITECTURE

AWARD TO RECOGNIZE INNOVATIVE HORTICULTURAL RESEARCH OR DESIGN AS IT RELATES TO THE PROFESSION OF LANDSCAPE ARCHITECTURE. OPEN TO GRADUATE AND UNDERGRADUATE STUDENTS.

WRITE FOR COMPLETE INFORMATION.

176

LANDSCAPE ARCHITECTURE FOUNDATION (LANDCADD INC SCHOLARSHIP FUND)

4401 CONNECTICUT AVE NW; SUITE 500
WASHINGTON DC 20008
202/686-0068

AMOUNT: $500

DEADLINE(S): MAY 4

FIELD(S): LANDSCAPE ARCHITECTURE

SCHOLARSHIPS OPEN TO UNDERGRADUATE & GRADUATE STUDENTS WHO WISH TO UTILIZE TECHNOLOGICAL ADVANCEMENTS SUCH AS COMPUTER-AIDED DESIGN; VIDEO IMAGING AND/OR TELECOMMUNICATIONS IN THEIR CAREER.

WRITE FOR COMPLETE INFORMATION.

177

LANDSCAPE ARCHITECTURE FOUNDATION (LESTER WALLS III ENDOWMENT SCHOLARSHIP)

4401 CONNECTICUT AVE NW; SUITE 500
WASHINGTON DC 20008
202/686-0068

AMOUNT: $500

DEADLINE(S): MAY 4

FIELD(S): LANDSCAPE ARCHITECTURE

SCHOLARSHIP OPEN TO HANDICAPPED STUDENTS PURSUING A DEGREE IN LANDSCAPE ARCHITECTURE OR FOR RESEARCH ON BARRIER-FREE DESIGN FOR THE DISABLED.

WRITE FOR COMPLETE INFORMATION.

178

LANDSCAPE ARCHITECTURE FOUNDATION (RAYMOND E.PAGE SCHOLARSHIP FUND)

4401 CONNECTICUT AVE NW; SUITE 500
WASHINGTON DC 20008
202/686-0068

AMOUNT: $500

DEADLINE(S): MAY 4

FIELD(S): LANDSCAPE ARCHITECTURE

SCHOLARSHIPS OPEN TO ANY UNDERGRADUATE OR GRADUATE STUDENT WHO IS IN NEED OF FINANCIAL ASSISTANCE.

WRITE FOR COMPLETE INFORMATION.

179

LANDSCAPE ARCHITECTURE FOUNDATION (STUDENT RESEARCH GRANTS)

4401 CONNECTICUT AVE NW; SUITE 500
WASHINGTON DC 20008
202/686-0068

AMOUNT: $1000

DEADLINE(S): MAY 4

FIELD(S): LANDSCAPE ARCHITECTURE

RESEARCH GRANTS TO ENCOURAGE STUDENT EFFORTS IN PRACTICAL RESEARCH & EXPAND THE KNOWLEDGE BASE OF THE PROFESSION. OPEN TO UNDERGRADUATE & GRADUATE STUDENTS.

WRITE FOR COMPLETE INFORMATION.

180

LANDSCAPE ARCHITECTURE FOUNDATION (THE COXE GROUP SCHOLARSHIP)

4401 CONNECTICUT AVE NW; SUITE 500
WASHINGTON DC 20008
202/686-0068

AMOUNT: $1000

DEADLINE(S): MAY 4

FIELD(S): LANDSCAPE ARCHITECTURE

SCHOLARSHIP OPEN TO 4TH; 5TH & 6TH YEAR LANDSCAPE ARCHITECTURE STUDENTS WHO HAVE DEMONSTRATED ABILITY & NEED.

WRITE FOR COMPLETE INFORMATION.

181

LANDSCAPE ARCHITECTURE FOUNDATION (THE EDITH H.HENDERSON SCHOLARSHIP)

4401 CONNECTICUT AVE NW; SUITE 500
WASHINGTON DC 20008
202/686-0068

AMOUNT: $500

DEADLINE(S): MAY 4

FIELD(S): LANDSCAPE ARCHITECTURE

SCHOLARSHIP OPEN TO FEMALE STUDENTS AT THE UNIVERSITY OF GEORGIA WHO ARE ENTERING THEIR FINAL YEAR OF UNDERGRADUATE STUDY OR ANY YEAR OF GRADUATE STUDY.

WRITE FOR COMPLETE INFORMATION.

182

LANDSCAPE ARCHITECTURE FOUNDATION (WILLIAM LOCKLIN SCHOLARSHIP)

4401 CONNECTICUT AVE NW; SUITE 500
WASHINGTON DC 20008
202/686-0068

AMOUNT: $500

DEADLINE(S): MAY 4

FIELD(S): LANDSCAPE ARCHITECTURE

SCHOLARSHIPS OPEN TO UNDERGRADUATE & GRADUATE STUDENTS WHO ARE ARE PURSUING A PROGRAM IN LIGHTING DESIGN. PURPOSE IS STRESS THE IMPORTANCE OF 24-HOUR LIGHTING IN LANDSCAPE DESIGNS.

WRITE FOR COMPLETE INFORMATION.

183

NATIONAL ENDOWMENT FOR THE ARTS/ AMERICAN ACADEMY IN ROME FELLOWSHIPS

41 EAST 65TH STREET
NEW YORK NY 10021
212/517-4200

AMOUNT: $5800 (INCLUDES STIPEND & TRAVEL ALLOWANCE)

DEADLINE(S): NOV 15

FIELD(S): ARCHITECTURE;LANDSCAPE ARCHITECTURE;DESIGN ARTS

OPEN TO USA CITIZENS WHO HAVE 7 YEARS OF PROFESSIONAL PRACTICE IN ABOVE FIELDS. AWARDS TENABLE AT THE ACADEMY IN ROME ITALY.

3 NEA/AAR FELLOWSHIPS PER YEAR FOR 6-MONTH TERM. NOT RENEWABLE. CONTACT ADDRESS ABOVE FOR COMPLETE INFORMATION.

184

NATIONAL INSTITUTE FOR ARCHITECTURAL EDUCATION (J.DINKELOO TRAVELING FELLOWSHIPS TO ROME)

30 WEST 22ND ST
NEW YORK NY 10010
212/924-7000

AMOUNT: $5000

DEADLINE(S): MAY 15

FIELD(S): ARCHITECTURAL DESIGN & TECHNOLOGY

TRAVELING FELLOWSHIPS TENABLE AT THE AMERICAN ACADEMY IN ROME ITALY. OPEN TO USA CITIZENS WHO HAVE OR ANTICIPATE RECEIVING THEIR FIRST PROFESSIONAL DEGREE IN ARCHITECTURE BETWEEN JUNE OF THE COMPETITION YEAR & JUNE 3 YEARS PRIOR.

WRITE FOR COMPLETE INFORMATION.

185

NATIONAL INSTITUTE FOR ARCHITECTURAL EDUCATION (LLOYD WARREN FELLOWSHIPS)

30 WEST 22ND ST
NEW YORK NY 10010
212/924-7000

AMOUNT: UP TO $6000

DEADLINE(S): FEB 28

FIELD(S): ARCHITECTURE

ARCHITECTURAL DESIGN COMPETITION OPEN TO STUDENTS WHO HAVE RECEIVED OR ANTICIPATE RECEIVING THEIR FIRST PROFESSIONAL DEGREE IN ARCHITECTURE FROM A USA SCHOOL BETWEEN JUNE OF COMPETITION YEAR & JUNE 3 YEARS PRIOR.

AWARDS ARE TO SUPPORT TRAVEL/STUDY TRIPS ABROAD. TRAVEL MUST COMMENCE WITHIN ONE YEAR OF AWARD. WRITE FOR COMPLETE INFORMATION.

186

NATIONAL INSTITUTE FOR ARCHITECTURAL EDUCATION (WILLIAM VAN ALEN ARCHITECT MEMORIAL FELLOWSHIP)

30 WEST 22ND STREET
NEW YORK NY 10010
212-924-7000

AMOUNT: UP TO $5000

DEADLINE(S): MAY 8

FIELD(S): ARCHITECTURE; CIVIL ENGINEERING

DESIGN COMPETITION OPEN TO UNDERGRADUATE & MASTER'S STUDENTS ENROLLED IN AN ACCREDITED ARCHITECTURAL OR ENGINEERING PROGRAM IN THE USA OR CANADA.

WINNERS WILL RECEIVE AWARDS FOR TRAVEL & STUDY ABROAD. CONTACT ADDRESS ABOVE FOR COMPLETE DETAILS.

187

NATIONAL ROOFING FOUNDATION (NRF SCHOLARSHIP AWARDS PROGRAM)

O'HARE INTERNATIONAL CENTER;
10255 W. HIGGINS RD. - SUITE 600
ROSEMONT IL 60018
708/299-9070

AMOUNT: $2000

ARCHITECTURE

DEADLINE(S): JAN 15

FIELD(S): ARCHITECTURE; CONSTRUCTION

OPEN TO HIGH SCHOOL SENIORS; UNDERGRADUATE AND GRADUATE ARCHITECTURAL STUDENTS OR STUDENTS OF ANOTHER CURRICULUM RELATED TO THE ROOFING INDUSTRY. APPLICANTS MUST BE USA CITIZENS.

FOR FULL TIME STUDY AT AN ACCREDITED 4 YEAR COLLEGE OR UNIVERSITY. SEND A SELF ADDRESSED STAMPED ENVELOPE (#10) TO RECEIVE AN APPLICATION.

188

NEW YORK CITY DEPT. OF PERSONNEL (URBAN FELLOWS PROGRAM)

2 WASHINGTON ST.; 15TH FLOOR
NEW YORK NY 10004
212/487-5698

AMOUNT: $17000 STIPEND

DEADLINE(S): JAN 26

FIELD(S): PUBLIC ADMINISTRATION; URBAN PLANNING; GOVERNMENT; PUBLIC SERVICE; URBAN AFFAIRS

FELLOWSHIP PROGRAM PROVIDES ONE ACADEMIC YEAR (9 MONTHS) OF FULL-TIME WORK EXPERIENCE IN URBAN GOVERNMENT. OPEN TO GRADUATING COLLEGE SENIORS AND RECENT COLLEGE GRADUATES. USA CITIZEN.

WRITE FOR COMPLETE INFORMATION.

189

NEW YORK FOUNDATION FOR THE ARTS (ARTIST'S FELLOWSHIPS & SERVICES)

155 AVE OF THE AMERICAS; 14TH FLOOR
NEW YORK NY 10013
212/366-6900; FAX 212/366-1778

AMOUNT: $7000

DEADLINE(S): SEP 30

FIELD(S): VISUAL ARTS; LITERATURE; ARCHITECTURE; MUSIC AND MEDIA

FELLOWSHIPS & SERVICES OPEN TO ORIGINATING ARTISTS OVER 18 WHO HAVE BEEN NY STATE RESIDENTS FOR 2 YEARS PREVIOUS TO APPLICATION DATE & ARE NOT ENROLLED IN A DEGREE AWARDING COURSE OF STUDY. AWARDS ARE TO ASSIST IN CREATION OF ONGOING WORK.

APPLICATIONS AVAILABLE IN SPRINT OF EACH YEAR. ABOUT 120 FELLOWSHIPS PER YEAR; MANY OTHER SERVICES ARE AVAILABLE. - NOT- FOR ACADEMIC STUDY. WRITE FOR COMPLETE INFORMATION.

190

ROBERT SCHRECK MEMORIAL FUND (GRANTS)

C/O TEXAS COMMERCE BANK-TRUST DEPT; PO DRAWER 140
EL PASO TX 79980
915/546-6515

AMOUNT: $500 - $1500

DEADLINE(S): JUL 15; NOV 15

FIELD(S): MEDICINE; VETERINARY MEDICINE; PHYSICS; CHEMISTRY; ARCHITECTURE; ENGINEERING; EPISCOPAL CLERGY

GRANTS TO UNDERGRADUATE JUNIORS OR SENIORS OR GRADUATE STUDENTS WHO HAVE BEEN RESIDENTS OF EL PASO COUNTY FOR AT LEAST TWO YEARS. MUST BE USA CITIZEN OR LEGAL RESIDENT AND HAVE A HIGH GRADE POINT AVERAGE. FINANCIAL NEED IS A CONSIDERATION.

WRITE FOR COMPLETE INFORMATION.

191

SKIDMORE OWINGS & MERRILL FOUNDATION (TRAVELLING FELLOWSHIP PROGRAM)

224 S MICHIGAN AVE; SUITE 1000
CHICAGO IL 60604
312/554-9090

AMOUNT: $10000 - $25000

DEADLINE(S): NONE SPECIFIED

FIELD(S): ARCHITECTURE

OPEN TO UNDERGRADUATE AND GRADUATE ARCHITECTURE STUDENTS. CANDIDATES MUST BE USA CITIZENS WHO ARE ATTENDING OR RECENTLY GRADUATED FROM AN ACCREDITED ARCHITECTURE SCHOOL.

WRITE FOR COMPLETE INFORMATION.

192

SMITHSONIAN INSTITUTION (MINORITY UNDERGRADUATE & GRADUATE INTERNSHIP)

OFFICE OF FELLOWSHIPS & GRANTS;
955 L'ENFANT PLAZA; SUITE 7300
WASHINGTON DC 20560
202/287-3271

AMOUNT: $250 - $300 PER WEEK STIPEND + TRAVEL

DEADLINE(S): FEB 15; JUN 15; OCT 15

FIELD(S): DESIGN; ARCHITECTURE; ART; MUSEUM STUDIES

INTERNSHIPS OPEN TO MINORITY STUDENTS FOR RESEARCH & STUDY AT THE SMITHSONIAN OR THE COOPER-HEWITT MUSEUM OF DESIGN IN NEW YORK CITY. THE MUSEUM'S COLLECTION SPANS 3000 YEARS OF DESIGN FROM ANCIENT POTTERY TO MODERN FASHION & ADVERTISING.

UNDERGRADUATES RECEIVE $250 PER WEEK STIPEND & GRADUATE STUDENTS RECEIVE $300 PER WEEK STIPEND. WRITE FOR COMPLETE INFORMATION.

193

SOCIETY OF ARCHITECTURAL HISTORIANS (ANNUAL DOMESTIC TOURS & ANNUAL MEETING)

1232 PINE ST
PHILADELPHIA PA 19107
215/735-0224; 215/635-0246

AMOUNT: VARIES

DEADLINE(S): NOT SPECIFIED

FIELD(S): ARCHITECTURE

GRADUATE STUDENT MEMBERS OF THE SOCIETY MAY APPLY TO PARTICIPATE IN AN ARCHITECTURAL STUDY TOUR LED BY EXPERT(S) OF THE REGION. COMPETITION TO AWARD ONE STUDENT SCHOLARSHIP FOR ATTENDANCE AT ANNUAL DOMESTIC TOURS.

TWO AWARDS PER YEAR. ADDRESS INQUIRIES TO EXECUTIVE DIRECTOR DAVID BAHLMAN.

194

SOCIETY OF NAVAL ARCHITECTS & MARINE ENGINEERS (SNAME GRADUATE SCHOLARSHIPS)

601 PAVONIA AVE
JERSEY CITY NJ 07306
201/798-4800

AMOUNT: VARIES

DEADLINE(S): FEB 1

FIELD(S): NAVAL ARCHITECTURE; NAVAL/MARINE ENGINEERING; RELATED AREAS

OPEN TO GRADUATE DEGREE CANDIDATES IN THE ABOVE AREAS AT ACCREDITED INSTITUTIONS. PREFERENCE TO APPLICANTS WHO PLAN A CAREER IN THE MARINE FIELD. USA OR CANADIAN CITIZEN.

ONE AWARD IS RESERVED FOR OLDER RE-ENTRY APPLICANTS WHO HAVE 5 OR MORE YEARS OF MARINE WORK EXPERIENCE AFTER RECIEVING THEIR B.S. DEGREE. WRITE FOR COMPLETE INFORMATION.

195

UNIVERSITY OF ILLINOIS AT URBANA-CHAMPAIGN (KATE N. KINLEY FELLOWSHIP)

COLLEGE OF FINE & APPLIED ARTS;
110 ARCHITECTURE BLDG;
608 E. LORADO TAFT DR.
CHAMPAIGN IL 61820
217/333-2723

AMOUNT: $7000

DEADLINE(S): FEB 15

FIELD(S): ART; MUSIC; ARCHITECTURE

GRADUATE FELLOWSHIP FOR ADVANCED STUDY IN THE USA OR ABROAD. OPEN TO APPLICANTS WITH A BACHELOR'S DEGREE IN THE ABOVE AREAS. PREFERENCE GIVEN TO (BUT NOT LIMITED TO) APPLICANTS UNDER 25 YEARS OF AGE.

TWO ADDITIONAL AWARDS OF A LESSER AMOUNT MAY BE GRANTED UPON COMMITTEE RECOMMENDATION. WRITE FOR COMPLETE INFORMATION.

196

VIRGINIA MUSEUM OF FINE ARTS (UNDERGRAD/GRADUATE & PROFESSIONAL FELLOWSHIPS)

2800 GROVE AVE
RICHMOND VA 23221
804/367-0824

AMOUNT: UP TO $4000 UNDERGRADS; $5000 GRADS; $8000 PROFESSIONALS

DEADLINE(S): MAR 1

FIELD(S): ART; FINE ARTS; ART HISTORY (GRADUATE ONLY); ARCHITECTURE; PHOTOGRAPHY; FILM; VIDEO

VIRGINIA RESIDENT FOR 1 YEAR PRIOR TO DEADLINE. US CITIZEN OR LEGAL RESIDENT. PROFESSIONAL ARTIST FELLOWSHIPS ALSO AVAILABLE. NEED IS CONSIDERED.

ART; FINE ARTS & ART HISTORY FOR GRADUATE STUDENTS ONLY. 9-12 AWARDS PER YEAR. WRITE FOR COMPLETE INFORMATION.

197

WASHINGTON UNIVERSITY IN ST LOUIS (JAMES HARRISON STEEDMAN MEMORIAL FELLOWSHIP IN ARCHITECTURE)

SCHOOL OF ARCHITECTURE; BOX 1079
ST LOUIS MO 63130
314/935-6200

AMOUNT: $20000

DEADLINE(S): DEC 1

FIELD(S): ARCHITECTURE

AWARD IS FOR 1 ACADEMIC YEAR OF TRAVEL &
STUDY ABROAD. APPLICANTS SHOULD HAVE
RECEIVED A PROFESSIONAL DEGREE IN
ARCHITECTURE FROM AN ACCREDITED
SCHOOL WITHIN THE LAST 8 YEARS AND
HAVE AT LEAST A YEAR OF EXPERIENCE IN
AN ARCHITECT'S OFFICE.

AWARDED IN EVEN NUMBERED YEARS. THERE IS
A $50 APPLICATION FEE. WRITE FOR
COMPLETE INFORMATION.

198

**WAVERLY COMMUNITY HOUSE INC (F.
LAMMONT BELIN ARTS SCHOLARSHIPS)**

SCHOLARSHIPS SELECTION COMMITTEE
WAVERLY PA 18471
717/586-8191

AMOUNT: $9000

DEADLINE(S): DEC 15

FIELD(S): PAINTING; SCULPTURE; MUSIC;
DRAMA; DANCE; LITERATURE;
ARCHITECTURE; PHOTOGRAPHY

APPLICANTS MUST RESIDE IN THE ABINGTONS OR
POCONO REGIONS OF NORTHEASTERN
PENNSYLVANIA. THEY MUST FURNISH
PROOF OF EXCEPTIONAL ABILITY IN THEIR
CHOSEN FIELD BUT NEED NO FORMAL
TRAINING IN ANY ACADEMIC OR
PROFESSIONAL PROGRAM.

USA CITIZENSHIP REQUIRED. FINALISTS MUST
APPEAR IN PERSON BEFORE THE SELECTION
COMMITTEE. WRITE FOR COMPLETE
INFORMATION.

CIVIL ENG

199

**AMERICAN PUBLIC WORKS ASSOC EDUCATION
FOUNDATION (APWA MATCHING
SCHOLARSHIP PROGRAM)**

1313 EAST 60TH ST
CHICAGO IL 60637
312/667-2200

AMOUNT: $2500

DEADLINE(S): VARIES

FIELD(S): PUBLIC WORKS ADMIN; CIVIL
ENGINEERING

MATCHING SCHOLARSHIP PROGRAM FOR
GRADUATE STUDY IN PUBLIC WORKS
MANAGEMENT WITHIN MASTERS OF PUBLIC
ADMIN OR MASTERS OF CIVIL ENGINEERING
DEGREES FROM INSTITUTIONS OFFICIALLY
RECOGNIZED BY APWA.

WRITE FOR COMPLETE INFORMATION AND A LIST
OF RECOGNIZED SCHOOLS.

200

**AMERICAN SOCIETY OF CIVIL ENGINEERS
(ARTHUR S. TUTTLE MEMORIAL
SCHOLARSHIP FUND)**

345 EAST 47TH ST
NEW YORK NY 10017
800/548-2723 OUTSIDE NY;
800/628-0041 INSIDE NY

AMOUNT: DETERMINED ANNUALLY

DEADLINE(S): FEB 1

FIELD(S): CIVIL ENGINEERING

OPEN TO FIRST YEAR GRADUATE STUDENTS WHO
ARE STUDENT MEMBERS OF ASCE IN GOOD
STANDING. AWARDS TENABLE AT ABET
ACCREDITED COLLEGES & UNIVERSITIES.
MUST DEMONSTRATE FINANCIAL NEED.

WRITE FOR COMPLETE INFORMATION.

201

**AMERICAN SOCIETY OF CIVIL ENGINEERS
(ASCE RESEARCH FELLOWSHIPS)**

345 EAST 47TH ST
NEW YORK NY 10017
800/548-2723 OUTSIDE NY;
800/628-0041 INSIDE NY

AMOUNT: $15000

DEADLINE(S): FEB 1

FIELD(S): CIVIL ENGINEERING

FELLOWSHIPS TO AID IN THE CREATION OF NEW
KNOWLEDGE FOR THE BENEFIT &
ADVANCEMENT OF THE SCIENCE &
PROFESSION OF CIVIL ENGINEERING. OPEN
TO ASCE MEMBERS IN ANY GRADE WHO ARE
GRADUATES OF AN ACCREDITED
INSTITUTION & A USA CITIZEN.

WRITE FOR COMPLETE INFORMATION.

202

**AMERICAN SOCIETY OF CIVIL ENGINEERS
(J.WALDO SMITH HYDRAULIC
FELLOWSHIP)**

345 EAST 47TH ST
NEW YORK NY 10017
800/548-2723 OUTSIDE NY;
800/628-0041 INSIDE NY

AMOUNT: $4000 - $5000

DEADLINE(S): FEB 1

FIELD(S): CIVIL ENGINEERING

FELLOWSHIPS TO ENCOURAGE RESEARCH IN
EXPERIMENTAL HYDRAULIC RESEARCH.
OPEN TO GRADUATE STUDENTS WHO ARE
STUDENT MEMBERS (PREFERABLY
ASSOCIATE MEMBERS) OF ASCE IN GOOD
STANDING. AWARDS TENABLE AT ABET
ACCREDITED COLLEGES & UNIVERSITIES.

THIS FELLOWSHIP IS OFFERED EVERY THIRD YEAR (1994; 1997; 2000; ETC). WRITE FOR COMPLETE INFORMATION.

203

AMERICAN SOCIETY OF CIVIL ENGINEERS (O.H.AMMANN RESEARCH FELLOWSHIP IN STRUCTURAL ENGINEERING)

345 EAST 47TH ST
NEW YORK NY 10017
800/548-2723 OUTSIDE NY;
800/628-0041 INSIDE NY

AMOUNT: $5000

DEADLINE(S): FEB 1

FIELD(S): STRUCTURAL ENGINEERING

FELLOWSHIPS TO ENCOURAGE RESEARCH IN STRUCTURAL DESIGN & CONSTRUCTION. OPEN TO GRADUATE STUDENTS WHO ARE NATIONAL MEMBERS (OR APPLICANTS FOR MEMBERSHIP) OF ASCE. AWARDS TENABLE AT ABET ACCREDITED COLLEGES & UNIVERSITIES.

WRITE FOR COMPLETE INFORMATION.

204

AMERICAN SOCIETY OF CIVIL ENGINEERS (THE FREEMAN FELLOWSHIP)

345 EAST 47TH ST
NEW YORK NY 10017
800/548-2723 OUTSIDE NY;
800/628-0041 INSIDE NY

AMOUNT: VARIES

DEADLINE(S): FEB 1

FIELD(S): CIVIL ENGINEERING

FELLOWSHIPS TO ENCOURAGE RESEARCH IN CIVIL ENGINEERING. OPEN TO YOUNG ENGINEERS (UNDER 45) WHO ARE MEMBERS OF ASCE. GRANTS ARE MADE TOWARD EXPENSES FOR EXPERIMENTS; OBSERVATIONS & COMPILATIONS TO DISCOVER NEW & ACCURATE DATA.

WRITE FOR COMPLETE INFORMATION.

205

ASSOCIATED GENERAL CONTRACTORS EDUCATION AND RESEARCH FOUNDATION (SAUL HOROWITZ JR. MEMORIAL GRADUATE SCHOLARSHIP)

1957 'E' ST NW
WASHINGTON DC 20006
202/393-2040

AMOUNT: $7500

DEADLINE(S): NOV 15

FIELD(S): CONSTRUCTION; CIVIL ENGINEERING

OPEN TO UNDERGRADUATE SENIOR OR DEGREE HOLDER WHO IS ENROLLED IN OR PLANNING TO ENROLL IN A FULL-TIME GRADUATE PROGRAM AT AN ACCREDITED INSTITUTION. USA CITIZEN OR LEGAL RESIDENT.

APPLICANTS MUST PLAN TO PURSUE A CAREER IN THE CONSTRUCTION INDUSTRY. WRITE FOR COMPLETE INFORMATION.

206

ASSOCIATED GENERAL CONTRACTORS EDUCATION AND RESEARCH FOUNDATION (OUTSTANDING EDUCATOR AWARD)

1957 'E' ST NW
WASHINGTON DC 20006
202/393-2040

AMOUNT: $5000

DEADLINE(S): DEC 1

FIELD(S): CONSTRUCTION; CIVIL ENGINEERING

ANNUAL AWARD TO RECOGNIZE ACCOMPLISHMENTS OF PERMANENT TEACHING FACULTY MEMBERS IN ACCREDITED COLLEGE OR UNIVERSITY LEVEL PROGRAMS IN CONSTRUCTION OR CIVIL ENGINEERING. USA CITIZEN OR LEGAL RESIDENT.

WINNER ALSO WILL RECEIVE TRIP TO AGC'S ANNUAL 5-DAY CONVENTION IN NEW ORLEANS. WRITE FOR NOMINATION DETAILS.

207

EPPLEY FOUNDATION FOR RESEARCH (POST-DOCTORAL RESEARCH GRANTS)

575 LEXINGTON AVE
NEW YORK NY 10022
WRITTEN INQUIRY

AMOUNT: UP TO $25000

DEADLINE(S): FEB 1; MAY 1; AUG 1; NOV 1

FIELD(S): PHYSICAL SCIENCES; BIOLOGICAL SCIENCES

POST-DOCTORAL GRANTS FOR ORIGINAL ADVANCED RESEARCH IN ANY OF THE PHYSICAL OR BIOLOGICAL SCIENCES. OPEN TO ESTABLISHED RESEARCH SCIENTISTS WHO ARE ATTACHED TO A RECOGNIZED INSTITUTION.

WRITE FOR COMPLETE INFORMATION.

208

NATIONAL ASSOCIATION OF WATER COMPANIES - NEW JERSEY CHAPTER (SCHOLARSHIP)

C/O NJ-AMERICAN WATER CO -
EASTERN DIV 661 SHREWSBURY AVE
SHREWSBURY NJ 07702
908/842-6900; FAX 908/842-7541

COMPUTER SCIENCE

AMOUNT: $2500

DEADLINE(S): APR 1 (POSTMARK)

FIELD(S): BUSINESS ADMINISTRATION;
BIOLOGY; CHEMISTRY; ENGINEERING

OPEN TO USA CITIZENS WHO HAVE LIVED IN NJ
AT LEAST 5 YEARS AND PLAN A CAREER IN
THE INVESTOR-OWNED WATER UTILITY
INDUSTRY IN DISCIPLINES SUCH AS THOSE
ABOVE. MUST BE UNDERGRAD OR
GRADUATE STUDENT IN A 2 OR 4 YEAR NJ
COLLEGE OR UNIVERSITY.

GPA OF 3.0 OR BETTER REQUIRED. WRITE FOR
COMPLETE INFORMATION.

209 ─────────────

NATIONAL ROOFING FOUNDATION (NRF
SCHOLARSHIP AWARDS PROGRAM)

O'HARE INTERNATIONAL CENTER;
10255 W. HIGGINS RD. - SUITE 600
ROSEMONT IL 60018
708/299-9070

AMOUNT: $2000

DEADLINE(S): JAN 15

FIELD(S): ARCHITECTURE; CONSTRUCTION

OPEN TO HIGH SCHOOL SENIORS;
UNDERGRADUATE AND GRADUATE
ARCHITECTURAL STUDENTS OR STUDENTS
OF ANOTHER CURRICULUM RELATED TO THE
ROOFING INDUSTRY. APPLICANTS MUST BE
USA CITIZENS.

FOR FULL TIME STUDY AT AN ACCREDITED 4
YEAR COLLEGE OR UNIVERSITY. SEND A
SELF ADDRESSED STAMPED ENVELOPE (#10)
TO RECEIVE AN APPLICATION.

210 ─────────────

ROYAL NORWEGIAN COUNCIL FOR SCIENTIFIC
& INDUSTRIAL RESEARCH (POST-
DOCTORAL RESEARCH FELLOWSHIPS)

PO BOX 70 TAASEN
N-0801 OSLO NORWAY
+4722 23 76 85

AMOUNT: NOK 132000 SINGLE; NOK 156000
MARRIED + EXPENSES

DEADLINE(S): MAR 1; SEP 1

FIELD(S): NATURAL SCIENCES; ENGINEERING

POST-DOCTORAL FELLOWSHIPS OPEN TO YOUNG
FOREIGN SCIENTISTS (UNDER AGE 40) WHO
WISH TO DO RESEARCH WORK IN NORWAY.
THEIR QUALIFICATIONS MUST CORRESPOND
AT LEAST TO A BRITISH OR AMERICAN PH.D
IN NATURAL SCIENCE OR ENGINEERING.

AWARDS ARE FOR ONE YEAR. 20 AWARDS PER
YEAR. RENEWALS CONSIDERED. WRITE FOR
COMPLETE INFORMATION.

COMPUTER SCIENCE

211 ─────────────

AMERICAN ASSOCIATION OF UNIVERSITY
WOMEN (SCIENCE & TECHNOLOGY GROUP
- SELECTED PROFESSIONS FELLOWSHIPS)

1111 16TH STREET NW
WASHINGTON DC 20036
202/728-7603; FAX 202/872-1430

AMOUNT: $5000 - $9500

DEADLINE(S): DEC 15 (POSTMARK)

FIELD(S): ARCHITECTURE; COMPUTER/
INFORMATION SCIENCE; ENGINEERING;
MATHEMATICS/STATISTICS

OPEN TO WOMEN WHO ARE USA CITIZENS OR
PERMANENT RESIDENTS WHO ARE IN THEIR
FINAL YEAR OF A MASTER'S DEGREE IN THE
ABOVE AREAS. APPLICATIONS AVAILABLE
AUG 1 - DEC 1.

WRITE FOR COMPLETE INFORMATION.

212 ─────────────

AMERICAN SOCIETY FOR ENGINEERING
EDUCATION (OFFICE OF NAVAL RESEARCH
GRADUATE FELLOWSHIP PROGRAM)

ELEVEN DUPONT CIRCLE #200
WASHINGTON DC 20036
202/745-3616

AMOUNT: $15000

DEADLINE(S): JAN 31

FIELD(S): ELEC ENG; MECH ENG; AEROSPACE
ENG; MATHEMATICS; PHYSICS; COMPUTER
SCIENCE; MATERIALS SCIENCE; BIOLOGICAL-
BIOMEDICAL SCIENCE; NAVAL
ARCHITECTURE & OCEAN ENG; RELATED
FIELDS

LIMITED TO INDIVIDUALS WHO HAVE 'NOT'
BEGUN GRADUATE PROGRAMS. FOR STUDY
AND RESEARCH LEADING TO DOCTORAL
DEGREE. FELLOWSHIPS ARE AWARDED ON
THE BASIS OF ABILITY. USA CITIZEN.

50 THREE-YEAR FELLOWSHIPS ARE OFFERED.
WRITE FOR COMPLETE INFORMATION.

213 ─────────────

ARGONNE NATIONAL LABORATORY (STUDENT
RESEARCH PARTICIPATION PROGRAM;
THESIS RESEARCH)

DIV OF EDUCATIONAL PROGRAMS;
9700 SOUTH CASS AVE
ARGONNE IL 60439
312/972-3366

AMOUNT: $200 PER WEEK STIPEND

DEADLINE(S): FEB 1; MAY 15; OCT 15

FIELD(S): PHYSICAL SCIENCES; LIFE SCIENCES; EARTH SCIENCES; MATHEMATICS; COMPUTER SCIENCES; ENGINEERING; FUSION & FISSION ENERGY

1-SEMESTER ACCREDITED INTERNSHIP PROGRAM TO PERMIT STUDENTS TO WORK IN ABOVE AREAS IN RELATION TO ENERGY DEVELOPMENT. OPEN TO FULL-TIME UNDERGRAD JUNIORS; SENIORS & 1ST YEAR GRAD STUDENTS. USA CITIZEN OR LEGAL RESIDENT.

THESIS RESEARCH AWARDS OPEN TO DOCTORAL CANDIDATES WORKING ON THEIR DISSERTATION. WRITE FOR COMPLETE INFORMATION.

214

AT&T BELL LABORATORIES (COOPERATIVE RESEARCH FELLOWSHIP PROGRAM FOR MINORITIES)

101 CRAWFORDS CORNER ROAD;
ROOM 1E-209; BOX 3030
HOLMDEL NJ 07733
WRITTEN INQUIRY

AMOUNT: FULL-TUITION & FEES + $13200 STIPEND PER YEAR

DEADLINE(S): JAN 15

FIELD(S): ENGINEERING; MATH; SCIENCES; COMPUTER SCIENCE

FELLOWSHIPS ARE AWARDED TO MINORITY STUDENTS WHO ARE ACCEPTED INTO AN ACCREDITED DOCTORAL PROGRAM FOR THE FOLLOWING FALL. USA CITIZEN OR PERMANENT RESIDENT.

10 AWARDS PER YEAR. RENEWABLE UP TO 4 YEARS. WRITE TO SPECIAL PROGRAMS MANAGER - CRFP FOR COMPLETE INFORMATION.

215

AT&T BELL LABORATORIES (GRADUATE RESEARCH PROGRAM FOR WOMEN)

101 CRAWFORDS CORNER ROAD;
ROOM 1E-209; BOX 3030
HOLMDEL NJ 07733
WRITTEN INQUIRY

AMOUNT: FULL TUITION & FEES + $13200 STIPEND PER YEAR

DEADLINE(S): JAN 15

FIELD(S): ENGINEERING; MATH; SCIENCES; COMPUTER SCIENCE

FOR WOMEN STUDENTS WHO HAVE BEEN ACCEPTED INTO AN ACCREDITED DOCTORAL PROGRAM FOR THE FOLLOWING FALL. USA CITIZEN OR PERMANENT RESIDENT.

FELLOWSHIPS ARE RENEWABLE FOR DURATION OF GRADUATE PROGRAM. WRITE TO SPECIAL PROGRAMS MANAGER - GRPW FOR COMPLETE INFORMATION.

216

BUSINESS AND PROFESSIONAL WOMEN'S FOUNDATION (CAREER ADVANCEMENT SCHOLARSHIPS)

2012 MASSACHUSETTS AVE NW
WASHINGTON DC 20036
202/293-1200

AMOUNT: $500 - $1000

DEADLINE(S): APR 15 POSTMARK (APPS AVAILABLE -ONLY- OCT 1 - APR 1)

FIELD(S): COMPUTER SCIENCE; EDUCATION; PARALEGAL; ENGINEERING; SCIENCE (EXCEPT HEALTH CARE)

OPEN TO WOMEN (30 OR OLDER) WITHIN 12-24 MONTHS OF COMPLETING UNDERGRAD OR GRAD STUDY IN USA (INCLUDING PUERTO RICO & THE VIRGIN ISLANDS). SHOULD LEAD TO ENTRY OR REENTRY INTO THE WORK FORCE OR IMPROVE CAREER ADVANCEMENT CHANCES.

MUST SHOW FINANCIAL NEED. SEND SELF-ADDRESSED STAMPED ($.52) #10 ENVELOPE FOR APPLICATION & COMPLETE INFORMATION. NOT FOR STUDY AT DOCTORAL LEVEL.

217

ELECTRONIC INDUSTRIES FOUNDATION (SCHOLARSHIP FUND)

919 18TH ST.; SUITE 900
WASHINGTON DC 20006
202/955-5814

AMOUNT: $2000

DEADLINE(S): FEB 1

FIELD(S): AERONAUTICS; COMPUTER SCIENCE; ELECTRICAL ENGINEERING; ENGINEERING TECHNOLOGY; APPLIED MATHEMATICS; MICROBIOLOGY

OPEN TO DISABLED STUDENTS WHO ARE PURSUING CAREERS IN HIGH-TECH AREAS THROUGH ACADEMIC OR TECHNICAL TRAINING. AWARDS TENABLE AT RECOGNIZED UNDERGRADUATE & GRADUATE COLLEGES & UNIVERSITIES. USA CITIZEN. FINANCIAL NEED IS A CONSIDERATION.

6 AWARDS PER YEAR. RENEWABLE. WRITE FOR COMPLETE INFORMATION.

218

FOUNDATION FOR SCIENCE & THE HANDICAPPED (GRANTS PROGRAM)

C/O REBECCA F. SMITH;
115 S. BRAINARD AVE.
LA GRANGE IL 60525
708/352-1091

AMOUNT: $1000

DEADLINE(S): DEC 1

FIELD(S): SCIENCE; MATHEMATICS; MEDICINE; COMPUTER SCIENCE; ENGINEERING

OPEN TO GRADUATE STUDENTS IN THE ABOVE AREAS WHO HAVE SOME PHYSICAL OR SENSORY DISABILITY. APPLICATIONS WILL ALSO BE ACCEPTED FROM UNDERGRADUATE SENIORS WHO HAVE BEEN ACCEPTED TO GRADUATE SCHOOL. USA CITIZEN OR LEGAL RESIDENT.

WRITE FOR COMPLETE INFORMATION.

219

NATIONAL RADIO ASTRONOMY OBSERVATORY (SUMMER RESEARCH ASSISTANTSHIPS)

EDGEMONT ROAD
CHARLOTTESVILLE VA 22903
804/296-0211

AMOUNT: $1000 - $1300 PER MONTH + TRAVEL EXPENSES

DEADLINE(S): FEB 1

FIELD(S): ASTRONOMY; PHYSICS; COMPUTER SCIENCE; ELECTRICAL ENGINEERING

SUMMER RESEARCH ASSISTANTSHIPS OPEN TO UNDERGRADUATES WHO HAVE COMPLETED AT LEAST 3 YEARS OF STUDY AND TO GRADUATE STUDENTS WHO HAVE COMPLETED NO MORE THAN 2 YEARS. TENABLE AT NRAO SITES.

APPROXIMATELY 20 AWARDS PER YEAR. WRITE FOR COMPLETE INFORMATION.

220

NATIONAL RESEARCH COUNCIL (NATIONAL SCIENCE FOUNDATION MINORITY GRADUATE FELLOWSHIPS)

2101 CONSTITUTION AVE.
WASHINGTON DC 20418
202/334-2872

AMOUNT: $14000 STIPEND (12 MONTHS) + UP TO $7500 FOR TUITION AND FEES

DEADLINE(S): NOV 6

FIELD(S): ENGINEERING; MATHEMATICS; COMPUTER SCIENCE; CHEMISTRY; EARTH SCIENCES; LIFE SCIENCES; PSYCHOLOGY; SOCIAL SCIENCES

OPEN MINORITY GRADUATE STUDENTS (MASTERS OR PH.D) WHO ARE USA CITIZENS OR LEGAL RESIDENTS & ARE AT OR NEAR THE BEGINNING OF THEIR GRADUATE STUDY. FELLOWSHIPS TENABLE AT ACCREDITED INSTITUTION OFFERING ADVANCED DEGREES IN THE FIELDS ABOVE.

APPROX 150 NEW 3-YEAR FELLOWSHIPS AWARDED EACH YEAR. WRITE FOR COMPLETE INFORMATION.

221

NATIONAL RESEARCH COUNCIL (NRC POSTDOCTORAL & SENIOR RESEARCH ASSOCIATESHIP AWARDS)

ASSOCIATESHIP PROGRAMS GR430/D3; 2101
CONSTITUTION AVE. NW
WASHINGTON DC 20418
202/334-2760

AMOUNT: ANNUAL STIPEND FROM 27750 TO 44000 + BENEFITS

DEADLINE(S): JAN 15; APR 15; AUG 15

FIELD(S): CHEMISTRY; EARTH & ATMOSPHERIC SCIENCES; ENGINEERING & APPLIED SCIENCES; COMPUTER SCIENCE; MATHEMATICS; BIOLOGICAL & MEDICAL SCIENCES SPACE & PLANETARY SCIENCES; PHYSICS

POSTDOCTORAL & SENIOR ASSOCIATESHIP AWARDS FOR RESEARCH AT ONE OF 38 PARTICIPATING SPONSOR FEDERAL LABORATORIES. USA CITIZENSHIP REQUIRED FOR SOME OF THE SPONSOR LABORATORIES; MANY ARE OPEN TO FOREIGN NATIONALS.

WRITE FOR COMPLETE INFORMATION AND APPLICATION MATERIALS.

222

ROYAL NORWEGIAN COUNCIL FOR SCIENTIFIC & INDUSTRIAL RESEARCH (POST-DOCTORAL RESEARCH FELLOWSHIPS)

PO BOX 70 TAASEN
N-0801 OSLO NORWAY
+4722 23 76 85

AMOUNT: NOK 132000 SINGLE; NOK 156000 MARRIED + EXPENSES

DEADLINE(S): MAR 1; SEP 1

FIELD(S): NATURAL SCIENCES; ENGINEERING

POST-DOCTORAL FELLOWSHIPS OPEN TO YOUNG FOREIGN SCIENTISTS (UNDER AGE 40) WHO WISH TO DO RESEARCH WORK IN NORWAY. THEIR QUALIFICATIONS MUST CORRESPOND AT LEAST TO A BRITISH OR AMERICAN PH.D IN NATURAL SCIENCE OR ENGINEERING.

AWARDS ARE FOR ONE YEAR. 20 AWARDS PER YEAR. RENEWALS CONSIDERED. WRITE FOR COMPLETE INFORMATION.

223

SIGMA DELTA EPSILON-GRADUATE WOMEN IN SCIENCE (SDE FELLOWSHIPS; ELOISE GERRY FELLOWSHIPS)

ONE ILLINOIS CENTER;
111 E. WACKER DR.
CHICAGO IL 60601
312/616-0800

AMOUNT: $2600 - $4000 (SDE); $2300 - $2700 (ELOISE GERRY)

DEADLINE(S): DEC 1 (POSTMARK)

FIELD(S): BIOLOGY; CHEMISTRY; NATURAL SCIENCES; PHYSICAL SCIENCES; BIOLOGICAL SCIENCES; COMPUTER SCIENCES

WOMEN ONLY. OPEN TO GRADUATE STUDENTS AND POST-DOCTORAL RESEARCHERS IN THE ABOVE AREAS. FELLOWSHIPS MAY ONLY BE USED TO SUPPORT SCIENTIFIC RESEARCH AND/OR PROJECTS. FINANCIAL NEED IS A MAJOR CONSIDERATION.

ELOISE GERRY FELLOWSHIPS ARE LIMITED TO THE CHEMICAL AND BIOLOGICAL SCIENCES. WRITE FOR COMPLETE INFORMATION.

ELECTRICAL ENG

224

AMERICAN RADIO RELAY LEAGUE FOUNDATION (DR. JAMES L. LAWSON MEMORIAL SCHOLARSHIP)

225 MAIN ST
NEWINGTON CT 06111
203/666-1541

AMOUNT: $500

DEADLINE(S): FEB 15

FIELD(S): ELECTRONICS; COMMUNICATIONS

OPEN TO RADIO AMATEURS HOLDING AT LEAST A GENERAL LICENSE AND RESIDING IN CT; MA; ME; NH; RI; VT; OR NY AND ATTENDING A SCHOOL IN ONE OF THOSE STATES.

WRITE FOR COMPLETE INFORMATION.

225

AMERICAN RADIO RELAY LEAGUE FOUNDATION (IRVING W. COOK WA0CGS SCHOLARSHIP)

225 MAIN ST
NEWINGTON CT 06111
203/666-1541

AMOUNT: $500

DEADLINE(S): FEB 15

FIELD(S): ELECTRONICS; COMMUNICATIONS

OPEN TO RESIDENTS OF KANSAS WHO HOLD ANY CLASS OF RADIO AMATEUR LICENSE AND ARE SEEKING A BACCALAUREATE OR HIGHER DEGREE. FOR STUDY IN ANY USA COLLEGE OR UNIVERSITY.

WRITE FOR COMPLETE INFORMATION.

226

AMERICAN RADIO RELAY LEAGUE FOUNDATION (L PHILIP & ALICE J WICKER SCHOLARSHIP FUND)

225 MAIN ST
NEWINGTON CT 06111
203/666-1541

AMOUNT: $1000

DEADLINE(S): FEB 15

FIELD(S): ELECTRICAL ENGINEERING; COMMUNICATIONS

OPEN TO STUDENTS WHO ARE RESIDENTS OF ARRL ROANOKE DIV (N.CAROLINA; S.CAROLINA; VIRGINIA; W.VIRGINIA); ATTEND A SCHOOL IN THE ROANOKE DIV AS AN UNDERGRADUATE OR GRADUATE STUDENT & ARE AT LEAST GENERAL CLASS LICENSED RADIO AMATEURS.

WRITE FOR COMPLETE INFORMATION.

227

AMERICAN RADIO RELAY LEAGUE FOUNDATION (PAUL & HELEN L GRAUER SCHOLARSHIP FUND)

225 MAIN ST
NEWINGTON CT 06111
203/666-1541

AMOUNT: $1000

DEADLINE(S): FEB 15

FIELD(S): ELECTRICAL ENGINEERING; COMMUNICATIONS

OPEN TO ARRL MIDWEST DIV RESIDENTS (IOWA; KANSAS; MISSOURI; NEBRASKA) WHO ARE LICENSED RADIO AMATEURS & ENROLLED FULL TIME AS AN UNDERGRADUATE OR GRADUATE STUDENT AT AN ACCREDITED INSTITUTION IN THE ARRL MIDWEST DIV.

WRITE FOR COMPLETE INFORMATION.

228

AMERICAN RADIO RELAY LEAGUE FOUNDATION (PERRY F HADLOCK MEMORIAL SCHOLARSHIP FUND)

225 MAIN ST
NEWINGTON CT 06111
203/666-1541

AMOUNT: $1000

DEADLINE(S): FEB 15

FIELD(S): ELECTRICAL ENGINEERING

OPEN TO STUDENTS WHO ARE GENERAL CLASS LICENSED RADIO AMATEURS; HAVE DEMONSTRATED ENTHUSIAM IN PROMOTING AMATEUR RADIO & ARE ENROLLED FULL TIME AS AN UNDERGRADUATE OR GRADUATE STUDENT AT AN ACCREDITED INSTITUTION.

WRITE FOR COMPLETE INFORMATION.

229

AMERICAN RADIO RELAY LEAGUE FOUNDATION (SENATOR BARRY GOLDWATER (#K7UGA) SCHOLARSHIP FUND)

225 MAIN ST
NEWINGTON CT 06111
203/666-1541

AMOUNT: $5000

DEADLINE(S): FEB 15

FIELD(S): COMMUNICATIONS

OPEN TO STUDENTS WHO ARE LICENSED RADIO AMATEURS & ENROLLED FULL TIME AS AN UNDERGRADUATE OR GRADUATE STUDENT AT AN ACCREDITED INSTITUTION IN A FIELD RELATED TO COMMUNICATIONS.

WRITE FOR COMPLETE INFORMATION.

230

AMERICAN SOCIETY FOR ENGINEERING EDUCATION (OFFICE OF NAVAL RESEARCH GRADUATE FELLOWSHIP PROGRAM)

ELEVEN DUPONT CIRCLE #200
WASHINGTON DC 20036
202/745-3616

AMOUNT: $15000

DEADLINE(S): JAN 31

FIELD(S): ELEC ENG; MECH ENG; AEROSPACE ENG; MATHEMATICS; PHYSICS; COMPUTER SCIENCE; MATERIALS SCIENCE; BIOLOGICAL-BIOMEDICAL SCIENCE; NAVAL ARCHITECTURE & OCEAN ENG; RELATED FIELDS

LIMITED TO INDIVIDUALS WHO HAVE 'NOT' BEGUN GRADUATE PROGRAMS. FOR STUDY AND RESEARCH LEADING TO DOCTORAL DEGREE. FELLOWSHIPS ARE AWARDED ON THE BASIS OF ABILITY. USA CITIZEN.

50 THREE-YEAR FELLOWSHIPS ARE OFFERED. WRITE FOR COMPLETE INFORMATION.

231

AMERICAN VACUUM SOCIETY (GRADUATE STUDENT PRIZE)

335 E. 45TH ST
NEW YORK NY 10017
212/661-9404

AMOUNT: $500

DEADLINE(S): MAR 31

FIELD(S): VACUUM SCIENCE

PRIZES AWARDED FOR GRADUATE WORK IN SCIENCES AND TECHNOLOGIES OF INTEREST TO THE SOCIETY. NOMINEES MUST BE GRADUATE STUDENTS IN ACCREDITED NORTH AMERICAN INSTITUTIONS. AWARDS ARE BASED ON RESEARCH EXCELLENCE AND STUDENT'S ACADEMIC RECORD.

APPROXIMATELY 10 PRIZES GIVEN ANNUALLY. WINNERS ALSO RECEIVE REASONABLE TRAVEL EXPENSES TO ATTEND THE NATIONAL SYMPOSIUM. WRITE FOR COMPLETE INFORMATION.

232

AMERICAN VACUUM SOCIETY (RUSSELL AND SIGURD VARIAN FELLOW AWARD)

335 E. 45TH ST
NEW YORK NY 10017
212/661-9404

AMOUNT: $1500

DEADLINE(S): MAR 31

FIELD(S): ELECTRIAL ENGINEERING-VACUUM SCIENCE

OPEN TO FULL TIME GRADUATE STUDENTS IN ACCREDITED ACADEMIC INSTITUTIONS IN NORTH AMERICA. FOR EXPERIMENTAL OR THEORETICAL RESEARCH IN ANY OF THE TECHNICAL AND SCIENTIFIC AREAS OF INTEREST TO THE SOCIETY.

APPLICANTS ARE NORMALLY EXPECTED TO GRADUATE AFTER SEP 30 OF THE YEAR FOLLOWING THE AWARD. WRITE FOR COMPLETE INFORMATION.

233

AT&T BELL LABORATORIES (COOPERATIVE RESEARCH FELLOWSHIP PROGRAM FOR MINORITIES)

101 CRAWFORDS CORNER ROAD;
ROOM 1E-209; BOX 3030
HOLMDEL NJ 07733
WRITTEN INQUIRY

AMOUNT: FULL-TUITION & FEES + $13200 STIPEND PER YEAR

DEADLINE(S): JAN 15

FIELD(S): ENGINEERING; MATH; SCIENCES; COMPUTER SCIENCE

FELLOWSHIPS ARE AWARDED TO MINORITY STUDENTS WHO ARE ACCEPTED INTO AN ACCREDITED DOCTORAL PROGRAM FOR THE FOLLOWING FALL. USA CITIZEN OR PERMANENT RESIDENT.

10 AWARDS PER YEAR. RENEWABLE UP TO 4 YEARS. WRITE TO SPECIAL PROGRAMS MANAGER - CRFP FOR COMPLETE INFORMATION.

234

AT&T BELL LABORATORIES (GRADUATE RESEARCH PROGRAM FOR WOMEN)

101 CRAWFORDS CORNER ROAD;
ROOM 1E-209; BOX 3030
HOLMDEL NJ 07733
WRITTEN INQUIRY

AMOUNT: FULL TUITION & FEES + $13200 STIPEND PER YEAR

DEADLINE(S): JAN 15

FIELD(S): ENGINEERING; MATH; SCIENCES; COMPUTER SCIENCE

FOR WOMEN STUDENTS WHO HAVE BEEN ACCEPTED INTO AN ACCREDITED DOCTORAL PROGRAM FOR THE FOLLOWING FALL. USA CITIZEN OR PERMANENT RESIDENT.

FELLOWSHIPS ARE RENEWABLE FOR DURATION OF GRADUATE PROGRAM. WRITE TO SPECIAL PROGRAMS MANAGER - GRPW FOR COMPLETE INFORMATION.

235

ELECTROCHEMICAL SOCIETY (SUMMER RESEARCH FELLOWSHIPS)

10 SOUTH MAIN ST
PENNINGTON NJ 08534
609/737-1902

AMOUNT: $2000 - $6000

DEADLINE(S): JAN 15

FIELD(S): ENERGY; CHEMICAL ENGINEERING; CHEMISTRY; ELECTRICAL ENGINEERING

SUMMER FELLOWSHIPS OPEN TO GRADUATE STUDENTS AT ACCREDITED COLLEGES & UNIVERSITIES IN THE USA & CANADA. PURPOSE IS TO SUPPORT RESEARCH OF INTEREST TO ELECTROCHEMICAL SOCIETY & RESEARCH AIMED AT REDUCING ENERGY CONSUMPTION.

WRITE FOR COMPLETE INFORMATION.

236

ELECTRONIC INDUSTRIES FOUNDATION (SCHOLARSHIP FUND)

919 18TH ST.; SUITE 900
WASHINGTON DC 20006
202/955-5814

AMOUNT: $2000

DEADLINE(S): FEB 1

FIELD(S): AERONAUTICS; COMPUTER SCIENCE; ELECTRICAL ENGINEERING; ENGINEERING TECHNOLOGY; APPLIED MATHEMATICS; MICROBIOLOGY

OPEN TO DISABLED STUDENTS WHO ARE PURSUING CAREERS IN HIGH-TECH AREAS THROUGH ACADEMIC OR TECHNICAL TRAINING. AWARDS TENABLE AT RECOGNIZED UNDERGRADUATE & GRADUATE COLLEGES & UNIVERSITIES. USA CITIZEN. FINANCIAL NEED IS A CONSIDERATION.

6 AWARDS PER YEAR. RENEWABLE. WRITE FOR COMPLETE INFORMATION.

237

EPPLEY FOUNDATION FOR RESEARCH (POST-DOCTORAL RESEARCH GRANTS)

575 LEXINGTON AVE
NEW YORK NY 10022
WRITTEN INQUIRY

AMOUNT: UP TO $25000

DEADLINE(S): FEB 1; MAY 1; AUG 1; NOV 1

FIELD(S): PHYSICAL SCIENCES; BIOLOGICAL SCIENCES

POST-DOCTORAL GRANTS FOR ORIGINAL ADVANCED RESEARCH IN ANY OF THE PHYSICAL OR BIOLOGICAL SCIENCES. OPEN TO ESTABLISHED RESEARCH SCIENTISTS WHO ARE ATTACHED TO A RECOGNIZED INSTITUTION.

WRITE FOR COMPLETE INFORMATION.

238

INSTITUTE OF ELECTRICAL & ELECTRONICS ENGINEERS (CHARLES LE GEYT FORTESCUE FELLOWSHIP)

345 EAST 47TH STREET
NEW YORK NY 10017
212/705-7882

AMOUNT: $24000

DEADLINE(S): JAN 31

FIELD(S): ELECTRICAL ENGINEERING

FELLOWSHIP IS OPEN TO FIRST YEAR GRADUATE STUDENTS AT RECOGNIZED ENGINEERING SCHOOLS LOCATED IN THE USA OR CANADA. AWARDS SUPPORT FULL-TIME STUDY FOR ONE ACADEMIC YEAR.

WRITE FOR COMPLETE INFORMATION.

239

INTERNATIONAL UNION FOR VACUUM SCIENCE (WELCH FOUNDATION RESEARCH SCHOLARSHIPS)

C/O BNR; PO BOX 3511 STATION C
OTTAWA ONTARIO K1Y 4H7 CANADA
613/763-3248; FAX 613/763-2404

AMOUNT: $12500 US

DEADLINE(S): APR 15

ELECTRICAL ENG

FIELD(S): VACUUM SCIENCE

OPEN TO PROMISING YOUNG SCHOLARS WHO WISH TO CONTRIBUTE TO THE STUDY OF VACUUM SCIENCE TECHNIQUES OR THEIR APPLICATION IN ANY FIELD. PREFERENCE TO APPLICANTS WHO PROPOSE RESEARCH IN A FOREIGN LAB IN WHICH THEY HAVE NOT YET STUDIED.

CANDIDATES SHOULD HAVE AT LEAST A BACHELOR'S DEGREE; A DOCTOR'S DEGREE IS PREFEREED. WRITE FOR COMPLETE INFORMATION.

240

NATIONAL RADIO ASTRONOMY OBSERVATORY (SUMMER RESEARCH ASSISTANTSHIPS)

EDGEMONT ROAD
CHARLOTTESVILLE VA 22903
804/296-0211

AMOUNT: $1000 - $1300 PER MONTH + TRAVEL EXPENSES

DEADLINE(S): FEB 1

FIELD(S): ASTRONOMY; PHYSICS; COMPUTER SCIENCE; ELECTRICAL ENGINEERING

SUMMER RESEARCH ASSISTANTSHIPS OPEN TO UNDERGRADUATES WHO HAVE COMPLETED AT LEAST 3 YEARS OF STUDY AND TO GRADUATE STUDENTS WHO HAVE COMPLETED NO MORE THAN 2 YEARS. TENABLE AT NRAO SITES.

APPROXIMATELY 20 AWARDS PER YEAR. WRITE FOR COMPLETE INFORMATION.

241

OPTICAL SOCIETY OF AMERICA (NEWPORT RESEARCH AWARD)

2010 MASSACHUSETTS AVE NW
WASHINGTON DC 20036
202-416-1404

AMOUNT: $16000

DEADLINE(S): FEB 15

FIELD(S): PHYSICS; ELECTRICAL ENGINEERING

GRANTS OPEN TO DOCTORAL CANDIDATES WHO ARE PURSUING THESIS RESEARCH ON LASERS AND ELECTRO-OPTICS OR RELATED FIELDS. AWARDS ARE TENABLE AT ACCREDITED INSTITUTIONS IN THE USA.

AWARDS ARE RENEWABLE FOR ONE YEAR. WRITE FOR COMPLETE INFORMATION.

242

RADIO FREE EUROPE/RADIO LIBERTY (ENGINEERING INTERN PROGRAM)

PERSONNEL DIVISION; 1201 CONNECTICUT AVE NW
WASHINGTON DC 20036
202/457-6936

AMOUNT: DAILY STIPEND OF 55 GERMAN MARKS + ACCOMMODATIONS

DEADLINE(S): FEB 22

FIELD(S): ELECTRICAL ENGINEERING

INTERNSHIP IN GERMANY OPEN TO GRADUATE OR EXCEPTIONALLY QUALIFIED UNDERGRAD ELECTRICAL ENGINEERING STUDENTS. PREFERENCE TO THOSE WHO HAVE COMPLETED COURSES IN SUBJECTS RELATED TO THE TECHNICAL ASPECTS OF INTERNATIONAL BROADCASTING.

AT LEAST BASIC ABILITY TO SPEAK GERMAN IS HIGHLY DESIRABLE. WRITE FOR COMPLETE INFORMATION.

243

ROYAL NORWEGIAN COUNCIL FOR SCIENTIFIC & INDUSTRIAL RESEARCH (POST-DOCTORAL RESEARCH FELLOWSHIPS)

PO BOX 70 TAASEN
N-0801 OSLO NORWAY
+4722 23 76 85

AMOUNT: NOK 132000 SINGLE; NOK 156000 MARRIED + EXPENSES

DEADLINE(S): MAR 1; SEP 1

FIELD(S): NATURAL SCIENCES; ENGINEERING

POST-DOCTORAL FELLOWSHIPS OPEN TO YOUNG FOREIGN SCIENTISTS (UNDER AGE 40) WHO WISH TO DO RESEARCH WORK IN NORWAY. THEIR QUALIFICATIONS MUST CORRESPOND AT LEAST TO A BRITISH OR AMERICAN PH.D IN NATURAL SCIENCE OR ENGINEERING.

AWARDS ARE FOR ONE YEAR. 20 AWARDS PER YEAR. RENEWALS CONSIDERED. WRITE FOR COMPLETE INFORMATION.

244

RTCA INC - RADIO TECHNICAL COMMISSION FOR AERONAUTICS (WILLIAM JACKSON AWARD)

1140 CONNECTICUT AVE NW #1020
WASHINGTON DC 20036
202/833-9339; FAX 202/833-9434

AMOUNT: $2000

DEADLINE(S): JUN 30

FIELD(S): AVIATION ELECTRONICS; AVIATION; TELECOMMUNICATIONS

OPEN TO GRADUATE STUDENTS STUDYING IN THE ABOVE FIELDS AND TO POSTGRADUATES WHO SUBMIT A THESIS; PROJECT REPORT OR TECHNICAL JOURNAL PAPER COMPLETED WITHIN THREE YEARS OF THE CLOSING DATE.

WRITE FOR COMPLETE INFORMATION.

245

SRC COMPETITIVENESS FOUNDATION (FELLOWSHIPS)

PO BOX 12053; 79 ALEXANDER DR;
BLDG 4401 #302
RESEARCH TRIANGLE PARK NC 27709
919/541-9400

AMOUNT: TUITION & FEES + $1400 PER MONTH STIPEND

DEADLINE(S): MAR 15

FIELD(S): MICROELECTRONICS

RESEARCH FELLOWSHIPS OPEN TO PH.D CANDIDATES IN AREAS RELEVANT TO MICROELECTRONICS. RESEARCH WILL BE PERFORMED UNDER THE GUIDANCE OF AN SRC-DESIGNATED FACULTY MEMBER. USA CITIZEN.

7-10 FELLOWSHIPS PER YEAR. CONTACT UNIVERSITY PROGRAM ADMINISTRATOR AT ADDRESS ABOVE FOR COMPLETE INFORMATION.

246

VERTICAL FLIGHT FOUNDATION (UNDERGRADUATE/GRADUATE SCHOLARSHIPS)

217 N.WASHINGTON ST
ALEXANDRIA VA 22314
703/684-6777

AMOUNT: UP TO $2000

DEADLINE(S): FEB 1

FIELD(S): MECHANICAL ENGINEERING; ELECTRICAL ENGINEERING; AEROSPACE ENGINEERING

ANNUAL SCHOLARSHIPS OPEN TO UNDERGRADUATE & GRADUATE STUDENTS IN THE ABOVE AREAS WHO ARE INTERESTED IN PURSUING CAREERS IN SOME ASPECT OF HELICOPTER OR VERTICAL FLIGHT. FOR FULL TIME STUDY AT ACCREDITED SCHOOL OF ENGINEERING.

WRITE FOR COMPLETE INFORMATION.

ENGINEERING TECH

247

AMERICAN NUCLEAR SOCIETY (GRADUATE SCHOLARSHIPS)

555 NORTH KENSINGTON AVE
LA GRANGE PARK IL 60525
312/352-6611

AMOUNT: $500 - $4000

DEADLINE(S): MAR 1

FIELD(S): NUCLEAR ENGINEERING

SCHOLARSHIPS OPEN TO FULL-TIME GRADUATE STUDENTS ENROLLED IN AN ACCREDITED PROGRAM LEADING TO AN ADVANCED DEGREE IN NUCLEAR SCIENCE OR NUCLEAR ENGINEERING AT AN INSTITUTION IN THE USA. USA CITIZEN OR LEGAL RESIDENT.

7 AWARDS PER YEAR. WRITE FOR COMPLETE INFORMATION.

248

AMERICAN NUCLEAR SOCIETY (JOHN & MURIEL LANDIS SCHOLARSHIPS)

555 NORTH KENSINGTON AVE
LA GRANGE PARK IL 60525
312/352-6611

AMOUNT: $3500

DEADLINE(S): MAR 1

FIELD(S): NUCLEAR ENGINEERING

OPEN TO ANY UNDERGRADUATE OR GRADUATE STUDENT THAT HAS GREATER THAN AVERAGE FINANCIAL NEED & IS PLANNING A CAREER IN NUCLEAR ENGINEERING OR A NUCLEAR RELATED FIELD. AWARDS TENABLE AT ACCREDITED INSTITUTIONS IN THE USA.

MUST BE USA CITIZEN OR HAVE A PERMANENT RESIDENT VISA. 8 AWARDS PER YEAR. WRITE FOR COMPLETE INFORMATION.

249

AMERICAN SOCIETY OF HEATING; REFRIGERATING & AIR-CONDITIONING ENGINEERS (ASHRAE GRADUATE GRANT IN AID)

1791 TULLIE CIRCLE NE
ATLANTA GA 30329
404/636-8400

AMOUNT: $7500

DEADLINE(S): DEC 15

FIELD(S): HEATING; REFRIGERATION & AIR-CONDITIONING; VENTILATION

OPEN TO FULL-TIME GRADUATE STUDENTS AT ACCREDITED COLLEGES & UNIVERSITIES IN THE USA & CANADA. GRANTS ARE INTENDED TO ENCOURAGE THE STUDENT TO CONTINUE PREPARATION FOR SERVICE IN THE HEATING; REFRIGERATING & AIR CONDITIONING INDUSTRY.

WRITE FOR COMPLETE INFORMATION.

250

AMERICAN SOCIETY OF MECHANICAL ENGINEERS (STUDENT ASSISTANCE LOAN PROGRAM)

345 E. 47TH ST
NEW YORK NY 10017
212/705-7375

ENGINEERING TECH

AMOUNT: UP TO $2500

DEADLINE(S): APR 1; NOV 1

FIELD(S): MECHANICAL ENGINEERING; ENGINEERING TECHNOLOGY (STUDENT ASSISTANCE LOAN PROGRAM)

LOANS TO STUDENT MEMBERS OF ASME WHO ARE UNDERGRADUATE OR GRADUATE STUDENTS ENROLLED IN SCHOOLS WITH ACCREDITED MECHANICAL ENGINEERING OR ENGINEERING TECHNOLOGYU CURRICULA. MINIMUM 2.0 GPA ON 4.0 SCALE. USA CITIZEN.

FIRST PREFERENCE GIVEN TO UNDERGRADUATE JUNIORS AND SENIORS. WRITE FOR COMPLETE INFORMATION.

251

AMERICAN WELDING SOCIETY (SCHOLARSHIP PROGRAM)

550 NW LEJEUNE RD; PO BOX 351040
MIAMI FL 33135
305/443-9353

AMOUNT: VARIES

DEADLINE(S): JUN 1

FIELD(S): WELDING TECHNOLOGY

OPEN TO USA CITIZENS WHO RESIDE IN THE USA & ARE ENROLLED IN AN ACCREDITED MATERIAL JOINING OR SIMILAR PROGRAM. AWARDS ARE TENABLE AT JUNIOR COLLEGES; COLLEGES; UNIVERSITIES & INSTITUTIONS IN THE USA.

WRITE FOR COMPLETE INFORMATION.

252

AT&T BELL LABORATORIES (COOPERATIVE RESEARCH FELLOWSHIP PROGRAM FOR MINORITIES)

101 CRAWFORDS CORNER ROAD;
ROOM 1E-209; BOX 3030
HOLMDEL NJ 07733
WRITTEN INQUIRY

AMOUNT: FULL-TUITION & FEES + $13200 STIPEND PER YEAR

DEADLINE(S): JAN 15

FIELD(S): ENGINEERING; MATH; SCIENCES; COMPUTER SCIENCE

FELLOWSHIPS ARE AWARDED TO MINORITY STUDENTS WHO ARE ACCEPTED INTO AN ACCREDITED DOCTORAL PROGRAM FOR THE FOLLOWING FALL. USA CITIZEN OR PERMANENT RESIDENT.

10 AWARDS PER YEAR. RENEWABLE UP TO 4 YEARS. WRITE TO SPECIAL PROGRAMS MANAGER - CRFP FOR COMPLETE INFORMATION.

253

AT&T BELL LABORATORIES (GRADUATE RESEARCH PROGRAM FOR WOMEN)

101 CRAWFORDS CORNER ROAD;
ROOM 1E-209; BOX 3030
HOLMDEL NJ 07733
WRITTEN INQUIRY

AMOUNT: FULL TUITION & FEES + $13200 STIPEND PER YEAR

DEADLINE(S): JAN 15

FIELD(S): ENGINEERING; MATH; SCIENCES; COMPUTER SCIENCE

FOR WOMEN STUDENTS WHO HAVE BEEN ACCEPTED INTO AN ACCREDITED DOCTORAL PROGRAM FOR THE FOLLOWING FALL. USA CITIZEN OR PERMANENT RESIDENT.

FELLOWSHIPS ARE RENEWABLE FOR DURATION OF GRADUATE PROGRAM. WRITE TO SPECIAL PROGRAMS MANAGER - GRPW FOR COMPLETE INFORMATION.

254

CHEMICAL MANUFACTURERS ASSOCIATION (TEACHER AWARDS)

2501 M STREET NW
WASHINGTON DC 20037
202/887-1223

AMOUNT: $2500 REGIONAL AWARD; $5000 NATIONAL

DEADLINE(S): JAN 29

FIELD(S): SCIENCE ; CHEMISTRY; CHEMICAL ENGINEERING

SIX NATIONAL AND 8 REGIONAL AWARDS WILL BE OFFERED TO COLLEGE AND HIGH SCHOOL CHEMISTRY OR CHEMICAL ENGINEERING TEACHERS IN THE USA OR CANADA. CRITERIA ARE EXCELLENCE IN TEACHING; DEDICATION & MOTIVATION OF STUDENTS TO SCIENCE CAREERS.

FOR TEACHERS OF GENERAL SCIENCE; CHEMISTRY AND CHEMICAL ENGINEERING - ONLY-. WRITE FOR COMPLETE INFORMATION.

255

ELECTROCHEMICAL SOCIETY (SUMMER RESEARCH FELLOWSHIPS)

10 SOUTH MAIN ST
PENNINGTON NJ 08534
609/737-1902

AMOUNT: $2000 - $6000

DEADLINE(S): JAN 15

FIELD(S): ENERGY; CHEMICAL ENGINEERING; CHEMISTRY; ELECTRICAL ENGINEERING

SUMMER FELLOWSHIPS OPEN TO GRADUATE STUDENTS AT ACCREDITED COLLEGES & UNIVERSITIES IN THE USA & CANADA. PURPOSE IS TO SUPPORT RESEARCH OF INTEREST TO ELECTROCHEMICAL SOCIETY & RESEARCH AIMED AT REDUCING ENERGY CONSUMPTION.

WRITE FOR COMPLETE INFORMATION.

256

ELECTRONIC INDUSTRIES FOUNDATION (SCHOLARSHIP FUND)

919 18TH ST.; SUITE 900
WASHINGTON DC 20006
202/955-5814

AMOUNT: $2000

DEADLINE(S): FEB 1

FIELD(S): AERONAUTICS; COMPUTER SCIENCE; ELECTRICAL ENGINEERING; ENGINEERING TECHNOLOGY; APPLIED MATHEMATICS; MICROBIOLOGY

OPEN TO DISABLED STUDENTS WHO ARE PURSUING CAREERS IN HIGH-TECH AREAS THROUGH ACADEMIC OR TECHNICAL TRAINING. AWARDS TENABLE AT RECOGNIZED UNDERGRADUATE & GRADUATE COLLEGES & UNIVERSITIES. USA CITIZEN. FINANCIAL NEED IS A CONSIDERATION.

6 AWARDS PER YEAR. RENEWABLE. WRITE FOR COMPLETE INFORMATION.

257

EPPLEY FOUNDATION FOR RESEARCH (POST-DOCTORAL RESEARCH GRANTS)

575 LEXINGTON AVE
NEW YORK NY 10022
WRITTEN INQUIRY

AMOUNT: UP TO $25000

DEADLINE(S): FEB 1; MAY 1; AUG 1; NOV 1

FIELD(S): PHYSICAL SCIENCES; BIOLOGICAL SCIENCES

POST-DOCTORAL GRANTS FOR ORIGINAL ADVANCED RESEARCH IN ANY OF THE PHYSICAL OR BIOLOGICAL SCIENCES. OPEN TO ESTABLISHED RESEARCH SCIENTISTS WHO ARE ATTACHED TO A RECOGNIZED INSTITUTION.

WRITE FOR COMPLETE INFORMATION.

258

INSTITUTE OF INDUSTRIAL ENGINEERS (IIE SCHOLARSHIPS)

25 TECHNOLOGY PARK/ATLANTA
NORCROSS GA 30092
404/449-0460

AMOUNT: VARIES

DEADLINE(S): NOV 15 (NOMINATIONS); FEB 15 (APPLICATIONS)

FIELD(S): INDUSTRIAL ENGINEERING

UNDERGRADUATE & GRADUATE SCHOLARSHIPS OPEN TO ACTIVE IIE MEMBERS WITH AT LEAST 1 FULL YEAR OF STUDY REMAINING AT AN ACCREDITED COLLEGE OR UNIVERSITY IN NORTH AMERICA. A GPA OF 3.4 OR BETTER IS REQUIRED.

APPLICATIONS WILL BE MAILED -ONLY- TO STUDENTS NOMINATED BY THEIR DEPARTMENT HEAD. WRITE FOR NOMINATION FORMS & COMPLETE INFORMATION.

259

INSTITUTE OF PAPER SCIENCE AND TECHNOLOGY (FELLOWSHIP PROGRAM)

575 14TH ST NW
ATLANTA GA 30318
404/853-9500

AMOUNT: FULL TUITION PLUS $11250 STIPEND

DEADLINE(S): MAR 15

FIELD(S): CHEMISTRY; CHEMICAL ENGINEERING; PHYSICS; BIOLOGY; MATHEMATICS; PULP AND PAPER TECHNOLOGY

OPEN TO GRADUATE STUDENTS WHO ARE USA OR CANADIAN CITIZENS WHO HOLD A B.S. DEGREE IN THE ABOVE FIELDS. FOR PURSUIT OF A MASTER OF SCIENCE OR PH.D. DEGREE AT THE INSTITUTE.

35 FELLOWSHIPS ANNUALLY. ADDRESS INQUIRIES TO DIRECTOR OF ADMISSIONS.

260

INTERNATIONAL SOCIETY FOR OPTICAL ENGINEERING (SCHOLARSHIPS & GRANTS)

PO BOX 10
BELLINGHAM WA 98227
206/676-3290

AMOUNT: $500 - $5000

DEADLINE(S): APR 3

FIELD(S): OPTICAL ENGINEERING

SCHOLARSHIP AWARDS ARE FOR EDUCATIONAL PURPOSES WITH FINAL SELECTIONS BASED UPON AN ASSESSMENT OF THE STUDENT'S POTENTIAL CONTRIBUTION TO OPTICS OR OPTICAL ENGINEERING.

30 TO 35 AWARDS PER YEAR. APPLICATIONS MAY BE OBTAINED BY WRITING TO MR. WARREN J. SMITH; CHAIRMAN; SPIE EDUCATION COMMITTEE; ADDRESS ABOVE.

261

**JAMES F. LINCOLN ARC WELDING
FOUNDATION (AWARDS PROGRAM)**

PO BOX 17035
CLEVELAND OH 44117
216/481-4300

AMOUNT: UP TO $2000

DEADLINE(S): JUN 15

FIELD(S): ARC WELDING TECHNOLOGY

OPEN TO UNDERGRADUATE & GRADUATE
ENGINEERING & TECHNOLOGY STUDENTS
WHO SOLVE DESIGN ENGINEERING OR
FABRICATION PROBLEMS INVOLVING THE
KNOWLEDGE OR APPLICATION OF ARC
WELDING.

TOTAL OF 29 AWARDS; 17 FOR UNDERGRADUATE
AND 12 FOR GRADUATE STUDENTS. WRITE
FOR COMPLETE INFORMATION.

262

LADIES OF NORTHANTS (SCHOLARSHIP)

PO BOX 6609
CODDINGTOWN CA 95406
WRITTEN INQUIRY

AMOUNT: $250

DEADLINE(S): FEB 8

FIELD(S): NUCLEAR ENGINEERING

THE LADIES OF NORTHANTS OFFERS A
SCHOLARSHIP TO A WOMAN OVER 40 WHO
MIGRATED TO THE UNITED STATES FROM
NORTHAMPTONSHIRE ENGLAND AND IS
COMMITTED TO A CAREER IN NUCLEAR
ENGINEERING. FOR UNDERGRADUATE OR
GRADUATE STUDY.

PREFERENCE TO NATIVES OF THE VILLAGE OF
PODINGTON WHO HAVE A 3.75 OR BETTER
GRADE POINT AVERAGE (4.0 SCALE) AND
CAN DEMONSTRATE FINANCIAL NEED.
WRITE FOR COMPLETE INFORMATION.

263

**NATIONAL ASSOCIATION OF WATER
COMPANIES - NEW JERSEY CHAPTER
(SCHOLARSHIP)**

C/O NJ-AMERICAN WATER CO - EASTERN DIV 661
SHREWSBURY AVE
SHREWSBURY NJ 07702
908/842-6900; FAX 908/842-7541

AMOUNT: $2500

DEADLINE(S): APR 1 (POSTMARK)

FIELD(S): BUSINESS ADMINISTRATION;
BIOLOGY; CHEMISTRY; ENGINEERING

OPEN TO USA CITIZENS WHO HAVE LIVED IN NJ
AT LEAST 5 YEARS AND PLAN A CAREER IN
THE INVESTOR-OWNED WATER UTILITY
INDUSTRY IN DISCIPLINES SUCH AS THOSE
ABOVE. MUST BE UNDERGRAD OR
GRADUATE STUDENT IN A 2 OR 4 YEAR NJ
COLLEGE OR UNIVERSITY.

GPA OF 3.0 OR BETTER REQUIRED. WRITE FOR
COMPLETE INFORMATION.

264

**NORTH AMERICAN DIE CASTING ASSOCIATION
(DAVID LAINE MEMORIAL SCHOLARSHIPS)**

2000 NORTH FIFTH AVE
RIVER GROVE IL 60171
312/452-0700

AMOUNT: VARIES

DEADLINE(S): MAY 1

FIELD(S): DIE CASTING TECHNOLOGY

OPEN TO STUDENTS ENROLLED AT AN
ENGINEERING COLLEGE AFFILIATED WITH
THE FOUNDRY EDUCATIONAL FOUNDATION
(FEF) & REGISTERED WITH FEF FOR THE
CURRENT YEAR. USA CITIZEN.

FOR UNDERGRADUATE OR GRADUATE STUDY.
WRITE FOR COMPLETE INFORMATION.

265

**OAK RIDGE ASSOCIATED UNIVERSITIES (US
DEPT OF ENERGY GRADUATE NUCLEAR &
FUSION ENERGY FELLOWSHIPS)**

SCIENCE/ENGINEERING EDUCATION DIVISION; PO
BOX 117
OAK RIDGE TN 37831
615/576-8503

AMOUNT: FULL TUITION & FEES; + $14400
STIPEND

DEADLINE(S): JAN 27

FIELD(S): NUCLEAR ENGINEERING; FUSION
ENGINEERING; FUSION SCIENCE

GRADUATE FELLOWSHIPS SPONSORED BY US
DEPT OF ENERGY FOR FIRST TIME GRAD
STUDENTS WHO HOLD BS DEGREE IN
PHYSICAL SCIENCES; ENGINEERING
SCIENCE; MATH OR ENGINEERING. USA
CITIZEN OR LEGAL RESIDENT.

AWARDS TENABLE AT PARTICIPATING
UNIVERSITIES IN USA. WRITE FOR LIST OF
UNIVERSITIES AND COMPLETE
INFORMATION.

266

**OAK RIDGE INSTITUTE FOR SCIENCE &
EDUCATION (GRADUATE FELLOWSHIPS)**

UNIV PROGRAMS DIV; PO BOX 117
OAK RIDGE TN 37831
WRITTEN INQUIRY

AMOUNT: $1200 - $1300 PER MONTH STIPEND + TUITION & FEES

DEADLINE(S): JAN 25

FIELD(S): NUCLEAR ENGINEERING; PHYSICS; RADIOACTIVE WASTE MANAGEMENT; FUSION ENERGY; INDUSTRIAL HYGIENE; ENVIRONMENTAL RESTORATION

OPEN TO ENTERING & OTHER GRADUATE STUDENTS FOR STUDY LEADING TO M.S. OR PH.D DEGREE. PROVIDES ACCESS TO STUDY AND RESEARCH AT DEPT. OF ENERGY LABORATORIES. RENEWABLE UP TO 48 MONTHS.

WRITE FOR COMPLETE INFORMATION.

267 ————————————————————

ROYAL NORWEGIAN COUNCIL FOR SCIENTIFIC & INDUSTRIAL RESEARCH (POST-DOCTORAL RESEARCH FELLOWSHIPS)

PO BOX 70 TAASEN
N-0801 OSLO NORWAY
+4722 23 76 85

AMOUNT: NOK 132000 SINGLE; NOK 156000 MARRIED + EXPENSES

DEADLINE(S): MAR 1; SEP 1

FIELD(S): NATURAL SCIENCES; ENGINEERING

POST-DOCTORAL FELLOWSHIPS OPEN TO YOUNG FOREIGN SCIENTISTS (UNDER AGE 40) WHO WISH TO DO RESEARCH WORK IN NORWAY. THEIR QUALIFICATIONS MUST CORRESPOND AT LEAST TO A BRITISH OR AMERICAN PH.D IN NATURAL SCIENCE OR ENGINEERING.

AWARDS ARE FOR ONE YEAR. 20 AWARDS PER YEAR. RENEWALS CONSIDERED. WRITE FOR COMPLETE INFORMATION.

268 ————————————————————

TECHNOLOGY STUDENT ASSOCIATION (SCHOLARSHIPS)

1914 ASSOCIATION DR
RESTON VA 22091
703/860-9000

AMOUNT: $250 - $500

DEADLINE(S): MAY 1

FIELD(S): TECHNOLOGY EDUCATION

OPEN TO STUDENT MEMBERS OF THE TECHNOLOGY STUDENT ASSOCIATION WHO CAN DEMONSTRATE FINANCIAL NEED. GRADE POINT AVERAGE IS -NOT- A CONSIDERATION BUT APPLICANTS MUST BE ACCEPTED TO A 4-YEAR COLLEGE OR UNIVERSITY.

FUNDS ARE SENT TO AND ADMINISTERED BY THE RECIPIENT'S COLLEGE OR UNIVERSITY. WRITE FOR COMPLETE INFORMATION.

MECHANICAL ENG

269 ————————————————————

AMERICAN ASSOCIATION OF PETROLEUM GEOLOGISTS (GRANTS-IN-AID)

C/O W.A. MORGAN; PO BOX 979
TULSA OK 74101
918/584-2555 EXT 239

AMOUNT: $2000 MAX ($500 - $1740 AVG)

DEADLINE(S): JAN 15

FIELD(S): PETROLEUM GEOLOGY; GEOLOGY; GEOPHYSICS; PALEONTOLOGY

GRANTS IN SUPPORT OF RESEARCH PROJECTS LEADING TO THE MASTERS OR DOCTORAL DEGREE. PREFERENCE TO PROJECTS RELATED TO THE SEARCH FOR HYDROCARBONS; ECONOMIC SEDIMENTARY MINERALS OR ENVIRONMENTAL GEOLOGY.

50 GRANTS PER YEAR. WRITE FOR COMPLETE INFORMATION.

270 ————————————————————

AMERICAN GEOLOGICAL INSTITUTE (MINORITY PARTICIPATION PROGRAM SCHOLARSHIPS)

4220 KING ST
ALEXANDRIA VA 22302
703/379-2480

AMOUNT: UP TO $10000 PER YEAR UNDERGRAD; $4000 PER YEAR GRAD

DEADLINE(S): FEB 1

FIELD(S): EARTH SCIENCES; SPACE SCIENCES; MARINE SCIENCES

FOR FULL TIME UNDERGRADUATE OR GRADUATE STUDY IN THE ABOVE FIELDS. OPEN TO AMERICAN BLACKS; NATIVE AMERICANS & HISPANIC AMERICANS. MUST BE USA CITIZEN AND DEMONSTRATE FINANCIAL NEED.

APPROX 80 AWARDS PER YEAR. RENEWALS POSSIBLE WITH REAPPLICATION. WRITE FOR COMPLETE INFORMATION.

271 ————————————————————

AMERICAN SOCIETY FOR ENGINEERING EDUCATION (OFFICE OF NAVAL RESEARCH GRADUATE FELLOWSHIP PROGRAM)

ELEVEN DUPONT CIRCLE #200
WASHINGTON DC 20036
202/745-3616

AMOUNT: $15000

DEADLINE(S): JAN 31

FIELD(S): ELEC ENG; MECH ENG; AEROSPACE ENG; MATHEMATICS; PHYSICS; COMPUTER SCIENCE; MATERIALS SCIENCE; BIOLOGICAL-BIOMEDICAL SCIENCE; NAVAL ARCHITECTURE & OCEAN ENG; RELATED FIELDS

LIMITED TO INDIVIDUALS WHO HAVE 'NOT' BEGUN GRADUATE PROGRAMS. FOR STUDY AND RESEARCH LEADING TO DOCTORAL DEGREE. FELLOWSHIPS ARE AWARDED ON THE BASIS OF ABILITY. USA CITIZEN.

50 THREE-YEAR FELLOWSHIPS ARE OFFERED. WRITE FOR COMPLETE INFORMATION.

272

AMERICAN SOCIETY OF MECHANICAL ENGINEERS (STUDENT ASSISTANCE LOAN PROGRAM)

345 E. 47TH ST
NEW YORK NY 10017
212/705-7375

AMOUNT: UP TO $2500

DEADLINE(S): APR 1; NOV 1

FIELD(S): MECHANICAL ENGINEERING; ENGINEERING TECHNOLOGY (STUDENT ASSISTANCE LOAN PROGRAM)

LOANS TO STUDENT MEMBERS OF ASME WHO ARE UNDERGRADUATE OR GRADUATE STUDENTS ENROLLED IN SCHOOLS WITH ACCREDITED MECHANICAL ENGINEERING OR ENGINEERING TECHNOLOGYU CURRICULA. MINIMUM 2.0 GPA ON 4.0 SCALE. USA CITIZEN.

FIRST PREFERENCE GIVEN TO UNDERGRADUATE JUNIORS AND SENIORS. WRITE FOR COMPLETE INFORMATION.

273

AMERICAN SOCIETY OF MECHANICAL ENGINEERS AUXILIARY INC (ELISABETH M & WINCHELL M PARSONS SCHOLARSHIP)

345 E 47TH ST
NEW YORK NY 10017
212/705-7746

AMOUNT: $1500

DEADLINE(S): FEB 15

FIELD(S): MECHANICAL ENGINEERING

OPEN TO A USA CITIZEN WHO IS WORKING TOWARD A DOCTORAL DEGREE IN MECHANICAL ENGINEERING. MUST BE A STUDENT MEMBER OF ASME AND HAVE A BACHELORS DEGREE IN MECHANICAL ENGINEERING.

5-6 SCHOLARSHIPS PER YEAR. ADDRESS INQUIRIES C/O MRS KENNETH O CARTWRIGHT; 910 RASIC RIDGE RD; GLENDALE CA 91207; 818/244-2369.

274

AMERICAN SOCIETY OF MECHANICAL ENGINEERS AUXILIARY INC (MARJORIE ROY ROTHERMEL SCHOLARSHIP)

345 E 47TH ST
NEW YORK NY 10017
212/705-7746

AMOUNT: $1500

DEADLINE(S): FEB 15

FIELD(S): MECHANICAL ENGINEERING

OPEN TO GRADUATE STUDENT ENROLLED IN A SCHOOL HAVING A MECHANICAL ENGINEERING CURRICULUM WHO IS WORKING TOWARD A MASTER'S DEGREE IN ENGINEERING. USA CITIZEN.

5-6 SCHOLARSHIPS PER YEAR. ADDRESS INQUIRIES C/O MRS ELIZABETH PROCHASKA; 332 VALENCIA ST; GULF BREEZE FL 32561; 904/932-3698.

275

ASSOCIATION OF ENGINEERING GEOLOGISTS (MARLIAVE FUND SCHOLARSHIPS)

323 BOSTON POST ROAD SUITE 2D
SUDBURY MA 01776
508/443-4639

AMOUNT: UP TO $1000

DEADLINE(S): FEB 1

FIELD(S): ENGINEERING GEOLOGY

GRADUATE SCHOLARSHIPS FOR AEG MEMBERS. AWARDS BASED ON ABILITY; SCHOLARSHIP; CHARACTER; EXTRACURRICULAR ACTIVITIES AND POTENTIAL FOR CONTRIBUTIONS TO THE PROFESSION.

WRITE FOR COMPLETE INFORMATION.

276

AT&T BELL LABORATORIES (COOPERATIVE RESEARCH FELLOWSHIP PROGRAM FOR MINORITIES)

101 CRAWFORDS CORNER ROAD;
ROOM 1E-209; BOX 3030
HOLMDEL NJ 07733
WRITTEN INQUIRY

AMOUNT: FULL-TUITION & FEES + $13200 STIPEND PER YEAR

DEADLINE(S): JAN 15

FIELD(S): ENGINEERING; MATH; SCIENCES; COMPUTER SCIENCE

FELLOWSHIPS ARE AWARDED TO MINORITY STUDENTS WHO ARE ACCEPTED INTO AN ACCREDITED DOCTORAL PROGRAM FOR THE FOLLOWING FALL. USA CITIZEN OR PERMANENT RESIDENT.

10 AWARDS PER YEAR. RENEWABLE UP TO 4 YEARS. WRITE TO SPECIAL PROGRAMS MANAGER - CRFP FOR COMPLETE INFORMATION.

277

AT&T BELL LABORATORIES (GRADUATE RESEARCH PROGRAM FOR WOMEN)

101 CRAWFORDS CORNER ROAD;
ROOM 1E-209; BOX 3030
HOLMDEL NJ 07733
WRITTEN INQUIRY

AMOUNT: FULL TUITION & FEES + $13200 STIPEND PER YEAR

DEADLINE(S): JAN 15

FIELD(S): ENGINEERING; MATH; SCIENCES; COMPUTER SCIENCE

FOR WOMEN STUDENTS WHO HAVE BEEN ACCEPTED INTO AN ACCREDITED DOCTORAL PROGRAM FOR THE FOLLOWING FALL. USA CITIZEN OR PERMANENT RESIDENT.

FELLOWSHIPS ARE RENEWABLE FOR DURATION OF GRADUATE PROGRAM. WRITE TO SPECIAL PROGRAMS MANAGER - GRPW FOR COMPLETE INFORMATION.

278

EPPLEY FOUNDATION FOR RESEARCH (POST-DOCTORAL RESEARCH GRANTS)

575 LEXINGTON AVE
NEW YORK NY 10022
WRITTEN INQUIRY

AMOUNT: UP TO $25000

DEADLINE(S): FEB 1; MAY 1; AUG 1; NOV 1

FIELD(S): PHYSICAL SCIENCES; BIOLOGICAL SCIENCES

POST-DOCTORAL GRANTS FOR ORIGINAL ADVANCED RESEARCH IN ANY OF THE PHYSICAL OR BIOLOGICAL SCIENCES. OPEN TO ESTABLISHED RESEARCH SCIENTISTS WHO ARE ATTACHED TO A RECOGNIZED INSTITUTION.

WRITE FOR COMPLETE INFORMATION.

279

INTERNATIONAL LEAD ZINC RESEARCH ORGANIZATION INC. (FELLOWSHIP PROGRAM)

PO BOX 12036; 2525 MERIDIAN PARKWAY
RESEARCH TRIANGLE PARK NC 27709
WRITTEN INQUIRY

AMOUNT: $15000 - $25000

DEADLINE(S): MAY

FIELD(S): CHEMISTRY; ENVIRONMENTAL HEALTH; ELECTROCHEMISTRY; METALLURGY

DOCTORAL AND POST-DOCTORAL FELLOWSHIPS FOR RESEARCH INVOLVING LEAD; ZINC AND CADMIUM COMPOUNDS IN CERAMICS; CHEMISTRY; METALLURGY; ELECTROCHEMISTRY; AND ENVIRONMENTAL HEALTH.

ONE YEAR FELLOWSHIPS RENEWABLE FOR TWO ADDITIONAL YEARS. WRITE FOR COMPLETE INFORMATION.

280

NATIONAL ASSOCIATION OF WATER COMPANIES - NEW JERSEY CHAPTER (SCHOLARSHIP)

C/O NJ-AMERICAN WATER CO -
EASTERN DIV 661 SHREWSBURY AVE
SHREWSBURY NJ 07702
908/842-6900; FAX 908/842-7541

AMOUNT: $2500

DEADLINE(S): APR 1 (POSTMARK)

FIELD(S): BUSINESS ADMINISTRATION; BIOLOGY; CHEMISTRY; ENGINEERING

OPEN TO USA CITIZENS WHO HAVE LIVED IN NJ AT LEAST 5 YEARS AND PLAN A CAREER IN THE INVESTOR-OWNED WATER UTILITY INDUSTRY IN DISCIPLINES SUCH AS THOSE ABOVE. MUST BE UNDERGRAD OR GRADUATE STUDENT IN A 2 OR 4 YEAR NJ COLLEGE OR UNIVERSITY.

GPA OF 3.0 OR BETTER REQUIRED. WRITE FOR COMPLETE INFORMATION.

281

ROYAL NORWEGIAN COUNCIL FOR SCIENTIFIC & INDUSTRIAL RESEARCH (POST-DOCTORAL RESEARCH FELLOWSHIPS)

PO BOX 70 TAASEN
N-0801 OSLO NORWAY
+4722 23 76 85

AMOUNT: NOK 132000 SINGLE; NOK 156000 MARRIED + EXPENSES

DEADLINE(S): MAR 1; SEP 1

FIELD(S): NATURAL SCIENCES; ENGINEERING

POST-DOCTORAL FELLOWSHIPS OPEN TO YOUNG FOREIGN SCIENTISTS (UNDER AGE 40) WHO WISH TO DO RESEARCH WORK IN NORWAY. THEIR QUALIFICATIONS MUST CORRESPOND AT LEAST TO A BRITISH OR AMERICAN PH.D IN NATURAL SCIENCE OR ENGINEERING.

AWARDS ARE FOR ONE YEAR. 20 AWARDS PER YEAR. RENEWALS CONSIDERED. WRITE FOR COMPLETE INFORMATION.

SCHOOL OF HUMANITIES

282

SOCIETY OF NAVAL ARCHITECTS & MARINE ENGINEERS (SNAME GRADUATE SCHOLARSHIPS)

601 PAVONIA AVE
JERSEY CITY NJ 07306
201/798-4800

AMOUNT: VARIES

DEADLINE(S): FEB 1

FIELD(S): NAVAL ARCHITECTURE; NAVAL/ MARINE ENGINEERING; RELATED AREAS

OPEN TO GRADUATE DEGREE CANDIDATES IN THE ABOVE AREAS AT ACCREDITED INSTITUTIONS. PREFERENCE TO APPLICANTS WHO PLAN A CAREER IN THE MARINE FIELD. USA OR CANADIAN CITIZEN.

ONE AWARD IS RESERVED FOR OLDER RE-ENTRY APPLICANTS WHO HAVE 5 OR MORE YEARS OF MARINE WORK EXPERIENCE AFTER RECIEVING THEIR B.S. DEGREE. WRITE FOR COMPLETE INFORMATION.

283

VERTICAL FLIGHT FOUNDATION (UNDERGRADUATE/GRADUATE SCHOLARSHIPS)

217 N.WASHINGTON ST
ALEXANDRIA VA 22314
703/684-6777

AMOUNT: UP TO $2000

DEADLINE(S): FEB 1

FIELD(S): MECHANICAL ENGINEERING; ELECTRICAL ENGINEERING; AEROSPACE ENGINEERING

ANNUAL SCHOLARSHIPS OPEN TO UNDERGRADUATE & GRADUATE STUDENTS IN THE ABOVE AREAS WHO ARE INTERESTED IN PURSUING CAREERS IN SOME ASPECT OF HELICOPTER OR VERTICAL FLIGHT. FOR FULL TIME STUDY AT ACCREDITED SCHOOL OF ENGINEERING.

WRITE FOR COMPLETE INFORMATION.

284

WOMAN'S AUXILIARY TO THE AMERICAN INSTITUTE OF MINING METALLURGICAL & PETROLEUM ENGINEERS (WAAIME SCHOLARSHIP LOAN FUND)

345 E.47TH ST; 14TH FLOOR
NEW YORK NY 10017
WRITTEN INQUIRY ONLY

AMOUNT: VARIES

DEADLINE(S): MAR 15

FIELD(S): EARTH SCIENCES; MINING ENGINEERING; PETROLEUM ENGINEERING

OPEN TO UNDERGRADUATE JUNIORS & SENIORS AND GRADUATE STUDENTS. ELIGIBLE APPLICANTS RECEIVE A SCHOLARSHIP LOAN FOR ALL OR PART OF THEIR EDUCATION. RECIPIENTS REPAY ONLY 50% WITH NO INTEREST CHARGES.

REPAYMENT TO BEGIN BY 6 MONTHS AFTER GRADUATION AND BE COMPLETED WITHIN 6 YEARS. WRITE TO WAAIME SCHOLARSHIP LOAN FUND; ADDRESS ABOVE; FOR COMPLETE INFORMATION.

SCHOOL OF HUMANITIES

285

ALPHA DELTA KAPPA (1995 ADK FINE ARTS GRANTS)

1615 WEST 92ND STREET
KANSAS CITY MO 64114
816/363-5525

AMOUNT: $5000 FIRST PLACE; $3000 SECOND

DEADLINE(S): JUN 1 1994

FIELD(S): INSTRUMENTAL MUSIC (STRINGS); VISUAL ARTS (FINE ARTS ORIGINAL CRAFTS)

OPEN TO ALL QUALIFIED UNDERGRADS; GRADS & POST GRADS. CATEGORIES CHANGE EVERY 2 YRS. CATEGORIES FOR 1995 ARE INSTRUMENTAL MUSIC (STRINGS) AND IN VISUAL ARTS (FINE ARTS ORIGINAL CRAFTS).

GRANTS ARE PAID OVER A TWO YEAR PERIOD. REQUEST APPLICATIONS AFTER JUL 1 1993 FROM KAREN LOONEY; ADK GRANTS COORDINATOR; ADDRESS ABOVE. YOU MUST SPECIFY CATEGORY.

286

AMERICAN COUNCIL OF LEARNED SOCIETIES (ACLS FELLOWSHIPS)

OFFICE OF FELLOWSHIPS & GRANTS;
228 E. 45TH ST.
NEW YORK NY 10017
WRITTEN INQUIRY

AMOUNT: UP TO $20000

DEADLINE(S): SEP 30

FIELD(S): HUMANITIES; SOCIAL SCIENCES; OTHER AREAS HAVING PREDOMINATELY HUMANISTIC EMPHASIS

OPEN TO USA CITIZENS OR LEGAL RESIDENTS WHO HOLD THE PH.D OR ITS EQUIVALENT. FELLOWSHIPS ARE DESIGNED TO HELP SCHOLARS DEVOTE 2 TO 12 CONTINUOUS MONTHS TO FULL TIME RESEARCH.

WRITE FOR COMPLETE INFORMATION.

287

AMERICAN INSTITUTE OF INDIAN STUDIES (SENIOR RESEARCH FELLOWSHIPS)

1130 E. 59TH ST.
CHICAGO IL 60637
312/702-8638

AMOUNT: $6000 - $11000 PLUS TRAVEL

DEADLINE(S): JUL 1

FIELD(S): HUMANITIES

POST-DOCTORAL FELLOWSHIPS OPEN TO USA CITIZENS OR FOREIGN NATIONALS IN RESIDENCE AT AMERICAN COLLEGES AND UNIVERSITIES. FELLOWS MUST HAVE PH.D. AND MUST AGREE TO BE FORMALLY AFFILIATED WITH AN INDIAN UNIVERSITY WHILE IN INDIA.

APPROXIMATELY 50 SENIOR AWARDS PER YEAR. WRITE FOR COMPLETE INFORMATION.

288

AMERICAN INSTITUTE OF PAKISTAN STUDIES (GRANT PROGRAM)

WAKE FOREST UNIV; PO BOX 7568
WINSTON-SALEM NC 27109
919/759-5453; FAX 919/759-6104

AMOUNT: VARIES

DEADLINE(S): JAN 1

FIELD(S): HUMANITIES; SOCIAL SCIENCES

FELLOWSHIPS TO SUPPORT STUDY & RESEARCH IN THE COUNTRY OF PAKISTAN. OPEN TO POST-DOCTORAL RESEARCHERS & PH.D CANDIDATES AT USA INSTITUTIONS WHO HAVE COMPLETED ALL COURSEWORK EXCEPT FOR THE DISSERTATION. USA OR CANADIAN CITIZEN.

7-10 AWARDS PER YEAR. WRITE FOR COMPLETE INFORMATION.

289

AMERICAN RESEARCH INSTITUTE IN TURKEY (DOCTORAL DISSERTATION RESEARCH FELLOWSHIPS)

C/O UNIVERSITY MUSEUM; 33RD & SPRUCE STREETS
PHILADELPHIA PA 19104
215/898-3474

AMOUNT: $1000 - $4000

DEADLINE(S): NOV 15

FIELD(S): HUMANITIES; SOCIAL SCIENCES

FELLOWSHIPS TO SUPPORT DOCTORAL DISSERTATION RESEARCH IN THE COUNTRY OF TURKEY. OPEN TO PH.D CANDIDATES AT USA & CANADIAN INSTITUTIONS WHO HAVE COMPLETED ALL COURSEWORK EXCEPT FOR THE DISSERTATION.

8-10 AWARDS PER YEAR. WRITE FOR COMPLETE INFORMATION.

290

ASSOCIATION FOR EDUCATION IN JOURNALISM & MASS COMMUNICATION (CORRESPONDENTS FUND SCHOLARSHIPS)

UNIV OF SOUTH CAROLINA
COLLEGE OF JOURNALISM
COLUMBIA SC 29208
803/777-2005

AMOUNT: UP TO $2000

DEADLINE(S): APR 30

FIELD(S): JOURNALISM; MASS COMMUNICATIONS; LIBERAL ARTS

OPEN TO CHILDREN OF PRINT OR BROADCAST JOURNALISTS WHO ARE FOREIGN CORRESPONDENTS FOR A USA NEWS MEDIUM. FOR UNDERGRADUATE; GRADUATE OR POST-GRADUATE STUDY AT ANY ACCREDITED COLLEGE OR UNIVERSITY IN THE USA.

PREFERENCE TO JOURNALISM OR COMMUNICATIONS MAJORS. 8-15 RENEWABLE AWARDS PER YEAR. WRITE FOR COMPLETE INFORMATION.

291

CHAUTAUQUA INSTITUTION (SCHOLARSHIPS)

SCHOOLS OFFICE; BOX 1098; DEPT. 6
CHAUTAUQUA NY 14722
716/357-6233

AMOUNT: VARIES

DEADLINE(S): APR 1

FIELD(S): ART; MUSIC; DANCE; THEATER

SCHOLARSHIPS FOR SUMMER SCHOOL ONLY. AWARDS ARE BASED ON AUDITIONS (PORTFOLIO IN ART) INDICATING PROFICIENCY; FINANCIAL NEED IS A CONSIDERATION.

SOME AUDITIONS ARE REQUIRED IN PERSON BUT TAPED AUDITIONS ALSO ARE ACCEPTABLE. 250 AWARDS PER YEAR. WRITE OR CALL FOR COMPLETE INFORMATION.

292

COMMITTEE ON SCHOLARLY COMMUNICATION WITH CHINA (CHINESE FELLOWSHIPS FOR SCHOLARLY DEVELOPMENT)

1055 THOMAS JEFFERSON ST NW;
SUITE 2013
WASHINGTON DC 20007
202/337-1250; FAX 202/337-3109

AMOUNT: VARIES

DEADLINE(S): LIVING AND TRAVEL EXPENSES FOR 1 SEMESTER (AUG - DEC)

FIELD(S): SOCIAL SCIENCES; HUMANITIES; CHINESE STUDIES

SCHOOL OF HUMANITIES

OPEN TO CHINESE SCHOLARS IN THE SOCIAL SCIENCES AND HUMANITIES WITH THE MA OR PH.D (OR EQUIVALENT) FROM A CHINESE INSTITUTION TO CONDUCT POSTGRADUATE RESEARCH AT A USA INSTITUTION. AN AMERICAN SCHOLAR MUST NOMINATE THE CHINESE CANDIDATE.

SCHOLARS ENROLLED IN USA DEGREE PROGRAMS ARE NOT ELIGIBLE. WRITE FOR COMPLETE INFORMATION.

293

COMMITTEE ON SCHOLARLY COMMUNICATION WITH CHINA (POSTDOCTORAL RESEARCH PROGRAM)

1055 THOMAS JEFFERSON ST NW;
SUITE 2013
WASHINGTON DC 20007
202/337-1250; FAX 202/337-3109

AMOUNT: VARIES

DEADLINE(S): OCT 16

FIELD(S): SOCIAL SCIENCES; HUMANITIES; CHINESE STUDIES

POST DOCTORAL GRANTS TO SUPPORT IN DEPTH RESEARCH ON THE PEOPLES REPUBLIC OF CHINA; THE CHINESE PORTION OF A COMPARATIVE STUDY OR EXPLORATORY RESEARCH ON AN ASPECT OF CONTEMPORARY CHINA. USA CITIZEN OR PERMANENT RESIDENT.

APPROX 15 AWARDS PER YEAR. WRITE FOR COMPLETE INFORMATION.

294

COMMITTEE ON SCHOLARLY COMMUNICATION WITH CHINA (GRADUATE PROGRAM)

1055 THOMAS JEFFERSON ST NW;
SUITE 2013
WASHINGTON DC 20007
202/337-1250; FAX 202/337-3109

AMOUNT: $15000 (APPROX)

DEADLINE(S): OCT 16

FIELD(S): SOCIAL SCIENCES; HUMANITIES; CHINESE STUDIES

GRANTS FOR INDIVIDUALS ENROLLED IN A GRADUATE PROGRAM IN THE SOCIAL SCIENCES OR HUMANITIES TO DO COURSEWORK IN AN ACADEMIC DISCIPLINE AT A CHINESE UNIVERSITY. ALSO SUPPORTS DISSERTATION RESEARCH. USA CITIZEN OR PERMANENT RESIDENT.

MUST HAVE CHINESE LANGUAGE PROFICIENCY. 15 AWARDS PER YEAR; RENEWABLE. WRITE FOR COMPLETE INFORMATION.

295

CORNELL UNIVERSITY (MELLON POST-DOCTORAL FELLOWSHIP PROGRAM)

A.D. WHITE HOUSE; 27 EAST AVE.
ITHACA NY 14853
607/255-9274

AMOUNT: $25000 STIPEND

DEADLINE(S): JAN

FIELD(S): HUMANITIES

FELLOWSHIPS OPEN TO NONTENURED SCHOLARS AND TEACHERS IN THE HUMANITIES. PROGRAM IS DESIGNED TO ENCOURAGE ACADEMIC GROWTH OF PROMISING HUMANISTS WITH RECENT PH.D DEGREES. USA OR CANADIAN CITIZENS OR PERMANENT RESIDENTS.

APPLICANTS MUST HAVE COMPLETED REQUIREMENTS FOR PH.D AFTER JUN 1987 AND BEFORE APPLYING. WHILE IN RESIDENCE AT CORNELL FELLOWS HAVE LIMITED TEACHING DUTIES AND OPPORTUNITY FOR SCHOLARLY WORK. WRITE FOR COMPLETE INFORMATION.

296

EMORY COLLEGE (ANDREW W. MELLON POST-DOCTORAL FELLOWSHIPS IN THE HUMANITIES)

DEAN ELEANOR MAIN; EMORY UNIVERSITY
ATLANTA GA 30322
404/727-0676

AMOUNT: VARIES

DEADLINE(S): VARIES

FIELD(S): HUMANITIES

FELLOWSHIPS AT EMORY ARE OPEN TO NON-TENURED JUNIOR SCHOLARS WHO HAVE HAD THEIR PH.D FOR LESS THAN THREE YEARS. LIMITED TEACHING & DEPARTMENTAL DUTIES. OPPORTUNITY TO DEVELOP SCHOLARLY RESEARCH. DURATION IS 1 YEAR.

WRITE FOR COMPLETE INFORMATION.

297

FLORIDA ENDOWMENT FUND FOR HIGHER EDUCATION (MCKNIGHT DOCTORAL FELLOWSHIP PROGRAM)

201 E.KENNEDY BLVD; SUITE 1525
TAMPA FL 33602
813/272-2772

AMOUNT: $11000 STIPEND + $5000 TUITION & FEES (PER YEAR)

DEADLINE(S): JAN 15

FIELD(S): ALL FIELDS (EXCEPT LAW; MEDICINE & EDUCATION)

OPEN TO ALL AFRICAN-AMERICANS WITH AT LEAST A BACHELOR'S DEGREE FROM AN ACCREDITED INSTITUTION WHO WISH TO PURSUE A DOCTORAL DEGREE. PROGRAM RECRUITS NATIONWIDE; HOWEVER FELLOWS MUST ENROLL IN A FLORIDA INSTITUTION. USA CITIZEN.

25 AWARDS PER YEAR. RENEWABLE FOR UP TO 5 YEARS. WRITE FOR COMPLETE INFORMATION.

298

GETTY CENTER FOR THE HISTORY OF ART & THE HUMANITIES (PREDOCTORAL & POSTDOCTORAL FELLOWSHIPS)

DR H.H.HYMANS;
401 WILSHIRE BLVD; #400
SANTA MONICA CA 90401
310/458-9811

AMOUNT: $15000 PREDOCTORAL; $20000 POSTDOCTORAL

DEADLINE(S): DEC 1

FIELD(S): HUMANITIES; SOCIAL SCIENCES; ANTHROPOLOGY; ART/SCIENCE HISTORY; LITERATURE; PHILOSOPHY ETC.

OPEN TO PRE & POSTDOCTORAL SCHOLARS WHOSE AREAS OF RESEARCH COMPLEMENT THE CENTER'S PROGRAMS & RESOURCES. PREDOCTORAL CANDIDATES SHOULD EXPECT TO COMPLETE DISSERTATIONS DURING THE FELLOWSHIP YEAR.

POSTDOCTORALS SHOULD HAVE RECEIVED DOCTORATE IN HUMANITIES OR SOCIAL SCIENCES WITHIN LAST 3 YEARS & BE REWRITING DISSERTATIONS FOR PUBLICATION. WRITE FOR COMPLETE INFORMATION.

299

GIRTON COLLEGE (FELLOWSHIPS)

SECRETARY TO THE ELECTORS
CAMBRIDGE CB3 OJG ENGLAND
338 999

AMOUNT: UP TO 10000 POUNDS STERLING PER YEAR

DEADLINE(S): OCT 14

FIELD(S): HUMANITIES; SCIENCE

APPLICATIONS ARE INVITED FOR RESEARCH FELLOWSHIPS AT GIRTON COLLEGE TENABLE FOR THREE YEARS BEGINNING OCT 1. THE FELLOWSHIPS ARE OPEN TO MEN AND WOMEN GRADUATES OF ANY UNIVERSITY.

A STATEMENT OF APPROXIMATELY 1000 WORDS OUTLINING THE RESEARCH TO BE UNDERTAKEN MUST BE SUBMITTED. WRITE FOR APPLICATION FORM AND COMPLETE INFORMATION.

300

HARVARD UNIVERSITY (ANDREW W. MELLON FACULTY FELLOWSHIPS IN THE HUMANITIES)

LAMONT LIBRARY 202
CAMBRIDGE MA 02138
617/495-2519

AMOUNT: $32000 PER YEAR

DEADLINE(S): NOV 1

FIELD(S): HUMANITIES

FELLOWSHIPS AT HARVARD. OPEN TO NON-TENURED JUNIOR SCHOLARS WHO HAVE THEIR PH.D & HAVE TAUGHT IN THE HUMANITIES FOR AT LEAST 2 YEARS. LIMITED TEACHING & DEPARTMENTAL DUTIES. OPPORTUNITY TO DEVELOP SCHOLARLY RESEARCH. DURATION IS 1 YEAR.

SPECIAL CONSIDERATION TO APPLICANTS WHO HAVE NOT RECENTLY HAD ACCESS TO RESOUCES OF MAJOR RESEARCH UNIVERSITY. 15 AWARDS PER YEAR. WRITE FOR COMPLETE INFORMATION.

301

NATIONAL ENDOWMENT FOR THE HUMANITIES (POST-GRADUATE FELLOWSHIPS; GRANTS & SUMMER SEMINARS)

DIV OF FELLOWSHIPS & SEMINARS;
1100 PENNSYLVANIA AVE NW; RM #316
WASHINGTON DC 20506
202/606-8466

AMOUNT: $30000 MAX STIPEND

DEADLINE(S): JUN 1; OCT 1 FOR SUMMER STIPENDS

FIELD(S): HUMANITIES

FOR POST-GRADUATE TEACHERS; WRITERS; RESEARCHERS; ETC. TO ENHANCE THEIR CAPACITIES AS SCHOLARS; TEACHERS OR INTERPRETERS OF THE HUMANITIES & TO ENABLE THEM TO MAKE SIGNIFICANT CONTRIBUTIONS TO THOUGHT & KNOWLEDGE IN THE HUMANITIES.

FELLOWSHIPS NORMALLY SUPPORT FULL-TIME WORK FOR 6-12 MONTHS. 2 MONTH SUMMER STIPENDS & SEMINARS ALSO AVAILABLE. US CITIZEN OR RESIDENT FOR 3 YEARS PRIOR TO APPLICATION. WRITE FOR COMPLETE INFORMATION.

302

NATIONAL HUMANITIES CENTER (POST-DOCTORAL FELLOWSHIPS)

PO BOX 12256; 7 ALEXANDER DR
RESEARCH TRIANGLE PARK NC 27709
919/549-0661

AMOUNT: STIPEND + TRAVEL EXPENSES

SCHOOL OF HUMANITIES

DEADLINE(S): OCT 15

FIELD(S): HISTORY; LANGUAGES & LITERATURE; PHILOSOPHY; OTHER FIELDS IN THE LIBERAL ARTS

POST-DOCTORAL RESEARCH FELLOWSHIPS OPEN TO YOUNG & SENIOR SCHOLARS FROM ANY NATION. AWARDS SUPPORT RESEARCH & WRITING AT THE CENTER. SCHOLARS FROM OTHER AREAS SUCH AS NATURAL SCIENCES; ARTS; PROFESSIONS & PUBLIC LIFE ALSO MAY APPLY.

30-35 FELLOWSHIPS PER YEAR. WRITE FOR COMPLETE INFORMATION.

303

NATIONAL LEAGUE OF AMERICAN PEN WOMEN INC. (SCHOLARSHIP GRANTS FOR MATURE WOMEN)

1300 SEVENTEENTH ST. N.W.
WASHINGTON DC 20036
202/785-1997

AMOUNT: $1000

DEADLINE(S): JAN

FIELD(S): ART; MUSIC; CREATIVE WRITING

THE NATIONAL LEAGUE OF AMERICAN PEN WOMEN GIVES THREE $1000 GRANTS IN EVEN NUMBERED YEARS TO WOMEN AGE 35 AND OVER. SHOULD SUBMIT SLIDES; MANUSCRIPTS OR MUSICAL COMPOSITIONS SUITED TO THE CRITERIA FOR THAT YEAR.

WRITE FOR COMPLETE INFORMATION.

304

NEWBERRY LIBRARY (FRANCES C. ALLEN FELLOWSHIPS)

60 W. WALTON ST
CHICAGO IL 60610
312/943-9090

AMOUNT: VARIES ACCORDING TO NEED

DEADLINE(S): AUG 1 AND FEB 1

FIELD(S): HUMANITIES & SOCIAL SCIENCES

FELLOWSHIPS ARE AVAILABLE TO WOMEN OF AMERICAN INDIAN HERITAGE WHO ARE STUDYING AT THE GRADUATE LEVEL. PURPOSE OF THE FELLOWSHIP IS TO ENCOURAGE STUDY IN THE HUMANITIES AND SOCIAL SCIENCES.

FELLOWS ARE EXPECTED TO SPEND A SIGNIFICANT PART OF THEIR RESIDENCE AT THE CENTER FOR THE HISTORY OF THE AMERICAN INDIAN. WRITE FOR COMPLETE INFORMATION.

305

NEWBERRY LIBRARY (MONTICELLO COLLEGE FOUNDATION FELLOWSHIP FOR WOMEN)

60 WEST WALTON STREET
CHICAGO IL 60610
312/943-9090

AMOUNT: $12500

DEADLINE(S): JAN 10

FIELD(S): HUMANITIES

OPEN TO WOMEN WITH THE PH.D DEGREE WHO ARE AT AN EARLY STAGE OF THEIR CAREER. PREFERENCE TO THOSE WHOSE SCHOLARSHIP IS CONCERNED WITH THE STUDY OF WOMEN. HOWEVER STUDY MAY BE PROPOSED IN ANY FIELD APPROPRIATE TO NEWBERRY'S COLLECTIONS.

FELLOWSHIP IS FOR 6 MONTHS STUDY IN RESIDENCE AT THE NEWBERRY LIBRARY. USA CITIZEN. WRITE FOR COMPLETE INFORMATION.

306

NEWBERRY LIBRARY (SHORT-TERM FELLOWSHIPS)

60 WEST WALTON STREET
CHICAGO IL 60610
312/943-9090

AMOUNT: $800 PER MONTH STIPEND

DEADLINE(S): MAR 1; OCT 15

FIELD(S): HUMANITIES

FELLOWSHIPS OPEN TO CANDIDATES WHO HOLD A PH.D OR WHO HAVE COMPLETED ALL PH.D REQUIREMENTS EXCEPT FOR THE DISSERTATION. FOR RESEARCH AT THE NEWBERRY FOR UP TO 2 MONTHS (3 MONTHS IF TRAVEL FROM A FOREIGN COUNTRY IS INVOLVED).

PREFERENCE TO APPLICANTS OUTSIDE CHICAGO AREA WHOSE RESEARCH PARTICULARLY REQUIRES STUDY AT THE NEWBERRY. WRITE FOR COMPLETE INFORMATION.

307

ORGANIZATION OF AMERICAN STATES DEPT OF FELLOWSHIPS & TRAINING (OAS PRA-FELLOWSHIPS)

TRAINEE SELECTION DIVISION
WASHINGTON DC 20006
202/789-3902

AMOUNT: TUITION + FEES; TRAVEL EXP & STIPEND

DEADLINE(S): APR 30; AUG 31

FIELD(S): ALL FIELDS EXCEPT MEDICINE & FOREIGN LANGUAGES

GRADUATE FELLOWSHIPS FOR USA CITIZENS OR PERMANENT RESIDENTS TO STUDY IN AN OAS MEMBER COUNTRY. MUST HAVE UNDERGRADUATE DEGREE AND HAVE DEMONSTRATED ABILITY TO PURSUE ADVANCED STUDIES IN CHOSEN FIELD.

APPLICANTS SHOULD BE FLUENT IN LANGUAGE OF COUNTRY OF INTENDED STUDY. PRIORITY IS GIVEN TO RESEARCH PROJECTS. WRITE FOR COMPLETE INFORMATION.

308

ROCKEFELLER FOUNDATION (POST-DOCTORAL RESIDENCY PROGRAM IN THE HUMANITIES)

1133 AVENUE OF THE AMERICAS
NEW YORK NY 10036
212/869-8500

AMOUNT: VARIES WITH INSTITUTION

DEADLINE(S): VARIES WITH INSTITUTION

FIELD(S): HUMANITIES

POST-DOCTORAL FELLOWSHIPS OFFERED FOR 1 YEAR OR 6 MONTHS. FOR THE SUPPORT OF SCHOLARS AND WRITERS WHOSE RESEARCH AIDS IN UNDERSTANDING CONTEMPORARY AND CULTURAL ISSUES AND EXTENDS INTERNATIONAL OR INTERCULTURAL SCHOLARSHIP.

WRITE TO THE ADDRESS ABOVE FOR A LIST OF HOST INSTITUTIONS OFFERING FELLOWSHIPS.

309

SOCIAL SCIENCE RESEARCH COUNCIL (POST-DOCTORAL GRANTS FOR ADVANCED AREA RESEARCH)

605 THIRD AVENUE
NEW YORK NY 10158
212/661-0280

AMOUNT: VARIES

DEADLINE(S): DEC 1

FIELD(S): HUMANITIES; SOCIAL SCIENCES

OPEN TO SCHOLARS WHOSE PREVIOUS WORK HAS DEMONSTRATED THEIR COMPETENCE FOR RESEARCH IN THE SOCIAL SCIENCE OR HUMANITIES AND WHO HOLD THE PH.D DEGREE OR HAVE EQUIVALENT RESEARCH EXPERIENCE.

PROGRAMS ARE TO SUPPORT RESEARCH IN ONE COUNTRY; COMPARATIVE RESEARCH BETWEEN COUNTRIES IN AN AREA; AND COMPARATIVE RESEARCH BETWEEN AREAS. WRITE FOR COMPLETE INFORMATION.

310

SOCIETY FOR THE HUMANITIES (FELLOWSHIPS)

C/O CORNELL UNIV; AD WHITE HOUSE;
27 EAST AVE
ITHACA NY 14853
607/255-9274

AMOUNT: $32000

DEADLINE(S): NOV 1

FIELD(S): HUMANITIES

ANNUAL POST-DOCTORAL FELLOWSHIPS AT CORNELL UNIVERSITY. EACH YEAR THERE IS A FOCAL THEME WITH FELLOWS WORKING ON TOPICS RELATED TO THAT THEME. THEIR APPROACH TO THE HUMANITIES SHOULD BE BROAD ENOUGH TO APPEAL TO STUDENTS & SCHOLARS ALIKE.

SIX FELLOWSHIPS PER YEAR. WRITE FOR COMPLETE INFORMATION.

311

SPACE FOUNDATION (SPACE INDUSTRIALIZATION FELLOWSHIP)

4800 RESEARCH FOREST DR
THE WOODLANDS TX 77381
713/363-7944; FAX 713/363-7914

AMOUNT: $4000

DEADLINE(S): OCT 1

FIELD(S): SCIENCES & ENGINEERING; BUSINESS; LAW; ECONOMICS; SOCIAL SCIENCES; ENVIRONMENTAL STUDIES; HUMANITIES

OPEN TO SUPERIOR GRADUATE STUDENTS IN THE ABOVE DISCIPLINES WHO INTEND TO DEVOTE THEIR CAREERS TO THE FURTHERANCE OF PRACTICAL SPACE RESEARCH; ENGINEERING; BUSINESS OR OTHER APPLICATION VENTURES.

CONTACT DR. DAVID J. NORTON; EDUCATIONAL GRANT PROGRAM CHAIRMAN; ADDRESS ABOVE; FOR COMPLETE INFORMATION.

312

U.S. DEPT. OF EDUCATION (JACOB K JAVITS FELLOWSHIP PROGRAM)

PO BOX 84
WASHINGTON DC 20044
800/4FED-AID

AMOUNT: $15000 PER YEAR ON AVERAGE

DEADLINE(S): MAR 15

FIELD(S): ARTS; HUMANITIES; SOCIAL SCIENCES

FELLOWSHIPS TO ASSIST STUDENTS OF SUPERIOR ABILITIES IN STUDIES FOR DOCTORAL-LEVEL DEGREES IN SPECIFIED SUBFIELDS OF THE ABOVE AREAS. USA CITIZEN OR LEGAL RESIDENT.

SCHOOL OF HUMANITIES

APPLICATION PACKAGE AVAILABLE LATE OCT OR EARLY NOV. APPROX 100 AWARDS PER YEAR; RENEWABLE UP TO 48 MONTHS. WRITE FOR COMPLETE INFORMATION.

313

UNITARIAN UNIVERSALIST ASSN (SCHOLARSHIPS AND AWARDS)

25 BEACON STREET
BOSTON MA 02108
617-742-2100

AMOUNT: $100 - $700

DEADLINE(S): MAR 15

FIELD(S): ART; POETRY; MUSIC

FOR GRADUATE OR UNDERGRADUATE STUDY. APPLICANTS MUST BE MEMBERS OF THE UNITARIAN CHURCH OR BE SPONSORED BY A UNITARIAN UNIVERSALIST SOCIETY.

SEND A SELF ADDRESSED STAMPED ENVELOPE TO ABOVE ADDRESS FOR COMPLETE INFORMATION.

314

UNIVERSITY OF PENNSYLVANIA (ANDREW W. MELLON POST-DOCTORAL FELLOWSHIPS IN THE HUMANITIES)

GRADUATE DIVISION; 16 COLLEGE HALL
PHILADELPHIA PA 19104
215/898-4940

AMOUNT: $30000

DEADLINE(S): OCT 15

FIELD(S): HUMANITIES

POST-DOCTORAL FELLOWSHIPS AT THE UNIV OF PENN. OPEN TO APPLICANTS WHO HAVE HELD THE PH.D DEGREE FOR 3-8 YEARS. PROPOSALS MAY REPRESENT ANY ASPECT OF HUMANISTIC STUDY & RESEARCH EXCEPT FOR EDUCATIONAL CURRICULUM BUILDING & PERFORMING ARTS.

DURATION OF AWARD IS ONE YEAR. WRITE TO CHAIR; HUMANITIES COORDINATING COMMITTEE; ADDRESS ABOVE; FOR COMPLETE INFORMATION.

315

UNIVERSITY OF SOUTHERN CALIFORNIA (MELLON POST-DOCTORAL FELLOWSHIP)

HUMANITIES DIV-OFFICE OF THE DEAN; UNIVERSITY PARK; MAIL CODE 4012
LOS ANGELES CA 90089
213/740-5294

AMOUNT: APPROX $27500

DEADLINE(S): VARIES - WRITE FOR DETAILS

FIELD(S): HUMANITIES

POST-DOCTORAL FELLOWSHIPS AT USC FOR JUNIOR SCHOLARS WITH CONCURRENT ONE YEAR APPOINTMENT AS LECTURER.

WRITE FOR COMPLETE INFORMATION.

316

WOODROW WILSON INTERNATIONAL CENTER FOR SCHOLARS (FELLOWSHIPS IN THE HUMANITIES AND SOCIAL SCIENCES)

FELLOWSHIPS OFFICE; WOODROW WILSON CENTER
WASHINGTON DC 20560
202/357-2841

AMOUNT: UP TO $52000

DEADLINE(S): OCT 1

FIELD(S): HUMANITIES; SOCIAL SCIENCES

OPEN TO INDIVIDUALS FROM ANY COUNTRY WHO HAVE OUTSTANDING CAPABILITIES AND EXPERIENCE FROM A WIDE VARIETY OF BACKGROUNDS. ACADEMIC PARTICIPANTS LIMITED TO POSTDOCTORAL LEVEL AND SHOULD HAVE PUBLISHED A MAJOR WORK BEYOND PH.D DISSERTATION.

APPROXIMATELY 30 FELLOWSHIPS ANNUALLY TO SCHOLARS WITH OUTSTANDING PROJECT PROPOSALS; ESPECIALLY THOSE TRANSCENDING NARROW SPECIALITIES. WRITE FOR COMPLETE INFORMATION.

317

WOODROW WILSON NATIONAL FELLOWSHIP FOUNDATION (NEWCOMBE DISSERTATION FELLOWSHIPS)

BOX 642
PRINCETON NJ 08542
609/924-4666

AMOUNT: $12000 STIPEND

DEADLINE(S): DEC 13

FIELD(S): SOCIAL SCIENCES; HUMANITIES; EDUCATION

OPEN TO PH.D; TH.D & ED.D CANDIDATES IN THE USA WHO WILL COMPLETE ALL DOCTORAL REQUIREMENTS EXCEPT THE DISSERTATION BY NOV 29. THESE AWARDS ARE NOT DESIGNED TO FINANCE FIELD WORK BUT RATHER THE COMPLETION OF DISSERTATION WRITING.

ELIGIBLE PROPOSALS WILL HAVE ETHICAL OR RELIGIOUS VALUES AS A CENTRAL CONCERN. REQUEST APPLICATION BY NOV. 29. WRITE FOR COMPLETE INFORMATION.

318

YALE CENTER FOR BRITISH ART (FELLOWSHIPS)

BOX 2120 YALE STATION
NEW HAVEN CT 06520
203/432-2800

AMOUNT: TRAVEL; ACCOMMODATION; PER DIEM

DEADLINE(S): DEC 31

FIELD(S): BRITISH ART; HISTORY; LITERATURE

FELLOWSHIPS ENABLE SCHOLARS ENGAGED IN POST-DOCTORAL OR EQUIVALENT RESEARCH IN BRITISH ART; HISTORY OR LITERATURE TO STUDY THE CENTER'S HOLDINGS OF PAINTINGS DRAWINGS PRINTS AND RARE BOOKS AND TO MAKE USE OF ITS RESEARCH FACILITIES.

GRANTS COVER TRAVEL AND PER DIEM AND NORMALLY RUN FOR A PERIOD OF 4 WEEKS. 10 AWARDS PER YEAR. WRITE FOR COMPLETE INFORMATION.

AREA STUDIES

319

AFRICAN STUDIES CENTER (AFRICAN LANGUAGE SCHOLARSHIPS - TITLE VI)

C/O UCLA; 10244 BUNCHE HALL
LOS ANGELES CA 90024
213/825-3686

AMOUNT: $8000 + TUITION & FEES

DEADLINE(S): FEB 1

FIELD(S): AFRICAN STUDIES

FOR STUDENTS IN GRADUATE PROGRAMS STUDYING AN AFRICAN LANGUAGE AT UCLA. USA CITIZEN OR PERMANENT RESIDENT.

5-10 AWARDS PER YEAR. AWARDS CAN BE RENEWED ONCE. WRITE FOR COMPLETE INFORMATION.

320

AMERICAN COUNCIL OF LEARNED SOCIETIES (ACLS FELLOWSHIPS)

OFFICE OF FELLOWSHIPS & GRANTS;
228 E. 45TH ST.
NEW YORK NY 10017
WRITTEN INQUIRY

AMOUNT: UP TO $20000

DEADLINE(S): SEP 30

FIELD(S): HUMANITIES; SOCIAL SCIENCES; OTHER AREAS HAVING PREDOMINATELY HUMANISTIC EMPHASIS

OPEN TO USA CITIZENS OR LEGAL RESIDENTS WHO HOLD THE PH.D OR ITS EQUIVALENT. FELLOWSHIPS ARE DESIGNED TO HELP SCHOLARS DEVOTE 2 TO 12 CONTINUOUS MONTHS TO FULL TIME RESEARCH.

WRITE FOR COMPLETE INFORMATION.

321

AMERICAN COUNCIL OF LEARNED SOCIETIES (DISSERTATION GRANTS IN EAST EUROPEAN STUDIES)

OFFICE OF FELLOWSHIPS & GRANTS;
228 E. 45TH ST.
NEW YORK NY 10017
WRITTEN INQUIRY

AMOUNT: UP TO $15000 + EXPENSES

DEADLINE(S): DEC 1

FIELD(S): EAST EUROPEAN STUDIES

OPEN TO DOCTORAL CANDIDATES FOR SUPPORT OF DISSERTATION RESEARCH OR WRITING TO BE UNDERTAKEN AT ANY UNIVERSITY OR INSTITUTION -OUTSIDE- OF EAST EUROPE. USA CITIZEN OR LEGAL RESIDENT.

WRITE FOR COMPLETE INFORMATION.

322

AMERICAN COUNCIL OF LEARNED SOCIETIES (FELLOWSHIPS FOR POSTDOCTORAL RESEARCH IN CHINESE STUDIES)

228 EAST 45TH ST; OFFICE OF FELLOWSHIPS & GRANTS
NEW YORK NY 10017
WRITTEN INQUIRY

AMOUNT: UP TO $25000

DEADLINE(S): DEC 1

FIELD(S): CHINESE STUDIES

POSTDOCTORAL FELLOWSHIPS FOR RESEARCH OR WRITING ON CHINESE CULTURE OR SOCIETY INCLUDING RESEARCH TO SYNTHESIZE OR REINTERPRET THE APPLICANT'S PAST RESEARCH AND PRODUCE A SCHOLARLY OVERVIEW OF A TOPIC IMPORTANT TO THE STUDY OF CHINA.

PROGRAM IS -NOT- INTENDED TO SUPPORT RESEARCH WITHIN THE PEOPLE'S REPUBLIC OF CHINA. WRITE FOR COMPLETE INFORMATION.

323

AMERICAN COUNCIL OF LEARNED SOCIETIES (FELLOWSHIPS FOR CHINESE STUDIES DISSERTATION RESEARCH ABROAD)

OFFICE OF FELLOWSHIPS & GRANTS;
228 E. 45TH ST.
NEW YORK NY 10017
WRITTEN INQUIRY

AREA STUDIES

AMOUNT: UP TO $20000 FOR FULL-YEAR PROGRAMS

DEADLINE(S): DEC 1

FIELD(S): CHINESE STUDIES

OPEN TO DOCTORAL DEGREE CANDIDATES FOR DISSERTATION RESEARCH OUTSIDE THE USA IN ANY COUNTRY 'EXCEPT' THE PEOPLES REPUBLIC OF CHINA. THE DISSERTATION MUST BE RELATED TO CHINA BUT MAY BE COMPARATIVE IN NATURE.

FOREIGN NATIONALS MUST BE ENROLLED AS FULL TIME PH.D CANDIDATES IN USA INSTITUTIONS. WRITE FOR COMPLETE INFORMATION.

324

AMERICAN COUNCIL OF LEARNED SOCIETIES (FELLOWSHIPS FOR POSTDOCTORAL RESEARCH IN EAST EUROPEAN STUDY)

OFFICE OF FELLOWSHIPS & GRANTS; 228 E. 45TH ST.
NEW YORK NY 10017
WRITTEN INQUIRY

AMOUNT: UP TO $30000

DEADLINE(S): DEC 1

FIELD(S): EAST EUROPEAN STUDIES

FELLOWSHIPS FOR RESEARCH IN THE SOCIAL SCIENCES AND HUMANITIES RELATING TO ALBANIA; BULGARIA; CZECHOSLOVAKIA; GERMANY; HUNGARY; POLAND; ROMANIA AND THE FORMER YUGOSLAVIA. FOR AT LEAST SIX MONTHS OF FULL TIME RESEARCH.

NOT INTENDED TO SUPPORT RESEARCH 'WITHIN' EAST EUROPE. USA CITIZEN OR LEGAL RESIDENT. WRITE FOR COMPLETE INFORMATION.

325

AMERICAN COUNCIL OF LEARNED SOCIETIES (FELLOWSHIPS FOR ADVANCED GRADUATE TRAINING IN EAST EUROPEAN STUDIES)

OFFICE OF FELLOWSHIPS & GRANTS;
228 E. 45TH ST.
NEW YORK NY 10017
WRITTEN INQUIRY ONLY

AMOUNT: UP TO $15000 PLUS EXPENSES

DEADLINE(S): DEC 1

FIELD(S): EAST EUROPEAN STUDIES

OPEN TO GRADUATE STUDENTS WHO HAVE COMPLETED AT LEAST TWO ACADEMIC YEARS OF WORK TOWARD A DOCTORATE DEGREE. INTENDED FOR STUDENTS WHO NEED EXTRA TRAINING BEFORE BEGINNING THE DISSERTATION.

USA CITIZEN OR LEGAL RESIDENT. WRITE FOR COMPLETE INFORMATION.

326

AMERICAN JEWISH ARCHIVES (DISSERTATION & POST-DOCTORAL RESEARCH FELLOWSHIPS)

3101 CLIFTON AVE
CINCINNATI OH 45220
513/221-1875

AMOUNT: $1000 - $2000

DEADLINE(S): APR 1

FIELD(S): JEWISH STUDIES

SEVEN FELLOWSHIP PROGRAMS ARE AVAILABLE FOR POST-DOCTORAL CANDIDATES OR PERSONS AT THE DOCTORAL DISSERTATION STAGE FOR UP TO ONE MONTH OF ACTIVE RESEARCH OR WRITING AT THE AMERICAN JEWISH ARCHIVES DURING THE STIPEND YEAR.

WRITE FOR COMPLETE INFORMATION.

327

AMERICAN ORIENTAL SOCIETY (FELLOWSHIP PROGRAM)

HARLAN HATCHER GRADUATE LIBRARY - RM 111E - UNIV OF MICHIGAN
ANN ARBOR MI 48109
313/747-4760

AMOUNT: $8000

DEADLINE(S): FEB 1

FIELD(S): CHINESE PAINTING / CHINESE ART

CHINESE PAINTING PROGRAM OPEN TO STUDENTS WHO HAVE COMPLETED ALL PH.D REQUIREMENTS EXCEPT RESEARCH TRAVEL; DISSERTATION AND ITS DEFENSE. CHINESE ART PROGRAM OPEN TO DOCTORAL & POST-DOCTORAL STUDENTS WHO ARE USA CITIZENS SHOWING APTITUDE.

APPLICANTS FOR EITHER FELLOWSHIP SHOULD HAVE COMPLETED THREE YEARS STUDY OF THE CHINESE LANGUAGE. WRITE FOR COMPLETE INFORMATION.

328

AMERICAN SCHOOL OF CLASSICAL STUDIES AT ATHENS (FELLOWSHIPS)

41 E.72ND ST
NEW YORK NY 10021
212/861-0302

AMOUNT: UP TO $5650 + ROOM & PARTIAL BOARD

DEADLINE(S): JAN 5

FIELD(S): CLASSICAL STUDIES; ARCHAEOLOGY; ANCIENT GREECE

FELLOWSHIPS FOR STUDY AT ASCSA IN GREECE. OPEN TO GRADUATE STUDENTS AT AMERICAN & CANADIAN COLLEGES & UNIVERSITIES. RECENT GRADUATES ALSO ARE ELIGIBLE.

WRITE FOR COMPLETE INFORMATION.

329 ─────────────

AMERICAN SCHOOL OF CLASSICAL STUDIES AT ATHENS (GENNADEION FELLOWSHIP)

41 EAST 72ND ST
NEW YORK NY 10021
212/861-0302

AMOUNT: $5650 + ROOM & PARTIAL BOARD

DEADLINE(S): JAN 15

FIELD(S): BYZANTINE STUDIES; GREEK STUDIES

OPEN TO GRADUATE STUDENTS & JUNIOR ACADEMICS. FELLOWSHIPS SUPPORT WORK & STUDY AT THE GENNADEION IN ATHENS GREECE.

WRITE FOR COMPLETE INFORMATION.

330 ─────────────

ARCHAEOLOGICAL INSTITUTE OF AMERICA (OLIVIA JAMES TRAVELING FELLOWSHIP)

675 COMMONWEALTH AVE
BOSTON MA 02215
617/353-9361; FAX 617/353-6550

AMOUNT: $11500 STIPEND

DEADLINE(S): NOV 15

FIELD(S): ARCHAEOLOGY; CLASSICS; SCULPTURE; HISTORY; ARCHITECTURE

FOR GRADUATE OR POST-GRADUATE STUDY IN GREECE; AEGEAN ISLANDS; SICILY; SOUTHERN ITALY; ASIA MINOR OR MESOPOTAMIA. PREFERENCE IS FOR DISSERTATION OR RECENT PH.D RESEARCH. WILL NOT SUPPORT FIELD EXCAVATION. USA CITIZEN OR LEGAL RESIDENT.

WRITE FOR COMPLETE INFORMATION.

331 ─────────────

ARMENIAN GENERAL BENEVOLENT UNION (GRADUATE SCHOLARSHIP PROGRAM)

585 SADDLE RIVER RD
SADDLE BROOK NJ 07662
201/797-7600

AMOUNT: $1000

DEADLINE(S): APR 30

FIELD(S): LAW; MEDICINE; INTERNATIONAL RELATIONS; ARMENIAN STUDIES

GRANTS AND LOANS OPEN TO FULLY MATRICULATED STUDENTS OF ARMENIAN DESCENT IN ACCREDITED COLLEGES AND UNIVERSITIES IN THE USA. REQUEST APPLICATIONS BETWEEN JAN 1 AND MAR 15. -WRITTEN REQUESTS ONLY-.

LOANS ARE WITHOUT INTEREST. REPAYMENT IS TO BEGIN 1 YEAR AFTER LEAVING SCHOOL AND MUST BE COMPLETED WITHIN 3 YEARS. WRITE FOR COMPLETE INFORMATION.

332 ─────────────

ASSOCIATION OF AMERICAN GEOGRAPHERS (HODGSON; VOURAS & STARKEY FUNDS)

1710 SIXTEENTH ST NW
WASHINGTON DC 20009
202/234-1450; FAX 202/234-2744

AMOUNT: NOT SPECIFIED

DEADLINE(S): DEC 31

FIELD(S): GEOGRAPHY

OPEN TO AAG -MEMBERS- OF AT LEAST 1 YEAR. FUND PROVIDES DISSSERTATION RESEARCH GRANTS TO PH.D CANDIDATES WHO HAVE COMPLETED ALL COURSE WORK. VOURAS FUND GIVES PREFERENCE TO MINORITY STUDENT APPLICANTS.

WRITE FOR COMPLETE INFORMATION.

333 ─────────────

AUSTRIAN CULTURAL INSTITUTE (GRANTS FOR AMERICAN GRADUATE STUDENTS)

11 EAST 52ND STREET
NEW YORK NY 10022
212/759-5165; FAX 212/319-9636

AMOUNT: AS 6.800 (APPROX US$566) PER MONTH (AS 7.500 -APPROX US$625- FOR THOSE WITH MASTER'S DEGREE)

DEADLINE(S): JAN 31

FIELD(S): AUSTRIAN STUDIES

OPEN TO DOCTORAL OR GRADUATE STUDENTS WHO ARE USA CITIZENS BETWEEN THE AGES OF 20 AND 35 AND HAVE A GOOD COMMAND OF THE GERMAN LANGUAGE. FOR RESEARCH OR STUDY PROJECTS IN AUSTRIA IN MODERN AUSTRIAN LITERATURE; HISTORY; ECONOMICS ETC.

WRITE FOR COMPLETE INFORMATION.

334 ─────────────

CANADIAN EMBASSY (CANADIAN STUDIES GRADUATE STUDENT FELLOWSHIP PROGRAM)

501 PENNSYLVANIA AVE NW
WASHINGTON DC 20001
202/682-1740

AMOUNT: $850 PER MONTH (UP TO 9 MONTHS)

DEADLINE(S): OCT 31

FIELD(S): CANADIAN STUDIES

GRANTS FOR FULL-TIME DOCTORAL STUDENTS AT ACCREDITED USA COLLEGES & UNIVERSITIES WHOSE DISSERTATIONS ARE RELATED IN SUBSTANTIAL PART TO THE STUDY OF CANADA. USA CITIZEN OR PERMANENT RESIDENT.

THERE ALSO ARE GRANTS FOR USA COLLEGE & UNIVERSITY FACULTY AND POST-DOCTORAL SCHOLARS. WRITE FOR COMPLETE INFORMATION.

335 ───────────────────

CENTER FOR HELLENIC STUDIES (RESIDENT JUNIOR FELLOWSHIPS)

3100 WHITEHAVEN STREET NW
WASHINGTON DC 20008
202/234-3738

AMOUNT: $18000

DEADLINE(S): NOV 1

FIELD(S): ANCIENT GREEK LITERATURE; HISTORY; PHILOSOPHY; LANGUAGE OR RELIGION

RESIDENT FELLOWSHIPS FOR POST-DOCTORAL SCHOLARS WITH PROFESSIONAL COMPETENCE AND SOME PUBLICATION IN ANCIENT GREEK AREAS SHOWN ABOVE.

8 RESIDENT FELLOWSHIPS PER YEAR. WRITE FOR COMPLETE INFORMATION.

336 ───────────────────

CHARLES A. LINDBERGH FUND INC. (GRANTS FOR RESEARCH PROJECTS)

708 S. THIRD ST.- SUITE 110
MINNEAPOLIS MN 55415
612/338-1703

AMOUNT: UP TO $10580

DEADLINE(S): JUN 15

FIELD(S): AVIATION/AEROSPACE; AGRICULTURE; ARTS & HUMANITIES; BIOMEDICAL RESEARCH; CONSERVATION; EXPLORATION; HEALTH & POPULATION SCIENCES; INTERCULTURAL COMMUNICATION; OCEANOGRAPHY; WASTE DISPOSAL MGMT; WATER RESOURCE MGMT; WILDLIFE PRESERVATION.

RESEARCH GRANTS ARE AWARDED ANNUALLY TO INDIVIDUALS WHOSE PROPOSED PROJECTS REPRESENT A SIGNIFICANT CONTRIBUTION TOWARD THE ACHIEVEMENT OF A BALANCE BETWEEN THE ADVANCE OF TECHNOLOGY & PRESERVATION OF THE NATURAL ENVIRONMENT.

WRITE FOR APPLICATION AND COMPLETE INFORMATION.

337 ───────────────────

COMMITTEE ON INSTITUTIONAL COOPERATION (CIC PREDOCTORAL FELLOWSHIPS)

KIRKWOOD HALL RM 111; INDIANA UNIV.
BLOOMINGTON IN 47405
812/855-0822

AMOUNT: $9500 + TUITION (5 YEARS)

DEADLINE(S): JAN 2

FIELD(S): HUMANITIES; SOCIAL SCIENCES; NATURAL SCIENCES; MATHEMATICS; ENGINEERING

PREDOCTORAL FELLOWSHIPS FOR USA CITIZENS OF AFRICAN AMERICAN; AMERICAN INDIAN; MEXICAN AMERICAN OR PUERTO RICAN HERITAGE. MUST HOLD OR EXPECT TO RECEIVE BACHELOR'S DEGREE BY LATE SUMMER FROM A REGIONALLY ACCREDITED COLLEGE OR UNIVERSITY.

AWARDS FOR SPECIFIED UNIVERSITIES IN IL; IN; IA; MI; MN; OH; WI; PA. WRITE FOR DETAILS.

338 ───────────────────

COMMITTEE ON SCHOLARLY COMMUNICATION WITH CHINA (CHINESE FELLOWSHIPS FOR SCHOLARLY DEVELOPMENT)

1055 THOMAS JEFFERSON ST NW;
SUITE 2013
WASHINGTON DC 20007
202/337-1250; FAX 202/337-3109

AMOUNT: VARIES

DEADLINE(S): LIVING AND TRAVEL EXPENSES FOR 1 SEMESTER (AUG - DEC)

FIELD(S): SOCIAL SCIENCES; HUMANITIES; CHINESE STUDIES

OPEN TO CHINESE SCHOLARS IN THE SOCIAL SCIENCES AND HUMANITIES WITH THE MA OR PH.D (OR EQUIVALENT) FROM A CHINESE INSTITUTION TO CONDUCT POSTGRADUATE RESEARCH AT A USA INSTITUTION. AN AMERICAN SCHOLAR MUST NOMINATE THE CHINESE CANDIDATE.

SCHOLARS ENROLLED IN USA DEGREE PROGRAMS ARE NOT ELIGIBLE. WRITE FOR COMPLETE INFORMATION.

339 ───────────────────

COMMITTEE ON SCHOLARLY COMMUNICATION WITH CHINA (POSTDOCTORAL RESEARCH PROGRAM)

1055 THOMAS JEFFERSON ST NW;
SUITE 2013
WASHINGTON DC 20007
202/337-1250; FAX 202/337-3109

AMOUNT: VARIES

DEADLINE(S): OCT 16

FIELD(S): SOCIAL SCIENCES; HUMANITIES; CHINESE STUDIES

POST DOCTORAL GRANTS TO SUPPORT IN DEPTH RESEARCH ON THE PEOPLES REPUBLIC OF CHINA; THE CHINESE PORTION OF A COMPARATIVE STUDY OR EXPLORATORY RESEARCH ON AN ASPECT OF CONTEMPORARY CHINA. USA CITIZEN OR PERMANENT RESIDENT.

APPROX 15 AWARDS PER YEAR. WRITE FOR COMPLETE INFORMATION.

340

COMMITTEE ON SCHOLARLY COMMUNICATION WITH CHINA (GRADUATE PROGRAM)

1055 THOMAS JEFFERSON ST NW; SUITE 2013
WASHINGTON DC 20007
202/337-1250; FAX 202/337-3109

AMOUNT: $15000 (APPROX)

DEADLINE(S): OCT 16

FIELD(S): SOCIAL SCIENCES; HUMANITIES; CHINESE STUDIES

GRANTS FOR INDIVIDUALS ENROLLED IN A GRADUATE PROGRAM IN THE SOCIAL SCIENCES OR HUMANITIES TO DO COURSEWORK IN AN ACADEMIC DISCIPLINE AT A CHINESE UNIVERSITY. ALSO SUPPORTS DISSERTATION RESEARCH. USA CITIZEN OR PERMANENT RESIDENT.

MUST HAVE CHINESE LANGUAGE PROFICIENCY. 15 AWARDS PER YEAR; RENEWABLE. WRITE FOR COMPLETE INFORMATION.

341

COMMITTEE ON THE STUDY OF THE JAPANESE ECONOMY (DOCTORAL & POSTDOCTORAL FELLOWSHIPS)

PROF. GARY SAXZENHOUSE; DEPT OF ECONOMICS; UNIV. OF MICHIGAN
ANN ARBOR MI 48109
313/764-3296

AMOUNT: VARIES

DEADLINE(S): NONE

FIELD(S): JAPANESE STUDIES - ECONOMICS

DOCTORAL AND SOME POST-DOCTORAL FELLOWSHIPS FOR ADVANCED STUDY OF THE JAPANESE ECONOMY. US CITIZEN OR LEGAL RESIDENT STUDYING IN USA.

FELLOWSHIPS ARE MADE AVAILABLE BY THE JAPAN-US FRIENDSHIP COMMISSION. WRITE FOR COMPLETE INFORMATION.

342

CONFERENCE ON LATIN AMERICAN HISTORY (JAMES R. SCOBIE MEMORIAL AWARD FOR PRELIMINARY PH.D. RESEARCH)

LATIN AMERICAN AREA CTR; U OF ARIZ; 1522 E. DRACHMAN
TUCSON AZ 85721
602/622-4002; FAX 602/622-0177

AMOUNT: $900

DEADLINE(S): MAR 15

FIELD(S): LATIN AMERICAN HISTORY

TRAVEL GRANT WILL BE AWARDED EACH YEAR FOR USE DURING THE FOLLOWING SUMMER FOR PRELIMINARY PH.D RESEARCH (NOT DISSERTATION RESEARCH).

WRITE FOR COMPLETE INFORMATION.

343

CREOLE-AMERICAN GENEALOGICAL SOCIETY INC. (CREOLE SCHOLARSHIPS)

PO BOX 2666 - CHURCH STREET STATION
NEW YORK NY 10008
WRITTEN INQUIRY ONLY

AMOUNT: $1500

DEADLINE(S): APPLY BETWEEN JAN 1 AND APR 30

FIELD(S): GENEALOGY OR LANGUAGE OR CREOLE CULTURE

AWARDS IN THE ABOVE AREAS OPEN TO INDIVIDUALS OF MIXED RACIAL ANCESTRY WHO SUBMIT A FOUR-GENERATION GENEAOLOGICAL CHART ATTESTING TO CREOLE ANCESTRY AND/OR INTERRACIAL PARENTAGE. FOR UNDERGRADUATE OR GRADUATE STUDY/RESEARCH.

FOR SCHOLARSHIP/AWARD INFORMATION SEND $2 MONEY ORDER AND SELF ADDRESSED STAMPED ENVELOPE TO ADDRESS ABOVE. CASH AND PERSONAL CHECKS ARE NOT ACCEPTED. LETTERS WITHOUT SASE AND HANDLING CHARGE WILL NOT BE ANSWERED.

344

DUMBARTON OAKS (AWARDS IN BYZANTINE STUDIES; PRECOLUMBIAN STUDIES; AND THE HISTORY OF LANDSCAPE ARCHITECTURE)

1703 32ND ST NW
WASHINGTON DC 20007
202/342-3232

AMOUNT: UP TO $31700 PER ACADEMIC YEAR

DEADLINE(S): NOV 1

FIELD(S): BYZANTINE STUDIES; PRECOLUMBIAN STUDIES; HISTORY OF LANDSCAPE ARCHITECTURE

DOCTORAL & POST-DOCTORAL FELLOWSHIPS; JUNIOR FELLOWSHIPS & SUMMER FELLOWSHIPS TO SUPPORT STUDY AND/OR RESEARCH IN THE ABOVE AREAS. ALL FELLOWS ARE EXPECTED TO BE ABLE TO COMMUNICATE SATISFACTORILY IN ENGLISH.

WRITE FOR COMPLETE INFORMATION.

345

DUMBARTON OAKS (SUMMER FELLOWSHIPS FOR BYZANTINE STUDIES)

1703 32ND STREET NW
WASHINGTON DC 20007
202/342-3232

AMOUNT: $150 PER WEEK FOR 6 TO 9 WEEKS

DEADLINE(S): NOV 15

FIELD(S): BYZANTINE STUDIES

SUMMER FELLOWSHIPS OPEN TO ADVANCED GRADUATE STUDENTS. QUALIFIED STUDENTS OF HISTORY; ARCHAEOLOGY; HISTORY OF ART; PHILOLOGY; THEOLOGY & OTHER DISCIPLINES ARE ELIGIBLE TO APPLY. POST-DOCTORAL FELLOWSHIPS ARE ALSO AVAILABLE.

10 AWARDS PER YEAR. WRITE FOR COMPLETE INFORMATION.

346

EAST-WEST CENTER (DOCTORAL & POST-DOCTORAL RESEARCH FELLOWSHIPS)

AWARD SERVICES OFFICER; ROOM 2066; 1777 EAST-WEST RD.
HONOLULU HI 96848
808-944-7736

AMOUNT: STIPEND + TRANSPORTATION

DEADLINE(S): JAN 15

FIELD(S): ASIAN PACIFIC AREA STUDIES

OPEN TO INDIVIDUALS AT THE PH.D DISSERTATION WRITING STAGE AND TO RECENT DOCTORAL RECIPIENTS INTERESTED IN PURSUING RESEARCH AT THE EAST-WEST CENTER.

USA; ASIAN OR PACIFIC CITIZEN. WRITE FOR COMPLETE INFORMATION.

347

GAMMA THETA UPSILON - INTERNAT'L GEOGRAPHIC HONOR SOCIETY (BUZZARD & RICHARDSON SCHOLARSHIPS)

C/O DR. O.O. MAXFIELD;
DEPT OF GEOGRAPHY; OZAR 108A;
UNIV OF ARKANSAS
TOWSON MD 21204
FAYETTEVILLE AR 72701

AMOUNT: $500

DEADLINE(S): AUG 1

FIELD(S): GEOGRAPHY

GRADUATE SCHOLARSHIPS OPEN TO GAMMA THETA UPSILON MEMBERS WHO MAINTAIN AT LEAST A 'B' GRADE POINT AVERAGE IN ANY ACCREDITED GRADUATE GEOGRAPHY PROGRAM.

WRITE FOR COMPLETE INFORMATION.

348

GETTY CENTER FOR THE HISTORY OF ART & THE HUMANITIES (PREDOCTORAL & POSTDOCTORAL FELLOWSHIPS)

DR H.H.HYMANS;
401 WILSHIRE BLVD; #400
SANTA MONICA CA 90401
310/458-9811

AMOUNT: $15000 PREDOCTORAL; $20000 POSTDOCTORAL

DEADLINE(S): DEC 1

FIELD(S): HUMANITIES; SOCIAL SCIENCES; ANTHROPOLOGY; ART/SCIENCE HISTORY; LITERATURE; PHILOSOPHY ETC.

OPEN TO PRE & POSTDOCTORAL SCHOLARS WHOSE AREAS OF RESEARCH COMPLEMENT THE CENTER'S PROGRAMS & RESOURCES. PREDOCTORAL CANDIDATES SHOULD EXPECT TO COMPLETE DISSERTATIONS DURING THE FELLOWSHIP YEAR.

POSTDOCTORALS SHOULD HAVE RECEIVED DOCTORATE IN HUMANITIES OR SOCIAL SCIENCES WITHIN LAST 3 YEARS & BE REWRITING DISSERTATIONS FOR PUBLICATION. WRITE FOR COMPLETE INFORMATION.

349

HENRY A.MURRAY RESEARCH CENTER AT RADCLIFFE COLLEGE (JEANNE HUMPHREY BLOCK DISSERTATION GRANTS)

10 GARDEN ST
CAMBRIDGE MA 02138
617/495-8140; FAX 617/495-8422

AMOUNT: $2500

DEADLINE(S): APR 1

FIELD(S): WOMEN'S ISSUES

WOMEN ONLY. OPEN TO PH.D CANDIDATES WHO HAVE COMPLETED ALL COURSEWORK. GRANT SUPPORTS DISSERTATION RESEARCH ON GIRL'S & WOMEN'S PSYCHOLOGICAL DEVELOPMENT.

PRIORITY WILL BE GIVEN TO PROJECTS THAT DRAW ON THE DATA RESOURCES OF THE MURRAY RESEARCH CENTER. WRITE FOR COMPLETE INFORMATION.

350

INSTITUTE FOR THE STUDY OF WORLD POLITICS (RESEARCH GRANTS)

1755 MASSACHUSETTS AVE NW -
SUITE 500
WASHINGTON DC 20036
WRITTEN INQUIRY ONLY

AMOUNT: VARIES

DEADLINE(S): FEB 15

FIELD(S): INTERNATIONAL RELATIONS; ENVIRONMENTAL ISSUES; POPULATION STUDIES (SOCIAL SCIENCE ASPECTS) HUMAN RIGHTS; ARMS CONTROL; THIRD WORLD DEVELOPMENT.

FOR DOCTORAL CANDIDATES CONDUCTING DISSERTATION RESEARCH IN ABOVE AREAS. FINANCIAL NEED IS A CONSIDERATION.

20-25 FELLOWSHIPS PER YEAR. WRITE FOR COMPLETE INFORMATION.

351

INSTITUTE OF AMERICAN CULTURES (UCLA FELLOWSHIP PROGRAM)

UCLA CENTER FOR AFRO-AMERICAN STUDIES;
160 HAINES HALL;
405 HILGARD AVE
LOS ANGELES CA 90024
213/825-7403

AMOUNT: $10000 PREDOCTORAL; UP TO $28000 POST-DOCTORAL

DEADLINE(S): DEC 31

FIELD(S): AFRO-AMERICAN STUDIES

PRE-DOCTORAL AND POST-DOCTORAL FELLOWSHIPS FOR RESEARCH AND WRITING AT UCLA CENTER FOR AFRO-AMERICAN STUDIES. PRE-DOCTORAL FELLOWSHIP OPEN TO UCLA STUDENTS ONLY AND INCLUDES TUITION AND FEES. POST-DOCTORAL RANGE IS $23000 TO $28000.

SECOND-YEAR FUNDING IS IN COMPETITION WITH OTHER APPLICANTS. WRITE FOR COMPLETE INFORMATION.

352

INTER-AMERICAN FOUNDATION (DOCTORAL DISSERTATION FELLOWSHIPS)

PO BOX 9486
ROSSLYN VA 22219
703/841-3864

AMOUNT: $3000 - $7000 AVERAGE

DEADLINE(S): DEC 1

FIELD(S): LATIN AMERICA & THE CARIBBEAN STUDIES

OPEN TO PH.D CANDIDATES (ENROLLED IN USA UNIV.'S) FROM THE SOCIAL SCIENCES/ PHYSICAL SCIENCES & THE PROFESSIONS WHO HAVE FULFILLED ALL DEGREE REQUIREMENTS OTHER THAN THE DISSERTATION BEFORE THEY TRAVEL TO THEIR COUNTRY OF INTENDED STUDY.

RESEARCH THEMES MUST DEAL DIRECTLY WITH DEVELOPMENT ACTIVITIES AMONG THE POOR. APPLICANTS REQUIRED TO SPEAK & WRITE LANGUAGE OF THEIR COUNTRY OF INTENDED STUDY. APPROX 15 AWARDS PER YEAR. WRITE FOR COMPLETE INFORMATION.

353

INTER-AMERICAN FOUNDATION (MASTER'S RESEARCH FELLOWSHIPS)

PO BOX 9486
ROSSLYN VA 22219
703/841-3864

AMOUNT: $1000 - $3000 AVERAGE RANGE

DEADLINE(S): MAR 1

FIELD(S): LATIN AMERICAN & CARIBBEAN STUDIES

OPEN TO MASTER'S STUDENTS (ENROLLED IN USA UNIV.'S) FOR FIELD RESEARCH IN LATIN AMERICA OR THE CARIBBEAN. APPLICANTS REQUIRED TO SPEAK & WRITE THE LANGUAGE OF THEIR COUNTRY OF INTENDED STUDY.

10-15 AWARDS PER YEAR. WRITE FOR COMPLETE INFORMATION.

354

JAPAN FOUNDATION (DISSERTATION FELLOWSHIPS)

142 W. 57TH STREET
NEW YORK NY 10019
212/949-6360

AMOUNT: APPROX 210000 YEN PER MONTH STIPEND + 100000 YEN FOR HOUSING

DEADLINE(S): NOV 1

FIELD(S): JAPANESE STUDIES

FELLOWSHIPS INTENDED TO PROVIDE PH.D CANDIDATES AN OPPORTUNITY TO CONDUCT DISSERTATION RESEARCH IN JAPAN. ALL PH.D REQUIREMENTS EXCEPT THE DISSERTATION MUST BE COMPLETED PRIOR TO RECEIVING AWARD. US CITIZEN OR LEGAL RESIDENT.

SHOULD BE SUFFICIENTLY PROFICIENT IN JAPANESE LANGUAGE TO PURSUE RESEARCH IN JAPAN. FELLOWSHIPS ARE AVAILABLE FOR PERIODS RANGING FROM 4 TO 14 MONTHS. WRITE FOR COMPLETE INFORMATION.

355

JEWISH BRAILLE INSTITUTE OF AMERICA (SCHOLARSHIPS)

110 E.30TH ST
NEW YORK NY 10016
212/889-2525

AMOUNT: VARIES

DEADLINE(S): NONE SPECIFIED

FIELD(S): JEWISH STUDIES

JEWISH FAITH. OPEN TO LEGALLY BLIND GRADUATE STUDENTS WHO ARE PURSUING STUDIES LEADING TO PROFESSIONAL CAREERS IN JEWISH SERVICE SUCH AS A RABBI; CANTOR; JEWISH COMMUNAL WORKER; ETC.

WRITE FOR COMPLETE INFORMATION.

356

JEWISH COMMUNITY CENTERS ASSOCIATION (JCCA SCHOLARSHIP PROGRAM)

SCHOLARSHIP COORDINATOR;
15 E. 26TH ST.
NEW YORK NY 10010
212/532-4949

AMOUNT: $7500

DEADLINE(S): FEB 1

FIELD(S): ADULT EDUCATION; EARLY CHILDHOOD EDUCATION; PHYSICAL EDUCATION; SOCIAL WORK; JEWISH STUDIES; BUSINESS ADMINISTRATION

OPEN TO INDIVIDUALS OF THE JEWISH FAITH WHO ARE ENROLLED IN A MASTERS DEGREE PROGRAM AND HAVE A STRONG DESIRE TO WORK IN THE JEWISH COMMUNITY CENTER FIELD. USA OR CANADIAN CITIZEN.

10 AWARDS PER YEAR. WRITE FOR COMPLETE INFORMATION.

357

JEWISH COMMUNITY CENTERS ASSOCIATION (SCHOLARSHIPS & LOANS)

15 EAST 26TH ST; GRANTS COORDINATOR
NEW YORK NY 10010
212/532-4949

AMOUNT: VARIES

DEADLINE(S): FEB 1

FIELD(S): JEWISH STUDIES; SOCIAL WORK; HEALTH; PHYSICAL EDUCATION; RECREATION

JEWISH FAITH. GRADUATE AWARDS TO ENRICH JEWISH LIFE IN AMERICA BY STRENGTHENING JEWISH IDENTITY & HELPING DEVELOP JEWISH LEADERSHIP FOR THE FUTURE. A COMMITMENT TO THE "CENTER FIELD" JEWISH COMMUNITY IS ESSENTIAL.

WRITE FOR COMPLETE INFORMATION.

358

MARY MCEWEN SCHIMKE SCHOLARSHIP (SUPPORT SCHOLARSHIPS)

C/O WELLESLEY COLLEGE;
SECRETARY GRADUATE FELLOWSHIPS; CAREER CENTER
WELLESLEY MA 02181
617/283-3525

AMOUNT: UP TO $1000 STIPEND

DEADLINE(S): DEC 1

FIELD(S): LITERATURE; AMERICAN HISTORY; PREFERENCE GIVEN TO AMERICAN STUDIES

SUPPLEMENTAL AWARD FOR THE PURPOSE OF AFFORDING RELIEF FROM HOUSEHOLD AND CHILD CARE WHILE PURSUING GRADUATE STUDY. AWARD IS BASED ON SCHOLARLY EXPECTATION AND IDENTIFIED NEED.

CANDIDATE MUST BE OVER 30 AND CURRENTLY ENGAGED IN GRADUATE STUDY IN GRADUATE STUDY IN LITERATURE AND/OR HISTORY WITH PREFERENCE GIVEN TO AMERICAN STUDIES. WRITE FOR COMPLETE INFORMATION.

359

MEMORIAL FOUNDATION FOR JEWISH CULTURE (INTERNATIONAL FELLOWSHIPS IN JEWISH STUDIES)

15 EAST 26TH ST - ROOM 1903
NEW YORK NY 10010
212/679-4074

AMOUNT: $1000 - $4000 PER YEAR

DEADLINE(S): OCT 31

FIELD(S): JEWISH STUDIES

PROGRAM IS TO ASSIST WELL QUALIFIED INDIVIDUALS IN CARRYING OUT AN INDEPENDENT SCHOLARLY LITERARY OR ART PROJECT IN A FIELD OF JEWISH SPECIALIZATION. APPLICANTS SHOULD POSSESS KNOWLEDGE & EXPERIENCE NECESSARY TO IMPLEMENT THE PROJECT.

GRANTS ARE FOR ONE ACADEMIC YEAR BUT MAY BE RENEWED. WRITE FOR COMPLETE INFORMATION.

360

MEMORIAL FOUNDATION FOR JEWISH CULTURE (INTERNATIONAL DOCTORAL SCHOLARSHIP)

15 EAST 26TH ST - ROOM 1903
NEW YORK NY 10010
212/679-4074

AMOUNT: $1000 - $5000 PER YEAR

DEADLINE(S): OCT 31

FIELD(S): JEWISH STUDIES

SCHOLARSHIPS OPEN TO GRADUATE STUDENTS ENROLLED IN A DOCTORAL PROGRAM AT A RECOGNIZED UNIVERSITY. PROGRAM IS TO HELP TRAIN QUALIFIED INDIVIDUALS FOR CAREERS IN JEWISH SCHOLARSHIP. PRIORITY IS GIVEN TO APPLICANTS AT THE DISSERTATION LEVEL.

SCHOLARSHIPS ARE RENEWABLE UP TO 4 YEARS. WRITE FOR COMPLETE INFORMATION.

361 ─────────────

MEMORIAL FOUNDATION FOR JEWISH CULTURE (POST-RABBINIC SCHOLARSHIPS)

15 EAST 26TH ST - ROOM 1903
NEW YORK NY 10010
212/679-4074

AMOUNT: UP TO $3000

DEADLINE(S): NOV 30

FIELD(S): RABBINICAL STUDIES

OPEN TO NEWLY ORDAINED RABBIS FOR ADVANCED TRAINING AS JUDGES ON RABBINICAL COURTS; HEADS OF INSTITUTIONS OF HIGHER LEARNING; OR OTHER ADVANCED RELIGIOUS LEADERSHIP POSITIONS.

APPLICANTS SHOULD BE ENROLLED FULL TIME IN A RABBINICAL SEMINARY; YESHIVA OR OTHER INSTITUTION OF HIGHER JEWISH LEARNING. WRITE FOR COMPLETE INFORMATION.

362 ─────────────

MINISTRY OF EDUCATION OF THE REPUBLIC OF CHINA (SCHOLARSHIPS FOR FOREIGN STUDENTS)

5 SOUTH CHUNG-SHAN ROAD
TAIPEI TAIWAN R.O.C.
321-6375; 321-7644

AMOUNT: NT$8000

DEADLINE(S): BETWEEN FEB 1 AND APR 30

FIELD(S): CHINESE STUDIES

UNDERGRADUATE & GRADUATE SCHOLARSHIPS ARE AVAILABLE TO FOREIGN STUDENTS WISHING TO STUDY IN TAIWAN R.O.C. MUST STUDY FULL TIME.

SCHOLARSHIPS ARE RENEWABLE. 300 AWARDS PER YEAR. WRITE FOR COMPLETE INFORMATION.

363 ─────────────

MONGOLIA SOCIETY (DR. GOMBOJAB HANGIN MEMORIAL SCHOLARSHIP)

321-322 GOODBODY HALL;
INDIANA UNIV.
BLOOMINGTON IN 47405
812/855-4078

AMOUNT: $3000 - $3500

DEADLINE(S): JAN 1

FIELD(S): MONGOLIAN STUDIES

OPEN TO STUDENTS OF MONGOLIAN NATIONALITY (PERMANENT RESIDENT OF MONGOLIA; CHINA OR THE FORMER SOVIET UNION) TO PURSUE MONGOLIAN STUDIES IN THE USA. RECIPIENT WILL RECEIVE MONEY IN ONE LUMP SUM UPON ARRIVAL IN THE USA.

REPORT ON RECIPIENT'S ACTIVITIES IS DUE AT CONCLUSION OF THE AWARD YEAR. WRITE FOR COMPLETE INFORMATION.

364 ─────────────

NATIONAL FOUNDATION FOR JEWISH CULTURE (DOCTORAL DISSERTATION FELLOWSHIPS)

330 SEVENTH AVE. - 21ST FLOOR
NEW YORK NY 10001
212/629-0500

AMOUNT: $4000 - $7000

DEADLINE(S): DEC 31

FIELD(S): JEWISH STUDIES

FOR DOCTORAL CANDIDATES WHO HAVE COMPLETED ALL ACADEMIC REQUIREMENTS FOR THEIR PH.D EXCEPT THE DISSERTATION. SHOULD GIVE EVIDENCE OF A PLAN LEADING TO A CAREER IN JEWISH SCHOLARSHIP OR RELATED FIELDS. USA CITIZEN OR PERMANENT RESIDENT.

5-10 FELLOWSHIPS PER YEAR. WRITE FOR COMPLETE INFORMATION.

365 ─────────────

PEN AMERICAN CENTER (RENATO POGGIOLI TRANSLATION PRIZE)

568 BROADWAY; SUITE 401
NEW YORK NY 10012
212/334-1660

AMOUNT: $3000

DEADLINE(S): JAN 15

FIELD(S): ITALIAN LITERATURE & TRANSLATION

THIS AWARD IS GIVEN TO A YOUNG OR DEVELOPING TRANSLATOR WHO HAS IN PROGRESS A BOOK-LENGTH TRANSLATION OF A WORK OF ITALIAN LITERATURE. APPLICANTS WHO PLAN A RESEARCH TRIP TO ITALY ARE FAVORED. USA CITIZEN.

WRITE FOR COMPLETE INFORMATION.

366 ─────────────

PHI BETA KAPPA (MARY ISABEL SIBLEY FELLOWSHIP)

1811 'Q' STREET NW
WASHINGTON DC 20009
202/265-3808

AREA STUDIES

AMOUNT: $10000

DEADLINE(S): JAN 15

FIELD(S): FRENCH STUDIES; GREEK STUDIES (LANGUAGE; LITERATURE; HISTORY OR ARCHAEOLOGY)

PH.D DISSERTATION OR POST-DOCTORAL RESEARCH FELLOWSHIPS FOR UNMARRIED WOMEN AGED 25-35 WHO HAVE DEMONSTRATED THEIR ABILITY TO CARRY ON ORIGINAL RESEARCH. APPLICANTS MUST PLAN TO DEVOTE FULL TIME TO RESEARCH DURING THE FELLOWSHIP YEAR.

FRENCH STUDIES IN EVEN NUMBERED YEARS; GREEK STUDIES IN ODD NUMBERED YEARS. ELIGIBILITY -NOT- RESTRICTED TO PHI BETA KAPPA MEMBERS. WRITE FOR COMPLETE INFORMATION.

367

PITT RIVERS MUSEUM (SWAN FUND)

SOUTH PARKS ROAD
OXFORD OX1 3PP ENGLAND
0865-270927

AMOUNT: 1000-2000 POUNDS STERLING

DEADLINE(S): NONE

FIELD(S): AFRICAN STUDIES

RESEARCH GRANTS FOR GRADUATE STUDENTS TO SUPPORT RESEARCH IN AFRICA RELATING TO THE 'SMALL PEOPLES' SUCH AS BUSHMEN; PYGMIES & OTHER HUNTER-GATHERERS.

APPROX 10 AWARDS PER YEAR. AWARDS RENEWABLE. CONTACT THE DIRECTOR AT THE ADDRESS ABOVE FOR COMPLETE INFORMATION.

368

POPULATION COUNCIL (FELLOWSHIPS)

FELLOWSHIP OFFICE; ONE DAG HAMMARSKJOLD PLAZA
NEW YORK NY 10017
212/644-1782

AMOUNT: TUITION; MONTHLY STIPEND; RESEARCH & TRAVEL EXPENSES

DEADLINE(S): NOV 15

FIELD(S): POPULATION STUDIES; DEMOGRAPHY; SOCIOLOGY

DOCTORAL; POST-DOCTORAL & MIDCAREER TRAINING FELLOWSHIPS IN THE ABOVE FIELDS. DOCTORAL CANDIDATES SHOULD HAVE MADE CONSIDERABLE PROGRESS TOWARD THEIR PH.D. OR AN EQUIVALENT DEGREE IN ONE OF THE SOCIAL SCIENCES.

20-25 AWARDS ARE MADE FOR UP TO ONE YEAR. SELECTION CRITERIA WILL STRESS ACADEMIC EXCELLENCE AND PROSPECTIVE CONTRIBUTION TO THE POPULATION FIELD. WRITE FOR COMPLETE INFORMATION.

369

RADIO FREE EUROPE/RADIO LIBERTY (MEDIA & OPINION RESEARCH ON EASTERN EUROPE & THE FORMER SOVIET UNION)

PERSONNEL DIVISION; 1201 CONNECTICUT AVE NW
WAHINGTON DC 20036
WRITTEN INQUIRY

AMOUNT: DAILY STIPEND OF 48 GERMAN MARKS PLUS ACCOMMODATIONS

DEADLINE(S): FEB 22

FIELD(S): COMMUNICATIONS; MARKET RESEARCH; STATISTICS; SOCIOLOGY; SOCIAL PSYCHOLOGY; EAST EUROPEAN STUDIES

INTERNSHIP OPEN TO GRADUATE STUDENT OR EXCEPTIONALLY QUALIFIED UNDERGRADUATE IN THE ABOVE AREAS WHO CAN DEMONSTRATE KNOWLEDGE OF QUANTITIVE RESEARCH METHODS; COMPUTER APPLICATIONS AND PUBLIC OPINION SURVEY TECHNIQUES.

EAST EUROPEAN LANGUAGE SKILLS WOULD BE AN ADVANTAGE. WRITE FOR COMPLETE INFORMATION.

370

RADIO FREE EUROPE/RADIO LIBERTY (RESEARCH INTERN PROGRAM)

1201 CONNECTICUT AVE
WASHINGTON DC 20036
WRITTEN INQUIRY

AMOUNT: DAILY STIPEND OF 55 GERMAN MARKS + ACCOMMODATIONS

DEADLINE(S): FEB 22

FIELD(S): AFFAIRS OF EASTERN EUROPE AND THE FORMER SOVIET UNION

OPEN TO GRADUATE STUDENTS SPECIALIZING IN SOME ASPECT OF RADIO FREE EUROPE/ RADIO LIBERTY BROADCAST AREAS. WHILE APPLICANTS ARE EXPECTED TO HAVE A THOROUGH GROUNDING IN HISTORY; RESEARCH INSTITUTE EFFORT GENERAL FOCUSES ON CURRENT AFFAIRS.

APPLICANTS NEED HIGH PROFICIENCY IN ENGLISH AND AT LEAST A GOOD READING KNOWLEDGE OF ONE OR MORE EAST EUROPEAN LANGUAGES. WRITE FOR COMPLETE INFORMATION.

371

ROCKEFELLER FOUNDATION (POPULATION SCIENCES FELLOWSHIPS)

1133 AVENUE OF THE AMERICAS
NEW YORK NY 10036
212/869-8500

AMOUNT: MONTHLY STIPEND

DEADLINE(S): NOV 15

FIELD(S): POPULATION STUDIES

DOCTORAL DISSERTATION FELLOWSHIPS FOR STUDENTS UNDER 36 YEARS OLD WHO HAVE COMPLETED ALL OTHER WORK TOWARD THEIR PH.D DEGREE (OR AN EQUIVALENT) IN ONE OF THE SOCIAL SCIENCES WITH A SPECIALIZATION IN POPULATION STUDIES.

PREFERENCE TO PERSONS FROM DEVELOPING COUNTRIES COMMITTED TO RETURNING TO HOME COUNTRY AFTER TRAINING. WRITE FOR COMPLETE INFORMATION.

372

SCHOOL OF ORIENTAL AND AFRICAN STUDIES (MASTER'S SCHOLARSHIPS)

THORNHAUGH ST.; RUSSELL SQUARE
LONDON WC1H 0XG ENGLAND
01/637-2388

AMOUNT: 5320 POUNDS STERLING

DEADLINE(S): MAY 1

FIELD(S): ORIENTAL STUDIES; AFRICAN STUDIES

SCHOLARSHIPS OPEN TO MASTER'S DEGREE STUDENTS IN THE ABOVE AREAS. AWARDS TENABLE AT THE SCHOOL OF ORIENTAL AND AFRICAN STUDIES IN LONDON.

EIGHT AWARDS PER YEAR. CONTACT T. HARVEY; REGISTRAR; ADDRESS ABOVE FOR COMPLETE INFORMATION.

373

SOCIAL SCIENCE RESEARCH COUNCIL (INTERNATIONAL PREDISSERTATION FELLOWSHIP PROGRAM)

ELLEN PERECMAN; 605 THIRD AVE.
NEW YORK NY 10158
212-661-0280

AMOUNT: VARIES

DEADLINE(S): TO BE ANNOUNCED BY PARTICIPATING UNIVERSITIES

FIELD(S): ECONOMICS; POLITICAL SCIENCE; PSYCHOLOGY SOCIOLOGY; OTHER SOCIAL SCIENCE DISCIPLINES

OPEN TO PH.D CANDIDATES ENROLLED IN SOCIAL SCIENCES PROGRAMS AT SELECTED UNIVERSITIES. STUDENTS SHOULD BE INTERESTED IN SUPPLEMENTING THEIR DISCIPLINARY SKILLS WITH AREA AND LANGUAGE STUDIES.

FELLOWS UNDERTAKE A PROGRAM OF STUDY IN OR ON AFRICA; CHINA; LATIN AMERICA; THE CARIBBEAN; THE NEAR & MIDDLE EAST; SOUTH ASIA OR SOUTHEAST ASIA. WRITE FOR COMPLETE INFORMATION.

374

SONS OF NORWAY FOUNDATION (KING OLAV V NORWGIAN-AMERICAN HERITAGE FUND)

1455 WEST LAKE STREET
MINNEAPOLIS MN 55408
612/827-3611

AMOUNT: $250 - $3000

DEADLINE(S): MAR 1

FIELD(S): NORWEGIAN STUDIES

OPEN TO USA CITIZENS 18 OR OLDER WHO HAVE DEMONSTRATED A KEEN AND SINCERE INTEREST IN THE NORWEGIAN HERITAGE. THE STUDENT MUST BE ENROLLED IN A RECOGNIZED EDUCATIONAL INSTITUTION AND BE STUDYING A SUBJECT RELATED TO THE NORWEGIAN HERITAGE.

FINANCIAL NEED IS A CONSIDERATION BUT IT IS SECONDARY TO SCHOLARSHIP. 12 AWARDS PER YEAR. WRITE FOR COMPLETE INFORMATION.

375

SWEDISH INFORMATION SERVICE (BICENTENNIAL FUND GRANTS)

ONE DAG HAMMARSKJOLD PLAZA;
45TH FLOOR
NEW YORK NY 10017
212/751-5900

AMOUNT: 20000 SWEDISH KRONA

DEADLINE(S): FEB 1

FIELD(S): POLITICAL SCIENCE; BUSINESS ADMIN; EDUCATION; COMMUNICATION; CULTURE; ENVIRONMENTAL STUDIES

GRANTS TO PROVIDE THE OPPORTUNITY FOR THOSE IN A POSITION TO INFLUENCE PUBLIC OPINION AND CONTRIBUTE TO THE DEVELOPMENT OF THEIR SOCIETY. 3-6 WEEK INTENSIVE STUDY VISITS IN SWEDEN IN ANY OF THE ABOVE AREAS OR THEIR RELATED FIELDS.

US CITIZEN OR LEGAL RESIDENT. APPROXIMATELY 10 GRANTS PER YEAR. WRITE FOR COMPLETE INFORMATION.

376

U.S. DEPT. OF EDUCATION (FLAS FELLOWSHIPS)

CENTER FOR INTERNATIONAL EDUCTION; ATRB
WASHINGTON DC 20202
202/708-7283

AMOUNT: TUITION & FEES + $8000 STIPEND

DEADLINE(S): VARIES

FIELD(S): FOREIGN LANGUAGE & AREA OR INTERNATIONAL STUDIES

ART

FELLOWSHIPS FOR GRADUATE STUDENTS AT
ACCREDITED INSTITUTIONS IN USA WHO
ARE PREPARING FOR CAREER AS SPECIALIST
IN UNCOMMON FOREIGN LANGUAGE & AREA
OR INTERNATIONAL STUDIES. USA CITIZEN
OR LEGAL RESIDENT.

APPROX 1000 FELLOWSHIPS PER YEAR.
RENEWABLE. CONTACT YOUR
INSTITUTION'S FINANCIAL AID OFFICE FOR
COMPLETE INFORMATION.

377

**WILLIAM ANDREWS CLARK MEMORIAL
LIBRARY AT UCLA (PRE-DOCTORAL &
POST-DOCTORAL SHORT TERM RESEARCH
FELLOWSHIPS)**

2520 CIMARRON STREET
LOS ANGELES CA 90018
213/735-7605

AMOUNT: $1500 PER MONTH

DEADLINE(S): MAR 15

FIELD(S): ENGLISH CULTURE 1640 - 1750

PRE-DOCTORAL AND POST-DOCTORAL
FELLOWSHIPS FOR ADVANCED STUDY AND
RESEARCH INTO THE ENGLISH CULTURE
BETWEEN THE YEARS OF 1640 AND 1750. FOR
STUDY AT THE WILLIAM ANDREWS CLARK
MEMORIAL LIBRARY AT UCLA.

A NUMBER OF THREE-MONTH PRE-DOCTORAL
AWARDS TO ADVANCED PH.D CANDIDATES
AND 6 TO 10 SHORT TERM AWARDS FOR
SHORT TERM POST-DOCTORAL RESEARCH.
WRITE FOR COMPLETE INFORMATION.

ART

378

**ACADEMY OF MOTION PICTURE ARTS AND
SCIENCES (STUDENT ACADEMY AWARDS
COMPETITION)**

8949 WILSHIRE BLVD
BEVERLY HILLS CA 90211
310/278-8990

AMOUNT: $2000; $1500; $1000

DEADLINE(S): APR 1

FIELD(S): FILMMAKING

STUDENT ACADEMY AWARDS COMPETITION IS
OPEN TO STUDENT FILMMAKERS WHO HAVE
NO PROFESSIONAL EXPERIENCE AND ARE
ENROLLED IN ACCREDITED COLLEGES AND
UNIVERSITIES. AWARDS ARE FOR -
COMPLETED- FILM PROJECTS ONLY.

WRITE FOR COMPLETE INFORMATION.

379

**ALASKA STATE COUNCIL ON THE ARTS
(INDIVIDUAL ARTIST FELLOWSHIPS &
GRANTS)**

411 W. 4TH AVE. SUITE 1E
ANCHORAGE AK 99501
907/279-1558

AMOUNT: $5000

DEADLINE(S): OCT 1

FIELD(S): VISUAL ARTS; CRAFTS; PHOTOGRAPHY
- ODD NUMBERED YEARS. MUSIC
COMPOSITION; CHOREOGRAPHY; MEDIA
ARTS; LITERATURE - EVEN NUMBERED
YEARS.

OPEN TO ALASKA RESIDENTS WHO ARE
ENGAGED IN THE CREATION OF NEW WORKS.
FULL TIME STUDENTS ARE -NOT- ELIGIBLE.

WRITE FOR COMPLETE INFORMATION.

380

**AMERICAN ACADEMY IN ROME (ROME PRIZE
FELLOWSHIPS)**

41 EAST 65TH STREET
NEW YORK NY 10021
212/535-4250

AMOUNT: $8300 (INCLUDES ROUND TRIP TRAVEL
TO ROME AND EUROPEAN TRAVEL
ALLOWANCE)

DEADLINE(S): NOV 15

FIELD(S): ARCHITECTURE; LANDSCAPE
ARCHITECTURE; MUSICAL COMPOSITION;
CLASSICS; ART HISTORY; PAINTING;
SCULPTURE AND THE VISUAL ARTS; POST
CLASSICAL HUMANISTIC STUDIES.

THE ACADEMY INVITES ARTISTS AND SCHOLARS
WHO ARE USA CITIZENS TO APPLY FOR A
LIMITED NUMBER OF ROME PRIZE
FELLOWSHIPS IN THE ARTS AND
HUMANITIES.

16 ROME PRIZE FELLOWSHIPS ANNUALLY. WRITE
FOR COMPLETE INFORMATION.

381

**AMERICAN COUNCIL OF LEARNED SOCIETIES
(ACLS FELLOWSHIPS)**

OFFICE OF FELLOWSHIPS & GRANTS;
228 E. 45TH ST.
NEW YORK NY 10017
WRITTEN INQUIRY

AMOUNT: UP TO $20000

DEADLINE(S): SEP 30

FIELD(S): HUMANITIES; SOCIAL SCIENCES;
OTHER AREAS HAVING PREDOMINATELY
HUMANISTIC EMPHASIS

OPEN TO USA CITIZENS OR LEGAL RESIDENTS WHO HOLD THE PH.D OR ITS EQUIVALENT. FELLOWSHIPS ARE DESIGNED TO HELP SCHOLARS DEVOTE 2 TO 12 CONTINUOUS MONTHS TO FULL TIME RESEARCH.

WRITE FOR COMPLETE INFORMATION.

382

AMERICAN COUNCIL OF LEARNED SOCIETIES (AMERICAN ART DOCTORAL DISSERTATION FELLOWSHIP)

OFFICE OF FELLOWSHIPS & GRANTS;
228 E. 45TH ST.
NEW YORK NY 10017
WRITTEN INQUIRY

AMOUNT: $15000

DEADLINE(S): NOV 15

FIELD(S): AMERICAN ART HISTORY

OPEN TO STUDENTS WHO ARE USA CITIZENS OR LEGAL RESIDENTS WHO ARE WORKING ON DOCTORAL DISSERTATIONS IN A DEPARTMENT OF ART HISTORY ON A TOPIC IN THE HISTORY OF THE VISUAL ARTS IN THE USA.

WRITE FOR COMPLETE INFORMATION.

383

AMERICAN NUMISMATIC SOCIETY (GRANTS & FELLOWSHIPS)

BROADWAY AT 155TH ST
NEW YORK NY 10032
212/234-3130

AMOUNT: $2000 GRANTS IN AID; $3500 FELLOWSHIP

DEADLINE(S): MAR 1

FIELD(S): NUMISMATICS

GRANTS IN AID OPEN TO STUDENTS WHO HAVE COMPLETED AT LEAST 1 YEAR OF GRADUATE STUDY AT A NORTH AMERICAN UNIVERSITY. FELLOWSHIP OF $3500 GOES TO GRAD STUDENT WHOSE DISSERTATION WILL MAKE SIGNIFICANT USE OF NUMISMATIC EVIDENCE.

WRITE FOR COMPLETE INFORMATION.

384

AMERICAN WOMEN IN RADIO & TELEVISION (HOUSTON INTERNSHIP PROGRAM)

APRILLE MEEK; AWRT-HOUSTON;
PO BOX 980908
HOUSTON TX 77098
WRITTEN INQUIRY

AMOUNT: $500 PER YEAR

DEADLINE(S): MAR 1

FIELD(S): RADIO; TELEVISION; FILM & VIDEO; ADVERTISING; MARKETING

INTERNSHIPS OPEN TO STUDENTS WHO ARE JUNIORS; SENIORS OR GRADUATE STUDENTS AT GREATER HOUSTON AREA COLLEGES & UNIVERSITIES.

WRITE FOR COMPLETE INFORMATION.

385

ARCHAEOLOGICAL INSTITUTE OF AMERICA (OLIVIA JAMES TRAVELING FELLOWSHIP)

675 COMMONWEALTH AVE
BOSTON MA 02215
617/353-9361; FAX 617/353-6550

AMOUNT: $11500 STIPEND

DEADLINE(S): NOV 15

FIELD(S): ARCHAEOLOGY; CLASSICS; SCULPTURE; HISTORY; ARCHITECTURE

FOR GRADUATE OR POST-GRADUATE STUDY IN GREECE; AEGEAN ISLANDS; SICILY; SOUTHERN ITALY; ASIA MINOR OR MESOPOTAMIA. PREFERENCE IS FOR DISSERTATION OR RECENT PH.D RESEARCH. WILL NOT SUPPORT FIELD EXCAVATION. USA CITIZEN OR LEGAL RESIDENT.

WRITE FOR COMPLETE INFORMATION.

386

ARTS INTERNATIONAL; INSTITUTE OF INTERNATIONAL EDUCATION (CINTAS FELLOWSHIP PROGRAM)

809 UNITED NATIONS PLAZA
NEW YORK NY 10017
212/984-5370

AMOUNT: $10000

DEADLINE(S): MAR 1

FIELD(S): ARCHITECTURE; PAINTING; PHOTOGRAPHY; SCULPTURE; PRINTMAKING; MUSIC COMPOSITION; CREATIVE WRITING

FELLOWSHIPS OPEN TO ARTISTS WHO ARE OF CUBAN ANCESTRY OR CUBAN CITIZENS LIVING OUTSIDE OF CUBA. THEY ARE INTENDED TO FOSTER & ENCOURAGE THE PROFESSIONAL DEVELOPMENT & RECOGNITION OF TALENTED CREATIVE ARTISTS IN THE ABOVE AREAS.

FELLOWSHIPS ARE NOT AWARDED FOR FURTHERANCE OF ACADEMIC STUDY. 5-10 AWARDS PER YEAR. WRITE FOR COMPLETE INFORMATION.

387

ASIAN CULTURAL COUNCIL (RESEARCH FELLOWSHIPS FOR USA CITIZENS TO STUDY IN ASIA; ASIANS TO STUDY IN USA)

1290 AVE OF THE AMERICAS
NEW YORK NY 10104
212/373-4300

AMOUNT: VARIES

DEADLINE(S): FEB 1; AUG 1

FIELD(S): VISUAL ARTS; PERFORMING ARTS

DOCTORAL & POST-DOCTORAL FELLOWSHIPS OPEN TO USA CITIZENS WHO WISH TO DO RESEARCH IN ASIA ON ASIAN VISUAL OR PERFORMING ARTS. FUNDS ALSO AVAILABLE FOR STUDENTS FROM ASIA FOR STUDY AND RESEARCH IN USA.

WRITE FOR COMPLETE INFORMATION.

388

BLACK AMERICAN CINEMA SOCIETY (FILMMAKERS GRANTS PROGRAM)

3617 MONTCLAIR STREET
LOS ANGELES CA 90018
213/737-3292; FAX 213/737-2842

AMOUNT: UP TO $3000

DEADLINE(S): FEB 22

FIELD(S): FILMMAKING

OPEN TO BLACK FILMMAKERS. APPLICATIONS ACCEPTED ONLY FROM THE INDIVIDUAL(S) WHO HAVE PRIMARY CREATIVE RESPONSIBILITY FOR THE FILM. PROJECT (1 PER GRANT CYCLE) MAY BE SUBMITTED IN 16MM FILM OR 3/4" VIDEO. USA CITIZEN OR LEGAL RESIDENT.

PROJECTS MUST BE MADE IN THE USA. CONTACT ADDRESS ABOVE FOR COMPLETE INFORMATION.

389

BUSH FOUNDATION (BUSH ARTIST FELLOWSHIPS)

E900 FIRST NATIONAL BANK BLDG; 322 MINNESOTA ST.
ST PAUL MN 55101
612/227-5222

AMOUNT: UP TO $26000 STIPEND + $7000 EXPENSES

DEADLINE(S): LATE OCT; EARLY NOV

FIELD(S): LITERATURE; MUSIC COMPOSITION; CHOREOGRAPHY; VISUAL ARTS; SCRIPTWORKS

OPEN TO WRITERS; VISUAL ARTISTS; COMPOSERS & CHOREOGRAPHERS WHO ARE RESIDENTS OF MN.; N.D.; S.D. OR WESTERN WI. & AT LEAST 25 YRS OLD. AWARDS ARE TO HELP ARTISTS WORK FULL-TIME IN THEIR CHOSEN FIELD; NOT FOR ACADEMIC STUDY.

15 FELLOWSHIPS PER YEAR; 6-18 MONTHS IN DURATION. WRITE FOR COMPLETE INFORMATION.

390

CALIFORNIA COLLEGE OF ARTS & CRAFTS (UNDERGRADUATE AND GRADUATE SCHOLARSHIPS)

5212 BROADWAY
OAKLAND CA 94618
510/653-8118

AMOUNT: VARIES

DEADLINE(S): MAR 1

FIELD(S): ART

OPEN TO UNDERGRADUATE AND GRADUATE STUDENTS ACCEPTED TO OR ENROLLED IN A DEGREE PROGRAM AT THE CALIFORNIA COLLEGE OF ARTS AND CRAFTS. MUST BE A USA CITIZEN OR LEGAL RESIDENT AND DEMONSTRATE FINANCIAL NEED.

APPROX 600 AWARDS PER YEAR. RENEWABLE. CONTACT OFFICE OF ENROLLMENT SERVICES FOR COMPLETE INFORMATION.

391

DISTRICT OF COLUMBIA COMMISSION ON THE ARTS & HUMANITIES (GRANTS)

410 EIGHTH ST. NW - 5TH FLOOR
WASHINGTON DC 20004
202/724-5613; TDD 202/727-318; FAX 202/727-4135

AMOUNT: $5000

DEADLINE(S): FEB 15

FIELD(S): ARTS; PERFORMING ARTS; LITERATURE

APPLICANTS FOR GRANTS MUST BE PROFESSIONAL ARTISTS AND RESIDENTS OF WASHINGTON D.C. FOR AT LEAST ONE YEAR PRIOR TO SUBMITTING APPLICATION. AWARDS INTENDED TO GENERATE ARTS ENDEAVORS WITHIN THE WASHINGTON D.C. COMMUNITY.

OPEN ALSO TO ARTS ORGANIZATIONS THAT TRAIN; EXHIBIT OR PERFORM WITHIN D.C. 150 GRANTS PER YEAR. WRITE FOR COMPLETE INFORMATION.

392

FLORIDA ARTS COUNCIL (INDIVIDUAL ARTISTS FELLOWSHIPS)

FLA DEPT OF STATE; DIV OF CULTURAL AFFAIRS; STATE CAPITOL
TALLAHASSEE FL 32399
904/487-2980

AMOUNT: UP TO $5000

DEADLINE(S): FEB 15 (APR 15 FOR VISUAL ARTS)

FIELD(S): VISUAL ARTS; DANCE; FOLK ARTS; MEDIA; MUSIC; THEATER; LITERARY ARTS

FELLOWSHIPS AWARDED TO INDIVIDUAL ARTISTS IN THE ABOVE AREAS. MUST BE FLORIDA RESIDENTS; USA CITIZENS AND OVER 18 YEARS OLD. MAY -NOT- BE A DEGREE SEEKING STUDENT; FUNDING IS FOR SUPPORT OF ARTISTIC ENDEAVORS ONLY.

FORTY AWARDS PER YEAR. WRITE FOR COMPLETE INFORMATION.

393

FONDATION DES ETATS UNIS (HARRIET HALE WOOLLEY SCHOLARSHIPS)

15 BOULEVARD JOURDAN
75690 PARIS-CEDEX 14 FRANCE
33-1/45-89-35-79

AMOUNT: $8500 STIPEND

DEADLINE(S): JAN 31

FIELD(S): PAINTING; PRINT-MAKING; SCULPTURE; INSTRUMENTAL MUSIC

USA CITIZEN. SCHOLARSHIPS FOR GRADUATE STUDY IN PARIS. PREFERENCE IS GIVEN TO STUDENTS WHO HAVE ALREADY DONE GRADUATE STUDY. MUST BE BETWEEN 21 AND 29 YEARS OF AGE AND BE SINGLE. SHOULD HAVE GOOD KNOWLEDGE OF FRENCH.

GRANTEES LIVE AT THE FONDATION DES ETATS-UNIS. CONTACT THE DIRECTOR ADDRESS ABOVE FOR COMPLETE INFORMATION.

394

GEORGIA COUNCIL FOR THE ARTS (INDIVIDUAL ARTIST GRANTS)

530 MEANS ST NW; SUITE 115
ATLANTA GA 30318
404/651-7920

AMOUNT: UP TO $5000

DEADLINE(S): APR 20

FIELD(S): THE ARTS

GRANTS TO SUPPORT ARTISTIC PROJECTS BY PROFESSIONAL ARTISTS WHO HAVE BEEN GEORGIA RESIDENTS AT LEAST ONE YEAR PRIOR TO APPLICATION. SELECTION IS BASED ON PROJECT'S ARTISTIC MERIT AND ITS POTENTIAL FOR CAREER DEVELOPMENT.

GRANTS -DO NOT- SUPPORT ACADEMIC STUDY. WRITE FOR COMPLETE INFORMATION.

395

GETTY CENTER FOR THE HISTORY OF ART & THE HUMANITIES (PREDOCTORAL & POSTDOCTORAL FELLOWSHIPS)

DR H.H.HYMANS;
401 WILSHIRE BLVD; #400
SANTA MONICA CA 90401
310/458-9811

AMOUNT: $15000 PREDOCTORAL; $20000 POSTDOCTORAL

DEADLINE(S): DEC 1

FIELD(S): HUMANITIES; SOCIAL SCIENCES; ANTHROPOLOGY; ART/SCIENCE HISTORY; LITERATURE; PHILOSOPHY ETC.

OPEN TO PRE & POSTDOCTORAL SCHOLARS WHOSE AREAS OF RESEARCH COMPLEMENT THE CENTER'S PROGRAMS & RESOURCES. PREDOCTORAL CANDIDATES SHOULD EXPECT TO COMPLETE DISSERTATIONS DURING THE FELLOWSHIP YEAR.

POSTDOCTORALS SHOULD HAVE RECEIVED DOCTORATE IN HUMANITIES OR SOCIAL SCIENCES WITHIN LAST 3 YEARS & BE REWRITING DISSERTATIONS FOR PUBLICATION. WRITE FOR COMPLETE INFORMATION.

396

GRAPHIC ARTS TECHNICAL FOUNDATION (SCHOLARSHIP TRUST FUND FELLOWSHIPS)

4615 FORBES AVE
PITTSBURGH PA 15213
412/621-6941

AMOUNT: $1500 - $4000

DEADLINE(S): JAN 10

FIELD(S): GRAPHIC ARTS; PRINTING; PRINTMAKING

GRADUATE FELLOWSHIPS FOR RESEARCH AND STUDY IN ONE OR MORE DISCIPLINES HAVING POTENTIAL APPLICATION IN THE PRINTING; PUBLISHING AND PACKAGING INDUSTRIES.

AWARDS ARE RENEWABLE. WRITE FOR COMPLETE INFORMATION.

397

HAYSTACK MOUNTAIN SCHOOL OF CRAFTS (SCHOLARSHIP PROGRAM)

ADMISSIONS OFFICE; PO BOX 518
DEER ISLE ME 04627
207/348-2306

AMOUNT: $400

DEADLINE(S): MAR 25

FIELD(S): CRAFTS; GRAPHIC ARTS

SCHOLARSHIPS ARE FOR STUDY IN GRAPHICS; CERAMICS; WEAVING; JEWELRY; GLASS; BLACKSMITHING; FABRIC & WOOD. LIMITED WORK SCHOLARSHIPS ALSO ARE AVAILABLE.

SCHOLARSHIPS ARE TENABLE AT THE SCHOOL OF CRAFTS FOR THE SIX SUMMER SESSIONS. EACH SESSION IS ONE; TWO OR THREE WEEKS LONG. WRITE FOR COMPLETE INFORMATION.

398

ILLINOIS ARTS COUNCIL (ARTISTS FELLOWSHIP AWARDS)

100 W. RANDOLPH; SUITE 10-500
CHICAGO IL 60601
312/814-6750

AMOUNT: $500 - $15000

DEADLINE(S): NOV 1

FIELD(S): CHOREOGRAPHY; VISUAL ARTS; LITERATURE; FILM; VIDEO; PLAYWRITING; MUSIC COMPOSITION; CRAFTS; ETHNIC & FOLK ARTS; PERFORMANCE ART; PHOTOGRAPHY

OPEN TO PROFESSIONAL ARTISTS WHO ARE ILLINOIS RESIDENTS. AWARDS ARE IN RECOGNITION OF WORK IN THE ABOVE AREAS; THEY ARE NOT FOR CONTINUING STUDY. STUDENTS ARE -NOT- ELIGIBLE.

WRITE TO ADDRESS ABOVE FOR APPLICATION FORM.

399

INSTITUTE OF BUSINESS DESIGNERS FOUNDATION (FELLOWSHIP PROGRAM)

341 MERCHANDISE MART
CHICAGO IL 60654
312/467-1950

AMOUNT: $10000

DEADLINE(S): MAY 1

FIELD(S): INTERIOR DESIGN

FELLOWSHIP GRANTS FOR DESIGNERS WHO WISH TO RETURN TO SCHOOL TO ADVANCE THEIR KNOWLEDGE OF DESIGN. MUST BE IN GRADUATE PROGRAM.

3 AWARDS PER YEAR. CONTACT ADM. DIR. TERRI CARLTON AT ADDRESS ABOVE FOR COMPLETE INFORMATION.

400

INTERNATIONAL FURNISHINGS & DESIGN ASSOCIATION (IFDA STUDENT DESIGN COMPETITION)

107 WORLD TRADE CENTER;
PO BOX 58045
DALLAS TX 75258
214/747-2406

AMOUNT: $2000 - $3500

DEADLINE(S): MAR 1

FIELD(S): STUDENT DESIGN COMPETITION

DESIGN COMPETITION OPEN TO GRADUATE STUDENTS; 2ND; 3RD OR 4TH YEAR UNDERGRAD STUDENTS ENROLLED IN AN ACCREDITED UNIVERSITY OR COLLEGE WITH SCHOOLS OF DESIGN; CRAFTS OR ARTS; AND 2ND YEAR STUDENTS IN A 2-YEAR SCHOOL OF DESIGN.

NATIONAL AND REGIONAL PRIZES. WRITE FOR COMPLETE INFORMATION.

401

JOHN F. AND ANNA LEE STACEY FOUNDATION (STACEY SCHOLARSHIP FUND)

C/O NAWA - 1700 NE 63RD ST
OKLAHOMA CITY OK 73111
WRITTEN INQUIRY

AMOUNT: $3000 (AVERAGE)

DEADLINE(S): DEC 1

FIELD(S): DRAWING AND PAINTING

GRADUATE SCHOLARSHIPS OPEN TO USA CITIZENS BETWEEN THE AGES OF 18 AND 35. MUST BE SKILLED AND DEVOTED TO THE CLASSICAL OR CONSERVATIVE TRADITION OF ART.

APPLICANTS MUST SUBMIT REPRESENTATIVE 35MM SLIDES OF THEIR WORK. WRITE TO ED MUNO AT ADDRESS ABOVE FOR COMPLETE INFORMATION.

402

LESLIE T. POSEY AND FRANCES U. POSEY FOUNDATION (SCHOLARSHIPS)

1800 SECOND ST.; SUITE 905
SARASOTA FL 34236
813/957-0442

AMOUNT: $1000 - $4000

DEADLINE(S): MAR 1

FIELD(S): ART (PAINTING OR SCULPTURE)

OPEN TO GRADUATE ART STUDENTS WHO MAJORED IN TRADITIONAL PAINTING OR SCULPTURE. THE SCHOOL OR ARTIST WITH WHOM THE STUDENT WISHES TO STUDY SHOULD BE KNOWN FOR TEACHING TRADITIONAL ART. FOR FULL TIME STUDY.

WRITE TO ROBERT E. PERKINS; EXEC. DIR.; ADDRESS ABOVE FOR COMPLETE INFORMATION.

403

MARYLAND INSTITUTE COLLEGE OF ART (FELLOWSHIP GRANTS)

1300 WEST MT ROYAL AVE
BALTIMORE MD 21217
301/225-2255

AMOUNT: TUITION

DEADLINE(S): MAR 1

FIELD(S): FINE ARTS

FELLOWSHIP GRANTS OPEN TO MASTER OF FINE ARTS CANDIDATES AT MARYLAND INSTITUTE COLLEGE OF ART. APPLICANTS MUST HAVE BA OR BFA DEGREE WITH AT LEAST 40 STUDIO CREDITS & 6 ART HISTORY CREDITS.

APPROX 60 GRANTS PER YEAR. FINANCIAL NEED IS A CONSIDERATION. WRITE FOR COMPLETE INFORMATION.

404

METROPOLITAN MUSEUM OF ART (ART HISTORY FELLOWSHIPS)

1000 FIFTH AVENUE
NEW YORK NY 10028
212/879-5500

AMOUNT: $15000 PRE-DOCTORAL; $25000 POST DOCTORAL (PLUS $2500 TRAVEL STIPEND)

DEADLINE(S): NOV 13

FIELD(S): ART HISTORY/CLASSICAL STUDIES

GRADUATE SCHOLARSHIPS; FELLOWSHIPS; AND POST-DOCTORAL FELLOWSHIPS FOR PROMISING YOUNG SCHOLARS IN THE FIELDS OF ART HISTORY AND THE CLASSICS.

WRITE FOR COMPLETE INFORMATION.

405

METROPOLITAN MUSEUM OF ART (INTERNSHIPS)

1000 FIFTH AVENUE
NEW YORK NY 10028
212/570-3710

AMOUNT: $2200; $2500; $8000; $12000 (DEPENDING ON INTERNSHIP)

DEADLINE(S): FEB 1

FIELD(S): ART CONSERVATION

INTERNSHIPS OPEN TO UNDERGRADUATE AND GRADUATE STUDENTS WHO INTEND TO PURSUE CAREERS IN ART MUSEUMS. THERE ARE PROGRAMS FOR GRAD AND UNDERGRAD STUDENTS; MINORITIES AND DISADVANTAGED INDIVIDUALS.

TYPED APPLICATION SHOULD INCLUDE NAME; HOME & SCHOOL ADDRESSES & TELEPHONE NUMBERS; EDUCATION & EMPLOYMENT RESUME; TWO ACADEMIC RECOMMENDATIONS; UNDERGRAD & GRADUATE TRANSCRIPTS; ESSAY. WRITE FOR COMPLETE INFORMATION.

406

METROPOLITAN MUSEUM OF ART (STARR FELLOWSHIP IN ASIAN PAINTINGS CONSERVATION)

1000 FIFTH AVENUE
NEW YORK NY 10028
212/879-5500

AMOUNT: STIPEND DEPENDS ON FUNDS AVAILABLE AND MAY VARY WITH CIRCUMSTANCES.

DEADLINE(S): NONE SPECIFIED

FIELD(S): CONSERVATION AND MOUNTING OF ASIAN PAINTINGS

FELLOWSHIP IS FOR INTENSIVE TRAINING IN THE CONSERVATION AND MOUNTING OF ASIAN PAINTINGS. THE PROGRAM IS COMPREHENSIVE AND IS INTENDED FOR A PERSON WHO MIGHT PURSUE THIS FIELD AS A LIFETIME CAREER.

WRITE FOR COMPLETE INFORMATION.

407

MILLAY COLONY FOR THE ARTS (RESIDENCIES)

STEEPLETOP; PO BOX 3
AUSTERLITZ NY 12017
518/392-3103

AMOUNT: RESIDENCY

DEADLINE(S): SEP 1; FEB 1; MAY 1

FIELD(S): CREATIVE WRITING; VISUAL ARTS; MUSIC COMPOSITION; SCULPTURE; GRAPHIC ARTS; POETRY

THE COLONY PROVIDES 60 RESIDENCIES PER YEAR FOR PROFESSIONALS IN THE ABOVE FIELDS. THERE IS NO APPLICATION FEE AND NO FEE FOR COLONY RESIDENCY.

RESIDENCIES ARE FOR ONE MONTH AND USUALLY COVER A PERIOD FROM THE FIRST TO THE 28TH OF EACH MONTH. WRITE FOR COMPLETE INFORMATION.

408

MINNESOTA STATE ARTS BOARD (GRANTS PROGRAM)

432 SUMMIT AVE
ST PAUL MN 55102
612/297-2603

AMOUNT: FELLOWSHIPS $6000; CAREER OPPORTUNITY GRANTS $100 - $1000 OR SPECIAL RESIDENCY STIPEND.

DEADLINE(S): SEP - VISUAL ARTS; OCT - MUSIC & DANCE; DEC - LITERATURE & THEATER

FIELD(S): LITERATURE; MUSIC; THEATER; DANCE; VISUAL ARTS

CAREER ADVANCEMENT GRANTS OPEN TO PROFESSIONAL ARTISTS WHO ARE RESIDENTS OF MINNESOTA. GRANTS ARE NOT INTENDED FOR SUPPORT OF TUITION OR WORK TOWARD ANY DEGREE.

CAREER OPPORTUNITY GRANTS AND FELLOWSHIPS ARE AVAILABLE. ARTISTS ALSO ARE ELIGIBLE FOR A SPECIAL RESIDENCE AT HEADLANDS CENTER FOR THE ARTS NEAR SAN FRANCISCO. WRITE FOR COMPLETE INFORMATION.

409

NATIONAL ENDOWMENT FOR THE ARTS (VISUAL ARTISTS FELLOWSHIPS)

1100 PENNSYLVANIA AVE NW
WASHINGTON DC 20506
202/682-5448

AMOUNT: $15000 - $20000

DEADLINE(S): VARIOUS IN JAN; FEB & MAR

FIELD(S): VISUAL ARTS

FELLOWSHIPS OPEN TO PRACTICING PROFESSIONAL ARTISTS OF EXCEPTIONAL TALENT IN ALL AREAS OF THE VISUAL ARTS. AWARDS ARE TO ASSIST CREATIVE DEVELOPMENT. THEY WILL NOT SUPPORT ACADEMIC STUDY. USA CITIZEN OR LEGAL RESIDENT.

STUDENTS ARE -NOT- ELIGIBLE TO APPLY. WRITE FOR COMPLETE INFORMATION.

410

NATIONAL GALLERY OF ART (FINLEY; PAUL MELLON; ANDREW MELON ; KRESS; DAVIS; WYETH; ITTLESON; SMITH & DALE DISSERTATION FELLOWSHIPS)

CENTER FOR ADVANCED STUDY IN THE VISUAL ARTS
WASHINGTON DC 20565
202/842-6482; FAX 202/408-8531

AMOUNT: $13000 STIPEND PER YEAR

DEADLINE(S): NOV 15

FIELD(S): ART HISTORY

PREDOCTORAL FELLOWSHIPS FOR SCHOLARLY WORK IN THE HISTORY; THEORY & CRITICISM OF ART; ARCHITECTURE; & URBANISM. FELLOWSHIPS ARE TO SUPPORT DOCTORAL DISSERTATION RESEARCH BY THOSE WHO HAVE COMPLETED RESIDENCE REQUIREMENTS & PH.D COURSEWORK.

APPLICANTS MUST BE USA CITIZENS OR A FOREIGN NATIONAL ENROLLED IN A USA UNIVERSITY. STUDENTS MUST KNOW TWO FOREIGN LANGUAGES RELATED TO THEIR DISSERTATION TOPIC. WRITE FOR COMPLETE INFORMATION.

411

NATIONAL SCULPTURE SOCIETY (YOUNG SCULPTOR AWARDS COMPETITION)

15 EAST 26TH STREET
NEW YORK NY 10010
212/889-6960

AMOUNT: $1000; $750; $500; $250

DEADLINE(S): MAY 15

FIELD(S): SCULPTURE

COMPETITION IS OPEN TO SCULPTORS UNDER AGE 36 WHO ARE RESIDENTS OF THE USA. A JURY OF PROFESSIONAL SCULPTORS WILL MAKE THEIR SELECTIONS BASED UPON 5-10 BLACK & WHITE 8 X 10 PHOTOS OF EACH ENTRANT'S WORKS.

IN ADDITION TO CASH AWARDS & PRIZES PHOTOS OF WINNERS' WORKS WILL BE PUBLISHED IN SCULPTURE REVIEW MAGAZINE. WRITE FOR COMPLETE INFORMATION ON OTHER PRIZES AND EXHIBITIONS.

412

NEW JERSEY STATE COUNCIL ON THE ARTS (FELLOWSHIP SUPPORT)

4 NORTH BROAD ST - CN 306
TRENTON NJ 08625
609/292-6130

AMOUNT: UP TO $12000

DEADLINE(S): VARIES (USUALLY JAN OR FEB)

FIELD(S): LITERATURE; CHOREOGRAPHY; COMPOSITION; VISUAL ARTS; PHOTOGRAPHY

NEW JERSEY RESIDENTS. FELLOWSHIP AWARDS ARE MADE TO PROFESSIONAL ARTISTS & GRADUATE STUDENTS TO ENABLE THEM TO COMPLETE EITHER NEW WORKS OR WORKS IN PROGRESS. UNDERGRADUATES ARE NOT ELIGIBLE.

FUNDS MAY -NOT- BE USED FOR TUITION OR DIRECT EXPENSES OF FORMAL EDUCATION. WRITE TO GRANTS COORDINATOR; ADDRESS ABOVE; FOR COMPLETE INFORMATION.

413

NEW YORK FOUNDATION FOR THE ARTS (ARTIST'S FELLOWSHIPS & SERVICES)

155 AVE OF THE AMERICAS; 14TH FLOOR
NEW YORK NY 10013
212/366-6900; FAX 212/366-1778

AMOUNT: $7000

DEADLINE(S): SEP 30

FIELD(S): VISUAL ARTS; LITERATURE; ARCHITECTURE; MUSIC AND MEDIA

FELLOWSHIPS & SERVICES OPEN TO ORIGINATING ARTISTS OVER 18 WHO HAVE BEEN NY STATE RESIDENTS FOR 2 YEARS PREVIOUS TO APPLICATION DATE & ARE NOT ENROLLED IN A DEGREE AWARDING COURSE OF STUDY. AWARDS ARE TO ASSIST IN CREATION OF ONGOING WORK.

APPLICATIONS AVAILABLE IN SPRINT OF EACH YEAR. ABOUT 120 FELLOWSHIPS PER YEAR; MANY OTHER SERVICES ARE AVAILABLE. -NOT- FOR ACADEMIC STUDY. WRITE FOR COMPLETE INFORMATION.

414

NEW YORK UNIVERSITY (SPIKE LEE/COLUMBIA PICTURES PRODUCTION FELLOWSHIP)

TISH SCHOOL OF FILM;
721 BROADWAY; 7TH FL
NEW YORK NY 10003
212/998-1900

AMOUNT: $5000

DEADLINE(S): OCT 11

FIELD(S): FILMMAKING; FILM PRODUCTION

FELLOWSHIPS OPEN TO 2ND AND 3RD YEAR GRADUATE STUDENTS AT NYU'S TISH SCHOOL OF FILM WHO DEMONSTRATE TALENT IN FILMMAKING AND FILM PRODUCTION.

CONTACT DIRECTOR OF STUDENT AFFAIRS AT ADDRESS ABOVE FOR COMPLETE INFORMATION.

415

NOVA SCOTIA COLLEGE OF ART AND DESIGN (SCHOLARSHIPS)

5163 DUKE STREET
HALIFAX NOVA SCOTIA B3J 3J6 CANADA
902/422-7381

AMOUNT: $100 - $1500

DEADLINE(S): NONE SPECIFIED

FIELD(S): ART/FINE ARTS

THE NOVA SCOTIA COLLEGE OF ART AND DESIGN ADMINISTERS A NUMBER OF SCHOLARSHIPS AND BURSARY AWARDS THAT ACKNOWLEDGE HIGH ACHIEVEMENT AND SPECIAL PROMISE OF STUDENTS AT THE COLLEGE. SOME AWARDS ARE NEED BASED.

CONTACT THE STUDENT SERVICES OFFICE AT ADDRESS ABOVE FOR COMPLETE INFORMATION.

416

PARAMOUNT PICTURES (PARAMOUNT INTERNSHIPS IN FILM & TELEVISION)

5555 MELROSE AVE
HOLLYWOOD CA 90038
213/956-5145

AMOUNT: APPROX $25000

DEADLINE(S): FEB 1

FIELD(S): FILM & VIDEO; SCREENWRITING

POST-GRADUATE PRODUCING; DIRECTING AND FILM & TV WRITING INTERNSHIPS AT PARAMOUNT PICTURES. OPEN TO NEW GRADUATES OF THE GRADUATE FILM PROGRAMS AT NEW YORK UNIV; COLUMBIA UNIV; UCLA; USC & THE AMERICAN FILM INSTITUTE.

APPLICATION IS THROUGH THE SCHOOL. -DO NOT- APPLY DIRECTLY TO PARAMOUNT. RENEWABLE. WRITE FOR COMPLETE INFORMATION.

417

PASTEL SOCIETY OF AMERICA (PSA SCHOLARSHIPS)

15 GRAMERCY PARK SOUTH
NEW YORK NY 10003
212/533-6931

AMOUNT: TUITION ONLY (NO CASH AWARDS)

DEADLINE(S): MAY 30 (FOR SUBMISSION OF SLIDES)

FIELD(S): PAINTING (PASTELS ONLY)

OPEN TO TALENTED PASTEL ARTISTS AT ALL LEVELS OF STUDY. AWARDS ARE FOR THE STUDY OF PASTEL ARTS AT THE ART STUDENTS LEAGUE; PSA STUDIO OR WITH A PRIVATE PSA TEACHER. DURATION RANGES FROM 1 WEEK TO 1 CLASS PER WEEK FOR 1 YEAR.

20 AWARDS PER YEAR. WRITE FOR COMPLETE INFORMATION.

418

SAMUEL H. KRESS FOUNDATION (FELLOWSHIPS)

174 EAST 80TH STREET
NEW YORK NY 10021
212/861-4993

AMOUNT: VARIES

DEADLINE(S): NOV 30 ART HISTORY; FEB 28 ART CONSERVATION

FIELD(S): ART HISTORY/ART CONSERVATION

DOCTORAL DISSERTATION FELLOWSHIPS IN ART HISTORY. MUST ANTICIPATE COMPLETION OF ALL REQUIREMENTS FOR PH.D. DEGREE EXCEPT DISSERATATION AT TIME GRANT WILL BE RECEIVED. GRANTS ARE MADE FOR TRAVEL TO PURSUE ESSENTIAL RESEARCH.

GRANTS ALSO FOR ART CONSERVATION AT THE ADVANCED LEVEL. 25-30 GRANTS FOR ART HISTORY; 25 FOR ART CONSERVATION. USA CITIZEN. WRITE TO PROGRAM DIRECTOR AT ADDRESS ABOVE FOR COMPLETE INFORMATION.

419

SAN FRANCISCO FOUNDATION (JAMES D PHELAN ART AWARDS)

685 MARKET ST; SUITE 910
SAN FRANCISCO CA 94105
415/495-3100 OR 510/436-3100

AMOUNT: $2500

DEADLINE(S): EARLY FALL

FIELD(S): PRINTMAKING; PHOTOGRAPHY; FILM & VIDEO

OPEN TO CALIFORNIA-BORN ARTISTS IN ABOVE AREAS. PRINTMAKING & PHOTOGRAPHY AWARDS IN ODD-NUMBERED YEARS AND FILM & VIDEO AWARDS IN EVEN NUMBERED YEARS. USA CITIZEN.

AWARDS WILL BE PRESENTED AT A PUBLIC RECEPTION AND SCREENING OF WINNERS' WORKS. WRITE FOR COMPLETE INFORMATION.

420

SCRIPPS HOWARD FOUNDATION (CHARLES M. SCHULZ AWARD)

312 WALNUT ST - 28TH FLOOR
CINCINNATI OH 45201
513/977-3035

AMOUNT: $2000

DEADLINE(S): JAN 14

FIELD(S): COLLEGE CARTOONIST

AWARD TO HONOR OUTSTANDING COLLEGE CARTOONISTS & TO ENCOURAGE THEM TO LAUNCH POST-GRADUATE PROFESSIONAL CAREERS. OPEN TO ANY STUDENT CARTOONIST AT A COLLEGE NEWSPAPER OR MAGAZINE IN THE USA & ITS TERRITORIES.

APPLICATIONS AVAILABLE DURING THE FALL MONTHS. WRITE FOR COMPLETE INFORMATION.

421

SCRIPPS HOWARD FOUNDATION (ROBERT P SCRIPPS GRAPHIC ARTS GRANTS)

312 WALNUT ST - 28TH FLOOR
CINCINNATI OH 45201
513/977-3035

AMOUNT: UP TO $3000

DEADLINE(S): DEC 20 FOR AN APPLICATION; FEB 25 FOR MAILING IN APPLICATION

FIELD(S): GRAPHIC ARTS (NEWSPAPER INDUSTRY)

PREFERENCE TO UNDERGRAD JUNIORS; SENIORS OR GRAD STUDENTS MAJORING IN GRAPHIC ARTS AS APPLIED TO NEWSPAPERS WHO HAVE POTENTIAL (IN COLLEGE AUTHORITIES' OPINION) OF BECOMING NEWSPAPER PRODUCTION ADMINISTRATORS. US CITIZEN OR LEGAL RESIDENT.

RENEWABLE WITH REAPPLICATION. QUALIFIED STUDENTS SHOULD SUBMIT A LETTER (BEFORE DEC 20) REQUESTING AN APPLICATION AND STATING COLLEGE MAJOR AND CAREER GOAL.

422

SMITHSONIAN INSTITUTION (MINORITY UNDERGRADUATE & GRADUATE INTERNSHIP)

OFFICE OF FELLOWSHIPS & GRANTS;
955 L'ENFANT PLAZA; SUITE 7300
WASHINGTON DC 20560
202/287-3271

AMOUNT: $250 - $300 PER WEEK STIPEND + TRAVELDEADLINE(S): FEB 15; JUN 15; OCT 15

FIELD(S): DESIGN; ARCHITECTURE; ART; MUSEUM STUDIES

INTERNSHIPS OPEN TO MINORITY STUDENTS FOR RESEARCH & STUDY AT THE SMITHSONIAN OR THE COOPER-HEWITT MUSEUM OF DESIGN IN NEW YORK CITY. THE MUSEUM'S COLLECTION SPANS 3000 YEARS OF DESIGN FROM ANCIENT POTTERY TO MODERN FASHION & ADVERTISING.

UNDERGRADUATES RECEIVE $250 PER WEEK STIPEND & GRADUATE STUDENTS RECEIVE $300 PER WEEK STIPEND. WRITE FOR COMPLETE INFORMATION.

423

SMITHSONIAN INSTITUTION (PETER KRUEGER SUMMER INTERNSHIP PROGRAM)

COOPER-HEWITT MUSEUM;
2 EAST 91ST ST.
NEW YORK NY 10128
212/860-6868; FAX 212/860-6909

AMOUNT: $2500

DEADLINE(S): MAR 31

FIELD(S): ART HISTORY; ARCHITECTURAL HISTORY; DESIGN

TEN WEEK SUMMER INTERNSHIPS OPEN TO GRADUATE AND UNDERGRADUATE STUDENTS CONSIDERING A CAREER IN THE MUSEUM PROFESSION. INTERNS WILL ASSIST ON SPECIAL RESEARCH OR EXHIBITION PROJECTS AND PARTICIPATE IN DAILY MUSEUM ACTIVITIES.

INTERNSHIP COMMENCES IN JUNE AND ENDS IN AUGUST. HOUSING IS NOT PROVIDED. WRITE FOR COMPLETE INFORMATION.

424

SOCIETY FOR IMAGING SCIENCE AND TECHNOLOGY (RAYMOND DAVIS SCHOLARSHIP)

7003 KILWORTH LANE
SPRINGFIELD VA 22151
703/642-9090; FAX 703/642-9094

AMOUNT: $1000

DEADLINE(S): DEC 15

FIELD(S): PHOTOGRAPHIC SCIENCE OR
ENGINEERING

SCHOLARSHIPS FOR UNDERGRADUATE JUNIORS
OR SENIORS OR GRADUATE STUDENTS FOR
FULL TIME CONTINUING STUDIES IN THE
THEORY OR PRACTICE OF PHOTOGRAPHIC
SCIENCE INCLUDING ANY KIND OF IMAGE
FORMATION INITIATED BY RADIANT
ENERGY.

WRITE FOR COMPLETE INFORMATION.

425

SOLOMON R. GUGGENHEIM MUSEUM
(FELLOWSHIP AND VOLUNTARY
INTERNSHIP PROGRAMS)

1071 FIFTH AVE.
NEW YORK NY 10128
212/423-3600

AMOUNT: STIPENDS VARY (SOME POSITIONS
NON-PAID)

DEADLINE(S): AUG 15; DEC 15; MAR 15

FIELD(S): ARTS ADMINISTRATION; ART HISTORY

TEN WEEK INTERNSHIP OPEN TO STUDENTS IN
THE ABOVE FIELDS WHO HAVE COMPLETED
AT LEAST TWO YEARS OF UNDERGRADUATE
STUDY; FELLOWSHIPS OPEN TO GRADUATE
STUDENTS HOLDING B.A. OR M.A. IN ART
HISTORY.

DIRECT INQUIRIES TO ADDRESS ABOVE; ATTN
INTERNSHIP PROGRAM.

426

TENNESSEE ARTS COMMISSION (INDIVIDUAL
ARTISTS' FELLOWSHIPS)

320 SIXTH AVE NORTH #100
NASHVILLE TN 37243
615/741-1701

AMOUNT: $2500 - $5000

DEADLINE(S): JAN 11

FIELD(S): VISUAL ARTS; PERFORMING ARTS;
CREATIVE ARTS

GRANTS OPEN TO ARTISTS WHO ARE RESIDENTS
OF THE STATE OF TENNESSEE. DURATION OF
AWARD IS ONE YEAR. APPLICANTS MUST BE
PROFESSIONAL ARTISTS. FULL TIME
STUDENTS ARE -NOT- ELIGIBLE.

WRITE FOR COMPLETE INFORMATION.

427

UNIVERSITY FILM AND VIDEO ASSN (GRANTS)

J.STEPHEN HANK; DEPT. OF DRAMA &
COMMUNICATIONS; UNIVERSITY OF NEW
ORLEANS; LAKEFRONT
NEW ORLEANS LA 70148
WRITTEN INQUIRY ONLY

AMOUNT: VARIES

DEADLINE(S): JAN 1

FIELD(S): FILM & VIDEO

OPEN TO UNDERGRADUATE & GRADUATE
STUDENTS WHO ARE SPONSORED BY A
FACULTY MEMBER WHO IS ACTIVE IN THE
FILM AND VIDEO ASSOCIATION. GRANTS FOR
STUDENT FILM OR VIDEO PRODUCTIONS OR
RESEARCH PROJECTS.

RESEARCH PROJECTS MAY BE IN HISTORICAL;
CRITICAL; THEORETICAL OR EXPERIMENTAL
STUDIES OF FILM OR VIDEO. WRITE FOR
COMPLETE INFORMATION.

428

UNIVERSITY OF ILLINOIS AT URBANA-
CHAMPAIGN (KATE N. KINLEY
FELLOWSHIP)

COLLEGE OF FINE & APPLIED ARTS;
110 ARCHITECTURE BLDG;
608 E. LORADO TAFT DR.
CHAMPAIGN IL 61820
217/333-2723

AMOUNT: $7000

DEADLINE(S): FEB 15

FIELD(S): ART; MUSIC; ARCHITECTURE

GRADUATE FELLOWSHIP FOR ADVANCED STUDY
IN THE USA OR ABROAD. OPEN TO
APPLICANTS WITH A BACHELOR'S DEGREE
IN THE ABOVE AREAS. PREFERENCE GIVEN
TO (BUT NOT LIMITED TO) APPLICANTS
UNDER 25 YEARS OF AGE.

TWO ADDITIONAL AWARDS OF A LESSER
AMOUNT MAY BE GRANTED UPON
COMMITTEE RECOMMENDATION. WRITE FOR
COMPLETE INFORMATION.

429

VIRGINIA MUSEUM OF FINE ARTS
(UNDERGRAD/GRADUATE &
PROFESSIONAL FELLOWSHIPS)

2800 GROVE AVE
RICHMOND VA 23221
804/367-0824

AMOUNT: UP TO $4000 UNDERGRADS; $5000
GRADS; $8000 PROFESSIONALS

DEADLINE(S): MAR 1

FIELD(S): ART; FINE ARTS; ART HISTORY
(GRADUATE ONLY); ARCHITECTURE;
PHOTOGRAPHY; FILM; VIDEO

VIRGINIA RESIDENT FOR 1 YEAR PRIOR TO
DEADLINE. US CITIZEN OR LEGAL RESIDENT.
PROFESSIONAL ARTIST FELLOWSHIPS ALSO
AVAILABLE. NEED IS CONSIDERED.

ART; FINE ARTS & ART HISTORY FOR GRADUATE
STUDENTS ONLY. 9-12 AWARDS PER YEAR.
WRITE FOR COMPLETE INFORMATION.

430

WAVERLY COMMUNITY HOUSE INC (F. LAMMONT BELIN ARTS SCHOLARSHIPS)

SCHOLARSHIPS SELECTION COMMITTEE
WAVERLY PA 18471
717/586-8191

AMOUNT: $9000

DEADLINE(S): DEC 15

FIELD(S): PAINTING; SCULPTURE; MUSIC; DRAMA; DANCE; LITERATURE; ARCHITECTURE; PHOTOGRAPHY

APPLICANTS MUST RESIDE IN THE ABINGTONS OR POCONO REGIONS OF NORTHEASTERN PENNSYLVANIA. THEY MUST FURNISH PROOF OF EXCEPTIONAL ABILITY IN THEIR CHOSEN FIELD BUT NEED NO FORMAL TRAINING IN ANY ACADEMIC OR PROFESSIONAL PROGRAM.

USA CITIZENSHIP REQUIRED. FINALISTS MUST APPEAR IN PERSON BEFORE THE SELECTION COMMITTEE. WRITE FOR COMPLETE INFORMATION.

ENGLISH LANG / LIT

431

ACADEMY OF MOTION PICTURE ARTS AND SCIENCES (DON & GEE NICHOLL FELLOWSHIPS IN SCREENWRITING)

8949 WILSHIRE BLVD
BEVERLY HILLS CA 90211
310/247-3059

AMOUNT: $20000

DEADLINE(S): JUN 1

FIELD(S): SCREENWRITING

FELLOWSHIPS OPEN TO ANY ENGLISH LANGUAGE WRITER WHO IS PREPARING FOR A CAREER AS A SCREENWRITER BUT HAS NOT AS YET BEEN PAID TO WRITE A SCREENPLAY OR TELEPLAY. AWARD MAY -NOT- BE USED TO CONTINUE OR COMPLETE FORMAL EDUCATION.

5 AWARDS PER YEAR. SEND SELF ADDRESSED STAMPED ENVELOPE FOR COMPLETE INFORMATION.

432

ALABAMA PUBLIC LIBRARY SERVICE (EDUCATIONAL GRANT PROGRAM)

6030 MONTICELLO DR
MONTGOMERY AL 36130
205/277-7330

AMOUNT: $5000 FULL TIME; UP TO $3000 CUMULATIVE TOTAL FOR PART TIME

DEADLINE(S): MAY 1

FIELD(S): LIBRARY SCIENCE

FULL TIME STUDENTS MUST BE ALABAMA RESIDENTS SEEKING MASTER OF LIBRARY SCIENCE DEGREE AT ANY ACCREDITED SCHOOL OF LIBRARY SCIENCE. RECIPIENTS AGREE TO WORK IN AN ALABAMA PUBLIC LIBRARY FOR TWO YEARS AFTER GRADUATION.

PART TIME STUDENTS MUST BE CURRENTLY EMPLOYED BY AN ALABAMA PUBLIC LIBRARY. PART TIME GRANTS ARE RENEWABLE. WRITE FOR COMPLETE INFORMATION.

433

ALASKA STATE COUNCIL ON THE ARTS (INDIVIDUAL ARTIST FELLOWSHIPS & GRANTS)

411 W. 4TH AVE. SUITE 1E
ANCHORAGE AK 99501
907/279-1558

AMOUNT: $5000

DEADLINE(S): OCT 1

FIELD(S): VISUAL ARTS; CRAFTS; PHOTOGRAPHY - ODD NUMBERED YEARS. MUSIC COMPOSITION; CHOREOGRAPHY; MEDIA ARTS; LITERATURE - EVEN NUMBERED YEARS.

OPEN TO ALASKA RESIDENTS WHO ARE ENGAGED IN THE CREATION OF NEW WORKS. FULL TIME STUDENTS ARE -NOT- ELIGIBLE.

WRITE FOR COMPLETE INFORMATION.

434

AMERICAN ACADEMY IN ROME (ROME PRIZE FELLOWSHIPS)

41 EAST 65TH STREET
NEW YORK NY 10021
212/535-4250

AMOUNT: $8300 (INCLUDES ROUND TRIP TRAVEL TO ROME AND EUROPEAN TRAVEL ALLOWANCE)

DEADLINE(S): NOV 15

FIELD(S): ARCHITECTURE; LANDSCAPE ARCHITECTURE; MUSICAL COMPOSITION; CLASSICS; ART HISTORY; PAINTING; SCULPTURE AND THE VISUAL ARTS; POST CLASSICAL HUMANISTIC STUDIES.

THE ACADEMY INVITES ARTISTS AND SCHOLARS WHO ARE USA CITIZENS TO APPLY FOR A LIMITED NUMBER OF ROME PRIZE FELLOWSHIPS IN THE ARTS AND HUMANITIES.

16 ROME PRIZE FELLOWSHIPS ANNUALLY. WRITE FOR COMPLETE INFORMATION.

435

AMERICAN ANTIQUARIAN SOCIETY (VISITING RESEARCH FELLOWSHIPS)

185 SALISBURY ST
WORCESTER MA 01609
508/755-5221

AMOUNT: $850 PER MONTH

DEADLINE(S): JAN 15

FIELD(S): AMERICAN HISTORY; BIBLIOGRAPHY; PRINTING & PUBLISHING (THROUGH 1876)

FELLOWSHIPS OF ONE TO THREE MONTHS DURATION AT THE SOCIETY LIBRARY. FOR DOCTORAL DISSERTATION RESEARCH AND POST-DOCTORAL RESEARCH IN THE ABOVE FIELDS.

RECIPIENTS ARE EXPECTED TO BE IN REGULAR AND CONTINUOUS RESIDENCE AT THE SOCIETY LIBRARY DURING THE PERIOD OF THE GRANT. WRITE FOR COMPLETE INFORMATION.

436

AMERICAN ASSOCIATION OF LAW LIBRARIES (LAW LIBRARIAN SCHOLARSHIPS - LAW SCHOOL GRADUATES)

53 W. JACKSON BLVD. SUITE 940
CHICAGO IL 60604
312/939-4764

AMOUNT: VARIES

DEADLINE(S): APR 1

FIELD(S): LAW LIBRARIANSHIP

OPEN TO GRADUATES OF ACCREDITED LAW SCHOOLS WHO ARE DEGREE CANDIDATES IN AN ACCREDITED LIBRARY SCHOOL AND PLAN TO PURSUE A CAREER IN LAW LIBRARIANSHIP.

WRITE FOR COMPLETE INFORMATION.

437

AMERICAN ASSOCIATION OF LAW LIBRARIES (MINORITY STIPEND GRANT)

53 W. JACKSON BLVD. SUITE 940
CHICAGO IL 60604
312/939-4764

AMOUNT: $3500 STIPEND

DEADLINE(S): APR 1

FIELD(S): LIBRARY SCIENCE - LAW

OPEN TO A MINORITY GROUP MEMBER WHO IS A COLLEGE GRADUATE WITH LIBRARY EXPERIENCE AND IS WORKING TOWARD AN ADVANCED DEGREE WHICH WOULD FURTHER HIS OR HER LAW LIBRARY CAREER.

WRITE FOR COMPLETE INFORMATION.

438

AMERICAN CATHOLIC HISTORICAL ASSOCIATION (THE PETER GUILDAY PRIZE)

C/O CATHOLIC UNIVERSITY OF AMERICA
WASHINGTON DC 20064
202/635-5079

AMOUNT: $100

DEADLINE(S): OCT 1

FIELD(S): CREATIVE WRITING - CATHOLIC CHURCH HISTORY

PRIZE FOR BEST ARTICLE OF 30 PAGES OR LESS (IN MANUSCRIPT FORM) ON THE HISTORY OF THE CATHOLIC CHURCH. MUST NOT HAVE HAD PREVIOUS WORKS PUBLISHED. PARTS OF DOCTORAL DISSERTATIONS ACCEPTED. USA OR CANADIAN CITIZEN OR LEGAL RESIDENT.

JUDGES ARE THE EDITORS OF THE CATHOLIC HISTORY REVIEW. WRITE FOR COMPLETE INFORMATION.

439

AMERICAN COUNCIL OF LEARNED SOCIETIES (ACLS FELLOWSHIPS)

OFFICE OF FELLOWSHIPS & GRANTS;
228 E. 45TH ST.
NEW YORK NY 10017
WRITTEN INQUIRY

AMOUNT: UP TO $20000

DEADLINE(S): SEP 30

FIELD(S): HUMANITIES; SOCIAL SCIENCES; OTHER AREAS HAVING PREDOMINATELY HUMANISTIC EMPHASIS

OPEN TO USA CITIZENS OR LEGAL RESIDENTS WHO HOLD THE PH.D OR ITS EQUIVALENT. FELLOWSHIPS ARE DESIGNED TO HELP SCHOLARS DEVOTE 2 TO 12 CONTINUOUS MONTHS TO FULL TIME RESEARCH.

WRITE FOR COMPLETE INFORMATION.

440

AMERICAN LIBRARY ASSN (GILES MINORITY SCHOLARSHIPS)

50 EAST HURON ST
CHICAGO IL 60611
312/944-6780 OR 800/545-2433 EXT 4277

AMOUNT: $3000

DEADLINE(S): DEC OR JAN (VARIES EACH YEAR)

FIELD(S): LIBRARY SCIENCE

GRADUATE SCHOLARSHIPS OPEN TO AMERICAN INDIAN; ALASKAN NATIVE; HISPANIC; BLACK; ASIAN; OR PACIFIC ISLANDER STUDENTS ENROLLED IN OR ACCEPTED TO AN ALA ACCREDITED GRADUATE LIBRARY EDUCATION PROGRAM. USA OR CANADIAN CITIZEN OR LEGAL RESIDENT.

WRITE FOR COMPLETE INFORMATION.

441

AMERICAN SCHOOL OF CLASSICAL STUDIES AT ATHENS (FELLOWSHIPS)

41 E.72ND ST
NEW YORK NY 10021
212/861-0302

AMOUNT: UP TO $5650 + ROOM & PARTIAL BOARD

DEADLINE(S): JAN 5

FIELD(S): CLASSICAL STUDIES; ARCHAEOLOGY; ANCIENT GREECE

FELLOWSHIPS FOR STUDY AT ASCSA IN GREECE. OPEN TO GRADUATE STUDENTS AT AMERICAN & CANADIAN COLLEGES & UNIVERSITIES. RECENT GRADUATES ALSO ARE ELIGIBLE.

WRITE FOR COMPLETE INFORMATION.

442

ARCHAEOLOGICAL INSTITUTE OF AMERICA (OLIVIA JAMES TRAVELING FELLOWSHIP)

675 COMMONWEALTH AVE
BOSTON MA 02215
617/353-9361; FAX 617/353-6550

AMOUNT: $11500 STIPEND

DEADLINE(S): NOV 15

FIELD(S): ARCHAEOLOGY; CLASSICS; SCULPTURE; HISTORY; ARCHITECTURE

FOR GRADUATE OR POST-GRADUATE STUDY IN GREECE; AEGEAN ISLANDS; SICILY; SOUTHERN ITALY; ASIA MINOR OR MESOPOTAMIA. PREFERENCE IS FOR DISSERTATION OR RECENT PH.D RESEARCH. WILL NOT SUPPORT FIELD EXCAVATION. USA CITIZEN OR LEGAL RESIDENT.

WRITE FOR COMPLETE INFORMATION.

443

ARTS INTERNATIONAL; INSTITUTE OF INTERNATIONAL EDUCATION (CINTAS FELLOWSHIP PROGRAM)

809 UNITED NATIONS PLAZA
NEW YORK NY 10017
212/984-5370

AMOUNT: $10000

DEADLINE(S): MAR 1

FIELD(S): ARCHITECTURE; PAINTING; PHOTOGRAPHY; SCULPTURE; PRINTMAKING; MUSIC COMPOSITION; CREATIVE WRITING

FELLOWSHIPS OPEN TO ARTISTS WHO ARE OF CUBAN ANCESTRY OR CUBAN CITIZENS LIVING OUTSIDE OF CUBA. THEY ARE INTENDED TO FOSTER & ENCOURAGE THE PROFESSIONAL DEVELOPMENT & RECOGNITION OF TALENTED CREATIVE ARTISTS IN THE ABOVE AREAS.

FELLOWSHIPS ARE NOT AWARDED FOR FURTHERANCE OF ACADEMIC STUDY. 5-10 AWARDS PER YEAR. WRITE FOR COMPLETE INFORMATION.

444

ASSOCIATION FOR INFORMATION AND IMAGE MANAGEMENT (JOHN P EAGER SCHOLARSHIP PROGRAM)

1100 WAYNE AVE #1100
SILVER SPRING MD 20910
301/587-8202

AMOUNT: $5000

DEADLINE(S): DEC 30

FIELD(S): LIBRARY SCIENCE

OPEN TO ANY STUDENT WITH 3.0 GRADE AVG OR HIGHER WHO IS ENROLLED IN AN ACCREDITED UNDERGRADUATE OR GRADUATE PROGRAM OF STUDY IN INFORMATION AND IMAGE MANAGEMENT.

WRITE FOR COMPLETE INFORMATION.

445

ASSOCIATION FOR LIBRARY & INFORMATION SCIENCE EDUCATION (ALISE RESEARCH GRANTS PROGRAM)

5623 PALM AIRE DR
SARASOTA FL 34243
813/355-1795

AMOUNT: $2500

DEADLINE(S): OCT 1

FIELD(S): LIBRARY SCIENCE

GRANTS TO HELP SUPPORT RESEARCH COSTS OPEN TO MEMBERS OF THE ASSOCIATION FOR LIBRARY & INFORMATION SCIENCE. MEMBERSHIP INFORMATION IS AVAILABLE FROM THE ABOVE ADDRESS.

WRITE FOR COMPLETE INFORMATION.

446

ASSOCIATION FOR LIBRARY SERVICE TO CHILDREN OF THE AMERICAN LIBRARY ASSN (MELCHER SCHOLARSHIPS)

50 EAST HURON ST
CHICAGO IL 60611
312/280-2163

AMOUNT: $5000 MAX

DEADLINE(S): MAR 1

FIELD(S): CHILDRENS LIBRARIANSHIP

SCHOLARSHIPS FOR GRADUATE STUDY OPEN TO STUDENTS ACCEPTED TO AN ALA ACCREDITED LIBRARY EDUCATION PROGRAM. USA OR CANADIAN CITIZEN.

WRITE FOR COMPLETE INFORMATION.

447

BETA PHI MU INTERNATIONAL LIBRARY SCIENCE HONOR SOCIETY (SARAH REBECCA REED SCHOLARSHIP; HAROLD LANCOUR SCHOLARSHIP FOR FOREIGN STUDY)

UNIVERSITY OF PITTSBURGH - SLIS
PITTSBURGH PA 15260
412/624-9435

AMOUNT: $1500 (REED); $1000 (LANCOUR)

DEADLINE(S): MAR 1

FIELD(S): LIBRARIANSHIP

OPEN TO STUDENTS ELIGIBLE FOR ADMITTANCE TO A GRADUATE LIBRARY SCHOOL PROGRAM ACCREDITED BY THE AMERICAN LIBRARY ASSOCIATION.

WRITE FOR COMPLETE INFORMATION AND APPLICATION FORM.

448

BETA PHI MU INTERNATIONAL LIBRARY SCIENCE HONOR SOCIETY (FRANK B. SESSA SCHOLARSHIP FOR CONTINUING EDUCATION)

UNIVERSITY OF PITTSBURGH - SLIS
PITTSBURGH PA 15260
412/624-9435

AMOUNT: $750

DEADLINE(S): MAR 1

FIELD(S): LIBRARIANSHIP

CONTINUING EDUCATION PROGRAM OPEN TO BETA PHI MU MEMBERS. APPLICANTS SHOULD SUBMIT RESUME AND AN EXPLANATION OF PROPOSED STUDY OR RESEARCH.

WRITE FOR COMPLETE INFORMATION AND APPLICATION FORM.

449

BEVERLY HILLS THEATRE GUILD (JULIE HARRIS PLAYWRIGHT AWARD COMPETITION)

2815 N. BEACHWOOD DR.
LOS ANGELES CA 90068
213/465-2703

AMOUNT: $1000; $2000; $5000

DEADLINE(S): NOV 1 (ENTRIES ACCEPTED AUG 1 - NOV 1)

FIELD(S): PLAYWRITING COMPETITION

ANNUAL COMPETITION OF FULL-LENGTH (90 MINUTES) UNPRODUCED & UNPUBLISHED PLAYS WRITTEN FOR THE THEATRE. MUSICALS; 1-ACT PLAYS; ADAPTATIONS; TRANSLATIONS & PLAYS ENTERED IN OTHER COMPETITIONS NOT ELIGIBLE. OPEN TO ANY USA CITIZEN.

CO-AUTHORSHIPS ARE PERMISSIBLE. $5000 FOR 1ST; $2000 FOR 2ND & $1000 FOR 3RD. SEND SELF ADDRESSED STAMPED ENVELOPE FOR COMPLETE INFORMATION.

450

BIBLIOGRAPHICAL SOCIETY OF AMERICA (FELLOWSHIP)

PO BOX 397 GRAND CENTRAL STATION
NEW YORK NY 10163
212/995-9151

AMOUNT: UP TO $1000 PER MONTH FOR UP TO 2 MONTHS

DEADLINE(S): JAN 31

FIELD(S): BIBLIOGRAPHY

GRADUATE RESEARCH FELLOWSHIPS. TOPICS MAY CONCENTRATE ON BOOKS & DOCUMENTS IN ANY FIELD BUT FOCUSING ON THE PHYSICAL BOOK OR MANUSCRIPT AS HISTORICAL EVIDENCE; HISTORY OF BOOK PRODUCTION; PUBLICATION; DISTRIBUTION; OR ESTABLISHING A TEXT.

8-10 AWARDS PER YEAR. WRITE FOR COMPLETE INFORMATION.

451

BUSH FOUNDATION (BUSH ARTIST FELLOWSHIPS)

E900 FIRST NATIONAL BANK BLDG;
322 MINNESOTA ST.
ST PAUL MN 55101
612/227-5222

AMOUNT: UP TO $26000 STIPEND + $7000 EXPENSES

DEADLINE(S): LATE OCT; EARLY NOV

FIELD(S): LITERATURE; MUSIC COMPOSITION; CHOREOGRAPHY; VISUAL ARTS; SCRIPTWORKS

OPEN TO WRITERS; VISUAL ARTISTS; COMPOSERS & CHOREOGRAPHERS WHO ARE RESIDENTS OF MN.; N.D.; S.D. OR WESTERN WI. & AT LEAST 25 YRS OLD. AWARDS ARE TO HELP ARTISTS WORK FULL-TIME IN THEIR CHOSEN FIELD; NOT FOR ACADEMIC STUDY.

15 FELLOWSHIPS PER YEAR; 6-18 MONTHS IN DURATION. WRITE FOR COMPLETE INFORMATION.

452

CALIFORNIA LIBRARY ASSOCIATION (EDNA YELLAND MEMORIAL SCHOLARSHIP)

717 'K' STREET; SUITE 300
SACRAMENTO CA 95814
916/447-8541

AMOUNT: $2000

DEADLINE(S): SPRING

FIELD(S): LIBRARY SCIENCE (MASTER'S)

OPEN TO MINORITY STUDENTS ENROLLED IN AN ALA ACCREDITED MASTER'S OF LIBRARY OR INFORMATION SCIENCE PROGRAM AT A COLLEGE OR UNIVERSITY IN CALIFORNIA. USA CITIZEN.

WRITE OR CALL FOR COMPLETE INFORMATION.

453

CALIFORNIA LIBRARY ASSOCIATION (REFERENCE SERVICE PRESS FELLOWSHIP)

717 K ST; SUITE 300
SACRAMENTO CA 95814
916/447-8541

AMOUNT: $2000

DEADLINE(S): MAY 31

FIELD(S): LIBRARY SCIENCE (MASTER'S)

OPEN TO COLLEGE SENIORS OR GRADUATES WHO HAVE BEEN ACCEPTED IN AN ACCREDITED MLS PROGRAM. FOR RESIDENTS OF CA ATTENDING LIBRARY SCHOOL IN ANY STATE OR RESIDENT OF ANY STATE ATTENDING A CA LIBRARY SCHOOL.

STUDENTS PURSUING AN MLS ON A PART TIME OR FULL TIME BASIS ARE EQUALLY ELIGIBLE. WRITE FOR COMPLETE INFORMATION.

454

CALIFORNIA STATE LIBRARY (MULTI-ETHNIC RECRUITMENT SCHOLARSHIP PROGRAM)

1001 SIXTH STREET SUITE 300
SACRAMENTO CA 95814
916/445-4730

AMOUNT: $1000 - $5000

DEADLINE(S): JUN 1

FIELD(S): LIBRARY SCIENCE

OPEN TO AMERICAN INDIAN; ASIAN; PACIFIC ISLANDER; BLACK OR HISPANIC STUDENTS ACCEPTED TO A MASTER'S PROGRAM AT ELIGIBLE ACCREDITED CALIF. GRADUATE LIBRARY SCHOOLS. PROGRAM SEEKS TO INCREASE POOL OF MINORITIES FOR STATE'S PUBLIC LIBRARIES.

APPLICATIONS AVAILABLE -ONLY- FROM PARTICIPATING CALIFORNIA LIBRARIES & LIBRARY SCHOOLS. CONTACT SCHOOL'S FINANCIAL AID OFFICE OR WRITE FOR COMPLETE INFORMATION.

455

CATHOLIC LIBRARY ASSOCIATION (BOUWHUIS SCHOLARSHIP IN LIBRARY SCIENCE)

461 WEST LANCASTER AVE
HAVERFORD PA 19041
215/649-5251

AMOUNT: $1500

DEADLINE(S): FEB 1

FIELD(S): LIBRARY SCIENCE

OPEN TO COLLEGE SENIOR WITH GPA OF 3.0 OR BETTER WHO IS ACCEPTED AS A MASTER'S CANDIDATE BY AN ACCREDITED GRADUATE LIBRARY SCHOOL. FINANCIAL NEED IS A CONSIDERATION.

WRITE FOR COMPLETE INFORMATION.

456

CATHOLIC LIBRARY ASSOCIATION (GRANT)

461 WEST LANCASTER AVENUE
HAVERFORD PA 19041
215/649-5251

AMOUNT: $1500

DEADLINE(S): FEB 1

FIELD(S): LIBRARY SCIENCE

OPEN TO MEMBERS OF NATIONAL CATHOLIC LIBRARY ASSOCIATION. PURPOSE OF AWARD IS TO ADD EXPERTISE IN THE FIELD OF CHILDREN'S OR SCHOOL LIBRARIANSHIP.

WRITE FOR COMPLETE INFORMATION.

457

CENTER FOR HELLENIC STUDIES (RESIDENT JUNIOR FELLOWSHIPS)

3100 WHITEHAVEN STREET NW
WASHINGTON DC 20008
202/234-3738

AMOUNT: $18000

DEADLINE(S): NOV 1

FIELD(S): ANCIENT GREEK LITERATURE; HISTORY; PHILOSOPHY; LANGUAGE OR RELIGION

RESIDENT FELLOWSHIPS FOR POST-DOCTORAL SCHOLARS WITH PROFESSIONAL COMPETENCE AND SOME PUBLICATION IN ANCIENT GREEK AREAS SHOWN ABOVE.

8 RESIDENT FELLOWSHIPS PER YEAR. WRITE FOR COMPLETE INFORMATION.

458

CONNECTICUT LIBRARY ASSOCIATION (PROGRAM FOR EDUCATION GRANTS)

638 PROSPECT AVE
HARTFORD CT 06105
203/232-4825

AMOUNT: VARIES

DEADLINE(S): NONE

FIELD(S): LIBRARIANSHIP

CONTINUING EDUCATION GRANTS FOR LIBRARY EMPLOYEES; VOLUNTEER TRUSTEES OR FRIENDS OF THE LIBRARY IN THE STATE OF CONNECTICUT. MUST JOIN CLA TO BE ELIGIBLE. TUITION COST IS NOT COVERED.

4-5 GRANTS PER YEAR. WRITE FOR COMPLETE INFORMATION.

459

CREOLE-AMERICAN GENEALOGICAL SOCIETY INC. (CREOLE SCHOLARSHIPS)

PO BOX 2666 - CHURCH STREET STATION
NEW YORK NY 10008
WRITTEN INQUIRY ONLY

AMOUNT: $1500

DEADLINE(S): APPLY BETWEEN JAN 1 AND APR 30

FIELD(S): GENEALOGY OR LANGUAGE OR CREOLE CULTURE

AWARDS IN THE ABOVE AREAS OPEN TO INDIVIDUALS OF MIXED RACIAL ANCESTRY WHO SUBMIT A FOUR-GENERATION GENEAOLOGICAL CHART ATTESTING TO CREOLE ANCESTRY AND/OR INTERRACIAL PARENTAGE. FOR UNDERGRADUATE OR GRADUATE STUDY/RESEARCH.

FOR SCHOLARSHIP/AWARD INFORMATION SEND $2 MONEY ORDER AND SELF ADDRESSED STAMPED ENVELOPE TO ADDRESS ABOVE. CASH AND PERSONAL CHECKS ARE NOT ACCEPTED. LETTERS WITHOUT SASE AND HANDLING CHARGE WILL NOT BE ANSWERED.

460

DISTRICT OF COLUMBIA COMMISSION ON THE ARTS & HUMANITIES (GRANTS)

410 EIGHTH ST. NW - 5TH FLOOR
WASHINGTON DC 20004
202/724-5613; TDD 202/727-318; FAX 202/727-4135

AMOUNT: $5000

DEADLINE(S): FEB 15

FIELD(S): ARTS; PERFORMING ARTS; LITERATURE

APPLICANTS FOR GRANTS MUST BE PROFESSIONAL ARTISTS AND RESIDENTS OF WASHINGTON D.C. FOR AT LEAST ONE YEAR PRIOR TO SUBMITTING APPLICATION. AWARDS INTENDED TO GENERATE ARTS ENDEAVORS WITHIN THE WASHINGTON D.C. COMMUNITY.

OPEN ALSO TO ARTS ORGANIZATIONS THAT TRAIN; EXHIBIT OR PERFORM WITHIN D.C. 150 GRANTS PER YEAR. WRITE FOR COMPLETE INFORMATION.

461

ETA SIGMA PHI (SUMMER SCHOLARSHIPS)

UNIVERSITY OF SOUTH DAKOTA
VERMILLION SD 57069
605/677-5468

AMOUNT: $2500 ROME; $3150 ATHENS

DEADLINE(S): DEC 15

FIELD(S): CLASSICS

OPEN TO MEMBERS OF ETA SIGMA PHI. SCHOLARSHIPS ARE FOR GRADUATE STUDY AT THE AMERICAN ACADEMY IN ROME OR THE AMERICAN SCHOOL OF CLASSICAL STUDIES IN ATHENS. ATTENTION WILL BE GIVEN TO WORK IN GREEK & LATIN AND INTENTION TO TEACH.

WRITE FOR COMPLETE INFORMATION.

462

FLORIDA ARTS COUNCIL (INDIVIDUAL ARTISTS FELLOWSHIPS)

FLA DEPT OF STATE; DIV OF CULTURAL AFFAIRS; STATE CAPITOL
TALLAHASSEE FL 32399
904/487-2980

AMOUNT: UP TO $5000

DEADLINE(S): FEB 15 (APR 15 FOR VISUAL ARTS)

FIELD(S): VISUAL ARTS; DANCE; FOLK ARTS; MEDIA; MUSIC; THEATER; LITERARY ARTS

FELLOWSHIPS AWARDED TO INDIVIDUAL ARTISTS IN THE ABOVE AREAS. MUST BE FLORIDA RESIDENTS; USA CITIZENS AND OVER 18 YEARS OLD. MAY -NOT- BE A DEGREE SEEKING STUDENT; FUNDING IS FOR SUPPORT OF ARTISTIC ENDEAVORS ONLY.

FORTY AWARDS PER YEAR. WRITE FOR COMPLETE INFORMATION.

463

FRIENDS OF THE LIBRARY OF HAWAII (GRANTS PROGRAM)

99-1151 IWAENA ST.
AIEA HI 96701
808/487-7449

AMOUNT: $1000 - $2000

DEADLINE(S): JUN 15

FIELD(S): LIBRARY SCIENCE

OPEN TO HAWAII RESIDENTS. GRANTS SUPPORT GRADUATE STUDY IN LIBRARY SCIENCE AT THE UNIVERSITY OF HAWAII. USA CITIZEN.

5-10 AWARDS PER YEAR. WRITE FOR COMPLETE INFORMATION.

464

GEORGE MASON UNIVERSITY (MARY ROBERTS RINEHART FUND)

GEORGE MASON UNIV.;
4400 UNIVERSITY DR.
FAIRFAX VA 22030
703/323-2220

AMOUNT: APPROX $900

DEADLINE(S): NOV 30

FIELD(S): CREATIVE WRITING

GRANTS AWARDED TO UNPUBLISHED CREATIVE WRITERS WHO NEED FINANCIAL AID TO COMPLETE WORKS OF FICTION; POETRY; DRAMA; BIOGRAPHY; AUTOBIOGRAPHY OR HISTORY. ONLY WORKS WRITTEN IN ENGLISH WILL BE CONSIDERED BUT USA CITIZENSHIP NOT REQUIRED.

CANDIDATE MUST BE NOMINATED BY WRITING PROGRAM FACULTY MEMBER OR A SPONSORING WRITER; AGENT; OR EDITOR. WRITE TO ROGER LATHBURY AT ADDRESS ABOVE FOR COMPLETE INFORMATION.

465

GEORGE WASHINGTON UNIVERSITY (GEORGE MC CANDLISH FELLOWSHIP IN AMERICAN LITERATURE)

GRADUATE STUDIES - ENGLISH DEPT
WASHINGTON DC 20052
202/994-6180

AMOUNT: APPROX $6000

DEADLINE(S): FEB 15

FIELD(S): AMERICAN LITERATURE

GRADUATE FELLOWSHIP AT GEORGE WASHINGTON UNIVERSITY OPEN TO THE MOST PROMISING STUDENT ENROLLING IN A GRADUATE DEGREE PROGRAM (MA OR PH.D) IN AMERICAN LITERATURE. GRADE POINT AVERAGE OF 3.25 OR BETTER ON 4.0 SCALE.

FELLOWSHIP IS FOR ONE YEAR. CONTACT DIRECTOR OF GRADUATE STUDIES ADDRESS ABOVE FOR COMPLETE INFORMATION.

466

GEORGIA LIBRARY ASSOCIATION (HUBBARD SCHOLARSHIP FUND)

PO BOX 39
YOUNG HARRIS GA 30582
WRITTEN INQUIRY ONLY

AMOUNT: $3000

DEADLINE(S): MAY 1

FIELD(S): LIBRARY SCIENCE

OPEN TO GRADUATING SENIORS & GRADUATES OF ACCREDITED COLLEGES WHO HAVE BEEN ACCEPTED INTO AN ALA ACCREDITED DEGREE PROGRAM. MUST BE READY TO BEGIN STUDY IN FALL TERM OF AWARD YEAR AND INTEND TO COMPLETE DEGREE REQUIREMENTS WITHIN 2 YEARS.

RECIPIENTS AGREE TO WORK (FOLLOWING GRADUATION) FOR ONE YEAR IN A LIBRARY OR LIBRARY-RELATED CAPACITY IN GEORGIA -OR- TO PAY BACK A PRORATED AMOUNT OF THE AWARD WITHIN 2 YEARS (WITH INTEREST). WRITE FOR COMPLETE INFORMATION.

467

GERMANISTIC SOCIETY OF AMERICA (FOREIGN STUDY SCHOLARSHIPS)

809 UNITED NATIONS PLAZA
NEW YORK NY 10017
212/984-5330

AMOUNT: $8500

DEADLINE(S): OCT 31

FIELD(S): HISTORY; POLITICAL SCIENCE; INT'L RELATIONS; PUBLIC AFFAIRS; LANGUAGE; PHILOSOPHY; LITERATURE

APPLICANTS MUST BE US CITIZENS WITH A BACHELORS DEGREE. AWARDS ARE FOR GRADUATE STUDY AT A WEST GERMAN UNIVERSITY.

SELECTION IS BASED UPON PROPOSED PROJECT; LANGUAGE FLUENCY; ACADEMIC ACHIEVEMENT; & REFERENCES. WRITE FOR COMPLETE INFORMATION.

468

GETTY CENTER FOR THE HISTORY OF ART & THE HUMANITIES (PREDOCTORAL & POSTDOCTORAL FELLOWSHIPS)

DR H.H.HYMANS;
401 WILSHIRE BLVD; #400
SANTA MONICA CA 90401
310/458-9811

AMOUNT: $15000 PREDOCTORAL; $20000 POSTDOCTORAL

DEADLINE(S): DEC 1

FIELD(S): HUMANITIES; SOCIAL SCIENCES; ANTHROPOLOGY; ART/SCIENCE HISTORY; LITERATURE; PHILOSOPHY ETC.

OPEN TO PRE & POSTDOCTORAL SCHOLARS WHOSE AREAS OF RESEARCH COMPLEMENT THE CENTER'S PROGRAMS & RESOURCES. PREDOCTORAL CANDIDATES SHOULD EXPECT TO COMPLETE DISSERTATIONS DURING THE FELLOWSHIP YEAR.

POSTDOCTORALS SHOULD HAVE RECEIVED DOCTORATE IN HUMANITIES OR SOCIAL SCIENCES WITHIN LAST 3 YEARS & BE REWRITING DISSERTATIONS FOR PUBLICATION. WRITE FOR COMPLETE INFORMATION.

469

HARTFORD PUBLIC LIBRARY (HEWINS SCHOLARSHIP PROGRAM)

HARTFORD PUBLIC LIBRARY CHIEF LIBRARIAN - 500 MAIN ST
HARTFORD CT 06103
203/293-6076

AMOUNT: $4000

DEADLINE(S): MAR 1

FIELD(S): CHILDRENS LIBRARIANSHIP

OPEN TO STUDENTS WHO HAVE BEEN ACCEPTED TO OR ARE ENROLLED IN A GRADUATE LEVEL LIBRARY SCHOOL ACCREDITED BY THE AMERICAN LIBRARY ASSOCIATION & INTEND TO SPECIALIZE CHILDREN'S LIBRARIANSHIP. USA CITIZEN OR LEGAL RESIDENT.

PREFERENCE TO APPLICANTS PURSUING A CAREER IN PUBLIC LIBRARY SERVICE. WRITE FOR COMPLETE INFORMATION.

470

ILLINOIS ARTS COUNCIL (ARTISTS FELLOWSHIP AWARDS)

100 W. RANDOLPH; SUITE 10-500
CHICAGO IL 60601
312/814-6750

AMOUNT: $500 - $15000

DEADLINE(S): NOV 1

FIELD(S): CHOREOGRAPHY; VISUAL ARTS; LITERATURE; FILM; VIDEO; PLAYWRITING; MUSIC COMPOSITION; CRAFTS; ETHNIC & FOLK ARTS; PERFORMANCE ART; PHOTOGRAPHY

OPEN TO PROFESSIONAL ARTISTS WHO ARE ILLINOIS RESIDENTS. AWARDS ARE IN RECOGNITION OF WORK IN THE ABOVE AREAS; THEY ARE NOT FOR CONTINUING STUDY. STUDENTS ARE -NOT- ELIGIBLE.

WRITE TO ADDRESS ABOVE FOR APPLICATION FORM.

471

INTERNATIONAL SOCIETY FOR GENERAL SEMANTICS (GENERAL SEMANTICS RESEARCH SCHOLARSHIP)

PO BOX 2469
SAN FRANCISCO CA 94126
415/543-1747

AMOUNT: $3000

DEADLINE(S): APR 15

FIELD(S): GENERAL SEMANTICS

OPEN TO GRADUATE STUDENTS ENROLLED AT ACCREDITED INSTITUTIONS. AWARDS ARE TO SUPPORT RESEARCH ON HOW USE OF LANGUAGE INFLUENCES THOUGHT; BEHAVIOR; COMMUNICATION; ADVANCEMENT OF KNOWLEDGE & FOR OTHER INVESTIGATIONS IN GENERAL SEMANTICS.

WRITE FOR COMPLETE INFORMATION.

472

JOHN FITZGERALD KENNEDY LIBRARY FOUNDATION (HEMINGWAY RESEARCH GRANTS)

COLUMBIA POINT
BOSTON MA 02125
617/929-4524

AMOUNT: $200 TO $1000

DEADLINE(S): FEB 15

FIELD(S): LITERATURE

OPEN TO PH.D CANDIDATES FOR DISSERTATION RESEARCH IN THE ERNEST HEMINGWAY COLLECTION. PREFERENCE TO THOSE RESEARCHING RECENTLY OPENED OR RELATIVELY UNUSED PORTIONS OF THE COLLECTION.

LIBRARY HOUSES 90-95% OF THE HEMINGWAY MANUSCRIPTS. WRITE FOR COMPLETE INFORMATION.

473

LOUISIANA LIBRARY ASSOCIATION (SCHOLARSHIPS)

PO BOX 3058
BATON ROUGE LA 70821
504/342-4928

AMOUNT: $2500

DEADLINE(S): MAY 1

FIELD(S): LIBRARY SCIENCE

LOUISIANA RESIDENT. SCHOLARSHIP IS OPEN TO STUDENTS WHO ARE ACCEPTED FOR ENROLLMENT AT LOUISIANA STATE UNIVERSITY AND WORKING TOWARD A GRADUATE DEGREE IN LIBRARY SCIENCE.

WRITE FOR COMPLETE INFORMATION.

474

MARY MCEWEN SCHIMKE SCHOLARSHIP (SUPPORT SCHOLARSHIPS)

C/O WELLESLEY COLLEGE;
SECRETARY GRADUATE FELLOWSHIPS; CAREER
CENTER
WELLESLEY MA 02181
617/283-3525

AMOUNT: UP TO $1000 STIPEND

DEADLINE(S): DEC 1

FIELD(S): LITERATURE; AMERICAN HISTORY;
PREFERENCE GIVEN TO AMERICAN STUDIES

SUPPLEMENTAL AWARD FOR THE PURPOSE OF
AFFORDING RELIEF FROM HOUSEHOLD AND
CHILD CARE WHILE PURSUING GRADUATE
STUDY. AWARD IS BASED ON SCHOLARLY
EXPECTATION AND IDENTIFIED NEED.

CANDIDATE MUST BE OVER 30 AND CURRENTLY
ENGAGED IN GRADUATE STUDY IN
GRADUATE STUDY IN LITERATURE AND/OR
HISTORY WITH PREFERENCE GIVEN TO
AMERICAN STUDIES. WRITE FOR COMPLETE
INFORMATION.

475

MEDICAL LIBRARY ASSOCIATION (CONTINUING EDUCATION AWARD)

6 N. MICHIGAN AVE. SUITE 300
CHICAGO IL 60602
312/419-9094

AMOUNT: $100 - $500

DEADLINE(S): FEB 1; OCT 1

FIELD(S): MEDICAL LIBRARIANSHIP

FOR CONTINUING EDUCATION; NOT WORK
TOWARD A DEGREE OR CERTIFICATE.
APPLICANTS MUST HOLD GRAD DEGREE IN
LIBRARY SCIENCE; BE A PRACTICING
MEDICAL LIBRARIAN WITH AT LEAST TWO
YEARS EXPERIENCE & BE A REGULAR
MEMBER OF THE ASSOCIATION.

USA OR CANADIAN CITIZEN OR LEGAL RESIDENT.
WRITE FOR COMPLETE INFORMATION.

476

MEDICAL LIBRARY ASSOCIATION (MINORITY SCHOLARSHIP)

6 N MICHIGAN AVE. SUITE 300
CHICAGO IL 60602
312/419-9094

AMOUNT: $2000

DEADLINE(S): FEB 1

FIELD(S): MEDICAL LIBRARIANSHIP

GRADUATE SCHOLARSHIP FOR MINORITY
STUDENTS JUST ENTERING FIELD OF
MEDICAL LIBRARIANSHIP AT AN ALA
ACCREDITED SCHOOL; OR HAVE AT LEAST 1/
2 OF ACADEMIC REQUIRENTS TO COMPLETE
DURING THE YEAR FOLLOWING GRANTING
OF SCHOLARSHIP.

USA OR CANADIAN CITIZEN OR LEGAL RESIDENT.
WRITE FOR COMPLETE INFORMATION.

477

METROPOLITAN MUSEUM OF ART (ART HISTORY FELLOWSHIPS)

1000 FIFTH AVENUE
NEW YORK NY 10028
212/879-5500

AMOUNT: $15000 PRE-DOCTORAL; $25000 POST
DOCTORAL (PLUS $2500 TRAVEL STIPEND)

DEADLINE(S): NOV 13

FIELD(S): ART HISTORY/CLASSICAL STUDIES

GRADUATE SCHOLARSHIPS; FELLOWSHIPS; AND
POST-DOCTORAL FELLOWSHIPS FOR
PROMISING YOUNG SCHOLARS IN THE
FIELDS OF ART HISTORY AND THE CLASSICS.

WRITE FOR COMPLETE INFORMATION.

478

MILLAY COLONY FOR THE ARTS (RESIDENCIES)

STEEPLETOP; PO BOX 3
AUSTERLITZ NY 12017
518/392-3103

AMOUNT: RESIDENCY

DEADLINE(S): SEP 1; FEB 1; MAY 1

FIELD(S): CREATIVE WRITING; VISUAL ARTS;
MUSIC COMPOSITION; SCULPTURE; GRAPHIC
ARTS; POETRY

THE COLONY PROVIDES 60 RESIDENCIES PER
YEAR FOR PROFESSIONALS IN THE ABOVE
FIELDS. THERE IS NO APPLICATION FEE AND
NO FEE FOR COLONY RESIDENCY.

RESIDENCIES ARE FOR ONE MONTH AND
USUALLY COVER A PERIOD FROM THE FIRST
TO THE 28TH OF EACH MONTH. WRITE FOR
COMPLETE INFORMATION.

479

MINNESOTA STATE ARTS BOARD (GRANTS PROGRAM)

432 SUMMIT AVE
ST PAUL MN 55102
612/297-2603

AMOUNT: FELLOWSHIPS $6000; CAREER
OPPORTUNITY GRANTS $100 - $1000 OR
SPECIAL RESIDENCY STIPEND.

DEADLINE(S): SEP - VISUAL ARTS; OCT - MUSIC & DANCE; DEC - LITERATURE & THEATER

FIELD(S): LITERATURE; MUSIC; THEATER; DANCE; VISUAL ARTS

CAREER ADVANCEMENT GRANTS OPEN TO PROFESSIONAL ARTISTS WHO ARE RESIDENTS OF MINNESOTA. GRANTS ARE NOT INTENDED FOR SUPPORT OF TUITION OR WORK TOWARD ANY DEGREE.

CAREER OPPORTUNITY GRANTS AND FELLOWSHIPS ARE AVAILABLE. ARTISTS ALSO ARE ELIGIBLE FOR A SPECIAL RESIDENCE AT HEADLANDS CENTER FOR THE ARTS NEAR SAN FRANCISCO. WRITE FOR COMPLETE INFORMATION.

480

NATIONAL COUNCIL OF TEACHERS OF ENGLISH RESEARCH FOUNDATION (GRANTS-IN-AID)

PROJECT ASSISTANT; 1111 KENYON RD.
URBANA IL 61801
217/328-3870

AMOUNT: UP TO $12500

DEADLINE(S): FEB 15

FIELD(S): TEACHING ENGLISH

OPEN TO RESEARCHERS AND ADVANCED GRADUATE STUDENTS FOR RESEARCH PROJECTS DEALING WITH SOME PHASE OF THE TEACHING OF ENGLISH. APPLICANTS MUST BE NCTE MEMBERS.

WRITE FOR COMPLETE INFORMATION.

481

NATIONAL HUMANITIES CENTER (POST-DOCTORAL FELLOWSHIPS)

PO BOX 12256; 7 ALEXANDER DR
RESEARCH TRIANGLE PARK NC 27709
919/549-0661

AMOUNT: STIPEND + TRAVEL EXPENSES

DEADLINE(S): OCT 15

FIELD(S): HISTORY; LANGUAGES & LITERATURE; PHILOSOPHY; OTHER FIELDS IN THE LIBERAL ARTS

POST-DOCTORAL RESEARCH FELLOWSHIPS OPEN TO YOUNG & SENIOR SCHOLARS FROM ANY NATION. AWARDS SUPPORT RESEARCH & WRITING AT THE CENTER. SCHOLARS FROM OTHER AREAS SUCH AS NATURAL SCIENCES; ARTS; PROFESSIONS & PUBLIC LIFE ALSO MAY APPLY.

30-35 FELLOWSHIPS PER YEAR. WRITE FOR COMPLETE INFORMATION.

482

NATIONAL SPEAKERS ASSOCIATION (NSA SCHOLARSHIP)

1500 S. PRIEST DR
TEMPE AZ 85281
602/968-2552; FAX 602/968-0911

AMOUNT: $2000

DEADLINE(S): JUN 1

FIELD(S): ORAL COMMUNICATIONS

OPEN TO COLLEGE JUNIORS; SENIORS OR GRADUATE STUDENTS WHO ARE MAJORING OR MINORING IN SPEECH OR A DIRECTLY RELATED FIELD. MUST BE FULL TIME STUDENT IN AN ACCREDITED COLLEGE OR UNIVERSITY. NEED AT LEAST 3.0 GPA.

FOUR AWARDS PER YEAR TO WELL ROUNDED STUDENTS CAPABLE OF LEADERSHIP AND HAVING POTENTIAL TO MAKE AN IMPACT BY USING ORAL COMMUNICATIONS.

483

NATIONAL SPEAKERS ASSOCIATION (OUTSTANDING PROFESSOR AWARDS)

1500 S. PRIEST DR
TEMPE AZ 85281
602/968-2552; FAX 602/968-0911

AMOUNT: $1000

DEADLINE(S): JUN 1

FIELD(S): ORAL COMMUNICATIONS

OPEN TO FULL TIME FACULTY MEMBERS IN THE DEPARTMENT OF SPEECH COMMUNICATION OF ACCREDITED USA COLLEGES OR UNIVERSITIES. NOMINATIONS TO BE FORWARDED THROUGH NOMINEE'S DEPARTMENT HEAD AND INCLUDE 2 LETTERS OF RECOMMENDATION FROM STUDENTS.

TWO AWARDS PER YEAR. WRITE FOR COMPLETE INFORMATION.

484

NEW JERSEY STATE COUNCIL ON THE ARTS (FELLOWSHIP SUPPORT)

4 NORTH BROAD ST - CN 306
TRENTON NJ 08625
609/292-6130

AMOUNT: UP TO $12000

DEADLINE(S): VARIES (USUALLY JAN OR FEB)

FIELD(S): LITERATURE; CHOREOGRAPHY; COMPOSITION; VISUAL ARTS; PHOTOGRAPHY

NEW JERSEY RESIDENTS. FELLOWSHIP AWARDS ARE MADE TO PROFESSIONAL ARTISTS & GRADUATE STUDENTS TO ENABLE THEM TO COMPLETE EITHER NEW WORKS OR WORKS IN PROGRESS. UNDERGRADUATES ARE NOT ELIGIBLE.

FUNDS MAY -NOT- BE USED FOR TUITION OR DIRECT EXPENSES OF FORMAL EDUCATION. WRITE TO GRANTS COORDINATOR; ADDRESS ABOVE; FOR COMPLETE INFORMATION.

485 ─────────────────

NEW YORK FOUNDATION FOR THE ARTS (ARTIST'S FELLOWSHIPS & SERVICES)

155 AVE OF THE AMERICAS; 14TH FLOOR
NEW YORK NY 10013
212/366-6900; FAX 212/366-1778

AMOUNT: $7000

DEADLINE(S): SEP 30

FIELD(S): VISUAL ARTS; LITERATURE; ARCHITECTURE; MUSIC AND MEDIA

FELLOWSHIPS & SERVICES OPEN TO ORIGINATING ARTISTS OVER 18 WHO HAVE BEEN NY STATE RESIDENTS FOR 2 YEARS PREVIOUS TO APPLICATION DATE & ARE NOT ENROLLED IN A DEGREE AWARDING COURSE OF STUDY. AWARDS ARE TO ASSIST IN CREATION OF ONGOING WORK.

APPLICATIONS AVAILABLE IN SPRINT OF EACH YEAR. ABOUT 120 FELLOWSHIPS PER YEAR; MANY OTHER SERVICES ARE AVAILABLE. -NOT- FOR ACADEMIC STUDY. WRITE FOR COMPLETE INFORMATION.

486 ─────────────────

PARAMOUNT PICTURES (PARAMOUNT INTERNSHIPS IN FILM & TELEVISION)

5555 MELROSE AVE
HOLLYWOOD CA 90038
213/956-5145

AMOUNT: APPROX $25000

DEADLINE(S): FEB 1

FIELD(S): FILM & VIDEO; SCREENWRITING

POST-GRADUATE PRODUCING; DIRECTING AND FILM & TV WRITING INTERNSHIPS AT PARAMOUNT PICTURES. OPEN TO NEW GRADUATES OF THE GRADUATE FILM PROGRAMS AT NEW YORK UNIV; COLUMBIA UNIV; UCLA; USC & THE AMERICAN FILM INSTITUTE.

APPLICATION IS THROUGH THE SCHOOL. -DO NOT- APPLY DIRECTLY TO PARAMOUNT. RENEWABLE. WRITE FOR COMPLETE INFORMATION.

487 ─────────────────

PARAMOUNT PICTURES - EDDIE MURPHY PRODUCTIONS (WRITING FELLOWSHIP)

5555 MELROSE AVE
HOLLYWOOD CA 90038
WRITTEN INQUIRY

AMOUNT: APPROX $25000

DEADLINE(S): FEB 1

FIELD(S): SCREENWRITING

POST-GRADUATE FILM & TV WRITING INTERNSHIPS AT PARAMOUNT PICTURES. OPEN TO RECENT BACHELOR'S DEGREE GRADUATES OF HAMPTON UNIVERSITY & HOWARD UNIVERSITY.

RENEWABLE. WRITE FOR COMPLETE INFORMATION.

488 ─────────────────

PENNSYLVANIA LIBRARY ASSOCIATION (GRADUATE STUDY-LIBRARY SCIENCE SCHOLARSHIP)

1919 NORTH FRONT ST
HARRISBURG PA 17102
717/233-3113

AMOUNT: $2000

DEADLINE(S): APR 1

FIELD(S): LIBRARY SCIENCE

FOR RESIDENTS OF PENNSYLVANIA WHO ARE ENROLLED IN AN AMERICAN LIBRARY ASSOCIATION APPROVED PROGRAM OF GRADUATE STUDY IN AN INSTITUTION OF HIGHER LEARNING. FUNDS TO BE APPLIED TOWARD TUITION AND FEES. USA CITIZEN OR LEGAL RESIDENT.

WRITE FOR COMPLETE INFORMATION.

489 ─────────────────

PLAYWRIGHTS' CENTER (MCKNIGHT ADVANCEMENT GRANT)

2301 FRANKLIN AVENUE EAST
MINNEAPOLIS MN 55406
612/332-7481; FAX 612/332-6037

AMOUNT: $8500

DEADLINE(S): JAN 6

FIELD(S): PLAYWRITING

OPEN TO PLAYWRIGHTS WHOSE WORK DEMONSTRATES EXCEPTIONAL ARTISTIC MERIT & POTENTIAL & WHOSE PRIMARY RESIDENCE IS IN MINNESOTA. TWO WORKS BY APPLICANT MUST HAVE BEEN FULLY PRODUCED BY PROFESSIONAL THEATERS.

RECIPIENTS MUST DESIGNATE TWO MONTHS OF THE GRANT YEAR IN WHICH THEY WILL ACTIVELY PARTICIPATE IN CENTER PROGRAMS. APPLICATIONS AVAILABLE NOV 2. WRITE FOR COMPLETE INFORMATION.

490 ─────────────────

PLAYWRIGHTS' CENTER (MIDWEST PLAYLABS)

2301 FRANKLIN AVENUE EAST
MINNEAPOLIS MN 55406
612/332-7481; FAX 612/332-6037

AMOUNT: HONORARIA; TRAVEL EXPENSES; ROOM AND BOARD

DEADLINE(S): DEC 1

FIELD(S): PLAYWRITING

TWO WEEK WORKSHOP OPEN TO USA CITIZENS WHO ARE AUTHORS OF UNPRODUCED; UNPUBLISHED FULL LENGTH PLAYS (NO ONE-ACTS). EACH PLAY RECEIVES A PUBLIC READING FOLLOWED BY AUDIENCE DISCUSSION OF THE WORK.

FOUR TO SIX PLAYWRIGHTS CHOSEN BY OPEN SCRIPT COMPETITION. CONFERENCE IS INTENDED TO ALLOW PLAYWRIGHTS TO TAKE RISKS FREE OF ARTISTIC RESTRAINT. APPLICATIONS AVAILABLE BY OCT 1. SEND SASE FOR COMPLETE INFORMATION.

491

PLAYWRIGHTS' CENTER (PLAYWRIGHT-IN-RESIDENCE FELLOWSHIPS)

2301 FRANKLIN AVENUE EAST
MINNEAPOLIS MN 55406
612/332-7481; FAX 612/332-6037

AMOUNT: $5000

DEADLINE(S): MAR 1

FIELD(S): PLAYWRITING

OPEN TO EMERGING PLAWRIGHTS WHO ARE USA CITIZENS OR PERMANENT RESIDENTS WHO HAVE NOT HAD MORE THAN TWO PRODUCTIONS OF THEIR WORK FULLY STAGED BY PROFESSIONAL THEATERS. FELLOWS SPEND 12 MONTHS AS CORE MEMBERS OF THE PLAYWRIGHTS' CENTER.

FELLOWSHIPS ARE TO PROVIDE PLAYWRIGHTS WITH FUNDS AND SERVICES TO AID THEM IN THE DEVELOPMENT OF THEIR CRAFT. APPLICATIONS AVAILABLE AFTER NOV 15. SEND SASE FOR COMPLETE INFORMATION.

492

POETRY SOCIETY OF AMERICA (CASH AWARDS)

15 GRAMERCY PARK
NEW YORK NY 10003
212-254-9628

AMOUNT: $100

DEADLINE(S): DEC 31

FIELD(S): POETRY

THE POETRY SOCIETY'S EXTENSIVE ANNUAL AWARDS COMPETITION IS AIMED AT ADVANCING EXCELLENCE IN POETRY & ENCOURAGING SKILL IN TRADITIONAL FORMS AS WELL AS EXPERIMENTATION IN CONTEMPORARY FORMS. THESE ARE CASH AWARDS NOT SCHOLARSHIPS.

SEND STAMPED SELF ADDRESSED ENVELOPE FOR CONTEST RULES AND BROCHURE.

493

POETRY SOCIETY OF AMERICA (CONTESTS OPEN TO PSA MEMBERS)

15 GRAMERCY PARK
NEW YORK NY 10003
WRITTEN INQUIRY

AMOUNT: VARIES WITH AWARD

DEADLINE(S): OCT 1 - DEC 31

FIELD(S): POETRY

VARIOUS CONTESTS OPEN TO PSA MEMBERS. ONLY 1 SUBMISSION MAY BE SENT FOR EACH CONTEST. ALL SUBMISSIONS MUST BE UNPUBLISHED ON DATE OF ENTRY & NOT SCHEDULED FOR PUBLICATION BY THE DATE OF THE PSA AWARDS CEREMONY HELD IN THE SPRING.

SEND SELF ADDRESSED STAMPED ENVELOPE FOR CONTEST RULES BROCHURE.

494

ROTARY FOUNDATION OF ROTARY INTERNATIONAL (CULTURAL AMBASSADORIAL SCHOLARSHIPS)

1 ROTARY CENTER; 1560 SHERMAN AV
EVANSTON IL 60201
313/866-3000

AMOUNT: TUITION; FEES; LIVING EXPENSES; TRAVEL

DEADLINE(S): CONTACT LOCAL ROTARY CLUB

FIELD(S): LANGUAGES (ENGLISH; FRENCH; GERMAN; ITALIAN; JAPANESE; POLISH; PORTUGUESE; RUSSIAN; SPANISH; SWAHILI)

SCHOLARSHIPS OF 3 TO 6 MONTHS FOR STUDY ABROAD OF LANGUAGES IN WHICH APPLICANT MAY BE SOMEWHAT COMPETENT. STUDY LOCATIONS ARE ASSIGNED BY ROTARY. AT LEAST 1 YEAR OF TRAINING IN PREFERRED LANGUAGE REQUIRED.

APPLICATION DEADLINES ARE SET BY LOCAL CLUBS AND MAY BE AS EARLY AS MARCH OR AS LATE AS JUL 15. CONTACT -LOCAL-ROTARY CLUB FOR COMPLETE INFORMATION.

495

SAN FRANCISCO FOUNDATION (JAMES D PHELAN LITERARY AWARD)

685 MARKET ST; SUITE 910
SAN FRANCISCO CA 94105
415/495-3100 OR 510/436-3100

AMOUNT: $2000

DEADLINE(S): JAN 15

FIELD(S): LITERATURE

OPEN TO CALIFORNIA-BORN AUTHORS OF AN UNPUBLISHED WORK-IN-PROGRESS (FICTION; NON-FICTION OR POETRY) WHO ARE BETWEEN 20-35 YEARS OF AGE AND ARE USA CITIZENS.

WRITERS OF NON-FICTION ARE ALSO ELIGIBLE FOR THE $1000 JOSEPH HENRY JACKSON HONORABLE MENTION AWARD. WRITE FOR COMPLETE INFORMATION.

496

SAN FRANCISCO FOUNDATION (JOSEPH HENRY JACKSON LITERARY AWARD)

685 MARKET ST; SUITE 910
SAN FRANCISCO CA 94105
415/495-3100 OR 510/436-3100

AMOUNT: $2000

DEADLINE(S): JAN 15

FIELD(S): LITERATURE

OPEN TO N.CALIFORNIA OR NEVADA RESIDENTS (FOR 3 CONSECUTIVE YEARS IMMEDIATELY PRIOR TO CLOSING DATE OF THE COMPETITION) WHO ARE AUTHORS OF UNPUBLISHED WORK-IN-PROGRESS (FICTION; NON-FICTION OR POETRY) & BETWEEN 20-35 YEARS OF AGE.

WRITERS OF NON-FICTION ARE ALSO ELIGIBLE FOR THE $1000 JOSEPH HENRY JACKSON HONORABLE MENTION AWARD. WRITE FOR COMPLETE INFORMATION.

497

SPECIAL LIBRARIES ASSOCIATION (AFFIRMATIVE ACTION SCHOLARSHIP PROGRAM)

1700 EIGHTEENTH ST NW
WASHINGTON DC 20009
202-234-4700

AMOUNT: TO BE ANNOUNCED

DEADLINE(S): OCT 31

FIELD(S): LIBRARY SCIENCE

OPEN TO MINORITY STUDENTS WHO ARE ACCEPTED TO OR ENROLLED IN AN ACCREDITED MASTER'S OF LIBRARY SCIENCE PROGRAM. USA OR CANADIAN CITIZEN. MUST SUBMIT EVIDENCE OF FINANCIAL NEED.

EXTRA CONSIDERATION WILL BE GIVEN TO MEMBERS OF SPECIAL LIBRARIES ASSN AND TO PERSONS WHO HAVE WORKED IN AND FOR SPECIAL LIBRARIES. WRITE FOR COMPLETE INFORMATION.

498

SPECIAL LIBRARIES ASSOCIATION (SLA SCHOLARSHIP PROGRAM)

1700 EIGHTEENTH ST NW
WASHINGTON DC 20009
202-234-4700

AMOUNT: TO BE ANNOUNCED

DEADLINE(S): OCT 31

FIELD(S): LIBRARY SCIENCE

OPEN TO GRADUATE STUDENTS PURSUING THEIR MASTER'S OR PH.D IN LIBRARY SCIENCE AT ACCREDITED COLLEGES & UNIVERSITIES. USA OR CANADIAN CITIZEN. MUST SUBMIT EVIDENCE OF FINANCIAL NEED.

SPECIAL CONSIDERATION GIVEN TO APPLICANTS WITH AN INTEREST IN SPECIAL LIBRARIANSHIP. WRITE FOR COMPLETE INFORMATION.

499

ST. JOHNS COLLEGE (HARPER-WOOD STUDENTSHIP)

THE MASTER
CAMBRIDGE CB2 1TP ENGLAND
WRITTEN INQUIRIES ONLY

AMOUNT: UP TO 4125 POUNDS STERLING

DEADLINE(S): MAY 31

FIELD(S): CREATIVE WRITING IN ENGLISH POETRY AND LITERATURE

STUDENTSHIP IS TENABLE FOR ONE YEAR OF GRADUATE STUDY IN A COUNTRY OF THE STUDENT'S CHOICE SPONSORED BY ST JOHNS . MUST BE A GRADUATE OF ANY UNIVERSITY OF THE UNITED KINGDOM/THE COMMONWEALTH OR THE USA AND NOT MORE THAN 30 YEARS OLD.

WRITE FOR COMPLETE INFORMATION.

500

STANLEY DRAMA AWARD (PLAYWRITING AWARDS COMPETITION)

C/O WAGNER COLLEGE DRAMA DEPT; HOWARD AVE & CAMPUS RD
STATEN ISLAND NY 10301
718/390-3256

AMOUNT: $2000

DEADLINE(S): SEP 1

FIELD(S): PLAYWRITING COMPETITION

ANNUAL AWARD FOR THE BEST PLAY OR MUSICAL SUBMITTED TO THE COMPETITION. SCRIPT MUST NOT HAVE BEEN COMMERCIALLY PRODUCED OR PUBLISHED AND SHOULD BE RECOMMENDED BY A THEATRE PROFESSIONAL.

APPLICATION MUST BE SUBMITTED WITH SCRIPT. PREVIOUS WINNERS ARE NOT ELIGIBLE. WRITE FOR COMPLETE INFORMATION.

501

TENNESSEE ARTS COMMISSION (INDIVIDUAL ARTISTS' FELLOWSHIPS)

320 SIXTH AVE NORTH #100
NASHVILLE TN 37243
615/741-1701

AMOUNT: $2500 - $5000

DEADLINE(S): JAN 11

FIELD(S): VISUAL ARTS; PERFORMING ARTS; CREATIVE ARTS

GRANTS OPEN TO ARTISTS WHO ARE RESIDENTS OF THE STATE OF TENNESSEE. DURATION OF AWARD IS ONE YEAR. APPLICANTS MUST BE PROFESSIONAL ARTISTS. FULL TIME STUDENTS ARE -NOT- ELIGIBLE.

WRITE FOR COMPLETE INFORMATION.

502

TEXAS LIBRARY ASSOCIATION (GRADUATE SCHOLARSHIPS)

3355 BEE CAVE RD #401
AUSTIN TX 78746
512/328-1518

AMOUNT: $500 - $2000

DEADLINE(S): FEB 15

FIELD(S): LIBRARY SCIENCE

TEXAS RESIDENT. AWARDS ARE FOR GRADUATE STUDY AT AN ALA ACCREDITED SCHOOL IN TEXAS LEADING TO A MASTER OF LIBRARY SCIENCE DEGREE. USA CITIZEN.

5 AWARDS PER YEAR. WRITE TO THE CHAIRPERSON OF THE TLA SCHOLARSHIP & RESEARCH COMMITTEE FOR COMPLETE INFORMATION.

503

U.S. DEPT. OF EDUCATION (FELLOWSHIPS & TRAINEESHIPS IN LIBRARY SCIENCE)

DISCRETIONARY LIBRARY PROGRAMS DIVISION; LP/OERI;
555 NEW JERSEY AVE NW
WASHINGTON DC 20208
202/219-1315

AMOUNT: VARIES

DEADLINE(S): VARIES

FIELD(S): LIBRARY SCIENCE

FUNDS ARE AWARDED ANNUALLY TO COLLEGES; UNIVERSITIES & LIBRARY AGENCIES TO FINANCE GRADUATE FELLOWSHIPS & TRAINEESHIPS IN LIBRARY & INFORMATION SCIENCES. APPLICATION MUST BE BE MADE TO THESE INSTITUTIONS. USA CITIZEN OR LEGAL RESIDENT.

WRITE THE ADDRESS ABOVE FOR A LIST OF THESE INSTITUTIONS.

504

UNIVERSITY OF VIRGINIA (HOYNS FELLOWSHIP)

107 WILSON HALL; DEPT OF ENGLISH
CHARLOTTESVILLE VA 22903
804/924-6675

AMOUNT: TUITION COSTS + STIPEND

DEADLINE(S): FEB 15

FIELD(S): CREATIVE WRITING

OPEN TO ANYONE WHO IS ACCEPTED INTO THE MASTERS OF FINE ARTS IN CREATIVE WRITING PROGRAM AT THE UNIVERSITY OF VIRGINIA. AN ORIGINAL 30-40 PAGE FICTION MANUSCRIPT OR 10 PAGES OF POETRY WILL BE REQUIRED.

3 FICTION AND 3 POETRY FELLOWSHIPS ARE AWARDED EACH YEAR. WRITE TO PROGRAM ADMINISTRATOR SYDNEY BLAIR FOR COMPLETE INFORMATION.

505

WAVERLY COMMUNITY HOUSE INC (F. LAMMONT BELIN ARTS SCHOLARSHIPS)

SCHOLARSHIPS SELECTION COMMITTEE
WAVERLY PA 18471
717/586-8191

AMOUNT: $9000

DEADLINE(S): DEC 15

FIELD(S): PAINTING; SCULPTURE; MUSIC; DRAMA; DANCE; LITERATURE; ARCHITECTURE; PHOTOGRAPHY

APPLICANTS MUST RESIDE IN THE ABINGTONS OR POCONO REGIONS OF NORTHEASTERN PENNSYLVANIA. THEY MUST FURNISH PROOF OF EXCEPTIONAL ABILITY IN THEIR CHOSEN FIELD BUT NEED NO FORMAL TRAINING IN ANY ACADEMIC OR PROFESSIONAL PROGRAM.

USA CITIZENSHIP REQUIRED. FINALISTS MUST APPEAR IN PERSON BEFORE THE SELECTION COMMITTEE. WRITE FOR COMPLETE INFORMATION.

506 —————————————

WISCONSIN LIBRARY ASSOCIATION (WLA LIBRARY CAREERS COMMITTEE)

4785 HAYES ROAD
MADISON WI 53704
608/242-2040

AMOUNT: VARIES

DEADLINE(S): JUN 15

FIELD(S): LIBRARY SCIENCE

WISCONSIN RESIDENT ADMITTED TO ACCREDITED GRADUATE LIBRARY SCHOOL IN WISCONSIN. US CITIZEN OR LEGAL RESIDENT.

WRITE FOR COMPLETE INFORMATION.

FOREIGN LANGUAGE

507 —————————————

AMERICAN COUNCIL OF LEARNED SOCIETIES (ACLS FELLOWSHIPS)

OFFICE OF FELLOWSHIPS & GRANTS;
228 E. 45TH ST.
NEW YORK NY 10017
WRITTEN INQUIRY

AMOUNT: UP TO $20000

DEADLINE(S): SEP 30

FIELD(S): HUMANITIES; SOCIAL SCIENCES; OTHER AREAS HAVING PREDOMINATELY HUMANISTIC EMPHASIS

OPEN TO USA CITIZENS OR LEGAL RESIDENTS WHO HOLD THE PH.D OR ITS EQUIVALENT. FELLOWSHIPS ARE DESIGNED TO HELP SCHOLARS DEVOTE 2 TO 12 CONTINUOUS MONTHS TO FULL TIME RESEARCH.

WRITE FOR COMPLETE INFORMATION.

508 —————————————

AMERICAN COUNCIL OF LEARNED SOCIETIES (EAST EUROPEAN LANGUAGE TRAINING GRANTS)

OFFICE OF FELLOWSHIPS & GRANTS;
228 E. 45TH ST.
NEW YORK NY 10017
WRITTEN INQUIRY

AMOUNT: $2000 - $2500

DEADLINE(S): MAR 1

FIELD(S): EAST EUROPEAN LANGUAGES

GRANTS OF $2000 EACH OFFERED FOR THE FIRST OR SECOND YEAR STUDY OF ANY EAST EUROPEAN LANGUAGE (EXCEPT RUSSIAN) IN THE USA. $2500 GRANTS OFFERED FOR INTERMEDIATE OR ADVANCED TRAINING IN THESE LANGUAGES IN EASTERN EUROPE.

USA CITIZEN OR LEGAL RESIDENT. FOR ADVANCED UNDERGRAD; GRAD OR POSTGRTAD STUDY. WRITE FOR COMPLETE INFORMATION.

509 —————————————

AMERICAN INSTITUTE OF INDIAN STUDIES (AIIS 9-MONTH LANGUAGE PROGRAM)

C/O UNIV OF CHICAGO; FOSTER HALL; 1130 E. 59TH ST.
CHICAGO IL 60637
312/702-8638

AMOUNT: $3000 PLUS TRAVEL

DEADLINE(S): JAN 31

FIELD(S): LANGUAGES OF INDIA

FELLOWSHIPS HELD IN INDIA OPEN TO GRADUATE STUDENTS WHO HAVE A MINIMUM OF 2 YEARS OR 240 HOURS OF CLASSROOM INSTRUCTION IN A LANGUAGE OF INDIA. USA CITIZEN.

10 FELLOWSHIPS PER YEAR. WRITE FOR COMPLETE INFORMATION.

510 —————————————

CENTER FOR ARABIC STUDY ABROAD (CASA FELLOWSHIPS)

C/O JOHNS-HOPKINS UNIV;
1619 MASSACHUSETTS AVE NW
WASHINGTON DC 20036
202/663-5750

AMOUNT: TUITION & ALLOWANCE + AIRFARE

DEADLINE(S): JAN 1

FIELD(S): ARABIC LANGUAGE

FELLOWSHIPS FOR SUMMER & FULL YEAR INTENSIVE ARABIC TRAINING AT THE AMERICAN UNIVERSITY IN CAIRO EGYPT OPEN TO USA GRADUATE STUDENTS AND A LIMITED NUMBER OF UNDERGRADS. MINIMUM OF 2 YRS OF ARABIC STUDY AND USA CITIZENSHIP REQUIRED.

25-30 FELLOWSHIPS PER YEAR. WRITE FOR COMPLETE INFORMATION.

511 —————————————

CENTER FOR HELLENIC STUDIES (RESIDENT JUNIOR FELLOWSHIPS)

3100 WHITEHAVEN STREET NW
WASHINGTON DC 20008
202/234-3738

AMOUNT: $18000

DEADLINE(S): NOV 1

FIELD(S): ANCIENT GREEK LITERATURE; HISTORY; PHILOSOPHY; LANGUAGE OR RELIGION

RESIDENT FELLOWSHIPS FOR POST-DOCTORAL SCHOLARS WITH -PROFESSIONAL COMPETENCE AND SOME PUBLICATION IN ANCIENT GREEK AREAS SHOWN ABOVE.

8 RESIDENT FELLOWSHIPS PER YEAR. WRITE FOR COMPLETE INFORMATION.

512

GERMANISTIC SOCIETY OF AMERICA (FOREIGN STUDY SCHOLARSHIPS)

809 UNITED NATIONS PLAZA
NEW YORK NY 10017
212/984-5330

AMOUNT: $8500

DEADLINE(S): OCT 31

FIELD(S): HISTORY; POLITICAL SCIENCE; INT'L RELATION; PUBLIC AFFAIRS; LANGUAGE; PHILOSOPHY; LITERATURE

APPLICANTS MUST BE US CITIZENS WITH A BACHELORS DEGREE. AWARDS ARE FOR GRADUATE STUDY AT A WEST GERMAN UNIVERSITY.

SELECTION IS BASED UPON PROPOSED PROJECT; LANGUAGE FLUENCY; ACADEMIC ACHIEVEMENT; & REFERENCES. WRITE FOR COMPLETE INFORMATION.

513

NATIONAL HUMANITIES CENTER (POST-DOCTORAL FELLOWSHIPS)

P.O. BOX 12256; 7 ALEXANDER DR
RESEARCH TRIANGLE PARK NC 27709
919/549-0661

AMOUNT: STIPEND + TRAVEL EXPENSES

DEADLINE(S): OCT 15

FIELD(S): HISTORY; LANGUAGES & LITERATURE; PHILOSOPHY; OTHER FIELDS IN THE LIBERAL ARTS

POST-DOCTORAL RESEARCH FELLOWSHIPS OPEN TO YOUNG & SENIOR SCHOLARS FROM ANY NATION. AWARDS SUPPORT RESEARCH & WRITING AT THE CENTER. SCHOLARS FROM OTHER AREAS SUCH AS NATURAL SCIENCES; ARTS; PROFESSIONS & PUBLIC LIFE ALSO MAY APPLY.

30-35 FELLOWSHIPS PER YEAR. WRITE FOR COMPLETE INFORMATION.

514

NORWICH JUBILEE ESPERANTO FOUNDATION (TRAVEL GRANTS)

37 GRANVILLE COURT
OXFORD OX OHS ENGLAND
0865-245509

AMOUNT: UP TO 1000 POUNDS STERLING

DEADLINE(S): NONE

FIELD(S): ESPERANTO-THE INTERNATIONAL LANGUAGE

TRAVEL GRANTS OPEN TO THOSE WHO SPEAK ESPERANTO AND WISH TO IMPROVE THEIR USE OF THE LANGUAGE THROUGH TRAVEL IN THE UNITED KINGDOM. CANDIDATES - MUST- BE UNDER AGE 26 AND ABLE TO LECTURE IN ESPERANTO.

INQUIRIES WITHOUT INDICATION OF FLUENCY AND INTEREST IN ESPERANTO WILL -NOT- BE ACKNOWLEDGED. UP TO 25 AWARDS PER YEAR. RENEWABLE. WRITE FOR COMPLETE INFORMATION.

515

PHI BETA KAPPA (MARY ISABEL SIBLEY FELLOWSHIP)

1811 'Q' STREET NW
WASHINGTON DC 20009
202/265-3808

AMOUNT: 10000

DEADLINE(S): JAN 15

FIELD(S): FRENCH STUDIES; GREEK STUDIES (LANGUAGE; LITERATURE; HISTORY OR ARCHAEOLOGY)

PH.D DISSERTATION OR POST-DOCTORAL RESEARCH FELLOWSHIPS FOR UNMARRIED WOMEN AGED 25-35 WHO HAVE DEMONSTRATED THEIR ABILITY TO CARRY ON ORIGINAL RESEARCH. APPLICANTS MUST PLAN TO DEVOTE FULL TIME TO RESEARCH DURING THE FELLOWSHIP YEAR.

FRENCH STUDIES IN EVEN NUMBERED YEARS; GREEK STUDIES IN ODD NUMBERED YEARS. ELIGIBILITY -NOT- RESTRICTED TO PHI BETA KAPPA MEMBERS. WRITE FOR COMPLETE INFORMATION.

516

PHI SIGMA IOTA-OFFICE OF THE PRESIDENT (SCHOLARSHIP PROGRAM)

UNIV OF NEVADA LAS VEGAS;
FOREIGN LANGUAGE DEPT.
LAS VEGAS NV 89154
702/739-3431; FAX 702/739-3850

AMOUNT: $500

DEADLINE(S): MAR 1

FIELD(S): FOREIGN LANGUAGES; LITERATURES; CULTURE

OPEN -ONLY- TO ACTIVE MEMBERS OF PHI SIGMA IOTA (FOREIGN LANGUAGES HONOR SOCIETY) WHO MEET STANDARDS OF EXCELLENCE IN SCHOLARSHIP IN ANY OF THE FOREIGN LANGUAGES. MAINTAIN 'B' OR BETTER GRADE AVERAGE.

WRITE FOR COMPLETE INFORMATION.

517

ROTARY FOUNDATION OF ROTARY INTERNATIONAL (CULTURAL AMBASSADORIAL SCHOLARSHIPS)

1 ROTARY CENTER; 1560 SHERMAN AV
EVANSTON IL 60201
313/866-3000

AMOUNT: TUITION; FEES; LIVING EXPENSES; TRAVEL

DEADLINE(S): CONTACT LOCAL ROTARY CLUB

FIELD(S): LANGUAGES (ENGLISH; FRENCH; GERMAN; ITALIAN; JAPANESE; POLISH; PORTUGUESE; RUSSIAN; SPANISH; SWAHILI)

SCHOLARSHIPS OF 3 TO 6 MONTHS FOR STUDY ABROAD OF LANGUAGES IN WHICH APPLICANT MAY BE SOMEWHAT COMPETENT. STUDY LOCATIONS ARE ASSIGNED BY ROTARY. AT LEAST 1 YEAR OF TRAINING IN PREFERRED LANGUAGE REQUIRED.

APPLICATION DEADLINES ARE SET BY LOCAL CLUBS AND MAY BE AS EARLY AS MARCH OR AS LATE AS JUL 15. CONTACT -LOCAL- ROTARY CLUB FOR COMPLETE INFORMATION.

518

U.S. DEPT. OF EDUCATION (FLAS FELLOWSHIPS)

CENTER FOR INTERNATIONAL EDUCTION; ATRB
WASHINGTON DC 20202
202/708-7283

AMOUNT: TUITION & FEES + $8000 STIPEND

DEADLINE(S): VARIES

FIELD(S): FOREIGN LANGUAGE & AREA OR INTERNATIONAL STUDIES

FELLOWSHIPS FOR GRADUATE STUDENTS AT ACCREDITED INSTITUTIONS IN USA WHO ARE PREPARING FOR CAREER AS SPECIALIST IN UNCOMMON FOREIGN LANGUAGE & AREA OR INTERNATIONAL STUDIES. USA CITIZEN OR LEGAL RESIDENT.

APPROX 1000 FELLOWSHIPS PER YEAR. RENEWABLE. CONTACT YOUR INSTITUTION'S FINANCIAL AID OFFICE FOR COMPLETE INFORMATION.

PERFORMING ARTS

519

ACADEMY OF VOCAL ARTS (SCHOLARSHIPS)

1920 SPRUCE ST.
PHILADELPHIA PA 19103
215/735-1685

AMOUNT: FULL TUITION

DEADLINE(S): 2 WEEKS PRIOR TO AUDITIONS IN SPRING

FIELD(S): VOCAL MUSIC; OPERATIC ACTING

TENABLE ONLY AT THE ACADEMY OF VOCAL ARTS. OPEN TO UNUSUALLY GIFTED SINGERS WITH 2 YRS COLLEGE VOCAL TRAINING OR EQUIVALENT. COLLEGE DEGREE RECOMMENDED. FULL TUITION SCHOLARSHIPS & COMPLETE TRAINING IN VOICE; OPERATIC ACTING; & REPERTOIRE.

WINNERS SELECTED IN SPRING COMPETITIVE AUDITIONS. TOTAL STUDENT ENROLMENT LIMITED TO 30. WRITE FOR COMPLETE INFORMATION.

520

ALASKA STATE COUNCIL ON THE ARTS (INDIVIDUAL ARTIST FELLOWSHIPS & GRANTS)

411 W. 4TH AVE. SUITE 1E
ANCHORAGE AK 99501
907/279-1558

AMOUNT: $5000

DEADLINE(S): OCT 1

FIELD(S): VISUAL ARTS; CRAFTS; PHOTOGRAPHY - ODD NUMBERED YEARS. MUSIC COMPOSITION; CHOREOGRAPHY; MEDIA ARTS; LITERATURE - EVEN NUMBERED YEARS.

OPEN TO ALASKA RESIDENTS WHO ARE ENGAGED IN THE CREATION OF NEW WORKS. FULL TIME STUDENTS ARE -NOT- ELIGIBLE.

WRITE FOR COMPLETE INFORMATION.

521

AMERICAN ACADEMY IN ROME (ROME PRIZE FELLOWSHIPS)

41 EAST 65TH STREET
NEW YORK NY 10021
212/535-4250

AMOUNT: $8300 (INCLUDES ROUND TRIP TRAVEL TO ROME AND EUROPEAN TRAVEL ALLOWANCE)

DEADLINE(S): NOV 15

FIELD(S): ARCHITECTURE; LANDSCAPE ARCHITECTURE; MUSICAL COMPOSITION; CLASSICS; ART HISTORY; PAINTING; SCULPTURE AND THE VISUAL ARTS; POST CLASSICAL HUMANISTIC STUDIES.

THE ACADEMY INVITES ARTISTS AND SCHOLARS WHO ARE USA CITIZENS TO APPLY FOR A LIMITED NUMBER OF ROME PRIZE FELLOWSHIPS IN THE ARTS AND HUMANITIES.

16 ROME PRIZE FELLOWSHIPS ANNUALLY. WRITE FOR COMPLETE INFORMATION.

522

AMERICAN ACCORDION MUSICOLOGICAL SOCIETY (CONTEST)

334 SOUTH BROADWAY
PITMAN NJ 08071
609/854-6628

AMOUNT: $100 - $250

DEADLINE(S): SEP 10

FIELD(S): MUSIC COMPOSITION

ANNUAL COMPETITION OPEN TO AMATEUR OR PROFESSIONAL MUSIC COMPOSERS WHO WRITE A SERIOUS PIECE MUSIC (OF SIX MINUTES OR MORE) FOR THE ACCORDION.

WRITE FOR COMPLETE INFORMATION.

523

ARTS INTERNATIONAL; INSTITUTE OF INTERNATIONAL EDUCATION (CINTAS FELLOWSHIP PROGRAM)

809 UNITED NATIONS PLAZA
NEW YORK NY 10017
212/984-5370

AMOUNT: $10000

DEADLINE(S): MAR 1

FIELD(S): ARCHITECTURE; PAINTING; PHOTOGRAPHY; SCULPTURE; PRINTMAKING; MUSIC COMPOSITION; CREATIVE WRITING

FELLOWSHIPS OPEN TO ARTISTS WHO ARE OF CUBAN ANCESTRY OR CUBAN CITIZENS LIVING OUTSIDE OF CUBA. THEY ARE INTENDED TO FOSTER & ENCOURAGE THE PROFESSIONAL DEVELOPMENT & RECOGNITION OF TALENTED CREATIVE ARTISTS IN THE ABOVE AREAS.

FELLOWSHIPS ARE NOT AWARDED FOR FURTHERANCE OF ACADEMIC STUDY. 5-10 AWARDS PER YEAR. WRITE FOR COMPLETE INFORMATION.

524

ASCAP FOUNDATION (THE) - (MUSIC COMPOSITION AWARDS PROGRAM)

ASCAP BUILDING; 1 LINCOLN PLAZA
NEW YORK NY 10023
212/621-6219

AMOUNT: $250 - $1500

DEADLINE(S): MAR 15

FIELD(S): MUSIC COMPOSITION COMPETITION

COMPETITION IS OPEN TO YOUNG COMPOSERS WHO ARE UNDER 30 YEARS OF AGE AS OF MARCH 15 OF THE YEAR OF APPLICATION. WINNING COMPOSITIONS SELECTED BY PANEL OF JUDGES.

AWARDS HELP YOUNG COMPOSERS CONTINUE THEIR STUDIES AND DEVELOP THEIR SKILLS. 15 AWARDS PER YEAR. WRITE FOR COMPLETE INFORMATION.

525

ASIAN CULTURAL COUNCIL (RESEARCH FELLOWSHIPS FOR USA CITIZENS TO STUDY IN ASIA; ASIANS TO STUDY IN USA)

1290 AVE OF THE AMERICAS
NEW YORK NY 10104
212/373-4300

AMOUNT: VARIES

DEADLINE(S): FEB 1; AUG 1

FIELD(S): VISUAL ARTS; PERFORMING ARTS

DOCTORAL & POST-DOCTORAL FELLOWSHIPS OPEN TO USA CITIZENS WHO WISH TO DO RESEARCH IN ASIA ON ASIAN VISUAL OR PERFORMING ARTS. FUNDS ALSO AVAILABLE FOR STUDENTS FROM ASIA FOR STUDY AND RESEARCH IN USA.

WRITE FOR COMPLETE INFORMATION.

526

BALTIMORE OPERA COMPANY (VOCAL COMPETITION FOR AMERICAN OPERAIC ARTISTS)

101 W. READ ST. SUITE 605
BALTIMORE MD 21201
301/727-0592

AMOUNT: $1000 - $12000

DEADLINE(S): MAY 15

FIELD(S): SINGING

ANNUAL CONTEST FOR OPERAIC SINGERS BETWEEN 20 AND 35 YEARS OF AGE WHO ARE USA CITIZENS AND CAN PRESENT 2 LETTERS OF RECOMMENDATION FROM RECOGNIZED MUSICAL AUTHORITIES.

EIGHT AWARDS ANNUALLY; RENEWABLE BY COMPETITION. THERE IS A $35 APPLICATION FEE. WRITE FOR COMPLETE INFORMATION.

527

BROADCAST MUSIC INC (BMI AWARDS TO STUDENT COMPOSERS)

320 W 57TH ST
NEW YORK NY 10019
212/586-2000

AMOUNT: $500 - $2500

DEADLINE(S): FEB 8

FIELD(S): MUSIC COMPOSITION AWARDS

CITIZENS OR PERMANENT RESIDENTS OF WESTERN HEMISPHERE; ENROLLED IN ACCREDITED SECONDARY SCHOOLS; COLLEGES OR CONSERVATORIES OF MUSIC; OR ENGAGED IN PRIVATE STUDY OF MUSIC WITH A RECOGNIZED ESTABLISHED TEACHER. MUST BE UNDER 26.

15 AWARDS PER YEAR. WRITE FOR COMPLETE INFORMATION.

528

BRYAN INTERNATIONAL STRING COMPETITION (MUSIC PERFORMANCE AWARDS)

NORTH CAROLINA SYMPHONY;
PO BOX 28026
RALEIGH NC 27611
919/733-2750

AMOUNT: $12000 1ST PRIZE; $6000 2ND PRIZE; $3000 3RD PRIZE

DEADLINE(S): JAN 2 -1996- AND EVERY FOR YEARS THEREAFTER

FIELD(S): MUSIC PERFORMANCE COMPETITION (VIOLIN; VIOLA; CELLO)

AUDITIONS FOR COMPETITION OPEN TO VIOLINISTS; VIOLISTS; CELLISTS BETWEEN THE AGES OF 18 AND 30. COMPETITION IS OPEN TO ALL NATIONALITIES AND IS HELD EVERY FOUR YEARS. -NEXT COMPETITION- WILL BE IN -1996-.

WRITE FOR COMPLETE INFORMATION.

529

BUSH FOUNDATION (BUSH ARTIST FELLOWSHIPS)

E900 FIRST NATIONAL BANK BLDG;
322 MINNESOTA ST.
ST PAUL MN 55101
612/227-5222

AMOUNT: UP TO $26000 STIPEND + $7000 EXPENSES

DEADLINE(S): LATE OCT; EARLY NOV

FIELD(S): LITERATURE; MUSIC COMPOSITION; CHOREOGRAPHY; VISUAL ARTS; SCRIPTWORKS

OPEN TO WRITERS; VISUAL ARTISTS; COMPOSERS & CHOREOGRAPHERS WHO ARE RESIDENTS OF MN.; N.D.; S.D. OR WESTERN WI. & AT LEAST 25 YRS OLD. AWARDS ARE TO HELP ARTISTS WORK FULL-TIME IN THEIR CHOSEN FIELD; NOT FOR ACADEMIC STUDY.

15 FELLOWSHIPS PER YEAR; 6-18 MONTHS IN DURATION. WRITE FOR COMPLETE INFORMATION.

530

COLUMBIA UNIVERSITY (JOSEPH H. BEARNS PRIZE IN MUSIC)

DEPT OF MUSIC; 703 DODGE HALL
NEW YORK NY 10027
212-854-3825

AMOUNT: $3000; $2000

DEADLINE(S): FEB 1 (OF ODD-NUMBERED YEARS)

FIELD(S): MUSIC COMPOSITION

COMPETITION OPEN TO YOUNG COMPOSERS AGED 18-25. THERE ARE TWO CATEGORIES FOR MUSIC COMPOSITION. ONE AWARD OF $3000 FOR LARGER FORMS & ONE AWARD OF $2000 FOR SMALLER FORMS. NO MORE THAN ONE ENTRY SHOULD BE SENT. USA CITIZEN.

WRITE TO ATTN OF BEARNS PRIZE COMMITTEE AT ADDRESS ABOVE FOR COMPLETE DETAILS.

531

CURTIS INSTITUTE OF MUSIC (TUITION SCHOLARSHIPS)

ADMISSIONS OFFICE; 1726 LOCUST ST.
PHILADELPHIA PA 19103
215/893-5252

AMOUNT: FULL TUITION

DEADLINE(S): JAN 15

FIELD(S): MUSIC; VOICE; OPERA; ACCOMPANYING

FULL-TUITION SCHOLARSHIPS OPEN TO STUDENTS IN THE ABOVE AREAS WHO ARE ACCEPTED FOR FULL-TIME STUDY AT THE CURTIS INSTITUTE OF MUSIC. (OPERA AND ACCOMPANYING ARE FOR MASTER OF MUSIC CANDIDATES ONLY.)

APPROX 50 AWARDS PER YEAR. SCHOLARSHIPS ARE RENEWABLE. WRITE FOR COMPLETE INFORMATION.

532

DELTA OMICRON INTERNATIONAL MUSIC FRATERNITY (COMPOSITION COMPETITION-TRIENNIAL)

12297 W. TENNESSEE PL.
LAKEWOOD CO 80228
606/266-1215

AMOUNT: $500 AND PREMIERE

DEADLINE(S): MAR 30 EVERY SECOND YEAR AFTER TRIENNIUM

FIELD(S): MUSIC COMPOSITION

CONTEST OPEN TO MUSIC COMPOSERS OF COLLEGE AGE OR ABOVE FOR A WORK OF 10 TO 15 MINUTES IN DURATION IN THE CATEGORY SELECTED FOR THE PARTICULAR COMPETITION. (FOR 1993 - AN INSTRUMENTAL TRIO.)

CONTACT JUDITH EIDSON AT ADDRESS ABOVE FOR COMPLETE INFORMATION.

533

DISTRICT OF COLUMBIA COMMISSION ON THE ARTS & HUMANITIES (GRANTS)

410 EIGHTH ST. NW - 5TH FLOOR
WASHINGTON DC 20004
202/724-5613; TDD 202/727-318; FAX 202/727-4135

AMOUNT: $5000

DEADLINE(S): FEB 15

FIELD(S): ARTS; PERFORMING ARTS; LITERATURE

APPLICANTS FOR GRANTS MUST BE PROFESSIONAL ARTISTS AND RESIDENTS OF WASHINGTON D.C. FOR AT LEAST ONE YEAR PRIOR TO SUBMITTING APPLICATION. AWARDS INTENDED TO GENERATE ARTS ENDEAVORS WITHIN THE WASHINGTON D.C. COMMUNITY.

OPEN ALSO TO ARTS ORGANIZATIONS THAT TRAIN; EXHIBIT OR PERFORM WITHIN D.C. 150 GRANTS PER YEAR. WRITE FOR COMPLETE INFORMATION.

534

ETUDE MUSIC CLUB OF SANTA ROSA (MUSIC COMPETITION FOR VOCALISTS)

PO BOX 823
SANTA ROSA CA 95402
707/538-5325

AMOUNT: $600 FIRST (5); $300 SECOND (5)

DEADLINE(S): DEC 25

FIELD(S): CLASSICAL VOCALISTS

COMPETITION IS OPEN TO VOCALISTS BETWEEN THE AGES OF 16 & 20 WHO ARE RESIDENTS OF SONOMA; NAPA OR MENDOCINO COUNTIES & ARE STUDYING MUSIC WITH A PRIVATE TEACHER OF MUSIC OR ARE RECOMMENDED BY THEIR SCHOOL'S MUSIC DEPARTMENT.

WRITE FOR COMPLETE INFORMATION.

535

FARGO-MOORHEAD SYMPHONY ORCHESTRAL ASSOCIATION (SIGWALD THOMPSON COMPOSITION AWARD COMPETITION)

PO BOX 1753
FARGO ND 58107
218/233-8397

AMOUNT: $2500

DEADLINE(S): SEP 30 (EVEN NUMBERED YEARS)

FIELD(S): MUSIC COMPOSITION

THIS AWARD WAS ESTABLISHED TO BIENNIALLY SELECT AMERICAN COMPOSERS FOR THE COMMISSIONING OF A WORK TO BE PREMIERED BY THE FARGO-MOORHEAD SYMPHONY ORCHESTRA DURING ITS CONCERT SEASON. USA CITIZEN.

PROGRAM IS UNDER REVIEW. PROGRAM'S FUTURE DIRECTION WILL BE ANNOUNCED AT END OF 1992-93 SEASON.

536

FLORIDA ARTS COUNCIL (INDIVIDUAL ARTISTS FELLOWSHIPS)

FLA DEPT OF STATE; DIV OF CULTURAL AFFAIRS; STATE CAPITOL
TALLAHASSEE FL 32399
904/487-2980

AMOUNT: UP TO $5000

DEADLINE(S): FEB 15 (APR 15 FOR VISUAL ARTS)

FIELD(S): VISUAL ARTS; DANCE; FOLK ARTS; MEDIA; MUSIC; THEATER; LITERARY ARTS

FELLOWSHIPS AWARDED TO INDIVIDUAL ARTISTS IN THE ABOVE AREAS. MUST BE FLORIDA RESIDENTS; USA CITIZENS AND OVER 18 YEARS OLD. MAY -NOT- BE A DEGREE SEEKING STUDENT; FUNDING IS FOR SUPPORT OF ARTISTIC ENDEAVORS ONLY.

FORTY AWARDS PER YEAR. WRITE FOR COMPLETE INFORMATION.

537

FONDATION DES ETATS UNIS (HARRIET HALE WOOLLEY SCHOLARSHIPS)

15 BOULEVARD JOURDAN
75690 PARIS-CEDEX 14 FRANCE
33-1/45-89-35-79

AMOUNT: $8500 STIPEND

DEADLINE(S): JAN 31

FIELD(S): PAINTING; PRINT-MAKING; SCULPTURE; INSTRUMENTAL MUSIC

USA CITIZEN. SCHOLARSHIPS FOR GRADUATE STUDY IN PARIS. PREFERENCE IS GIVEN TO STUDENTS WHO HAVE ALREADY DONE GRADUATE STUDY. MUST BE BETWEEN 21 AND 29 YEARS OF AGE AND BE SINGLE. SHOULD HAVE GOOD KNOWLEDGE OF FRENCH.

GRANTEES LIVE AT THE FONDATION DES ETATS-UNIS. CONTACT THE DIRECTOR ADDRESS ABOVE FOR COMPLETE INFORMATION.

PERFORMING ARTS

538

GEORGIA COUNCIL FOR THE ARTS (INDIVIDUAL ARTIST GRANTS)

530 MEANS ST NW; SUITE 115
ATLANTA GA 30318
404/651-7920

AMOUNT: UP TO $5000

DEADLINE(S): APR 20

FIELD(S): THE ARTS

GRANTS TO SUPPORT ARTISTIC PROJECTS BY PROFESSIONAL ARTISTS WHO HAVE BEEN GEORGIA RESIDENTS AT LEAST ONE YEAR PRIOR TO APPLICATION. SELECTION IS BASED ON PROJECT'S ARTISTIC MERIT AND ITS POTENTIAL FOR CAREER DEVELOPMENT.

GRANTS -DO NOT- SUPPORT ACADEMIC STUDY. WRITE FOR COMPLETE INFORMATION.

539

ILLINOIS ARTS COUNCIL (ARTISTS FELLOWSHIP AWARDS)

100 W. RANDOLPH; SUITE 10-500
CHICAGO IL 60601
312/814-6750

AMOUNT: $500 - $15000

DEADLINE(S): NOV 1

FIELD(S): CHOREOGRAPHY; VISUAL ARTS; LITERATURE; FILM; VIDEO; PLAYWRITING; MUSIC COMPOSITION; CRAFTS; ETHNIC & FOLK ARTS; PERFORMANCE ART; PHOTOGRAPHY

OPEN TO PROFESSIONAL ARTISTS WHO ARE ILLINOIS RESIDENTS. AWARDS ARE IN RECOGNITION OF WORK IN THE ABOVE AREAS; THEY ARE NOT FOR CONTINUING STUDY. STUDENTS ARE -NOT- ELIGIBLE.

WRITE TO ADDRESS ABOVE FOR APPLICATION FORM.

540

INTERNATIONAL COMPETITION FOR SYMPHONIC COMPOSITION (PREMIO CITTA DI TRIESTE)

PIAZZA DELL'UNITA D'ITALIA 4 - PALAZZO MUNICIPALE
34121 TRIESTE ITALY
040-6751-68844

AMOUNT: 5 MIL. LIRA-1ST; 2.5 MIL. LIRA-2ND; 1.5 MIL. LIRA-3RD

DEADLINE(S): AUG 31

FIELD(S): MUSIC COMPOSITION

OPEN TO ANYONE WHO SUBMITS AN ORIGINAL COMPOSITION FOR FULL ORCHESTRA (NORMAL SYMPHONIC INSTRUMENTATION). COMPOSITION MAY HAVE BEEN PERFORMED AND PUBLISHED BUT NOT BEFORE JAN 1 1988.

PREVIOUS FIRST PRIZE WINNERS ARE EXCLUDED FROM COMPETITION. WRITE TO SECRETARIAT OF THE MUSIC AWARD AT ADDRESS ABOVE FOR COMPLETE INFORMATION.

541

INTERNATIONAL VOCAL COMPETITION 'S-HERTOGENBOSCH

PO BOX 1225
5200 BG 'S-HERTOGENBOSCH
THE NETHERLANDS
0/73-136569

AMOUNT: $20000 TOTAL PRIZES

DEADLINE(S): JUL 1

FIELD(S): SINGING COMPETITION

ANNUAL VOCAL COMPETITION TO REWARD EXCEPTIONAL SINGING TALENT OF ALL NATIONALITIES (UP TO 32 YEARS OLD). PRIZES FOR OPERA; ORATORIO AND LIED CATEGORIES; VARIOUS OTHER PRIZES. ENTRY FEE OF 175 DUTCH GUILDERS IS REQUIRED.

WRITE FOR COMPLETE INFORMATION.

542

KURT WEILL FOUNDATION FOR MUSIC (DISSERTATION FELLOWSHIPS & TRAVEL GRANTS)

7 EAST 20TH ST
NEW YORK NY 10003
212/505-5240

AMOUNT: VARIES

DEADLINE(S): NOV 1

FIELD(S): MUSIC

FELLOWSHIPS & TRAVEL GRANTS OPEN TO DOCTORAL CANDIDATES TO SUPPORT DISSERTATION RESEARCH ON 'KURT WEILL AND HIS MUSIC'. WILL ALSO SUPPORT TRAVEL ANYWHERE IN THE WORLD TO STUDY PRIMARY DOCUMENTS.

GRANTS ALSO AVAILABLE TO FUND PRODUCTIONS & PERFORMANCES OF KURT WEILL'S MUSIC. WRITE FOR COMPLETE INFORMATION.

543

LABAN/BARTENIEFF INSTITUTE OF MOVEMENT STUDIES (WORKSTUDY PROGRAMS)

11 E. 4TH ST.; 3RD FLOOR
NEW YORK NY 10003
212/477-4299

AMOUNT: $500 - $2500

DEADLINE(S): MAY 1

FIELD(S): HUMAN MOVEMENT STUDIES

OPEN TO GRADUATE STUDENTS & PROFESSIONALS IN DANCE; EDUCATION; HEALTH FIELDS; BEHAVIORAL SCIENCES; FITNESS; ATHLETIC TRAINING; ETC. FOR WORK STUDY -ONLY- AT THE LABAN/ BARTENIEFF INSTITUTE IN THE LABAN MOVEMENT STUDIES CERTIFICATE PROGRAM.

WRITE FOR COMPLETE INFORMATION.

544

LIEDERKRANZ FOUNDATION (SCHOLARSHIP AWARDS)

6 EAST 87TH STREET
NEW YORK NY 10128
212/534-0880

AMOUNT: $1000 - $4000

DEADLINE(S): DEC 1

FIELD(S): VOCAL MUSIC

12-15 SCHOLARSHIPS AWARDED BY COMPETITION EACH YEAR. AWARDS CAN BE USED ANYWHERE. THERE IS A $25 APPLICATION FEE AND A LOWER AGE LIMIT OF 20.

CONTACT COMPETITION DIRECTOR JOHN BALME AT ADDRESS ABOVE FOR APPLICATION REGULATIONS; AUDITION SCHEDULES AND OTHER DETAILS.

545

LITTLE EMO AWARD (POST-DOCTORAL AWARDS)

PO BOX 3155
PALOS VERDES ESTATES CA 90274
WRITTEN INQUIRY

AMOUNT: VARIES

DEADLINE(S): NONE

FIELD(S): PERFORMING ARTS

AWARDS SUPPORT INDIVIDUALS OF EXTREMELY HIGH ABILITY & PROJECTS OF UNUSUAL DIRECTION & EXTRAORDINARY INNOVATION. 1993-94 PROJECTS COVER MUSICAL/THEATRICAL REPRESENTATIONS OF WORLD ECOLOGY; EMPHASIS ON RAIN FORESTS & USA WILDERNESS AREAS.

SEND PROJECT DESCRIPTION; BUDGET PROPOSAL AND SUBSTANTIAL DOCUMENTATION OF ARTISTIC EXCELLENCE TO ADDRESS ABOVE.

546

LOREN L. ZACHARY SOCIETY FOR THE PERFORMING ARTS (ANNUAL NATIONAL VOCAL COMPETITION FOR YOUNG OPERA SINGERS)

2250 GLOAMING WAY
BEVERLY HILLS CA 90210
310/276-2731

AMOUNT: $1000 - $3000 + ROUND-TRIP AIR TRANSPORTATION FOR AUDITIONS IN EUROPE

DEADLINE(S): FEB 7 (NY); MAR 16 (LA); MAY (FINAL COMPETITION)

FIELD(S): SINGING-OPERA

ANNUAL VOCAL COMPETITION OPEN TO YOUNG (AGED 21-33 FEMALES; 21-35 MALES) OPERA SINGERS. THE COMPETITION IS GEARED TOWARD FINDING EMPLOYMENT FOR THEM IN EUROPEAN OPERA HOUSES.

APPROX 10 AWARDS PER YEAR. APPLICATIONS AVAILABLE IN NOVEMBER. SEND SELF ADDRESSED STAMPED ENVELOPE TO ADDRESS ABOVE FOR APPLICATION & COMPLETE INFORMATION.

547

MARTIN MUSICAL SCHOLARSHIP FUND (SCHOLARSHIPS)

76 GREAT PORTLAND ST
LONDON W1N 5AL ENGLAND
01/580-9961

AMOUNT: VARIABLE

DEADLINE(S): OCT 1

FIELD(S): INSTRUMENTAL MUSIC

GRADUATE SCHOLARSHIPS OPEN TO APPLICANTS OF EXCEPTIONAL TALENT UNDER AGE 25. AWARDS ARE FOR STUDY AT ANY APPROVED INSTITUTION IN ENGLAND OR ON THE EUROPEAN CONTINENT. PREFERENCE TO CITIZENS OF THE UNITED KINGDOM ALTHOUGH ANYONE CAN APPLY.

APPLICANTS SHOULD BE PREPARING FOR A CAREER ON THE CONCERT STAGE AS INSTRUMENTAL SOLOIST OR ORCHESTRAL PLAYER. NOT OPEN TO ORGANISTS. WRITE FOR COMPLETE INFORMATION.

548

MERCYHURST COLLEGE (D'ANGELO YOUNG ARTIST COMPETITION)

GLENWOOD HILLS
ERIE PA 16546
814/825-0363

AMOUNT: $10000; $5000; $3000

DEADLINE(S): JAN 15

FIELD(S): VOICE; STRINGS; PIANO

FOR MUSICIANS AGED 18-30. ROTATING CYCLE OF AREAS (VOICE 1993; STRINGS 1994; PIANO 1995). DOLLAR AWARDS & PERFORMANCE CONTRACTS. WRITE FOR APPLICATION & REPERTOIRE REQUIREMENTS IN THE FALL OF THE YEAR PRECEDING YEAR OF COMPETITION.

WRITE FOR COMPLETE INFORMATION.

549

MILLAY COLONY FOR THE ARTS (RESIDENCIES)

STEEPLETOP; PO BOX 3
AUSTERLITZ NY 12017
518/392-3103

AMOUNT: RESIDENCY

DEADLINE(S): SEP 1; FEB 1; MAY 1

FIELD(S): CREATIVE WRITING; VISUAL ARTS; MUSIC COMPOSITION; SCULPTURE; GRAPHIC ARTS; POETRY

THE COLONY PROVIDES 60 RESIDENCIES PER YEAR FOR PROFESSIONALS IN THE ABOVE FIELDS. THERE IS NO APPLICATION FEE AND NO FEE FOR COLONY RESIDENCY.

RESIDENCIES ARE FOR ONE MONTH AND USUALLY COVER A PERIOD FROM THE FIRST TO THE 28TH OF EACH MONTH. WRITE FOR COMPLETE INFORMATION.

550

MINNESOTA STATE ARTS BOARD (GRANTS PROGRAM)

432 SUMMIT AVE
ST PAUL MN 55102
612/297-2603

AMOUNT: FELLOWSHIPS $6000; CAREER OPPORTUNITY GRANTS $100 - $1000 OR SPECIAL RESIDENCY STIPEND.

DEADLINE(S): SEP - VISUAL ARTS; OCT - MUSIC & DANCE; DEC - LITERATURE & THEATER

FIELD(S): LITERATURE; MUSIC; THEATER; DANCE; VISUAL ARTS

CAREER ADVANCEMENT GRANTS OPEN TO PROFESSIONAL ARTISTS WHO ARE RESIDENTS OF MINNESOTA. GRANTS ARE NOT INTENDED FOR SUPPORT OF TUITION OR WORK TOWARD ANY DEGREE.

CAREER OPPORTUNITY GRANTS AND FELLOWSHIPS ARE AVAILABLE. ARTISTS ALSO ARE ELIGIBLE FOR A SPECIAL RESIDENCE AT HEADLANDS CENTER FOR THE ARTS NEAR SAN FRANCISCO. WRITE FOR COMPLETE INFORMATION.

551

NAPA VALLEY SYMPHONY ASSOCIATION (ROBERT MONDAVI MUSIC ACHIEVEMENT AWARDS)

ELLE WHEELER; 2407 CALIFORNIA BLVD.
NAPA CA 94558
707/226-6872

AMOUNT: $2000 AND $1000 CASH PRIZES

DEADLINE(S): FEB 12

FIELD(S): MUSIC PERFORMANCE

CONTEST HELD IN ODD-NUMBERED YEARS FOR MUSICIANS AGE 18 TO 25. COMPETITION IS IN THE FOLLOWING SEQUENCE OF INSTRUMENTS—1993 PIANO; 1995 WOODWINDS; 1997 CELLO AND BASS; 1999 BRASS; 2001 VIOLINS AND VIOLAS.

APPLICANTS SUBMIT AUDITION CASETTE RECORDING AND A NON-REFUNDABLE $25 ENTRANCE FEE WITH THE APPLICATION. WRITE FOR COMPLETE INFORMATION.

552

NATIONAL ASSOCIATION OF TEACHERS OF SINGING (ARTIST AWARDS COMPETITION)

2800 UNIVERSITY BLVD NORTH
JACKSONVILLE FL 32211
904/744-9022

AMOUNT: $2500 TO $5000

DEADLINE(S): VARIES

FIELD(S): SINGING

PURPOSE OF THE PROGRAM IS TO SELECT YOUNG SINGERS WHO ARE READY FOR PROFESSIONAL CAREERS AND TO ENCOURAGE THEM TO CARRY ON THE TRADITION OF FINE SINGING.

APPLICANTS SHOULD BE BETWEEN 21 AND 35 YEARS OLD AND HAVE STUDIED WITH A N.A.T.S. TEACHER FOR AT LEAST ONE ACADEMIC YEAR. 6 AWARDS EVERY 18 MONTHS. WRITE FOR COMPLETE INFORMATION.

553

NATIONAL FEDERATION OF MUSIC CLUBS SCHOLARSHIP AND AWARDS PROGRAM (STUDENT AWARDS)

1336 N.DELAWARE ST
INDIANAPOLIS IN 46202
317/638-4003

AMOUNT: $100 - $5000

DEADLINE(S): VARIOUS

FIELD(S): MUSIC PERFORMANCE; MUSIC COMPOSITION

NUMEROUS SCHOLARSHIP & AWARD PROGRAMS OPEN TO YOUNG MUSICIANS AGED 16-35 WHO ARE EITHER GROUP OR INDIVIDUAL MEMBERS OF THE NAT'L FED OF MUSIC CLUBS. THE PROGRAMS PROVIDE OPPORTUNITIES FOR STUDENTS INTERESTED IN PROFESSIONAL MUSIC CAREERS.

REQUEST SCHOLARSHIP & AWARDS CHART FROM THE ADDRESS ABOVE. INCLUDE SELF-ADDRESSED BUSINESS SIZE ENVELOPE WITH 52 CENTS POSTAGE.

554

NATIONAL GUILD OF COMMUNITY SCHOOLS OF THE ARTS (YOUNG COMPOSERS AWARDS)

40 NORTH VAN BRUNT ST; SUITE 32
ENGLEWOOD NJ 07631
201/871-3337

AMOUNT: $1000; $750; $500; $250

DEADLINE(S): APR 1

FIELD(S): MUSIC COMPOSITION

COMPETITION OPEN TO STUDENTS AGED 13-18 (AS OF JUN 30 OF AWARD YEAR) WHO ARE ENROLLED IN A PUBLIC OR PRIVATE SECONDARY SCHOOL; RECOGNIZED MUSICAL SCHOOL OR ENGAGED IN PRIVATE STUDY OF MUSIC WITH AN ESTABLISHED TEACHER IN THE USA OR CANADA.

USA OR CANADIAN CITIZEN OR LEGAL RESIDENT. WRITE FOR COMPLETE INFORMATION.

555

NEW JERSEY STATE COUNCIL ON THE ARTS (FELLOWSHIP SUPPORT)

4 NORTH BROAD ST - CN 306
TRENTON NJ 08625
609/292-6130

AMOUNT: UP TO $12000

DEADLINE(S): VARIES (USUALLY JAN OR FEB)

FIELD(S): LITERATURE; CHOREOGRAPHY; COMPOSITION; VISUAL ARTS; PHOTOGRAPHY

NEW JERSEY RESIDENTS. FELLOWSHIP AWARDS ARE MADE TO PROFESSIONAL ARTISTS & GRADUATE STUDENTS TO ENABLE THEM TO COMPLETE EITHER NEW WORKS OR WORKS IN PROGRESS. UNDERGRADUATES ARE NOT ELIGIBLE.

FUNDS MAY -NOT- BE USED FOR TUITION OR DIRECT EXPENSES OF FORMAL EDUCATION. WRITE TO GRANTS COORDINATOR; ADDRESS ABOVE; FOR COMPLETE INFORMATION.

556

NEW JERSEY STATE OPERA (CASH AWARDS)

1020 BROAD STREET
NEWARK NJ 07102
201/623-5757

AMOUNT: AWARDS TOTAL $10000

DEADLINE(S): VARIES EACH YEAR

FIELD(S): OPERA

PROFESSIONAL SINGERS BETWEEN THE AGES OF 22 AND 34 CAN APPLY FOR THIS COMPETITION. SINGERS COMPETING SHOULD HAVE BEEN REPRESENTED BY AN ARTISTS' MANAGEMENT FIRM FOR NO MORE THAN ONE YEAR. MANAGEMENT REPRESENTATION NOT REQUIRED FOR ENTRY.

CONTACT ADDRESS ABOVE FOR COMPLETE INFORMATION.

557

NEW YORK CITY OPERA (JULIUS RUDEL AWARD)

NEW YORK STATE THEATER;
20 LINCOLN CENTER
NEW YORK NY 10023
212/870-5600

AMOUNT: $12000

DEADLINE(S): NONE

FIELD(S): OPERA & MUSIC MANAGEMENT (CAREER SUPPORT)

APPLICANTS SHOULD PRESENT EVIDENCE OF ARTISTIC ACCOMPLISHMENTS ALONG WITH A RESUME AND LETTERS OF RECOMMENDATION; ALSO A STATEMENT OUTLINING HOW AFFILIATION WITH THE NYC OPERA WILL FURTHER APPLICANT'S ARTISTIC AND CAREER GOALS.

AWARD RECIPIENT PERFORMS ADMINISTRATIVE TASKS FOR NYC OPERA BUT RECIPIENT IS ENCOURAGED TO CONTINUE OUTSIDE ARTISTIC WORK. WRITE FOR COMPLETE INFORMATION.

558

NEW YORK FOUNDATION FOR THE ARTS (ARTIST'S FELLOWSHIPS & SERVICES)

155 AVE OF THE AMERICAS; 14TH FLOOR
NEW YORK NY 10013
212/366-6900; FAX 212/366-1778

AMOUNT: $7000

DEADLINE(S): SEP 30

FIELD(S): VISUAL ARTS; LITERATURE; ARCHITECTURE; MUSIC AND MEDIA

FELLOWSHIPS & SERVICES OPEN TO ORIGINATING ARTISTS OVER 18 WHO HAVE BEEN NY STATE RESIDENTS FOR 2 YEARS PREVIOUS TO APPLICATION DATE & ARE NOT ENROLLED IN A DEGREE AWARDING COURSE OF STUDY. AWARDS ARE TO ASSIST IN CREATION OF ONGOING WORK.

APPLICATIONS AVAILABLE IN SPRINT OF EACH YEAR. ABOUT 120 FELLOWSHIPS PER YEAR; MANY OTHER SERVICES ARE AVAILABLE. -NOT- FOR ACADEMIC STUDY. WRITE FOR COMPLETE INFORMATION.

559

NEW YORK PHILHARMONIC (MUSIC ASSISTANCE FUND SCHOLARSHIPS)

AVERY FISCHER HALL;
BROADWAY AT 65TH ST
NEW YORK NY 10023
212/580-8700

PERFORMING ARTS

AMOUNT: UP TO $2500

DEADLINE(S): JAN 15

FIELD(S): ORCHESTRAL MUSIC STUDY

OPEN TO USA CITIZENS OF AFRICAN DESCENT WHO ARE PURSUING DEGREES AT CONSERVATORIES AND UNIVERSITY SCHOOLS OF MUSIC. FOR ORCHESTRAL INSTRUMENTS ONLY; PIANO NOT INCLUDED.

AWARDS ARE RENEWABLE AND BASED ON RECOMMENDATIONS; PERSONAL AUDITIONS AND FINANCIAL NEED. WRITE FOR COMPLETE INFORMATION.

560

PHI MU ALPHA-SINFONIA FOUNDATION (RESEARCH ASSISTANCE GRANTS)

10600 OLD STATE ROAD;
GRANT COMMITTEE
EVANSVILLE IN 47711
812/867-2433

AMOUNT: UP TO $1000

DEADLINE(S): APR 1

FIELD(S): MUSIC

GRADUATE GRANTS FOR RESEARCH RELATED TO AMERICAN MUSIC OR MUSIC IN AMERICA. SHOW EVIDENCE OF PREVIOUS SUCCESSFUL WRITING AND RESEARCH OR SHOW EVIDENCE OF UNUSUAL KNOWLEDGE OR COMPETENCE IN THE FIELD TO BE RESEARCHED.

WRITE FOR COMPLETE INFORMATION.

561

PITTSBURGH NEW MUSIC ENSEMBLE (HARVEY GAUL BI-ANNUAL COMPOSITION CONTEST)

600 FORBES AVE
PITTSBURGH PA 15219
412/261-0554

AMOUNT: $1500

DEADLINE(S): APR 15

FIELD(S): MUSIC COMPOSITION

OPEN TO USA CITIZENS. PRIZES ARE GIVEN FOR NEW WORKS SCORED FOR SIX TO FIFTEEN INSTRUMENTS. AN ENTRY FEE OF $10 MUST ACCOMPANY EACH COMPOSITION SUBMITTED. COMPOSERS MAY ENTER MORE THAN ONE COMPOSITION.

WRITE FOR COMPLETE INFORMATION.

562

QUEEN MARIE JOSE (MUSICAL PRIZE CONTEST)

CASE POSTALE 19; 1252 MEINIER
GENEVA SWITZERLAND
WRITTEN INQUIRY

AMOUNT: 10000 SWISS FRANCS

DEADLINE(S): MAY 31

FIELD(S): MUSIC COMPOSITION COMPETITION

THIS CONTEST IS OPEN TO COMPOSERS OF ALL NATIONALITIES WITHOUT AGE LIMIT. MUSICAL SCORES PREFERABLY WRITTEN IN INK TOGETHER WITH A TAPE RECORDING OF THE WORK WILL BE REQUIRED.

WRITE FOR COMPLETE INFORMATION.

563

QUEEN SONJA INTERNATIONAL MUSIC COMPETITION (PIANO/VOICE COMPETITION)

PO BOX 1568 VIKA
N-0116 OSLO 1 NORWAY
+47 2 46 40 55

AMOUNT: APPROX $40000 TOTAL PRIZE MONEY

DEADLINE(S): FEB 1 - EVERY 3 YEARS

FIELD(S): PIANO; VOICE

THE NEXT COMPETITION WILL BE FOR SINGERS IN 1995. IN ADDITION TO CASH AWARDS FOR THE 4 FINALISTS (PLACES 1-4) THE BOARD OF DIRECTORS WILL ENDEAVOUR TO PROVIDE THEM WITH SOLO ENGAGEMENTS IN VARIOUS NORDIC CITIES.

WRITE FOR COMPLETE INFORMATION.

564

SANTA BARBARA FOUNDATION (MARY & EDITH PILLSBURY FOUNDATION SCHOLARSHIPS)

15 E.CARRILLO ST
SANTA BARBARA CA 93101
805/963-1873

AMOUNT: VARIES

DEADLINE(S): MAY 15

FIELD(S): MUSIC PERFORMANCE; MUSIC COMPOSITION

OPEN TO TALENTED MUSIC STUDENTS WHO ARE SANTA BARBARA COUNTY RESIDENTS OR HAVE STRONG SANTA BARBARA TIES. AWARDS MAY BE USED FOR MUSIC LESSONS; CAMPS OR COLLEGE TUITION. USA CITIZEN. FINANCIAL NEED IS A CONSIDERATION.

APPROXIMATELY 30 SCHOLARSHIPS PER YEAR; RENEWABLE. WRITE FOR COMPLETE INFORMATION.

565

TENNESSEE ARTS COMMISSION (INDIVIDUAL ARTISTS' FELLOWSHIPS)

320 SIXTH AVE NORTH #100
NASHVILLE TN 37243
615/741-1701

AMOUNT: $2500 - $5000

DEADLINE(S): JAN 11

FIELD(S): VISUAL ARTS; PERFORMING ARTS; CREATIVE ARTS

GRANTS OPEN TO ARTISTS WHO ARE RESIDENTS OF THE STATE OF TENNESSEE. DURATION OF AWARD IS ONE YEAR. APPLICANTS MUST BE PROFESSIONAL ARTISTS. FULL TIME STUDENTS ARE -NOT- ELIGIBLE.

WRITE FOR COMPLETE INFORMATION.

566

UNIVERSITY OF ILLINOIS AT URBANA-CHAMPAIGN (KATE N. KINLEY FELLOWSHIP)

COLLEGE OF FINE & APPLIED ARTS;
110 ARCHITECTURE BLDG;
608 E. LORADO TAFT DR.
CHAMPAIGN IL 61820
217/333-2723

AMOUNT: $7000

DEADLINE(S): FEB 15

FIELD(S): ART; MUSIC; ARCHITECTURE

GRADUATE FELLOWSHIP FOR ADVANCED STUDY IN THE USA OR ABROAD. OPEN TO APPLICANTS WITH A BACHELOR'S DEGREE IN THE ABOVE AREAS. PREFERENCE GIVEN TO (BUT NOT LIMITED TO) APPLICANTS UNDER 25 YEARS OF AGE.

TWO ADDITIONAL AWARDS OF A LESSER AMOUNT MAY BE GRANTED UPON COMMITTEE RECOMMENDATION. WRITE FOR COMPLETE INFORMATION.

567

VIRGIN ISLANDS BOARD OF EDUCATION (MUSIC SCHOLARSHIPS)

PO BOX 11900
ST THOMAS VI 00801
809/774-4546

AMOUNT: $2000

DEADLINE(S): MAR 31

FIELD(S): MUSIC

OPEN TO BONAFIDE RESIDENTS OF THE VIRGIN ISLANDS WHO ARE ENROLLED IN AN ACCREDITED MUSIC PROGRAM AT AN INSTITUTION OF HIGHER LEARNING.

THIS SCHOLARSHIP IS GRANTED FOR THE DURATION OF THE COURSE PROVIDED THE RECIPIENTS MAINTAIN AT LEAST A 'C' AVERAGE. WRITE FOR COMPLETE INFORMATION.

568

WAMSO (YOUNG ARTIST COMPETITION)

1111 NICOLLET MALL
MINNEAPOLIS MN 55403
612/371-5654

AMOUNT: $2500 1ST PRIZE PLUS PERFORMANCE WITH MN ORCHESTRA

DEADLINE(S): NOV 1 (COMPETITION USUALLY HELD IN JAN)

FIELD(S): PIANO & ORCHESTRAL INSTRUMENTS

COMPETITION OFFERS 4 PRIZES & POSSIBLE SCHOLARSHIPS TO H.S & COLLEGE STUDENTS IN SCHOOLS IN IA; MN; MO; NE; ND; SD; WI & THE CANDAIAN PROVINCES OF MANITOBA & ONTARIO. ENTRANTS MAY NOT HAVE PASSED THEIR 26TH BIRTHDAY ON DATE OF COMPETITION.

FOR LIST OF REPERTOIRES & COMPLETE INFORMATION SPECIFY YOUR INSTRUMENT & WRITE TO ADDRESS ABOVE.

569

WAVERLY COMMUNITY HOUSE INC (F. LAMMONT BELIN ARTS SCHOLARSHIPS)

SCHOLARSHIPS SELECTION COMMITTEE
WAVERLY PA 18471
717/586-8191

AMOUNT: $9000

DEADLINE(S): DEC 15

FIELD(S): PAINTING; SCULPTURE; MUSIC; DRAMA; DANCE; LITERATURE; ARCHITECTURE; PHOTOGRAPHY

APPLICANTS MUST RESIDE IN THE ABINGTONS OR POCONO REGIONS OF NORTHEASTERN PENNSYLVANIA. THEY MUST FURNISH PROOF OF EXCEPTIONAL ABILITY IN THEIR CHOSEN FIELD BUT NEED NO FORMAL TRAINING IN ANY ACADEMIC OR PROFESSIONAL PROGRAM.

USA CITIZENSHIP REQUIRED. FINALISTS MUST APPEAR IN PERSON BEFORE THE SELECTION COMMITTEE. WRITE FOR COMPLETE INFORMATION.

PHILOSOPHY

570

AMERICAN CATHOLIC HISTORICAL ASSOCIATION (THE JOHN GILMARY SHEA PRIZE)

C/O CATHOLIC UNIVERSITY OF AMERICA
WASHINGTON DC 20064
201/635-5079

AMOUNT: $300

DEADLINE(S): OCT 1

FIELD(S): CREATIVE WRITING - CATHOLIC CHURCH

PHILOSOPHY

PRIZE FOR THE BOOK PUBLISHED WITHIN LAST YEAR JUDGED TO HAVE MADE THE MOST SIGNIFICANT CONTRIBUTION TO THE HISTORY OF THE CATHOLIC CHURCH. MUST BE CITIZEN OR PERMANENT RESIDENT OF USA OR CANADA.

PUBLISHERS OR AUTHORS SHOULD SEND 3 COPIES OF THE WORK TO THE JUDGES AT THE ADDRESS ABOVE.

571

AMERICAN COUNCIL OF LEARNED SOCIETIES (ACLS FELLOWSHIPS)

OFFICE OF FELLOWSHIPS & GRANTS;
228 E. 45TH ST.
NEW YORK NY 10017
WRITTEN INQUIRY

AMOUNT: UP TO $20000

DEADLINE(S): SEP 30

FIELD(S): HUMANITIES; SOCIAL SCIENCES; OTHER AREAS HAVING PREDOMINATELY HUMANISTIC EMPHASIS

OPEN TO USA CITIZENS OR LEGAL RESIDENTS WHO HOLD THE PH.D OR ITS EQUIVALENT. FELLOWSHIPS ARE DESIGNED TO HELP SCHOLARS DEVOTE 2 TO 12 CONTINUOUS MONTHS TO FULL TIME RESEARCH.

WRITE FOR COMPLETE INFORMATION.

572

AMERICAN SOCIETY OF CHURCH HISTORY (ALBERT C. OUTLER PRIZE IN ECUMENICAL CHURCH HISTORY)

328 DELAND AVENUE
INDIALANTIC FL 32903
WRITTEN INQUIRY

AMOUNT: $1000 - $3000

DEADLINE(S): JUN 1

FIELD(S): CREATIVE WRITING - THEOLOGY

AWARD OF $1000 TO THE AUTHOR OF A BOOK-LENGTH MANUSCRIPT ON ECUMENICAL CHURCH HISTORY & A POSSIBLE GRANT OF UP TO $3000 FOR PUBLICATION. SHOULD BE CHIEFLY CONCERNED WITH THE PROBLEMS OF CHRISTIAN UNITY & DISUNITY IN ANY PERIOD.

WRITE FOR COMPLETE INFORMATION.

573

AMERICAN SOCIETY OF CHURCH HISTORY (BREWER PRIZE)

328 DELAND AVENUE
INDIALANTIC FL 32903
WRITTEN INQUIRY

AMOUNT: $1000

DEADLINE(S): NOV 1

FIELD(S): CREATIVE WRITING - THEOLOGY

AWARD FOR BEST BOOK LENGTH MANUSCRIPT OR ESSAY WRITTEN ON TOPICS DEALING WITH CHURCH HISTORY. PRIZE IS FOR THE PURPOSE OF PUBLISHING WORK.

NO MANUSCRIPT PREVIOUSLY SUMMITTED WILL BE CONSIDERED. WRITE FOR COMPLETE INFORMATION.

574

AMERICAN SOCIETY OF CHURCH HISTORY (JANE DEMPSEY DOUGLASS PRIZE)

DR. S.J. STEIN; 1420 E. MAXWELL LN.
BLOOMINGTON IN 47401
WRITTEN INQUIRY

AMOUNT: $250

DEADLINE(S): AUG 1

FIELD(S): CREATIVE WRITING - THEOLOGY

PRIZE FOR THE BEST UNPUBLISHED ESSAY ON SOME ASPECT OF THE ROLE OF WOMEN IN THE HISTORY OF CHRISTIANITY. THE MANUSCRIPT WILL BE PUBLISHED IN CHURCH HISTORY.

WRITE FOR COMPLETE INFORMATION.

575

AMERICAN SOCIETY OF CHURCH HISTORY (PHILIP SCHAFF PRIZE)

328 DELAND AVENUE
INDIALANTIC FL 32903
WRITTEN INQUIRY

AMOUNT: $1000

DEADLINE(S): MAR 1 1993 FOR BOOKS PUBLISHED DURING 1991 OR 1992

FIELD(S): CREATIVE WRITING - THEOLOGY

PRIZE FOR BEST PUBLISHED BOOK WRITTEN WITHIN NORTHERN AMERICAN SCHOLARLY COMMUNITY. WORK MUST PRESENT ORIGINAL RESEARCH ON HISTORY OF CHRISTIANITY.

BOOKS MUST HAVE BEEN PUBLISHED WITHIN 2 YEARS OF AWARD YEAR.

576

AMERICAN SOCIETY OF CHURCH HISTORY (SIDNEY E MEAD PRIZE)

DR. S.J. STEIN; 1420 E. MAXWELL LN.
BLOOMINGTON IN 47401
WRITTEN INQUIRY

AMOUNT: $250

DEADLINE(S): JUL 1

FIELD(S): CREATIVE WRITING- THEOLOGY

PRIZE FOR BEST ESSAY IN ANY FIELD OF CHURCH HISTORY WRITTEN BY A DOCTORAL CANDIDATE OR RECENT PH.D WHOSE ESSAY STEMS DIRECTLY FROM DOCTORAL RESEARCH. WINNER WILL BE PUBLISHED IN CHURCH HISTORY.

WRITE FOR COMPLETE INFORMATION.

577

CHRISTIAN CHURCH (DISCIPLES OF CHRIST - DISCIPLE CHAPLIN SCHOLARSHIP FUND)

PO BOX 1986
INDIANAPOLIS IN 46206
317/353-1491

AMOUNT: VARIES

DEADLINE(S): MAR 15

FIELD(S): THEOLOGY

OPEN TO MEMBERS OF THE CHRISTIAN CHURCH (DISCIPLES OF CHRIST) WHO ARE FIRST YEAR SEMINARIANS PREPARING FOR THE MINISTRY. ABOVE AVERAGE GPA; FINANCIAL NEED.

WRITE FOR COMPLETE INFORMATION.

578

CHRISTIAN CHURCH (DISCIPLES OF CHRIST - MINISTERIAL EDUCATION SCHOLARSHIP GRANT)

PO BOX 1986
INDIANAPOLIS IN 46206
317/353-1491

AMOUNT: VARIES

DEADLINE(S): MAR 15

FIELD(S): THEOLOGY

OPEN TO CHRISTIAN CHURCH (DISCIPLES OF CHRIST) MEMBERS WHO ARE ENROLLED IN AN ACCREDITED GRADUATE SCHOOL OR SEMINARY IN PREPARATION FOR THE MINISTRY. ABOVE AVERAGE ACADEMIC STANDING; FINANCIAL NEED.

RENEWABLE. WRITE FOR COMPLETE INFORMATION.

579

CHRISTIAN CHURCH (DISCIPLES OF CHRIST - BLACK 'STAR SUPPORTER' SCHOLARSHIP FUND)

PO BOX 1986
INDIANAPOLIS IN 46206
317/353-1491

AMOUNT: VARIES

DEADLINE(S): APR 15

FIELD(S): THEOLOGY

OPEN TO CHRISTIAN CHURCH (DISCIPLES OF CHRIST) MEMBERS WHO ARE BLACK OR AFRO AMERICAN AND ARE ENROLLED IN AN ACCREDITED BACHELORS DEGREE OR GRADUATE PROGRAM IN PREPARATION FOR THE MINISTRY. ABOVE AVERAGE GPA; FINANCIAL NEED.

RENEWABLE. WRITE FOR COMPLETE INFORMATION.

580

CHRISTIAN CHURCH (DISCIPLES OF CHRIST - HISPANIC SCHOLARSHIP)

PO BOX 1986
INDIANAPOLIS IN 46206
317/353-1491

AMOUNT: VARIES

DEADLINE(S): MAR 15

FIELD(S): THEOLOGY

OPEN TO CHRISTIAN CHURCH (DISCIPLES OF CHRIST) MEMBERS OF HISPANIC DESCENT WHO ARE ENROLLED IN AN ACCREDITED GRADUATE SCHOOL OR SEMINARY IN PREPARATION FOR THE MINISTRY. ABOVE AVERAGE GPA; FINANCIAL NEED.

RENEWABLE. WRITE FOR COMPLETE INFORMATION.

581

CHRISTIAN CHURCH (DISCIPLES OF CHRIST - DAVID TAMOTSU KAGIWADA MEMORIAL FUND)

PO BOX 1986
INDIANAPOLIS IN 46206
317/353-1491

AMOUNT: VARIES

DEADLINE(S): APR 15

FIELD(S): THEOLOGY

OPEN TO CHRISTIAN CHURCH (DISCIPLES OF CHRIST) MEMBERS OF ASIAN DESCENT WHO ARE ENROLLED IN AN ACCREDITED GRADUATE SCHOOL OR SEMINARY IN PREPARATION FOR THE MINISTRY. ABOVE AVERAGE GPA; FINANCIAL NEED.

RENEWABLE. WRITE FOR COMPLETE INFORMATION.

582

CHRISTIAN CHURCH (DISCIPLES OF CHRIST - ROWLEY FUND)

PO BOX 1986
INDIANAPOLIS IN 46206
317/353-1491

AMOUNT: VARIES

DEADLINE(S): MAR 15

FIELD(S): THEOLOGY

PHILOSOPHY

OPEN TO CHRISTIAN CHURCH (DISCIPLES OF CHRIST) MEMBERS WHO ARE ENROLLED IN AN ACCREDITED GRADUATE SCHOOL OR SEMINARY IN PREPARATION FOR THE MINISTRY. ABOVE AVERAGE ACADEMIC STANDING; FINANCIAL NEED.

RENEWABLE. WRITE FOR COMPLETE INFORMATION.

583

CHRISTIAN CHURCH (DISCIPLES OF CHRIST - JAMES M. PHILPUTT MEMORIAL SCHOLARSHIP / LOAN FUND)

PO BOX 1986
INDIANAPOLIS IN 46206
317/353-1491

AMOUNT: VARIES

DEADLINE(S): MAR 15

FIELD(S): THEOLOGY

OPEN TO CHRISTIAN CHURCH (DISCIPLES OF CHRIST) MEMBERS WHO ARE PREPARING FOR THE MINISTRY AT THE UNIVERSITY OF CHICAGO DIVINITY SCHOOL; UNION THEOLOGICAL SEMINARY (NEW YORK CITY); OR VANDERBILT OR YALE UNIVERSITY DIVINITY SCHOOL.

ABOVE AVERAGE GPA; FINANCIAL NEED. WRITE FOR COMPLETE INFORMATION.

584

CHURCH OF THE BRETHREN GENERAL BOARD (GRANTS PROGRAM)

1451 DUNDEE AVENUE
ELGIN IL 60120
708/742-5100

AMOUNT: UP TO $500

DEADLINE(S): NONE SPECIFIED

FIELD(S): THEOLOGY

GRADUATE GRANTS OPEN TO MEMBERS OF THE CHURCH OF THE BRETHREN WHO ARE PURSUING A COURSE OF STUDY AT BETHANY THEOLOGICAL SEMINARY LEADING TO THE PASTORAL MINISTRY IN THE CHURCH OF THE BRETHREN.

UP TO 20 AWARDS PER YEAR. RENEWABLE. WRITE FOR COMPLETE INFORMATION.

585

CLEM JAUNICH EDUCATION TRUST (SCHOLARSHIPS)

5353 GAMBLE DR; SUITE 110
MINNEAPOLIS MN 55416
612/546-1555

AMOUNT: $750 - $3000

DEADLINE(S): JUL 15

FIELD(S): THEOLOGY; MEDICINE

OPEN TO STUDENTS WHO HAVE ATTENDED PUBLIC OR PAROCHIAL SCHOOL IN THE DELANO (MN) SCHOOL DISTRICT OR CURRENTLY RESIDE WITHIN 7 MILES OF THE CITY OF DELANO MN. AWARDS SUPPORT UNDERGRADUATE OR GRADUATE STUDY IN THEOLOGY OR MEDICINE.

4-6 SCHOLARSHIPS PER YEAR. WRITE FOR COMPLETE INFORMATION.

586

EPISCOPAL CHURCH FOUNDATION (GRADUATE FELLOWSHIP PROGRAM)

815 SECOND AVE; 4TH FLOOR
NEW YORK NY 10017
212/697-2858

AMOUNT: UP TO $17500

DEADLINE(S): NOV 1

FIELD(S): THEOLOGY

FELLOWSHIPS TO ENCOURAGE DOCTORAL STUDY BY RECENT SEMINARY GRADUATES. OPEN TO APPLICANTS WHO WISH TO QUALIFY FOR THE TEACHING MINISTRY OF THE EPISCOPAL CHURCH IN THE USA. MUST BE RECOMMENDED BY DEAN.

4 TO 8 AWARDS PER YEAR. CONTACT DEAN'S OFFICE AT ANY ACCREDITED EPISCOPAL SEMINARY FOR APPLICATION MATERIALS. (UPDATED MATERIALS AVAILABLE BEGINNING JUNE 1).

587

FUND FOR THEOLOGICAL EDUCATION (BENJAMIN E. MAYS SCHOLARSHIPS FOR MINISTRY)

475 RIVERSIDE DR #832
NEW YORK NY 10115
212/870-2058

AMOUNT: VARIES

DEADLINE(S): NOV 10

FIELD(S): THEOLOGY

OPEN TO AFRO-AMERICAN NOMINEES WHO ARE ORDAINED OR ARE OFFICIAL CANDIDATES FOR ORDINATION & ARE ENROLLED OR PREPARING TO ENROLL FULL OR PART TIME IN A MASTER OF DIVINITY PROGRAM AT AN ACCREDITED USA OR CANADIAN THEOLOGICAL SCHOOL.

MUST BE NOMINATED BY A CHURCH OR SCHOOL OFFICIAL AND A CITIZEN OF THE USA OR CANADA. WRITE FOR COMPLETE INFORMATION.

588

FUND FOR THEOLOGICAL EDUCATION (DISSERTATION YEAR SCHOLARSHIPS FOR AFRO-AMERICANS)

475 RIVERSIDE DR #832
NEW YORK NY 10115
212/870-2058

AMOUNT: VARIES

DEADLINE(S): FEB 10

FIELD(S): THEOLOGY; CHRISTIAN EDUCATION

OPEN TO AFRO-AMERICANS WHO ARE USA OR CANADIAN CITIZENS COMPLETING THEIR PH.D ED.D OR TH.D DISSERTATIONS IN RELIGIOUS STUDIES. MUST BE MEMBERS OF A CHRISTIAN CHURCH AND NOMINATED BY THE COLLEGE.

RECIPIENTS ARE EXPECTED TO COMPLETE DISSERTATIONS BY THE END OF THE SCHOLARSHIP YEAR. WRITE FOR COMPLETE INFORMATION.

589

FUND FOR THEOLOGICAL EDUCATION (HISPANIC AMERICAN SCHOLARSHIPS FOR MINISTRY)

475 RIVERSIDE DR #832
NEW YORK NY 10115
212/870-2058

AMOUNT: VARIES

DEADLINE(S): NOV 10

FIELD(S): THEOLOGY

GRADUATE FELLOWSHIPS OPEN TO HISPANIC AMERICANS WHO ARE ORDAINED MINISTERS OR CANDIDATES FOR ORDINATION. MUST BE ENROLLED OR PREPARED TO ENROLL FULL TIME IN A MASTER OF DIVINITY PROGRAM AT AN ACCREDITED THEOLOGICAL SCHOOL IN USA OR CANADA.

MUST HAVE A COMMITMENT TO THE PRACTICE OF MINISTRY IN SPANISH SPEAKING COMMUNITIES IN THE USA; CANADA OR PUERTO RICO AND BE NOMINATED BY A CHURCH OFFICIAL OR FACULTY MEMBER. WRITE FOR COMPLETE INFORMATION.

590

FUND FOR THEOLOGICAL EDUCATION (MINORITY DOCTORAL SCHOLARSHIPS)

475 RIVERSIDE DR #832
NEW YORK NY 10115
212/870-2058

AMOUNT: VARIES

DEADLINE(S): FEB 10

FIELD(S): THEOLOGY; CHRISTIAN EDUCATION

OPEN TO AFRO-AMERICANS & HISPANIC AMERICANS WHO ARE USA OR CANADIAN CITIZENS AND ARE ENROLLED IN OR APPLYING TO A PH.D TH.D OR ED.D PROGRAM IN A FIELD OF RELIGIOUS STUDY. APPLICANTS SHOULD HAVE COMPLETED NO MORE THAN 1 YEAR OF COURSEWORK.

MUST BE MEMBERS OF A CHRISTIAN CHURCH AND NOMINATED BY THE COLLEGE. WRITE FOR COMPLETE INFORMATION.

591

FUND FOR THEOLOGICAL EDUCATION (NORTH AMERICAN MINISTERIAL SCHOLARSHIPS)

475 RIVERSIDE DR #832
NEW YORK NY 10115
212/870-2058

AMOUNT: VARIES

DEADLINE(S): NOV 10

FIELD(S): THEOLOGY

OPEN TO USA OR CANADIAN CITIZENS WHO ARE PREPARED TO ENROLL FULL TIME IN A MASTER OF DIVINITY PROGRAM AT AN ACCREDITED THEOLOGICAL SCHOOL IN THE USA OR CANADA. MUST BE MEMBER OF A CHRISTIAN CHURCH & PLAN TO ENTER ORDAINED MINISTRY.

MUST BE NOMINATED BY A MINISTER OR A FACULTY OR SCHOOL ADMINISTRATION MEMBER. WRITE FOR COMPLETE INFORMATION.

592

GERMANISTIC SOCIETY OF AMERICA (FOREIGN STUDY SCHOLARSHIPS)

809 UNITED NATIONS PLAZA
NEW YORK NY 10017
212/984-5330

AMOUNT: $8500

DEADLINE(S): OCT 31

FIELD(S): HISTORY; POLITICAL SCIENCE; INT'L RELATIONS; PUBLIC AFFAIRS; LANGUAGE; PHILOSOPHY; LITERATURE

APPLICANTS MUST BE US CITIZENS WITH A BACHELORS DEGREE. AWARDS ARE FOR GRADUATE STUDY AT A WEST GERMAN UNIVERSITY.

SELECTION IS BASED UPON PROPOSED PROJECT; LANGUAGE FLUENCY; ACADEMIC ACHIEVEMENT; & REFERENCES. WRITE FOR COMPLETE INFORMATION.

593

GETTY CENTER FOR THE HISTORY OF ART & THE HUMANITIES (PREDOCTORAL & POSTDOCTORAL FELLOWSHIPS)

DR H.H.HYMANS;
401 WILSHIRE BLVD; #400
SANTA MONICA CA 90401
310/458-9811

AMOUNT: $15000 PREDOCTORAL; $20000 POSTDOCTORAL

DEADLINE(S): DEC 1

FIELD(S): HUMANITIES; SOCIAL SCIENCES; ANTHROPOLOGY; ART/SCIENCE HISTORY; LITERATURE; PHILOSOPHY ETC.

OPEN TO PRE & POSTDOCTORAL SCHOLARS WHOSE AREAS OF RESEARCH COMPLEMENT THE CENTER'S PROGRAMS & RESOURCES. PREDOCTORAL CANDIDATES SHOULD EXPECT TO COMPLETE DISSERTATIONS DURING THE FELLOWSHIP YEAR.

POSTDOCTORALS SHOULD HAVE RECEIVED DOCTORATE IN HUMANITIES OR SOCIAL SCIENCES WITHIN LAST 3 YEARS & BE REWRITING DISSERTATIONS FOR PUBLICATION. WRITE FOR COMPLETE INFORMATION.

594

HARDING FOUNDATION (GRANTS)

BOX 130
RAYMONDVILLE TX 78580
512/689-2706

AMOUNT: $1200 PER SEMESTER OR TERM

DEADLINE(S): NONE

FIELD(S): THEOLOGY

GRANTS OPEN TO MINISTERIAL STUDENTS WHO ARE ENROLLED IN A GRADUATE PROGRAM OF STUDY AT ANY RECOGNIZED SEMINARY; COLLEGE OR UNIVERSITY.

CONTACT MRS. GLENN HARDING CORRESPONDING SECRETARY ADDRESS ABOVE FOR COMPLETE INFORMATION.

595

HASTINGS CENTER (INTERNATIONAL FELLOWSHIP PROGRAM)

255 ELM ROAD
BRIARCLIFF MANOR NY 10510
914/762-8500

AMOUNT: $500 - $1000 STIPEND

DEADLINE(S): NONE GIVEN

FIELD(S): BIOMEDICAL ETHICS

OPEN TO ADVANCED SCHOLARS FROM FOREIGN COUNTRIES WHO HAVE MADE A SIGNIFICANT CONTRIBUTION TO BIOETHICS IN THEIR OWN COUNTRIES. FELLOWSHIP FOR TWO TO SIX WEEK STAY AT HASTINGS CENTER. STIPEND LIMITED TO THOSE REQUIRING FINANCIAL ASSISTANCE.

WRITE FOR COMPLETE INFORMATION.

596

JIMMIE ULLERY CHARITABLE TRUST (SCHOLARSHIP GRANT)

SCHOLARSHIP COMMITTEE; CHRISTIAN EDUCATION DEPT; 1ST PREBYTERIAN CHURCH; 709 S. BOSTON
TULSA OK 74193
918/586-5845

AMOUNT: $1000 - $1200

DEADLINE(S): JUN 1

FIELD(S): THEOLOGY

OPEN TO PRESBYTERIAN STUDENTS IN FULL-TIME CHRISTIAN SERVICE. SCHOLARSHIPS ARE USUALLY (BUT NOT ALWAYS) AWARDED FOR STUDY AT PRESBYTERIAN THEOLOGICAL SEMINARIES. USA CITIZEN OR LEGAL RESIDENT.

6-8 SCHOLARSHIPS PER YEAR. WRITE FOR COMPLETE INFORMATION.

597

NATIONAL HUMANITIES CENTER (POST-DOCTORAL FELLOWSHIPS)

PO BOX 12256; 7 ALEXANDER DR
RESEARCH TRIANGLE PARK NC 27709
919/549-0661

AMOUNT: STIPEND + TRAVEL EXPENSES

DEADLINE(S): OCT 15

FIELD(S): HISTORY; LANGUAGES & LITERATURE; PHILOSOPHY; OTHER FIELDS IN THE LIBERAL ARTS

POST-DOCTORAL RESEARCH FELLOWSHIPS OPEN TO YOUNG & SENIOR SCHOLARS FROM ANY NATION. AWARDS SUPPORT RESEARCH & WRITING AT THE CENTER. SCHOLARS FROM OTHER AREAS SUCH AS NATURAL SCIENCES; ARTS; PROFESSIONS & PUBLIC LIFE ALSO MAY APPLY.

30-35 FELLOWSHIPS PER YEAR. WRITE FOR COMPLETE INFORMATION.

598

NORTH AMERICAN BAPTIST SEMINARY (FINANCIAL AID GRANTS)

1321 WEST 22ND STREET
SIOUX FALLS SD 57105
605/336-6588

AMOUNT: UP TO $1900

DEADLINE(S): NONE

FIELD(S): THEOLOGY

FINANCIAL AID GRANTS ARE OPEN TO STUDENTS WHO ARE ENROLLED FULL TIME AT NORTH AMERICAN BAPTIST SEMINARY. FINANCIAL NEED IS A CONSIDERATION.

APPROX 70 AWARDS PER YEAR. WRITE FOR COMPLETE INFORMATION.

599

PRESBYTERIAN CHURCH-USA (GRADUATE STUDY GRANTS)

CHURCH VOCATIONS UNIT;
100 WITHERSPOON ST
LOUISVILLE KY 40202
502/569-5760

AMOUNT: $500 TO $1000

DEADLINE(S): NONE SPECIFIED

FIELD(S): THEOLOGY

OPEN TO COMMUNICANT MEMBERS OF THE PRESBYTERIAN CHURCH (USA) WHO ARE GRADUATE STUDENTS IN PURSUIT OF ORDINATION OR OTHER PROFESSIONAL CHURCH OCCUPATIONS. MUST BE USA CITIZEN OR PERMANENT RESIDENT AND DEMONSTRATE FINANCIAL NEED.

NO GRANTS ARE AVAILABLE FOR DOCTORAL STUDY. WRITE FOR COMPLETE INFORMATION.

600

PRESBYTERIAN CHURCH-USA (NATIVE AMERICAN SEMINARY SCHOLARSHIPS)

CHURCH VOCATIONS UNIT;
100 WITHERSPOON ST
LOUISVILLE KY 40202
502/569-5760

AMOUNT: UP TO $1000

DEADLINE(S): NONE SPECIFIED

FIELD(S): THEOLOGY

OPEN TO USA CITIZENS OR PERMANENT RESIDENTS WHO ARE PRESBYTERIAN AND CAN DEMONSTRATE SIGNIFICANT FINANCIAL NEED. FOR FULL TIME GRADUATE STUDY IN PREPARATION FOR A CHURCH OCCUPATION.

WRITE FOR COMPLETE INFORMATION.

601

PRESBYTERIAN CHURCH-USA (RACIAL/ETHNIC LEADERSHIP SUPPLEMENTAL GRANTS)

CHURCH VOCATIONS UNIT;
100 WITHERSPOON ST.
LOUISVILLE KY 40202
502/569-5760

AMOUNT: $1000 MAXIMUM

DEADLINE(S): NONE SPECIFIED

FIELD(S): THEOLOGY

OPEN TO COMMUNICANT MEMBERS OF THE PRESBYTERIAN CHURCH WHO ARE OF ASIAN; BLACK; HISPANIC OR NATIVE AMERICAN HERITAGE. FOR GRADUATE STUDY AT A PC PRESBYTERY IN PURSUIT OF FIRST PROFESSIONAL DEGREE AND A CHURCH OCCUPATION.

MUST BE USA CITIZEN OR PERMANENT RESIDENT AND DEMONSTRATE UNUSUAL FINANCIAL NEED. WRITE FOR COMPLETE INFORMATION.

602

ROBERT SCHRECK MEMORIAL FUND (GRANTS)

C/O TEXAS COMMERCE BANK-TRUST DEPT; PO DRAWER 140
EL PASO TX 79980
915/546-6515

AMOUNT: $500 - $1500

DEADLINE(S): JUL 15; NOV 15

FIELD(S): MEDICINE; VETERINARY MEDICINE; PHYSICS; CHEMISTRY; ARCHITECTURE; ENGINEERING; EPISCOPAL CLERGY

GRANTS TO UNDERGRADUATE JUNIORS OR SENIORS OR GRADUATE STUDENTS WHO HAVE BEEN RESIDENTS OF EL PASO COUNTY FOR AT LEAST TWO YEARS. MUST BE USA CITIZEN OR LEGAL RESIDENT AND HAVE A HIGH GRADE POINT AVERAGE. FINANCIAL NEED IS A CONSIDERATION.

WRITE FOR COMPLETE INFORMATION.

603

SANDEE THOMPSON MEMORIAL SCHOLARSHIP FOUNDATION (SCHOLARSHIPS)

1211 NAPOLEON MANOR NE
LAWRENCEVILLE GA 30243
WRITTEN INQUIRY ONLY

AMOUNT: $500

DEADLINE(S): MAR 15

FIELD(S): MEDICINE; NURSING; PHYSICAL THERAPY; RELIGION

OPEN TO UNDERGRADUATE AND GRADUATE STUDENTS HAVING AN INTEREST IN SERVING HUMANINTY AND RELIEVING HUMAN SUFFERING. MUST HAVE MEDICAL OR RELIGIOUS ORIENTED CAREER GOAL WITH PHYSICAL THERAPY A HIGH PREFERENCE.

STUDENTS SHOULD BE ENTERING AT LEAST JUNIOR YEAR AT AN ACCREDITED COLEGE OR UNIVERSITY. FINANCIAL INFORMATION REQUIRED. SEND STAMPED; SELF ADDRESSED ENVELOPE FOR COMPLETE INFORMATION.

PHILOSOPHY

604

UNITARIAN UNIVERSALIST ASSN (GRADUATE THEOLOGICAL SCHOLARSHIPS)

25 BEACON ST
BOSTON MASS 02108
617-742-2100

AMOUNT: $1000 - $1500

DEADLINE(S): APR 15

FIELD(S): THEOLOGY

FINANCIAL AID TO STUDENTS WHO HAVE COMPLETED FIRST YEAR OF THEOLOGICAL PROGRAM AT GRAD LEVEL. MUST HAVE REGISTERED THEIR INTENTIONS WITH THE UNITARIAN UNIVERSALIST ASSOCIATION TO BECOME UNITARIAN UNIVERSALIST MINISTERS.

55 AWARDS PER YEAR. WRITE FOR COMPLETE INFORMATION.

605

VERNE CATT MCDOWELL CORPORATION (SCHOLARSHIPS FOR GRADUATE THEOLOGICAL EDUCATION)

PO BOX 128
ALBANY OR 97321
503/928-5955

AMOUNT: VARIES

DEADLINE(S): NONE

FIELD(S): THEOLOGY

OPEN TO MEN & WOMEN FOR GRADUATE THEOLOGICAL STUDIES. APPLICANTS MUST BE MEMBERS OF THE CHRISTIAN CHURCH (DISCIPLES OF CHRIST) & PLAN TO BE ORDAINED IN THE CHURCH. MEMBERS OF THE ALBANY ORE. FIRST CHRISTIAN CHURCH WILL BE GIVEN PREFERENCE.

RECIPIENTS AGREE TO REPAY THE FUNDS IF THEY DO NOT COMPLETE SEMINARY AND ENTER THE ORDAINED MINISTRY OF THE CHRISTIAN CHURCH (DISCIPLES OF CHRIST). WRITE FOR COMPLETE INFORMATION.

606

VIRGINIA BAPTIST GENERAL BOARD (JULIAN A HUDGENS TRUST FUND)

PO BOX 8568
RICHMOND VA 23226
WRITTEN INQUIRY

AMOUNT: VARIES

DEADLINE(S): AUG 1

FIELD(S): THEOLOGY

LOANS TO VIRGINIA RESIDENTS WHO ARE ENROLLED AS A GRADUATE STUDENT AT A SOUTHERN BAPTIST CONVENTION SCHOOL; STUDYING TO BECOME A SOUTHERN BAPTIST MINISTER & A MEMBER OF A CHURCH ASSOCIATED WITH BAPTIST GENERAL ASSOCIATION OF VIRGINIA.

LOANS DO NOT HAVE TO BE REPAID IF RECIPIENT WORKS IN THE MINISTRY FOR TWO YEARS. WRITE FOR COMPLETE INFORMATION.

607

WOMAN'S NATIONAL AUXILIARY CONVENTION (MEMORIAL STUDENT LOAN FUND)

PO BOX 1088
NASHVILLE TN 37202
615/361-1010

AMOUNT: VARIES

DEADLINE(S): NONE

FIELD(S): BIBLE

LOANS AT 7% INTEREST OPEN TO STUDENTS IN THE SECOND AND FOLLOWING YEARS AT FREE WILL BAPTIST BIBLE COLLEGE. INTEREST PAYMENTS BEGIN 1 YEAR FROM DATE OF LOAN AND PAYMENTS ON PRINCIPAL 3 MONTHS AFTER GRADUATION OR WITHDRAWAL FROM COLLEGE.

WRITE TO EXECUTIVE SECRETARY-TREASURER MARY R. WISEHART AT ADDRESS ABOVE FOR COMPLETE INFORMATION.

608

WORLD VISION INTERNATIONAL (INTERNATIONAL SCHOLARSHIPS)

919 WEST HUNTINGTON DR
MONROVIA CA 91016
818/303-8811

AMOUNT: $1000 - $4000

DEADLINE(S): MAR 31

FIELD(S): THEOLOGY; DEVELOPMENT; HOLISTIC EDUCATION

CHRISTIAN FAITH. INTERNATIONAL SCHOLARSHIPS FOR GRADUATE STUDY OPEN TO STUDENTS WHO WISH TO STUDY FOR THE MINISTRY IN A COUNTRY OTHER THAN THEIR OWN. PREFERENCE TO (BUT NOT LIMITED TO) CITIZENS OF DEVELOPING COUNTRIES.

APPROX 40 AWARDS PER YEAR. FINANCIAL NEED IS A CONSIDERATION. WRITE FOR COMPLETE INFORMATION.

SCHOOL OF NATURAL RESOURCES

609

CONGRESSIONAL FELLOWSHIP PROGRAM (MORRIS K. UDALL FELLOWSHIPS)

CONGRESS OF THE UNITED STATES; OFFICE OF
TECHNOLOGY ASSESSMENT
WASHINGTON DC 20510
202/224-8713

AMOUNT: $35000 - $70000

DEADLINE(S): JAN 31

FIELD(S): PHYSICAL OR BIOLOGICAL SCIENCES;
ENGINEERING; LAW; ECONOMICS;
ENVIRONMENTAL OR SOCIAL SCIENCES;
PUBLIC POLICY

ONE YEAR FELLOWSHIP PROGRAM HELD -ONLY-
IN WASHINGTO DC. CANDIDATES MUST
HAVE EXTENSIVE EXPERIENCE IN SCIENCE
OR TECHNOLOGY ISSUES OR HAVE
COMPLETED DOCTORAL LEVEL RESEARCH.
EXCEPTIONAL COMPETENCY IN ABOVE
AREAS REQUIRED.

CONSIDERATIONS INCLUDE ACHIEVEMENT
RECORDS AND CANDIDATE'S POTENTIAL IN
ONE OR MORE OF OTA'S ASSESSMENT
STUDIES. WRITE FOR COMPLETE
INFORMATION.

610

FLORIDA ENDOWMENT FUND FOR HIGHER EDUCATION (MCKNIGHT DOCTORAL FELLOWSHIP PROGRAM)

201 E.KENNEDY BLVD; SUITE 1525
TAMPA FL 33602
813/272-2772

AMOUNT: $11000 STIPEND + $5000 TUITION &
FEES (PER YEAR)

DEADLINE(S): JAN 15

FIELD(S): ALL FIELDS (EXCEPT LAW; MEDICINE
& EDUCATION)

OPEN TO ALL AFRICAN-AMERICANS WITH AT
LEAST A BACHELOR'S DEGREE FROM AN
ACCREDITED INSTITUTION WHO WISH TO
PURSUE A DOCTORAL DEGREE. PROGRAM
RECRUITS NATIONWIDE; HOWEVER
FELLOWS MUST ENROLL IN A FLORIDA
INSTITUTION. USA CITIZEN.

25 AWARDS PER YEAR. RENEWABLE FOR UP TO 5
YEARS. WRITE FOR COMPLETE
INFORMATION.

611

INSTITUTE FOR ADVANCED STUDY (POST-DOCTORAL FELLOWSHIP AWARDS)

OLDEN LANE
PRINCETON NJ 08540
609-734-8000

AMOUNT: VARIES ACCORDING TO SCHOOL

DEADLINE(S): CHECK WITH SCHOOL

FIELD(S): HISTORICAL STUDIES; SOCIAL
SCIENCES; NATURAL SCIENCES;
MATHEMATICS

POST-DOCTORAL FELLOWSHIPS AT THE
INSTITUTE FOR ADVANCED STUDY FOR
THOSE WHOSE TERM CAN BE EXPECTED TO
RESULT IN A WORK OF SIGNIFICANCE AND
INDIVIDUALITY.

150-160 FELLOWSHIPS PER ACADEMIC YEAR
ALTHOUGH SOME CAN BE EXTENDED.
REQUEST APPLICATION MATERIALS FROM
SCHOOL'S ADMINISTRATIVE OFFICER.

612

NATIONAL FEDERATION OF THE BLIND (HOWARD BROWN RICKARD SCHOLARSHIP)

814 4TH AVE #200
GRINNELL IA 50112
515/236-3366

AMOUNT: $2500

DEADLINE(S): MAR 31

FIELD(S): NATURAL SCIENCES; ARCHITECTURE;
ENGINEERING; MEDICINE; LAW

SCHOLARSHIPS FOR UNDERGRADUATE OR
GRADUATE STUDY IN THE ABOVE AREAS.
OPEN TO LEGALLY BLIND STUDENTS
ENROLLED FULL TIME AT ACCREDITED POST
SECONDARY INSTITUTIONS.

AWARDS BASED ON ACADEMIC EXCELLENCE;
SERVICE TO THE COMMUNITY AND
FINANCIAL NEED. WRITE FOR COMPLETE
INFORMATION.

613

NATIONAL RESEARCH COUNCIL (NATIONAL SCIENCE FOUNDATION MINORITY GRADUATE FELLOWSHIPS)

2101 CONSTITUTION AVE.
WASHINGTON DC 20418
202/334-2872

AMOUNT: $14000 STIPEND (12 MONTHS) + UP TO
$7500 FOR TUITION AND FEES

DEADLINE(S): NOV 6

FIELD(S): ENGINEERING; MATHEMATICS;
COMPUTER SCIENCE; CHEMISTRY; EARTH
SCIENCES; LIFE SCIENCES; PSYCHOLOGY;
SOCIAL SCIENCES

OPEN MINORITY GRADUATE STUDENTS
(MASTERS OR PH.D) WHO ARE USA CITIZENS
OR LEGAL RESIDENTS & ARE AT OR NEAR
THE BEGINNING OF THEIR GRADUATE
STUDY. FELLOWSHIPS TENABLE AT
ACCREDITED INSTITUTION OFFERING
ADVANCED DEGREES IN THE FIELDS ABOVE.

SCHOOL OF NATURAL RESOURCES

APPROX 150 NEW 3-YEAR FELLOWSHIPS AWARDED EACH YEAR. WRITE FOR COMPLETE INFORMATION.

614

NORTH ATLANTIC TREATY ORGANIZATION (NATO SCIENCE FELLOWSHIPS FOR USA CITIZENS)

B-1110; SCIENCE AFFAIRS DIV
BRUSSELS BELGIUM
2 728-41-11

AMOUNT: VARIES WITH COUNTRY

DEADLINE(S): NOV 1

FIELD(S): SCIENCES

GRADUATE & POST-DOCTORAL FELLOWSHIPS IN ALMOST ALL SCIENTIFIC AREAS; INCLUDING INTERDISCIPLINARY AREAS. OPEN TO USA CITIZENS WHO WISH TO STUDY AND/OR DO RESEARCH IN ANOTHER NATO MEMBER COUNTRY.

THE PROGRAM IS ADMINISTERED IN EACH NATO COUNTRY BY A NATIONAL ADMINISTRATOR. WRITE FOR COMPLETE INFORMATION.

615

ORGANIZATION OF AMERICAN STATES DEPT OF FELLOWSHIPS & TRAINING (OAS PRA-FELLOWSHIPS)

TRAINEE SELECTION DIVISION
WASHINGTON DC 20006
202/789-3902

AMOUNT: TUITION + FEES; TRAVEL EXP & STIPEND

DEADLINE(S): APR 30; AUG 31

FIELD(S): ALL FIELDS EXCEPT MEDICINE & FOREIGN LANGUAGES

GRADUATE FELLOWSHIPS FOR USA CITIZENS OR PERMANENT RESIDENTS TO STUDY IN AN OAS MEMBER COUNTRY. MUST HAVE UNDERGRADUATE DEGREE AND HAVE DEMONSTRATED ABILITY TO PURSUE ADVANCED STUDIES IN CHOSEN FIELD.

APPLICANTS SHOULD BE FLUENT IN LANGUAGE OF COUNTRY OF INTENDED STUDY. PRIORITY IS GIVEN TO RESEARCH PROJECTS. WRITE FOR COMPLETE INFORMATION.

616

RESOURCES FOR THE FUTURE (GILBERT F. WHITE FELLOWSHIP PROGRAM)

1616 'P' STREET NW
WASHINGTON DC 20036
202/328-5067

AMOUNT: $35000 STIPEND + $1000 MOVING/ LIVING EXPENSES

DEADLINE(S): MAR 1

FIELD(S): SOCIAL SCIENCES; NATURAL RESOURCES; ENERGY; ENVIRONMENT

POST-DOCTORAL RESIDENT FELLOWSHIPS FOR YOUNG PROFESSIONALS WHO WISH TO DEVOTE A YEAR TO SCHOLARLY WORK ON A SOCIAL OR POLICY PROBLEM IN AREAS OF NATURAL RESOURCES; ENERGY OR ENVIRONMENT. FACULTY MEMBERS ON SABBATICAL ENCOURAGED TO APPLY.

FELLOWSHIPS AWARDED FOR A MINIMUM OF 9 MOS.; MAXIMUM OF 12 MOS. ADDRESS INQUIRIES TO FELLOWSHIP DIRECTOR.

617

RESOURCES FOR THE FUTURE (SMALL GRANTS PROGRAM)

1616 'P' STREET NW
WASHINGTON DC 20036
202/328-5067

AMOUNT: $30000 MAXIMUM

DEADLINE(S): MAR 1

FIELD(S): NATURAL RESOURCES; ENERGY; ENVIRONMENTAL ISSUES

POST-DOCTORAL RESEARCH GRANTS OPEN TO RESEARCHERS OF ALL NATIONALITIES. PROPOSALS MAY ORIGINATE IN THE HUMANITIES; SOCIAL OR NATURAL SCIENCES & MAY BE THEORETICAL OR APPLIED RESEARCH. 2 MONTHS - 2 YEARS. ONGOING PROJECTS ALSO CONSIDERED.

GRANTS CAN ONLY BE MADE THROUGH TAX-EXEMPT INSTITUTIONS. WRITE FOR COMPLETE INFORMATION.

618

SIGMA DELTA EPSILON-GRADUATE WOMEN IN SCIENCE (SDE FELLOWSHIPS; ELOISE GERRY FELLOWSHIPS)

ONE ILLINOIS CENTER;
111 E. WACKER DR.
CHICAGO IL 60601
312/616-0800

AMOUNT: $2600 - $4000 (SDE); $2300 - $2700 (ELOISE GERRY)

DEADLINE(S): DEC 1 (POSTMARK)

FIELD(S): BIOLOGY; CHEMISTRY; NATURAL SCIENCES; PHYSICAL SCIENCES; BIOLOGICAL SCIENCES; COMPUTER SCIENCES

WOMEN ONLY. OPEN TO GRADUATE STUDENTS AND POST-DOCTORAL RESEARCHERS IN THE ABOVE AREAS. FELLOWSHIPS MAY ONLY BE USED TO SUPPORT SCIENTIFIC RESEARCH AND/OR PROJECTS. FINANCIAL NEED IS A MAJOR CONSIDERATION.

ELOISE GERRY FELLOWSHIPS ARE LIMITED TO THE CHEMICAL AND BIOLOGICAL SCIENCES. WRITE FOR COMPLETE INFORMATION.

619

SLOCUM-LUNZ FOUNDATION (SCHOLARSHIPS & GRANTS)

PO BOX 12559; 205 FORT JOHNSON
CHARLESTON SC 29422
803/762-5052

AMOUNT: UP TO $2000

DEADLINE(S): APR 1

FIELD(S): NATURAL SCIENCES; MARINE SCIENCES

OPEN TO BEGINNING GRADUATE STUDENTS & PH.D CANDIDATES ENROLLED AT INSTITUTIONS LOCATED IN SOUTH CAROLINA. AWARDS SUPPORT RESEARCH STUDIES IN THE ABOVE AREAS.

ACADEMIC WORK MUST BE PERFORMED IN SOUTH CAROLINA. WRITE FOR COMPLETE INFORMATION.

620

SOIL AND WATER CONSERVATION SOCIETY (KENNETH E GRANT RESEARCH SCHOLARSHIP)

7515 NORTHEAST ANKENY ROAD
ANKENY IA 50021
515/289-2331; FAX 515/289-1227

AMOUNT: $1000

DEADLINE(S): APR 1

FIELD(S): CONSERVATION

RESEARCH GRANT FOR MEMBERS OF THE SOCIETY FOR GRADUATE-LEVEL RESEARCH ON A SPECIFIC TOPIC OF INTEREST TO THE SOCIETY THAT WILL CONTRIBUTE TO THE SCIENCE AND ART OF GOOD LAND OR WATER USE.

STUDY MAY BE DEVELOPED AS PART OR ALL OF THE REQUIREMENTS FOR A MASTERS OR PH.D. THESIS OR IT MAY BE SEPARATE FROM FORMAL COURSE WORK. WRITE FOR THIS YEAR'S TOPIC AND COMPLETE INFORMATION.

621

U.S. DEPT. OF EDUCATION (INDIAN FELLOWSHIP PROGRAM)

400 MARYLAND AVENUE SW; RM 2177; MAIL STOP 6335
WASHINGTON DC 20202
202/401-1902

AMOUNT: $1000 - $34000 (AVERAGE $13000)

DEADLINE(S): FEB 7

FIELD(S): BUSINESS ADMIN; ENGINEERING; NATURAL RESOURCES & RELATED AREAS

FELLOWSHIPS FOR AMERICAN INDIANS OR ALASKAN NATIVES WHO ARE US CITIZENS AND SEEKING UNDERGRADUATE OR GRADUATE DEGREES IN THE ABOVE FIELDS AT ACCREDITED INSTITUTIONS IN USA.

APPROXIMATELY 90 CONTINUATION AND 35 NEW AWARDS PER YEAR. WRITE FOR COMPLETE INFORMATION.

AGRICULTURE

622

ABBIE SARGENT MEMORIAL SCHOLARSHIP INC (SCHOLARSHIPS)

295 SHEEP DAVIS ROAD
CONCORD NH 03301
603/224-1934

AMOUNT: $200

DEADLINE(S): MAR 15

FIELD(S): AGRICULTURE; VETERINARY MEDICINE; HOME ECONOMICS

OPEN TO NEW HAMPSHIRE RESIDENT WHO IS HIGH SCHOOL GRADUATE WITH GOOD GRADES AND CHARACTER. FOR UNDERGRADUATE OR GRADUATE STUDY. USA LEGAL RESIDENT. DEMONSTRATE FINANCIAL NEED.

RENEWABLE WITH REAPPLICATION. WRITE FOR COMPLETE INFORMATION.

623

AMERICAN ORCHID SOCIETY (GRANTS FOR ORCHID RESEARCH)

6000 SOUTH OLIVE AVE
WEST PALM BEACH FL 33405
407/585-8666

AMOUNT: UP TO $10000 PER YEAR FOR UP TO 3 YEARS

DEADLINE(S): JAN 1; AUG 1

FIELD(S): BOTANY; HORTICULTURE

GRANTS FOR EXPERIMENTAL PROJECTS AND FUNDAMENTAL & APPLIED RESEARCH ON ORCHIDS. QUALIFIED GRADUATE STUDENTS WITH APPROPRIATE INTERESTS MAY APPLY FOR GRANTS IN SUPPORT OF THEIR RESEARCH IF IT INVOLVES OR APPLIES TO ORCHIDS.

POST GRADUATES MAY APPLY -ONLY- ON BEHALF OF THE ACCREDITED INSTITUTION OF HIGHER LEARNING OR APPROPRIATE RESEARCH INSTITUTE THEY REPRESENT. WRITE FOR COMPLETE INFORMATION.

624

ANIMAL HEALTH TRUST (BLOUNT MEMORIAL FUND SCHOLARSHIP)

HEAD OF FINANCE; PO BOX 5
NEWMARKET SUFFOLK C88 7DW ENGLAND
0638-661111

AMOUNT: 5000 POUNDS STERLING

DEADLINE(S): MAR 31

FIELD(S): ANIMAL HEALTH

SCHOLARSHIPS TO STUDY ALL ASPECTS OF ANIMAL HEALTH. FOR GRADUATE STUDY AT AGREED CENTERS IN THE UNITED KINGDOM.

SCHOLARSHIP RENEWABLE FOR UP TO THREE YEARS. WRITE FOR COMPLETE INFORMATION.

625

BEDDING PLANTS FOUNDATION INC (HAROLD BETTINGER MEMORIAL SCHOLARSHIP)

PO BOX 27241
LANSING MI 48909
517/694-8537

AMOUNT: $1000

DEADLINE(S): APR 1

FIELD(S): HORTICULTURE

OPEN TO UNDERGRADUATE & GRADUATE HORTICULTURE MAJORS WITH BUSINESS AND/OR MARKETING EMPHASIS OR BUSINESS AND/OR MARKETING MAJORS WITH HORTICULTURE EMPHASIS. AWARDS TENABLE AT ACCREDITED 4-YEAR COLLEGES & UNIVERSITIES IN THE USA OR CANADA.

RENEWABLE. FINANCIAL NEED IS A CONSIDERATION. WRITE FOR COMPLETE INFORMATION.

626

BEDDING PLANTS FOUNDATION INC (JAMES K. RATHMELL JR. MEMORIAL SCHOLARSHIP)

PO BOX 27241
LANSING MI 48909
517/694-8537

AMOUNT: UP TO $2000

DEADLINE(S): APR 1

FIELD(S): HORTICULTURE

OPEN TO SERIOUS UNDERGRADUATE OR GRADUATE COLLEGE STUDENTS FOR WORK/ STUDY PROGRAMS OUTSIDE THE USA OR CANADA IN THE FIELD OF FLORICULTURE OR HORTICULTURE. PREFERENCE TO THOSE PLANNING PROGRAMS OF SIX MONTHS OR MORE.

USA CITIZEN. FINANCIAL NEED IS A CONSIDERATION. WRITE FOR COMPLETE INFORMATION.

627

BEDDING PLANTS FOUNDATION INC (JOHN CAREW MEMORIAL SCHOLARSHIP)

PO BOX 27241
LANSING MI 48909
517/694-8537

AMOUNT: $1500

DEADLINE(S): APR 1

FIELD(S): HORTICULTURE

OPEN TO GRADUATE STUDENTS MAJORING IN HORTICULTURE OR A RELATED FIELD WHO HAVE A SPECIFIC INTEREST IN BEDDING OR FLOWERING POTTED PLANTS. FOR STUDY IN THE USA OR CANADA.

RENEWABLE. FINANCIAL NEED IS A CONSIDERATION. WRITE FOR COMPLETE INFORMATION.

628

CHARLES A. LINDBERGH FUND INC. (GRANTS FOR RESEARCH PROJECTS)

708 S. THIRD ST.- SUITE 110
MINNEAPOLIS MN 55415
612/338-1703

AMOUNT: UP TO $10580

DEADLINE(S): JUN 15

FIELD(S): AVIATION/AEROSPACE; AGRICULTURE; ARTS & HUMANITIES; BIOMEDICAL RESEARCH; CONSERVATION; EXPLORATION; HEALTH & POPULATION SCIENCES; INTERCULTURAL COMMUNICATION; OCEANOGRAPHY; WASTE DISPOSAL MGMT; WATER RESOURCE MGMT; WILDLIFE PRESERVATION.

RESEARCH GRANTS ARE AWARDED ANNUALLY TO INDIVIDUALS WHOSE PROPOSED PROJECTS REPRESENT A SIGNIFICANT CONTRIBUTION TOWARD THE ACHIEVEMENT OF A BALANCE BETWEEN THE ADVANCE OF TECHNOLOGY & PRESERVATION OF THE NATURAL ENVIRONMENT.

WRITE FOR APPLICATION AND COMPLETE INFORMATION.

629

COMMITTEE ON INSTITUTIONAL COOPERATION (CIC PREDOCTORAL FELLOWSHIPS)

KIRKWOOD HALL RM 111; INDIANA UNIV.
BLOOMINGTON IN 47405
812/855-0822

AMOUNT: $9500 + TUITION (5 YEARS)

DEADLINE(S): JAN 2

FIELD(S): HUMANITIES; SOCIAL SCIENCES; NATURAL SCIENCES; MATHEMATICS; ENGINEERING

PREDOCTORAL FELLOWSHIPS FOR USA CITIZENS OF AFRICAN AMERICAN; AMERICAN INDIAN; MEXICAN AMERICAN OR PUERTO RICAN HERITAGE. MUST HOLD OR EXPECT TO RECEIVE BACHELOR'S DEGREE BY LATE SUMMER FROM A REGIONALLY ACCREDITED COLLEGE OR UNIVERSITY.

AWARDS FOR SPECIFIED UNIVERSITIES IN IL; IN; IA; MI; MN; OH; WI; PA. WRITE FOR DETAILS.

630

DOG WRITERS' EDUCATIONAL TRUST (SCHOLARSHIPS)

BERTA I PICKETT; PO BOX 2220
PAYSON AZ 85547
602/474-8867

AMOUNT: $1000

DEADLINE(S): DEC 31

FIELD(S): VETERINARY MEDICINE; ANIMAL BEHAVIOR; JOURNALISM

OPEN TO APPLICANTS WHOSE PARENTS; GRANDPARENTS OR OTHER CLOSE RELATIVES (OR THE APPLICANT) ARE OR HAVE BEEN INVOLVED IN THE WORLD OF DOGS AS EXHIBITORS; BREEDERS; HANDLERS; JUDGES; CLUB OFFICERS OR OTHER ACTIVITIES.

SCHOLARSHIPS SUPPORT UNDERGRADUATE OR GRADUATE STUDY. 10 AWARDS PER YEAR. SEND SELF ADDRESSED STAMPED ENVELOPE FOR COMPLETE INFORMATION AND APPLICATION.

631

GOLF COURSE SUPERINTENDENTS ASSOCIATION OF AMERICA (GCSAA SCHOLARSHIPS)

1421 RESEARCH PARK DRIVE
LAWRENCE KS 66049
913/841-2240

AMOUNT: $1000 - $5000

DEADLINE(S): OCT 1

FIELD(S): TURFGRASS MANAGEMENT

OPEN TO APPLICANTS WHO HAVE COMPLETED THE 1ST YEAR OF A 2-YEAR PROGRAM; THE 2ND YEAR OF A 4-YEAR PROGRAM OR ARE ENROLLED IN A GRADUATE PROGRAM. USA CITIZEN OR LEGAL RESIDENT.

5-10 SCHOLARSHIPS PER YEAR. RENEWABLE. WRITE FOR COMPLETE INFORMATION.

632

INTERNATIONAL SOCIETY OF ARBORICULTURE (RESEARCH TRUST)

DR FRANCIS W HOLMES;
24 BERKSHIRE TERRACE
AMHERST MA 01002
413/549-1226

AMOUNT: $2500

DEADLINE(S): DEC 1

FIELD(S): HORTICULTURE; BOTANY; ENTOMOLOGY; PHYTOPATHOLOGY

OPEN TO HORTICULTURISTS; PLANT PATHOLOGISTS; ENTOMOLOGISTS; SOIL SPECIALISTS AND OTHERS ENGAGING IN THE SCIENTIFIC STUDY OF SHADE TREES.

PROPOSALS MUST BE RECEIVED BY DEC 1. WRITE FOR COMPLETE INFORMATION.

633

NATIONAL COUNCIL OF FARMER COOPERATIVES (GRADUATE AWARDS)

50 'F' STREET NW; SUITE 900
WASHINGTON DC 20001
202/626-8700

AMOUNT: $1000; $800 & $600

DEADLINE(S): APR 15

FIELD(S): AGRICULTURE

NCFC OFFERS 3 AWARDS FOR GRAD THESES AND DISSERTATIONS ON TOPICS CONCERNED WITH AGRICULTURAL COOPERATIVES. AWARD INCLUDES EXPENSE PAID TRIP TO THE NATIONAL INSTITUTE ON COOPERATIVE EDUCATION IN JULY TO RECEIVE AWARD; PRESENT PAPER.

EACH ENTRY MUST BE ACCOMPANIED BY A REGISTRATION FORM WHICH IS AVAILABLE FROM NCFC AND MUST BE POSTMARKED BY APRIL 15.

634

NATIONAL JUNIOR HORTICULTURAL ASSOCIATION (SCOTTISH GARDENING SCHOLARSHIP)

401 N. 4TH
DURANT OK 74701
WRITTEN INQUIRY

AMOUNT: TRANSPORTATION; STIPEND; FOOD AND LODGING

DEADLINE(S): OCT 1

FIELD(S): HORTICULTURE

PROGRAM PROVIDES A 1-YEAR HORTICULTURAL STUDY & WORK EXPERIENCE PROGRAM IN SCOTLAND AT THE THREAVE SCHOOL OF PRACTICAL GARDENING. PREVIOUS WORK IN HORTICULTURE IS ESSENTIAL. MUST BE BETWEEN 18 AND 21 AND A USA CITIZEN.

WRITE FOR PROGRAM OUTLINE AND COMPLETE INFORMATION.

AGRICULTURE

635

PROFESSIONAL GROUNDS MANAGEMENT SOCIETY (SCHOLARSHIPS)

10402 RIDGELAND ROAD; SUITE 4
COCKEYSVILLE MD 21030
410/667-1833

AMOUNT: UP TO $1000

DEADLINE(S): JUL 1

FIELD(S): GROUNDS MANAGEMENT OR A CLOSELY RELATED FIELD

OPEN TO UNDERGRADUATE OR GRADUATE STUDENTS INTERESTED IN THE GREENS INDUSTRY; GROUNDS MANAGEMENT OR A CLOSELY RELATED FIELD. SOCIETY MEMBERSHIP IS NOT REQUIRED. USA OR CANADIAN CITIZEN.

WRITE FOR COMPLETE INFORMATION.

636

PURINA RESEARCH AWARDS COMMITTEE (PURINA MILLS RESEARCH FELLOWSHIP)

PO BOX 66812
ST LOUIS MO 63166-6812
314/768-4614

AMOUNT: $12500

DEADLINE(S): FEB 1

FIELD(S): ANIMAL; DAIRY OR POULTRY SCIENCE

OPEN TO ANY GRADUATE STUDENT AT ANY RECOGNIZED AGRICULTURAL SCHOOL IN THE USA. AWARDS SUPPORT ANIMAL NUTRITION & PHYSIOLOGY RESEARCH AS APPLIED TO DAIRY; POULTRY OR ANIMAL SCIENCE.

4 AWARDS PER YEAR. WRITE FOR COMPLETE INFORMATION.

637

UNITED AGRIBUSINESS LEAGUE (UAL SCHOLARSHIP PROGRAM)

54 CORPORATE PARK
IRVINE CA 92714
714/975-1424

AMOUNT: $2000 - $3500

DEADLINE(S): MAR 31

FIELD(S): AGRICULTURE; AGRIBUSINESS

OPEN TO UAL MEMBER EMPLOYEES & THEIR DEPENDENT CHILDREN. AWARDS SUPPORT UNDERGRADUATE OR GRADUATE STUDY IN THE ABOVE AREAS AT RECOGNIZED COLLEGES & UNIVERSITIES.

AWARDS RENEWABLE. WRITE FOR COMPLETE INFORMATION.

638

UNIVERSITY OF DELAWARE (LONGWOOD GRADUATE PROGRAM FELLOWSHIPS)

153 TOWNSEND HALL
NEWARK DE 19717
302/831-2517

AMOUNT: $9471 - $9945

DEADLINE(S): DEC 31

FIELD(S): PUBLIC HORTICULTURE ADMINISTRATION

OPEN TO GRADUATE STUDENTS AT THE UNIVERSITY OF DELAWARE WHO ARE SEEKING A MASTER'S DEGREE IN PUBLIC HORTICULTURE ADMINISTRATION. A GRADE POINT AVERAGE OF 3.0 OR BETTER IS REQUIRED. PRACTICAL EXPERIENCE IS OFFERED AT LONGWOOD GARDENS.

UP TO 5 FELLOWSHIPS PER YEAR. WRITE FOR COMPLETE INFORMATION.

639

WOMAN'S NATIONAL FARM AND GARDEN ASSOCIATION (SARAH TYSON MEMORIAL FELLOWSHIPS)

C/O MRS ELMER BRAUN; 13 DAVIS DR
SAGINAW MI 48602
517/793-1714

AMOUNT: $500

DEADLINE(S): APR 1

FIELD(S): AGRICULTURE; HORTICULTURE & ALLIED SUBJECTS

WOMEN ONLY. FELLOWSHIPS FOR GRADUATE RESEARCH IN THE ABOVE AREAS AT AN ACCREDITED INSTITUTION OF HIGHER LEARNING IN THE USA. MUST DEMONSTRATE FINANCIAL NEED.

WRITE FOR COMPLETE INFORMATION.

640

WORCESTER COUNTY HORTICULTURAL SOCIETY (SCHOLARSHIP PROGRAM)

TOWER HILL BOTANIC GARDEN
BOYLSTON MA 01505
508/869-6111

AMOUNT: $500 - $2000

DEADLINE(S): MAY 1

FIELD(S): HORTICULTURE

OPEN TO UNDERGRADUATES IN THEIR JUNIOR OR SENIOR YEAR AND TO GRADUATE STUDENTS WHO RESIDE IN NEW ENGLAND OR ATTEND A NEW ENGLAND COLLEGE OR UNIVERSITY AND ARE MAJORING IN HORTICULTURE OR A HORTICULTURE RELATED FIELD.

SELECTIONS BASED ON INTEREST IN
HORTICULTURE; SINCERITY OF PURPOSE;
ACADEMIC PERFORMANCE; FINANCIAL
NEED. WRITE FOR COMPLETE INFORMATION.

EARTH SCIENCE

641 ——————————————

**AMERICAN ASSOCIATION OF PETROLEUM
GEOLOGISTS (GRANTS-IN-AID)**

C/O W.A. MORGAN; PO BOX 979
TULSA OK 74101
918/584-2555 EXT 239

AMOUNT: $2000 MAX ($500 - $1740 AVG)

DEADLINE(S): JAN 15

FIELD(S): PETROLEUM GEOLOGY; GEOLOGY;
GEOPHYSICS; PALEONTOLOGY

GRANTS IN SUPPORT OF RESEARCH PROJECTS
LEADING TO THE MASTERS OR DOCTORAL
DEGREE. PREFERENCE TO PROJECTS
RELATED TO THE SEARCH FOR
HYDROCARBONS; ECONOMIC SEDIMENTARY
MINERALS OR ENVIRONMENTAL GEOLOGY.

50 GRANTS PER YEAR. WRITE FOR COMPLETE
INFORMATION.

642 ——————————————

**AMERICAN ASSOCIATION OF UNIVERSITY
WOMEN - HONOLULU BRANCH (HARTT
FELLOWSHIP FOR GRADUATE WOMEN IN
SCIENCE)**

1802 KEEAUMOKU ST
HONOLULU HI 96822
808/537-4702

AMOUNT: $2000

DEADLINE(S): MAY 1

FIELD(S): NATURAL OR PHYSICAL SCIENCES

OPEN TO A FEMALE WHO IS A BONA FIDE
RESIDENT OF HAWAII AND IS ENROLLED IN
AN ADVANCED DEGREE (PH.D) PROGRAM IN
THE NATURAL OR PHYSICAL SCIENCES.
MUST SHOW OUTSTANDING ABILITY AND
DEMONSTRATE FINANCIAL NEED.

WRITE FOR COMPLETE INFORMATION.

643 ——————————————

**AMERICAN GEOLOGICAL INSTITUTE
(MINORITY PARTICIPATION PROGRAM
SCHOLARSHIPS)**

4220 KING ST
ALEXANDRIA VA 22302
703/379-2480

AMOUNT: UP TO $10000 PER YEAR UNDERGRAD;
$4000 PER YEAR GRAD

DEADLINE(S): FEB 1

FIELD(S): EARTH SCIENCES; SPACE SCIENCES;
MARINE SCIENCES

FOR FULL TIME UNDERGRADUATE OR GRADUATE
STUDY IN THE ABOVE FIELDS. OPEN TO
AMERICAN BLACKS; NATIVE AMERICANS &
HISPANIC AMERICANS. MUST BE USA
CITIZEN AND DEMONSTRATE FINANCIAL
NEED.

APPROX 80 AWARDS PER YEAR. RENEWALS
POSSIBLE WITH REAPPLICATION. WRITE FOR
COMPLETE INFORMATION.

644 ——————————————

**AMERICAN GEOPHYSICAL UNION (HORTON
RESEARCH GRANT)**

2000 FLORIDA AVE NW
WASHINGTON DC 20009
202/462-6900

AMOUNT: $9000

DEADLINE(S): MAR 1

FIELD(S): HYDROLOGY

OPEN TO MEMBER OR STUDENT MEMBER OF AGU.
AWARDED ANNUALLY TO PH.D CANDIDATE
FOR SUPPORT OF DISSERTATION RESEARCH
ON HYDROLOGY & WATER RESOURCES.

WRITE FOR COMPLETE INFORMATION.

645 ——————————————

**AMERICAN PHILOSOPHICAL SOCIETY (JOHN
CLARKE SLATER FELLOWSHIP)**

LIBRARY; 105 S. FIFTH ST.
PHILADELPHIA PA 19106
WRITTEN INQUIRY ONLY

AMOUNT: $12000

DEADLINE(S): DEC 1

FIELD(S): HISTORY OF PHYSICAL SCIENCE

OPEN TO DOCTORAL CANDIDATES WHO HAVE
PASSED THEIR PRELIMINARY
EXAMINATIONS AND ARE WRITING
DISSERTATIONS ON THE HISTORY OF 20TH
CENTURY PHYSICAL SCIENCES.

WRITE FOR COMPLETE INFORMATION.

646 ——————————————

**AMERICAN PHILOSOPHICAL SOCIETY
(MICHAUX GRANTS IN FOREST BOTANY)**

104 S. 5TH ST.
PHILADELPHIA PA 19106
WRITTEN INQUIRY

AMOUNT: $1000 TO $5000

DEADLINE(S): FEB 1

FIELD(S): FORESTRY & SILVICULTURE

GRANTS FOR POST-DOCTORAL RESEARCH IN
SILVICULTURE AND FOREST BOTANY OR THE
HISTORY THEREOF.

WRITE FOR COMPLETE INFORMATION.

647

AMERICAN WATER WORKS ASSOCIATION (ACADEMIC ACHIEVEMENT AWARD)

6666 WEST QUINCY AVE
DENVER CO 80235
303/794-7711

AMOUNT: $500 - $1000

DEADLINE(S): OCT 1

FIELD(S): HYDROLOGY

AWARD FOR ANY MASTER'S THESIS OR DOCTORAL DISSERTATION THAT HAS POTENTIAL VALUE TO THE WATER SUPPLY INDUSTRY. THIS IS NOT A SCHOLARSHIP BUT A CASH AWARD FOR OUTSTANDING WORK THAT HAS BEEN COMPLETED.

WRITE FOR COMPLETE INFORMATION.

648

AMERICAN WATER WORKS ASSOCIATION (LARS SCHOLARSHIP)

6666 W. QUINCY
DENVER CO 80235
303/794-7711

AMOUNT: $3000 MASTERS; $5000 PH.D

DEADLINE(S): NOV 15 MASTERS; FEB 15 PH.D

FIELD(S): HYDROLOGY (WATER SUPPLY AND/OR TREATMENT)

OPEN TO CITIZENS OR PERMANENT RESIDENTS OF THE USA; MEXICO OR CANADA WHO ANTICIPATE COMPLETION OF THE REQUIREMENTS FOR A MASTER'S OR PH.D DEGREE WITHIN TWO YEARS OF THE AWARD. FOR STUDY OR RESEARCH INTO WATER SUPPLY AND/OR TREATMENT.

WRITE FOR COMPLETE INFORMATION.

649

ARGONNE NATIONAL LABORATORY (STUDENT RESEARCH PARTICIPATION PROGRAM; THESIS RESEARCH)

DIV OF EDUCATIONAL PROGRAMS;
9700 SOUTH CASS AVE
ARGONNE IL 60439
312/972-3366

AMOUNT: $200 PER WEEK STIPEND

DEADLINE(S): FEB 1; MAY 15; OCT 15

FIELD(S): PHYSICAL SCIENCES; LIFE SCIENCES; EARTH SCIENCES; MATHEMATICS; COMPUTER SCIENCES; ENGINEERING; FUSION & FISSION ENERGY

1-SEMESTER ACCREDITED INTERNSHIP PROGRAM TO PERMIT STUDENTS TO WORK IN ABOVE AREAS IN RELATION TO ENERGY DEVELOPMENT. OPEN TO FULL-TIME UNDERGRAD JUNIORS; SENIORS & 1ST YEAR GRAD STUDENTS. USA CITIZEN OR LEGAL RESIDENT.

THESIS RESEARCH AWARDS OPEN TO DOCTORAL CANDIDATES WORKING ON THEIR DISSERTATION. WRITE FOR COMPLETE INFORMATION.

650

ASSOCIATION OF ENGINEERING GEOLOGISTS (MARLIAVE FUND SCHOLARSHIPS)

323 BOSTON POST ROAD SUITE 2D
SUDBURY MA 01776
508/443-4639

AMOUNT: UP TO $1000

DEADLINE(S): FEB 1

FIELD(S): ENGINEERING GEOLOGY

GRADUATE SCHOLARSHIPS FOR AEG MEMBERS. AWARDS BASED ON ABILITY; SCHOLARSHIP; CHARACTER; EXTRACURRICULAR ACTIVITIES AND POTENTIAL FOR CONTRIBUTIONS TO THE PROFESSION.

WRITE FOR COMPLETE INFORMATION.

651

CAVE RESEARCH FOUNDATION (KARST RESEARCH FELLOWSHIP PROGRAM)

C/O DR.JOHN C. TINSLEY; US GEOLOGICAL SURVEY;
345 MIDDLEFIELD RD; M/S 975
MENLO PARK CA 94025
415/329-4928

AMOUNT: $3500

DEADLINE(S): JAN 31

FIELD(S): CAVE RESEARCH (KARST)

FELLOWSHIPS TO SUPPORT GRADUATE STUDY IN ANY KARST-RELATED DISCIPLINE; ANYWHERE IN THE WORLD. MERITORIOUS PROPOSALS THAT DO NOT RECEIVE FELLOWSHIPS MAY RECEIVE SMALLER GRANTS. ALL AWARDS MADE DIRECTLY TO STUDENT.

2-3 AWARDS PER YEAR. WRITE FOR COMPLETE INFORMATION.

652

CHARLES A. LINDBERGH FUND INC. (GRANTS FOR RESEARCH PROJECTS)

708 S. THIRD ST.- SUITE 110
MINNEAPOLIS MN 55415
612/338-1703

AMOUNT: UP TO $10580

DEADLINE(S): JUN 15

FIELD(S): AVIATION/AEROSPACE; AGRICULTURE; ARTS & HUMANITIES; BIOMEDICAL RESEARCH; CONSERVATION; EXPLORATION; HEALTH & POPULATION SCIENCES; INTERCULTURAL COMMUNICATION; OCEANOGRAPHY; WASTE DISPOSAL MGMT; WATER RESOURCE MGMT; WILDLIFE PRESERVATION.

RESEARCH GRANTS ARE AWARDED ANNUALLY TO INDIVIDUALS WHOSE PROPOSED PROJECTS REPRESENT A SIGNIFICANT CONTRIBUTION TOWARD THE ACHIEVEMENT OF A BALANCE BETWEEN THE ADVANCE OF TECHNOLOGY & PRESERVATION OF THE NATURAL ENVIRONMENT.

WRITE FOR APPLICATION AND COMPLETE INFORMATION.

653

ELECTROCHEMICAL SOCIETY (SUMMER RESEARCH FELLOWSHIPS)

10 SOUTH MAIN ST
PENNINGTON NJ 08534
609/737-1902

AMOUNT: $2000 - $6000

DEADLINE(S): JAN 15

FIELD(S): ENERGY; CHEMICAL ENGINEERING; CHEMISTRY; ELECTRICAL ENGINEERING

SUMMER FELLOWSHIPS OPEN TO GRADUATE STUDENTS AT ACCREDITED COLLEGES & UNIVERSITIES IN THE USA & CANADA. PURPOSE IS TO SUPPORT RESEARCH OF INTEREST TO ELECTROCHEMICAL SOCIETY & RESEARCH AIMED AT REDUCING ENERGY CONSUMPTION.

WRITE FOR COMPLETE INFORMATION.

654

EPPLEY FOUNDATION FOR RESEARCH (POST-DOCTORAL RESEARCH GRANTS)

575 LEXINGTON AVE
NEW YORK NY 10022
WRITTEN INQUIRY

AMOUNT: UP TO $25000

DEADLINE(S): FEB 1; MAY 1; AUG 1; NOV 1

FIELD(S): PHYSICAL SCIENCES; BIOLOGICAL SCIENCES

POST-DOCTORAL GRANTS FOR ORIGINAL ADVANCED RESEARCH IN ANY OF THE PHYSICAL OR BIOLOGICAL SCIENCES. OPEN TO ESTABLISHED RESEARCH SCIENTISTS WHO ARE ATTACHED TO A RECOGNIZED INSTITUTION.

WRITE FOR COMPLETE INFORMATION.

655

GEOLOGICAL SOCIETY OF AMERICA (RESEARCH GRANTS PROGRAM)

PO BOX 9140; 3300 PENROSE PLACE
BOULDER CO 80301
303/447-2020; FAX 303/447-1133

AMOUNT: $394 - $2500 (AVERAGE $1273)

DEADLINE(S): FEB 15

FIELD(S): GEOLOGY

OPEN TO MASTER'S & PH.D CANDIDATES AT COLLEGES & UNIVERSITIES IN THE USA; CANADA; MEXICO & CENTRAL AMERICA. AWARD IS TO HELP SUPPORT MASTER'S AND DOCTORAL THESIS RESEARCH. GSA MEMBERSHIP IS -NOT- REQUIRED.

APPROX 200 AWARDS PER YEAR. WRITE TO THE ATTN OF THE RESEARCH GRANTS ADMINISTRATOR FOR COMPLETE INFORMATION.

656

INTERNATIONAL ASTRONOMICAL UNION (EXCHANGE OF ASTRONOMERS TRAVEL GRANT)

PROF. F.GRAHAM SMITH; NRAL;
JODRELL BANK
MACCLESFIELD CHESHIRE SK11 9DL ENGLAND
WRITTEN INQUIRY ONLY

AMOUNT: COST OF TRAVEL ONLY

DEADLINE(S): NOV - AUG

FIELD(S): ASTRONOMY

TRAVEL GRANTS FOR GRADUATE STUDENTS; POST-DOCTORAL FELLOWS OR FACULTY-STAFF MEMBERS AT ANY RECOGNIZED EDUCATIONAL RESEARCH INSTITUTION OR OBSERVATORY. THE PROGRAM IS DESIGNED TO ENABLE QUALIFIED PERSONS TO VISIT INSTITUTIONS ABROAD.

TRIP SHOULD BE AT LEAST 3 MONTHS TO ALLOW AMPLE TIME TO INTERACT WITH THE HOST INSTITUTION AND FOR BENEFITS TO ASTRONOMY ON BOTH SIDES. WRITE FOR COMPLETE INFORMATION.

657

INTERNATIONAL DESALINATION ASSN (CHANNABASAPPA MEMORIAL SCHOLARSHIP FUND)

PO BOX 387
TOPSFIELD MA 01983
508/356-2727

AMOUNT: $6000

DEADLINE(S): VARIES

FIELD(S): DESALINATION

OPEN TO APPLICANTS WHO HAVE THEIR BACHELOR'S DEGREE FROM A RECOGNIZED UNIVERSITY & GRADUATED IN TOP 5% OF THEIR CLASS. SCHOLARSHIPS SUPPORT GRADUATE STUDY & RESEARCH IN DESALINATION & WATER RE-USE.

FOR COMPLETE INFORMATION CONTACT ADDRESS ABOVE OR DR.SHIGEKI TOYAMA; PROFESSOR OF CHEMICAL ENGINEERING; NAGOYA UNIV; FURO-CHO; CHIKUSA-KU; NAGOYA 464-01; JAPAN. MATCHING GRANTS FROM AN ACCREDITED UNIVERSITY ARE REQUIRED.

658

LINK FOUNDATION (ENERGY FELLOWSHIP PROGRAM)

PROVOST B.J. THOMPSON - ADMINISTRATOR - UNIV OF ROCHESTER - 200 ADMINISTRATION BLDG.
ROCHESTER NY 14627
WRITTEN INQUIRY

AMOUNT: $17000

DEADLINE(S): DEC 1

FIELD(S): ENERGY RESEARCH

AWARDS WILL BE MADE TO DOCTORAL STUDENTS IN ACADEMIC OR OTHER NON-PROFIT INSTITUTIONS FOR ENERGY RESEARCH.

CONTACT ADDRESS ABOVE FOR COMPLETE INFORMATION.

659

NATIONAL CENTER FOR ATMOSPHERIC RESEARCH (GRADUATE FELLOWSHIPS)

P.O. BOX 3000
BOULDER CO 80307
303/497-1602

AMOUNT: $12400 - $13150 STIPEND + EXPENSES

DEADLINE(S): JAN 1; APR 1; JUL 1; OCT 1

FIELD(S): ATMOSPHERIC SCIENCE; OCEAN DYNAMICS

THIS PROGRAM IS DESIGNED TO FOSTER COOPERATIVE RESEARCH BETWEEN NCAR AND ACADEMIC INSTITUTIONS BY PROVIDING SUPPORT FOR DOCTORAL CANDIDATES WHO ARE WILLING TO WORK ON THEIR THESIS IN COOPERATION WITH AN NCAR PROGRAM.

WRITE TO COORDINATOR BARBARA MCDONALD; ADDRESS ABOVE; FOR COMPLETE INFORMATION.

660

NATIONAL CENTER FOR ATMOSPHERIC RESEARCH (POST-DOCTORAL RESEARCH FELLOWSHIPS)

PO BOX 3000
BOULDER CO 80307
303/497-1602

AMOUNT: $29800 - $31200 STIPEND PER YEAR + BENEFITS

DEADLINE(S): JAN 10

FIELD(S): ATMOSPHERIC SCIENCES

OPEN TO SCIENTISTS JUST RECEIVING THE PH.D OR EQUIVALENT AND TO THOSE WITH NO MORE THAN 4 YEARS EXPERIENCE PAST THE PH.D. CRITERIA INCLUDE SCIENTIFIC CAPABILITY & POTENTIAL; ORIGINALITY & INDEPENDENCE & ABILITY TO UNDERTAKE RESEARCH.

CONTACT ADMINISTRATOR BARBARA MCDONALD AT ADDRESS ABOVE FOR COMPLETE INFORMATION.

661

NATIONAL CONSORTIUM FOR GRADUATE DEGREES FOR MINORITIES IN ENGINEERING & SCIENCE INC. (FELLOWSHIPS)

PO BOX 537
NOTRE DAME IN 46556
219/287-1097; FAX 219/287-1486

AMOUNT: FULL TUITION & FEES + ANNUAL STIPEND

DEADLINE(S): DEC 1

FIELD(S): ENGINEERING; NATURAL SCIENCES

MASTERS & DOCTORATE FELLOWSHIPS FOR ETHNIC/RACIAL MINORITIES (BLACK AMERICAN; MEXICAN AMERICAN; PUERTO RICAN; AMERICAN INDIAN). MUST BE USA CITIZEN AT TIME OF APPLICATION.

250 FELLOWSHIPS PER YEAR. ADDRESS INQUIRIES TO HOWARD G. ADAMS; EXECUTIVE DIRECTOR.

662

NATIONAL RADIO ASTRONOMY OBSERVATORY (SUMMER RESEARCH ASSISTANTSHIPS)

EDGEMONT ROAD
CHARLOTTESVILLE VA 22903
804/296-0211

AMOUNT: $1000 - $1300 PER MONTH + TRAVEL EXPENSES

DEADLINE(S): FEB 1

FIELD(S): ASTRONOMY; PHYSICS; COMPUTER SCIENCE; ELECTRICAL ENGINEERING

SUMMER RESEARCH ASSISTANTSHIPS OPEN TO UNDERGRADUATES WHO HAVE COMPLETED AT LEAST 3 YEARS OF STUDY AND TO GRADUATE STUDENTS WHO HAVE COMPLETED NO MORE THAN 2 YEARS. TENABLE AT NRAO SITES.

APPROXIMATELY 20 AWARDS PER YEAR. WRITE FOR COMPLETE INFORMATION.

663 ─────────────

NATIONAL RESEARCH COUNCIL (NATIONAL SCIENCE FOUNDATION MINORITY GRADUATE FELLOWSHIPS)

2101 CONSTITUTION AVE.
WASHINGTON DC 20418
202/334-2872

AMOUNT: $14000 STIPEND (12 MONTHS) + UP TO $7500 FOR TUITION AND FEES

DEADLINE(S): NOV 6

FIELD(S): ENGINEERING; MATHEMATICS; COMPUTER SCIENCE; CHEMISTRY; EARTH SCIENCES; LIFE SCIENCES; PSYCHOLOGY; SOCIAL SCIENCES

OPEN MINORITY GRADUATE STUDENTS (MASTERS OR PH.D) WHO ARE USA CITIZENS OR LEGAL RESIDENTS & ARE AT OR NEAR THE BEGINNING OF THEIR GRADUATE STUDY. FELLOWSHIPS TENABLE AT ACCREDITED INSTITUTION OFFERING ADVANCED DEGREES IN THE FIELDS ABOVE.

APPROX 150 NEW 3-YEAR FELLOWSHIPS AWARDED EACH YEAR. WRITE FOR COMPLETE INFORMATION.

664 ─────────────

NATIONAL RESEARCH COUNCIL (NATIONAL SCIENCE FOUNDATION GRADUATE FELLOWSHIPS)

2101 CONSTITUTION AVE
WASHINGTON DC 20418
202/334-2872

AMOUNT: $14000 STIPEND + $7000 TUITION ALLOWANCE

DEADLINE(S): NOV 10

FIELD(S): SOCIAL SCIENCES; PHYSICAL SCIENCES; MATHEMATICS; BIOLOGY; ENGINEERING

DOCTORAL) WHO HAVE NOT COMPLETED MORE THAN 1 YEAR OF GRAD STUDY. FELLOWSHIPS TENABLE AT ANY ACCREDITED INSTITUTION OFFERING ADVANCED DEGREES IN THE AREAS ABOVE. USA CITIZEN OR PERMANENT RESIDENT.

OPEN TO HISTORY & PHILOSOPHY OF SCIENCE STUDENTS ALSO. 950 NEW 3-YEAR FELLOWSHIPS AWARDED EACH YEAR. WRITE FOR COMPLETE INFORMATION.

665 ─────────────

NATIONAL RESEARCH COUNCIL (NRC POSTDOCTORAL & SENIOR RESEARCH ASSOCIATESHIP AWARDS)

ASSOCIATESHIP PROGRAMS GR430/D3; 2101 CONSTITUTION AVE. NW
WASHINGTON DC 20418
202/334-2760

AMOUNT: ANNUAL STIPEND FROM 27750 TO 44000 + BENEFITS

DEADLINE(S): JAN 15; APR 15; AUG 15

FIELD(S): CHEMISTRY; EARTH & ATMOSPHERIC SCIENCES; ENGINEERING & APPLIED SCIENCES; COMPUTER SCIENCE; MATHEMATICS; BIOLOGICAL & MEDICAL SCIENCES SPACE & PLANETARY SCIENCES; PHYSICS

POSTDOCTORAL & SENIOR ASSOCIATESHIP AWARDS FOR RESEARCH AT ONE OF 38 PARTICIPATING SPONSOR FEDERAL LABORATORIES. USA CITIZENSHIP REQUIRED FOR SOME OF THE SPONSOR LABORATORIES; MANY ARE OPEN TO FOREIGN NATIONALS.

WRITE FOR COMPLETE INFORMATION AND APPLICATION MATERIALS.

666 ─────────────

NATIONAL SPELEOLOGICAL SOCIETY (RALPH W STONE RESEARCH GRANT)

CAVE AVENUE
HUNTSVILLE AL 35810
205/852-1300

AMOUNT: $500

DEADLINE(S): MAY 1

FIELD(S): SPELEOLOGY (CAVE-RELATED RESEARCH)

OPEN TO MEMBERS OF NATIONAL SPELEOLOGICAL SOCIETY ONLY. GRANT FOR CAVE-RELATED GRADUATE THESIS RESEARCH IN THE BIOLOGICAL; SOCIAL OR EARTH SCIENCES.

TELEPHONE AWARD CHAIRMAN DR. DAVID J. DESMARAIS (415) 322-0778 OR WRITE TO ADDRESS ABOVE FOR COMPLETE INFORMATION.

667 ─────────────

NEWBERRY LIBRARY (HERMON DUNLAP SMITH CENTER FOR THE HISTORY OF CARTOGRAPHY)

60 WEST WALTON
CHICAGO IL 60610
312/943-9090

AMOUNT: UP TO $30000

DEADLINE(S): MAR 1; OCT 15

FIELD(S): HISTORY OF CARTOGRAPHY

THE HERMON DUNLAP SMITH CENTER FOR THE HISTORY OF CARTOGRAPHY OFFERS SHORT-TERM (1-3 MONTHS) & LONG-TERM (6-12 MONTHS) FELLOWSHIPS TO QUALIFIED GRADUATE & POST-GRADUATE APPLICANTS. AWARDS ARE TENABLE AT THE NEWBERRY LIBRARY.

8 AWARDS PER YEAR. WRITE FOR COMPLETE INFORMATION.

668

OAK RIDGE ASSOCIATED UNIVERSITIES (LABORATORY GRADUATE PARTICIPATION PROGRAM)

UNIV PROGRAMS DIV; PO BOX 117
OAK RIDGE TN 37831
615/576-3426

AMOUNT: $1000 - $1200 (MONTHLY STIPEND)

DEADLINE(S): VARIES

FIELD(S): ENERGY RESEARCH

RESEARCH APPOINTMENTS FOR MASTERS THESIS OR DOCTORAL DISSERTATION AT DEPT OF ENERGY FACILITIES. MASTERS APPOINTMENTS ARE FOR SIX MONTHS; PH.D FOR ONE YEAR; BOTH RENEWABLE. USA CITIZEN.

WRITE FOR COMPLETE INFORMATION.

669

OAK RIDGE INSTITUTE FOR SCIENCE AND EDUCATION (HOLLAENDER POSTDOCTORAL RESEARCH FELLOWSHIPS)

SCIENCE/ENGINEERING EDUCATION DIV.; PO BOX 117
OAK RIDGE TN 37831
615/576-9975

AMOUNT: $37500

DEADLINE(S): JAN 15

FIELD(S): ENERGY RELATED LIFE; BIOMEDICAL AND ENVIRONMENTAL SCIENCES

POSTDOCTORAL FELLOWSHIPS FOR RESEARCH PROGRAMS SPONSORED BY THE OFFICE OF HEALTH & ENVIRONMENTAL RESEARCH. TENABLE AT VARIOUS NATIONAL LABORATORIES. MUST BE USA CITIZEN OR LEGAL RESIDENT AND HAVE RECEIVED DOCTORAL DEGREE AFTER MAY 1 1991.

WRITE FOR COMPLETE INFORMATION.

670

RESOURCES FOR THE FUTURE (GILBERT F. WHITE FELLOWSHIP PROGRAM)

1616 'P' STREET NW
WASHINGTON DC 20036
202/328-5067

AMOUNT: $35000 STIPEND + $1000 MOVING/ LIVING EXPENSES

DEADLINE(S): MAR 1

FIELD(S): SOCIAL SCIENCES; NATURAL RESOURCES; ENERGY; ENVIRONMENT

POST-DOCTORAL RESIDENT FELLOWSHIPS FOR YOUNG PROFESSIONALS WHO WISH TO DEVOTE A YEAR TO SCHOLARLY WORK ON A SOCIAL OR POLICY PROBLEM IN AREAS OF NATURAL RESOURCES; ENERGY OR ENVIRONMENT. FACULTY MEMBERS ON SABBATICAL ENCOURAGED TO APPLY.

FELLOWSHIPS AWARDED FOR A MINIMUM OF 9 MOS.; MAXIMUM OF 12 MOS. ADDRESS INQUIRIES TO FELLOWSHIP DIRECTOR.

671

RESOURCES FOR THE FUTURE (SMALL GRANTS PROGRAM)

1616 'P' STREET NW
WASHINGTON DC 20036
202/328-5067

AMOUNT: $30000 MAXIMUM

DEADLINE(S): MAR 1

FIELD(S): NATURAL RESOURCES; ENERGY; ENVIRONMENTAL ISSUES

POST-DOCTORAL RESEARCH GRANTS OPEN TO RESEARCHERS OF ALL NATIONALITIES. PROPOSALS MAY ORIGINATE IN THE HUMANITIES; SOCIAL OR NATURAL SCIENCES & MAY BE THEORETICAL OR APPLIED RESEARCH. 2 MONTHS - 2 YEARS. ONGOING PROJECTS ALSO CONSIDERED.

GRANTS CAN ONLY BE MADE THROUGH TAX-EXEMPT INSTITUTIONS. WRITE FOR COMPLETE INFORMATION.

672

ROYAL NORWEGIAN COUNCIL FOR SCIENTIFIC & INDUSTRIAL RESEARCH (POST-DOCTORAL RESEARCH FELLOWSHIPS)

PO BOX 70 TAASEN
N-0801 OSLO NORWAY
+4722 23 76 85

AMOUNT: NOK 132000 SINGLE; NOK 156000 MARRIED + EXPENSES

DEADLINE(S): MAR 1; SEP 1

FIELD(S): NATURAL SCIENCES; ENGINEERING

POST-DOCTORAL FELLOWSHIPS OPEN TO YOUNG FOREIGN SCIENTISTS (UNDER AGE 40) WHO WISH TO DO RESEARCH WORK IN NORWAY. THEIR QUALIFICATIONS MUST CORRESPOND AT LEAST TO A BRITISH OR AMERICAN PH.D IN NATURAL SCIENCE OR ENGINEERING.

AWARDS ARE FOR ONE YEAR. 20 AWARDS PER YEAR. RENEWALS CONSIDERED. WRITE FOR COMPLETE INFORMATION.

673

SMITHSONIAN INSTITUTION (NATIONAL AIR & SPACE MUSEUM GUGGENHEIM FELLOWSHIPS)

INTERPRETIVE PROGRAMS; ROOM 3341; MRC-313;
6TH & INDEPENDENCE AVE SW
WASHINGTON DC 20560
WRITTEN INQUIRY

AMOUNT: $13000 - $21000 STIPEND + TRAVEL ALLOWANCE

DEADLINE(S): JAN 15

FIELD(S): AVIATION; AERONAUTICS; SPACE SCIENCE & EXPLORATION; EARTH & PLANETARY SCIENCES; LIFE SCIENCES

PRE-DOCTORAL APPLICANTS SHOULD HAVE COMPLETED PRELIMINARY COURSE WORK & EXAMS AND BE ENGAGED IN DISSERTATION RESEARCH. POST-DOCTORAL APPLICANTS SHOULD HAVE RECEIVED THEIR PH.D WITHIN THE PAST SEVEN YEARS.

OPEN TO ALL NATIONALITIES. FLUENCY IN ENGLISH REQUIRED. DURATION IS 6-12 MONTHS. WRITE FOR COMPLETE INFORMATION.

674

SOCIETY OF EXPLORATION GEOPHYSICISTS EDUCATION FOUNDATION (SCHOLARSHIP PROGRAM)

PO BOX 702740
TULSA OK 74170
918/493-3516

AMOUNT: $500 - $3000

DEADLINE(S): MAR 1

FIELD(S): GEOPHYSICS & RELATED EARTH SCIENCES

UNDERGRADUATE & GRADUATE SCHOLARSHIPS OPEN TO STUDENTS WHO ARE ACCEPTED TO OR ENROLLED IN AN ACCREDITED PROGRAM IN THE USA OR ITS POSSESSIONS & INTEND TO PURSUE A CAREER IN EXPLORATION GEOPHYSICS.

60-100 AWARDS PER YEAR. RENEWABLE. INTEREST IN AND APTITUDE FOR PHYSICS; MATHEMATICS AND GEOLOGY REQUIRED. WRITE FOR COMPLETE INFORMATION.

675

VANDERBILT UNIVERSITY (A.J. DYER OBSERVATORY RESEARCH ASSISTANTSHIP)

C/O DYER OBSERVATORY; 1000 OMAN DR
BRENTWOOD TN 37027
615/373-4897

AMOUNT: FULL-TUITION + $9500 STIPEND

DEADLINE(S): FEB 1

FIELD(S): ASTRONOMY

RESEARCH ASSISTANTSHIPS IN OBSERVATIONAL ASTRONOMY AT ARTHUR J DYER OBSERVATORY. INCLUDES STIPEND PLUS FULL-TUITION COSTS FOR GRADUATE STUDY AT VANDERBILT UNIVERSITY.

WRITE FOR COMPLETE INFORMATION.

676

WOMAN'S AUXILIARY TO THE AMERICAN INSTITUTE OF MINING METALLURGICAL & PETROLEUM ENGINEERS (WAAIME SCHOLARSHIP LOAN FUND)

345 E.47TH ST; 14TH FLOOR
NEW YORK NY 10017
WRITTEN INQUIRY ONLY

AMOUNT: VARIES

DEADLINE(S): MAR 15

FIELD(S): EARTH SCIENCES; MINING ENGINEERING; PETROLEUM ENGINEERING

OPEN TO UNDERGRADUATE JUNIORS & SENIORS AND GRADUATE STUDENTS. ELIGIBLE APPLICANTS RECEIVE A SCHOLARSHIP LOAN FOR ALL OR PART OF THEIR EDUCATION. RECIPIENTS REPAY ONLY 50% WITH NO INTEREST CHARGES.

REPAYMENT TO BEGIN BY 6 MONTHS AFTER GRADUATION AND BE COMPLETED WITHIN 6 YEARS. WRITE TO WAAIME SCHOLARSHIP LOAN FUND; ADDRESS ABOVE; FOR COMPLETE INFORMATION.

ENVIRO STUDIES

677

ARGONNE NATIONAL LABORATORY (STUDENT RESEARCH PARTICIPATION PROGRAM; THESIS RESEARCH)

DIV OF EDUCATIONAL PROGRAMS;
9700 SOUTH CASS AVE
ARGONNE IL 60439
312/972-3366

AMOUNT: $200 PER WEEK STIPEND

DEADLINE(S): FEB 1; MAY 15; OCT 15

FIELD(S): PHYSICAL SCIENCES; LIFE SCIENCES; EARTH SCIENCES; MATHEMATICS; COMPUTER SCIENCES; ENGINEERING; FUSION & FISSION ENERGY

1-SEMESTER ACCREDITED INTERNSHIP PROGRAM TO PERMIT STUDENTS TO WORK IN ABOVE AREAS IN RELATION TO ENERGY DEVELOPMENT. OPEN TO FULL-TIME UNDERGRAD JUNIORS; SENIORS & 1ST YEAR GRAD STUDENTS. USA CITIZEN OR LEGAL RESIDENT.

THESIS RESEARCH AWARDS OPEN TO DOCTORAL CANDIDATES WORKING ON THEIR DISSERTATION. WRITE FOR COMPLETE INFORMATION.

678

CENTER FOR INDOOR AIR RESEARCH (FELLOWSHIP GRANTS PROGRAM)

1099 WINTERSON ROAD - SUITE 280
LINTHICUM MD 21090
301/684-3777

AMOUNT: $30000 MAXIMUM

DEADLINE(S): OCT 31

FIELD(S): INDOOR AIR RESEARCH

POSTDOCTORAL FELLOWSHIP GRANTS FOR RESEARCH INTO FACTORS AFFECTING THE QUALITY OF INDOOR AIR AND METHODS OF PREVENTING AND ABATING INDOOR AIR CONTAMINANTS. MUST HOLD M.D. OR PH.D. DEGREE OR EQUIVALENT.

SPONSORSHIP OF FELLOW BY AN ESTABLISHED INVESTIGATOR IS REQUIRED. AWARDS ARE FOR ONE YEAR; RENEWABLE FOR A SECOND. WRITE FOR COMPLETE INFORMATION.

679

CHARLES A. LINDBERGH FUND INC. (GRANTS FOR RESEARCH PROJECTS)

708 S. THIRD ST.- SUITE 110
MINNEAPOLIS MN 55415
612/338-1703

AMOUNT: UP TO $10580

DEADLINE(S): JUN 15

FIELD(S): AVIATION/AEROSPACE; AGRICULTURE; ARTS & HUMANITIES; BIOMEDICAL RESEARCH; CONSERVATION; EXPLORATION; HEALTH & POPULATION SCIENCES; INTERCULTURAL COMMUNICATION; OCEANOGRAPHY; WASTE DISPOSAL MGMT; WATER RESOURCE MGMT; WILDLIFE PRESERVATION.

RESEARCH GRANTS ARE AWARDED ANNUALLY TO INDIVIDUALS WHOSE PROPOSED PROJECTS REPRESENT A SIGNIFICANT CONTRIBUTION TOWARD THE ACHIEVEMENT OF A BALANCE BETWEEN THE ADVANCE OF TECHNOLOGY & PRESERVATION OF THE NATURAL ENVIRONMENT.

WRITE FOR APPLICATION AND COMPLETE INFORMATION.

680

CONGRESSIONAL FELLOWSHIP PROGRAM (MORRIS K. UDALL FELLOWSHIPS)

CONGRESS OF THE UNITED STATES; OFFICE OF TECHNOLOGY ASSESSMENT
WASHINGTON DC 20510
202/224-8713

AMOUNT: $35000 - $70000

DEADLINE(S): JAN 31

FIELD(S): PHYSICAL OR BIOLOGICAL SCIENCES; ENGINEERING; LAW; ECONOMICS; ENVIRONMENTAL OR SOCIAL SCIENCES; PUBLIC POLICY

ONE YEAR FELLOWSHIP PROGRAM HELD -ONLY- IN WASHINGTO DC. CANDIDATES MUST HAVE EXTENSIVE EXPERIENCE IN SCIENCE OR TECHNOLOGY ISSUES OR HAVE COMPLETED DOCTORAL LEVEL RESEARCH. EXCEPTIONAL COMPETENCY IN ABOVE AREAS REQUIRED.

CONSIDERATIONS INCLUDE ACHIEVEMENT RECORDS AND CANDIDATE'S POTENTIAL IN ONE OR MORE OF OTA'S ASSESSMENT STUDIES. WRITE FOR COMPLETE INFORMATION.

681

EDMUND NILES HUYCK PRESERVE (GRADUATE AND POST-GRADUATE RESEARCH GRANTS)

MAIN ST
RENSSELAERVILLE NY 12147
518/797-3440

AMOUNT: UP TO $3500

DEADLINE(S): FEB 1

FIELD(S): ECOLOGY; BEHAVIOR; EVOLUTION; NATURAL HISTORY

GRANTS TO SUPPORT GRADUATE AND POST GRADUATE SCIENTISTS CONDUCTING RESEARCH ON THE NATURAL RESOURCES OF THE HUYCK PRESERVE. FUNDS ARE -NOT- AVAILABLE TO HELP STUDENTS DEFRAY COLLEGE EXPENSES.

HOUSING AND LAB SPACE ARE PROVIDED AT THE PRESERVE. WRITE FOR COMPLETE INFORMATION.

682

GARDEN CLUB OF AMERICA (CLARA CARTER HIGGINS SCHOLARSHIP)

598 MADISON AVE
NEW YORK NY 10022
212/753-8287

AMOUNT: $1000 TO $1500 (VARIES YEARLY)

DEADLINE(S): FEB 15

FIELD(S): ENVIRONMENTAL STUDIES

ANNUAL SCHOLARSHIP FOR A SUMMER COURSE IN ENVIRONMENTAL STUDIES. AWARD TENABLE AT ANY ACCREDITED COLLEGE OR UNIVERSITY IN USA. OPEN TO UNDERGRADUATE OR GRADUATE STUDENTS WHO ARE USA CITIZENS OR LEGAL RESIDENTS.

CONTACT CONSERVATION CHAIRMAN ADDRESS ABOVE.

683

INSTITUTE FOR THE STUDY OF WORLD POLITICS (RESEARCH GRANTS)

1755 MASSACHUSETTS AVE NW -
SUITE 500
WASHINGTON DC 20036
WRITTEN INQUIRY ONLY

AMOUNT: VARIES

DEADLINE(S): FEB 15

FIELD(S): INTERNATIONAL RELATIONS; ENVIRONMENTAL ISSUES; POPULATION STUDIES (SOCIAL SCIENCE ASPECTS) HUMAN RIGHTS; ARMS CONTROL; THIRD WORLD DEVELOPMENT.

FOR DOCTORAL CANDIDATES CONDUCTING DISSERTATION RESEARCH IN ABOVE AREAS. FINANCIAL NEED IS A CONSIDERATION.

20-25 FELLOWSHIPS PER YEAR. WRITE FOR COMPLETE INFORMATION.

684

INTERNATIONAL LEAD ZINC RESEARCH ORGANIZATION INC. (FELLOWSHIP PROGRAM)

PO BOX 12036; 2525 MERIDIAN PARKWAY
RESEARCH TRIANGLE PARK NC 27709
WRITTEN INQUIRY

AMOUNT: $15000 - $25000

DEADLINE(S): MAY

FIELD(S): CHEMISTRY; ENVIRONMENTAL HEALTH; ELECTROCHEMISTRY; METALLURGY

DOCTORAL AND POST-DOCTORAL FELLOWSHIPS FOR RESEARCH INVOLVING LEAD; ZINC AND CADMIUM COMPOUNDS IN CERAMICS; CHEMISTRY; METALLURGY; ELECTROCHEMISTRY; AND ENVIRONMENTAL HEALTH.

ONE YEAR FELLOWSHIPS RENEWABLE FOR TWO ADDITIONAL YEARS. WRITE FOR COMPLETE INFORMATION.

685

NATIONAL CONSORTIUM FOR GRADUATE DEGREES FOR MINORITIES IN ENGINEERING & SCIENCE INC. (FELLOWSHIPS)

PO BOX 537
NOTRE DAME IN 46556
219/287-1097; FAX 219/287-1486

AMOUNT: FULL TUITION & FEES + ANNUAL STIPEND

DEADLINE(S): DEC 1

FIELD(S): ENGINEERING; NATURAL SCIENCES

MASTERS & DOCTORATE FELLOWSHIPS FOR ETHNIC/RACIAL MINORITIES (BLACK AMERICAN; MEXICAN AMERICAN; PUERTO RICAN; AMERICAN INDIAN). MUST BE USA CITIZEN AT TIME OF APPLICATION.

250 FELLOWSHIPS PER YEAR. ADDRESS INQUIRIES TO HOWARD G. ADAMS; EXECUTIVE DIRECTOR.

686

NATIONAL RIFLE ASSOC (NRA-GRANTS IN AID PROGRAM)

HUNTER SERVICES DIV;
1600 RHODE ISLAND AVE NW
WASHINGTON DC 20036
202/828-6241

AMOUNT: $5000

DEADLINE(S): JUN 1

FIELD(S): SPORTS MEDICINE; GAME MANAGEMENT; CONSERVATION

GRADUATE RESEARCH GRANTS-IN-AID OPEN TO NRA MEMBERS DOING RESEARCH IN THE ABOVE FIELDS. MOST GRANTS GO TO GRADUATE LEVEL STUDENTS AT ACCREDITED COLLEGES OR UNIVERSITIES IN THE USA.

QUALITY OF PROJECT; ABILITY OF APPLICANT AND INTEREST TO SPONSORING ORGANIZATION ARE THE MAIN CRITERIA FOR SELECTION BY NRA GRANTS-IN-AID COMMITTEE. WRITE FOR COMPLETE INFORMATION.

687

OAK RIDGE INSTITUTE FOR SCIENCE AND EDUCATION (HOLLAENDER POSTDOCTORAL RESEARCH FELLOWSHIPS)

SCIENCE/ENGINEERING EDUCATION DIV.; PO BOX 117
OAK RIDGE TN 37831
615/576-9975

AMOUNT: $37500

DEADLINE(S): JAN 15

FIELD(S): ENERGY RELATED LIFE; BIOMEDICAL AND ENVIRONMENTAL SCIENCES

POSTDOCTORAL FELLOWSHIPS FOR RESEARCH PROGRAMS SPONSORED BY THE OFFICE OF HEALTH & ENVIRONMENTAL RESEARCH. TENABLE AT VARIOUS NATIONAL LABORATORIES. MUST BE USA CITIZEN OR LEGAL RESIDENT AND HAVE RECEIVED DOCTORAL DEGREE AFTER MAY 1 1991.

WRITE FOR COMPLETE INFORMATION.

688

RESOURCES FOR THE FUTURE (GILBERT F. WHITE FELLOWSHIP PROGRAM)

1616 'P' STREET NW
WASHINGTON DC 20036
202/328-5067

AMOUNT: $35000 STIPEND + $1000 MOVING/ LIVING EXPENSES

DEADLINE(S): MAR 1

FIELD(S): SOCIAL SCIENCES; NATURAL RESOURCES; ENERGY; ENVIRONMENT

POST-DOCTORAL RESIDENT FELLOWSHIPS FOR YOUNG PROFESSIONALS WHO WISH TO DEVOTE A YEAR TO SCHOLARLY WORK ON A SOCIAL OR POLICY PROBLEM IN AREAS OF NATURAL RESOURCES; ENERGY OR ENVIRONMENT. FACULTY MEMBERS ON SABBATICAL ENCOURAGED TO APPLY.

FELLOWSHIPS AWARDED FOR A MINIMUM OF 9 MOS.; MAXIMUM OF 12 MOS. ADDRESS INQUIRIES TO FELLOWSHIP DIRECTOR.

689

RESOURCES FOR THE FUTURE (SMALL GRANTS PROGRAM)

1616 'P' STREET NW
WASHINGTON DC 20036
202/328-5067

AMOUNT: $30000 MAXIMUM

DEADLINE(S): MAR 1

FIELD(S): NATURAL RESOURCES; ENERGY; ENVIRONMENTAL ISSUES

POST-DOCTORAL RESEARCH GRANTS OPEN TO RESEARCHERS OF ALL NATIONALITIES. PROPOSALS MAY ORIGINATE IN THE HUMANITIES; SOCIAL OR NATURAL SCIENCES & MAY BE THEORETICAL OR APPLIED RESEARCH. 2 MONTHS - 2 YEARS. ONGOING PROJECTS ALSO CONSIDERED.

GRANTS CAN ONLY BE MADE THROUGH TAX-EXEMPT INSTITUTIONS. WRITE FOR COMPLETE INFORMATION.

690

ROB AND BESSIE WELDER WILDLIFE FOUNDATION (SCHOLARSHIP PROGRAM)

PO DRAWER 1400
SINTON TX 78387
512/364-2643

AMOUNT: $750 PER MONTH-MASTERS; $800 PER MONTH-PH.D

DEADLINE(S): OCT 15

FIELD(S): WILDLIFE ECOLOGY & MANAGEMENT

OPEN TO GRADUATE STUDENTS WHO ARE APPROVED CANDIDATES FOR M.S. OR PH.D. DEGREES AT ACCREDITED INSTITUTIONS IN USA.

15-20 SCHOLARSHIPS PER YEAR. RENEWABLE. WRITE FOR COMPLETE INFORMATION.

691

ROYAL NORWEGIAN COUNCIL FOR SCIENTIFIC & INDUSTRIAL RESEARCH (POST-DOCTORAL RESEARCH FELLOWSHIPS)

PO BOX 70 TAASEN
N-0801 OSLO NORWAY
+4722 23 76 85

AMOUNT: NOK 132000 SINGLE; NOK 156000 MARRIED + EXPENSES

DEADLINE(S): MAR 1; SEP 1

FIELD(S): NATURAL SCIENCES; ENGINEERING

POST-DOCTORAL FELLOWSHIPS OPEN TO YOUNG FOREIGN SCIENTISTS (UNDER AGE 40) WHO WISH TO DO RESEARCH WORK IN NORWAY. THEIR QUALIFICATIONS MUST CORRESPOND AT LEAST TO A BRITISH OR AMERICAN PH.D IN NATURAL SCIENCE OR ENGINEERING.

AWARDS ARE FOR ONE YEAR. 20 AWARDS PER YEAR. RENEWALS CONSIDERED. WRITE FOR COMPLETE INFORMATION.

692

SIGURD OLSON ENVIRONMENTAL INSTITUTE - LOONWATCH (SIGURD T. OLSON RESEARCH FUND)

NORTHLAND COLLEGE
ASHLAND WI 54806
715/682-4531

AMOUNT: UP TO $1000

DEADLINE(S): JAN 6

FIELD(S): RESEARCH ON THE COMMON LOON (GAVIA IMMER)

OPEN TO STUDENTS AT ALL LEVELS FOR STUDY OF LOON POPULATIONS IN THE UPPER GREAT LAKES.

RENEWABLE. WRITE FOR COMPLETE INFORMATION.

693

SMITHSONIAN INSTITUTION ENVIRONMENTAL RESEARCH CENTER (WORK/LEARN CENTER)

PO BOX 28
EDGEWATER MD 21037
301/798-4424; 202/287-3321

AMOUNT: STIPEND

DEADLINE(S): MAR 1; JUL 1; DEC 1

FIELD(S): ENVIRONMENTAL STUDIES

WORK/LEARN INTERNSHIPS AT THE CENTER OPEN TO UNDERGRADUATE & GRADUATE STUDENTS. COMPETITIVE PROGRAM WHICH OFFERS UNIQUE OPPORTUNITY TO GAIN EXPOSURE TO & EXPERIENCE IN ENVIRONMENTAL RESEARCH.

PROJECTS GENERALLY COINCIDE WITH ACADEMIC SEMESTERS & SUMMER SESSIONS AND ARE NORMALLY 12 - 15 WEEKS. WRITE FOR COMPLETE INFORMATION.

694 ─────────

SPACE FOUNDATION (SPACE INDUSTRIALIZATION FELLOWSHIP)

4800 RESEARCH FOREST DR
THE WOODLANDS TX 77381
713/363-7944; FAX 713/363-7914

AMOUNT: $4000

DEADLINE(S): OCT 1

FIELD(S): SCIENCES & ENGINEERING; BUSINESS; LAW; ECONOMICS; SOCIAL SCIENCES; ENVIRONMENTAL STUDIES; HUMANITIES

OPEN TO SUPERIOR GRADUATE STUDENTS IN THE ABOVE DISCIPLINES WHO INTEND TO DEVOTE THEIR CAREERS TO THE FURTHERANCE OF PRACTICAL SPACE RESEARCH; ENGINEERING; BUSINESS OR OTHER APPLICATION VENTURES.

CONTACT DR. DAVID J. NORTON; EDUCATIONAL GRANT PROGRAM CHAIRMAN; ADDRESS ABOVE; FOR COMPLETE INFORMATION.

695 ─────────

SWEDISH INFORMATION SERVICE (BICENTENNIAL FUND GRANTS)

ONE DAG HAMMARSKJOLD PLAZA;
45TH FLOOR
NEW YORK NY 10017
212/751-5900

AMOUNT: 20000 SWEDISH KRONA

DEADLINE(S): FEB 1

FIELD(S): POLITICAL SCIENCE; BUSINESS ADMIN; EDUCATION; COMMUNICATION; CULTURE; ENVIRONMENTAL STUDIES

GRANTS TO PROVIDE THE OPPORTUNITY FOR THOSE IN A POSITION TO INFLUENCE PUBLIC OPINION AND CONTRIBUTE TO THE DEVELOPMENT OF THEIR SOCIETY. 3-6 WEEK INTENSIVE STUDY VISITS IN SWEDEN IN ANY OF THE ABOVE AREAS OR THEIR RELATED FIELDS.

US CITIZEN OR LEGAL RESIDENT. APPROXIMATELY 10 GRANTS PER YEAR. WRITE FOR COMPLETE INFORMATION.

696 ─────────

TUSKEGEE INSTITUTE (GRADUATE RESEARCH FELLOWSHIPS AND ASSISTANTSHIPS)

ADMISSIONS OFFICE
TUSKEGEE INSTITUTE AL 36088
205/727-8500

AMOUNT: TUITION

DEADLINE(S): MAR 15

FIELD(S): CHEMISTRY; ENGINEERING; ENVIRONMENTAL SCIENCE; LIFE SCIENCES; NUTRITION; EDUCATION

GRADUATE RESEARCH FELLOWSHIPS AND GRADUATE ASSISTANTSHIPS ARE AVAILABLE TO QUALIFIED INDIVIDUALS WHO WISH TO ENTER TUSKEGEE INSTITUTE'S GRADUATE PROGRAM IN PURSUIT OF A MASTER'S DEGREE.

WRITE FOR COMPLETE INFORMATION.

697 ─────────

WATER ENVIRONMENT FEDERATION (STUDENT PAPER COMPETITION)

SUSAN PHILLIPS; 601 WYTHE ST
ALEXANDRIA VA 22314
703/684-2407

AMOUNT: $1000 FIRST PRIZE; $500 SECOND; $250 THIRD IN EACH OF 4 CATEGORIES

DEADLINE(S): JAN 1

FIELD(S): WATER POLLUTION

AWARDS FOR 500 TO 1000 WORD ABSTRACTS DEALING WITH WATER POLLUTION CONTROL; WATER QUALITY PROBLEMS; WATER RELATED CONCERNS OR HAZARDOUS WASTES. OPEN TO OPERATIONS STUDENTS (AA DEGREE CANDIDATES) AS WELL AS UNDERGRAD AND GRAD STUDENTS.

ALSO OPEN TO RECENTLY GRADUATED STUDENTS (WITHIN 1 CALENDAR YEAR OF JAN 1 DEADLINE). WRITE FOR COMPLETE INFORMATION.

MARINE SCIENCE

698 ─────────

AMERICAN ASSOCIATION OF UNIVERSITY WOMEN - HONOLULU BRANCH (HARTT FELLOWSHIP FOR GRADUATE WOMEN IN SCIENCE)

1802 KEEAUMOKU ST
HONOLULU HI 96822
808/537-4702

AMOUNT: $2000

DEADLINE(S): MAY 1

FIELD(S): NATURAL OR PHYSICAL SCIENCES

MARINE SCIENCE

OPEN TO A FEMALE WHO IS A BONA FIDE RESIDENT OF HAWAII AND IS ENROLLED IN AN ADVANCED DEGREE (PH.D) PROGRAM IN THE NATURAL OR PHYSICAL SCIENCES. MUST SHOW OUTSTANDING ABILITY AND DEMONSTRATE FINANCIAL NEED.

WRITE FOR COMPLETE INFORMATION.

699

AMERICAN FISHING TACKLE MANUFACTURERS ASSN (ANDREW J. BOEHM GRADUATE FELLOWSHIP)

1250 GROVE AVENUE - SUITE 300
BARRINGTON IL 60010
708/381-9490

AMOUNT: $1000 TO $10000

DEADLINE(S): MAR 15

FIELD(S): FISH CONSERVATION AND MANAGEMENT

GRADUATE STIPENDS FOR STUDENTS WITH A COMMITMENT TO A PROFESSIONAL CAREER IN FISH CONSERVATION. APPLICANTS MUST SUBMIT A RESEARCH PROPOSAL FOR EITHER THE M.S. OR PH.D. DEGREE. APPLICATIONS TO BE MADE THROUGH SUPERVISING PROFESSOR.

DIRECT APPLICATIONS BY STUDENTS WILL NOT BE CONSIDERED. WRITE FOR COMPLETE INFORMATION.

700

AMERICAN GEOLOGICAL INSTITUTE (MINORITY PARTICIPATION PROGRAM SCHOLARSHIPS)

4220 KING ST
ALEXANDRIA VA 22302
703/379-2480

AMOUNT: UP TO $10000 PER YEAR UNDERGRAD; $4000 PER YEAR GRAD

DEADLINE(S): FEB 1

FIELD(S): EARTH SCIENCES; SPACE SCIENCES; MARINE SCIENCES

FOR FULL TIME UNDERGRADUATE OR GRADUATE STUDY IN THE ABOVE FIELDS. OPEN TO AMERICAN BLACKS; NATIVE AMERICANS & HISPANIC AMERICANS. MUST BE USA CITIZEN AND DEMONSTRATE FINANCIAL NEED.

APPROX 80 AWARDS PER YEAR. RENEWALS POSSIBLE WITH REAPPLICATION. WRITE FOR COMPLETE INFORMATION.

701

AMERICAN SOCIETY FOR ENGINEERING EDUCATION (OFFICE OF NAVAL RESEARCH GRADUATE FELLOWSHIP PROGRAM)

ELEVEN DUPONT CIRCLE #200
WASHINGTON DC 20036
202/745-3616

AMOUNT: $15000

DEADLINE(S): JAN 31

FIELD(S): ELEC ENG; MECH ENG; AEROSPACE ENG; MATHEMATICS; PHYSICS; COMPUTER SCIENCE; MATERIALS SCIENCE; BIOLOGICAL-BIOMEDICAL SCIENCE; NAVAL ARCHITECTURE & OCEAN ENG; RELATED FIELDS

LIMITED TO INDIVIDUALS WHO HAVE 'NOT' BEGUN GRADUATE PROGRAMS. FOR STUDY AND RESEARCH LEADING TO DOCTORAL DEGREE. FELLOWSHIPS ARE AWARDED ON THE BASIS OF ABILITY. USA CITIZEN.

50 THREE-YEAR FELLOWSHIPS ARE OFFERED. WRITE FOR COMPLETE INFORMATION.

702

ATLANTIC SALMON FEDERATION (BENSINGER-LIDDELL SALMON FELLOWSHIP)

PO DRAWER C
CALAIS ME 04619
WRITTEN INQUIRY

AMOUNT: $10000

DEADLINE(S): MAR 1

FIELD(S): FISHERIES; MARINE BIOLOGY

GRADUATE FELLOWSHIP AWARDED IN ALTERNATE YEARS TO CITIZENS OF NORTH AMERICA AND EUROPE FOR OVERSEAS TRAVEL; STUDY & RESEARCH BENEFITING ATLANTIC SALMON BIOLOGY; MANAGEMENT OR CONSERVATION.

APPLICATIONS SHOULD ADDRESS THE BENEFITS OF THE PROPOSED PROGRAM TO THE ATLANTIC SALMON RESOURCE. WRITE FOR COMPLETE INFORMATION.

703

BROOKHAVEN NATIONAL LABORATORY (POSTDOCTORAL RESEARCH ASSOCIATESHIPS)

BROOKHAVEN NATIONAL LABORATORY; ASSOCIATED UNIVERSITIES INC.
UPTON L.I. NY 11973
516/282-7813

AMOUNT: $27000 MINIMUM

DEADLINE(S): THROUGHOUT THE YEAR.

FIELD(S): CHEMISTRY; PHYSICS; MATERIALS SCIENCE; BIOLOGY; OCEANOGRAPHY; MEDICAL SCIENCE

POST-DOCTORAL RESEARCH ASSOCIATESHIPS TENABLE AT BROOKHAVEN NATIONAL LABORATORY FOR RESEARCH TO PROMOTE FUNDAMENTAL AND APPLIED RESEARCH IN THE ABOVE FIELDS. A RECENT DOCTORAL DEGREE IS REQUIRED.

25 ASSOCIATESHIPS PER YEAR. RENEWABLE FOR TWO ADDITIONAL YEARS. WRITE TO MS. E.E. THORNHILL; OFFICE OF SCIENTIFIC PERSONNEL; ADDRESS ABOVE.

704

CHARLES A. LINDBERGH FUND INC. (GRANTS FOR RESEARCH PROJECTS)

708 S. THIRD ST.- SUITE 110
MINNEAPOLIS MN 55415
612/338-1703

AMOUNT: UP TO $10580

DEADLINE(S): JUN 15

FIELD(S): AVIATION/AEROSPACE; AGRICULTURE; ARTS & HUMANITIES; BIOMEDICAL RESEARCH; CONSERVATION; EXPLORATION; HEALTH & POPULATION SCIENCES; INTERCULTURAL COMMUNICATION; OCEANOGRAPHY; WASTE DISPOSAL MGMT; WATER RESOURCE MGMT; WILDLIFE PRESERVATION.

RESEARCH GRANTS ARE AWARDED ANNUALLY TO INDIVIDUALS WHOSE PROPOSED PROJECTS REPRESENT A SIGNIFICANT CONTRIBUTION TOWARD THE ACHIEVEMENT OF A BALANCE BETWEEN THE ADVANCE OF TECHNOLOGY & PRESERVATION OF THE NATURAL ENVIRONMENT.

WRITE FOR APPLICATION AND COMPLETE INFORMATION.

705

EPPLEY FOUNDATION FOR RESEARCH (POST-DOCTORAL RESEARCH GRANTS)

575 LEXINGTON AVE
NEW YORK NY 10022
WRITTEN INQUIRY

AMOUNT: UP TO $25000

DEADLINE(S): FEB 1; MAY 1; AUG 1; NOV 1

FIELD(S): PHYSICAL SCIENCES; BIOLOGICAL SCIENCES

POST-DOCTORAL GRANTS FOR ORIGINAL ADVANCED RESEARCH IN ANY OF THE PHYSICAL OR BIOLOGICAL SCIENCES. OPEN TO ESTABLISHED RESEARCH SCIENTISTS WHO ARE ATTACHED TO A RECOGNIZED INSTITUTION.

WRITE FOR COMPLETE INFORMATION.

706

HOUSTON UNDERWATER CLUB (SEASPACE SCHOLARSHIPS)

PO BOX 3753
HOUSTON TX 77253
713/467-6675

AMOUNT: $1000 (AVERAGE)

DEADLINE(S): MAR 15

FIELD(S): MARINE SCIENCES; MARINE BIOLOGY OR GEOLOGY; NAUTICAL ARCHEOLOGY; BIOLOGICAL OCEANOGRAPHY; OCEAN & FISHERY SCIENCES; NAVAL/MARINE ENGINEERING; NAVAL SCIENCE

OPEN TO COLLEGE JUNIORS; SENIORS AND GRADUATE STUDENTS WHO ASPIRE TO A CAREER IN THE MARINE SCIENCES AND ATTEND A USA SCHOOL. UNDERGRADS SHOULD HAVE AT LEAST A 3.5 GPA; GRADUATES AT LEAST 3.0. MUST DEMONSTRATE FINANCIAL NEED.

AVERAGE OF 9 AWARDS PER YEAR. APPLICATIONS MUST BE RECEIVED BY MAR 15 DEADLINE TO BE CONSIDERED. WRITE FOR COMPLETE INFORMATION.

707

INTERNATIONAL WOMEN'S FISHING ASSOCIATION (SCHOLARSHIPS)

PO DRAWER 3125
PALM BEACH FL 33480
407/746-0547

AMOUNT: UP TO $3000

DEADLINE(S): MAR 1

FIELD(S): MARINE SCIENCE

OPEN TO GRADUATE STUDENTS IN MARINE SCIENCE WHO ARE MATRICULATED IN USA COLLEGES OR UNIVERSITIES. CONSIDERATIONS INCLUDE ACADEMIC ACHIEVEMENT; CHARACTER; FINANCIAL NEED.

WRITE FOR COMPLETE INFORMATION.

708

NATIONAL CAPITAL SHELL CLUB (CARL I. ASLAKSON SCHOLARSHIP AWARD)

DONN L. TIPPETT; MD;
10281 GAINSBOROUGH RD
POTOMAC MD 20854
WRITTEN INQUIRY

AMOUNT: $1000

DEADLINE(S): APR 15

FIELD(S): MARINE BIOLOGY-MALACOLOGY (STUDY OF MOLLUSKS)

GRADUATE MALACOLOGY STUDENTS AT COLLEGES OR UNIVERSITIES IN THE EASTERN UNITED STATES MAY COMPETE FOR THIS AWARD. STUDENTS IN ALLIED FIELDS OF MARINE SCIENCE WILL BE CONSIDERED IF NO APPLICANT IN THE FIELD OF MALACOLOGY IS CHOSEN.

ANNOUNCEMENTS ARE SENT TO APPROPRIATE EDUCATIONAL INSTITUTIONS IN EARLY FEBRUARY; -NOT- TO INDIVIDUALS. APPLICATIONS MUST BE OBTAINED THROUGH SCHOOL.

709

NATIONAL CENTER FOR ATMOSPHERIC RESEARCH (GRADUATE FELLOWSHIPS)

P.O. BOX 3000
BOULDER CO 80307
303/497-1602

AMOUNT: $12400 - $13150 STIPEND + EXPENSES

DEADLINE(S): JAN 1; APR 1; JUL 1; OCT 1

FIELD(S): ATMOSPHERIC SCIENCE; OCEAN DYNAMICS

THIS PROGRAM IS DESIGNED TO FOSTER COOPERATIVE RESEARCH BETWEEN NCAR AND ACADEMIC INSTITUTIONS BY PROVIDING SUPPORT FOR DOCTORAL CANDIDATES WHO ARE WILLING TO WORK ON THEIR THESIS IN COOPERATION WITH AN NCAR PROGRAM.

WRITE TO COORDINATOR BARBARA MCDONALD; ADDRESS ABOVE; FOR COMPLETE INFORMATION.

710

NATIONAL CENTER FOR ATMOSPHERIC RESEARCH (POST-DOCTORAL RESEARCH FELLOWSHIPS)

PO BOX 3000
BOULDER CO 80307
303/497-1602

AMOUNT: $29800 - $31200 STIPEND PER YEAR + BENEFITS

DEADLINE(S): JAN 10

FIELD(S): ATMOSPHERIC SCIENCES

OPEN TO SCIENTISTS JUST RECEIVING THE PH.D OR EQUIVALENT AND TO THOSE WITH NO MORE THAN 4 YEARS EXPERIENCE PAST THE PH.D. CRITERIA INCLUDE SCIENTIFIC CAPABILITY & POTENTIAL; ORIGINALITY & INDEPENDENCE & ABILITY TO UNDERTAKE RESEARCH.

CONTACT ADMINISTRATOR BARBARA MCDONALD AT ADDRESS ABOVE FOR COMPLETE INFORMATION.

711

NATIONAL CONSORTIUM FOR GRADUATE DEGREES FOR MINORITIES IN ENGINEERING & SCIENCE INC. (FELLOWSHIPS)

PO BOX 537
NOTRE DAME IN 46556
219/287-1097; FAX 219/287-1486

AMOUNT: FULL TUITION & FEES + ANNUAL STIPEND

DEADLINE(S): DEC 1

FIELD(S): ENGINEERING; NATURAL SCIENCES

MASTERS & DOCTORATE FELLOWSHIPS FOR ETHNIC/RACIAL MINORITIES (BLACK AMERICAN; MEXICAN AMERICAN; PUERTO RICAN; AMERICAN INDIAN). MUST BE USA CITIZEN AT TIME OF APPLICATION.

250 FELLOWSHIPS PER YEAR. ADDRESS INQUIRIES TO HOWARD G. ADAMS; EXECUTIVE DIRECTOR.

712

NATIONAL OCEANIC AND ATMOSPHERIC ADMINISTRATION (NATIONAL SEA GRANT COLLEGE PROGRAM)

1335 EAST-WEST HIGHWAY
SILVER SPRING MD 20910
WRITTEN INQUIRY

AMOUNT: $24000 (SALARY & LIVING EXPENSES)

DEADLINE(S): APPLY DURING SPRING/SUMMER MONTHS

FIELD(S): MARINE SCIENCE

OPEN TO STUDENTS WITH ADVANCED STANDING IN AN ACCREDITED GRADUATE OR PROFESSIONAL DEGREE PROGRAM IN A MARINE RELATED FIELD. PROGRAM MATCHES STUDENT WITH HOST IN THE EXECUTIVE OR LEGISLATIVE BRANCH OR DC BASED ASSOCIATIONS.

ONE-YEAR PAID FELLOWSHIP IN WASHINGTON. NON-RENEWABLE. UNDERGRADUATE INQUIRIES WILL -NOT- BE ACKNOWLEDGED. WRITE FOR COMPLETE INFORMATION.

713

NATIONAL RESEARCH COUNCIL (NATIONAL SCIENCE FOUNDATION GRADUATE FELLOWSHIPS)

2101 CONSTITUTION AVE
WASHINGTON DC 20418
202/334-2872

AMOUNT: $14000 STIPEND + $7000 TUITION ALLOWANCE

DEADLINE(S): NOV 10

FIELD(S): SOCIAL SCIENCES; PHYSICAL SCIENCES; MATHEMATICS; BIOLOGY; ENGINEERING

DOCTORAL) WHO HAVE NOT COMPLETED MORE THAN 1 YEAR OF GRAD STUDY. FELLOWSHIPS TENABLE AT ANY ACCREDITED INSTITUTION OFFERING ADVANCED DEGREES IN THE AREAS ABOVE. USA CITIZEN OR PERMANENT RESIDENT.

OPEN TO HISTORY & PHILOSOPHY OF SCIENCE STUDENTS ALSO. 950 NEW 3-YEAR FELLOWSHIPS AWARDED EACH YEAR. WRITE FOR COMPLETE INFORMATION.

714

SPORT FISHERY RESEARCH PROGRAM (GRADUATE FELLOWSHIPS)

1010 MASSACHUSETTS AVE NW #320
WASHINGTON DC 20001
202/898-0770

AMOUNT: $500 - $5000

DEADLINE(S): MAR 1

FIELD(S): RECREATIONAL FISHERIES; AQUATIC RESOURCE CONSERVATION

FELLOWSHIPS FOR GRADUATE LEVEL RESEARCH IN VARIOUS PHASES OF RECREATIONAL FISHERIES INCLUDING LIFE HISTORIES; ENVIRONMENTAL CONCERNS ETC. USA CITIZEN OR LEGAL RESIDENT.

20 AWARDS PER YEAR. WRITE FOR COMPLETE INFORMATION AND APPLICATION FORMS. CONTACT MS. CHRISTINE ALTMAN; GRANTS ADMINISTRATOR.

NATURAL HISTORY

715

AMERICAN ASSOCIATION OF PETROLEUM GEOLOGISTS (GRANTS-IN-AID)

C/O W.A. MORGAN; PO BOX 979
TULSA OK 74101
918/584-2555 EXT 239

AMOUNT: $2000 MAX ($500 - $1740 AVG)

DEADLINE(S): JAN 15

FIELD(S): PETROLEUM GEOLOGY; GEOLOGY; GEOPHYSICS; PALEONTOLOGY

GRANTS IN SUPPORT OF RESEARCH PROJECTS LEADING TO THE MASTERS OR DOCTORAL DEGREE. PREFERENCE TO PROJECTS RELATED TO THE SEARCH FOR HYDROCARBONS; ECONOMIC SEDIMENTARY MINERALS OR ENVIRONMENTAL GEOLOGY.

50 GRANTS PER YEAR. WRITE FOR COMPLETE INFORMATION.

716

AMERICAN COUNCIL OF LEARNED SOCIETIES (ACLS FELLOWSHIPS)

OFFICE OF FELLOWSHIPS & GRANTS;
228 E. 45TH ST.
NEW YORK NY 10017
WRITTEN INQUIRY

AMOUNT: UP TO $20000

DEADLINE(S): SEP 30

FIELD(S): HUMANITIES; SOCIAL SCIENCES; OTHER AREAS HAVING PREDOMINATELY HUMANISTIC EMPHASIS

OPEN TO USA CITIZENS OR LEGAL RESIDENTS WHO HOLD THE PH.D OR ITS EQUIVALENT. FELLOWSHIPS ARE DESIGNED TO HELP SCHOLARS DEVOTE 2 TO 12 CONTINUOUS MONTHS TO FULL TIME RESEARCH.

WRITE FOR COMPLETE INFORMATION.

717

AMERICAN MUSEUM OF NATURAL HISTORY (THEODORE ROOSEVELT MEMORIAL FUND GRANT)

CENTRAL PARK WEST AT 79TH STREET
NEW YORK NY 10024
212/873-4225

AMOUNT: $200 - $1000

DEADLINE(S): FEB 15

FIELD(S): NATURAL HISTORY

GRANTS MAY BE OBTAINED TO COVER RESEARCH INVESTIGATIONS AT ANY LOCATION ON THE NORTH AMERICAN CONTINENT; INCLUDING TRIPS TO STUDY THE COLLECTIONS AT THE AMERICAN MUSEUM OF NATURAL HISTORY OR FOR WORK AT ANY OF THE MUSEUM'S FIELD STATIONS.

GRANTS DO NOT SUPPORT TUITION EXPENSES. WRITE FOR COMPLETE INFORMATION.

718

AMERICAN SCHOOL OF CLASSICAL STUDIES AT ATHENS (FELLOWSHIPS)

41 E.72ND ST
NEW YORK NY 10021
212/861-0302

AMOUNT: UP TO $5650 + ROOM & PARTIAL BOARD

DEADLINE(S): JAN 5

FIELD(S): CLASSICAL STUDIES; ARCHAEOLOGY; ANCIENT GREECE

FELLOWSHIPS FOR STUDY AT ASCSA IN GREECE. OPEN TO GRADUATE STUDENTS AT AMERICAN & CANADIAN COLLEGES & UNIVERSITIES. RECENT GRADUATES ALSO ARE ELIGIBLE.

WRITE FOR COMPLETE INFORMATION.

719

ARCHAEOLOGICAL INSTITUTE OF AMERICA (HARRIET POMERANCE FELLOWSHIP)

675 COMMONWEALTH AVE
BOSTON MA 02215
617/353-9361; FAX 617/353-6550

AMOUNT: $3000

DEADLINE(S): NOV 15

FIELD(S): ARCHAEOLOGY

GRADUATE FELLOWSHIP TO ENABLE A PERSON
TO WORK ON A SCHOLARLY PROJECT
RELATING TO AEGEAN BRONZE AGE
ARCHAEOLOGY. PREFERENCE TO PERSONS
WHOSE PROJECT REQUIRES TRAVEL TO THE
MEDITERRANEAN. USA OR CANADIAN
LEGAL RESIDENT.

WRITE FOR COMPLETE INFORMATION.

720

ARCHAEOLOGICAL INSTITUTE OF AMERICA (OLIVIA JAMES TRAVELING FELLOWSHIP)

675 COMMONWEALTH AVE
BOSTON MA 02215
617/353-9361; FAX 617/353-6550

AMOUNT: $11500 STIPEND

DEADLINE(S): NOV 15

FIELD(S): ARCHAEOLOGY; CLASSICS;
SCULPTURE; HISTORY; ARCHITECTURE

FOR GRADUATE OR POST-GRADUATE STUDY IN
GREECE; AEGEAN ISLANDS; SICILY;
SOUTHERN ITALY; ASIA MINOR OR
MESOPOTAMIA. PREFERENCE IS FOR
DISSERTATION OR RECENT PH.D RESEARCH.
WILL NOT SUPPORT FIELD EXCAVATION. USA
CITIZEN OR LEGAL RESIDENT.

WRITE FOR COMPLETE INFORMATION.

721

COMMITTEE ON INSTITUTIONAL COOPERATION (CIC PREDOCTORAL FELLOWSHIPS)

KIRKWOOD HALL RM 111; INDIANA UNIV.
BLOOMINGTON IN 47405
812/855-0822

AMOUNT: $9500 + TUITION (5 YEARS)

DEADLINE(S): JAN 2

FIELD(S): HUMANITIES; SOCIAL SCIENCES;
NATURAL SCIENCES; MATHEMATICS;
ENGINEERING

PREDOCTORAL FELLOWSHIPS FOR USA CITIZENS
OF AFRICAN AMERICAN; AMERICAN INDIAN;
MEXICAN AMERICAN OR PUERTO RICAN
HERITAGE. MUST HOLD OR EXPECT TO
RECEIVE BACHELOR'S DEGREE BY LATE
SUMMER FROM A REGIONALLY ACCREDITED
COLLEGE OR UNIVERSITY.

AWARDS FOR SPECIFIED UNIVERSITIES IN IL; IN;
IA; MI; MN; OH; WI; PA. WRITE FOR DETAILS.

722

COUNCIL FOR EUROPEAN STUDIES (PRE-DISSERTATION FELLOWSHIP PROGRAM)

C/O COLUMBIA UNIV; BOX 44 SCHERMERHORN
HALL
NEW YORK NY 10027
212/854-4172

AMOUNT: $3000

DEADLINE(S): FEB 1

FIELD(S): EUROPEAN HISTORY; SOCIOLOGY;
POLITICAL SCIENCE; ANTHROPOLOGY;
ECONOMICS

GRANTS FOR EXPLORATORY RESEARCH IN
EUROPE FOR GRAD STUDENTS WHO HAVE
COMPLETED AT LEAST TWO YEARS
GRADUATE STUDY AND INTEND TO PURSUE
A PH.D. USA OR CANADIAN CITIZEN OR
LEGAL RESIDENT.

APPLICANTS SHOULD HAVE AT LEAST ONE YEAR
OF STUDY IN AN APPROPRIATE FOREIGN
LANGUAGE OR MUST SHOW WHY THE
REQUIREMENT IS INAPPROPRIATE. WRITE
FOR COMPLETE INFORMATION.

723

CREOLE-AMERICAN GENEALOGICAL SOCIETY INC. (CREOLE SCHOLARSHIPS)

PO BOX 2666 - CHURCH STREET STATION
NEW YORK NY 10008
WRITTEN INQUIRY ONLY

AMOUNT: $1500

DEADLINE(S): APPLY BETWEEN JAN 1 AND APR
30

FIELD(S): GENEALOGY OR LANGUAGE OR
CREOLE CULTURE

AWARDS IN THE ABOVE AREAS OPEN TO
INDIVIDUALS OF MIXED RACIAL ANCESTRY
WHO SUBMIT A FOUR-GENERATION
GENEAOLOGICAL CHART ATTESTING TO
CREOLE ANCESTRY AND/OR INTERRACIAL
PARENTAGE. FOR UNDERGRADUATE OR
GRADUATE STUDY/RESEARCH.

FOR SCHOLARSHIP/AWARD INFORMATION SEND
$2 MONEY ORDER AND SELF ADDRESSED
STAMPED ENVELOPE TO ADDRESS ABOVE.
CASH AND PERSONAL CHECKS ARE NOT
ACCEPTED. LETTERS WITHOUT SASE AND
HANDLING CHARGE WILL NOT BE
ANSWERED.

724

EDMUND NILES HUYCK PRESERVE (GRADUATE AND POST-GRADUATE RESEARCH GRANTS)

MAIN ST
RENSSELAERVILLE NY 12147
518/797-3440

AMOUNT: UP TO $3500

DEADLINE(S): FEB 1

FIELD(S): ECOLOGY; BEHAVIOR; EVOLUTION; NATURAL HISTORY

GRANTS TO SUPPORT GRADUATE AND POST GRADUATE SCIENTISTS CONDUCTING RESEARCH ON THE NATURAL RESOURCES OF THE HUYCK PRESERVE. FUNDS ARE -NOT- AVAILABLE TO HELP STUDENTS DEFRAY COLLEGE EXPENSES.

HOUSING AND LAB SPACE ARE PROVIDED AT THE PRESERVE. WRITE FOR COMPLETE INFORMATION.

725 ─────────────

GETTY CENTER FOR THE HISTORY OF ART & THE HUMANITIES (PREDOCTORAL & POSTDOCTORAL FELLOWSHIPS)

DR H.H.HYMANS;
401 WILSHIRE BLVD; #400
SANTA MONICA CA 90401
310/458-9811

AMOUNT: $15000 PREDOCTORAL; $20000 POSTDOCTORAL

DEADLINE(S): DEC 1

FIELD(S): HUMANITIES; SOCIAL SCIENCES; ANTHROPOLOGY; ART/SCIENCE HISTORY; LITERATURE; PHILOSOPHY ETC.

OPEN TO PRE & POSTDOCTORAL SCHOLARS WHOSE AREAS OF RESEARCH COMPLEMENT THE CENTER'S PROGRAMS & RESOURCES. PREDOCTORAL CANDIDATES SHOULD EXPECT TO COMPLETE DISSERTATIONS DURING THE FELLOWSHIP YEAR.

POSTDOCTORALS SHOULD HAVE RECEIVED DOCTORATE IN HUMANITIES OR SOCIAL SCIENCES WITHIN LAST 3 YEARS & BE REWRITING DISSERTATIONS FOR PUBLICATION. WRITE FOR COMPLETE INFORMATION.

726 ─────────────

L.S.B. LEAKEY FOUNDATION (FELLOWSHIP FOR GREAT APE RESEARCH AND CONSERVATION)

77 JACK LONDON SQUARE - SUITE M
OAKLAND CA 94607
510/834-3636; FAX 510/834-3640

AMOUNT: $20000 (USUALLY)

DEADLINE(S): OCT 15

FIELD(S): ANTHROPOLOGY (PRIMATOLOGY)

AWARD TO PROMOTE LONG-TERM RESEARCH ON WILD GREAT APE POPULATIONS. PREFERENCE TO PROPOSALS PROMISING TO IMPROVE CONSERVATION OF A POPULATION OR SPECIES; ELUCIDATE CAUSES OF APE BEHAVIOR VARIATION &/OR INCREASE HUMAN BEHAVIOR UNDERSTANDING.

PRIORITY TO RESEARCH IN PREVIOUSLY UNSTUDIED HABITATS. AWARDS WILL BE MADE FOR FIELD EXPENSES ONLY. WRITE FOR COMPLETE INFORMATION.

727 ─────────────

L.S.B. LEAKEY FOUNDATION (GENERAL GRANTS)

77 JACK LONDON SQUARE
OAKLAND CA 94607
510/834-3636; FAX 510/834-3640

AMOUNT: UP TO $10000; USUALLY $3000 TO $5000

DEADLINE(S): AUG 15; JAN 2

FIELD(S): ARCHEOLOGY; PALEONTOLOGY; PRIMATOLOGY

OPEN TO DOCTORAL AND POST-DOCTORAL STUDENTS AND SENIOR SCIENTISTS FOR EXPLORATORY RESEARCH INTO HUMAN ORIGINS; BEHAVIOR AND SURVIVAL. AWARDS ARE PRIMARLY FOR FIELD WORK EXPENSES; INCLUDING MUSEUM STUDIES.

WRITE FOR COMPLETE INFORMATION.

728 ─────────────

L.S.B. LEAKEY FOUNDATION GRANTS (FELLOWSHIP FOR THE STUDY OF FORAGING PEOPLES)

77 JACK LONDON SQUARE - SUITE M
OAKLAND CA 94607
510/834-3636; FAX 510/834-3640

AMOUNT: UP TO $20000

DEADLINE(S): OCT 15

FIELD(S): ANTHROPOLOGY

OPEN TO DOCTORAL OR POST-DOCTORAL STUDENTS & SENIOR SCIENTISTS FOR RESEARCH AMONG CONTEMPORARY FORAGING PEOPLES. MAY STUDY A LARGE GEOGRAPHICAL REGION OR A PARTICULAR AREA.

FOR FIELD EXPENSES ONLY. PROPOSALS ESPECIALLY SOUGHT FOR RESEARCH THAT OTHER AGENCIES ORDINARILY WOULD NOT FUND. WRITE FOR COMPLETE INFORMATION.

729 ─────────────

NATIONAL RESEARCH COUNCIL (NATIONAL SCIENCE FOUNDATION GRADUATE FELLOWSHIPS)

2101 CONSTITUTION AVE
WASHINGTON DC 20418
202/334-2872

AMOUNT: $14000 STIPEND + $7000 TUITION ALLOWANCE

DEADLINE(S): NOV 10

FIELD(S): SOCIAL SCIENCES; PHYSICAL
SCIENCES; MATHEMATICS; BIOLOGY;
ENGINEERING

DOCTORAL) WHO HAVE NOT COMPLETED MORE
THAN 1 YEAR OF GRAD STUDY.
FELLOWSHIPS TENABLE AT ANY
ACCREDITED INSTITUTION OFFERING
ADVANCED DEGREES IN THE AREAS ABOVE.
USA CITIZEN OR PERMANENT RESIDENT.

OPEN TO HISTORY & PHILOSOPHY OF SCIENCE
STUDENTS ALSO. 950 NEW 3-YEAR
FELLOWSHIPS AWARDED EACH YEAR. WRITE
FOR COMPLETE INFORMATION.

730

SMITHSONIAN INSTITUTION (MINORITY
UNDERGRADUATE & GRADUATE
INTERNSHIP)

OFFICE OF FELLOWSHIPS & GRANTS;
955 L'ENFANT PLAZA; SUITE 7300
WASHINGTON DC 20560
202/287-3271

AMOUNT: $250 - $300 PER WEEK STIPEND +
TRAVEL

DEADLINE(S): FEB 15; JUN 15; OCT 15

FIELD(S): DESIGN; ARCHITECTURE; ART;
MUSEUM STUDIES

INTERNSHIPS OPEN TO MINORITY STUDENTS FOR
RESEARCH & STUDY AT THE SMITHSONIAN
OR THE COOPER-HEWITT MUSEUM OF
DESIGN IN NEW YORK CITY. THE MUSEUM'S
COLLECTION SPANS 3000 YEARS OF DESIGN
FROM ANCIENT POTTERY TO MODERN
FASHION & ADVERTISING.

UNDERGRADUATES RECEIVE $250 PER WEEK
STIPEND & GRADUATE STUDENTS RECEIVE
$300 PER WEEK STIPEND. WRITE FOR
COMPLETE INFORMATION.

731

SMITHSONIAN INSTITUTION (PETER KRUEGER
SUMMER INTERNSHIP PROGRAM)

COOPER-HEWITT MUSEUM;
2 EAST 91ST ST.
NEW YORK NY 10128
212/860-6868; FAX 212/860-6909

AMOUNT: $2500

DEADLINE(S): MAR 31

FIELD(S): ART HISTORY; ARCHITECTURAL
HISTORY; DESIGN

TEN WEEK SUMMER INTERNSHIPS OPEN TO
GRADUATE AND UNDERGRADUATE
STUDENTS CONSIDERING A CAREER IN THE
MUSEUM PROFESSION. INTERNS WILL ASSIST
ON SPECIAL RESEARCH OR EXHIBITION
PROJECTS AND PARTICIPATE IN DAILY
MUSEUM ACTIVITIES.

INTERNSHIP COMMENCES IN JUNE AND ENDS IN
AUGUST. HOUSING IS NOT PROVIDED. WRITE
FOR COMPLETE INFORMATION.

732

SOCIETY OF VERTEBRATE PALEONTOLOGY
(BRYAN PATTERSON AWARD)

W436 NEBRASKA HALL;
UNIV OF NEBRASKA
LINCOLN NE 68588
WRITTEN INQUIRY

AMOUNT: $500

DEADLINE(S): APR 15

FIELD(S): PALEONTOLOGY

RESEARCH GRANT OPEN TO GRADUATE
STUDENTS WHO ARE SOCIETY OF
VERTEBRATE PALEONTOLOGY MEMBERS.
PROPOSALS SHOULD BE FOR FIELDWORK ON
VERTEBRATE PALEONTOLOGY THAT IS
IMAGINATIVE - NOT PEDESTRIAN;
VENTURESOME - NOT RUN OF THE MILL.

WRITE FOR COMPLETE INFORMATION.

733

WENNER-GREN FOUNDATION FOR
ANTHROPOLOGICAL RESEARCH (PRE-
DOCTORAL & REGULAR GRANTS)

220 FIFTH AVE
NEW YORK NY 10001
212/683-5000

AMOUNT: UP TO $12000

DEADLINE(S): MAY 1; NOV 1

FIELD(S): ANTHROPOLOGY; ARCHEOLOGY &
RELATED AREAS

PRE-DOCTORAL GRANTS ARE AWARDED TO
INDIVIDUALS TO SUPPORT DISSERTAION OR
THESIS RESEARCH. REGULAR RESEARCH
GRANTS ARE AWARDED TO QUALIFIED POST-
DOCTORAL SCHOLARS WHO ARE AFFILIATED
WITH ACCREDITED INSTITUTIONS &
ORGANIZATIONS.

APPROX 160 AWARDS PER YEAR. WRITE FOR
COMPLETE INFORMATION.

SCHOOL OF SCIENCE

734

AEROSPACE EDUCATION FOUNDATION
(CHRISTA MCAULIFFE MEMORIAL AWARD)

1501 LEE HIGHWAY
ARLINGTON VA 22209
703/247-5839

AMOUNT: $1000 CASH AWARD

DEADLINE(S): JUN 30

FIELD(S): SCIENCE; MATHEMATICS (TEACHER)

CASH AWARD TO RECOGNIZE AN OUTSTANDING MATHEMATICS OR SCIENCE TEACHER (K-12 ONLY) WHO BRINGS ABOUT A FUNDAMENTAL AWARENESS OF AEROSPACE ACTIVITIES TO HIS OR HER STUDENTS. MUST BE NOMINATED BY AIR FORCE ASSOCIATION REPRESENTATIVE.

USA CITIZEN OR LEGAL RESIDENT. WRITE FOR COMPLETE INFORMATION.

735

AEROSPACE EDUCATION FOUNDATION (THEODORE VON KARMAN GRADUATE SCHOLARSHIP PROGRAM)

1501 LEE HIGHWAY
ARLINGTON VA 22209
703/247-5839

AMOUNT: $5000

DEADLINE(S): MAR 1

FIELD(S): SCIENCE; MATHEMATICS; ENGINEERING

OPEN TO AIR FORCE ROTC GRADUATE STUDENTS WHO WILL PURSUE ADVANCED DEGREES IN THE FIELDS OF SCIENCE; MATHEMATICS; PHYSICS; OR ENGINEERING. USA CITIZEN OR LEGAL RESIDENT.

10 AWARDS PER YEAR BASED ON APTITUDE; ATTITUDE AND CAREER PLANS. WRITE FOR COMPLETE INFORMATION.

736

AMERICAN ASSOCIATION OF UNIVERSITY WOMEN - HONOLULU BRANCH (HARTT FELLOWSHIP FOR GRADUATE WOMEN IN SCIENCE)

1802 KEEAUMOKU ST
HONOLULU HI 96822
808/537-4702

AMOUNT: $2000

DEADLINE(S): MAY 1

FIELD(S): NATURAL OR PHYSICAL SCIENCES

OPEN TO A FEMALE WHO IS A BONA FIDE RESIDENT OF HAWAII AND IS ENROLLED IN AN ADVANCED DEGREE (PH.D) PROGRAM IN THE NATURAL OR PHYSICAL SCIENCES. MUST SHOW OUTSTANDING ABILITY AND DEMONSTRATE FINANCIAL NEED.

WRITE FOR COMPLETE INFORMATION.

737

AMERICAN UROLOGICAL ASSN & NATIONAL KIDNEY FOUNDATION (RESIDENT RESEARCH FELLOWSHIPS)

C/O NATIONAL KIDNEY FOUNDATION;
30 E. 33RD ST.
NEW YORK NY 10016
212/889-2210

AMOUNT: $25000 STIPEND

DEADLINE(S): SEP 15

FIELD(S): NEPHROLOGY; UROLOGY

RESEARCH FELLOWSHIPS FOR UROLOGY AND NEPHROLOGY RESIDENTS IN TRAINING WITH NO MORE THAN 1 YEAR OF RESEARCH EXPERIENCE ABOVE DOCTORATE LEVEL. NEED STRONG INTEREST IN CLINICAL OR LAB RESEARCH WITHIN BROAD FIELDS OF NEPHROLOGY AND UROLOGY.

WRITE FOR COMPLETE INFORMATION.

738

CARMELA GAGLIARDI FOUNDATION (HEALTH SCIENCES SCHOLARSHIP)

PO BOX 8396
BLOOMFIELD HILLS MI 48302
313/332-6223

AMOUNT: $1000 - $10000

DEADLINE(S): MAR 1

FIELD(S): HEALTH SCIENCES

OPEN TO STUDENTS OF ITALIAN DESCENT WHO ARE ENROLLED IN OR ACCEPTED TO AN ACCREDITED POST GRADUATE PROGRAM AND ARE IN THE TOP 25% OF THEIR CLASS. FINANCIAL NEED VERIFICATION BY SCHOOL FINANCIAL AID OFFICE IS NEEDED.

RENEWABLE. WRITE FOR COMPLETE INFORMATION.

739

CHEMICAL MANUFACTURERS ASSOCIATION (TEACHER AWARDS)

2501 M STREET NW
WASHINGTON DC 20037
202/887-1223

AMOUNT: $2500 REGIONAL AWARD; $5000 NATIONAL

DEADLINE(S): JAN 29

FIELD(S): SCIENCE ; CHEMISTRY; CHEMICAL ENGINEERING

SIX NATIONAL AND 8 REGIONAL AWARDS WILL BE OFFERED TO COLLEGE AND HIGH SCHOOL CHEMISTRY OR CHEMICAL ENGINEERING TEACHERS IN THE USA OR CANADA. CRITERIA ARE EXCELLENCE IN TEACHING; DEDICATION & MOTIVATION OF STUDENTS TO SCIENCE CAREERS.

FOR TEACHERS OF GENERAL SCIENCE; CHEMISTRY AND CHEMICAL ENGINEERING - ONLY-. WRITE FOR COMPLETE INFORMATION.

740 ——————————————

GIRTON COLLEGE (FELLOWSHIPS)

SECRETARY TO THE ELECTORS
CAMBRIDGE CB3 OJG ENGLAND
338 999

AMOUNT: UP TO 10000 POUNDS STERLING PER YEAR

DEADLINE(S): OCT 14

FIELD(S): HUMANITIES; SCIENCE

APPLICATIONS ARE INVITED FOR RESEARCH FELLOWSHIPS AT GIRTON COLLEGE TENABLE FOR THREE YEARS BEGINNING OCT 1. THE FELLOWSHIPS ARE OPEN TO MEN AND WOMEN GRADUATES OF ANY UNIVERSITY.

A STATEMENT OF APPROXIMATELY 1000 WORDS OUTLINING THE RESEARCH TO BE UNDERTAKEN MUST BE SUBMITTED. WRITE FOR APPLICATION FORM AND COMPLETE INFORMATION.

741 ——————————————

KNIGHT SCIENCE JOURNALISM FELLOWSHIPS

BUILDING 9; ROOM 315; MASSACHUSETTS INSTITUTE OF TECHNOLOGY
CAMBRIDGE MA 02139
617/253-3442

AMOUNT: $26000 + $2000 RELOCATION ALLOWANCE

DEADLINE(S): MAR 1

FIELD(S): SCIENCE JOURNALISM

PROGRAM AT MIT OPEN TO SCIENCE JOURNALISTS (PRINT OR BROADCAST) WITH AT LEAST 3 YEARS EXPERIENCE. FELLOWS ATTEND SEMINARS WITH LEADING SCIENTISTS & ENGINEERS; VISIT LABORATORIES; AUDIT CLASSES & ATTEND WORKSHOPS ON SCIENCE JOURNALISM.

FELLOWSHIPS OPEN TO SCIENCE & TECHNOLOGY JOURNALISTS FROM THE USA. FOREIGN JOURNALISTS MAY APPLY IF THEY CAN OBTAIN FUNDING IN THEIR OWN COUNTRIES. WRITE FOR COMPLETE INFORMATION.

742 ——————————————

NATIONAL CONSORTIUM FOR GRADUATE DEGREES FOR MINORITIES IN ENGINEERING & SCIENCE INC. (FELLOWSHIPS)

PO BOX 537
NOTRE DAME IN 46556
219/287-1097; FAX 219/287-1486

AMOUNT: FULL TUITION & FEES + ANNUAL STIPEND

DEADLINE(S): DEC 1

FIELD(S): ENGINEERING; NATURAL SCIENCES

MASTERS & DOCTORATE FELLOWSHIPS FOR ETHNIC/RACIAL MINORITIES (BLACK AMERICAN; MEXICAN AMERICAN; PUERTO RICAN; AMERICAN INDIAN). MUST BE USA CITIZEN AT TIME OF APPLICATION.

250 FELLOWSHIPS PER YEAR. ADDRESS INQUIRIES TO HOWARD G. ADAMS; EXECUTIVE DIRECTOR.

743 ——————————————

NATIONAL FEDERATION OF THE BLIND (HOWARD BROWN RICKARD SCHOLARSHIP)

814 4TH AVE #200
GRINNELL IA 50112
515/236-3366

AMOUNT: $2500

DEADLINE(S): MAR 31

FIELD(S): NATURAL SCIENCES; ARCHITECTURE; ENGINEERING; MEDICINE; LAW

SCHOLARSHIPS FOR UNDERGRADUATE OR GRADUATE STUDY IN THE ABOVE AREAS. OPEN TO LEGALLY BLIND STUDENTS ENROLLED FULL TIME AT ACCREDITED POST SECONDARY INSTITUTIONS.

AWARDS BASED ON ACADEMIC EXCELLENCE; SERVICE TO THE COMMUNITY AND FINANCIAL NEED. WRITE FOR COMPLETE INFORMATION.

744 ——————————————

NORTH ATLANTIC TREATY ORGANIZATION (NATO SCIENCE FELLOWSHIPS FOR USA CITIZENS)

B-1110; SCIENCE AFFAIRS DIV
BRUSSELS BELGIUM
2 728-41-11

AMOUNT: VARIES WITH COUNTRY

DEADLINE(S): NOV 1

FIELD(S): SCIENCES

GRADUATE & POST-DOCTORAL FELLOWSHIPS IN ALMOST ALL SCIENTIFIC AREAS; INCLUDING INTERDISCIPLINARY AREAS. OPEN TO USA CITIZENS WHO WISH TO STUDY AND/OR DO RESEARCH IN ANOTHER NATO MEMBER COUNTRY.

THE PROGRAM IS ADMINISTERED IN EACH NATO COUNTRY BY A NATIONAL ADMINISTRATOR. WRITE FOR COMPLETE INFORMATION.

745 ——————————————

NORTH CAROLINA STUDENT LOAN PROGRAM FOR HEALTH; SCIENCE; & MATHEMATICS (LOANS)

3824 BARRETT DR.; SUITE 304
RALEIGH NC 27619
919/733-2164

AMOUNT: $2500 - $7500 PER YEAR

DEADLINE(S): JAN 8 - MAY 5

FIELD(S): HEALTH PROFESSIONS; SCIENCES; ENGINEERING

LOW-INTEREST SCHOLARSHIP LOANS OPEN TO NORTH CAROLINA RESIDENTS OF AT LEAST 1 YEAR WHO ARE PURSUING AN ASSOCIATES; UNDERGRADUATE OR GRADUATE DEGREE IN THE ABOVE FIELDS AT AN ACCREDITED INSTITUTION IN THE USA.

LOANS MAY BE RETIRED AFTER GRADUATION BY WORKING (1 YEAR FOR EACH YEAR FUNDED) AT DESIGNATED INSTITUTIONS. WRITE FOR COMPLETE DETAILS.

746

OREGON STATE SCHOLARSHIP COMMISSION (MEDICAL; DENTAL & VETERINARY LOANS)

1445 WILLAMETTE STREET
EUGENE OR 97401
503/346-1240

AMOUNT: UP TO $4000

DEADLINE(S): NONE SPECIFIED

FIELD(S): MEDICINE; DENTISTRY; VETERINARY MEDICINE

LOANS AVAILABLE TO OREGON RESIDENTS ENROLLED FULL TIME AT OREGON HEALTH SCIENCES UNIV OR VET PROGRAM OF OREGON STATE UNIV. MUST SHOW SATISFACTORY ACADEMIC PROGRESS AND DEMONSTRATE FINANCIAL NEED.

CONTACT EDUCATIONAL INSTITUTION'S FINANCIAL AID OFFICE FOR COMPLETE INFORMATION.

747

SAN JOAQUIN MEDICAL SOCIETY (SCHOLARSHIP-LOAN FUND)

PO BOX 230; 110 W. WEBER AVE
STOCKTON CA 95201
209/948-1334

AMOUNT: VARIES

DEADLINE(S): EARLY SPRING

FIELD(S): MEDICINE/NURSING

APPLICANTS MUST BE RESIDENTS OF SAN JOAQUIN COUNTY AND ENROLLED IN A GRADUATE PROGRAM AT A USA SCHOOL. LOANS ARE INTEREST FREE IF REPAID UPON RECEIPT OF PROFESSIONAL DEGREE. MUST STUDY FULL TIME.

NUMBER OF LOANS VARIES. MUST SUBMIT TRANSCRIPTS WITH APPLICATION. CONTACT MICHAEL A. MONNICH EXEC. SECRETARY ADDRESS ABOVE FOR COMPLETE INFORMATION.

748

SIGMA DELTA EPSILON-GRADUATE WOMEN IN SCIENCE (SDE FELLOWSHIPS; ELOISE GERRY FELLOWSHIPS)

ONE ILLINOIS CENTER;
111 E. WACKER DR.
CHICAGO IL 60601
312/616-0800

AMOUNT: $2600 - $4000 (SDE); $2300 - $2700 (ELOISE GERRY)

DEADLINE(S): DEC 1 (POSTMARK)

FIELD(S): BIOLOGY; CHEMISTRY; NATURAL SCIENCES; PHYSICAL SCIENCES; BIOLOGICAL SCIENCES; COMPUTER SCIENCES

WOMEN ONLY. OPEN TO GRADUATE STUDENTS AND POST-DOCTORAL RESEARCHERS IN THE ABOVE AREAS. FELLOWSHIPS MAY ONLY BE USED TO SUPPORT SCIENTIFIC RESEARCH AND/OR PROJECTS. FINANCIAL NEED IS A MAJOR CONSIDERATION.

ELOISE GERRY FELLOWSHIPS ARE LIMITED TO THE CHEMICAL AND BIOLOGICAL SCIENCES. WRITE FOR COMPLETE INFORMATION.

749

SIGMA XI-THE SCIENTIFIC RESEARCH SOCIETY (RESEARCH GRANTS)

PO BOX 13975; 99 ALEXANDER DR.
RESEARCH TRIANGLE PARK NC 27709
919/549-4691

AMOUNT: UP TO $2500 IN ASTRONOMY OR EYE/VISION RESEARCH; UP TO $1000 IN ANY OTHER SCIENTIFIC FIELD

DEADLINE(S): FEB 1; MAY 1; NOV 1

FIELD(S): SCIENCE RESEARCH

GRANTS TO SUPPORT SCIENTIFIC INVESTIGATION IN ANY FIELD. ALL FUNDS MUST BE EXPENDED DIRECTLY IN SUPPORT OF THE PROPOSED INVESTIGATION. PRIORITY IS GIVEN TO RESEARCH SCIENTISTS IN EARLY STAGE OF CAREER.

WRITE FOR COMPLETE INFORMATION.

750

SOCIETY OF HISPANIC PROFESSIONAL ENGINEERS FOUNDATION (SHPE SCHOLARSHIPS)

5400 E. OLYMPIC BLVD. SUITE 306
LOS ANGELES CA 90022
213/888-2080

AMOUNT: $500 - $3000

DEADLINE(S): APR 15

FIELD(S): ENGINEERING & SCIENCE

BIOLOGY

OPEN TO DESERVING STUDENTS OF HISPANIC DESCENT WHO ARE SEEKING CAREERS IN ENGINEERING AND SCIENCE. FOR FULL TIME UNDERGRADUATE OR GRADUATE STUDY AT A COLLEGE OR UNIVERSITY. ACADEMIC ACHIEVEMENT AND FINANCIAL NEED ARE CONSIDERATIONS.

WRITE FOR COMPLETE INFORMATION.

---

751 —————————————

SPACE FOUNDATION (SPACE INDUSTRIALIZATION FELLOWSHIP)

4800 RESEARCH FOREST DR
THE WOODLANDS TX 77381
713/363-7944; FAX 713/363-7914

AMOUNT: $4000

DEADLINE(S): OCT 1

FIELD(S): SCIENCES & ENGINEERING; BUSINESS; LAW; ECONOMICS; SOCIAL SCIENCES; ENVIRONMENTAL STUDIES; HUMANITIES

OPEN TO SUPERIOR GRADUATE STUDENTS IN THE ABOVE DISCIPLINES WHO INTEND TO DEVOTE THEIR CAREERS TO THE FURTHERANCE OF PRACTICAL SPACE RESEARCH; ENGINEERING; BUSINESS OR OTHER APPLICATION VENTURES.

CONTACT DR. DAVID J. NORTON; EDUCATIONAL GRANT PROGRAM CHAIRMAN; ADDRESS ABOVE; FOR COMPLETE INFORMATION.

---

752 —————————————

WILLIAM M. GRUPE FOUNDATION INC (SCHOLARSHIPS)

PO BOX 775
LIVINGSTON NJ 07039
201/661-9387

AMOUNT: $500 - $2000

DEADLINE(S): MAR 1

FIELD(S): MEDICINE; NURSING

FOR RESIDENTS OF BERGEN; ESSEX OR HUDSON COUNTY NJ. ANNUAL SCHOLARSHIP AID TO GOOD STUDENTS IN NEED OF FINANCIAL SUPPORT IN THE ABOVE FIELDS. USA CITIZEN.

50-100 AWARDS PER YEAR. STUDENTS MAY APPLY EVERY YEAR. WRITE FOR COMPLETE INFORMATION.

BIOLOGY

---

753 —————————————

AMERICAN ASSOCIATION FOR THE ADVANCEMENT OF SCIENCE (SCIENCE & ENGINEERING FELLOWSHIPS)

1333 'H' STREET NW
WASHINGTON DC 20005
202/326-6600

AMOUNT: UP TO $38500

DEADLINE(S): JAN 15

FIELD(S): SCIENCE; ENGINEERING

POST-DOCTORAL FELLOWSHIPS OPEN TO AAAS MEMBERS OR APPLICANTS CONCURRENTLY APPLYING FOR MEMBERSHIP. PROSPECTIVE FELLOWS MUST DEMONSTRATE EXCEPTIONAL COMPETENCE IN AN AREA OF SCIENCE OR HAVE A BROAD SCIENTIFIC OR TECHNICAL BACKGROUND.

ONE-YEAR FELLOWSHIPS. SEND INQUIRIES TO PROGRAM DIRECTOR; CONGRESSIONAL SCIENCE FELLOWS PROGRAM; ADDRESS ABOVE.

---

754 —————————————

AMERICAN MUSEUM OF NATURAL HISTORY (FRANK M. CHAPMAN MEMORIAL FUND)

CENTRAL PARK AT 79TH STREET
NEW YORK NY 10024
212/769-5775

AMOUNT: GRANTS AVERAGE $500; RANGE $200 - $1000. 1 OR 2 YEAR POST-DOCTORAL FELLOWSHIPS IN RESIDENCE.

DEADLINE(S): JAN 15

FIELD(S): ORNITHOLOGY

FOR GRADUATE STUDENTS AND POST-DOCTORAL SCHOLARS OR DISTINGUISHED ORNITHOLOGISTS. FUNDS ARE NOT AWARDED FOR TUITION OR BOOKS. APPLICATIONS MUST BE ON PRESCRIBED FORMS.

FOR DETAILS WRITE TO OFFICE OF GRANTS AND FELLOWSHIPS AT THE ADDRESS ABOVE.

---

755 —————————————

AMERICAN MUSEUM OF NATURAL HISTORY (FRANK M. CHAPMAN MEMORIAL GRANTS)

CENTRAL PARK WEST AT 79TH ST
NEW YORK NY 10024
212/769-5775

AMOUNT: $1000 MAX

DEADLINE(S): JAN 15

FIELD(S): ORNITHOLOGY

GRANTS TO ENCOURAGE RESEARCH IN ORNITHOLOGY. OPEN TO GRADUATE STUDENTS & YOUNG SCIENTISTS. GRANTS PROVIDE MODEST SUPPORT FOR MUSEUM; FIELD OR LABORATORY RESEARCH PROJECTS.

WRITE FOR COMPLETE INFORMATION.

756

AMERICAN ORCHID SOCIETY (GRANTS FOR ORCHID RESEARCH)

6000 SOUTH OLIVE AVE
WEST PALM BEACH FL 33405
407/585-8666

AMOUNT: UP TO $10000 PER YEAR FOR UP TO 3 YEARS

DEADLINE(S): JAN 1; AUG 1

FIELD(S): BOTANY; HORTICULTURE

GRANTS FOR EXPERIMENTAL PROJECTS AND FUNDAMENTAL & APPLIED RESEARCH ON ORCHIDS. QUALIFIED GRADUATE STUDENTS WITH APPROPRIATE INTERESTS MAY APPLY FOR GRANTS IN SUPPORT OF THEIR RESEARCH IF IT INVOLVES OR APPLIES TO ORCHIDS.

POST GRADUATES MAY APPLY -ONLY- ON BEHALF OF THE ACCREDITED INSTITUTION OF HIGHER LEARNING OR APPROPRIATE RESEARCH INSTITUTE THEY REPRESENT. WRITE FOR COMPLETE INFORMATION.

757

AMERICAN SOCIETY FOR ENGINEERING EDUCATION (OFFICE OF NAVAL RESEARCH GRADUATE FELLOWSHIP PROGRAM)

ELEVEN DUPONT CIRCLE #200
WASHINGTON DC 20036
202/745-3616

AMOUNT: $15000

DEADLINE(S): JAN 31

FIELD(S): ELEC ENG; MECH ENG; AEROSPACE ENG; MATHEMATICS; PHYSICS; COMPUTER SCIENCE; MATERIALS SCIENCE; BIOLOGICAL-BIOMEDICAL SCIENCE; NAVAL ARCHITECTURE & OCEAN ENG; RELATED FIELDS

LIMITED TO INDIVIDUALS WHO HAVE 'NOT' BEGUN GRADUATE PROGRAMS. FOR STUDY AND RESEARCH LEADING TO DOCTORAL DEGREE. FELLOWSHIPS ARE AWARDED ON THE BASIS OF ABILITY. USA CITIZEN.

50 THREE-YEAR FELLOWSHIPS ARE OFFERED. WRITE FOR COMPLETE INFORMATION.

758

AMERICAN SOCIETY FOR ENOLOGY AND VITICULTURE (SCHOLARSHIP)

PO BOX 1855
DAVIS CA 95617
916/753-3142

AMOUNT: NO PREDETERMINED AMOUNTS

DEADLINE(S): MAR 1

FIELD(S): ENOLOGY (WINE MAKING); VITICULTURE (GRAPE GROWING)

FOR COLLEGE JUNIORS; SENIORS OR GRAD STUDENTS ENROLLED IN AN ACCREDITED NORTH AMERICAN COLLEGE OR UNIVERSITY IN A SCIENCE CURRICULUM BASIC TO THE WINE AND GRAPE INDUSTRY. NORTH AMERICAN RESIDENT.

UNDERGRADS NEED 3.0 OR BETTER OVERALL GPA; GRADS 3.2 OR BETTER OVERALL GPA. SCHOLARSHIPS ARE RENEWABLE; FINANCIAL NEED IS CONSIDERED. WRITE FOR COMPLETE INFORMATION.

759

AMERICAN SOCIETY OF ZOOLOGISTS (LIBBIE H HYMAN SCHOLARSHIP FUND)

104 SIRIUS CIRCLE
THOUSAND OAKS CA 91360
WRITTEN INQUIRY ONLY

AMOUNT: VARIES

DEADLINE(S): MAR 30

FIELD(S): ZOOLOGY - SUMMER RESEARCH

OPEN TO COLLEGE SENIORS AND BEGINNING GRADUATE STUDENTS. MODEST GRANTS-IN-AID INTENDED TO PARTIALLY SUPPORT SUMMER FIELD STATION RESEARCH.

REQUEST APPLICATIONS FROM DR. JOSEPH L. SIMON; DEPT. OF BIOLOGY; UNIV. OF SOUTH FLA.; TAMPA FL 33620

760

ASSOCIATION FOR WOMEN IN SCIENCE EDUCATIONAL FOUNDATION (AWIS PRE-DOCTORAL AWARDS)

1522 K STREET NW SUITE 820
WASHINGTON DC 20005
202/408-0742

AMOUNT: $500

DEADLINE(S): JAN 15

FIELD(S): ENGINEERING; LIFE SCIENCES; MATHEMATICS; PHYSICAL SCIENCES; BEHAVIORAL SCIENCES; SOCIAL SCIENCES

SCHOLARSHIP AID & INCENTIVE AWARDS OPEN TO WOMEN WHO ARE WORKING ACTIVELY TOWARDS A DOCTORAL DEGREE IN THE ABOVE AREAS. USA CITIZENS MAY STUDY IN USA OR ABROAD; NON-CITIZENS MUST BE ENROLLED IN USA INSTITUTION.

APPLICATIONS ARE AVAILABLE OCT 1 - DEC 15. WRITE FOR COMPLETE INFORMATION.

761

BROOKHAVEN NATIONAL LABORATORY (POSTDOCTORAL RESEARCH ASSOCIATESHIPS)

BROOKHAVEN NATIONAL LABORATORY;
ASSOCIATED UNIVERSITIES INC.
UPTON L.I. NY 11973
516/282-7813

BIOLOGY

AMOUNT: $27000 MINIMUM

DEADLINE(S): THROUGHOUT THE YEAR.

FIELD(S): CHEMISTRY; PHYSICS; MATERIALS SCIENCE; BIOLOGY; OCEANOGRAPHY; MEDICAL SCIENCE

POST-DOCTORAL RESEARCH ASSOCIATESHIPS TENABLE AT BROOKHAVEN NATIONAL LABORATORY FOR RESEARCH TO PROMOTE FUNDAMENTAL AND APPLIED RESEARCH IN THE ABOVE FIELDS. A RECENT DOCTORAL DEGREE IS REQUIRED.

25 ASSOCIATESHIPS PER YEAR. RENEWABLE FOR TWO ADDITIONAL YEARS. WRITE TO MS. E.E. THORNHILL; OFFICE OF SCIENTIFIC PERSONNEL; ADDRESS ABOVE.

762

BUSINESS AND PROFESSIONAL WOMEN'S FOUNDATION (CAREER ADVANCEMENT SCHOLARSHIPS)

2012 MASSACHUSETTS AVE NW
WASHINGTON DC 20036
202/293-1200

AMOUNT: $500 - $1000

DEADLINE(S): APR 15 POSTMARK (APPS AVAILABLE -ONLY- OCT 1 - APR 1)

FIELD(S): COMPUTER SCIENCE; EDUCATION; PARALEGAL; ENGINEERING; SCIENCE (EXCEPT HEALTH CARE)

OPEN TO WOMEN (30 OR OLDER) WITHIN 12-24 MONTHS OF COMPLETING UNDERGRAD OR GRAD STUDY IN USA (INCLUDING PUERTO RICO & THE VIRGIN ISLANDS). SHOULD LEAD TO ENTRY OR REENTRY INTO THE WORK FORCE OR IMPROVE CAREER ADVANCEMENT CHANCES.

MUST SHOW FINANCIAL NEED. SEND SELF-ADDRESSED STAMPED ($.52) #10 ENVELOPE FOR APPLICATION & COMPLETE INFORMATION. NOT FOR STUDY AT DOCTORAL LEVEL.

763

COMMITTEE ON INSTITUTIONAL COOPERATION (CIC PREDOCTORAL FELLOWSHIPS)

KIRKWOOD HALL RM 111; INDIANA UNIV.
BLOOMINGTON IN 47405
812/855-0822

AMOUNT: $9500 + TUITION (5 YEARS)

DEADLINE(S): JAN 2

FIELD(S): HUMANITIES; SOCIAL SCIENCES; NATURAL SCIENCES; MATHEMATICS; ENGINEERING

PREDOCTORAL FELLOWSHIPS FOR USA CITIZENS OF AFRICAN AMERICAN; AMERICAN INDIAN; MEXICAN AMERICAN OR PUERTO RICAN HERITAGE. MUST HOLD OR EXPECT TO RECEIVE BACHELOR'S DEGREE BY LATE SUMMER FROM A REGIONALLY ACCREDITED COLLEGE OR UNIVERSITY.

AWARDS FOR SPECIFIED UNIVERSITIES IN IL; IN; IA; MI; MN; OH; WI; PA. WRITE FOR DETAILS.

764

CONGRESSIONAL FELLOWSHIP PROGRAM (MORRIS K. UDALL FELLOWSHIPS)

CONGRESS OF THE UNITED STATES; OFFICE OF TECHNOLOGY ASSESSMENT
WASHINGTON DC 20510
202/224-8713

AMOUNT: $35000 - $70000

DEADLINE(S): JAN 31

FIELD(S): PHYSICAL OR BIOLOGICAL SCIENCES; ENGINEERING; LAW; ECONOMICS; ENVIRONMENTAL OR SOCIAL SCIENCES; PUBLIC POLICY

ONE YEAR FELLOWSHIP PROGRAM HELD -ONLY- IN WASHINGTO DC. CANDIDATES MUST HAVE EXTENSIVE EXPERIENCE IN SCIENCE OR TECHNOLOGY ISSUES OR HAVE COMPLETED DOCTORAL LEVEL RESEARCH. EXCEPTIONAL COMPETENCY IN ABOVE AREAS REQUIRED.

CONSIDERATIONS INCLUDE ACHIEVEMENT RECORDS AND CANDIDATE'S POTENTIAL IN ONE OR MORE OF OTA'S ASSESSMENT STUDIES. WRITE FOR COMPLETE INFORMATION.

765

ELECTRONIC INDUSTRIES FOUNDATION (SCHOLARSHIP FUND)

919 18TH ST.; SUITE 900
WASHINGTON DC 20006
202/955-5814

AMOUNT: $2000

DEADLINE(S): FEB 1

FIELD(S): AERONAUTICS; COMPUTER SCIENCE; ELECTRICAL ENGINEERING; ENGINEERING TECHNOLOGY; APPLIED MATHEMATICS; MICROBIOLOGY

OPEN TO DISABLED STUDENTS WHO ARE PURSUING CAREERS IN HIGH-TECH AREAS THROUGH ACADEMIC OR TECHNICAL TRAINING. AWARDS TENABLE AT RECOGNIZED UNDERGRADUATE & GRADUATE COLLEGES & UNIVERSITIES. USA CITIZEN. FINANCIAL NEED IS A CONSIDERATION.

6 AWARDS PER YEAR. RENEWABLE. WRITE FOR COMPLETE INFORMATION.

766

EPPLEY FOUNDATION FOR RESEARCH (POST-DOCTORAL RESEARCH GRANTS)

575 LEXINGTON AVE
NEW YORK NY 10022
WRITTEN INQUIRY

AMOUNT: UP TO $25000

DEADLINE(S): FEB 1; MAY 1; AUG 1; NOV 1

FIELD(S): PHYSICAL SCIENCES; BIOLOGICAL SCIENCES

POST-DOCTORAL GRANTS FOR ORIGINAL ADVANCED RESEARCH IN ANY OF THE PHYSICAL OR BIOLOGICAL SCIENCES. OPEN TO ESTABLISHED RESEARCH SCIENTISTS WHO ARE ATTACHED TO A RECOGNIZED INSTITUTION.

WRITE FOR COMPLETE INFORMATION.

767

FLORIDA ENDOWMENT FUND FOR HIGHER EDUCATION (MCKNIGHT DOCTORAL FELLOWSHIP PROGRAM)

201 E.KENNEDY BLVD; SUITE 1525
TAMPA FL 33602
813/272-2772

AMOUNT: $11000 STIPEND + $5000 TUITION & FEES (PER YEAR)

DEADLINE(S): JAN 15

FIELD(S): ALL FIELDS (EXCEPT LAW; MEDICINE & EDUCATION)

OPEN TO ALL AFRICAN-AMERICANS WITH AT LEAST A BACHELOR'S DEGREE FROM AN ACCREDITED INSTITUTION WHO WISH TO PURSUE A DOCTORAL DEGREE. PROGRAM RECRUITS NATIONWIDE; HOWEVER FELLOWS MUST ENROLL IN A FLORIDA INSTITUTION. USA CITIZEN.

25 AWARDS PER YEAR. RENEWABLE FOR UP TO 5 YEARS. WRITE FOR COMPLETE INFORMATION.

768

FOUNDATION FOR SCIENCE & THE HANDICAPPED (GRANTS PROGRAM)

C/O REBECCA F. SMITH;
115 S. BRAINARD AVE.
LA GRANGE IL 60525
708/352-1091

AMOUNT: $1000

DEADLINE(S): DEC 1

FIELD(S): SCIENCE; MATHEMATICS; MEDICINE; COMPUTER SCIENCE; ENGINEERING

OPEN TO GRADUATE STUDENTS IN THE ABOVE AREAS WHO HAVE SOME PHYSICAL OR SENSORY DISABILITY. APPLICATIONS WILL ALSO BE ACCEPTED FROM UNDERGRADUATE SENIORS WHO HAVE BEEN ACCEPTED TO GRADUATE SCHOOL. USA CITIZEN OR LEGAL RESIDENT.

WRITE FOR COMPLETE INFORMATION.

769

INSTITUTE OF PAPER SCIENCE AND TECHNOLOGY (FELLOWSHIP PROGRAM)

575 14TH ST NW
ATLANTA GA 30318
404/853-9500

AMOUNT: FULL TUITION PLUS $11250 STIPEND

DEADLINE(S): MAR 15

FIELD(S): CHEMISTRY; CHEMICAL ENGINEERING; PHYSICS; BIOLOGY; MATHEMATICS; PULP AND PAPER TECHNOLOGY

OPEN TO GRADUATE STUDENTS WHO ARE USA OR CANADIAN CITIZENS WHO HOLD A B.S. DEGREE IN THE ABOVE FIELDS. FOR PURSUIT OF A MASTER OF SCIENCE OR PH.D. DEGREE AT THE INSTITUTE.

35 FELLOWSHIPS ANNUALLY. ADDRESS INQUIRIES TO DIRECTOR OF ADMISSIONS.

770

INTERNATIONAL SOCIETY OF ARBORICULTURE (RESEARCH TRUST)

DR FRANCIS W HOLMES;
24 BERKSHIRE TERRACE
AMHERST MA 01002
413/549-1226

AMOUNT: $2500

DEADLINE(S): DEC 1

FIELD(S): HORTICULTURE; BOTANY; ENTOMOLOGY; PHYTOPATHOLOGY

OPEN TO HORTICULTURISTS; PLANT PATHOLOGISTS; ENTOMOLOGISTS; SOIL SPECIALISTS AND OTHERS ENGAGING IN THE SCIENTIFIC STUDY OF SHADE TREES.

PROPOSALS MUST BE RECEIVED BY DEC 1. WRITE FOR COMPLETE INFORMATION.

771

MUSCULAR DYSTROPHY ASSOCIATION (POST-DOCTORAL FELLOWSHIP PROGRAM)

3561 E SUNRISE BLVD
TUCSON AZ 85718
602/529-2000

AMOUNT: $25000 AND $28000

DEADLINE(S): JUL 10; JAN 10

FIELD(S): MEDICINE; BIOLOGICAL SCIENCES; LIFE SCIENCES

GRANTS & FELLOWSHIPS FOR POST-DOCTORAL RESEARCH INTO CAUSES; DIAGNOSIS & TREATMENT OF NEUROMUSCULAR DISEASES. PREFERENCE TO THOSE WHO RECEIVED M.D.; PH.D.; D.SC. OR EQUIVALENT DEGREE WITHIN 3 YEARS OF STARTING DATE OF SUPPORT PERIOD.

100 RESEARCH FELLOWSHIPS PER YEAR. WRITE FOR COMPLETE INFORMATION.

772

MYCOLOGICAL SOCIETY OF AMERICA (GRADUATE FELLOWSHIPS)

RM. 329; B-011A - BARC WEST
BELTSVILLE MD 20705
301/504-5327

AMOUNT: $1000

DEADLINE(S): MAR 1

FIELD(S): MYCOLOGY

FELLOWSHIPS FOR THE STUDY OF FUNGUS BY PH.D CANDIDATES AT ACCREDITED USA OR CANADIAN UNIVERSITIES. MSA FELLOWSHIPS ARE AWARDED ONLY TO STUDENT MEMBERS OF THE MYCOLOGICAL SOCIETY OF AMERICA. PREVIOUS RECIPIENTS ARE NOT ELIGIBLE.

WRITE FOR COMPLETE INFORMATION.

773

NATIONAL ASSOCIATION OF WATER COMPANIES - NEW JERSEY CHAPTER (SCHOLARSHIP)

C/O NJ-AMERICAN WATER CO -
EASTERN DIV 661 SHREWSBURY AVE
SHREWSBURY NJ 07702
908/842-6900; FAX 908/842-7541

AMOUNT: $2500

DEADLINE(S): APR 1 (POSTMARK)

FIELD(S): BUSINESS ADMINISTRATION; BIOLOGY; CHEMISTRY; ENGINEERING

OPEN TO USA CITIZENS WHO HAVE LIVED IN NJ AT LEAST 5 YEARS AND PLAN A CAREER IN THE INVESTOR-OWNED WATER UTILITY INDUSTRY IN DISCIPLINES SUCH AS THOSE ABOVE. MUST BE UNDERGRAD OR GRADUATE STUDENT IN A 2 OR 4 YEAR NJ COLLEGE OR UNIVERSITY.

GPA OF 3.0 OR BETTER REQUIRED. WRITE FOR COMPLETE INFORMATION.

774

NATIONAL RESEARCH COUNCIL (HOWARD HUGHES MEDICAL INSTITUTE PREDOCTORAL FELLOWHIPS IN BIOLOGICAL SCIENCES)

FELLOWSHIP OFFC;
2101 CONSTITUTION AV NW
WASHINGTON DC 20418
202/334-2872

AMOUNT: $14000 ANNUAL STIPEND + $11700 COST OF EDUCATION ALLOWANCE

DEADLINE(S): NOV 1

FIELD(S): BIOLOGICAL SCIENCES

OPEN TO COLLEGE SENIORS OR GRADUATES AT OR NEAR THE BEGINNING OF THEIR STUDY TOWARD A PH.D OR SC.D IN BIOLOGICAL SCIENCES. USA CITIZENS MAY STUDY IN THE USA OR ABROAD; FOREIGN NATIONALS MAY STUDY ONLY IN THE USA.

WRITE FOR COMPLETE INFORMATION.

775

NATIONAL RESEARCH COUNCIL (NATIONAL SCIENCE FOUNDATION GRADUATE FELLOWSHIPS)

2101 CONSTITUTION AVE
WASHINGTON DC 20418
202/334-2872

AMOUNT: $14000 STIPEND + $7000 TUITION ALLOWANCE

DEADLINE(S): NOV 10

FIELD(S): SOCIAL SCIENCES; PHYSICAL SCIENCES; MATHEMATICS; BIOLOGY; ENGINEERING

DOCTORAL) WHO HAVE NOT COMPLETED MORE THAN 1 YEAR OF GRAD STUDY. FELLOWSHIPS TENABLE AT ANY ACCREDITED INSTITUTION OFFERING ADVANCED DEGREES IN THE AREAS ABOVE. USA CITIZEN OR PERMANENT RESIDENT.

OPEN TO HISTORY & PHILOSOPHY OF SCIENCE STUDENTS ALSO. 950 NEW 3-YEAR FELLOWSHIPS AWARDED EACH YEAR. WRITE FOR COMPLETE INFORMATION.

776

NATIONAL RESEARCH COUNCIL (NRC POSTDOCTORAL & SENIOR RESEARCH ASSOCIATESHIP AWARDS)

ASSOCIATESHIP PROGRAMS GR430/D3; 2101 CONSTITUTION AVE. NW
WASHINGTON DC 20418
202/334-2760

AMOUNT: ANNUAL STIPEND FROM 27750 TO 44000 + BENEFITS

DEADLINE(S): JAN 15; APR 15; AUG 15

FIELD(S): CHEMISTRY; EARTH & ATMOSPHERIC SCIENCES; ENGINEERING & APPLIED SCIENCES; COMPUTER SCIENCE; MATHEMATICS; BIOLOGICAL & MEDICAL SCIENCES SPACE & PLANETARY SCIENCES; PHYSICS

POSTDOCTORAL & SENIOR ASSOCIATESHIP AWARDS FOR RESEARCH AT ONE OF 38 PARTICIPATING SPONSOR FEDERAL LABORATORIES. USA CITIZENSHIP REQUIRED FOR SOME OF THE SPONSOR LABORATORIES; MANY ARE OPEN TO FOREIGN NATIONALS.

WRITE FOR COMPLETE INFORMATION AND APPLICATION MATERIALS.

777

ORGANIZATION OF AMERICAN STATES DEPT OF FELLOWSHIPS & TRAINING (OAS PRA-FELLOWSHIPS)

TRAINEE SELECTION DIVISION
WASHINGTON DC 20006
202/789-3902

AMOUNT: TUITION + FEES; TRAVEL EXP & STIPEND

DEADLINE(S): APR 30; AUG 31

FIELD(S): ALL FIELDS EXCEPT MEDICINE & FOREIGN LANGUAGES

GRADUATE FELLOWSHIPS FOR USA CITIZENS OR PERMANENT RESIDENTS TO STUDY IN AN OAS MEMBER COUNTRY. MUST HAVE UNDERGRADUATE DEGREE AND HAVE DEMONSTRATED ABILITY TO PURSUE ADVANCED STUDIES IN CHOSEN FIELD.

APPLICANTS SHOULD BE FLUENT IN LANGUAGE OF COUNTRY OF INTENDED STUDY. PRIORITY IS GIVEN TO RESEARCH PROJECTS. WRITE FOR COMPLETE INFORMATION.

778

ROYAL NORWEGIAN COUNCIL FOR SCIENTIFIC & INDUSTRIAL RESEARCH (POST-DOCTORAL RESEARCH FELLOWSHIPS)

PO BOX 70 TAASEN
N-0801 OSLO NORWAY
+4722 23 76 85

AMOUNT: NOK 132000 SINGLE; NOK 156000 MARRIED + EXPENSES

DEADLINE(S): MAR 1; SEP 1

FIELD(S): NATURAL SCIENCES; ENGINEERING

POST-DOCTORAL FELLOWSHIPS OPEN TO YOUNG FOREIGN SCIENTISTS (UNDER AGE 40) WHO WISH TO DO RESEARCH WORK IN NORWAY. THEIR QUALIFICATIONS MUST CORRESPOND AT LEAST TO A BRITISH OR AMERICAN PH.D IN NATURAL SCIENCE OR ENGINEERING.

AWARDS ARE FOR ONE YEAR. 20 AWARDS PER YEAR. RENEWALS CONSIDERED. WRITE FOR COMPLETE INFORMATION.

779

SIGMA DELTA EPSILON-GRADUATE WOMEN IN SCIENCE (SDE FELLOWSHIPS; ELOISE GERRY FELLOWSHIPS)

ONE ILLINOIS CENTER;
111 E. WACKER DR.
CHICAGO IL 60601
312/616-0800

AMOUNT: $2600 - $4000 (SDE); $2300 - $2700 (ELOISE GERRY)

DEADLINE(S): DEC 1 (POSTMARK)

FIELD(S): BIOLOGY; CHEMISTRY; NATURAL SCIENCES; PHYSICAL SCIENCES; BIOLOGICAL SCIENCES; COMPUTER SCIENCES

WOMEN ONLY. OPEN TO GRADUATE STUDENTS AND POST-DOCTORAL RESEARCHERS IN THE ABOVE AREAS. FELLOWSHIPS MAY ONLY BE USED TO SUPPORT SCIENTIFIC RESEARCH AND/OR PROJECTS. FINANCIAL NEED IS A MAJOR CONSIDERATION.

ELOISE GERRY FELLOWSHIPS ARE LIMITED TO THE CHEMICAL AND BIOLOGICAL SCIENCES. WRITE FOR COMPLETE INFORMATION.

780

TERATOLOGY SOCIETY (STUDENT TRAVEL GRANTS)

9650 ROCKVILLE PIKE
BETHESDA MD 20814
301/571-1841

AMOUNT: $250

DEADLINE(S): MAY 1

FIELD(S): TERATOLOGY

TRAVEL ASSISTANCE GRANTS OPEN TO UNDERGRADUATES; GRADUATES & POST-GRADUATES FOR ATTENDANCE AT THE TERATOLOGY SOCIETY'S ANNUAL MEETING FOR ABSTRACT PRESENTATION. PURPOSE IS TO PROMOTE INTEREST IN & ADVANCE STUDY OF BIOLOGICAL ABNORMALITIES.

10 AWARDS PER YEAR. WRITE FOR COMPLETE INFORMATION.

781

TUSKEGEE INSTITUTE (GRADUATE RESEARCH FELLOWSHIPS AND ASSISTANTSHIPS)

ADMISSIONS OFFICE
TUSKEGEE INSTITUTE AL 36088
205/727-8500

AMOUNT: TUITION

DEADLINE(S): MAR 15

FIELD(S): CHEMISTRY; ENGINEERING; ENVIRONMENTAL SCIENCE; LIFE SCIENCES; NUTRITION; EDUCATION

CHEMISTRY

GRADUATE RESEARCH FELLOWSHIPS AND GRADUATE ASSISTANTSHIPS ARE AVAILABLE TO QUALIFIED INDIVIDUALS WHO WISH TO ENTER TUSKEGEE INSTITUTE'S GRADUATE PROGRAM IN PURSUIT OF A MASTER'S DEGREE.

WRITE FOR COMPLETE INFORMATION.

782

WHITEHALL FOUNDATION INC (RESEARCH GRANTS-IN-AID)

249 ROYAL PALM WAY; SUITE 202
PALM BEACH FL 33480
407/655-4474; FAX 407/659-4978

AMOUNT: $15000 MAXIMUM

DEADLINE(S): ASSIGNED WHEN APPLICATION IS ISSUED

FIELD(S): INVERTEBRATE & VERTEBRATE NEUROBIOLOGY (EXCEPT HUMANS)

GRANTS-IN-AID OPEN TO ASSISTANT PROFESSORS & SENIOR SCIENTISTS FOR INVESTIGATIONS OF NEURAL MECHNAMISMS INVOLVED IN SENSORY; MOTOR OR OTHER COMPLEX FUNCTIONS OF THE WHOLE ORGANISM.

INITIAL APPROACH SHOULD BE A ONE PAGE LETTER SUMMARIZING THE PROJECT. WRITE FOR COMPLETE INFORMATION.

783

WHITEHALL FOUNDATION INC. (RESEARCH GRANTS)

249 ROYAL PALM WAY; SUITE 202
PALM BEACH FL 33480
407-655-4474 OR FAX 407-659-4978

AMOUNT: $40000 PER YEAR (AVERAGE)

DEADLINE(S): MAR 1; SEP 1; DEC 1

FIELD(S): INVERTEBRATE & VERTEBRATE NEUROBIOLOGY (EXCEPT HUMAN BEINGS)

OPEN TO ESTABLISHED SCIENTISTS OF ALL AGES WORKING AT ACCREDITED INSTITUTIONS. FOR INVESTIGATIONS OF NEURAL MECHANISMS INVOLVED IN SENSORY; MOTOR OR OTHER COMPLEX FUNCTIONS OF THE WHOLE ORGANISM AS THEY RELATE TO BEHAVIOR.

APPLICANTS MAY NOT BE SEEKING SALARY. WRITE FOR COMPLETE INFORMATION.

784

WILSON ORNITHOLOGICAL SOCIETY (FUERTES; NICE & STEWART GRANTS)

C/O MUSEUM OF ZOOLOGY;
UNIV OF MICHIGAN
ANN ARBOR MI 48109
WRITTEN INQUIRY ONLY

AMOUNT: $200

DEADLINE(S): JAN 15

FIELD(S): ORNITHOLOGY

GRANTS TO SUPPORT AVIAN RESEARCH. OPEN TO ANYONE PRESENTING A SUITABLE RESEARCH PROBLEM IN ORNITHOLOGY. RESEARCH PROPOSAL REQUIRED.

5-6 GRANTS PER YEAR. NOT RENEWABLE. WRITE FOR COMPLETE INFORMATION.

CHEMISTRY

785

AMERICAN ASSOCIATION FOR THE ADVANCEMENT OF SCIENCE (SCIENCE & ENGINEERING FELLOWSHIPS)

1333 'H' STREET NW
WASHINGTON DC 20005
202/326-6600

AMOUNT: UP TO $38500

DEADLINE(S): JAN 15

FIELD(S): SCIENCE; ENGINEERING

POST-DOCTORAL FELLOWSHIPS OPEN TO AAAS MEMBERS OR APPLICANTS CONCURRENTLY APPLYING FOR MEMBERSHIP. PROSPECTIVE FELLOWS MUST DEMONSTRATE EXCEPTIONAL COMPETENCE IN AN AREA OF SCIENCE OR HAVE A BROAD SCIENTIFIC OR TECHNICAL BACKGROUND.

ONE-YEAR FELLOWSHIPS. SEND INQUIRIES TO PROGRAM DIRECTOR; CONGRESSIONAL SCIENCE FELLOWS PROGRAM; ADDRESS ABOVE.

786

AMERICAN PHILOSOPHICAL SOCIETY (JOHN CLARKE SLATER FELLOWSHIP)

LIBRARY; 105 S. FIFTH ST.
PHILADELPHIA PA 19106
WRITTEN INQUIRY ONLY

AMOUNT: $12000

DEADLINE(S): DEC 1

FIELD(S): HISTORY OF PHYSICAL SCIENCE

OPEN TO DOCTORAL CANDIDATES WHO HAVE PASSED THEIR PRELIMINARY EXAMINATIONS AND ARE WRITING DISSERTATIONS ON THE HISTORY OF 20TH CENTURY PHYSICAL SCIENCES.

WRITE FOR COMPLETE INFORMATION.

787

AMERICAN SOCIETY FOR ENGINEERING EDUCATION (OFFICE OF NAVAL RESEARCH GRADUATE FELLOWSHIP PROGRAM)

ELEVEN DUPONT CIRCLE #200
WASHINGTON DC 20036
202/745-3616

AMOUNT: $15000

DEADLINE(S): JAN 31

FIELD(S): ELEC ENG; MECH ENG; AEROSPACE ENG; MATHEMATICS; PHYSICS; COMPUTER SCIENCE; MATERIALS SCIENCE; BIOLOGICAL-BIOMEDICAL SCIENCE; NAVAL ARCHITECTURE & OCEAN ENG; RELATED FIELDS

LIMITED TO INDIVIDUALS WHO HAVE 'NOT' BEGUN GRADUATE PROGRAMS. FOR STUDY AND RESEARCH LEADING TO DOCTORAL DEGREE. FELLOWSHIPS ARE AWARDED ON THE BASIS OF ABILITY. USA CITIZEN.

50 THREE-YEAR FELLOWSHIPS ARE OFFERED. WRITE FOR COMPLETE INFORMATION.

788

ASSOCIATION FOR WOMEN IN SCIENCE EDUCATIONAL FOUNDATION (AWIS PRE-DOCTORAL AWARDS)

1522 K STREET NW SUITE 820
WASHINGTON DC 20005
202/408-0742

AMOUNT: $500

DEADLINE(S): JAN 15

FIELD(S): ENGINEERING; LIFE SCIENCES; MATHEMATICS; PHYSICAL SCIENCES; BEHAVIORAL SCIENCES; SOCIAL SCIENCES

SCHOLARSHIP AID & INCENTIVE AWARDS OPEN TO WOMEN WHO ARE WORKING ACTIVELY TOWARDS A DOCTORAL DEGREE IN THE ABOVE AREAS. USA CITIZENS MAY STUDY IN USA OR ABROAD; NON-CITIZENS MUST BE ENROLLED IN USA INSTITUTION.

APPLICATIONS ARE AVAILABLE OCT 1 - DEC 15. WRITE FOR COMPLETE INFORMATION.

789

AT&T BELL LABORATORIES (COOPERATIVE RESEARCH FELLOWSHIP PROGRAM FOR MINORITIES)

101 CRAWFORDS CORNER ROAD;
ROOM 1E-209; BOX 3030
HOLMDEL NJ 07733
WRITTEN INQUIRY

AMOUNT: FULL-TUITION & FEES + $13200 STIPEND PER YEAR

DEADLINE(S): JAN 15

FIELD(S): ENGINEERING; MATH; SCIENCES; COMPUTER SCIENCE

FELLOWSHIPS ARE AWARDED TO MINORITY STUDENTS WHO ARE ACCEPTED INTO AN ACCREDITED DOCTORAL PROGRAM FOR THE FOLLOWING FALL. USA CITIZEN OR PERMANENT RESIDENT.

10 AWARDS PER YEAR. RENEWABLE UP TO 4 YEARS. WRITE TO SPECIAL PROGRAMS MANAGER - CRFP FOR COMPLETE INFORMATION.

790

AT&T BELL LABORATORIES (GRADUATE RESEARCH PROGRAM FOR WOMEN)

101 CRAWFORDS CORNER ROAD;
ROOM 1E-209; BOX 3030
HOLMDEL NJ 07733
WRITTEN INQUIRY

AMOUNT: FULL TUITION & FEES + $13200 STIPEND PER YEAR

DEADLINE(S): JAN 15

FIELD(S): ENGINEERING; MATH; SCIENCES; COMPUTER SCIENCE

FOR WOMEN STUDENTS WHO HAVE BEEN ACCEPTED INTO AN ACCREDITED DOCTORAL PROGRAM FOR THE FOLLOWING FALL. USA CITIZEN OR PERMANENT RESIDENT.

FELLOWSHIPS ARE RENEWABLE FOR DURATION OF GRADUATE PROGRAM. WRITE TO SPECIAL PROGRAMS MANAGER - GRPW FOR COMPLETE INFORMATION.

791

BROOKHAVEN NATIONAL LABORATORY (POSTDOCTORAL RESEARCH ASSOCIATESHIPS)

BROOKHAVEN NATIONAL LABORATORY;
ASSOCIATED UNIVERSITIES INC.
UPTON L.I. NY 11973
516/282-7813

AMOUNT: $27000 MINIMUM

DEADLINE(S): THROUGHOUT THE YEAR.

FIELD(S): CHEMISTRY; PHYSICS; MATERIALS SCIENCE; BIOLOGY; OCEANOGRAPHY; MEDICAL SCIENCE

POST-DOCTORAL RESEARCH ASSOCIATESHIPS TENABLE AT BROOKHAVEN NATIONAL LABORATORY FOR RESEARCH TO PROMOTE FUNDAMENTAL AND APPLIED RESEARCH IN THE ABOVE FIELDS. A RECENT DOCTORAL DEGREE IS REQUIRED.

25 ASSOCIATESHIPS PER YEAR. RENEWABLE FOR TWO ADDITIONAL YEARS. WRITE TO MS. E.E. THORNHILL; OFFICE OF SCIENTIFIC PERSONNEL; ADDRESS ABOVE.

792

BUSINESS AND PROFESSIONAL WOMEN'S FOUNDATION (CAREER ADVANCEMENT SCHOLARSHIPS)

2012 MASSACHUSETTS AVE NW
WASHINGTON DC 20036
202/293-1200

CHEMISTRY

AMOUNT: $500 - $1000

DEADLINE(S): APR 15 POSTMARK (APPS AVAILABLE -ONLY- OCT 1 - APR 1)

FIELD(S): COMPUTER SCIENCE; EDUCATION; PARALEGAL; ENGINEERING; SCIENCE (EXCEPT HEALTH CARE)

OPEN TO WOMEN (30 OR OLDER) WITHIN 12-24 MONTHS OF COMPLETING UNDERGRAD OR GRAD STUDY IN USA (INCLUDING PUERTO RICO & THE VIRGIN ISLANDS). SHOULD LEAD TO ENTRY OR REENTRY INTO THE WORK FORCE OR IMPROVE CAREER ADVANCEMENT CHANCES.

MUST SHOW FINANCIAL NEED. SEND SELF-ADDRESSED STAMPED ($.52) #10 ENVELOPE FOR APPLICATION & COMPLETE INFORMATION. NOT FOR STUDY AT DOCTORAL LEVEL.

793

CHEMICAL MANUFACTURERS ASSOCIATION (TEACHER AWARDS)

2501 M STREET NW
WASHINGTON DC 20037
202/887-1223

AMOUNT: $2500 REGIONAL AWARD; $5000 NATIONAL

DEADLINE(S): JAN 29

FIELD(S): SCIENCE ; CHEMISTRY; CHEMICAL ENGINEERING

SIX NATIONAL AND 8 REGIONAL AWARDS WILL BE OFFERED TO COLLEGE AND HIGH SCHOOL CHEMISTRY OR CHEMICAL ENGINEERING TEACHERS IN THE USA OR CANADA. CRITERIA ARE EXCELLENCE IN TEACHING; DEDICATION & MOTIVATION OF STUDENTS TO SCIENCE CAREERS.

FOR TEACHERS OF GENERAL SCIENCE; CHEMISTRY AND CHEMICAL ENGINEERING -ONLY-. WRITE FOR COMPLETE INFORMATION.

794

CONGRESSIONAL FELLOWSHIP PROGRAM (MORRIS K. UDALL FELLOWSHIPS)

CONGRESS OF THE UNITED STATES; OFFICE OF TECHNOLOGY ASSESSMENT
WASHINGTON DC 20510
202/224-8713

AMOUNT: $35000 - $70000

DEADLINE(S): JAN 31

FIELD(S): PHYSICAL OR BIOLOGICAL SCIENCES; ENGINEERING; LAW; ECONOMICS; ENVIRONMENTAL OR SOCIAL SCIENCES; PUBLIC POLICY

ONE YEAR FELLOWSHIP PROGRAM HELD -ONLY- IN WASHINGTO DC. CANDIDATES MUST HAVE EXTENSIVE EXPERIENCE IN SCIENCE OR TECHNOLOGY ISSUES OR HAVE COMPLETED DOCTORAL LEVEL RESEARCH. EXCEPTIONAL COMPETENCY IN ABOVE AREAS REQUIRED.

CONSIDERATIONS INCLUDE ACHIEVEMENT RECORDS AND CANDIDATE'S POTENTIAL IN ONE OR MORE OF OTA'S ASSESSMENT STUDIES. WRITE FOR COMPLETE INFORMATION.

795

COOPERATIVE INSTITUTE FOR RESEARCH IN ENVIRONMENTAL SCIENCES (CIRES VISITING FELLOWSHIP)

UNIV OF COLORADO; CAMPUS BOX 216
BOULDER CO 80309
303/492-8020

AMOUNT: VARIES

DEADLINE(S): FEB 15

FIELD(S): ATMOSPHERIC CHEMISTRY

1-YEAR VISITING FELLOWSHIPS IN THE AREAS OF ATMOSPHERIC CHEMISTRY; ATMOSPHERIC & CLIMATE DYNAMICS; ENVIRONMENTAL CHEMISTRY & BIOLOGY; ENVIRONMENTAL MEASUREMENTS AND INSTRUMENTATION; GOLBAL CHANGE & REMOTE SENSING.

OPEN TO RECENT PH.D'S AND SENIOR SCIENTISTS INCLUDING FACULTY ON SABBATICAL. 5 FELLOWSHIPS PER YEAR. WRITE FOR COMPLETE INFORMATION.

796

ELECTROCHEMICAL SOCIETY (SUMMER RESEARCH FELLOWSHIPS)

10 SOUTH MAIN ST
PENNINGTON NJ 08534
609/737-1902

AMOUNT: $2000 - $6000

DEADLINE(S): JAN 15

FIELD(S): ENERGY; CHEMICAL ENGINEERING; CHEMISTRY; ELECTRICAL ENGINEERING

SUMMER FELLOWSHIPS OPEN TO GRADUATE STUDENTS AT ACCREDITED COLLEGES & UNIVERSITIES IN THE USA & CANADA. PURPOSE IS TO SUPPORT RESEARCH OF INTEREST TO ELECTROCHEMICAL SOCIETY & RESEARCH AIMED AT REDUCING ENERGY CONSUMPTION.

WRITE FOR COMPLETE INFORMATION.

797

EPPLEY FOUNDATION FOR RESEARCH (POST-DOCTORAL RESEARCH GRANTS)

575 LEXINGTON AVE
NEW YORK NY 10022
WRITTEN INQUIRY

AMOUNT: UP TO $25000

DEADLINE(S): FEB 1; MAY 1; AUG 1; NOV 1

FIELD(S): PHYSICAL SCIENCES; BIOLOGICAL SCIENCES

POST-DOCTORAL GRANTS FOR ORIGINAL ADVANCED RESEARCH IN ANY OF THE PHYSICAL OR BIOLOGICAL SCIENCES. OPEN TO ESTABLISHED RESEARCH SCIENTISTS WHO ARE ATTACHED TO A RECOGNIZED INSTITUTION.

WRITE FOR COMPLETE INFORMATION.

798

FANNIE AND JOHN HERTZ FOUNDATION (DOCTORAL FELLOWSHIP PROGRAM)

BOX 5032
LIVERMORE CA 94551
510/373-1642

AMOUNT: UP TO $10000 FOR TUITION + $16000 STIPEND

DEADLINE(S): NOV 1

FIELD(S): ENGINEERING; APPLIED PHYSICS; MATHEMATICS; CHEMISTRY

FELLOWSHIPS OPEN TO STUDENTS PURSUING A PH.D OR A PROFESSIONAL DEGREE IN THE ABOVE AREAS WITH A 3.75 OR BETTER GPA. STUDENTS PURSUING A JOINT DEGREE SUCH AS PH.D/MD ARE NOT ELIGIBLE TO APPLY. USA CITIZEN.

25 FELLOWSHIPS PER YEAR RENEWABLE UP TO FIVE YEARS. WRITE FOR COMPLETE INFORMATION.

799

FLORIDA ENDOWMENT FUND FOR HIGHER EDUCATION (MCKNIGHT DOCTORAL FELLOWSHIP PROGRAM)

201 E.KENNEDY BLVD; SUITE 1525
TAMPA FL 33602
813/272-2772

AMOUNT: $11000 STIPEND + $5000 TUITION & FEES (PER YEAR)

DEADLINE(S): JAN 15

FIELD(S): ALL FIELDS (EXCEPT LAW; MEDICINE & EDUCATION)

OPEN TO ALL AFRICAN-AMERICANS WITH AT LEAST A BACHELOR'S DEGREE FROM AN ACCREDITED INSTITUTION WHO WISH TO PURSUE A DOCTORAL DEGREE. PROGRAM RECRUITS NATIONWIDE; HOWEVER FELLOWS MUST ENROLL IN A FLORIDA INSTITUTION. USA CITIZEN.

25 AWARDS PER YEAR. RENEWABLE FOR UP TO 5 YEARS. WRITE FOR COMPLETE INFORMATION.

800

FOUNDATION FOR SCIENCE & THE HANDICAPPED (GRANTS PROGRAM)

C/O REBECCA F. SMITH;
115 S. BRAINARD AVE.
LA GRANGE IL 60525
708/352-1091

AMOUNT: $1000

DEADLINE(S): DEC 1

FIELD(S): SCIENCE; MATHEMATICS; MEDICINE; COMPUTER SCIENCE; ENGINEERING

OPEN TO GRADUATE STUDENTS IN THE ABOVE AREAS WHO HAVE SOME PHYSICAL OR SENSORY DISABILITY. APPLICATIONS WILL ALSO BE ACCEPTED FROM UNDERGRADUATE SENIORS WHO HAVE BEEN ACCEPTED TO GRADUATE SCHOOL. USA CITIZEN OR LEGAL RESIDENT.

WRITE FOR COMPLETE INFORMATION.

801

GEORGETOWN UNIVERSITY (DOCTORAL PROGRAM IN CHEMISTRY)

DEPARTMENT OF CHEMISTRY
WASHINGTON DC 20057
202/687-6073

AMOUNT: TUITION + $13560 STIPEND/12 MONTHS

DEADLINE(S): MAR 1

FIELD(S): CHEMISTRY

DOCTORAL FELLOWSHIPS AT GEORGETOWN UNIVERSITY. OPEN TO STUDENTS WHO HAVE THEIR BA OR BS OR EQUIVALENT DEGREE & HAVE BEEN ACCEPTED BY THE UNIVERSITY AS A PH.D CANDIDATE IN CHEMISTRY.

45-55 AWARDS PER YEAR. RENEWABLE. WRITE FOR COMPLETE INFORMATION.

802

H. FLETCHER BROWN FUND (SCHOLARSHIPS)

C/O BANK OF DELAWARE; TRUST DEPT; PO BOX 791
WILMINGTON DE 19899
302/429-2827

AMOUNT: VARIES

DEADLINE(S): APR 15

CHEMISTRY

FIELD(S): MEDICINE; DENTISTRY; LAW;
ENGINEERING; CHEMISTRY

OPEN TO STUDENTS BORN IN DELAWARE;
GRADUATED FROM A DELAWARE HIGH
SCHOOL & STILL RESIDING IN DELAWARE.
FOR FOUR YEARS OF STUDY (UNDERGRAD
OR GRAD) LEADING TO A DEGREE THAT
ENABLES APPLICANT TO PRACTICE IN
CHOSEN FIELD.

SCHOLARSHIPS ARE BASED ON NEED;
SCHOLASTIC ACHIEVEMENT; GOOD MORAL
CHARACTER. RENEWABLE. WRITE FOR
COMPLETE INFORMATION.

803

INSTITUTE OF PAPER SCIENCE AND TECHNOLOGY (FELLOWSHIP PROGRAM)

575 14TH ST NW
ATLANTA GA 30318
404/853-9500

AMOUNT: FULL TUITION PLUS $11250 STIPEND

DEADLINE(S): MAR 15

FIELD(S): CHEMISTRY; CHEMICAL
ENGINEERING; PHYSICS; BIOLOGY;
MATHEMATICS; PULP AND PAPER
TECHNOLOGY

OPEN TO GRADUATE STUDENTS WHO ARE USA
OR CANADIAN CITIZENS WHO HOLD A B.S.
DEGREE IN THE ABOVE FIELDS. FOR PURSUIT
OF A MASTER OF SCIENCE OR PH.D. DEGREE
AT THE INSTITUTE.

35 FELLOWSHIPS ANNUALLY. ADDRESS
INQUIRIES TO DIRECTOR OF ADMISSIONS.

804

INTERNATIONAL LEAD ZINC RESEARCH ORGANIZATION INC. (FELLOWSHIP PROGRAM)

PO BOX 12036; 2525 MERIDIAN PARKWAY
RESEARCH TRIANGLE PARK NC 27709
WRITTEN INQUIRY

AMOUNT: $15000 - $25000

DEADLINE(S): MAY

FIELD(S): CHEMISTRY; ENVIRONMENTAL
HEALTH; ELECTROCHEMISTRY;
METALLURGY

DOCTORAL AND POST-DOCTORAL FELLOWSHIPS
FOR RESEARCH INVOLVING LEAD; ZINC AND
CADMIUM COMPOUNDS IN CERAMICS;
CHEMISTRY; METALLURGY;
ELECTROCHEMISTRY; AND
ENVIRONMENTAL HEALTH.

ONE YEAR FELLOWSHIPS RENEWABLE FOR TWO
ADDITIONAL YEARS. WRITE FOR COMPLETE
INFORMATION.

805

INTERNATIONAL ORDER OF THE KING'S DAUGHTERS AND SONS (HEALTH CAREERS SCHOLARSHIPS)

PO BOX 1017
CHAUTAUQUA NY 14722
716/357-4951

AMOUNT: UP TO $1000

DEADLINE(S): APR 1

FIELD(S): MEDICINE; DENTISTRY; NURSING;
PHYSICAL THERAPY; OCCUPATIONAL
THERAPY; MEDICAL TECHNOLOGIES;
PHARMACY

OPEN TO STUDENTS ACCEPTED TO/ENROLLED IN
AN ACCREDITED USA OR CANADIAN 4-YR OR
GRADUATE SCHOOL. RN CANDIDATES MUST
HAVE COMPLETED 1ST YEAR; BA
CANDIDATES IN AT LEAST 3RD YEAR. PRE
MED STUDENTS -NOT- ELIGIBLE.

USA OR CANADIAN CITIZEN. THOSE SEEKING MD
OR DDS DEGREES MUST BE IN 2ND YEAR OF
MED OR DENTAL SCHOOL. FOR APPLICATION
SEND SASE TO MRS. MERLE RABER; 6024 E.
CHICAGO RD; JONESVILLE MI 49250.

806

NATIONAL ASSOCIATION OF WATER COMPANIES - NEW JERSEY CHAPTER (SCHOLARSHIP)

C/O NJ-AMERICAN WATER CO -
EASTERN DIV 661 SHREWSBURY AVE
SHREWSBURY NJ 07702
908/842-6900; FAX 908/842-7541

AMOUNT: $2500

DEADLINE(S): APR 1 (POSTMARK)

FIELD(S): BUSINESS ADMINISTRATION;
BIOLOGY; CHEMISTRY; ENGINEERING

OPEN TO USA CITIZENS WHO HAVE LIVED IN NJ
AT LEAST 5 YEARS AND PLAN A CAREER IN
THE INVESTOR-OWNED WATER UTILITY
INDUSTRY IN DISCIPLINES SUCH AS THOSE
ABOVE. MUST BE UNDERGRAD OR
GRADUATE STUDENT IN A 2 OR 4 YEAR NJ
COLLEGE OR UNIVERSITY.

GPA OF 3.0 OR BETTER REQUIRED. WRITE FOR
COMPLETE INFORMATION.

807

NATIONAL CENTER FOR ATMOSPHERIC RESEARCH (GRADUATE FELLOWSHIPS)

P.O. BOX 3000
BOULDER CO 80307
303/497-1602

AMOUNT: $12400 - $13150 STIPEND + EXPENSES

DEADLINE(S): JAN 1; APR 1; JUL 1; OCT 1

FIELD(S): ATMOSPHERIC SCIENCE; OCEAN
DYNAMICS

THIS PROGRAM IS DESIGNED TO FOSTER COOPERATIVE RESEARCH BETWEEN NCAR AND ACADEMIC INSTITUTIONS BY PROVIDING SUPPORT FOR DOCTORAL CANDIDATES WHO ARE WILLING TO WORK ON THEIR THESIS IN COOPERATION WITH AN NCAR PROGRAM.

WRITE TO COORDINATOR BARBARA MCDONALD; ADDRESS ABOVE; FOR COMPLETE INFORMATION.

808

NATIONAL CENTER FOR ATMOSPHERIC RESEARCH (POST-DOCTORAL RESEARCH FELLOWSHIPS)

PO BOX 3000
BOULDER CO 80307
303/497-1602

AMOUNT: $29800 - $31200 STIPEND PER YEAR + BENEFITS

DEADLINE(S): JAN 10

FIELD(S): ATMOSPHERIC SCIENCES

OPEN TO SCIENTISTS JUST RECEIVING THE PH.D OR EQUIVALENT AND TO THOSE WITH NO MORE THAN 4 YEARS EXPERIENCE PAST THE PH.D. CRITERIA INCLUDE SCIENTIFIC CAPABILITY & POTENTIAL; ORIGINALITY & INDEPENDENCE & ABILITY TO UNDERTAKE RESEARCH.

CONTACT ADMINISTRATOR BARBARA MCDONALD AT ADDRESS ABOVE FOR COMPLETE INFORMATION.

809

NATIONAL RESEARCH COUNCIL (NATIONAL SCIENCE FOUNDATION MINORITY GRADUATE FELLOWSHIPS)

2101 CONSTITUTION AVE.
WASHINGTON DC 20418
202/334-2872

AMOUNT: $14000 STIPEND (12 MONTHS) + UP TO $7500 FOR TUITION AND FEES

DEADLINE(S): NOV 6

FIELD(S): ENGINEERING; MATHEMATICS; COMPUTER SCIENCE; CHEMISTRY; EARTH SCIENCES; LIFE SCIENCES; PSYCHOLOGY; SOCIAL SCIENCES

OPEN MINORITY GRADUATE STUDENTS (MASTERS OR PH.D) WHO ARE USA CITIZENS OR LEGAL RESIDENTS & ARE AT OR NEAR THE BEGINNING OF THEIR GRADUATE STUDY. FELLOWSHIPS TENABLE AT ACCREDITED INSTITUTION OFFERING ADVANCED DEGREES IN THE FIELDS ABOVE.

APPROX 150 NEW 3-YEAR FELLOWSHIPS AWARDED EACH YEAR. WRITE FOR COMPLETE INFORMATION.

810

NATIONAL RESEARCH COUNCIL (NATIONAL SCIENCE FOUNDATION GRADUATE FELLOWSHIPS)

2101 CONSTITUTION AVE
WASHINGTON DC 20418
202/334-2872

AMOUNT: $14000 STIPEND + $7000 TUITION ALLOWANCE

DEADLINE(S): NOV 10

FIELD(S): SOCIAL SCIENCES; PHYSICAL SCIENCES; MATHEMATICS; BIOLOGY; ENGINEERING

DOCTORAL) WHO HAVE NOT COMPLETED MORE THAN 1 YEAR OF GRAD STUDY. FELLOWSHIPS TENABLE AT ANY ACCREDITED INSTITUTION OFFERING ADVANCED DEGREES IN THE AREAS ABOVE. USA CITIZEN OR PERMANENT RESIDENT.

OPEN TO HISTORY & PHILOSOPHY OF SCIENCE STUDENTS ALSO. 950 NEW 3-YEAR FELLOWSHIPS AWARDED EACH YEAR. WRITE FOR COMPLETE INFORMATION.

811

NATIONAL RESEARCH COUNCIL (NATIONAL SCIENCE FOUNDATION POST-DOCTORAL RESEARCH FELLOWSHIPS IN CHEMISTRY)

CHEMISTRY DIVISION; 1800 G ST. NW; ROOM 340
WASHINGTON DC 20550
202/357-7947

AMOUNT: $40000

DEADLINE(S): NOV 1

FIELD(S): CHEMISTRY

RESEARCH FELLOWSHIPS OPEN TO APPLICANTS WHO WILL FULFILL THE REQUIREMENTS FOR THE DOCTORAL DEGREE IN CHEMISTRY (OR A CLOSELY RELATED DISCIPLINE) BETWEEN JUN 1 & SEP 30 OF THE AWARD YEAR. USA CITIZEN OR PERMANENT RESIDENT.

WRITE FOR COMPLETE INFORMATION.

812

NATIONAL RESEARCH COUNCIL (NRC POSTDOCTORAL & SENIOR RESEARCH ASSOCIATESHIP AWARDS)

ASSOCIATESHIP PROGRAMS GR430/D3; 2101 CONSTITUTION AVE. NW
WASHINGTON DC 20418
202/334-2760

AMOUNT: ANNUAL STIPEND FROM 27750 TO 44000 + BENEFITS

DEADLINE(S): JAN 15; APR 15; AUG 15

CHEMISTRY

FIELD(S): CHEMISTRY; EARTH & ATMOSPHERIC SCIENCES; ENGINEERING & APPLIED SCIENCES; COMPUTER SCIENCE; MATHEMATICS; BIOLOGICAL & MEDICAL SCIENCES SPACE & PLANETARY SCIENCES; PHYSICS

POSTDOCTORAL & SENIOR ASSOCIATESHIP AWARDS FOR RESEARCH AT ONE OF 38 PARTICIPATING SPONSOR FEDERAL LABORATORIES. USA CITIZENSHIP REQUIRED FOR SOME OF THE SPONSOR LABORATORIES; MANY ARE OPEN TO FOREIGN NATIONALS.

WRITE FOR COMPLETE INFORMATION AND APPLICATION MATERIALS.

813

ORGANIZATION OF AMERICAN STATES DEPT OF FELLOWSHIPS & TRAINING (OAS PRA-FELLOWSHIPS)

TRAINEE SELECTION DIVISION
WASHINGTON DC 20006
202/789-3902

AMOUNT: TUITION + FEES; TRAVEL EXP & STIPEND

DEADLINE(S): APR 30; AUG 31

FIELD(S): ALL FIELDS EXCEPT MEDICINE & FOREIGN LANGUAGES

GRADUATE FELLOWSHIPS FOR USA CITIZENS OR PERMANENT RESIDENTS TO STUDY IN AN OAS MEMBER COUNTRY. MUST HAVE UNDERGRADUATE DEGREE AND HAVE DEMONSTRATED ABILITY TO PURSUE ADVANCED STUDIES IN CHOSEN FIELD.

APPLICANTS SHOULD BE FLUENT IN LANGUAGE OF COUNTRY OF INTENDED STUDY. PRIORITY IS GIVEN TO RESEARCH PROJECTS. WRITE FOR COMPLETE INFORMATION.

814

ROBERT SCHRECK MEMORIAL FUND (GRANTS)

C/O TEXAS COMMERCE BANK-
TRUST DEPT; PO DRAWER 140
EL PASO TX 79980
915/546-6515

AMOUNT: $500 - $1500

DEADLINE(S): JUL 15; NOV 15

FIELD(S): MEDICINE; VETERINARY MEDICINE; PHYSICS; CHEMISTRY; ARCHITECTURE; ENGINEERING; EPISCOPAL CLERGY

GRANTS TO UNDERGRADUATE JUNIORS OR SENIORS OR GRADUATE STUDENTS WHO HAVE BEEN RESIDENTS OF EL PASO COUNTY FOR AT LEAST TWO YEARS. MUST BE USA CITIZEN OR LEGAL RESIDENT AND HAVE A HIGH GRADE POINT AVERAGE. FINANCIAL NEED IS A CONSIDERATION.

WRITE FOR COMPLETE INFORMATION.

815

ROYAL NORWEGIAN COUNCIL FOR SCIENTIFIC & INDUSTRIAL RESEARCH (POST-DOCTORAL RESEARCH FELLOWSHIPS)

PO BOX 70 TAASEN
N-0801 OSLO NORWAY
+4722 23 76 85

AMOUNT: NOK 132000 SINGLE; NOK 156000 MARRIED + EXPENSES

DEADLINE(S): MAR 1; SEP 1

FIELD(S): NATURAL SCIENCES; ENGINEERING

POST-DOCTORAL FELLOWSHIPS OPEN TO YOUNG FOREIGN SCIENTISTS (UNDER AGE 40) WHO WISH TO DO RESEARCH WORK IN NORWAY. THEIR QUALIFICATIONS MUST CORRESPOND AT LEAST TO A BRITISH OR AMERICAN PH.D IN NATURAL SCIENCE OR ENGINEERING.

AWARDS ARE FOR ONE YEAR. 20 AWARDS PER YEAR. RENEWALS CONSIDERED. WRITE FOR COMPLETE INFORMATION.

816

SALES ASSOCIATION OF THE CHEMICAL INDUSTRY (ONE-YEAR SCHOLARSHIP)

ONE GAIL COURT
PISCATAWAY NJ 08854
908/463-1540

AMOUNT: $500

DEADLINE(S): MAY 30

FIELD(S): CHEMISTRY

OPEN TO RESIDENTS OF CT; NY; NJ; PA OR DE OR TO THOSE WHO ARE RELATED TO A SACI MEMBER. FOR UNDERGRADUATE OR GRADUATE STUDY AT ACCREDITED COLLEGES OR UNIVERSITIES. USA CITIZEN OR LEGAL RESIDENT.

CRITERIA ARE ACADEMIC ACHIEVEMENT AND EXTRACURRICULAR ACTIVITIES. SEND SELF ADDRESSED STAMPED ENVELOPE (BUSINESS SIZE) FOR COMPLETE INFORMATION.

817

SIGMA DELTA EPSILON-GRADUATE WOMEN IN SCIENCE (SDE FELLOWSHIPS; ELOISE GERRY FELLOWSHIPS)

ONE ILLINOIS CENTER;
111 E. WACKER DR.
CHICAGO IL 60601
312/616-0800

AMOUNT: $2600 - $4000 (SDE); $2300 - $2700 (ELOISE GERRY)

DEADLINE(S): DEC 1 (POSTMARK)

FIELD(S): BIOLOGY; CHEMISTRY; NATURAL SCIENCES; PHYSICAL SCIENCES; BIOLOGICAL SCIENCES; COMPUTER SCIENCES

WOMEN ONLY. OPEN TO GRADUATE STUDENTS AND POST-DOCTORAL RESEARCHERS IN THE ABOVE AREAS. FELLOWSHIPS MAY ONLY BE USED TO SUPPORT SCIENTIFIC RESEARCH AND/OR PROJECTS. FINANCIAL NEED IS A MAJOR CONSIDERATION.

ELOISE GERRY FELLOWSHIPS ARE LIMITED TO THE CHEMICAL AND BIOLOGICAL SCIENCES. WRITE FOR COMPLETE INFORMATION.

818

SMITHSONIAN INSTITUTION (NATIONAL AIR & SPACE MUSEUM GUGGENHEIM FELLOWSHIPS)

INTERPRETIVE PROGRAMS; ROOM 3341; MRC-313; 6TH & INDEPENDENCE AVE SW
WASHINGTON DC 20560
WRITTEN INQUIRY

AMOUNT: $13000 - $21000 STIPEND + TRAVEL ALLOWANCE

DEADLINE(S): JAN 15

FIELD(S): AVIATION; AERONAUTICS; SPACE SCIENCE & EXPLORATION; EARTH & PLANETARY SCIENCES; LIFE SCIENCES

PRE-DOCTORAL APPLICANTS SHOULD HAVE COMPLETED PRELIMINARY COURSE WORK & EXAMS AND BE ENGAGED IN DISSERTATION RESEARCH. POST-DOCTORAL APPLICANTS SHOULD HAVE RECEIVED THEIR PH.D WITHIN THE PAST SEVEN YEARS.

OPEN TO ALL NATIONALITIES. FLUENCY IN ENGLISH REQUIRED. DURATION IS 6-12 MONTHS. WRITE FOR COMPLETE INFORMATION.

819

TUSKEGEE INSTITUTE (GRADUATE RESEARCH FELLOWSHIPS AND ASSISTANTSHIPS)

ADMISSIONS OFFICE
TUSKEGEE INSTITUTE AL 36088
205/727-8500

AMOUNT: TUITION

DEADLINE(S): MAR 15

FIELD(S): CHEMISTRY; ENGINEERING; ENVIRONMENTAL SCIENCE; LIFE SCIENCES; NUTRITION; EDUCATION

GRADUATE RESEARCH FELLOWSHIPS AND GRADUATE ASSISTANTSHIPS ARE AVAILABLE TO QUALIFIED INDIVIDUALS WHO WISH TO ENTER TUSKEGEE INSTITUTE'S GRADUATE PROGRAM IN PURSUIT OF A MASTER'S DEGREE.

WRITE FOR COMPLETE INFORMATION.

MATHEMATICS

820

AEROSPACE EDUCATION FOUNDATION (CHRISTA MCAULIFFE MEMORIAL AWARD)

1501 LEE HIGHWAY
ARLINGTON VA 22209
703/247-5839

AMOUNT: $1000 CASH AWARD

DEADLINE(S): JUN 30

FIELD(S): SCIENCE; MATHEMATICS (TEACHER)

CASH AWARD TO RECOGNIZE AN OUTSTANDING MATHEMATICS OR SCIENCE TEACHER (K-12 ONLY) WHO BRINGS ABOUT A FUNDAMENTAL AWARENESS OF AEROSPACE ACTIVITIES TO HIS OR HER STUDENTS. MUST BE NOMINATED BY AIR FORCE ASSOCIATION REPRESENTATIVE.

USA CITIZEN OR LEGAL RESIDENT. WRITE FOR COMPLETE INFORMATION.

821

AEROSPACE EDUCATION FOUNDATION (THEODORE VON KARMAN GRADUATE SCHOLARSHIP PROGRAM)

1501 LEE HIGHWAY
ARLINGTON VA 22209
703/247-5839

AMOUNT: $5000

DEADLINE(S): MAR 1

FIELD(S): SCIENCE; MATHEMATICS; ENGINEERING

OPEN TO AIR FORCE ROTC GRADUATE STUDENTS WHO WILL PURSUE ADVANCED DEGREES IN THE FIELDS OF SCIENCE; MATHEMATICS; PHYSICS; OR ENGINEERING. USA CITIZEN OR LEGAL RESIDENT.

10 AWARDS PER YEAR BASED ON APTITUDE; ATTITUDE AND CAREER PLANS. WRITE FOR COMPLETE INFORMATION.

822

AMERICAN ASSOCIATION FOR THE ADVANCEMENT OF SCIENCE (SCIENCE & ENGINEERING FELLOWSHIPS)

1333 'H' STREET NW
WASHINGTON DC 20005
202/326-6600

AMOUNT: UP TO $38500

DEADLINE(S): JAN 15

FIELD(S): SCIENCE; ENGINEERING

MATHEMATICS

POST-DOCTORAL FELLOWSHIPS OPEN TO AAAS MEMBERS OR APPLICANTS CONCURRENTLY APPLYING FOR MEMBERSHIP. PROSPECTIVE FELLOWS MUST DEMONSTRATE EXCEPTIONAL COMPETENCE IN AN AREA OF SCIENCE OR HAVE A BROAD SCIENTIFIC OR TECHNICAL BACKGROUND.

ONE-YEAR FELLOWSHIPS. SEND INQUIRIES TO PROGRAM DIRECTOR; CONGRESSIONAL SCIENCE FELLOWS PROGRAM; ADDRESS ABOVE.

823

AMERICAN ASSOCIATION OF UNIVERSITY WOMEN (SCIENCE & TECHNOLOGY GROUP - SELECTED PROFESSIONS FELLOWSHIPS)

1111 16TH STREET NW
WASHINGTON DC 20036
202/728-7603; FAX 202/872-1430

AMOUNT: $5000 - $9500

DEADLINE(S): DEC 15 (POSTMARK)

FIELD(S): ARCHITECTURE; COMPUTER/ INFORMATION SCIENCE; ENGINEERING; MATHEMATICS/STATISTICS

OPEN TO WOMEN WHO ARE USA CITIZENS OR PERMANENT RESIDENTS WHO ARE IN THEIR FINAL YEAR OF A MASTER'S DEGREE IN THE ABOVE AREAS. APPLICATIONS AVAILABLE AUG 1 - DEC 1.

WRITE FOR COMPLETE INFORMATION.

824

AMERICAN MATHEMATICAL SOCIETY (CENTENNIAL FELLOWSHIPS)

PO BOX 6248
PROVIDENCE RI 02940
401/445-4000

AMOUNT: $41500

DEADLINE(S): DEC 1

FIELD(S): MATHEMATICS

FELLOWSHIP TO PROVIDE ENHANCED RESEARCH OPPORTUNITIES TO MATHEMATICIANS WHO ARE 7 TO 12 YEARS PAST THE PH.D WHO HAVE A STRONG RESEARCH RECORD BUT HAVE NOT PREVIOUSLY HAD EXTENSIVE POSTDOCTORAL RESEARCH SUPPORT.

MUST BE CITIZEN OR PERMANENT RESIDENT OF A COUNTRY IN NORTH AMERICA. WRITE FOR COMPLETE INFORMATION.

825

AMERICAN PHILOSOPHICAL SOCIETY (JOHN CLARKE SLATER FELLOWSHIP)

LIBRARY; 105 S. FIFTH ST.
PHILADELPHIA PA 19106
WRITTEN INQUIRY ONLY

AMOUNT: $12000

DEADLINE(S): DEC 1

FIELD(S): HISTORY OF PHYSICAL SCIENCE

OPEN TO DOCTORAL CANDIDATES WHO HAVE PASSED THEIR PRELIMINARY EXAMINATIONS AND ARE WRITING DISSERTATIONS ON THE HISTORY OF 20TH CENTURY PHYSICAL SCIENCES.

WRITE FOR COMPLETE INFORMATION.

826

AMERICAN SOCIETY FOR ENGINEERING EDUCATION (OFFICE OF NAVAL RESEARCH GRADUATE FELLOWSHIP PROGRAM)

ELEVEN DUPONT CIRCLE #200
WASHINGTON DC 20036
202/745-3616

AMOUNT: $15000

DEADLINE(S): JAN 31

FIELD(S): ELEC ENG; MECH ENG; AEROSPACE ENG; MATHEMATICS; PHYSICS; COMPUTER SCIENCE; MATERIALS SCIENCE; BIOLOGICAL-BIOMEDICAL SCIENCE; NAVAL ARCHITECTURE & OCEAN ENG; RELATED FIELDS

LIMITED TO INDIVIDUALS WHO HAVE 'NOT' BEGUN GRADUATE PROGRAMS. FOR STUDY AND RESEARCH LEADING TO DOCTORAL DEGREE. FELLOWSHIPS ARE AWARDED ON THE BASIS OF ABILITY. USA CITIZEN.

50 THREE-YEAR FELLOWSHIPS ARE OFFERED. WRITE FOR COMPLETE INFORMATION.

827

ARGONNE NATIONAL LABORATORY (STUDENT RESEARCH PARTICIPATION PROGRAM; THESIS RESEARCH)

DIV OF EDUCATIONAL PROGRAMS;
9700 SOUTH CASS AVE
ARGONNE IL 60439
312/972-3366

AMOUNT: $200 PER WEEK STIPEND

DEADLINE(S): FEB 1; MAY 15; OCT 15

FIELD(S): PHYSICAL SCIENCES; LIFE SCIENCES; EARTH SCIENCES; MATHEMATICS; COMPUTER SCIENCES; ENGINEERING; FUSION & FISSION ENERGY

1-SEMESTER ACCREDITED INTERNSHIP PROGRAM TO PERMIT STUDENTS TO WORK IN ABOVE AREAS IN RELATION TO ENERGY DEVELOPMENT. OPEN TO FULL-TIME UNDERGRAD JUNIORS; SENIORS & 1ST YEAR GRAD STUDENTS. USA CITIZEN OR LEGAL RESIDENT.

THESIS RESEARCH AWARDS OPEN TO DOCTORAL CANDIDATES WORKING ON THEIR DISSERTATION. WRITE FOR COMPLETE INFORMATION.

828

ASSOCIATION FOR WOMEN IN SCIENCE EDUCATIONAL FOUNDATION (AWIS PRE-DOCTORAL AWARDS)

1522 K STREET NW SUITE 820
WASHINGTON DC 20005
202/408-0742

AMOUNT: $500

DEADLINE(S): JAN 15

FIELD(S): ENGINEERING; LIFE SCIENCES; MATHEMATICS; PHYSICAL SCIENCES; BEHAVIORAL SCIENCES; SOCIAL SCIENCES

SCHOLARSHIP AID & INCENTIVE AWARDS OPEN TO WOMEN WHO ARE WORKING ACTIVELY TOWARDS A DOCTORAL DEGREE IN THE ABOVE AREAS. USA CITIZENS MAY STUDY IN USA OR ABROAD; NON-CITIZENS MUST BE ENROLLED IN USA INSTITUTION.

APPLICATIONS ARE AVAILABLE OCT 1 - DEC 15. WRITE FOR COMPLETE INFORMATION.

829

AT&T BELL LABORATORIES (COOPERATIVE RESEARCH FELLOWSHIP PROGRAM FOR MINORITIES)

101 CRAWFORDS CORNER ROAD;
ROOM 1E-209; BOX 3030
HOLMDEL NJ 07733
WRITTEN INQUIRY

AMOUNT: FULL-TUITION & FEES + $13200 STIPEND PER YEAR

DEADLINE(S): JAN 15

FIELD(S): ENGINEERING; MATH; SCIENCES; COMPUTER SCIENCE

FELLOWSHIPS ARE AWARDED TO MINORITY STUDENTS WHO ARE ACCEPTED INTO AN ACCREDITED DOCTORAL PROGRAM FOR THE FOLLOWING FALL. USA CITIZEN OR PERMANENT RESIDENT.

10 AWARDS PER YEAR. RENEWABLE UP TO 4 YEARS. WRITE TO SPECIAL PROGRAMS MANAGER - CRFP FOR COMPLETE INFORMATION.

830

AT&T BELL LABORATORIES (GRADUATE RESEARCH PROGRAM FOR WOMEN)

101 CRAWFORDS CORNER ROAD;
ROOM 1E-209; BOX 3030
HOLMDEL NJ 07733
WRITTEN INQUIRY

AMOUNT: FULL TUITION & FEES + $13200 STIPEND PER YEAR

DEADLINE(S): JAN 15

FIELD(S): ENGINEERING; MATH; SCIENCES; COMPUTER SCIENCE

FOR WOMEN STUDENTS WHO HAVE BEEN ACCEPTED INTO AN ACCREDITED DOCTORAL PROGRAM FOR THE FOLLOWING FALL. USA CITIZEN OR PERMANENT RESIDENT.

FELLOWSHIPS ARE RENEWABLE FOR DURATION OF GRADUATE PROGRAM. WRITE TO SPECIAL PROGRAMS MANAGER - GRPW FOR COMPLETE INFORMATION.

831

BROOKHAVEN NATIONAL LABORATORY (POSTDOCTORAL RESEARCH ASSOCIATESHIPS)

BROOKHAVEN NATIONAL LABORATORY;
ASSOCIATED UNIVERSITIES INC.
UPTON L.I. NY 11973
516/282-7813

AMOUNT: $27000 MINIMUM

DEADLINE(S): THROUGHOUT THE YEAR.

FIELD(S): CHEMISTRY; PHYSICS; MATERIALS SCIENCE; BIOLOGY; OCEANOGRAPHY; MEDICAL SCIENCE

POST-DOCTORAL RESEARCH ASSOCIATESHIPS TENABLE AT BROOKHAVEN NATIONAL LABORATORY FOR RESEARCH TO PROMOTE FUNDAMENTAL AND APPLIED RESEARCH IN THE ABOVE FIELDS. A RECENT DOCTORAL DEGREE IS REQUIRED.

25 ASSOCIATESHIPS PER YEAR. RENEWABLE FOR TWO ADDITIONAL YEARS. WRITE TO MS. E.E. THORNHILL; OFFICE OF SCIENTIFIC PERSONNEL; ADDRESS ABOVE.

832

BUSINESS AND PROFESSIONAL WOMEN'S FOUNDATION (CAREER ADVANCEMENT SCHOLARSHIPS)

2012 MASSACHUSETTS AVE NW
WASHINGTON DC 20036
202/293-1200

AMOUNT: $500 - $1000

DEADLINE(S): APR 15 POSTMARK (APPS AVAILABLE -ONLY- OCT 1 - APR 1)

FIELD(S): COMPUTER SCIENCE; EDUCATION; PARALEGAL; ENGINEERING; SCIENCE (EXCEPT HEALTH CARE)

OPEN TO WOMEN (30 OR OLDER) WITHIN 12-24 MONTHS OF COMPLETING UNDERGRAD OR GRAD STUDY IN USA (INCLUDING PUERTO RICO & THE VIRGIN ISLANDS). SHOULD LEAD TO ENTRY OR REENTRY INTO THE WORK FORCE OR IMPROVE CAREER ADVANCEMENT CHANCES.

MUST SHOW FINANCIAL NEED. SEND SELF-ADDRESSED STAMPED ($.52) #10 ENVELOPE FOR APPLICATION & COMPLETE INFORMATION. NOT FOR STUDY AT DOCTORAL LEVEL.

MATHEMATICS

833

COMMITTEE ON INSTITUTIONAL COOPERATION (CIC PREDOCTORAL FELLOWSHIPS)

KIRKWOOD HALL RM 111; INDIANA UNIV.
BLOOMINGTON IN 47405
812/855-0822

AMOUNT: $9500 + TUITION (5 YEARS)

DEADLINE(S): JAN 2

FIELD(S): HUMANITIES; SOCIAL SCIENCES; NATURAL SCIENCES; MATHEMATICS; ENGINEERING

PREDOCTORAL FELLOWSHIPS FOR USA CITIZENS OF AFRICAN AMERICAN; AMERICAN INDIAN; MEXICAN AMERICAN OR PUERTO RICAN HERITAGE. MUST HOLD OR EXPECT TO RECEIVE BACHELOR'S DEGREE BY LATE SUMMER FROM A REGIONALLY ACCREDITED COLLEGE OR UNIVERSITY.

AWARDS FOR SPECIFIED UNIVERSITIES IN IL; IN; IA; MI; MN; OH; WI; PA. WRITE FOR DETAILS.

834

CONGRESSIONAL FELLOWSHIP PROGRAM (MORRIS K. UDALL FELLOWSHIPS)

CONGRESS OF THE UNITED STATES; OFFICE OF TECHNOLOGY ASSESSMENT
WASHINGTON DC 20510
202/224-8713

AMOUNT: $35000 - $70000

DEADLINE(S): JAN 31

FIELD(S): PHYSICAL OR BIOLOGICAL SCIENCES; ENGINEERING; LAW; ECONOMICS; ENVIRONMENTAL OR SOCIAL SCIENCES; PUBLIC POLICY

ONE YEAR FELLOWSHIP PROGRAM HELD -ONLY- IN WASHINGTO DC. CANDIDATES MUST HAVE EXTENSIVE EXPERIENCE IN SCIENCE OR TECHNOLOGY ISSUES OR HAVE COMPLETED DOCTORAL LEVEL RESEARCH. EXCEPTIONAL COMPETENCY IN ABOVE AREAS REQUIRED.

CONSIDERATIONS INCLUDE ACHIEVEMENT RECORDS AND CANDIDATE'S POTENTIAL IN ONE OR MORE OF OTA'S ASSESSMENT STUDIES. WRITE FOR COMPLETE INFORMATION.

835

ELECTRONIC INDUSTRIES FOUNDATION (SCHOLARSHIP FUND)

919 18TH ST.; SUITE 900
WASHINGTON DC 20006
202/955-5814

AMOUNT: $2000

DEADLINE(S): FEB 1

FIELD(S): AERONAUTICS; COMPUTER SCIENCE; ELECTRICAL ENGINEERING; ENGINEERING TECHNOLOGY; APPLIED MATHEMATICS; MICROBIOLOGY

OPEN TO DISABLED STUDENTS WHO ARE PURSUING CAREERS IN HIGH-TECH AREAS THROUGH ACADEMIC OR TECHNICAL TRAINING. AWARDS TENABLE AT RECOGNIZED UNDERGRADUATE & GRADUATE COLLEGES & UNIVERSITIES. USA CITIZEN. FINANCIAL NEED IS A CONSIDERATION.

6 AWARDS PER YEAR. RENEWABLE. WRITE FOR COMPLETE INFORMATION.

836

EPPLEY FOUNDATION FOR RESEARCH (POST-DOCTORAL RESEARCH GRANTS)

575 LEXINGTON AVE
NEW YORK NY 10022
WRITTEN INQUIRY

AMOUNT: UP TO $25000

DEADLINE(S): FEB 1; MAY 1; AUG 1; NOV 1

FIELD(S): PHYSICAL SCIENCES; BIOLOGICAL SCIENCES

POST-DOCTORAL GRANTS FOR ORIGINAL ADVANCED RESEARCH IN ANY OF THE PHYSICAL OR BIOLOGICAL SCIENCES. OPEN TO ESTABLISHED RESEARCH SCIENTISTS WHO ARE ATTACHED TO A RECOGNIZED INSTITUTION.

WRITE FOR COMPLETE INFORMATION.

837

FANNIE AND JOHN HERTZ FOUNDATION (DOCTORAL FELLOWSHIP PROGRAM)

BOX 5032
LIVERMORE CA 94551
510/373-1642

AMOUNT: UP TO $10000 FOR TUITION + $16000 STIPEND

DEADLINE(S): NOV 1

FIELD(S): ENGINEERING; APPLIED PHYSICS; MATHEMATICS; CHEMISTRY

FELLOWSHIPS OPEN TO STUDENTS PURSUING A PH.D OR A PROFESSIONAL DEGREE IN THE ABOVE AREAS WITH A 3.75 OR BETTER GPA. STUDENTS PURSUING A JOINT DEGREE SUCH AS PH.D/MD ARE NOT ELIGIBLE TO APPLY. USA CITIZEN.

25 FELLOWSHIPS PER YEAR RENEWABLE UP TO FIVE YEARS. WRITE FOR COMPLETE INFORMATION.

838

FLORIDA ENDOWMENT FUND FOR HIGHER EDUCATION (MCKNIGHT DOCTORAL FELLOWSHIP PROGRAM)

201 E.KENNEDY BLVD; SUITE 1525
TAMPA FL 33602
813/272-2772

AMOUNT: $11000 STIPEND + $5000 TUITION & FEES (PER YEAR)

DEADLINE(S): JAN 15

FIELD(S): ALL FIELDS (EXCEPT LAW; MEDICINE & EDUCATION)

OPEN TO ALL AFRICAN-AMERICANS WITH AT LEAST A BACHELOR'S DEGREE FROM AN ACCREDITED INSTITUTION WHO WISH TO PURSUE A DOCTORAL DEGREE. PROGRAM RECRUITS NATIONWIDE; HOWEVER FELLOWS MUST ENROLL IN A FLORIDA INSTITUTION. USA CITIZEN.

25 AWARDS PER YEAR. RENEWABLE FOR UP TO 5 YEARS. WRITE FOR COMPLETE INFORMATION.

839

FOUNDATION FOR SCIENCE & THE HANDICAPPED (GRANTS PROGRAM)

C/O REBECCA F. SMITH; 115 S. BRAINARD AVE.
LA GRANGE IL 60525
708/352-1091

AMOUNT: $1000

DEADLINE(S): DEC 1

FIELD(S): SCIENCE; MATHEMATICS; MEDICINE; COMPUTER SCIENCE; ENGINEERING

OPEN TO GRADUATE STUDENTS IN THE ABOVE AREAS WHO HAVE SOME PHYSICAL OR SENSORY DISABILITY. APPLICATIONS WILL ALSO BE ACCEPTED FROM UNDERGRADUATE SENIORS WHO HAVE BEEN ACCEPTED TO GRADUATE SCHOOL. USA CITIZEN OR LEGAL RESIDENT.

WRITE FOR COMPLETE INFORMATION.

840

INSTITUTE FOR ADVANCED STUDY (POST-DOCTORAL FELLOWSHIP AWARDS)

OLDEN LANE
PRINCETON NJ 08540
609-734-8000

AMOUNT: VARIES ACCORDING TO SCHOOL

DEADLINE(S): CHECK WITH SCHOOL

FIELD(S): HISTORICAL STUDIES; SOCIAL SCIENCES; NATURAL SCIENCES; MATHEMATICS

POST-DOCTORAL FELLOWSHIPS AT THE INSTITUTE FOR ADVANCED STUDY FOR THOSE WHOSE TERM CAN BE EXPECTED TO RESULT IN A WORK OF SIGNIFICANCE AND INDIVIDUALITY.

150-160 FELLOWSHIPS PER ACADEMIC YEAR ALTHOUGH SOME CAN BE EXTENDED. REQUEST APPLICATION MATERIALS FROM SCHOOL'S ADMINISTRATIVE OFFICER.

841

INSTITUTE OF PAPER SCIENCE AND TECHNOLOGY (FELLOWSHIP PROGRAM)

575 14TH ST NW
ATLANTA GA 30318
404/853-9500

AMOUNT: FULL TUITION PLUS $11250 STIPEND

DEADLINE(S): MAR 15

FIELD(S): CHEMISTRY; CHEMICAL ENGINEERING; PHYSICS; BIOLOGY; MATHEMATICS; PULP AND PAPER TECHNOLOGY

OPEN TO GRADUATE STUDENTS WHO ARE USA OR CANADIAN CITIZENS WHO HOLD A B.S. DEGREE IN THE ABOVE FIELDS. FOR PURSUIT OF A MASTER OF SCIENCE OR PH.D. DEGREE AT THE INSTITUTE.

35 FELLOWSHIPS ANNUALLY. ADDRESS INQUIRIES TO DIRECTOR OF ADMISSIONS.

842

NATIONAL RADIO ASTRONOMY OBSERVATORY (SUMMER RESEARCH ASSISTANTSHIPS)

EDGEMONT ROAD
CHARLOTTESVILLE VA 22903
804/296-0211

AMOUNT: $1000 - $1300 PER MONTH + TRAVEL EXPENSES

DEADLINE(S): FEB 1

FIELD(S): ASTRONOMY; PHYSICS; COMPUTER SCIENCE; ELECTRICAL ENGINEERING

SUMMER RESEARCH ASSISTANTSHIPS OPEN TO UNDERGRADUATES WHO HAVE COMPLETED AT LEAST 3 YEARS OF STUDY AND TO GRADUATE STUDENTS WHO HAVE COMPLETED NO MORE THAN 2 YEARS. TENABLE AT NRAO SITES.

APPROXIMATELY 20 AWARDS PER YEAR. WRITE FOR COMPLETE INFORMATION.

843

NATIONAL RESEARCH COUNCIL (NATIONAL SCIENCE FOUNDATION MINORITY GRADUATE FELLOWSHIPS)

2101 CONSTITUTION AVE.
WASHINGTON DC 20418
202/334-2872

AMOUNT: $14000 STIPEND (12 MONTHS) + UP TO $7500 FOR TUITION AND FEES

DEADLINE(S): NOV 6

FIELD(S): ENGINEERING; MATHEMATICS; COMPUTER SCIENCE; CHEMISTRY; EARTH SCIENCES; LIFE SCIENCES; PSYCHOLOGY; SOCIAL SCIENCES

OPEN MINORITY GRADUATE STUDENTS (MASTERS OR PH.D) WHO ARE USA CITIZENS OR LEGAL RESIDENTS & ARE AT OR NEAR THE BEGINNING OF THEIR GRADUATE STUDY. FELLOWSHIPS TENABLE AT ACCREDITED INSTITUTION OFFERING ADVANCED DEGREES IN THE FIELDS ABOVE.

APPROX 150 NEW 3-YEAR FELLOWSHIPS AWARDED EACH YEAR. WRITE FOR COMPLETE INFORMATION.

844

NATIONAL RESEARCH COUNCIL (NATIONAL SCIENCE FOUNDATION GRADUATE FELLOWSHIPS)

2101 CONSTITUTION AVE
WASHINGTON DC 20418
202/334-2872

AMOUNT: $14000 STIPEND + $7000 TUITION ALLOWANCE

DEADLINE(S): NOV 10

FIELD(S): SOCIAL SCIENCES; PHYSICAL SCIENCES; MATHEMATICS; BIOLOGY; ENGINEERING

DOCTORAL) WHO HAVE NOT COMPLETED MORE THAN 1 YEAR OF GRAD STUDY. FELLOWSHIPS TENABLE AT ANY ACCREDITED INSTITUTION OFFERING ADVANCED DEGREES IN THE AREAS ABOVE. USA CITIZEN OR PERMANENT RESIDENT.

OPEN TO HISTORY & PHILOSOPHY OF SCIENCE STUDENTS ALSO. 950 NEW 3-YEAR FELLOWSHIPS AWARDED EACH YEAR. WRITE FOR COMPLETE INFORMATION.

845

NATIONAL RESEARCH COUNCIL (NRC POSTDOCTORAL & SENIOR RESEARCH ASSOCIATESHIP AWARDS)

ASSOCIATESHIP PROGRAMS GR430/D3;
2101 CONSTITUTION AVE. NW
WASHINGTON DC 20418
202/334-2760

AMOUNT: ANNUAL STIPEND FROM 27750 TO 44000 + BENEFITS

DEADLINE(S): JAN 15; APR 15; AUG 15

FIELD(S): CHEMISTRY; EARTH & ATMOSPHERIC SCIENCES; ENGINEERING & APPLIED SCIENCES; COMPUTER SCIENCE; MATHEMATICS; BIOLOGICAL & MEDICAL SCIENCES SPACE & PLANETARY SCIENCES; PHYSICS

POSTDOCTORAL & SENIOR ASSOCIATESHIP AWARDS FOR RESEARCH AT ONE OF 38 PARTICIPATING SPONSOR FEDERAL LABORATORIES. USA CITIZENSHIP REQUIRED FOR SOME OF THE SPONSOR LABORATORIES; MANY ARE OPEN TO FOREIGN NATIONALS.

WRITE FOR COMPLETE INFORMATION AND APPLICATION MATERIALS.

846

OAK RIDGE INSTITUTE FOR SCIENCE & EDUCATION (GRADUATE FELLOWSHIPS)

UNIV PROGRAMS DIV; PO BOX 117
OAK RIDGE TN 37831
WRITTEN INQUIRY

AMOUNT: $1200 - $1300 PER MONTH STIPEND + TUITION & FEES

DEADLINE(S): JAN 25

FIELD(S): NUCLEAR ENGINEERING; PHYSICS; RADIOACTIVE WASTE MANAGEMENT; FUSION ENERGY; INDUSTRIAL HYGIENE; ENVIRONMENTAL RESTORATION

OPEN TO ENTERING & OTHER GRADUATE STUDENTS FOR STUDY LEADING TO M.S. OR PH.D DEGREE. PROVIDES ACCESS TO STUDY AND RESEARCH AT DEPT. OF ENERGY LABORATORIES. RENEWABLE UP TO 48 MONTHS.

WRITE FOR COMPLETE INFORMATION.

847

OPTICAL SOCIETY OF AMERICA (NEWPORT RESEARCH AWARD)

2010 MASSACHUSETTS AVE NW
WASHINGTON DC 20036
202-416-1404

AMOUNT: $16000

DEADLINE(S): FEB 15

FIELD(S): PHYSICS; ELECTRICAL ENGINEERING

GRANTS OPEN TO DOCTORAL CANDIDATES WHO ARE PURSUING THESIS RESEARCH ON LASERS AND ELECTRO-OPTICS OR RELATED FIELDS. AWARDS ARE TENABLE AT ACCREDITED INSTITUTIONS IN THE USA.

AWARDS ARE RENEWABLE FOR ONE YEAR. WRITE FOR COMPLETE INFORMATION.

848

ORGANIZATION OF AMERICAN STATES DEPT OF FELLOWSHIPS & TRAINING (OAS PRA-FELLOWSHIPS)

TRAINEE SELECTION DIVISION
WASHINGTON DC 20006
202/789-3902

AMOUNT: TUITION + FEES; TRAVEL EXP & STIPEND

DEADLINE(S): APR 30; AUG 31

FIELD(S): ALL FIELDS EXCEPT MEDICINE & FOREIGN LANGUAGES

GRADUATE FELLOWSHIPS FOR USA CITIZENS OR PERMANENT RESIDENTS TO STUDY IN AN OAS MEMBER COUNTRY. MUST HAVE UNDERGRADUATE DEGREE AND HAVE DEMONSTRATED ABILITY TO PURSUE ADVANCED STUDIES IN CHOSEN FIELD.

APPLICANTS SHOULD BE FLUENT IN LANGUAGE OF COUNTRY OF INTENDED STUDY. PRIORITY IS GIVEN TO RESEARCH PROJECTS. WRITE FOR COMPLETE INFORMATION.

849

RADIO FREE EUROPE/RADIO LIBERTY (MEDIA & OPINION RESEARCH ON EASTERN EUROPE & THE FORMER SOVIET UNION)

PERSONNEL DIVISION;
1201 CONNECTICUT AVE NW
WAHINGTON DC 20036
WRITTEN INQUIRY

AMOUNT: DAILY STIPEND OF 48 GERMAN MARKS PLUS ACCOMMODATIONS

DEADLINE(S): FEB 22

FIELD(S): COMMUNICATIONS; MARKET RESEARCH; STATISTICS; SOCIOLOGY; SOCIAL PSYCHOLOGY; EAST EUROPEAN STUDIES

INTERNSHIP OPEN TO GRADUATE STUDENT OR EXCEPTIONALLY QUALIFIED UNDERGRADUATE IN THE ABOVE AREAS WHO CAN DEMONSTRATE KNOWLEDGE OF QUANTITIVE RESEARCH METHODS; COMPUTER APPLICATIONS AND PUBLIC OPINION SURVEY TECHNIQUES.

EAST EUROPEAN LANGUAGE SKILLS WOULD BE AN ADVANTAGE. WRITE FOR COMPLETE INFORMATION.

850

ROYAL NORWEGIAN COUNCIL FOR SCIENTIFIC & INDUSTRIAL RESEARCH (POST-DOCTORAL RESEARCH FELLOWSHIPS)

PO BOX 70 TAASEN
N-0801 OSLO NORWAY
+4722 23 76 85

AMOUNT: NOK 132000 SINGLE; NOK 156000 MARRIED + EXPENSES

DEADLINE(S): MAR 1; SEP 1

FIELD(S): NATURAL SCIENCES; ENGINEERING

POST-DOCTORAL FELLOWSHIPS OPEN TO YOUNG FOREIGN SCIENTISTS (UNDER AGE 40) WHO WISH TO DO RESEARCH WORK IN NORWAY. THEIR QUALIFICATIONS MUST CORRESPOND AT LEAST TO A BRITISH OR AMERICAN PH.D IN NATURAL SCIENCE OR ENGINEERING.

AWARDS ARE FOR ONE YEAR. 20 AWARDS PER YEAR. RENEWALS CONSIDERED. WRITE FOR COMPLETE INFORMATION.

851

SMITHSONIAN INSTITUTION (NATIONAL AIR & SPACE MUSEUM GUGGENHEIM FELLOWSHIPS)

INTERPRETIVE PROGRAMS; ROOM 3341; MRC-313;
6TH & INDEPENDENCE AVE SW
WASHINGTON DC 20560
WRITTEN INQUIRY

AMOUNT: $13000 - $21000 STIPEND + TRAVEL ALLOWANCE

DEADLINE(S): JAN 15

FIELD(S): AVIATION; AERONAUTICS; SPACE SCIENCE & EXPLORATION; EARTH & PLANETARY SCIENCES; LIFE SCIENCES

PRE-DOCTORAL APPLICANTS SHOULD HAVE COMPLETED PRELIMINARY COURSE WORK & EXAMS AND BE ENGAGED IN DISSERTATION RESEARCH. POST-DOCTORAL APPLICANTS SHOULD HAVE RECEIVED THEIR PH.D WITHIN THE PAST SEVEN YEARS.

OPEN TO ALL NATIONALITIES. FLUENCY IN ENGLISH REQUIRED. DURATION IS 6-12 MONTHS. WRITE FOR COMPLETE INFORMATION.

MEDICAL DOCTOR

852

AMERICAN ACADEMY OF FAMILY PHYSICIANS (MEAD JOHNSON AWARDS)

8880 WARD PKWY
KANSAS CITY MO 64114
816/333-9700

AMOUNT: $2000

DEADLINE(S): NONE SPECIFIED

FIELD(S): FAMILY PRACTICE MEDICINE

MEAD JOHNSON AWARDS ARE OPEN TO MD'S WHO ARE CURRENTLY IN THEIR SECOND YEAR OF AN ACCREDITED FAMILY PRACTICE RESIDENCY PROGRAM IN THE USA.

20 GRANTS PER YEAR. WRITE FOR COMPLETE INFORMATION.

853

AMERICAN ACADEMY OF PEDIATRICS (POST-DOCTORAL FELLOWSHIPS)

141 NW POINT BLVD; PO BOX 927
ELK GROVE VILLAGE IL 60009
708/228-5005

AMOUNT: $1000 - $5000

DEADLINE(S): FEB 28

FIELD(S): PEDIATRICS

MEDICAL DOCTOR

POST-DOCTORAL FELLOWSHIPS OPEN TO YOUNG PHYSICIANS WHO HAVE COMPLETED THEIR INTERNSHIP & HAVE AT LEAST 1 YEAR REMAINING IN AN ACCREDITED PEDIATRIC RESIDENT PROGRAM. USA OR CANADIAN CITIZEN OR LEGAL RESIDENT.

30 OR MORE FELLOWSHIPS PER YEAR. WRITE FOR COMPLETE INFORMATION.

854

AMERICAN COLLEGE OF LEGAL MEDICINE (STUDENT WRITING COMPETITION)

JAY A. GOLD; EXECUTIVE DIRECTOR;
611 E. WELLS ST.
MILWAUKEE WI 53202
414/276-1881

AMOUNT: $1000

DEADLINE(S): FEB 1

FIELD(S): LEGAL MEDICINE

AWARD FOR THE BEST PAPER ON ANY ASPECT OF LEGAL MEDICINE OPEN TO STUDENTS ENROLLED IN AN ACCREDITED SCHOOL OF LAW; MEDICINE; DENTISTRY; PODIATRY; NURSING; PHARMACY; HEALTH SCIENCE OR HEALTH CARE ADMINISTRATION IN THE USA OR CANADA.

AWARDS ARE GIVEN TO FIRST PLACE WINNER IN EACH OF THREE CATEGORIES. WRITE FOR COMPLETE INFORMATION.

855

AMERICAN COLLEGE OF OBSTETRICIANS AND GYNECOLOGISTS (HIGHER EDUCATION LOAN PROGRAM)

409 12TH ST SW
WASHINGTON DC 20024
202/638-5577

AMOUNT: UP TO $5000

DEADLINE(S): APR 1 AND OCT 1

FIELD(S): OBSTETRICS & GYNECOLOGY

OPEN TO JUNIOR FELLOWS OF THE COLLEGE WHO ARE APPROVED RESIDENTS AND HAVE COMPLETED ONE YEAR OF TRAINING PROGRAMS IN OBSTETRICS AND GYNECOLOGY. APPLICANTS MAY RECEIVE MORE THAN ONE LOAN BUT AGGREGATE AMOUNT MAY NOT EXCEED $5000.

MUST BE USA CITIZEN AND DEMONSTRATE FINANCIAL NEED. WRITE FOR COMPLETE INFORMATION.

856

AMERICAN COLLEGE OF PHYSICIANS (LATIN AMERICAN SCHOLARSHIP)

INDEPENDENCE MALL WEST;
6TH ST. AT RACE
PHILADELPHIA PA 19106
215/351-2732

AMOUNT: $5000

DEADLINE(S): JUN 30

FIELD(S): INTERNAL MEDICINE & ALLIED SPECIALTIES

OPEN TO LATIN AMERICAN PHYSICIANS WHO HOLD AN ACADEMIC APPOINTMENT AT A LATIN AMERICAN MEDICAL SCHOOL AND ARE PROFICIENT IN ENGLISH. FOR TRAVEL TO THE USA OR CANADA FOR A SHORT TERM OF ADVANCED STUDY IN A LIMITED FIELD.

WRITE FOR COMPLETE INFORMATION.

857

AMERICAN LIVER FOUNDATION (STUDENT RESEARCH FELLOWSHIPS)

1425 POMPTON AVE
CEDAR GROVE NJ 07009
201/256-2550

AMOUNT: $2500 STIPEND

DEADLINE(S): DEC 15

FIELD(S): MEDICAL RESEARCH

FELLOWSHIPS OPEN TO MEDICAL STUDENTS; VETERINARY STUDENTS & PH.D CANDIDATES. PURPOSE IS TO ENCOURAGE THEM TO GAIN EXPOSURE IN THE RESEARCH LABORATORY & POSSIBLY CONSIDER LIVER RESEARCH AS A CAREER OPTION.

DURATION IS 3 MONTHS. WRITE FOR COMPLETE INFORMATION.

858

AMERICAN MEDICAL STUDENT ASSOCIATION (LOAN PROGRAM)

1890 PRESTON WHITE DR
RESTON VA 22091
703/620-6600; 800/767-2266; FAX 703/620-5873

AMOUNT: REVOLVING LINE OF CREDIT

DEADLINE(S): NONE

FIELD(S): MEDICAL SCIENCES

UNSECURED PERSONAL LOANS FOR SENIOR MEDICAL STUDENTS; RESIDENTS AND PRACTICING PHYSICIANS. LOANS NOT AVAILABLE IN HI; AK OR PR DUE TO DIFFERING STATE LAWS OR OTHER TECHNICALITIES. USA CITIZEN OR LEGAL RESIDENT.

WRITE FOR COMPLETE INFORMATION.

859

AMERICAN MEDICAL WOMEN'S ASSOCIATION INC (SCHOLARSHIP LOAN FUND)

801 N.FAIRFAX ST; SUITE 400
ALEXANDRIA VA 22314
703/838-0500

AMOUNT: $1000 OR $2000

DEADLINE(S): JAN 1 - APR 15

FIELD(S): MEDICINE

SCHOLARSHIP/LOAN PROGRAM OPEN TO WOMEN WHO ARE STUDENT MEMBERS OF AMERICAN MEDICAL WOMEN'S ASSN & IN THEIR 1ST; 2ND; OR 3RD YEAR AT AN ACCREDITED MEDICAL OR OSTEOPATHIC SCHOOL IN THE USA. USA CITIZEN OR PERMANENT RESIDENT.

WRITE FOR COMPLETE INFORMATION.

860

AMERICAN OSTEOPATHIC ASSOCIATION AUXILIARY (SCHOLARSHIP PROGRAM)

SCHOLARSHIP CHAIRMAN;
142 E. ONTARIO ST.
CHICAGO IL 60611
312/280-5819

AMOUNT: $3000 MAXIMUM

DEADLINE(S): JUN 1

FIELD(S): OSTEOPATHIC MEDICINE

OPEN TO CITIZENS OF USA OR CANADA WHO ARE ENTERING SOPHOMORE YEAR IN APPROVED COLLEGE OF OSTEOPATHIC MEDICINE. MUST BE IN TOP 20% OR HAVE HONORS FROM 1ST YEAR AND SHOW EVIDENCE OF FINANCIAL NEED AND MOTIVATION TOWARDS OSTEOPATHIC MEDICINE.

UNSPECIFIED NUMBER OF SCHOLARSHIPS PER YEAR. WRITE FOR COMPLETE INFORMATION.

861

AMERICAN PSYCHIATRIC ASSOCIATION (BURROUGHS WELLCOME FELLOWSHIP)

1400 'K' STREET NW
WASHINGTON DC 20005
202/682-6097

AMOUNT: VARIES

DEADLINE(S): APR 1

FIELD(S): PSYCHIATRY

TWO-YEAR FELLOWSHIP PROGRAM TO ACQUAINT SELECTED PSYCHIATRY RESIDENTS WITH WORK OF APA & WITH NATIONAL ISSUES AFFECTING PSYCHIATRY. APA BENEFITS FROM THE IDEAS & PERSPECTIVES OF FUTURE LEADERS IN PSYCHIATRY.

10 AWARDS PER YEAR. WRITE FOR COMPLETE INFORMATION.

862

ARMENIAN GENERAL BENEVOLENT UNION (GRADUATE SCHOLARSHIP PROGRAM)

585 SADDLE RIVER RD
SADDLE BROOK NJ 07662
201/797-7600

AMOUNT: $1000

DEADLINE(S): APR 30

FIELD(S): LAW; MEDICINE; INTERNATIONAL RELATIONS; ARMENIAN STUDIES

GRANTS AND LOANS OPEN TO FULLY MATRICULATED STUDENTS OF ARMENIAN DESCENT IN ACCREDITED COLLEGES AND UNIVERSITIES IN THE USA. REQUEST APPLICATIONS BETWEEN JAN 1 AND MAR 15. -WRITTEN REQUESTS ONLY-.

LOANS ARE WITHOUT INTEREST. REPAYMENT IS TO BEGIN 1 YEAR AFTER LEAVING SCHOOL AND MUST BE COMPLETED WITHIN 3 YEARS. WRITE FOR COMPLETE INFORMATION.

863

BERKSHIRE DISTRICT MEDICAL SOCIETY (INTEREST-FREE LOANS)

741 NORTH STREET
PITTSFIELD MA 01201
413/442-9900

AMOUNT: UP TO $4000

DEADLINE(S): APR 1

FIELD(S): MEDICINE

INTEREST-FREE LOANS OPEN TO RESIDENTS OF BERKSHIRE COUNTY MASSACHUSETTS WHO HAVE BEEN ACCEPTED TO OR ARE ENROLLED AT AN ACCREDITED MEDICAL SCHOOL IN THE USA OR CANADA.

LOANS ARE RENEWABLE. WRITE FOR COMPLETE INFORMATION.

864

CENTRAL NEUROPSYCHIATRIC ASSOCIATION (WILLIAM C. MENNINGER AWARD)

3707 GASTON AVE #418
DALLAS TX 75246
214/824-2273

AMOUNT: $300-WINNER; 2-$50 EACH HONORABLE MENTION (TOTAL-$400)

DEADLINE(S): MAY 30

FIELD(S): NEUROLOGY; NEUROSURGERY; ADULT & CHILD PSYCHIATRY

ELIGIBILITY IS LIMITED TO RESIDENTS IN THE ABOVE FIELDS. THE ESSAY OR RESEARCH STUDY MUST BE COMPLETED DURING THE CANDIDATE'S RESIDENCY AND SUBMITTED WITHIN 1 YEAR AFTER COMPLETION OF RESIDENCY.

WRITE FOR COMPLETE INFORMATION.

865

CHARLES A LAUFFER SCHOLARSHIP TRUST FUND (MEDICAL STUDENT SCHOLARSHIP-LOANS)

NATIONSBANK -
ATTN LAUFFER SCHOLARSHIP
ST PETERSBURG FL 33733
813/892-6363

AMOUNT: $1500 - $3000

DEADLINE(S): JUN 15

FIELD(S): MEDICINE

SPECIAL LOW-INTEREST (2%) SCHOLARSHIP-LOANS OPEN TO MD DEGREE CANDIDATES IN GOOD STANDING AT ACCREDITED MEDICAL SCHOOLS IN THE USA. LIMITED TO 3RD & 4TH YEAR STUDENTS.

NON-CITIZENS MAY APPLY -ONLY- IF THEY PLAN TO PRACTICE MEDICINE IN THE USA. 12-15 AWARDS PER YEAR. RENEWABLE. WRITE FOR COMPLETE INFORMATION.

866

CHARLES RIVER DISTRICT MEDICAL SOCIETY (SCHOLARSHIP PROGRAM)

1440 MAIN STREET
WALTHAM MA 02154
617/891-8570

AMOUNT: $1000

DEADLINE(S): APR 1

FIELD(S): MEDICINE

THIS PROGRAM IS OPEN TO ANY MEDICAL SCHOOL STUDENT ENROLLED AT AN APPROVED U.S. INSTITUTION WHO IS A LEGAL RESIDENT OF ONE OF THE FIVE TOWNS IN THE DISTRICT- NEEDHAM; NEWTON; WALTHAM; WELLESLEY AND WESTON. FOR GRADUATE STUDY ONLY.

4 SCHOLARSHIPS PER YEAR. WRITE FOR COMPLETE INFORMATION.

867

CHEMICAL INDUSTRY INSTITUTE OF TOXICOLOGY (POST-DOCTORAL FELLOWSHIPS)

PO BOX 12137
RESEARCH TRIANGLE PARK NC 27709
919/541-2070

AMOUNT: VARIES

DEADLINE(S): NONE

FIELD(S): TOXICOLOGY; PATHOLOGY

CIIT PROVIDES STIPENDS & SUPPORT TO POST-DOCTORAL RESEARCH FELLOWS WHO DO ORGINAL RESEARCH RELATED TO CHEMICAL TOXICITY AND/OR PATHOLOGY. AWARD TENABLE AT CIIT'S LABORATORY ONLY.

20-30 AWARDS PER YEAR. RENEWABLE FOR A MAXIMUM OF 2 YEARS. CONTACT ADDRESS ABOVE FOR COMPLETE INFORMATION.

868

CLEM JAUNICH EDUCATION TRUST (SCHOLARSHIPS)

5353 GAMBLE DR; SUITE 110
MINNEAPOLIS MN 55416
612/546-1555

AMOUNT: $750 - $3000

DEADLINE(S): JUL 15

FIELD(S): THEOLOGY; MEDICINE

OPEN TO STUDENTS WHO HAVE ATTENDED PUBLIC OR PAROCHIAL SCHOOL IN THE DELANO (MN) SCHOOL DISTRICT OR CURRENTLY RESIDE WITHIN 7 MILES OF THE CITY OF DELANO MN. AWARDS SUPPORT UNDERGRADUATE OR GRADUATE STUDY IN THEOLOGY OR MEDICINE.

4-6 SCHOLARSHIPS PER YEAR. WRITE FOR COMPLETE INFORMATION.

869

COMMANDER; NAVY RECRUITING COMMAND (ARMED FORCES HEALTH PROFESSIONS SCHOLARSHIPS)

4015 WILSON BLVD.
ARLINGTON VA 22203
WRITTEN INQURIY

AMOUNT: $749 PER MONTH STIPEND + TUITION; FEES; BOOKS; LAB FEES ETC.

DEADLINE(S): NONE SPECIFIED

FIELD(S): MEDICINE; DENTISTRY; OPTOMETRY AND NURSE ANESTHESIA (MASTER'S DEGREE)

OPEN TO USA CITIZENS ENROLLED OR ACCEPTED FOR ENROLLMENT IN ANY OF THE ABOVE FIELDS AT AN ACCREDITED INSTITUTION IN THE USA OR PUERTO RICO. MUST QUALIFY FOR APPOINTMENT AS A NAVY OFFICER AND SIGN A CONTRACTUAL AGREEMENT.

WRITE FOR COMPLETE INFORMATION.

870

COMMUNITY FOUNDATION OF GREATER LORAIN COUNTY (ROY E. HAYES M.D. MEMORIAL FUND)

1865 N. RIDGE RD E. - SUITE A
LORAIN OH 44055
216/277-0142 OR 216/323-4445

AMOUNT: $1000

DEADLINE(S): MAY 1

FIELD(S): MEDICAL DOCTOR OR OSTEOPATHIC PHYSICIAN

MEDICAL DOCTOR

OPEN TO LORAIN COUNTY RESIDENTS WHO ARE ENTERING OR ENROLLED IN A USA MEDICAL SCHOOL WHO ARE CANDIDATES FOR M.D. OR D.O. DEGREE AND ARE IN NEED OF FINANCIAL ASSISTANCE. ACCEPTANCE OF APPLICATIONS BEGINS ON OR AROUND JAN 30.

AWARDS ARE FOR ONE YEAR RENEWABLE WITH REAPPLICATION. WRITE FOR COMPLETE INFORMATION.

871

COMMUNITY FOUNDATION OF GREATER LORAIN COUNTY (MARY J. AND PAUL J. KOPSCH FUND)

1865 N. RIDGE RD. E. - SUITE A
LORAIN OH 44055
216/277-0142 OR 216/323-4445

AMOUNT: $2000

DEADLINE(S): MAY 1

FIELD(S): MEDICAL DOCTOR OR OSTEOPATHIC PHYSICIAN

OPEN TO LORAIN COUNTY RESIDENTS WHO HAVE COMPLETED AT LEAST 1 YEAR IN A USA MEDICAL SCHOOL AND ARE SEEKING EITHER AN M.D. OR D.O. DEGREE. MUST DEMONSTRATE FINANCIAL NEED AND SHOW PROMISE OF SATISFACTORY PERFORMANCE.

APPLICATIONS ACCEPTED STARTING AROUND JAN 30. WRITE FOR COMPLETE INFORMATION.

872

CUYAHOGA COUNTY MEDICAL FOUNDATION (SCHOLARSHIP GRANT PROGRAM)

11001 CEDAR AVE
CLEVELAND OH 44106
216/229-2200

AMOUNT: $500 - $1500

DEADLINE(S): JUN 1

FIELD(S): MEDICINE; DENTISTRY; PHARMACY; NURSING; OSTEOPATHY

GRANTS OPEN TO RESIDENTS OF CUYAHOGA COUNTY WHO ARE ACCEPTED TO OR ENROLLED IN AN ACCREDITED PROFESSIONAL SCHOOL IN ONE OF THE ABOVE AREAS. USA CITIZEN.

APPROX 40 AWARDS PER YEAR. WRITE FOR COMPLETE INFORMATION.

873

DEKALB COUNTY PRODUCERS SUPPLY & FARM BUREAU (MEDICAL SCHOLARSHIP)

315 N. 6TH ST
DEKALB IL 60115
815/756-6361

AMOUNT: VARIES

DEADLINE(S): VARIES

FIELD(S): MEDICAL DOCTOR; NURSING

APPLICANTS OR THEIR PARENTS MUST HAVE BEEN VOTING OR ASSOCIATE MEMBERS OF DEKALB COUNTY FARM BUREAU FOR AT LEAST 2 YEARS PRIOR TO APPLICATION. MUST AGREE TO PRACTICE IN RURAL ILLINOIS COMMUNITY FOR 3 YEARS UPON COMPLETION OF TRAINING.

MUST HAVE BEEN ACCEPTED TO OR BE ATTENDING MEDICAL SCHOOL OR NURSING PROGRAM. WRITE TO VIRGINIA FLEETWOOD; ADDRESS ABOVE; FOR COMPLETE INFORMATION.

874

DELAWARE ACADEMY OF MEDICINE (STUDENT FINANCIAL AID-LOANS)

1925 LOVERING AVE
WILMINGTON DE 19806
302/656-1629

AMOUNT: $1000 - $5000

DEADLINE(S): MAY 15

FIELD(S): MEDICINE; DENTISTRY; ALLIED HEALTH FIELDS

DELAWARE RESIDENT. FOR FULL-TIME GRADUATE STUDY IN THE ABOVE AREAS AT ACCREDITED COLLEGES & UNIVERSITIES. USA CITIZEN OR LEGAL RESIDENT.

WRITE FOR COMPLETE INFORMATION.

875

EDWARD BANGS AND ELZA KELLEY FOUNDATION (SCHOLARSHIP PROGRAM)

243 SOUTH ST
HYANNIS MA 02601
508/775-3117

AMOUNT: UP TO $4000

DEADLINE(S): APR 30

FIELD(S): MEDICINE; NURSING; HEALTH SCIENCES; RELATED FIELDS

OPEN TO RESIDENTS OF BARNSTABLE COUNTY MASS. SCHOLARSHIPS ARE INTENDED TO BENEFIT HEALTH AND WELFARE OF BARNSTABLE COUNTY RESIDENTS. AWARDS SUPPORT STUDY AT RECOGNIZED UNDERGRADUATE; GRADUATE AND PROFESSIONAL INSTITUTIONS.

FINANCIAL NEED IS A CONSIDERATION. WRITE FOR COMPLETE INFORMATION.

876

EPILEPSY FOUNDATION OF AMERICA (MEDICAL STUDENT FELLOWSHIPS)

4351 GARDEN CITY DR.
LANDOVER MD 20785
301/459-3700

165

MEDICAL DOCTOR

AMOUNT: $2000

DEADLINE(S): MAR 2

FIELD(S): MEDICINE - EPILEPSY PROJECT

MEDICAL STUDENTS MAY PROPOSE A 3-MONTH PROJECT TO BE UNDERTAKEN IN A CLINICAL OR LABORATORY SETTING WHERE THERE ARE ONGOING PROGRAMS OF RESEARCH; SERVICE OR TRANING IN THE FIELD OF EPILEPSY.

PROJECT MAY BE CONDUCTED DURING ANY FREE PERIOD OF THE STUDENT'S YEAR AT A USA INSTITUTION OF THE STUDENT'S CHOICE. WRITE FOR COMPLETE INFORMATION.

877

FAIRFAX COUNTY MEDICAL SOCIETY FOUNDATION (SCHOLARSHIPS)

8100 OAK STREET
DUNN LORING VA 22027
703/560-4855

AMOUNT: $1500

DEADLINE(S): MAY 25

FIELD(S): MEDICAL DOCTOR; MEDICAL RELATED DISCIPLINES; MEDICAL TECHNOLGOIES; NURSING

OPEN TO UNDERGRADUATE AND GRADUATE STUDENTS WHO ARE USA CITIZENS AND ARE RESIDENTS OF FAIRFAX COUNTY; VA. FOR STUDIES RELATED TO HUMAN HEALTH. MUST DEMONSTRATE FINANCIAL NEED.

11 AWARDS PER YEAR; RENEWABLE. WRITE FOR COMPLETE INFORMATION.

878

FLORIDA DEPT. OF HEALTH & REHABILITATIVE SERVICES (MEDICAL EDUCATION LOAN REIMBURSEMENT PROGRAM)

RECRUITMENT/RETENTION PROGRAM; 1317 WINEWOOD BLVD.
TALLAHASSEE FL 32399
904/487-2044

AMOUNT: $20000 PER YEAR

DEADLINE(S): NONE

FIELD(S): MEDICINE

PROGRAM TO ENCOURAGE QUALIFIED MEDICAL PERSONNEL TO PRACTICE IN UNDERSERVED AREAS (AS IDENTIFIED BY DEPT OF HEALTH) IN FLORIDA. OPEN TO BOARD ELIGIBLE/ BOARD CERTIFIED PRIMARY CARE PHYSICIANS.

UP TO $20000 PER YEAR FOR THREE YEARS IN REPAYMENT CREDITS FOR OUTSTANDING MEDICAL SCHOOL LOANS. WRITE FOR COMPLETE INFORMATION.

879

FOUNDATION FOR SCIENCE & THE HANDICAPPED (GRANTS PROGRAM)

C/O REBECCA F. SMITH;
115 S. BRAINARD AVE.
LA GRANGE IL 60525
708/352-1091

AMOUNT: $1000

DEADLINE(S): DEC 1

FIELD(S): SCIENCE; MATHEMATICS; MEDICINE; COMPUTER SCIENCE; ENGINEERING

OPEN TO GRADUATE STUDENTS IN THE ABOVE AREAS WHO HAVE SOME PHYSICAL OR SENSORY DISABILITY. APPLICATIONS WILL ALSO BE ACCEPTED FROM UNDERGRADUATE SENIORS WHO HAVE BEEN ACCEPTED TO GRADUATE SCHOOL. USA CITIZEN OR LEGAL RESIDENT.

WRITE FOR COMPLETE INFORMATION.

880

FRESNO-MADERA COUNTY MEDICAL SOCIETY (SCHOLARSHIP FOUNDATION)

3425 N.FIRST STREET; PO BOX 31
FRESNO CA 93707
209/224-4224

AMOUNT: UP TO $1500

DEADLINE(S): MAY 15

FIELD(S): MEDICINE

OPEN TO STUDENTS WHO HAVE LIVED IN FRESNO OR MADERA COUNTY FOR A YEAR OR MORE AND HAVE BEEN APPROVED FOR MATRICULATION IN A MEDICAL SCHOOL. FUNDS MAY NOT BE USED FOR ROOM AND BOARD OR PERSONAL EXPENSES.

FINANCIAL NEED; SCHOLASTIC ACHIEVEMENT AND PROSPECTS FOR COMPLETION OF STUDIES ARE CONSIDERATIONS. WRITE FOR COMPLETE INFORMATION.

881

GEORGIA STATE MEDICAL EDUCATION BOARD ('COUNTRY DOCTOR' SCHOLARSHIP PROGRAM)

244 WASHINGTON STREET SW;
ROOM 574J
ATLANTA GA 30334
404/656-2226

AMOUNT: $8000 PER YEAR FOR 4 YEARS

DEADLINE(S): MAY 15

FIELD(S): MEDICINE - MD AND DO

FOR LEGAL RESIDENTS OF GEORGIA ENROLLED IN OR ACCEPTED FOR ADMISSION TO AN ACCREDITED MEDICAL SCHOOL IN USA. MUST BE WILLING TO PRACTICE IN A RURAL GEORGIA TOWN WITH A POPULATION OF 15000 OR LESS AND DEMONSTRATE FINANCIAL NEED.

30-35 SCHOLARSHIPS PER YEAR RENEWABLE FOR UP TO 4 YEARS. WRITE FOR COMPLETE INFORMATION.

882

GRASS FOUNDATION (ROBERT S. MORISON FELLOWSHIP)

77 RESERVOIR ROAD
QUINCY MA 02170
617/773-0002

AMOUNT: $30000 STIPEND PER YEAR + $700 PER DEPENDENT & $3000 FOR RESEARCH EXPENSES

DEADLINE(S): NOV 1 OF EVEN NUMBERED YEARS

FIELD(S): NEUROLOGY; NEUROSURGERY; NEUROSCIENCE

OPEN TO MD'S PREPARING FOR AN ACADEMIC CAREER WHO HAVE BEEN ACCEPTED INTO OR JUST COMPLETED A RESIDENCY IN ABOVE AREAS & WISH TO UNDERTAKE A 2-YEAR PROGRAM OF BASIC RESEARCH TRAINING AT A RECOGNIZED INSTITUTION IN NORTH AMERICA.

THIS IS A 2-YEAR PROGRAM WHICH STARTS IN JULY OF ODD-NUMBERED YEARS. WRITE FOR COMPLETE INFORMATION.

883

H. FLETCHER BROWN FUND (SCHOLARSHIPS)

C/O BANK OF DELAWARE; TRUST DEPT; PO BOX 791
WILMINGTON DE 19899
302/429-2827

AMOUNT: VARIES

DEADLINE(S): APR 15

FIELD(S): MEDICINE; DENTISTRY; LAW; ENGINEERING; CHEMISTRY

OPEN TO STUDENTS BORN IN DELAWARE; GRADUATED FROM A DELAWARE HIGH SCHOOL & STILL RESIDING IN DELAWARE. FOR FOUR YEARS OF STUDY (UNDERGRAD OR GRAD) LEADING TO A DEGREE THAT ENABLES APPLICANT TO PRACTICE IN CHOSEN FIELD.

SCHOLARSHIPS ARE BASED ON NEED; SCHOLASTIC ACHIEVEMENT; GOOD MORAL CHARACTER. RENEWABLE. WRITE FOR COMPLETE INFORMATION.

884

HEADQUARTERS; DEPT. OF THE ARMY (ARMED FORCES HEALTH PROFESSIONS SCHOLARSHIPS)

ATTN; SGPS-PDE; 5109 LEESBURG PIKE
FALLS CHURCH VA 22041
WRITTEN INQURIY

AMOUNT: $749 PER MONTH STIPEND + TUITION; FEES; BOOKS; LAB FEES ETC.

DEADLINE(S): NONE SPECIFIED

FIELD(S): MEDICINE; DENTISTRY; OPTOMETRY AND NURSE ANESTHESIA (MASTER'S DEGREE); CLINICAL PSYCHOLOGY (PH.D)

OPEN TO USA CITIZENS ENROLLED OR ACCEPTED FOR ENROLLMENT IN ANY OF THE ABOVE FIELDS AT AN ACCREDITED INSTITUTION IN THE USA OR PUERTO RICO. MUST QUALIFY FOR APPOINTMENT AS AN ARMY OFFICER AND SIGN A CONTRACTUAL AGREEMENT.

WRITE FOR COMPLETE INFORMATION.

885

HEADQUARTERS; USAF RECRUITING SERVICE (ARMED FORCES HEALTH PROFESSIONS SCHOLARSHIPS)

MEDICAL RECRUITING DIVISION
RANDOLPH AFB TX 78150
WRITTEN INQURIY

AMOUNT: $749 PER MONTH STIPEND + TUITION; FEES; BOOKS; LAB FEES ETC.

DEADLINE(S): NONE SPECIFIED

FIELD(S): MEDICINE; DENTISTRY; OPTOMETRY AND NURSE ANESTHESIA (MASTER'S DEGREE); CLINICAL PSYCHOLOGY (PH.D)

OPEN TO USA CITIZENS ENROLLED OR ACCEPTED FOR ENROLLMENT IN ANY OF THE ABOVE FIELDS AT AN ACCREDITED INSTITUTION IN THE USA OR PUERTO RICO. MUST QUALIFY FOR APPOINTMENT AS AN AIR FORCE OFFICER AND SIGN A CONTRACTUAL AGREEMENT.

WRITE FOR COMPLETE INFORMATION.

886

IMS EDUCATION FUND (LOAN PROGRAM)

1001 GRAND AVENUE
WEST DES MOINES IA 50265
515/223-1401

AMOUNT: $6000

DEADLINE(S): NONE SPECIFIED

FIELD(S): MEDICINE

LOANS OPEN TO RESIDENTS OF IOWA WHO ARE IN THEIR JUNIOR OR SENIOR YEAR OF MEDICAL COLLEGE. COLLEGE OF MEDICINE MUST CERTIFY STUDENT'S GOOD STANDING AND FINANCIAL NEED. COPY OF FINANCIAL AID FORM REQUIRED.

RENEWABLE. REPAYMENT BEGINS 3 YEARS AFTER GRADUATION. WRITE FOR COMPLETE INFORMATION.

887

INSTITUTO NACIONAL DE CARDIOLOGIA (RESIDENCY FELLOWSHIPS)

JUAN BADIANO #1
TLALPAN MEXICO 14080 DF MEXICO
573-04-80

AMOUNT: STIPEND PLUS ROOM AND BOARD

DEADLINE(S): SEP 30

FIELD(S): CARDIOLOGY; NEPHROLOGY; PATHOLOGY; ANESTHESIOLOGY (1 YEAR); SURGERY (3 YEARS)

A ROTATING RESIDENCY DESIGNED TO ACQUAINT THE FELLOW WITH ALL ASPECTS OF HIS OR HER SPECIALTY DURING A 2 TO 3 MONTH STAY IN EACH DEPARTMENT OF THE 270 BED INSTITUTE.

PROGRAM CONDUCTED IN ACCORDANCE WITH THE NATIONAL UNIVERSITY OF MEXICO. IT IS OPEN TO ALL MEDICAL SCHOOL GRADUATES HAVING 2 YEARS OF TRAINING IN A HOSPITAL DEVOTED TO GENERAL MEDICINE. WRITE FOR COMPLETE INFORMATION.

888

INTERNATIONAL ORDER OF THE KING'S DAUGHTERS AND SONS (HEALTH CAREERS SCHOLARSHIPS)

PO BOX 1017
CHAUTAUQUA NY 14722
716/357-4951

AMOUNT: UP TO $1000

DEADLINE(S): APR 1

FIELD(S): MEDICINE; DENTISTRY; NURSING; PHYSICAL THERAPY; OCCUPATIONAL THERAPY; MEDICAL TECHNOLOGIES; PHARMACY

OPEN TO STUDENTS ACCEPTED TO/ENROLLED IN AN ACCREDITED USA OR CANADIAN 4-YR OR GRADUATE SCHOOL. RN CANDIDATES MUST HAVE COMPLETED 1ST YEAR; BA CANDIDATES IN AT LEAST 3RD YEAR. PRE MED STUDENTS -NOT- ELIGIBLE.

USA OR CANADIAN CITIZEN. THOSE SEEKING MD OR DDS DEGREES MUST BE IN 2ND YR OF MED OR DENTAL SCHOOL. FOR APPLICATION SEND SASE TO MRS. MERLE RABER; 6024 E. CHICAGO RD; JONESVILLE MI 49250.

889

JEWISH VOCATIONAL SERVICE (MARCUS & THERESA LEVIE EDUCATIONAL FUND SCHOLARSHIPS)

1 SOUTH FRANKLIN STREET
CHICAGO IL 60606
312/346-6700 EXT 2214

AMOUNT: $5000

DEADLINE(S): MAR 1

FIELD(S): SOCIAL WORK; MEDICINE; DENTISTRY; NURSING & OTHER RELATED PROFESSIONS & VOCATIONS

OPEN TO COOK COUNTY RESIDENTS OF THE JEWISH FAITH WHO PLAN CAREERS IN THE HELPING PROFESSIONS. MUST SHOW FINANCIAL NEED. FOR UNDERGRADUATE; GRADUATE OR VOCATIONAL STUDY. APPLICATIONS AVAILABLE BEGINNING DEC 1 FROM SCHOLARSHIP SECRETARY.

85-100 AWARDS PER YEAR. RENEWAL POSSIBLE WITH REAPPLICATION. WRITE FOR COMPLETE INFORMATION.

890

JOHN FREDERICK STEINMAN FUND (PSYCHIATRY FELLOWSHIPS)

8 WEST KING STREET
LANCASTER PA 17603
WRITTEN INQUIRY

AMOUNT: $3500

DEADLINE(S): FEB 1

FIELD(S): PSYCHIATRY

FELLOWSHIPS FOR APPLICANTS WITH MD OR DO DEGREE WHO WANT TO CONTINUE STUDY FOR TWO MORE YEARS AND BECOME A TRAINED PSYCHIATRIST OR FOR PYSCHIATRISTS WHO WANT TO BECOME A CHILD PSYCHIATRIST OR COMPARABLE PSYCHIATRIC SUBSPECIALIST.

SELECTION WILL BE MADE ON THE BASIS OF SCHOLASTIC RECORD; PERSONAL QUALIFICATIONS; PERFORMANCE AND FUTURE PROMISE. PREFERENCE TO THOSE WHO AGREE TO PRACTICE IN THE LANCASTER PA AREA. WRITE FOR COMPLETE INFORMATION.

891

JOSEPH COLLINS FOUNDATION (JOSEPH COLLINS GRANTS)

153 EAST 53RD ST.
NEW YORK NY 10022
WRITTEN INQUIRY

AMOUNT: UP TO $3000

DEADLINE(S): MAR 1

FIELD(S): MEDICINE; PSYCHIATRY; NEUROLOGY

GRANTS OPEN TO NEEDY GRADUATE STUDENTS IN THE ABOVE AREAS WHO HAVE BROAD CULTURAL INTERESTS & LIVE WITHIN 200 MILES OF THE SCHOOL THEY ATTEND. AWARDS ARE TENABLE AT ACCREDITED MEDICAL SCHOOLS IN THE USA.

WRITE FOR COMPLETE INFORMATION.

892 ──────────────

KENT MEDICAL FOUNDATION (STUDENT LOAN PROGRAM)

220 CHERRY STREET SE
GRAND RAPIDS MI 49503
616/458-4157

AMOUNT: $6000

DEADLINE(S): NONE

FIELD(S): MEDICINE

INTEREST-FREE LOANS UNTIL DATE OF COMPLETION OF INTERNSHIP. OPEN TO RESIDENTS OF KENT COUNTY MI WHO HAVE SUCCESSFULLY COMPLETED THEIR FIRST YEAR OF MEDICAL SCHOOL.

WRITE FOR COMPLETE INFORMATION.

893 ──────────────

M.A. CARTLAND SHACKFORD MEDICAL FELLOWSHIPS

C/O WELLESLEY COLLEGE;
SECRETARY GRADUATE FELLOWSHIPS; CAREER CENTER
WELLESLEY MA 02181
617/283-3525

AMOUNT: UP TO $3500 STIPEND

DEADLINE(S): DEC 1

FIELD(S): MEDICINE (WITH A VIEW TOGENERAL PRACTICE; NOT PSYCHIATRY)

OPEN TO WOMEN WHO ARE USA CITIZEN OR LEGAL RESIDENT & HAVE BACHELORS DEGREE FROM USA INSTITUTION. AWARD IS FOR GRADUATE STUDY AT ACCREDITED AN ACCREDITED MEDICAL SCHOOL.

WRITE FOR COMPLETE INFORMATION.

894 ──────────────

MARYLAND HIGHER EDUCATION COMMISSION (FAMILY PRACTICE MEDICAL SCHOLARSHIPS)

STATE SCHOLARSHIP ADMINISTRATION; 16 FRANCIS ST.
ANNAPOLIS MD 21401
410/974-5370

AMOUNT: $7500

DEADLINE(S): MAR 1 & APR 15

FIELD(S): MEDICINE (FAMILY PRACTICE)

OPEN TO MARYLAND RESIDENTS WHO HAVE BEEN ADMITTED TO THE SCHOOL OF MEDICINE AT THE UNIV. OF MARYLAND - BALTIMORE. MUST AGREE TO DO RESIDENCY IN FAMILY PRACTICE AND WORK AS FAMILY PRACTITIONER 1 YEAR FOR EACH YEAR OF AWARD.

RENEWABLE UP TO 4 YEARS. WRITE FOR COMPLETE INFORMATION.

895 ──────────────

MARYLAND HIGHER EDUCATION COMMISSION (PROFESSIONAL SCHOOL SCHOLARSHIPS)

STATE SCHOLARSHIP ADMINISTRATION; 16 FRANCIS ST
ANNAPOLIS MD 21401
410/974-5370

AMOUNT: $200 - $1000

DEADLINE(S): MAR 1

FIELD(S): DENTISTRY; PHARMACY; MEDICINE; LAW; NURSING

OPEN TO MARYLAND RESIDENTS WHO HAVE BEEN ADMITTED AS FULL-TIME STUDENTS AT A PARTICIPATING GRADUATE INSTITUTION OF HIGHER LEARNING IN MARYLAND OR AN UNDERGRADUATE NURSING PROGRAM.

RENEWABLE UP TO 4 YEARS. WRITE FOR COMPLETE INFORMATION AND A LIST OF PARTICIPATING MARYLAND INSTITUTIONS.

896 ──────────────

MEDICAL SOCIETIES OF THE COUNTIES OF CHENANGO AND OTSEGO (LEE C. VAN WAGNER SCHOLARSHIP FUND)

210 CLINTON RD.; PO BOX 620
NEW HARTFORD NY 13413
315/735-2204

AMOUNT: $1000 - $2500

DEADLINE(S): JUN 1

FIELD(S): MEDICINE

FOR CHENANGO OR OTSEGO COUNTY (NEW YORK) RESIDENTS WHO ATTEND A MEDICAL OR OSTEOPATHIC SCHOOL APPROVED BY THE ASSOCIATION OF MEDICAL COLLEGES.

4-6 SCHOLARSHIPS PER YEAR. RENEWABLE. MUST STUDY FULL-TIME. WRITE FOR COMPLETE INFORMATION.

897 ──────────────

MICHIGAN OSTEOPATHIC COLLEGE FOUNDATION (STUDENT LOAN PROGRAM)

33100 FREEDOM RD
FARMINGTON MI 48336
313/335-7782

AMOUNT: $2000 PER ACADEMIC YEAR

MEDICAL DOCTOR

DEADLINE(S): NONE

FIELD(S): OSTEOPATHIC MEDICINE

LOANS ARE OPEN TO STUDENTS IN GOOD STANDING AT ACCREDITED OSTEOPATHIC COLLEGES. STUDENT MUST AGREE TO PRACTICE MEDICINE IN MICHIGAN FOR FIVE YEARS AFTER COMPLETION OF INTERNSHIP. US CITIZEN OR LEGAL RESIDENT.

MUST BE RESIDENT OF MICHIGAN FOR SIX MONTHS BEFORE APPLICATION. LOAN AVAILABLE ONLY FOR THE LAST TWO YEARS OF MEDICAL SCHOOL. WRITE FOR COMPLETE INFORMATION.

898

MINNESOTA HEART ASSOCIATION (HELEN N. AND HAROLD B. SHAPIRA SCHOLARSHIP)

4701 WEST 77TH STREET
MINNEAPOLIS MN 55435
612/835-3300

AMOUNT: $1000

DEADLINE(S): MAY 1

FIELD(S): MEDICINE

OPEN TO PRE-MED UNDERGRADUATE STUDENTS & MEDICAL STUDENTS WHO ARE ACCEPTED TO OR ENROLLED IN AN ACCREDITED MINNESOTA COLLEGE OR UNIVERSITY. MEDICAL STUDENTS SHOULD BE IN A CURRICULUM THAT IS RELATED TO THE HEART AND CIRCULATORY SYSTEM.

MAY BE RENEWED ONCE. USA CITIZEN OR LEGAL RESIDENT. WRITE FOR COMPLETE INFORMATION.

899

MINNESOTA PHYSICIANS FOUNDATION OF THE MMA (MEDICAL STUDENT FINANCIAL ASSISTANCE PROGRAM)

2221 UNIVERSITY AVE S.E.; SUITE 400
MINNEAPOLIS MN 55414
612/378-1875

AMOUNT: $3000 MAX PER SCHOOL YEAR

DEADLINE(S): MAR 15; OCT 15

FIELD(S): MEDICINE/MINN RESIDENTS

LOANS AVAILABLE TO STUDENTS WHO HAVE COMPLETED AT LEAST ONE SEMESTER AT A MINNESOTA MEDICAL SCHOOL. MUST DEMONSTRATE FINANCIAL NEED.

NOT RENEWABLE. WRITE FOR COMPLETE INFORMATION.

900

MINORITY MEDICAL FACULTY DEVELOPMENT PROGRAM (FELLOWSHIPS)

HAROLD AMOS PHD;
NATL PROGRAM OFFC; 68 HARVARD ST.
BROOKLINE MA 02146
617/732-1947

AMOUNT: $50000 PER YEAR STIPEND; $25000 PER YEAR RESEARCH SUPPORT

DEADLINE(S): APR 30

FIELD(S): MEDICINE/EDUCATION

OPEN TO MINORITY PHYSICIANS WHO ARE USA CITIZENS; HAVE EXCELLED IN THEIR EDUCATION; ARE COMPLETING OR HAVE COMPLETED THEIR FORMAL CLINICAL TRAINING AND ARE COMMITTED TO ACADEMIC CAREERS.

UP TO 12 FELLOWS ARE SELECTED EACH YEAR. WRITE FOR COMPLETE INFORMATION.

901

MISSISSIPPI BOARD OF TRUSTEES OF STATE INSTITUTIONS OF HIGHER LEARNING (MEDICAL EDUCATION LOAN PROGRAM)

3825 RIDGEWOOD RD
JACKSON MS 39211
601/982-6570

AMOUNT: UP TO $24000

DEADLINE(S): JUN 30

FIELD(S): INTERNAL MEDICINE; OBSTETRICS; GYNECOLOGY; PEDIATRICS

LOAN PROGRAM OPEN TO MISSISSIPPI RESIDENTS WHO HAVE BEEN ADMITTED TO THE UNIVERSITY OF MISSISSIPPI MEDICAL CENTER FOR GRADUATE STUDY IN THE ABOVE AREAS.

LOANS ARE RENEWABLE EACH YEAR. RECIPIENTS MUST AGREE TO PRACTICE IN A SMALL MISSISSIPPI COMMUNITY; AT THE STATE HEALTH AGENCY OR A MISSISSIPPI COMUNITY HEALTH CENTER FOR 4 YEARS UPON COMPLETION OF TRAINING.

902

MISSOURI STATE MEDICAL FOUNDATION (MEDICAL SCHOOL LOW-INTEREST LOANS)

PO BOX 1028; 113 MADISON ST
JEFFERSON CITY MO 65102
314-636-5151

AMOUNT: $4000

DEADLINE(S): AUG 1

FIELD(S): MEDICINE (MISSOURI RESIDENTS)

OPEN TO USA CITIZENS WHO ARE MISSOURI
RESIDENTS AND ARE REGISTERED AS A FULL
TIME STUDENT AT AN AMERICAN MEDICAL
ASSOCIATION ACCREDITED SCHOOL OF
MEDICINE IN THE USA. APPLICANTS MUST
HAVE COMPLETED AT LEAST ONE YEAR
TOWARD M.D. DEGREE.

APPROX 100 LOANS PER YEAR. WRITE FOR
COMPLETE INFORMATION.

903

**MUSCULAR DYSTROPHY ASSOCIATION (POST-
DOCTORAL FELLOWSHIP PROGRAM)**

3561 E SUNRISE BLVD
TUCSON AZ 85718
602/529-2000

AMOUNT: $25000 AND $28000

DEADLINE(S): JUL 10; JAN 10

FIELD(S): MEDICINE; BIOLOGICAL SCIENCES;
LIFE SCIENCES

GRANTS & FELLOWSHIPS FOR POST-DOCTORAL
RESEARCH INTO CAUSES; DIAGNOSIS &
TREATMENT OF NEUROMUSCULAR
DISEASES. PREFERENCE TO THOSE WHO
RECEIVED M.D.; PH.D.; D.SC. OR EQUIVALENT
DEGREE WITHIN 3 YEARS OF STARTING DATE
OF SUPPORT PERIOD.

100 RESEARCH FELLOWSHIPS PER YEAR. WRITE
FOR COMPLETE INFORMATION.

904

**MUTUAL ASSOCIATION FOR PROFESSIONAL
SERVICES (MAPS SCHOLARSHIP FUND)**

11828 RANCHO BERNARDO RD #209
SAN DIEGO CA 92128
619/451-7618

AMOUNT: VARIABLE

DEADLINE(S): MAR 31

FIELD(S): LAW; MEDICINE; DENTISTRY;
PODIATRY; VETERINARY MEDICINE;
OPTOMETRY

PROGRAM IS FOR GRADUATE STUDENTS IN THE
ABOVE AREAS. NOMINATION BY A MEMBER
OF MAPS HELPFUL BUT NOT REQUIRED.
CONSIDERATIONS ARE FINANCIAL NEED;
CHARACTER AND ACHIEVEMENT.
APPLICATIONS ARE ACCEPTED BEGINNING
JAN 1.

ONLY THE FIRST 50 APPLICATIONS RECEIVED
WILL BE CONSIDERED. IF FEWER THAN 50
APPLICATIONS ARE RECEIVED MAR 31
DEADLINE APPLIES. WRITE FOR COMPLETE
INFORMATION.

905

**NATIONAL INSTITUTES OF HEALTH (MINORITY
ACCESS TO RESEARCH CAREERS
PROGRAM-MARC PREDOCTORAL
FELLOWSHIP)**

NATIONAL INSTITUTE OF GENERAL MEDICAL
SCIENCES; WESTWOOD BLDG; ROOM 950
BETHESDA MD 20892
301/496-7941

AMOUNT: $8800 PER YEAR STIPEND

DEADLINE(S): JAN 10; MAY 10; SEPT 10

FIELD(S): MEDICINE-BIOMEDICAL RESEARCH

OPEN TO MINORITY STUDENTS WHO ARE
GRADUATES OF MARC HONORS
UNDERGRADUATE PROGRAM. FELLOWSHIP
IS TO PROVIDE RESEARCH TRAINING
LEADING TO A PH.D DEGREE. USA CITIZEN.

APPROX 11 AWARDS PER YEAR. RENEWABLE UP
TO 5 YEARS. FELLOWS ARE SELECTED ON A
HIGHLY COMPETITIVE BASIS. WRITE FOR
COMPLETE INFORMATION.

906

NATIONAL MEDICAL FELLOWSHIPS INC

254 W. 31ST ST - 7TH FLOOR
NEW YORK NY 10001
212/714-1007

AMOUNT: VARIES

DEADLINE(S): MAY 31 FOR RENEWAL; AUG 31
FOR NEW APPLICANT

FIELD(S): MEDICINE; OSTEOPATHY

AWARDS AND FELLOWSHIPS ARE OFFERED TO
AMERICAN BLACKS; MAINLAND PUERTO
RICANS; MEXICAN AMERICANS AND
AMERICAN INDIANS IN THEIR FIRST OR
SECOND YEAR AT AN ACCREDITED SCHOOL
OF ALLOPATHIC OR OSTEOPATHIC MEDICINE
IN THE USA.

MUST BE USA CITIZEN AND DEMONSTRATE
FINANCIAL NEED. WRITE FOR COMPLETE
INFORMATION.

907

**NATIONAL OSTEOPATHIC FOUNDATION
(EDUCATIONAL GRANTS)**

5775-G PEACHTREE DUNWOODY;
SUITE 500
ATLANTA GA 30342
404/705-9999

AMOUNT: $5000

DEADLINE(S): APR 15

FIELD(S): OSTEOPATHY

GRANTS OPEN TO DOCTORS OF OSTEOPATHY WHO ARE PURSUING POST-DOCTORAL TRAINING TO BECOME FULL-TIME FACULTY MEMBERS; OR THOSE SEEKING ADVANCED SPECIALTY TRAINING. USA CITIZEN.

6 AWARDS PER YEAR. ADDRESS INQUIRIES TO COMMITTEE ON EDUCATIONAL GRANTS.

908

NATIONAL OSTEOPATHIC FOUNDATION (MEAD JOHNSON FELLOWSHIP GRANT)

5775-G PEACHTREE DUNWOODY;
SUITE 500
ATLANTA GA 30342
404/705-9999

AMOUNT: $5000

DEADLINE(S): APR 15

FIELD(S): OSTEOPATHY

APPLICANTS MUST HAVE HELD THE DOCTOR OF OSTEOPATHY DEGREE FOR FOUR YEARS OR LESS AND HAVE DEMONSTRATED APTITUDE FOR ADVANCED TRAINING IN APPROVED SPECIALTIES.

RECIPIENT MAY PURSUE POSTDOCTORAL TRAINING IN ANY HOSPITAL OR AMBULATORY PROGRAM APPROVED FOR RESIDENCY TRAINING BY THE AOA. WRITE FOR COMPLETE INFORMATION.

909

NATIONAL RESEARCH COUNCIL (NRC POSTDOCTORAL & SENIOR RESEARCH ASSOCIATESHIP AWARDS)

ASSOCIATESHIP PROGRAMS GR430/D3; 2101 CONSTITUTION AVE. NW
WASHINGTON DC 20418
202/334-2760

AMOUNT: ANNUAL STIPEND FROM 27750 TO 44000 + BENEFITS

DEADLINE(S): JAN 15; APR 15; AUG 15

FIELD(S): CHEMISTRY; EARTH & ATMOSPHERIC SCIENCES; ENGINEERING & APPLIED SCIENCES; COMPUTER SCIENCE; MATHEMATICS; BIOLOGICAL & MEDICAL SCIENCES SPACE & PLANETARY SCIENCES; PHYSICS

POSTDOCTORAL & SENIOR ASSOCIATESHIP AWARDS FOR RESEARCH AT ONE OF 38 PARTICIPATING SPONSOR FEDERAL LABORATORIES. USA CITIZENSHIP REQUIRED FOR SOME OF THE SPONSOR LABORATORIES; MANY ARE OPEN TO FOREIGN NATIONALS.

WRITE FOR COMPLETE INFORMATION AND APPLICATION MATERIALS.

910

NEW JERSEY OSTEOPATHIC EDUCATION FOUNDATION (SCHOLARSHIPS AND LOANS)

1212 STUYVESANT AVE
TRENTON NJ 08618
609/393-8114

AMOUNT: $2500

DEADLINE(S): APR 30

FIELD(S): OSTEOPATHIC MEDICINE

GRANTS OPEN TO NEW JERSEY RESIDENTS WHO ARE ABOUT TO BEGIN THEIR FIRST YEAR OF OSTEOPATHIC EDUCATION. RECIPIENTS AGREE TO PRACTICE IN NEW JERSEY FOR 2 YEARS FOLLOWING THEIR INTERNSHIP OR RESIDENCY. USA CITIZEN.

5-8 AWARDS PER YEAR. WRITE FOR COMPLETE INFORMATION.

911

OKLAHOMA EDUCATIONAL FOUNDATION FOR OSTEOPATHIC MEDICINE (STUDENT LOAN PROGRAM)

4848 NORTH LINCOLN BLVD
OKLAHOMA CITY OK 73105
405/528-4848

AMOUNT: VARIES ACCORDING TO NEED

DEADLINE(S): 1ST THURS OF MAR JUN SEP & DEC

FIELD(S): OSTEOPATHY

OPEN TO OSTEOPATHIC MEDICINE STUDENTS IN GOOD SCHOLASTIC STANDING WITH THE RECOMMENDATION OF TWO OKLAHOMA OSTEOPATHS. PREFERENCE TO THOSE WHO WILL PRACTICE IN OKLAHOMA UPON COMPLETION OF INTERNSHIP & RESIDENCY.

LOANS BECOME DUE AND PAYABLE IF STUDENT LEAVES SCHOOL OR LEAVES OKLAHOMA TO PRACTICE ELSEWHERE AFTER INTERNSHIP & RESIDENCY. WRITE FOR COMPLETE INFORMATION.

912

PENNSYLVANIA MEDICAL SOCIETY - EDUCATIONAL AND SCIENTIFIC TRUST (LOAN PROGRAM)

777 EAST PARK DRIVE - PO BOX 8820
HARRISBURG PA 17105
717/558-7750 EXT 424

AMOUNT: $1500 - $3000

DEADLINE(S): APR 1 TO JUL 1

FIELD(S): MEDICINE AND ALLIED HEALTH FIELDS

OPEN TO PENNSYLVANIA RESIDENTS WITH DEMONSTRATED FINANCIAL NEED WHO ARE SEEKING A MEDICAL DEGREE OR ARE ENROLLED IN 4-YEAR OR 2-YEAR PROGRAMS IN THE HEALTH FIELD. FOR STUDY IN USA.

APPROX 300 LOANS PER YEAR. WRITE FOR COMPLETE INFORMATION.

913

PHARMACEUTICAL MANUFACTURERS ASSOCIATION FOUNDATION (MEDICAL/ DENTAL STUDENT RESEARCH FELLOWSHIPS)

1100 15TH STREET NW
WASHINGTON DC 20005
202/835-3400

AMOUNT: $500 PER MONTH

DEADLINE(S): JAN 15

FIELD(S): PHARMACOLOGY; CLINICAL PHARMACOLOGY

OPEN TO MEDIAL OR DENTAL STUDENTS WHO HAVE COMPLETED AT LEAST ONE YEAR AT A USA SCHOOL & ARE INTERESTED IN COMPLETING THEIR MEDICAL/DENTAL TRAINING & SUBSEQUENT CLINICAL TRAINING FOLLOWING THE FELLOWSHIP.

AWARDS ARE FOR 3-12 MONTHS OF FULL-TIME CLINICAL RESEARCH TRAINING. WRITE FOR COMPLETE INFORMATION.

914

PHI RHO SIGMA MEDICAL SOCIETY (ELLIOTT DOLLAR STUDENT LOAN FUND)

PO BOX 90264
INDIANAPOLIS IN 46290
317/255-4379 OR 317/255-9384

AMOUNT: VARIES

DEADLINE(S): NONE

FIELD(S): MEDICINE

OPEN ONLY TO PHI RHO SIGMA MEMBERS. APPLICATION IS MADE IN TRIPLICATE WITH RECOMMENDATIONS FROM YOUR CHAPTER PRESIDENT; CHAPTER COUNSELOR & THE DEAN OR OTHER ADMINISTRATIVE OFFICER OF THE MEDICAL SCHOOL IN WHICH YOU ARE ENROLLED.

THE MAXIMUM LOAN ALLOWED IS THE AMOUNT OF THE APPLICANT'S ANNUAL TUITION.

915

RHODE ISLAND MEDICAL SOCIETY (FISKE PRIZE)

106 FRANCIS STREET
PROVIDENCE RI 02903
WRITTEN INQUIRY

AMOUNT: $2500 MAXIMUM

DEADLINE(S): VARIES (USUALLY IN FALL)

FIELD(S): MEDICINE - BEST PAPER(S)

AWARD OPEN TO RHODE ISLAND PHYSICIANS FOR THE BEST PAPER(S) ON A MEDICALLY-RELATED TOPIC SELECTED ANNUALLY BY THE FUNDS' TRUSTEES. PAPERS MUST BE DOUBLE-SPACED AND SHOULD NOT EXCEED 10000 WORDS.

WRITE FOR COMPLETE INFORMATION.

916

ROBERT SCHRECK MEMORIAL FUND (GRANTS)

C/O TEXAS COMMERCE BANK-
TRUST DEPT; PO DRAWER 140
EL PASO TX 79980
915/546-6515

AMOUNT: $500 - $1500

DEADLINE(S): JUL 15; NOV 15

FIELD(S): MEDICINE; VETERINARY MEDICINE; PHYSICS; CHEMISTRY; ARCHITECTURE; ENGINEERING; EPISCOPAL CLERGY

GRANTS TO UNDERGRADUATE JUNIORS OR SENIORS OR GRADUATE STUDENTS WHO HAVE BEEN RESIDENTS OF EL PASO COUNTY FOR AT LEAST TWO YEARS. MUST BE USA CITIZEN OR LEGAL RESIDENT AND HAVE A HIGH GRADE POINT AVERAGE. FINANCIAL NEED IS A CONSIDERATION.

WRITE FOR COMPLETE INFORMATION.

917

SANDEE THOMPSON MEMORIAL SCHOLARSHIP FOUNDATION (SCHOLARSHIPS)

1211 NAPOLEON MANOR NE
LAWRENCEVILLE GA 30243
WRITTEN INQUIRY ONLY

AMOUNT: $500

DEADLINE(S): MAR 15

FIELD(S): MEDICINE; NURSING; PHYSICAL THERAPY; RELIGION

OPEN TO UNDERGRADUATE AND GRADUATE STUDENTS HAVING AN INTEREST IN SERVING HUMANINTY AND RELIEVING HUMAN SUFFERING. MUST HAVE MEDICAL OR RELIGIOUS ORIENTED CAREER GOAL WITH PHYSICAL THERAPY A HIGH PREFERENCE.

STUDENTS SHOULD BE ENTERING AT LEAST JUNIOR YEAR AT AN ACCREDITED COLEGE OR UNIVERSITY. FINANCIAL INFORMATION REQUIRED. SEND STAMPED; SELF ADDRESSED ENVELOPE FOR COMPLETE INFORMATION.

918

SANTA BARBARA FOUNDATION (MEDICAL STUDENT LOAN PROGRAM)

15 E.CARRILLO ST
SANTA BARBARA CA 93101
805/963-1873

MEDICAL DOCTOR

AMOUNT: VARIES

DEADLINE(S): APPLICATIONS ACCEPTED OCT 1 - JAN 15

FIELD(S): MEDICINE

OPEN TO SANTA BARBARA COUNTY HIGH SCHOOL GRADUATES OR STUDENTS WITH STRONG SANTA BARBARA TIES. AWARDS TENABLE AT ACCREDITED MEDICAL SCHOOLS. USA CITIZEN OR PERMANENT RESIDENT. FINANCIAL NEED IS A CONSIDERATION.

APPLICANTS SHOULD HAVE ATTENDED SANTA BARBARA COUNTY SCHOOLS SINCE THE 7TH GRADE. WRITE FOR COMPLETE INFORMATION.

919

SOCIETY OF BIOLOGICAL PSYCHIATRY (A.E. BENNETT RESEARCH AWARDS)

C/O A. JOHN RUSH MD; DEPT OF PSYCHIATRY;UT SOUTHWESTERN MEDICAL CENTER;
5323 HARRY HINES BLVD.
DALLAS TX 75235
214/688-8766

AMOUNT: $1500

DEADLINE(S): JAN 31

FIELD(S): BIOLOGICAL PSYCHIATRY

AWARDS ARE GIVEN IN BASIC SCIENCE AND CLINICAL SCIENCE FOR PURPOSE OF STIMULATING INTERNATIONAL RESEARCH IN BIOLOGICAL PSYCHIATRY BY YOUNG INVESTIGATORS UNDER THE AGE OF 35.

ALL COAUTHORS ALSO MUST BE UNDER 35. CANDIDATE MUST BE ACTIVELY INVOLVED IN THE AREA OF RESEARCH DESCRIBED IN SUBMISSION AND THE STUDIES AND DATA MUST NOT HAVE BEEN PUBLISHED ELSEWHERE.

920

SOCIETY OF BIOLOGICAL PSYCHIATRY (DISTA FELLOWSHIP AWARD)

C/O A. JOHN RUSH MD; DEPT OF PSYCHIATRY;UT SOUTHWESTERN MEDICAL CTR; 5323 HARRY HINES BLVD.
DALLAS TX 75235
214/688-8766

AMOUNT: $1500

DEADLINE(S): DEC 15

FIELD(S): BIOLOGICAL PSYCHIATRY

OPEN TO MEDICAL GRADUATES IN THEIR THIRD; FOURTH OR FIFTH YEAR OF RESIDENCY OR FELLOWSHIP TRAINING. SELECTION WILL BE BASED ON PAST EXCELLENCE & POTENTIAL FOR PROFESSIONAL GROWTH IN THE AREA OF BIOLOGICAL PSYCHIATRY OR CLINICAL NEUROSCIENC

NOMINATIONS ARE MADE BY UNIVERSITY DEPARTMENT OF PSYCHIATRY. WRITE FOR COMPLETE INFORMATION.

921

SOCIETY OF BIOLOGICAL PSYCHIATRY (ZISKIND-SOMERFIELD RESEARCH AWARD)

C/O A. JOHN RUSH MD; UT SOUTHWESTERN MEDICAL CENTER;
5323 HARRY HINES BLVD.
DALLAS TX 75235
214/688-8766

AMOUNT: $2500

DEADLINE(S): MAR 31

FIELD(S): BIOLOGICAL PSYCHIATRY

OPEN TO SENIOR INVESTIGATORS WHO ARE MEMBERS OF THE SOCIETY OF BIOLOGICAL PSYCHIATRY. AWARD IS FOR BASIC OR CLINICAL RESEARCH BY SENIOR INVESTIGATORS 35 OR OLDER.

CANDIDATES MUST BE MEMBERS IN GOOD STANDING OF THE SOCIETY OF BIOLOGICAL PSYCHIATRY. WRITE FOR COMPLETE INFORMATION.

922

SOUTH CAROLINA OPTOMETRIC ASSOCIATION (LOAN PROGRAM)

2730 DEVINE STREET
COLUMBIA SC 29205
803/799-6721

AMOUNT: $1000

DEADLINE(S): AUG 1 - SEP 1

FIELD(S): OPTOMETRY

PROGRAM OPEN TO RESIDENTS OF SOUTH CAROLINA WHO ARE ACCEPTED BY AN ACCREDITED SCHOOL OF OPTOMETRY & ARE IN THE UPPER 1/3 OF THEIR CLASS OR HAVE MAINTAINED AT LEAST A 'C' GPA.

6-10 LOANS PER YEAR. RENEWABLE. WRITE FOR COMPLETE INFORMATION.

923

TY COBB EDUCATIONAL FOUNDATION (GRADUATE SCHOLARSHIP PROGRAM)

P.O. BOX 725
FOREST PARK GA 30051
WRITTEN INQUIRY

AMOUNT: $3000

DEADLINE(S): JUN 15

FIELD(S): MEDICINE; DENTISTRY; VETERINARY MEDICINE; LAW

OPEN TO GRADUATE STUDENTS IN THE ABOVE FIELDS WHO ARE RESIDENTS OF GEORGIA; HAVE SATISFACTORY GRADES AND ARE ABLE TO DEMONSTRATE FINANCIAL NEED.

WRITE FOR COMPLETE INFORMATION.

924

U.S. DEPT. OF EDUCATION (INDIAN GRADUATE PROFESSIONAL FELLOWSHIPS)

400 MARYLAND AVENUE SW; RM 2177; MAIL STOP 6335
WASHINGTON DC 20202
202/401-1902

AMOUNT: $1000 - $34000 (AVERAGE $13000)

DEADLINE(S): FEB 7

FIELD(S): MEDICINE; PSYCHOLOGY; LAW; EDUCATION; RELATED FIELDS

FELLOWSHIPS FOR AMERICAN INDIANS OR ALASKAN NATIVES WHO ARE US CITZENS AND SEEKING GRADUATE DEREEES IN THE ABOVE FIELDS AT ACCREDITED INSTITUTIONS IN USA.

APPROXIMATELY 90 CONTINUATION AND 35 NEW AWARDS. WRITE FOR COMPLETE INFORMATION.

925

U.S. DEPT. OF HEALTH AND HUMAN SERVICES (NATIONAL HEALTH SERVICE CORPS SCHOLARSHIP PROGRAM)

1201 GREENSBORO DR.; SUITE 600
MCLEAN VA 22102
703/734-6855; 800/221-9393

AMOUNT: TUITION; FEES; EDUCATIONAL EXPENSES; MONTHLY STIPEND

DEADLINE(S): VARIES ANNUALLY

FIELD(S): MEDICINE (MD OR DO); DENTISTRY

OPEN TO USA CITIZENS ACCEPTED OR ENROLLED IN USA SCHOOLS OF ALLOPATHIC (MD) OR OSTEOPATHIC (DO) MEDICINE OR DENTISTRY. RECIPIENTS AGREE TO WORK 1 YEAR IN DESIGNATED HEALTH PROFESSIONS SHORTAGE AREAS FOR EACH YEAR OF AWARD.

THE MINIMUM SERVICE OBLIGATION IS TWO YEARS. WRITE OR CALL FOR INFORMATION ONE YEAR PRIOR TO APPLYING.

926

VIRGIN ISLANDS BOARD OF EDUCATION (NURSING & OTHER HEALTH SCHOLARSHIPS)

PO BOX 11900
ST THOMAS VI 00801
809/774-4546

AMOUNT: UP TO $1800

DEADLINE(S): MAR 31

FIELD(S): NURSING; MEDICINE; HEALTH RELATED AREAS

OPEN TO BONAFIDE RESIDENTS OF THE VIRGIN ISLANDS WHO ARE ACCEPTED BY AN ACCREDITED SCHOOL OF NURSING OR AN ACCREDITED INSTITUTION OFFERING COURSES IN ONE OF THE HEALTH RELATED FIELDS.

THIS SCHOLARSHIP IS GRANTED FOR ONE ACADEMIC YEAR. RECIPIENTS MAY REAPPLY WITH AT LEAST A 'C' AVERAGE. WRITE FOR COMPLETE INFORMATION.

927

WASHINGTON OSTEOPATHIC FOUNDATION (STUDENT LOAN PROGRAM)

PO BOX 16486
SEATTLE WA 98116
206-937-5358

AMOUNT: $3000 (TOWARD TUITION ONLY)

DEADLINE(S): APR 15; AUG 15; NOV 15; FEB 15

FIELD(S): OSTEOPATHIC MEDICINE-DOCTORAL LEVEL

WASHINGTON RESIDENTS. LOW INTEREST LOANS TO STUDENTS WHO ARE USA CITIZENS AND AGREE TO PRACTICE FOR 3 YEARS IN WASHINGTON STATE FOLLOWING TRAINING.

8-12 AWARDS PER YEAR. ADDRESS INQUIRIES TO KATHLEEN ITTER; EXEC DIRECTOR.

MEDICAL RELATED DISCIPLINES

928

ABBIE SARGENT MEMORIAL SCHOLARSHIP INC (SCHOLARSHIPS)

295 SHEEP DAVIS ROAD
CONCORD NH 03301
603/224-1934

AMOUNT: $200

DEADLINE(S): MAR 15

FIELD(S): AGRICULTURE; VETERINARY MEDICINE; HOME ECONOMICS

OPEN TO NEW HAMPSHIRE RESIDENT WHO IS HIGH SCHOOL GRADUATE WITH GOOD GRADES AND CHARACTER. FOR UNDERGRADUATE OR GRADUATE STUDY. USA LEGAL RESIDENT. DEMONSTRATE FINANCIAL NEED.

RENEWABLE WITH REAPPLICATION. WRITE FOR COMPLETE INFORMATION.

929

AMERICAN ACADEMY OF FIXED PROSTHODONTICS (TYLMAN RESEARCH GRANTS)

DEPT OF PROSTHETIC DENTISTRY; HARVARD SCHOOL OF DENTAL MEDICINE; 188 LONGWOOD AV
BOSTON MA 02115
617/432-2489; FAX 617/432-4266

AMOUNT: $1500

DEADLINE(S): MAR 1

FIELD(S): PROSTHODONTICS

GRANTS OFFERED ANNUALLY TO SUPPORT STUDENT RESEARCH IN THE FIELD OF FIXED PROSTHODONTICS. STUDENTS IN ACCREDITED GRADUATE AND POSTGRADUATE PROGRAMS MAY APPLY WITH THE APPROVAL OF THEIR PROGRAM DIRECTOR.

EIGHT GRANTS PER YEAR. WRITE FOR COMPLETE INFORMATION.

930

AMERICAN ACADEMY OF OPTOMETRY (JULIUS F. NEUMUELLER AWARD)

4330 EAST WEST HIGHWAY #1113
BETHESDA MD 20817
301/781-6500

AMOUNT: $500

DEADLINE(S): JUN 1

FIELD(S): OPTOMETRY

CASH AWARD OFFERED EACH YEAR FOR PAPER SELECTED BY COMMITTEE IN FIELD OR GEOMETRIC OPTICS. OPEN TO STUDENTS WHO ARE ENROLLED IN AN ACCREDITED SCHOOL OR COLLEGE OF OPTOMETRY AND ARE NOMINATED BY THE DEAN.

WRITE FOR COMPLETE INFORMATION.

931

AMERICAN ACADEMY OF THE HISTORY OF DENTISTRY (M.D.K. BREMNER DENTAL HISTORY ESSAY CONTEST)

DAVID O. MOLINE; RM 3202 GH; DEPT OF HOSP DENTISTRY; UNIV OF IOWA HOSPITALS & CLINICS; NEWTON RD
IOWA CITY IA 52242
319/356-2743

AMOUNT: $500

DEADLINE(S): JUN 1

FIELD(S): HISTORY OF DENTISTRY

OPEN TO ANY PRE-DOCTORAL STUDENT ENROLLED IN AN ACCREDITED SCHOOL OF DENTISTRY. ESSAYS MUST BE ORIGINAL & UNPUBLISHED. AWARDS CONFERRED AT ANNUAL MEETING OF ACADEMY IN YEAR FOLLOWING SUBMISSION OF ESSAYS.

WRITE FOR COMPLETE INFORMATION.

932

AMERICAN ASSOCIATION OF WOMEN DENTISTS (GILLETTE HAYDEN MEMORIAL FOUNDATION)

95 WEST BROADWAY
SALEM NJ 08079
609/935-0467

AMOUNT: $2000

DEADLINE(S): AUG 1

FIELD(S): DENTISTRY

LOANS AVAILABLE TO WOMEN WHO ARE 3RD & 4TH YEAR PRE-DENTAL STUDENTS OR ARE GRADUATE DEGREE CANDIDATES. SCHOLARSHIP; NEED FOR ASSISTANCE AND AMOUNG OF DEBT CURRENTLY ACCUMULATED ARE MAIN POINTS CONSIDERED.

WRITE FOR COMPLETE INFORMATION.

933

AMERICAN COLLEGE OF HEALTHCARE EXECUTIVES (ALBERT W DENT SCHOLARSHIP FUND)

840 N LAKE SHORE DR
CHICAGO IL 60611
312/943-0544

AMOUNT: $3000

DEADLINE(S): MAR 31

FIELD(S): HEALTH CARE ADMINISTRATION

OPEN TO ACHE STUDENT ASSOCIATES WHO ARE HANDICAPPED OR ARE MEMBERS OF A MINORITY GROUP & HAVE BEEN ACCEPTED TO OR ARE ENROLLED FULL TIME IN AN ACCREDITED GRADUATE PROGRAM. USA OR CANADIAN CITIZEN. PREVIOUS RECIPIENTS ARE NOT ELIGIBLE.

MUST DEMONSTRATE FINANCIAL NEED. APPLY BETWEEN JAN 1 AND MAR 31. WRITE FOR COMPLETE INFORMATION.

934

AMERICAN COLLEGE OF HEALTHCARE EXECUTIVES (FOSTER G MCGAW STUDENT LOAN FUND)

840 NORTH LAKE SHORE DRIVE
CHICAGO IL 60611
312/943-0544

AMOUNT: $4000 MAXIMUM

DEADLINE(S): MAR 31

FIELD(S): HEALTH CARE ADMINISTRATION

SPECIAL LOW-INTEREST LOANS OPEN TO ACHE STUDENT ASSOCIATES WHO ARE ENROLLED IN A GRADUATE PROGRAM ACCREDITED BY THE ACCREDITING COMMISSION ON EDUCATION FOR HEALTH SERVICES ADMINISTRATION. USA OR CANADIAN CITIZEN.

MUST DEMONSTRATE FINANCIAL NEED. LOAN IS INTEREST FREE THE FIRST 3 YRS; THEN REPAYABLE AT A PRE-ESTABLISHED INTEREST RATE. APPLICATIONS ARE ACCEPTED BETWEEN JAN 1 AND MAR 31. WRITE FOR COMPLETE INFORMATION.

935 ──────────────────

AMERICAN COLLEGE OF LEGAL MEDICINE (STUDENT WRITING COMPETITION)

JAY A. GOLD; EXECUTIVE DIRECTOR;
611 E. WELLS ST.
MILWAUKEE WI 53202
414/276-1881

AMOUNT: $1000

DEADLINE(S): FEB 1

FIELD(S): LEGAL MEDICINE

AWARD FOR THE BEST PAPER ON ANY ASPECT OF LEGAL MEDICINE OPEN TO STUDENTS ENROLLED IN AN ACCREDITED SCHOOL OF LAW; MEDICINE; DENTISTRY; PODIATRY; NURSING; PHARMACY; HEALTH SCIENCE OR HEALTH CARE ADMINISTRATION IN THE USA OR CANADA.

AWARDS ARE GIVEN TO FIRST PLACE WINNER IN EACH OF THREE CATEGORIES. WRITE FOR COMPLETE INFORMATION.

936 ──────────────────

AMERICAN FOUNDATION FOR PHARMACEUTICAL EDUCATION (FELLOWSHIP PROGRAM)

PO BOX 7126; 618 SOMERSET ST
NORTH PLAINFIELD NJ 07060
908/561-8077

AMOUNT: $6000; $7500; $10000

DEADLINE(S): MAR 1

FIELD(S): PHARMACY

OPEN TO STUDENTS WHO HAVE COMPLETED AT LEAST ONE SEMESTER OF GRADUATE SCHOOL AND ARE SEEKING THE PH.D DEGREE IN A GRADUATE PROGRAM ADMINISTERED BY OR AFFILIATED WITH A COLLEGE OF PHARMACY. MUST BE USA CITIZEN OR LEGAL RESIDENT.

A VARIETY OF FELLOWSHIPS ARE AWARDED ANNUALLY. WRITE FOR COMPLETE INFORMATION.

937 ──────────────────

AMERICAN FOUNDATION FOR PHARMACEUTICAL EDUCATION (SPRINGBOARD TO TEACHING FELLOWSHIP PROGRAM)

618 SOMERSET ST - PO BOX 7126
NORTH PLAINFIELD NJ 07060
908/561-8077

AMOUNT: $7500

DEADLINE(S): MAR 1

FIELD(S): TEACHING - COLLEGE OF PHARMACY

OPEN TO COLLEGE OF PHARMACY STUDENTS IN THEIR LAST YEAR OF STUDY TOWARD THE PH.D. PURPOSE IS TO ENCOURAGE PHARMACY GRADUATE STUDENTS TO CONSIDER A TEACHING CAREER IN A COLLEGE OF PHARMACY.

AN ADDITIONAL $15000 IS AWARDED OVER TWO YEARS FOR A RESEARCH PROJECT WHEN THE STUDENT ACCEPTS A TEACHING APPOINTMENT IN A PHARMACY COLLEGE. USA CITIZEN OR LEGAL RESIDENT. WRITE FOR COMPLETE INFORMATION.

938 ──────────────────

AMERICAN FOUNDATION FOR VISION AWARENESS (EDUCATION/RESEARCH GRANTS)

243 NORTH LINDBERGH BLVD
ST LOUIS MO 63141
314/991-4100

AMOUNT: $1000 SCHOLARSHIPS; $5000 - $10000 RESEARCH GRANTS

DEADLINE(S): FEB 1

FIELD(S): OPTOMETRY

SCHOLARSHIPS OPEN TO OPTOMETRY STUDENTS. RESEARCH GRANTS OPEN TO SCIENTISTS DOING RESEARCH IN THE FIELD OF VISION.

WRITE FOR COMPLETE INFORMATION.

939 ──────────────────

AMERICAN FOUNDATION FOR VISION AWARENESS OF WASHINGTON (SCHOLARSHIPS)

C/O MRS. CHRIS CASH;
28923 15TH PLACE SOUTH
FEDERAL WAY WA 98003
206/941-7554

AMOUNT: $700 - $1000

DEADLINE(S): DEC 15

FIELD(S): OPTOMETRY

WASHINGTON STATE RESIDENT. AWARDS ARE GRANTED WHEN STUDENT IS ACCEPTED AND ENROLLS IN AN ACCREDITED SCHOOL OF OPTOMETRY.

AWARDS ARE RENEWABLE. WRITE FOR COMPLETE INFORMATION.

940

AMERICAN FUND FOR DENTAL HEALTH (DENTAL SCHOLARSHIPS FOR MINORITY STUDENTS)

211 EAST CHICAGO AVE. SUITE 820
CHICAGO IL 60611
312/787-6270

AMOUNT: $1000

DEADLINE(S): MAY 1

FIELD(S): DENTISTRY

OPEN TO ETHNIC MINORITIES WHO ARE UNDERREPRESENTED IN DENTISTRY - AFRICAN AMERICAN; MEXICAN AMERICAN; PUERTO RICAN; NATIVE AMERICAN. MUST BE ENTERING FIRST YEAR OF DENTAL SCHOOL AND RESIDE IN AND BE A CITIZEN OF USA.

20-30 AWARDS PER YEAR. MUST DEMONSTRATE FINANCIAL NEED. WRITE FOR COMPLETE INFORMATION.

941

AMERICAN FUND FOR DENTAL HEALTH (DENTAL TEACHER TRAINING FELLOWSHIPS)

211 E. CHICAGO AVE. SUITE 820
CHICAGO IL 60611
312/787-6270

AMOUNT: $20000 STIPEND

DEADLINE(S): SEP 1

FIELD(S): TEACHING DENTISTRY

POST-DOCTORAL FELLOWSHIPS FOR DENTISTS WHO WISH TO TEACH DENTISTRY & FACULTY WHO WISH TO ENHANCE THEIR KNOWLEDGE & SKILLS. OPEN TO USA CITIZENS WHO HOLD DDS OR DMD. AWARD IS FOR 1 YEAR AT AN ACCREDITED USA INSTITUTION.

FELLOWS MUST AGREE TO TEACH FULL TIME FOR 2 CONSECUTIVE YEARS AT AN ACCREDITED DENTAL SCHOOL UPON COMPLETION OF FELLOWSHIP YEAR. WRITE FOR COMPLETE INFORMATION.

942

AMERICAN FUND FOR DENTAL HEALTH (HILLENBRAND FELLOWSHIP)

211 EAST CHICAGO AVE #820
CHICAGO IL 60611
312/787-6270

AMOUNT: $40000 STIPEND + TRAVEL EXPENSES

DEADLINE(S): DEC 1 (ODD NUMBERED YEARS)

FIELD(S): DENTAL ADMINISTRATION

APPLICANTS WILL BE JUDGED ON THE BASIS OF THEIR ACADEMIC RECORDS; QUALIFICATIONS; POTENTIAL FOR DENTAL ADMINISTRATION & PERSONAL ATTRIBUTES. SHOULD BE A GRADUATE OF AN ACCREDITED USA DENTAL SCHOOL. USA CITIZEN.

AWARDED EVERY TWO YEARS. WRITE FOR COMPLETE INFORMATION.

943

AMERICAN LIVER FOUNDATION (STUDENT RESEARCH FELLOWSHIPS)

1425 POMPTON AVE
CEDAR GROVE NJ 07009
201/256-2550

AMOUNT: $2500 STIPEND

DEADLINE(S): DEC 15

FIELD(S): MEDICAL RESEARCH

FELLOWSHIPS OPEN TO MEDICAL STUDENTS; VETERINARY STUDENTS & PH.D CANDIDATES. PURPOSE IS TO ENCOURAGE THEM TO GAIN EXPOSURE IN THE RESEARCH LABORATORY & POSSIBLY CONSIDER LIVER RESEARCH AS A CAREER OPTION.

DURATION IS 3 MONTHS. WRITE FOR COMPLETE INFORMATION.

944

AMERICAN OPTOMETRIC ASSN (STUDENT LOAN PROGRAM)

243 NORTH LINDBERGH BLVD
ST LOUIS MO 63141
WRITTEN INQUIRY

AMOUNT: $7500 ANNUALLY TO A MAX OF $54750 (INCLUDING UNDERGRAD LOANS)

DEADLINE(S): NONE

FIELD(S): OPTOMETRY

OPEN TO STUDENT MEMBERS OF AOA WHO ARE IN GOOD ACADEMIC STANDING AND PURSUING A DOCTOR OF OPTOMETRY DEGREE IN AN ACCREDITED COLLEGE OF OPTOMETRY.

WRITE FOR COMPLETE INFORMATION.

945

AMERICAN OPTOMETRIC FOUNDATION (WILLIAM EZELL O.D. FELLOWSHIP)

4330 EAST WEST HWY - SUITE 1117
BETHESDA MD 20814
301/718-6514

AMOUNT: MAXIMUM OF $6000 ANNUALLY

DEADLINE(S): APR 15

FIELD(S): OPTOMETRY

OPEN TO APPLICANTS WITH A DEGREE IN OPTOMETRY WHO ARE PURSUING THEIR PH.D & PLAN TO MAKE OPTOMETRIC TEACHING AND/OR RESEARCH THEIR CAREER.

WRITE FOR COMPLETE INFORMATION.

946

AMERICAN PHARMACEUTICAL ASSN AUXILIARY (IRENE A. PARKS STUDENT LOAN FUND)

C/O MRS. PEGGY GAWRONSKI;
6127 W. MT. PARKWAY
PRESTONBURG KY 41653
606/886-0249

AMOUNT: UP TO $500

DEADLINE(S): OCT 15

FIELD(S): PHARMACY

LOANS ARE AVAILABLE FOR PHARMACY STUDENTS IN THEIR LAST TWO YEARS OF PHARMACY SCHOOL. REPAYMENT OF LOAN PLUS INTEREST TO BEGIN 60 DAYS AFTER GRADUATION. MUST SHOW FINANCIAL NEED.

COMPLETE INFORMATION IS AVAILABLE FROM THE ADDRESS ABOVE OR FROM PHARMACY COLLEGE DEANS.

947

AMERICAN PODIATRIC MEDICAL ASSN (SCHOLARSHIPS AND LOANS)

9312 OLD GEORGETOWN RD
BETHESDA MD 20814
301/571-9200

AMOUNT: $7500

DEADLINE(S): APR 30

FIELD(S): PODIATRIC MEDICINE

SCHOLARSHIPS AND LOANS OPEN TO FOURTH-YEAR PODIATRY STUDENTS OR GRADUATE STUDENTS WHO WISH TO CONTINUE THEIR STUDIES FULL TIME. RECIPIENT MUST TAKE AT LEAST 12 CREDITS PER SEMESTER.

SELECTION IS BASED ON LEADERSHIP QUALITIES; PROFESSIONAL ATTITUDES & CHARACTER. AVAILABLE -ONLY- THROUGH SCHOOL'S FINANCIAL AID OFFICE.

948

AMERICAN SOCIETY FOR MEDICAL TECHNOLOGY (EDUCATION & RESEARCH FUND-RUTH I. HEINEMANN MEMORIAL TRUSTEE AWARD)

2021 'L' STREET NW; SUITE 400
WASHINGTON DC 20036
202/785-3311

AMOUNT: UP TO $500

DEADLINE(S): FEB 1

FIELD(S): CLINICAL LABORATORY SCIENCE

AWARD TO ASSIST INDIVIDUALS IN DEVELOPING EDUCATIONAL STRATEGIES; PREPARING EDUCATIONAL MEDIA OR DESIGNING INNOVATIVE METHODS OF INSTRUCTION. OPEN TO EDUCATORS & GRAD STUDENTS STUDYING TO BECOME EDUCATORS. USA CITIZEN.

WRITE TO EXECUTIVE DIRECTOR AT ADDRESS AABOVE FOR COMPLETE INFORMATION. ENCLOSE STAMPED SELF ADDRESSED BUSINESS SIZE ENVELOPE.

949

AMERICAN SOCIETY FOR MEDICAL TECHNOLOGY (EDUCATION & RESEARCH FUND-JOHN C. LANG MEMORIAL AWARD)

2021 'L' STREET NW; SUITE 400
WASHINGTON DC 20036
202-785-3311

AMOUNT: $250

DEADLINE(S): FEB 1

FIELD(S): HEALTH CARE ADMINISTRATION

AWARD TO RECOGNIZE OUTSTANDING PERFORMANCE IN ADMINISTRATION & LABORATORY MANAGEMENT & TO ENCOURAGE INDIVIDUALS TO DESSIMATE THEIR KNOWLEDGE TO THE PROFESSION. ANYONE IN THE PROFESSION MAY APPLY OR BE NOMINATED.

WRITE TO EXECUTIVE DIRECTOR AT ADDRESS ABOVE FOR COMPLETE INFORMATION. ENCLOSE STAMPED SELF ADDRESSED BUSINESS SIZE ENVELOPE.

950

AMERICAN SPEECH-LANGUAGE-HEARING FOUNDATION (GRADUATE STUDENT SCHOLARSHIPS)

10801 ROCKVILLE PIKE
ROCKVILLE MD 20852
301/897-5700; FAX 301/571-0457

AMOUNT: $2000 - $4000

DEADLINE(S): JUN 15

FIELD(S): COMMUNICATION DISORDERS

OPEN TO FULL TIME GRADUATE STUDENTS IN COMMUNICATION SCIENCES AND DISORDERS PROGRAMS. $2000 AWARDS GO TO FOREIGN OR MINORITY STUDENT STUDYING IN THE USA AND TO A DISABLED STUDENT PURSUING GRADUATE STUDIES IN THE FIELD.

THERE ARE UP TO FOUR $4000 GENERAL GRADUATE STUDENT SCHOLARSHIPS. WRITE FOR COMPLETE INFORMATION.

MEDICAL RELATED DISCIPLINES

951

ANIMAL HEALTH TRUST (AHT RESEARCH TRAINING SCHOLARSHIP)

HEAD OF FINANCE; PO BOX 5
NEWMARKET SUFFOLK C88 7DW ENGLAND
0638-661111

AMOUNT: UP TO 5000 POUNDS STERLING

DEADLINE(S): MAR 31

FIELD(S): VETERINARY AND ALLIED SCIENCES

SCHOLARSHIPS AWARDED TO CANDIDATES WITH AT LEAST 2ND CLASS HONORS DEGREE IN SCIENCE OR VETERINARY MEDICINE FOR TRAINING IN VETERINARY RESEARCH. FOR STUDY AT APPROVED INSTITUTIONS IN THE UNITED KINGDOM.

WRITE FOR COMPLETE INFORMATION.

952

ANIMAL HEALTH TRUST (BLOUNT MEMORIAL FUND SCHOLARSHIP)

HEAD OF FINANCE; PO BOX 5
NEWMARKET SUFFOLK C88 7DW ENGLAND
0638-661111

AMOUNT: 5000 POUNDS STERLING

DEADLINE(S): MAR 31

FIELD(S): ANIMAL HEALTH

SCHOLARSHIPS TO STUDY ALL ASPECTS OF ANIMAL HEALTH. FOR GRADUATE STUDY AT AGREED CENTERS IN THE UNITED KINGDOM.

SCHOLARSHIP RENEWABLE FOR UP TO THREE YEARS. WRITE FOR COMPLETE INFORMATION.

953

ASSOCIATION FOR WOMEN VETERINARIANS (STUDENT SCHOLARSHIP)

32205 ALLISON DRIVE
UNION CITY CA 94587
510/471-8379

AMOUNT: $1000

DEADLINE(S): FEB 10

FIELD(S): VETERINARY MEDICINE

OPEN TO SECOND OR THIRD YEAR VETERINARY MEDICINE STUDENTS IN THE USA OR CANADA WHO ARE USA OR CANADIAN CITIZENS. BOTH WOMEN AND MEN ARE ELIGIBLE. ESSAY IS REQUIRED.

WRITE FOR COMPLETE INFORMATION OR CONTACT DEAN OF VETERINARY SCHOOL.

954

AUXILIARY TO THE MICHIGAN OPTOMETRIC ASSOCIATION (SCHOLARSHIP PROGRAM)

511 ASHMUN SUITE 201
SAULT STE. MARIE MI 49783
906/635-0861

AMOUNT: $400 - $1000

DEADLINE(S): MAR 1

FIELD(S): OPTOMETRY

MICHIGAN RESIDENT & STUDENT MEMBER OF MICHIGAN OPTOMETRIC ASSN. APPLY IN 3RD YEAR OF STUDY AT A RECOGNIZED SCHOOL OF OPTOMETRY. MAINTAIN 'B' AVERAGE. US CITIZEN.

2-5 SCHOLARSHIPS PER YEAR. APPLICATIONS AVAILABLE IN NOVEMBER AT ALL OPTOMETRIC COLLEGES. WRITE FOR COMPLETE INFORMATION.

955

BRITISH DENTAL ASSOCIATION (THE DENTSPLY FUND)

64 WIMPOLE STREET
LONDON W1M 8AL ENGLAND
01-935-0875

AMOUNT: 200 - 500 POUNDS

DEADLINE(S): MAY 31

FIELD(S): DENTISTRY

LOANS & GRANTS TO PROVIDE FINANCIAL ASSISTANCE TOWARDS THE SPECIAL EDUCATION AND TRAINING FOR A CAREER IN DENTISTRY. U.K. CITIZENS MAY STUDY AT ANY ACCREDITED INSTITUTION IN ANY COUNTRY. NON-U.K. CITIZENS MUST STUDY AT A U.K. INSTITUTION.

15 AWARDS PER YEAR. AWARDS RENEWABLE. WRITE FOR COMPLETE INFORMATION.

956

CALIFORNIA PHARMACISTS ASSN EDUCATIONAL FOUNDATION TRUST FUND (PHARMACY STUDENT LOANS)

1112 'I' ST; SUITE 300
SACRAMENTO CA 95814
916/444-7811

AMOUNT: $500 - $3000

DEADLINE(S): NONE

FIELD(S): PHARMACY

OPEN TO CALIFORNIA RESIDENTS WHO HAVE COMPLETED AT LEAST 1 YEAR OF PHARMACY SCHOOL AND ARE ENROLLED IN THE SCHOOL OF PHARMACY AT THE UNIVERSITY OF CALIFORNIA; THE UNIVERSITY OF SOUTHERN CALIFORNIA OR THE UNIVERSITY OF THE PACIFIC.

USA CITIZEN. LOANS RENEWABLE. CONTACT THE FINANCIAL AID DEPT AT THE ABOVE SCHOOLS FOR COMPLETE INFORMATION.

957

COMMANDER; NAVY RECRUITING COMMAND (ARMED FORCES HEALTH PROFESSIONS SCHOLARSHIPS)

4015 WILSON BLVD.
ARLINGTON VA 22203
WRITTEN INQURIY

AMOUNT: $749 PER MONTH STIPEND + TUITION; FEES; BOOKS; LAB FEES ETC.

DEADLINE(S): NONE SPECIFIED

FIELD(S): MEDICINE; DENTISTRY; OPTOMETRY AND NURSE ANESTHESIA (MASTER'S DEGREE)

OPEN TO USA CITIZENS ENROLLED OR ACCEPTED FOR ENROLLMENT IN ANY OF THE ABOVE FIELDS AT AN ACCREDITED INSTITUTION IN THE USA OR PUERTO RICO. MUST QUALIFY FOR APPOINTMENT AS A NAVY OFFICER AND SIGN A CONTRACTUAL AGREEMENT.

WRITE FOR COMPLETE INFORMATION.

958

CONNECTICUT STATE DENTAL ASSOCIATION (DR. CHARLES A. VERNALE STUDENT LOAN AWARD)

62 RUSS STREET
HARTFORD CT 06106
203-278-5550

AMOUNT: $2000 - $2500

DEADLINE(S): JUN 30

FIELD(S): DENTISTRY

THIS LOAN IS AWARDED TO A CONNECTICUT RESIDENT ENGAGED IN THE STUDY OF DENTISTRY AT RECOGNIZED SCHOOL OF DENTISTRY WHO IS DEEMED QUALIFIED BY SCHOLASTIC ACHIEVEMENT & FINANCIAL NEED.

MUST STUDY FULL TIME. CONTACT DR. W. JOHNSTON CHAIRMAN SCHOLARSHIPS & AWARDS.

959

CUYAHOGA COUNTY MEDICAL FOUNDATION (SCHOLARSHIP GRANT PROGRAM)

11001 CEDAR AVE
CLEVELAND OH 44106
216/229-2200

AMOUNT: $500 - $1500

DEADLINE(S): JUN 1

FIELD(S): MEDICINE; DENTISTRY; PHARMACY; NURSING; OSTEOPATHY

GRANTS OPEN TO RESIDENTS OF CUYAHOGA COUNTY WHO ARE ACCEPTED TO OR ENROLLED IN AN ACCREDITED PROFESSIONAL SCHOOL IN ONE OF THE ABOVE AREAS. USA CITIZEN.

APPROX 40 AWARDS PER YEAR. WRITE FOR COMPLETE INFORMATION.

960

DELAWARE ACADEMY OF MEDICINE (STUDENT FINANCIAL AID-LOANS)

1925 LOVERING AVE
WILMINGTON DE 19806
302/656-1629

AMOUNT: $1000 - $5000

DEADLINE(S): MAY 15

FIELD(S): MEDICINE; DENTISTRY; ALLIED HEALTH FIELDS

DELAWARE RESIDENT. FOR FULL-TIME GRADUATE STUDY IN THE ABOVE AREAS AT ACCREDITED COLLEGES & UNIVERSITIES. USA CITIZEN OR LEGAL RESIDENT.

WRITE FOR COMPLETE INFORMATION.

961

DELAWARE STATE DENTAL SOCIETY (G. LAYTON GRIER SCHOLARSHIP)

1925 LOVERING AVE
WILMINGTON DE 19806
301/427-9412

AMOUNT: $1000

DEADLINE(S): FEB 1

FIELD(S): DENTISTRY

SCHOLARSHIPS OPEN TO DELAWARE RESIDENTS WHO HAVE COMPLETED AT LEAST 1 YEAR OF STUDY AT AN ACCREDITED DENTAL SCHOOL. AWARDS ARE FOR FULL-TIME STUDY. SCHOLARSHIPS ALSO AVAILABLE FOR POST-DOCTORAL TRAINING. DEMONSTRATE FINANCIAL NEED.

WRITE FOR COMPLETE INFORMATION.

962

DOG WRITERS' EDUCATIONAL TRUST (SCHOLARSHIPS)

BERTA I PICKETT; PO BOX 2220
PAYSON AZ 85547
602/474-8867

AMOUNT: $1000

DEADLINE(S): DEC 31

FIELD(S): VETERINARY MEDICINE; ANIMAL BEHAVIOR; JOURNALISM

OPEN TO APPLICANTS WHOSE PARENTS; GRANDPARENTS OR OTHER CLOSE RELATIVES (OR THE APPLICANT) ARE OR HAVE BEEN INVOLVED IN THE WORLD OF DOGS AS EXHIBITORS; BREEDERS; HANDLERS; JUDGES; CLUB OFFICERS OR OTHER ACTIVITIES.

MEDICAL RELATED DISCIPLINES

SCHOLARSHIPS SUPPORT UNDERGRADUATE OR GRADUATE STUDY. 10 AWARDS PER YEAR. SEND SELF ADDRESSED STAMPED ENVELOPE FOR COMPLETE INFORMATION AND APPLICATION.

963 ───────────────

EDWARD BANGS AND ELZA KELLEY FOUNDATION (SCHOLARSHIP PROGRAM)

243 SOUTH ST
HYANNIS MA 02601
508/775-3117

AMOUNT: UP TO $4000

DEADLINE(S): APR 30

FIELD(S): MEDICINE; NURSING; HEALTH SCIENCES; RELATED FIELDS

OPEN TO RESIDENTS OF BARNSTABLE COUNTY MASS. SCHOLARSHIPS ARE INTENDED TO BENEFIT HEALTH AND WELFARE OF BARNSTABLE COUNTY RESIDENTS. AWARDS SUPPORT STUDY AT RECOGNIZED UNDERGRADUATE; GRADUATE AND PROFESSIONAL INSTITUTIONS.

FINANCIAL NEED IS A CONSIDERATION. WRITE FOR COMPLETE INFORMATION.

964 ───────────────

FAIRFAX COUNTY MEDICAL SOCIETY FOUNDATION (SCHOLARSHIPS)

8100 OAK STREET
DUNN LORING VA 22027
703/560-4855

AMOUNT: $1500

DEADLINE(S): MAY 25

FIELD(S): MEDICAL DOCTOR; MEDICAL RELATED DISCIPLINES; MEDICAL TECHNOLGOIES; NURSING

OPEN TO UNDERGRADUATE AND GRADUATE STUDENTS WHO ARE USA CITIZENS AND ARE RESIDENTS OF FAIRFAX COUNTY; VA. FOR STUDIES RELATED TO HUMAN HEALTH. MUST DEMONSTRATE FINANCIAL NEED.

11 AWARDS PER YEAR; RENEWABLE. WRITE FOR COMPLETE INFORMATION.

965 ───────────────

FLORIDA DENTAL ASSOCIATION (STUDENT LOAN FUND)

3021 SWANN AVE
TAMPA FL 33609
813/877-7597

AMOUNT: $2000 - $4000

DEADLINE(S): MAY 31

FIELD(S): DENTISTRY

OPEN TO RESIDENTS OF FLORIDA WHO HAVE SUCCESSFULLY COMPLETED AT LEAST 1 ACADEMIC YEAR IN AN ACCREDITED DENTAL SCHOOL. ACADEMIC STANDING; FINANCIAL NEED & POTENTIAL WILL BE CONSIDERED IN GRANTING A LOAN.

WRITE FOR COMPLETE INFORMATION.

966 ───────────────

FOUNDATION FOR CHIROPRACTIC EDUCATION AND RESEARCH (FCER RESEARCH FELLOWSHIP)

1701 CLARENDON BLVD
ARLINGTON VA 22209
703/276-7445

AMOUNT: UP TO $10000 PER YEAR; $30000 OVER 5 YEARS

DEADLINE(S): MAR 1; OCT 1

FIELD(S): CHIROPRACTICS

FELLOWSHIPS ARE AWARDED PRIMARILY TO CHIROPRACTORS PURSUING RESEARCH TRAINING LEADING TO A DOCTORATE IN A BASIC SCIENCE OR NON-CLINICAL AREA.

NUMBER OF AWARDS PER YEAR VARIES. AWARDS ARE RENEWABLE. CONTACT ADDRESS ABOVE FOR COMPLETE INFORMATION.

967 ───────────────

H. FLETCHER BROWN FUND (SCHOLARSHIPS)

C/O BANK OF DELAWARE; TRUST DEPT; PO BOX 791
WILMINGTON DE 19899
302/429-2827

AMOUNT: VARIES

DEADLINE(S): APR 15

FIELD(S): MEDICINE; DENTISTRY; LAW; ENGINEERING; CHEMISTRY

OPEN TO STUDENTS BORN IN DELAWARE; GRADUATED FROM A DELAWARE HIGH SCHOOL & STILL RESIDING IN DELAWARE. FOR FOUR YEARS OF STUDY (UNDERGRAD OR GRAD) LEADING TO A DEGREE THAT ENABLES APPLICANT TO PRACTICE IN CHOSEN FIELD.

SCHOLARSHIPS ARE BASED ON NEED; SCHOLASTIC ACHIEVEMENT; GOOD MORAL CHARACTER. RENEWABLE. WRITE FOR COMPLETE INFORMATION.

968 ───────────────

HEADQUARTERS; DEPT. OF THE ARMY (ARMED FORCES HEALTH PROFESSIONS SCHOLARSHIPS)

ATTN; SGPS-PDE; 5109 LEESBURG PIKE
FALLS CHURCH VA 22041
WRITTEN INQURIY

AMOUNT: $749 PER MONTH STIPEND + TUITION; FEES; BOOKS; LAB FEES ETC.

DEADLINE(S): NONE SPECIFIED

FIELD(S): MEDICINE; DENTISTRY; OPTOMETRY AND NURSE ANESTHESIA (MASTER'S DEGREE); CLINICAL PSYCHOLOGY (PH.D)

OPEN TO USA CITIZENS ENROLLED OR ACCEPTED FOR ENROLLMENT IN ANY OF THE ABOVE FIELDS AT AN ACCREDITED INSTITUTION IN THE USA OR PUERTO RICO. MUST QUALIFY FOR APPOINTMENT AS AN ARMY OFFICER AND SIGN A CONTRACTUAL AGREEMENT.

WRITE FOR COMPLETE INFORMATION.

969

HEADQUARTERS; USAF RECRUITING SERVICE (ARMED FORCES HEALTH PROFESSIONS SCHOLARSHIPS)

MEDICAL RECRUITING DIVISION
RANDOLPH AFB TX 78150
WRITTEN INQURIY

AMOUNT: $749 PER MONTH STIPEND + TUITION; FEES; BOOKS; LAB FEES ETC.

DEADLINE(S): NONE SPECIFIED

FIELD(S): MEDICINE; DENTISTRY; OPTOMETRY AND NURSE ANESTHESIA (MASTER'S DEGREE); CLINICAL PSYCHOLOGY (PH.D)

OPEN TO USA CITIZENS ENROLLED OR ACCEPTED FOR ENROLLMENT IN ANY OF THE ABOVE FIELDS AT AN ACCREDITED INSTITUTION IN THE USA OR PUERTO RICO. MUST QUALIFY FOR APPOINTMENT AS AN AIR FORCE OFFICER AND SIGN A CONTRACTUAL AGREEMENT.

WRITE FOR COMPLETE INFORMATION.

970

INDIANA DENTAL ASSOCIATION (LOAN PROGRAM)

INB NATIONAL BANK -
ONE VIRGINIA AVE.
INDIANAPOLIS IN 46204
317/266-5263

AMOUNT: UP TO $3000

DEADLINE(S): NONE SPECIFIED

FIELD(S): DENTISTRY

LOANS ARE MADE TO DENTAL STUDENTS (UNDERGRADUATE AND GRADUATE) WHO ARE RESIDENTS OF INDIANA ARE ENROLLED IN THE INDIANA UNIVERSITY SCHOOL OF DENTISTRY AND HAVE DEMONSTRATED A NEED FOR FINANCIAL ASSISTANCE.

CONTACT ROBERT D. GODFREY - BRANCH OFFICER - AT ADDRESS ABOVE FOR COMPLETE INFORMATION.

971

INTERNATIONAL CHIROPRACTORS ASSOCIATION (KING KOIL SPINAL GUARD/ STUDENT (SICA); AUXILIARY (AICA) SCHOLARSHIPS)

1110 N. GLEBE RD. STE 1000
ARLINGTON VA 22201
703/528-5000

AMOUNT: $100 - $1000

DEADLINE(S): SPRING

FIELD(S): CHIROPRACTIC

OPEN TO STUDENT MEMBERS OF ICA BASED ON ACADEMIC ACHIEVEMENT & SERVICE. AWARDS ARE TENABLE AT SCHOOLS WITH ICA CHAPTERS. AWARDS ARE NOT AVAILABLE FOR FRESHMAN YEAR OF STUDY.

CONTACT YOUR ICA CHAPTER OR ADDRESS ABOVE FOR COMPLETE INFORMATION.

972

INTERNATIONAL ORDER OF THE KING'S DAUGHTERS AND SONS (HEALTH CAREERS SCHOLARSHIPS)

PO BOX 1017
CHAUTAUQUA NY 14722
716/357-4951

AMOUNT: UP TO $1000

DEADLINE(S): APR 1

FIELD(S): MEDICINE; DENTISTRY; NURSING; PHYSICAL THERAPY; OCCUPATIONAL THERAPY; MEDICAL TECHNOLOGIES; PHARMACY

OPEN TO STUDENTS ACCEPTED TO/ENROLLED IN AN ACCREDITED USA OR CANADIAN 4-YR OR GRADUATE SCHOOL. RN CANDIDATES MUST HAVE COMPLETED 1ST YEAR; BA CANDIDATES IN AT LEAST 3RD YEAR. PRE MED STUDENTS -NOT- ELIGIBLE.

USA OR CANADIAN CITIZEN. THOSE SEEKING MD OR DDS DEGREES MUST BE IN 2ND YR OF MED OR DENTAL SCHOOL. FOR APPLICATION SEND SASE TO MRS. MERLE RABER; 6024 E. CHICAGO RD; JONESVILLE MI 49250.

973

JEWISH VOCATIONAL SERVICE (MARCUS & THERESA LEVIE EDUCATIONAL FUND SCHOLARSHIPS)

1 SOUTH FRANKLIN STREET
CHICAGO IL 60606
312/346-6700 EXT 2214

AMOUNT: $5000

DEADLINE(S): MAR 1

FIELD(S): SOCIAL WORK; MEDICINE; DENTISTRY; NURSING & OTHER RELATED PROFESSIONS & VOCATIONS

MEDICAL RELATED DISCIPLINES

OPEN TO COOK COUNTY RESIDENTS OF THE JEWISH FAITH WHO PLAN CAREERS IN THE HELPING PROFESSIONS. MUST SHOW FINANCIAL NEED. FOR UNDERGRADUATE; GRADUATE OR VOCATIONAL STUDY. APPLICATIONS AVAILABLE BEGINNING DEC 1 FROM SCHOLARSHIP SECRETARY.

85-100 AWARDS PER YEAR. RENEWAL POSSIBLE WITH REAPPLICATION. WRITE FOR COMPLETE INFORMATION.

974
LABAN/BARTENIEFF INSTITUTE OF MOVEMENT STUDIES (WORKSTUDY PROGRAMS)

11 E. 4TH ST.; 3RD FLOOR
NEW YORK NY 10003
212/477-4299

AMOUNT: $500 - $2500

DEADLINE(S): MAY 1

FIELD(S): HUMAN MOVEMENT STUDIES

OPEN TO GRADUATE STUDENTS & PROFESSIONALS IN DANCE; EDUCATION; HEALTH FIELDS; BEHAVIORAL SCIENCES; FITNESS; ATHLETIC TRAINING; ETC. FOR WORK STUDY -ONLY- AT THE LABAN/ BARTENIEFF INSTITUTE IN THE LABAN MOVEMENT STUDIES CERTIFICATE PROGRAM.

WRITE FOR COMPLETE INFORMATION.

975
MAINE DENTAL ASSOCIATION (LOAN PROGRAM)

PO BOX 215
MANCHESTER ME 04351
207/622-7900

AMOUNT: UP $1500 PER SEMESTER

DEADLINE(S): NONE

FIELD(S): DENTISTRY

MAINE RESIDENT. STUDENT BECOMES ELIGIBLE TO RECEIVE 1ST $1000 LOAN FOLLOWING COMPLETION OF THE 1ST YEAR OF DENTAL SCHOOL. $3000 WILL BE AVAILABLE DURING EACH OF THE FOLLOWING 2 YEARS. STUDENT MAY ATTEND ANY ACCREDITED DENTAL SCHOOL.

WRITE FOR COMPLETE INFORMATION.

976
MARYLAND HIGHER EDUCATION COMMISSION (PROFESSIONAL SCHOOL SCHOLARSHIPS)

STATE SCHOLARSHIP ADMINISTRATION; 16 FRANCIS ST
ANNAPOLIS MD 21401
410/974-5370

AMOUNT: $200 - $1000

DEADLINE(S): MAR 1

FIELD(S): DENTISTRY; PHARMACY; MEDICINE; LAW; NURSING

OPEN TO MARYLAND RESIDENTS WHO HAVE BEEN ADMITTED AS FULL-TIME STUDENTS AT A PARTICIPATING GRADUATE INSTITUTION OF HIGHER LEARNING IN MARYLAND OR AN UNDERGRADUATE NURSING PROGRAM.

RENEWABLE UP TO 4 YEARS. WRITE FOR COMPLETE INFORMATION AND A LIST OF PARTICIPATING MARYLAND INSTITUTIONS.

977
MISSISSIPPI BOARD OF TRUSTEES OF STATE INSTITUTIONS OF HIGHER LEARNING (GRADUATE AND PROFESSIONAL SCHOLARSHIP PROGRAM)

3825 RIDGEWOOD ROAD
JACKSON MS 39211
601/982-6570

AMOUNT: VARIES

DEADLINE(S): JUN 30

FIELD(S): CHIROPRACTIC MEDICINE; PODIATRIC MEDICINE; ORTHOTICS/PROSTHETICS

OPEN TO GRADUATE STUDENTS WHO HAVE BEEN LEGAL RESIDENTS OF MISSISSIPPI PRIOR TO DATE OF APPLICATION. MUST BE ATTENDING AN OUT-OF-STATE INSTITUTION AND BE STUDYING FOR A DEGREE IN A FIELD NOT OFFERED IN MISSISSIPPI.

LOANS ARE RENEWABLE EACH YEAR. RECIPIENTS MUST AGREE TO PRACTICE IN MISSISSIPPI UPON COMPLETION OF TRAINING. WRITE FOR COMPLETE INFORMATION.

978
MUTUAL ASSOCIATION FOR PROFESSIONAL SERVICES (MAPS SCHOLARSHIP FUND)

11828 RANCHO BERNARDO RD #209
SAN DIEGO CA 92128
619/451-7618

AMOUNT: VARIABLE

DEADLINE(S): MAR 31

FIELD(S): LAW; MEDICINE; DENTISTRY; PODIATRY; VETERINARY MEDICINE; OPTOMETRY

PROGRAM IS FOR GRADUATE STUDENTS IN THE ABOVE AREAS. NOMINATION BY A MEMBER OF MAPS HELPFUL BUT NOT REQUIRED. CONSIDERATIONS ARE FINANCIAL NEED; CHARACTER AND ACHIEVEMENT. APPLICATIONS ARE ACCEPTED BEGINNING JAN 1.

ONLY THE FIRST 50 APPLICATIONS RECEIVED WILL BE CONSIDERED. IF FEWER THAN 50 APPLICATIONS ARE RECEIVED MAR 31 DEADLINE APPLIES. WRITE FOR COMPLETE INFORMATION.

979

NATIONAL INSTITUTE OF DENTAL RESEARCH (INDIVIDUAL FELLOWS)

EXTRAMURAL PROGRAM WESTWOOD BLDG. ROOM 510
BETHESDA MD 20892
301/496-6324

AMOUNT: $18600 - $32300

DEADLINE(S): JAN 10; MAY 10; SEP 10

FIELD(S): DENTAL RESEARCH

POST-DOCTORAL FELLOWSHIP PROVIDES HEALTH SCIENTISTS AN OPPORTUNITY FOR FULL-TIME RESEARCH TRAINING IN AREAS THAT REFLECT THE NATIONAL NEED FOR BIOMEDICAL AND BEHAVIORAL RESEARCH. MUST HOLD A DDS; DMD OR PH.D DEGREE.

MUST ARRANGE TO WORK WITH A SPONSOR WHO IS AFFLIATED WITH AND HAS THE STAFF AND FACILITIES NEEDED FOR THE PROPOSED TRAINING. US CITIZEN OR LEGAL RESIDENT.

980

NATIONAL INSTITUTE OF DENTAL RESEARCH (SHORT-TERM TRAINING FOR DENTAL RESEARCH)

WESTWOOD BLDG. ROOM 510
BETHESDA MD 20205
301-496-6324

AMOUNT: $733 PER MONTH

DEADLINE(S): NONE SPECIFIED

FIELD(S): DENTAL RESEARCH

OPEN TO STUDENTS ENROLLED IN A USA DENTAL SCHOOL. AWARD IS DESIGNED TO INTEREST DENTAL STUDENTS IN PURSUING A CAREER IN BIOMEDICAL/DENTAL RESEARCH. APPLY THROUGH INSTITUTION. USA CITIZENSHIP REQUIRED.

INSTITUTIONS AND INDIVIDUALS SEEKING ADDITIONAL INFORMATION ON SHORT TERM TRAINING PROGRAMS AND A LIST OF PARTICIPATING DENTAL SCHOOLS SHOULD CONTACT ADDRESS ABOVE.

981

NATIONAL RIFLE ASSOC (NRA-GRANTS IN AID PROGRAM)

HUNTER SERVICES DIV;
1600 RHODE ISLAND AVE NW
WASHINGTON DC 20036
202/828-6241

AMOUNT: $5000

DEADLINE(S): JUN 1

FIELD(S): SPORTS MEDICINE; GAME MANAGEMENT; CONSERVATION

GRADUATE RESEARCH GRANTS-IN-AID OPEN TO NRA MEMBERS DOING RESEARCH IN THE ABOVE FIELDS. MOST GRANTS GO TO GRADUATE LEVEL STUDENTS AT ACCREDITED COLLEGES OR UNIVERSITIES IN THE USA.

QUALITY OF PROJECT; ABILITY OF APPLICANT AND INTEREST TO SPONSORING ORGANIZATION ARE THE MAIN CRITERIA FOR SELECTION BY NRA GRANTS-IN-AID COMMITTEE. WRITE FOR COMPLETE INFORMATION.

982

NATIONAL STRENGTH & CONDITIONING ASSN (CHALLENGE SCHOLARSHIPS)

PO BOX 81410
LINCOLN NE 68501
402/472-3000

AMOUNT: $1000

DEADLINE(S): APR 17

FIELD(S): FIELDS RELATED TO STRENGTH & CONDITIONING

OPEN TO NATIONAL STRENGTH & CONDITIONING ASSN MEMBERS. AWARDS ARE FOR UNDERGRADUATE OR GRADUATE STUDY.

WRITE FOR COMPLETE INFORMATION.

983

NEVADA DENTAL ASSOCIATION (STUDENT LOAN FUND)

6889 W. CHARLESTON BLVD; SUITE B
LAS VEGAS NV 89117
702/255-4211

AMOUNT: $1000

DEADLINE(S): NONE

FIELD(S): DENTISTRY

LOANS AVAILABLE TO NEVADA RESIDENTS WHO HAVE MATRICULATED IN AN ACCREDITED DENTAL SCHOOL OR COLLEGE. MUST BE STUDYING FULL TIME.

NUMBER OF LOANS PER YEAR VARIES. WRITE FOR COMPLETE INFORMATION.

984

ORGANIZATION OF AMERICAN STATES DEPT OF FELLOWSHIPS & TRAINING (OAS PRA-FELLOWSHIPS)

TRAINEE SELECTION DIVISION
WASHINGTON DC 20006
202/789-3902

AMOUNT: TUITION + FEES; TRAVEL EXP & STIPEND

DEADLINE(S): APR 30; AUG 31

FIELD(S): ALL FIELDS EXCEPT MEDICINE & FOREIGN LANGUAGES

GRADUATE FELLOWSHIPS FOR USA CITIZENS OR PERMANENT RESIDENTS TO STUDY IN AN OAS MEMBER COUNTRY. MUST HAVE UNDERGRADUATE DEGREE AND HAVE DEMONSTRATED ABILITY TO PURSUE ADVANCED STUDIES IN CHOSEN FIELD.

APPLICANTS SHOULD BE FLUENT IN LANGUAGE OF COUNTRY OF INTENDED STUDY. PRIORITY IS GIVEN TO RESEARCH PROJECTS. WRITE FOR COMPLETE INFORMATION.

985

PHARMACEUTICAL MANUFACTURERS ASSOCIATION FOUNDATION (FELLOWSHIPS FOR ADVANCED PRE-DOCTORAL TRAINING IN PHARMACOLOGY OR TOXICOLOGY)

1100 15TH STREET NW
WASHINGTON DC 20005
202/835-3400

AMOUNT: $6552 STIPEND + TUITION

DEADLINE(S): SEP 15

FIELD(S): PHARMACOLOGY/TOXICOLOGY

OPEN TO FULL-TIME IN-RESIDENCE PH.D CANDIDATES IN FIELDS OF PHARMACOLOGY OR TOXICOLOGY WHO HAVE COMPLETED AT LEAST 2 YEARS OF MEDICAL; PHARMACY; DENTAL OR VETERINARY SCHOOL IN USA.

APPROX 14 AWARDS PER YEAR. RENEWABLE. WRITE FOR COMPLETE INFORMATION.

986

PHARMACEUTICAL MANUFACTURERS ASSOCIATION FOUNDATION (FELLOWSHIP AWARDS IN PHARMACOLOGY-MORPHOLOGY)

1100 15TH STREET NW
WASHINGTON DC 20005
202/835-3400

AMOUNT: VARIES

DEADLINE(S): JAN 15

FIELD(S): PHARMACOLOGY-MORPHOLOGY

POST-DOCTORAL FELLOWSHIPS DESIGNED FOR STUDENTS WHO ARE TRAINED IN ONE OF THE ABOVE FIELDS & SEEK TRAINING IN THE OTHER.

THE AWARDS COVER STIPENDS FOR 2 YEARS AT USA INSTITUTION WITH APPROPRIATE TRAINING FACILITIES. WRITE FOR COMPLETE INFORMATION.

987

PHARMACEUTICAL MANUFACTURERS ASSOCIATION FOUNDATION (FELLOWSHIPS FOR ADVANCED PRE-DOCTORAL TRAINING IN PHARMACEUTICS)

1100 15TH STREET NW
WASHINGTON DC 20005
202/835-3400

AMOUNT: $6552 STIPEND + TUITION

DEADLINE(S): FEB 1

FIELD(S): PHARMACY

OPEN TO FULL-TIME IN-RESIDENCE PH.D CANDIDATES WHO HAVE COMPLETED AT LEAST 2 YEARS OF STUDY AT USA SCHOOL OF PHARMACY & ARE ABOUT TO BEGIN THESIS RESEARCH.

RENEWABLE. WRITE FOR COMPLETE INFORMATION.

988

PHARMACEUTICAL MANUFACTURERS ASSOCIATION FOUNDATION (FACULTY DEVELOPMENT AWARDS)

1100 15TH STREET NW
WASHINGTON DC 20005
201/835-3400

AMOUNT: UP TO $30000 PER YEAR

DEADLINE(S): OCT 1

FIELD(S): CLINICAL PHARMACOLOGY

OPEN TO CANDIDATES WITH DOCTORAL DEGREE WHO HAVE BEEN APPOINTED OR ARE UNDER CONSIDERATION FOR FULL-TIME APPOINTMENTS AS INSTRUCTORS OR ASST. PROFESSORS IN PHARMACOLOGY. MUST DESIRE FULL-TIME CAREER IN HUMAN CLINICAL PHARMACOLOGY.

AWARDS ARE FOR 2 YEARS. WRITE FOR COMPLETE INFORMATION.

989

PHARMACEUTICAL MANUFACTURERS ASSOCIATION FOUNDATION (FELLOWSHIPS FOR CAREERS IN CLINICAL PHARMACOLOGY)

1100 15TH STREET NW
WASHINGTON DC 20005
202/835-3400

AMOUNT: VARIES

DEADLINE(S): OCT 1

FIELD(S): CLINICAL PHARMACOLOGY

CLINICAL TRAINING FELLOWSHIPS OPEN TO PHYSICIANS; DENTISTS & VETERINARIANS CURRENTLY ENGAGED IN CLINICAL TRAINING OR WHO HAVE RECENTLY COMPLETED SUCH TRAINING. MUST HAVE COMPLETED 2 YRS OF CLINICAL TRAINING BEYOND THE DOCTORAL DEGREE.

FELLOWSHIPS FOR ONE OR TWO YEARS. RENEWABLE. FOR STUDY AT USA INSTITUTION. WRITE FOR COMPLETE INFORMATION.

990 ─────────────────────────

PHARMACEUTICAL MANUFACTURERS ASSOCIATION FOUNDATION (MEDICAL/DENTAL STUDENT RESEARCH FELLOWSHIPS)

1100 15TH STREET NW
WASHINGTON DC 20005
202/835-3400

AMOUNT: $500 PER MONTH

DEADLINE(S): JAN 15

FIELD(S): PHARMACOLOGY; CLINICAL PHARMACOLOGY

OPEN TO MEDICAL OR DENTAL STUDENTS WHO HAVE COMPLETED AT LEAST ONE YEAR AT A USA SCHOOL & ARE INTERESTED IN COMPLETING THEIR MEDICAL/DENTAL TRAINING & SUBSEQUENT CLINICAL TRAINING FOLLOWING THE FELLOWSHIP.

AWARDS ARE FOR 3-12 MONTHS OF FULL-TIME CLINICAL RESEARCH TRAINING. WRITE FOR COMPLETE INFORMATION.

991 ─────────────────────────

PHARMACEUTICAL MANUFACTURERS ASSOCIATION FOUNDATION (RESEARCH STARTER GRANTS)

1100 15TH STREET NW
WASHINGTON DC 20005
202/835-3400

AMOUNT: $10000 PER YEAR FOR 2 YEARS

DEADLINE(S): SEP 1

FIELD(S): PHARMACOLOGY; TOXICOLOGY; MORPHOLOGY; PHARMACEUTICS

RESEARCH STARTER GRANTS OPEN TO POST-DOCTORAL INSTRUCTORS; ASSISTANT PROFESSORS & INVESTIGATORS. PROGRAM INTENDED TO ASSIST THEM IN ESTABLISHING CAREERS AS INDEPENDENT INVESTIGATORS IN THE FIELDS ABOVE.

20 GRANTS PER YEAR. TENABLE AT USA INSTITUTIONS. WRITE FOR COMPLETE INFORMATION.

992 ─────────────────────────

ROBERT SCHRECK MEMORIAL FUND (GRANTS)

C/O TEXAS COMMERCE BANK-TRUST DEPT; PO DRAWER 140
EL PASO TX 79980
915/546-6515

AMOUNT: $500 - $1500

DEADLINE(S): JUL 15; NOV 15

FIELD(S): MEDICINE; VETERINARY MEDICINE; PHYSICS; CHEMISTRY; ARCHITECTURE; ENGINEERING; EPISCOPAL CLERGY

GRANTS TO UNDERGRADUATE JUNIORS OR SENIORS OR GRADUATE STUDENTS WHO HAVE BEEN RESIDENTS OF EL PASO COUNTY FOR AT LEAST TWO YEARS. MUST BE USA CITIZEN OR LEGAL RESIDENT AND HAVE A HIGH GRADE POINT AVERAGE. FINANCIAL NEED IS A CONSIDERATION.

WRITE FOR COMPLETE INFORMATION.

993 ─────────────────────────

SANDEE THOMPSON MEMORIAL SCHOLARSHIP FOUNDATION (SCHOLARSHIPS)

1211 NAPOLEON MANOR NE
LAWRENCEVILLE GA 30243
WRITTEN INQUIRY ONLY

AMOUNT: $500

DEADLINE(S): MAR 15

FIELD(S): MEDICINE; NURSING; PHYSICAL THERAPY; RELIGION

OPEN TO UNDERGRADUATE AND GRADUATE STUDENTS HAVING AN INTEREST IN SERVING HUMANINTY AND RELIEVING HUMAN SUFFERING. MUST HAVE MEDICAL OR RELIGIOUS ORIENTED CAREER GOAL WITH PHYSICAL THERAPY A HIGH PREFERENCE.

STUDENTS SHOULD BE ENTERING AT LEAST JUNIOR YEAR AT AN ACCREDITED COLEGE OR UNIVERSITY. FINANCIAL INFORMATION REQUIRED. SEND STAMPED; SELF ADDRESSED ENVELOPE FOR COMPLETE INFORMATION.

994 ─────────────────────────

TY COBB EDUCATIONAL FOUNDATION (GRADUATE SCHOLARSHIP PROGRAM)

P.O. BOX 725
FOREST PARK GA 30051
WRITTEN INQUIRY

AMOUNT: $3000

DEADLINE(S): JUN 15

FIELD(S): MEDICINE; DENTISTRY; VETERINARY MEDICINE; LAW

MEDICAL RESEARCH

OPEN TO GRADUATE STUDENTS IN THE ABOVE FIELDS WHO ARE RESIDENTS OF GEORGIA; HAVE SATISFACTORY GRADES AND ARE ABLE TO DEMONSTRATE FINANCIAL NEED.

WRITE FOR COMPLETE INFORMATION.

995

U.S. DEPT. OF EDUCATION (INDIAN GRADUATE PROFESSIONAL FELLOWSHIPS)

400 MARYLAND AVENUE SW; RM 2177; MAIL STOP 6335
WASHINGTON DC 20202
202/401-1902

AMOUNT: $1000 - $34000 (AVERAGE $13000)

DEADLINE(S): FEB 7

FIELD(S): MEDICINE; PSYCHOLOGY; LAW; EDUCATION; RELATED FIELDS

FELLOWSHIPS FOR AMERICAN INDIANS OR ALASKAN NATIVES WHO ARE US CITIZENS AND SEEKING GRADUATE DEREEES IN THE ABOVE FIELDS AT ACCREDITED INSTITUTIONS IN USA.

APPROXIMATELY 90 CONTINUATION AND 35 NEW AWARDS. WRITE FOR COMPLETE INFORMATION.

996

U.S. DEPT. OF HEALTH AND HUMAN SERVICES (NATIONAL HEALTH SERVICE CORPS SCHOLARSHIP PROGRAM)

1201 GREENSBORO DR.; SUITE 600
MCLEAN VA 22102
703/734-6855; 800/221-9393

AMOUNT: TUITION; FEES; EDUCATIONAL EXPENSES; MONTHLY STIPEND

DEADLINE(S): VARIES ANNUALLY

FIELD(S): MEDICINE (MD OR DO); DENTISTRY

OPEN TO USA CITIZENS ACCEPTED OR ENROLLED IN USA SCHOOLS OF ALLOPATHIC (MD) OR OSTEOPATHIC (DO) MEDICINE OR DENTISTRY. RECIPIENTS AGREE TO WORK 1 YEAR IN DESIGNATED HEALTH PROFESSIONS SHORTAGE AREAS FOR EACH YEAR OF AWARD.

THE MINIMUM SERVICE OBLIGATION IS TWO YEARS. WRITE OR CALL FOR INFORMATION ONE YEAR PRIOR TO APPLYING.

997

U.S. DEPT. OF HEALTH AND HUMAN SERVICES-AHCPR (DOCTORAL DISSERTATION RESEARCH GRANTS)

2101 E. JEFFERSON ST. SUITE 602
ROCKVILLE MD 20852
301/227-8449

AMOUNT: UP TO $20000

DEADLINE(S): JAN 24 (VARIES EACH YEAR)

FIELD(S): HEALTH SERVICES RESEARCH

DOCTORAL DISSERTATION GRANTS FOR RESEARCH ON ANY ASPECT OF HEALTH CARE SERVICES (ORGANIZATION; DELIVERY; FINANCING; QUALITY; ETC). OPEN TO SOCIAL; MANAGEMENT; MEDICAL OR HEALTH SCIENCES DOCTORAL CANDIDATES.

AWARDS ARE MADE ON A COMPETITIVE BASIS. WRITE FOR COMPLETE INFORMATION.

MEDICAL RESEARCH

998

ALCOHOLIC BEVERAGE MEDICAL RESEARCH FOUNDATION (GRANTS FOR ALCOHOL RESEARCH)

2013 E. MONUMENT ST.
BALTIMORE MD 21205
410/327-0361

AMOUNT: UP TO $40000 PER YEAR

DEADLINE(S): FEB 1 AND SEP 15

FIELD(S): BIOMEDICAL AND PSYCHOSOCIAL RESEARCH ON ALCOHOL EFFECTS

OPEN TO THE STAFF OR FACULTY OF PUBLIC OR PRIVATE NON PROFIT ORGANIZATIONS IN THE USA AND CANADA FOR RESEARCH INTO THE BIOMEDICAL AND PSYCHOSOCIAL EFFECTS OF ALCOHOLIC BEVERAGES.

APPROXIMATELY 35 AWARDS PER YEAR. WRITE FOR COMPLETE INFORMATION.

999

AMERICAN ACADEMY OF ALLERGY AND IMMUNOLOGY (SUMMER FELLOWSHIPS)

611 EAST WELLS ST
MILWAUKEE WI 53202
414/272-6071

AMOUNT: $1500

DEADLINE(S): APR 1

FIELD(S): ALLERGY; IMMUNOLOGY

FELLOWSHIP PROGRAM OPEN TO MEDICAL STUDENTS INTERESTED IN PURSUING RESEARCH IN ALLERGY & IMMUNOLOGY DURING THEIR SUMMER RECESS. WORK IN BASIC OR CLINICAL RESEARCH WILL BE SUPPORTED. USA OR CANADIAN CITIZEN.

10-15 FELLOWSHIPS PER YEAR. WRITE FOR COMPLETE INFORMATION.

1000

AMERICAN ACADEMY OF IMPLANT DENTISTRY (RESEARCH GRANTS)

211 E. CHICAGO AVE
CHICAGO IL 60611
312/335-1550

AMOUNT: $10000 MAXIMUM

DEADLINE(S): OCT 31

FIELD(S): DENTAL RESEARCH

POST-DOCTORAL GRANTS OPEN TO APPLICANTS WITH DDS DEGREE. AWARDS SUPPORT WORTHY DENTAL RESEARCH PROJECTS.

WRITE FOR COMPLETE INFORMATION.

1001 —————————————————————

AMERICAN ACADEMY OF PERIODONTOLOGY (BALINT ORBAN PRIZE)

737 N MICHIGAN AVE - SUITE 800
CHICAGO IL 60611
312-787-5518

AMOUNT: $500

DEADLINE(S): MAR 15

FIELD(S): DENTAL RESEARCH

OPEN TO APPLICANTS ENROLLED IN GRADUATE OR POST-GRADUATE TRAINING IN PERIODONTOLOGY. AWARD IS FOR THE BEST RESEARCH PAPER ON PERIODONTOLOGY.

THE ACADEMY ALSO AWARDS A GOLD MEDAL & CASH PAYMENT OF $1000 TO PEOPLE WHO HAVE MADE OUTSTANDING CONTRIBUTIONS TO UNDERSTANDING & TREATMENT OF PERIODONTAL DISEASE. WRITE FOR COMPLETE INFORMATION.

1002 —————————————————————

AMERICAN ASSOCIATION FOR DENTAL RESEARCH (STUDENT RESEARCH FELLOWSHIPS)

1111 14TH STREET NW #1000
WASHINGTON DC 20005
202/898-1050

AMOUNT: $1600 STIPEND + $300 FOR EXPENSES

DEADLINE(S): JAN 6

FIELD(S): DENTAL RESEARCH

OPEN TO DENTAL STUDENTS AT ACCREDITED DENTAL SCHOOLS IN THE USA WHO ARE SPONSORED BY A FACULTY MEMBER AT THEIR SCHOOL. SHOULD NOT BE DUE TO RECEIVE THEIR DEGREE IN THE YEAR OF THE AWARD. USA LEGAL RESIDENT.

APPLICANTS MUST HAVE AN ADVANCED DEGREE IN A BASIC SCIENCE SUBJECT. UP TO 30 AWARDS PER YEAR. WRITE FOR COMPLETE INFORMATION.

1003 —————————————————————

AMERICAN CANCER SOCIETY (RESEARCH GRANTS)

1599 CLIFTON RD NE
ATLANTA GA 30329
404/329-7558

AMOUNT: $22000 - $26000

DEADLINE(S): OCT 1; MAR 1

FIELD(S): CANCER RESEARCH

POST-DOCTORAL GRANTS & FELLOWSHIPS. ALL APPLICATIONS MUST ORIGINATE FROM & BE RECOMMENDED BY APPLICANT'S PARENT INSTITUTION. AWARDS ARE TO SUPPORT RESEARCH/CLINICAL INVESTIGATIONS & PERSONNEL.

USA CITIZEN OR PERMANENT RESIDENT. WRITE FOR COMPLETE INFORMATION.

1004 —————————————————————

AMERICAN COLLEGE OF CHEST PHYSICIANS (LILLY PULMONARY RESEARCH FELLOWSHIP)

3300 DUNDEE ROAD
NORTHBROOK IL 60062
708/498-1400

AMOUNT: $35000

DEADLINE(S): JAN 4

FIELD(S): PULMONARY MEDICINE

OPEN TO THOSE ENTERING THE SIXTH OR LATER YEAR OF FULL TIME POSTGRADUATE MEDICAL TRAINING IN PULMONARY MEDICINE. LIMITED TO PHYSICIANS WHO ARE USA OR CANADA CITIZENS OR HOLD VALID PERMANENT US VISAS AND PLAN CAREERS IN ACADEMIC MEDICINE.

WRITE FOR COMPLETE INFORMATION.

1005 —————————————————————

AMERICAN FOUNDATION FOR AGING RESEARCH (SCHOLARSHIP PROGRAM)

C/O NC STATE UNIV; BIOCHEM DEPT; BOX 7622
RALEIGH NC 27695
919/515-5679

AMOUNT: $500 - $1000

DEADLINE(S): NONE

FIELD(S): GERONTOLOGY; AGING; CANCER

SCHOLARSHIPS FOR RESEARCH ON AGE-RELATED DISEASES OR THE BIOLOGY OF AGING. OPEN TO UNDERGRADUATE & GRADUATE STUDENTS AT ACCREDITED INSTITUTIONS IN THE USA. USA CITIZEN.

6 TO 10 SCHOLARSHIPS PER YEAR. WRITE FOR COMPLETE INFORMATION.

1006 —————————————————————

AMERICAN FOUNDATION FOR UROLOGIC DISEASE (RESEARCH SCHOLAR PROGRAM)

300 W. PRATT ST.
BALTIMORE MD 21201
410/727-2908; FAX 410/625-2390

AMOUNT: $44000 PER YEAR

DEADLINE(S): NOV 1

MEDICAL RESEARCH

FIELD(S): UROLOGIC RESEARCH

OPEN TO UROLOGISTS (IN RESIDENCY OR WITHIN 5 YEARS OF POST RESIDENCY) WHO ASPIRE TO LEARN SCIENTIFIC TECHNIQUES AND CAN DEMONSTRATE RESEARCH CAPABILITIES. A TWO YEAR COMMITMENT AS A FULL TIME RESEARCHER IS REQUIRED.

CONTINUED SUPPORT IS SUBJECT TO YEARLY REVIEW. WRITE FOR COMPLETE INFORMATION.

1007

AMERICAN FOUNDATION FOR UROLOGIC DISEASE INC. (AFUD PH.D RESEARCH SCHOLARS PROGRAM)

300 W. PRATT ST.
BALTIMORE MD 21201
410/727-2908; FAX 410/625-2390

AMOUNT: $46000 PER YEAR

DEADLINE(S): NOV 1

FIELD(S): UROLOGY RESEARCH

OPEN TO POSTDOCTORAL BASIC SCIENTIST WITH A RESEARCH INTEREST IN UROLOGIC OR RELATED DYSFUNCTIONS. A COMMITMENT TO DEDICATE TWO YEARS IN THE AFUD/PH.D PROGRAM AS A FULL TIME RESEARCHER IS REQUIRED.

WRITE FOR COMPLETE INFORMATION.

1008

AMERICAN FUND FOR DENTAL HEALTH (GRANTS FOR DENTAL RESEARCH)

211 EAST CHICAGO AVE #820
CHICAGO IL 60611
312/787-6270

AMOUNT: $35000 (MAX)

DEADLINE(S): SEP 15

FIELD(S): DENTAL RESEARCH

PROPOSALS - TO INCREASE PATIENT ACCESS TO & UTILIZATION OF DENTAL CARE; TO ENHANCE QUALITY OF CARE AVAILABLE; TO ACCELERATE TRANSFER OF KNOWLEDGE FROM RESEARCH LAB TO PRACTICE OR TO ASSIST DENTAL EDUCATION QUALITY ARE PREFERRED.

PROPOSALS MUST BE SUBMITTED BY NON PROFIT TAX EXEMPT ORGANIZATIONS OR BY INDIVIDUALS EMPLOYED BY SUCH ORGANIZATIONS. WRITE FOR COMPLETE INFORMATION.

1009

AMERICAN GERIATRICS SOCIETY (HENDERSON MEMORIAL STUDENT AWARD)

770 LEXINGTON AVE #400
NEW YORK NY 10021
212/308-1414

AMOUNT: $1000

DEADLINE(S): APR 10

FIELD(S): GERONTOLOGY; AGING

OPEN TO MEDICAL STUDENTS. SPECIAL CONSIDERATION GIVEN TO STUDENTS WHO HAVE ENGAGED IN RESEARCH OR CLINICAL INVESTIGATION IN GERIATRICS OR ARE PARTICIPATING IN AN ONGOING CLINICAL PROJECT. FORMAL PAPER IS NOT REQUIRED BUT IS WELCOME.

THE AWARD INCLUDES AN HONORARIUM AND IS PRESENTED AT THE SOCIETY'S ANNUAL MEETING. THE RECIPIENT ATTENDS AS AN INVITED GUEST.

1010

AMERICAN HEART ASSOCIATION; DIVISION OF RESEARCH AWARDS (CLINICIAN-SCIENTIST AWARD)

7272 GREENVILLE AVE
DALLAS TX 75231
214/706-1453

AMOUNT: $40000 TO $44000 STIPEND

DEADLINE(S): JUN 1

FIELD(S): HEART RESEARCH

OPEN TO USA CITIZENS OR PERMANENT RESIDENTS WHO HOLD THE MD; DO OR EQUIVALENT MEDICAL DEGREE FOR RESEARCH IN THE BROAD FIELD OF CARDIOVASCULAR FUNCTION AND DISEASE AND STROKE.

CANDIDATES MUST DEMONSTRATE A STRONG COMMITMENT TO A CAREER IN INVESTIGATIVE MEDICINE BUT DO -NOT- NEED SIGNIFICANT RESEARCH EXPERIENCE. WRITE FOR COMPLETE INFORMATION.

1011

AMERICAN HEART ASSOCIATION; DIVISION OF RESEARCH AWARDS (GRANT-IN-AID)

7272 GREENVILLE AVE
DALLAS TX 75231
214/706-1453

AMOUNT: $40000 (MAXIMUM)

DEADLINE(S): JUL 1

FIELD(S): HEART RESEARCH

AWARDS ARE MADE TO SUPPORT RESEARCH ACTIVIES BROADLY RELATED TO CARDIOVASCULAR FUNCTION AND DISEASE; STROKE; OR RELATED CLINICAL; BASIC SCIENCE AND PUBLIC HEALTH PROBLEMS.

AWARDS ARE TO ENCOURAGE DEVELOPMENT OF RESEARCH PROJECTS BY -JUNIOR- INVESTIGATORS AND NEW AREAS OF RESEARCH BY -ESTABLISHED- INVESTIGATORS. WRITE FOR COMPLETE INFORMATION.

1012

AMERICAN HEART ASSOCIATION; DIVISION OF RESEARCH AWARDS (MEDICAL STUDENT RESEARCH FELLOWSHIPS)

7272 GREENVILLE AVE
DALLAS TX 75231
214/706-1453

AMOUNT: $12000 STIPEND + $1800 TO INSTITUTION

DEADLINE(S): JUN 1

FIELD(S): HEART RESEARCH

THIS IS AN INSTITUTIONAL AWARD FOR ACCREDITED MEDICAL SCHOOLS. PURPOSE IS TO ENCOURAGE MEDICAL STUDENTS TO ENGAGE IN FULL-TIME RESEARCH FOR 1 OR MORE YEARS PRIOR TO GRADUATION. LOCATION OF TRAINING IS DECIDED BY THE FACULTY COMMITTEE.

EACH MEDICAL SCHOOL CAN HOLD FROM 1 TO 6 MEDICAL STUDENT RESEARCH FELLOWSHIPS PER YEAR. -NOT- A SCHOLARSHIP FOR MEDICAL SCHOOL ACADEMIC CREDIT. CONTACT YOUR MEDICAL SCHOOL OR WRITE TO ADDRESS ABOVE FOR COMPLETE INFORMATION.

1013

AMERICAN LIVER FOUNDATION (POST-DOCTORAL RESEARCH FELLOW PROGRAM)

1425 POMPTON AVE
CEDAR GROVE NJ 07009
201/256-2550

AMOUNT: $7500

DEADLINE(S): DEC 15

FIELD(S): LIVER RESEARCH

RESEARCH TRAINING FELLOWSHIPS OPEN TO RECENT MD'S; PH.D'S & MD/PH.D'S. PURPOSE IS TO ENCOURAGE DEVELOPMENT OF INDIVIDUALS WITH RESEARCH POTENTIAL WHO REQUIRE ADDITIONAL RESEARCH TRAINING & EXPERIENCE.

AWARDS TENABLE AT ELIGIBLE INSTITUTIONS IN USA OR ITS POSSESSIONS. WRITE FOR COMPLETE INFORMATION.

1014

AMERICAN LIVER FOUNDATION (STUDENT RESEARCH FELLOWSHIPS)

1425 POMPTON AVE
CEDAR GROVE NJ 07009
201/256-2550

AMOUNT: $2500 STIPEND

DEADLINE(S): DEC 15

FIELD(S): MEDICAL RESEARCH

FELLOWSHIPS OPEN TO MEDICAL STUDENTS; VETERINARY STUDENTS & PH.D CANDIDATES. PURPOSE IS TO ENCOURAGE THEM TO GAIN EXPOSURE IN THE RESEARCH LABORATORY & POSSIBLY CONSIDER LIVER RESEARCH AS A CAREER OPTION.

DURATION IS 3 MONTHS. WRITE FOR COMPLETE INFORMATION.

1015

AMERICAN LUNG ASSOCIATION (CAREER INVESTIGATOR AWARD)

MEDICAL AFFAIRS DIVISION;
1740 BROADWAY
NEW YORK NY 10019
212-315-8700

AMOUNT: $35000

DEADLINE(S): OCT 1

FIELD(S): LUNG DISEASE

OPEN TO MD'S AND DO'S OR THOSE WITH A DOCTORAL DEGREE IN A DISCIPLINE RELEVANT TO LUNG DISEASE. FOR FULL TIME RESEARCH BY ESTABLISHED INVESTIGATORS WHO HAVE A SUBSTANTIAL RESEARCH RECORD. USA OR CANADIAN CITIZENS OR PERMANENT RESIDENTS.

AWARDS ARE FOR FIVE YEARS SUBJECT TO ANNUAL REVIEWS. WRITE FOR COMPLETE INFORMATION.

1016

AMERICAN LUNG ASSOCIATION (DALSEMER RESEARCH SCHOLAR AWARD)

MEDICAL AFFAIRS DIVISION;
1740 BROADWAY
NEW YORK NY 10019
212-315-8700

AMOUNT: $30000

DEADLINE(S): OCT 1

FIELD(S): INTERSTITIAL LUNG DISEASE

OPEN TO PHYSICIANS WHO HAVE COMPLETED GRADUATE TRAINING IN INTERSTITIAL LUNG DISEASE AND ARE BEGINNING A FACULTY TRACK IN A SCHOOL OF MEDICINE. LIMITED TO USA CITIZENS OR PERMANENT RESIDENTS.

WRITE FOR COMPLETE INFORMATION.

1017

AMERICAN LUNG ASSOCIATION (NURSING RESEARCH TRAINING AWARD)

MEDICAL AFFAIRS DIVISION;
1740 BROADWAY
NEW YORK NY 10019
212-315-8700

AMOUNT: $11000 PER YEAR

DEADLINE(S): OCT 1

FIELD(S): RESPIRATORY OR LUNG DISEASE RESEARCH

OPEN TO PROFESSIONAL NURSES HOLDING MASTER'S DEGREES WHO ARE MATRICULATED IN FULL-TIME DOCTORAL PROGRAMS WITH A FOCUS RELEVANT TO LUNG DISEASE. PRIORITY TO THOSE WHO WILL PURSUE AN ACADEMIC CAREER.

USA OR CANADIAN CITIZEN OR PERMANENT USA RESIDENT TRAINING IN A USA INSTITUTION. AWARDS ARE FOR TWO YEARS. WRITE FOR COMPLETE INFORMATION.

1018

AMERICAN LUNG ASSOCIATION (RESEARCH GRANTS)

MEDICAL AFFAIRS DIVISION;
1740 BROADWAY
NEW YORK NY 10019
212-315-8700

AMOUNT: UP TO $25000 PER YEAR

DEADLINE(S): NOV 1

FIELD(S): LUNG DISEASE

OPEN TO NEW INVESTIGATORS WHO ARE WORKING IN AREAS RELEVANT TO THE CONQUEST OF LUNG DISEASE & THE PROMOTION OF LUNG HEALTH. MUST HOLD DOCTORAL DEGREE; FACULTY POSITION AND HAVE COMPLETED 2 YEARS OF RESEARCH TRAINING AT TIME OF APPLICATION.

USA OR CANADIAN CITIZEN OR PERMANENT RESIDENT TRAINING IN A USA INSTITUTION. WRITE FOR COMPLETE INFORMATION.

1019

AMERICAN LUNG ASSOCIATION (RESEARCH TRAINING FELLOWSHIPS)

MEDICAL AFFAIRS DIVISION;
1740 BROADWAY
NEW YORK NY 10019
212/315-8700

AMOUNT: $19000 FIRST YEAR; $20000 SECOND YEAR

DEADLINE(S): OCT 1

FIELD(S): LUNG DISEASE

OPEN TO USA CITIZENS OR PERMANENT RESIDENTS WHO HOLD M.D.; D.O.; PH.D; SC.D OR COMPARABLE DEGREES AND ARE SEEKING FURTHER TRAINING AS SCIENTIFIC INVESTIGATORS. MUST HAVE COMPLETED RESIDENCY IN SPECIALTY RELEVANT TO LUNG DISEASE.

AWARDS ARE FOR TWO YEARS SUBJECT TO ANNUAL REVIEW. WRITE FOR COMPLETE INFORMATION.

1020

AMERICAN LUNG ASSOCIATION (V. DALSEMER RESEARCH SCHOLAR AWARD)

1740 BROADWAY
NEW YORK NY 10019
212-315-8700

AMOUNT: $30000

DEADLINE(S): OCT 1

FIELD(S): PULMONARY DISEASE RESEARCH

OPEN TO PHYSICIANS WHO HAVE COMPLETED GRADUATE TRAINING IN PULMONARY DISEASE AND WHO HOLD A FACULTY POSITION IN A SCHOOL OF MEDICINE. A DALSEMER SCHOLAR IS EXPECTED TO DEVOTE AT LEAST 75% OF TIME TO RESEARCH.

USA CITIZEN OR PERMANENT RESIDENT. WRITE FOR COMPLETE INFORMATION.

1021

AMERICAN LUNG ASSOCIATION OF OREGON (PULMONARY RESEARCH FUND GRANTS)

1776 S.W. MADISON - SUITE 200
PORTLAND OR 97205-1798
503/224-5145

AMOUNT: UP TO $15000

DEADLINE(S): OCT 15

FIELD(S): LUNG DISEASE

OPEN TO OREGON RESIDENTS WHO HOLD M.D. OR PH.D DEGREE OR EQIVALENT FOR RESEARCH PROJECTS RELEVANT TO THE LUNG AND TO THE PREVENTION; CONTROL AND TREATMENT OF LUNG DISEASES. RESEARCH MAY BE LABORATORY; EPIDEMOLOGIC; BEHAVORIAL; OR CLINICAL.

WRITE FOR COMPLETE INFORMATION.

1022

AMERICAN PHILOSOPHICAL SOCIETY (DALAND FELLOWSHIPS FOR RESEARCH IN CLINICAL MEDICINE)

104 S. 5TH ST.
PHILADELPHIA PA 19106
WRITTEN INQUIRY ONLY

AMOUNT: $30000 OVER TWO YEARS

DEADLINE(S): SEP 1

FIELD(S): CLINICAL MEDICINE

CLINICAL MEDICINE RESEARCH FELLOWSHIPS OPEN TO THOSE WHO HAVE HELD THE M.D. PH.D OR D.O. DEGREE FOR LESS THAN 6 YEARS. CLINICAL MEDICINE IS BROADLY INTERPRETED.

WRITE FOR COMPLETE INFORMATION.

1023

AMERICAN SOCIETY FOR ENGINEERING EDUCATION (OFFICE OF NAVAL RESEARCH GRADUATE FELLOWSHIP PROGRAM)

ELEVEN DUPONT CIRCLE #200
WASHINGTON DC 20036
202/745-3616

AMOUNT: $15000

DEADLINE(S): JAN 31

FIELD(S): ELEC ENG; MECH ENG; AEROSPACE ENG; MATHEMATICS; PHYSICS; COMPUTER SCIENCE; MATERIALS SCIENCE; BIOLOGICAL-BIOMEDICAL SCIENCE; NAVAL ARCHITECTURE & OCEAN ENG; RELATED FIELDS

LIMITED TO INDIVIDUALS WHO HAVE 'NOT' BEGUN GRADUATE PROGRAMS. FOR STUDY AND RESEARCH LEADING TO DOCTORAL DEGREE. FELLOWSHIPS ARE AWARDED ON THE BASIS OF ABILITY. USA CITIZEN.

50 THREE-YEAR FELLOWSHIPS ARE OFFERED. WRITE FOR COMPLETE INFORMATION.

1024

AMERICAN SPEECH-LANGUAGE-HEARING FOUNDATION (RESEARCH GRANTS)

10801 ROCKVILLE PIKE
ROCKVILLE MD 20852
301/897-5700; FAX 301/571-0457

AMOUNT: $2000

DEADLINE(S): JUL 16

FIELD(S): SPEECH/LANGUAGE PATHOLOGY; AUDIOLOGY

RESEARCH GRANT FOR NEW INVESTIGATORS TO SUPPORT CLINICAL RESEARCH IN THE ABOVE AREAS. GRANTS ARE DESIGNED TO ENCOURAGE RESEARCH ACTVITIES OF NEW SCIENTISTS EARNING THEIR LATEST DEGREE WITHIN THE LAST 5 YEARS.

WRITE FOR COMPLETE INFORMATION.

1025

AMERICAN SPEECH-LANGUAGE-HEARING FOUNDATION (RESEARCH GRANT COMPETITION FOR NEW INVESTIGATORS)

10801 ROCKVILLE PIKE
ROCKVILLE MD 20852
301/897-5700; FAX 301/571-0457

AMOUNT: $4000

DEADLINE(S): JUL 19

FIELD(S): SPEECH/LANGUAGE PATHOLOGY; AUDIOLOGY

OPEN TO NEW RESEARCHERS WHO HAVE RECEIVED THEIR MASTER'S OR DOCTORAL DEGREE WITHIN THE PAST 5 YEARS. PROPOSAL MUST BE FOR RESEARCH TO BE INITIATED. STUDENTS ENROLLED IN A DEGREE PROGRAM ARE -NOT- ELIGIBLE.

WRITE FOR COMPLETE INFORMATION.

1026

AMYOTROPHIC LATERAL SCLEROSIS ASSOCIATION (RESEARCH GRANT PROGRAM)

21021 VENTURA BLVD; SUITE 321
WOODLAND HILLS CA 91364
818/340-7500

AMOUNT: VARIES

DEADLINE(S): SEP 15

FIELD(S): AMYOTROPHIC LATERAL SCLEROSIS

RESEARCH GRANTS ARE AVAILABLE FOR RESEARCH RELEVANT TO AMYOTROPHIC LATERAL SCLEROSIS. OPEN TO QUALIFIED POST-DOCTORAL RESEARCHERS. CURRICULUM VITAE REQUIRED.

ASSOCIATION DOES -NOT- OFFER GRANTS TO STUDENTS FOR THEIR EDUCATION. SCIENTISTS RESEARCHING ALS SHOULD WRITE FOR COMPLETE INFORMATION.

1027

ASTHMA AND ALLERGY FOUNDATION OF AMERICA (FELLOWSHIP GRANTS)

1125 FIFTEENTH ST NW - SUITE 502
WASHINGTON DC 20036
202/466-7643

AMOUNT: $5000 - $15000

DEADLINE(S): VARIES

FIELD(S): IMMUNOLOGY; ALLERGY; ASTHMA

POST-DOCTORAL RESEARCH GRANTS. CITIZEN OR PERMANENT RESIDENT OF UNITED STATES OR CANADA. MUST HOLD M.D. DEGREE.

4 FELLOWSHIPS PER YEAR. WRITE FOR COMPLETE INFORMATION.

1028

BROOKHAVEN NATIONAL LABORATORY (POSTDOCTORAL RESEARCH ASSOCIATESHIPS)

BROOKHAVEN NATIONAL LABORATORY; ASSOCIATED UNIVERSITIES INC.
UPTON L.I. NY 11973
516/282-7813

AMOUNT: $27000 MINIMUM

DEADLINE(S): THROUGHOUT THE YEAR.

FIELD(S): CHEMISTRY; PHYSICS; MATERIALS SCIENCE; BIOLOGY; OCEANOGRAPHY; MEDICAL SCIENCE

MEDICAL RESEARCH

POST-DOCTORAL RESEARCH ASSOCIATESHIPS TENABLE AT BROOKHAVEN NATIONAL LABORATORY FOR RESEARCH TO PROMOTE FUNDAMENTAL AND APPLIED RESEARCH IN THE ABOVE FIELDS. A RECENT DOCTORAL DEGREE IS REQUIRED.

25 ASSOCIATESHIPS PER YEAR. RENEWABLE FOR TWO ADDITIONAL YEARS. WRITE TO MS. E.E. THORNHILL; OFFICE OF SCIENTIFIC PERSONNEL; ADDRESS ABOVE.

1029 ────────────────

BURROUGHS WELLCOME FUND (EXPERIMENTAL THERAPEUTICS AWARD)

3030 CORNWALLIS ROAD
RESEARCH TRIANGLE PARK NC 27709
909/248-4136

AMOUNT: $70000 PER YEAR FOR 5 YEARS

DEADLINE(S): NOV 2

FIELD(S): EXPERIMENTAL THERAPEUTICS

CANDIDATE MUST HAVE MD OR MD/PHD DEGREE & HAVE AN APPOINTMENT IN PROGRAMS OF CLINICAL PHARMACOLOGY OR ONE OF THE CLINICAL MEDICINE SUBSPECIALTIES. APPLICATION TO BE MADE THROUGH MEDICAL SCHOOL DEAN OR DEPT CHAIR WHERE AWARD WILL BE USED.

PROGRAM AIM IS TO SUPPORT CAREER DEVELOPMENT; STIMULATE TEACHING & TRAINING IN THE SCIENTIFIC BASIS OF THERAPEUTICS. USA CITIZEN OR LEGAL RESIDENT. WRITE FOR COMPLETE INFORMATION.

1030 ────────────────

CANCER RESEARCH FUND OF THE DAMON RUYON-WALTER WINCHELL FOUNDATION (POST DOCTORAL RESEARCH FELLOWSHIPS)

131 EAST 36TH ST
NEW YORK NY 10016
212/532-3888

AMOUNT: $23000 TO $44000 DEPENDING ON TRAINING

DEADLINE(S): AUG 15; DEC 15; MAR 15

FIELD(S): CANCER RESEARCH

POST-DOCTORAL FELLOWSHIPS FOR BASIC AND PHYSICIAN SCIENTISTS TO ADVANCE CANCER RESEARCH. COVERS ALL AREAS OF THEORETICAL AND EXPERIMENTAL RESEARCH RELEVANT TO THE STUDY OF CANCER AND THE SEARCH FOR ITS CAUSES; THERAPIES AND PREVENTIONS.

CANDIDATES MUST HAVE A SPONSOR & HOLD A RECENT MD; PH.D; DDS; DVM OR EQUIVALENT DEGREE. RESEARCH USUALLY TO BE DONE IN USA. 60 AWARDS PER YEAR. DURATION IS 3 YEARS. WRITE FOR COMPLETE INFORMATION.

1031 ────────────────

CHARLES A. LINDBERGH FUND INC. (GRANTS FOR RESEARCH PROJECTS)

708 S. THIRD ST. - SUITE 110
MINNEAPOLIS MN 55415
612/338-1703

AMOUNT: UP TO $10580

DEADLINE(S): JUN 15

FIELD(S): AVIATION/AEROSPACE; AGRICULTURE; ARTS & HUMANITIES; BIOMEDICAL RESEARCH; CONSERVATION; EXPLORATION; HEALTH & POPULATION SCIENCES; INTERCULTURAL COMMUNICATION; OCEANOGRAPHY; WASTE DISPOSAL MGMT; WATER RESOURCE MGMT; WILDLIFE PRESERVATION.

RESEARCH GRANTS ARE AWARDED ANNUALLY TO INDIVIDUALS WHOSE PROPOSED PROJECTS REPRESENT A SIGNIFICANT CONTRIBUTION TOWARD THE ACHIEVEMENT OF A BALANCE BETWEEN THE ADVANCE OF TECHNOLOGY & PRESERVATION OF THE NATURAL ENVIRONMENT.

WRITE FOR COMPLETE INFORMATION.

1032 ────────────────

CHEMICAL INDUSTRY INSTITUTE OF TOXICOLOGY (POST-DOCTORAL FELLOWSHIPS)

PO BOX 12137
RESEARCH TRIANGLE PARK NC 27709
919/541-2070

AMOUNT: VARIES

DEADLINE(S): NONE

FIELD(S): TOXICOLOGY; PATHOLOGY

CIIT PROVIDES STIPENDS & SUPPORT TO POST-DOCTORAL RESEARCH FELLOWS WHO DO ORIGINAL RESEARCH RELATED TO CHEMICAL TOXICITY AND/OR PATHOLOGY. AWARD TENABLE AT CIIT'S LABORATORY ONLY.

20-30 AWARDS PER YEAR. RENEWABLE FOR A MAXIMUM OF 2 YEARS. CONTACT ADDRESS ABOVE FOR COMPLETE INFORMATION.

1033 ────────────────

CROHN'S & COLITIS FOUNDATION OF AMERICA INC (RESEARCH GRANTS)

444 PARK AVENUE S. - 11TH FLOOR
NEW YORK NY 10016
212/685-3440; 800/343/3637;
FAX 212/779-4098

AMOUNT: $80000 PER YEAR FOR 2 YEARS

DEADLINE(S): JAN 1 & JUL 1

FIELD(S): INFLAMMATORY BOWEL DISEASE

POST-DOCTORAL RESEARCH GRANTS OPEN TO MD'S & PH.D'S EMPLOYED BY A PUBLIC OR PRIVATE NON-PROFIT INSTITUTION OR GOVERNMENT AGENCY. PEER REVIEW CONSIDERATIONS WILL INCLUDE SCIENTIFIC MERIT OF THE PROPOSED RESEARCH.

MUST DISCLOSE ALL OTHER FUNDING SOURCES. APPROXIMATELY 20 AWARDS PER YEAR. WRITE FOR COMPLETE INFORMATION.

1034

CROHN'S & COLITIS FOUNDATION OF AMERICA INC (RESEARCH FELLOWSHIP AWARD)

444 PARK AVENUE S. - 11TH FLOOR
NEW YORK NY 10016
800/343-3637 OR 212/685-3440;
FAX 212/779-4098

AMOUNT: $30000 PER YEAR FOR 1 TO 3 YEARS

DEADLINE(S): JAN 1 & JUL 1

FIELD(S): INFLAMMATORY BOWEL DISEASE

POST DOCTORAL RESEARCH FELLOWSHIPS OPEN TO MD'S AND PH.D'S WITH A DEMONSTRATED INTEREST AND CAPABILITY IN RESEARCH. AWARDS ARE TO ENCOURAGE RESEARCH AND DEVELOP THE POTENTIAL OF YOUNG BASIC AND/OR CLINICAL SCIENTISTS.

MUST BE EMPLOYED BY A PUBLIC OR PRIVATE NON-PROFIT INSTITUTION OR GOVERNMENT AGENCY. WRITE FOR COMPLETE INFORMATION.

1035

CROHN'S & COLITIS FOUNDATION OF AMERICA INC. (RESEARCH TRAINING AWARDS PROGAM)

444 PARK AVENUE S. - 11TH FLOOR
NEW YORK NY 10016
800/343-3637 OR 212/685-3440;
FAX 212/779-4098

AMOUNT: $40000 PER YEAR SALARY + $20000/YR SUPPLIES

DEADLINE(S): JAN 1 AND JUL 1

FIELD(S): INFLAMMATORY BOWEL DISEASE

OPEN TO HOLDERS OF AN M.D. OR PH.D DEGREE FOR RESEARCH PROJECTS IN THE FIELD OF INFLAMMATORY BOWEL DISEASE. MD'S NEED 5 YEARS POST-DOCTORAL EXPERIENCE; PHD'S 2 YEARS.

CANDIDATES MUST BE SPONSORED BY A PUBLIC OR PRIVATE NON-PROFIT INSTITUTION OR A GOVERNMENT AGENCY ENGAGED IN HEALTH CARE OR HEALTH RELATED RESEARCH IN THE USA. WRITE FOR COMPLETE INFORMATION.

1036

CYSTIC FIBROSIS FOUNDATION (STUDENT TRAINEESHIP RESEARCH GRANTS)

6931 ARLINGTON RD
BETHESDA MD 20814
301/951-4422

AMOUNT: $1500

DEADLINE(S): NONE

FIELD(S): CYSTIC FIBROSIS RESEARCH

DOCTORAL (MD/OR PH.D) RESEARCH GRANTS FOR STUDENTS THAT PLAN CAREER IN RESEARCH AND HAVE A LAB PROJECT THAT CAN BE COMPLETED IN LESS THAN 1 YEAR. AWARD INTENDED TO INTEREST STUDENT IN CYSTIC FIBROSIS RESEARCH & OFFSET COSTS OF THE PROJECT.

CONTACT THE FOUNDATION FOR FURTHER INFORMATION ON APPLICATION PROCEDURE.

1037

DELAWARE ACADEMY OF MEDICINE (STUDENT FINANCIAL AID-LOANS)

1925 LOVERING AVE
WILMINGTON DE 19806
302/656-1629

AMOUNT: $1000 - $5000

DEADLINE(S): MAY 15

FIELD(S): MEDICINE; DENTISTRY; ALLIED HEALTH FIELDS

DELAWARE RESIDENT. FOR FULL-TIME GRADUATE STUDY IN THE ABOVE AREAS AT ACCREDITED COLLEGES & UNIVERSITIES. USA CITIZEN OR LEGAL RESIDENT.

WRITE FOR COMPLETE INFORMATION.

1038

DERMATOLOGY FOUNDATION (POST-DOCTORAL FELLOWSHIP AWARD PROGRAM)

1560 SHERMAN AVE
EVANSTON IL 60201
312/328-2256

AMOUNT: $25000

DEADLINE(S): AUG 1

FIELD(S): DERMATOLOGY & CUTANEOUS BIOLOGY

AVAILABLE TO POST-DOCTORAL FELLOWS WITH A COMMITMENT TO A CAREER IN ACADEMIC DERMATOLOGY WHO DESIRE RESEARCH TRAINING. MUST HOLD MD OR PHD OR EQUIVALENT. THOSE WITH MORE THAN 2 YEARS TRAINING IN SKIN RESEARCH ARE NOT ELIGIBLE.

MEDICAL RESEARCH

RESEARCH MUST BE CONDUCTED IN USA OR CANADA. CONTACT SANDRA RAHN GOLDMAN - EXEC DIRECTOR - ADDRESS ABOVE FOR COMPLETE INFORMATION.

1039 —————————————————

DERMATOLOGY FOUNDATION (POST-DOCTORAL GRANT PROGRAM)

1560 SHERMAN AVE
EVANSTON IL 60201
312/328-2256

AMOUNT: $10000

DEADLINE(S): AUG 1

FIELD(S): DERMATOLOGY & CUTANEOUS BIOLOGY

GRANTS AWARDED TO INITIATE POST DOCTORATE RESEARCH PROJECTS IN DERMATOLOGY AND CUTANEOUS BIOLOGY. GRANT APPLICATIONS ARE CAREFULLY REVIEWED AND AWARDED ON A COMPETITIVE BASIS. AWARDS CANNOT BE USED FOR PAYMENT OF INDIRECT COSTS.

RESEARCH TO BE DONE IN USA OR CANADA. FUNDING IS FOR 1 YEAR. WRITE TO SANDRA RAHN AT ADDRESS ABOVE FOR COMPLETE INFORMATION.

1040 —————————————————

DIABETES RESEARCH & EDUCATION FOUNDATION (HOECHST-ROUSSEL GRANTS)

PO BOX 6168; EXECUTIVE DIRECTOR
BRIDGEWATER NJ 08807
908/658-9322

AMOUNT: UP TO $20000

DEADLINE(S): MAR 30; SEP 30

FIELD(S): DIABETES RESEARCH

SEED GRANTS TO ENCOURAGE NOVEL INITIATIVES IN BASIC RESEARCH; CLINICAL RESEARCH & EDUCATION. OPEN TO MD'S; PH.D'S; PHARMACISTS; NURSES; EDUCATORS & OTHER HEALTH CARE PROFESSIONALS CONDUCTING PROJECTS IN USA. USA CITIZEN OR LEGAL RESIDENT.

WRITE TO DR. H.C. ROSENKILDE AT ADDRESS ABOVE FOR COMPLETE INFORMATION.

1041 —————————————————

EPILEPSY FOUNDATION OF AMERICA (BEHAVORIAL SCIENCES STUDENT FELLOWSHIPS)

4351 GARDEN CITY DR. SUITE 406
LANDOVER MD 20785
301/459-3700

AMOUNT: $1500

DEADLINE(S): MAR 2

FIELD(S): EPILEPSY RELATED STUDY OR TRAINING PROJECTS.

OPEN TO UNDERGRAD AND GRAD STUDENTS IN NURSING; PSYCHOLOGY AND RELATED AREAS WHO PROPOSE A 3-MONTH EPILEPSY-RELATED PROJECT TO BE CARRIED OUT IN A USA INSTITUTION AT WHICH THERE ARE ONGOING EPILEPSY RESEARCH; SERVICE OR TRAINING PROGRAMS.

FELLOWSHIP MUST BE UNDERTAKEN DURING A FREE PERIOD IN THE STUDENT'S YEAR. WRITE FOR COMPLETE INFORMATION.

1042 —————————————————

EPILEPSY FOUNDATION OF AMERICA (GRADUATE RESEARCH GRANTS)

4351 GARDEN CITY DR; SUITE 406
LANDOVER MD 20785
301/459-3700

AMOUNT: $30000

DEADLINE(S): SEP 1

FIELD(S): EPILEPSY RESEARCH

RESEARCH GRANTS FOR GRADUATE STUDENTS WHO ARE IN THE BIOLOGICAL; BEHAVIORAL OR SOCIAL SCIENCES. FOR PROJECTS (CONDUCTED IN THE USA) WHICH WILL ADVANCE THE UNDERSTANDING; TREATMENT AND PREVENTION OF EPILEPSY.

AWARDS ARE FOR A ONE-YEAR PERIOD RENEWABLE FOR A SECOND YEAR ON A COMPETITIVE BASIS. WRITE FOR COMPLETE INFORMATION.

1043 —————————————————

EPILEPSY FOUNDATION OF AMERICA (MEDICAL STUDENT FELLOWSHIPS)

4351 GARDEN CITY DR.
LANDOVER MD 20785
301/459-3700

AMOUNT: $2000

DEADLINE(S): MAR 2

FIELD(S): MEDICINE - EPILEPSY PROJECT

MEDICAL STUDENTS MAY PROPOSE A 3-MONTH PROJECT TO BE UNDERTAKEN IN A CLINICAL OR LABORATORY SETTING WHERE THERE ARE ONGOING PROGRAMS OF RESEARCH; SERVICE OR TRANING IN THE FIELD OF EPILEPSY.

PROJECT MAY BE CONDUCTED DURING ANY FREE PERIOD OF THE STUDENT'S YEAR AT A USA INSTITUTION OF THE STUDENT'S CHOICE. WRITE FOR COMPLETE INFORMATION.

1044

EPILEPSY FOUNDATION OF AMERICA (POST-DOCTORAL RESEARCH GRANTS & FELLOWSHIPS)

4351 GARDEN CITY DR. SUITE 406
LANDOVER MD 20785
301/459-3700

AMOUNT: VARIES

DEADLINE(S): SEP 1

FIELD(S): EPILEPSY RESEARCH

VARIOUS POST-DOCTORAL RESEARCH GRANTS & FELLOWSHIPS TO SUPPORT RESEARCH PROJECTS; CLINICAL TRAINING & CLINICAL RESEARCH WHICH WILL ADVANCE THE UNDERSTANDING; TREATMENT & PREVENTION OF EPILEPSY.

WRITE FOR COMPLETE INFORMATION.

1045

FIGHT FOR SIGHT (RESEARCH FELLOWSHIPS AND GRANTS-IN-AID)

160 EAST 56TH STREET
NEW YORK NY 10022
212/751-1118

AMOUNT: $14000 POST-DOCTORAL FELLOWSHIP; GRANTS FROM $1000 TO $12000

DEADLINE(S): VARIES

FIELD(S): OPHTHALMOLOGY

FIGHT FOR SIGHT FUNDS STUDENT FELLOWSHIPS; POST-DOCTORAL RESEARCH FELLOWSHIPS AND GRANTS-IN-AID WITH EMPHASIS ON PILOT PROJECTS. THE PROGRAM IS ADMINISTERED BY THE NATIONAL SOCIETY TO PREVENT BLINDNESS.

FOR APPLICATION FORMS AND BROCHURE DETAILING THE AWARDS PROGRAM WRITE THE NATIONAL SOCIETY TO PREVENT BLINDNESS; 500 E. REMINGTON RD.; SCHAUMBURG IL 60173-4557.

1046

GRASS FOUNDATION (GRASS FELLOWSHIPS IN NEUROPHYSIOLOGY)

77 RESERVOIR ROAD
QUINCY MA 02170
617/773-0002

AMOUNT: TRAVEL; RESEARCH & LIVING EXPENSES

DEADLINE(S): DEC 1

FIELD(S): NEUROSCIENCE

OPEN TO LATE PRE-DOCTORAL (MD OR PH.D) & EARLY POST-DOCTORAL (USUALLY NO MORE THAN 3 YEARS) RESEARCHERS. FELLOWSHIPS SUPPORT NEUROPHYSIOLOGICAL RESEARCH DURING THE SUMMER (10-14 WEEKS) AT THE MARINE BIOLOGICAL LABORATORY IN WOODS HOLE; MA.

APPROX 10 FELLOWSHIPS PER YEAR. WRITE FOR BULLETIN FA-294 WHICH CONTAINS DETAILED APPLICATION INSTRUCTIONS & APPROPRIATE FORMS.

1047

GRASS FOUNDATION (ROBERT S. MORISON FELLOWSHIP)

77 RESERVOIR ROAD
QUINCY MA 02170
617/773-0002

AMOUNT: $30000 STIPEND PER YEAR + $700 PER DEPENDENT & $3000 FOR RESEARCH EXPENSES

DEADLINE(S): NOV 1 OF EVEN NUMBERED YEARS

FIELD(S): NEUROLOGY; NEUROSURGERY; NEUROSCIENCE

OPEN TO MD'S PREPARING FOR AN ACADEMIC CAREER WHO HAVE BEEN ACCEPTED INTO OR JUST COMPLETED A RESIDENCY IN ABOVE AREAS & WISH TO UNDERTAKE A 2-YEAR PROGRAM OF BASIC RESEARCH TRAINING AT A RECOGNIZED INSTITUTION IN NORTH AMERICA.

THIS IS A 2-YEAR PROGRAM WHICH STARTS IN JULY OF ODD-NUMBERED YEARS. WRITE FOR COMPLETE INFORMATION.

1048

HEALTH RESEARCH COUNCIL OF NEW ZEALAND (POST-DOCTORAL FELLOWSHIPS)

PO BOX 5541; WELLESLEY ST
AUCKLAND 1036 NEW ZEALAND
09/3798-227; FAX 09/3779-988

AMOUNT: NZ$37440 + NZ$1750 RESEARCH EXPENSES & AIR FARE

DEADLINE(S): APR 1; OCT 1

FIELD(S): BIOMEDICAL & PUBLIC HEALTH RESEARCH

AWARDS ARE BASED ON THE ACADEMIC STANDING AND RESEARCH CAPABILITIES OF APPLICANTS WHO SHOULD HAVE DOCTOR OF PHILOSOPHY OR EQUIVALENT DEGREE. MUST BE NEW ZEALAND CITIZEN OR RESIDENT FOR AT LEAST ONE YEAR.

MEDICAL RESEARCH

FELLOWSHIPS ARE TENABLE WITHIN NEW ZEALAND. FELLOWSHIPS ARE NORMALLY AWARDED FOR PERIOD OF 12 MONTHS AND MAY BE EXTENDED FOR AN ADDITIONAL 12 MONTHS. WRITE FOR COMPLETE INFORMATION.

1049 ────────────────────

HEALTH SERVICES IMPROVEMENT FUND INC (DISSERTATION GRANT)

622 THIRD AVENUE
NEW YORK NY 10017
212/476-6649

AMOUNT: $15000

DEADLINE(S): DEC 1

FIELD(S): MEDICAL RESEARCH (HEALTH SERVICES)

OPEN TO DOCTORAL CANDIDATES WHO HAVE COMPLETED ALL QUALIFYING EXAMINATIONS EXCEPT FOR DISSERTATION. SPECIAL CONSIDERATION TO STUDENTS FROM NEW YORK SCHOOLS AND TOPICS RELEVANT TO NEW YORK HEALTH CARE DELIVERY.

CANDIDATES MUST BE NOMINATED BY THE DEAN OF THEIR SCHOOL. WRITE FOR COMPLETE INFORMATION.

1050 ────────────────────

HEART AND STROKE FOUNDATION OF CANADA (RESEARCH FELLOWSHIP)

160 GEORGE ST. SUITE 200
OTTAWA K1N 9M2 CANADA
613-237-4361

AMOUNT: VARIES

DEADLINE(S): NOV 15

FIELD(S): HEART RESEARCH

A LIMITED NUMBER OF CANADIAN HEART RESEARCH FELLOWSHIPS ARE AVAILABLE TO HIGHLY QUALIFIED POST-GRADUATE STUDENTS WHO ARE UNDERTAKING FULL-TIME TRAINING RESEARCH IN THE CARDIOVASCULAR; STROKE AND HEALTH EDUCATION FIELDS.

FELLOWSHIPS ARE NORMALLY TENABLE AT CANADIAN UNIVERSITIES. WRITE FOR COMPLETE INFORMATION.

1051 ────────────────────

HEISER PROGRAM FOR RESEARCH IN LEPROSY AND/OR TUBERCULOSIS (POST DOCTORAL FELLOWSHIPS AND RESEARCH GRANTS)

450 E. 63RD ST
NEW YORK NY 10021
212/751-6233

AMOUNT: UP TO $25000 PER YEAR PLUS TRAVEL ALLOWANCE

DEADLINE(S): FEB 1

FIELD(S): LEPROSY; TUBERCULOSIS RESEARCH

FELLOWSHIPS FOR RESEARCHERS WHO HOLD M.D./PH.D OR EQUIVALENT DEGREE. CANDIDATES SHOULD BE INTERESTED IN OBTAINING RESEARCH TRAINING DIRECTLY RELATED TO THE STUDY OF LEPROSY AND/OR TUBERCULOSIS.

WRITE FOR COMPLETE INFORMATION.

1052 ────────────────────

INTERMURAL RESEARCH TRAINING AWARD (SUMMER INTERN PROGRAM)

OFFICE OF EDUCATION; BLDG 10;
RM 1C-129
BETHESDA MD 20892
301/496-2427

AMOUNT: STIPEND

DEADLINE(S): FEB 1

FIELD(S): RESEARCH TRAINING (BIOMEDICAL RESEARCH)

SUMMER INTERN PROGRAM IS DESIGNED TO PROVIDE 'ACADEMICALLY TALENTED' UNDERGRADUATE; GRADUATE OR MEDICAL STUDENTS A UNIQUE OPPORTUNITY TO ACQUIRE VALUABLE HANDS-ON RESEARCH TRAINING AND EXPERIENCE IN THE NEUROSCIENCES.

WRITE FOR COMPLETE INFORMATION.

1053 ────────────────────

JANE COFFIN CHILDS MEMORIAL FUND FOR MEDICAL RESEARCH (POST-DOCTORAL FELLOWSHIPS)

333 CEDAR STREET
NEW HAVEN CT 06510
203/785-4612

AMOUNT: $22000 - $24000 + ALLOWANCES

DEADLINE(S): FEB 1

FIELD(S): CANCER RESEARCH

OPEN TO APPLICANTS WITH PH.D; MD OR EQUAL EXPERIENCE IN FIELD OF PROPOSED STUDY. USA CITIZENS MAY HOLD FELLOWSHIP IN USA OR FOREIGN COUNTRY. FOREIGN CITIZENS MAY HOLD FELLOWSHIP IN USA ONLY. PREFERENCE TO AGES 30 & YOUNGER.

20-25 FELLOWSHIPS PER YEAR. RENEWABLE. WRITE FOR COMPLETE INFORMATION.

1054

JUVENILE DIABETES FOUNDATION INTERNATIONAL (RESEARCH GRANTS; CAREER DEVELOPMENT AWARDS; POST-DOCTORAL FELLOWSHIPS)

432 PARK AVE SOUTH;
GRANT ADMINISTRATOR
NEW YORK NY 10016
212/889-7575

AMOUNT: VARIES

DEADLINE(S): FEB 15 FOR GRANTS; OCT 1 FOR AWARDS & FELLOWSHIPS

FIELD(S): DIABETES RESEARCH

POST DOCTORAL GRANTS; AWARDS & FELLOWSHIPS TO SUPPORT RESEARCH INTO THE CAUSES; TREATMENT; PREVENTION AND CURE OF DIABETES AND ITS COMPLICATIONS.

APPROXIMATELY 350 AWARDS PER YEAR. WRITE FOR COMPLETE INFORMATION.

1055

LALOR FOUNDATION (POST-DOCTORAL GRANTS)

3801 KENNETT PIKE; BLD6 C-100F
WILMINGTON DE 19807
302/571-1262

AMOUNT: $20000

DEADLINE(S): JAN 15

FIELD(S): MAMMALIAN REPRODUCTIVE PHYSIOLOGY

POST-DOCTORAL GRANTS TO SUPPORT RESEARCH IN THE ABOVE AREA; BEARING ON STERILIZATION AND/OR PREVENTION OR TERMINATION OF PREGNANCY.

10-15 GRANTS PER YEAR. RENEWABLE FOR UP TO ONE YEAR. WRITE FOR COMPLETE INFORMATION.

1056

LEUKEMIA SOCIETY OF AMERICA INC (SCHOLARSHIPS; SPECIAL FELLOWSHIPS AND FELLOWSHIPS)

733 THIRD AVE.
NEW YORK NY 10017
212/573-8484

AMOUNT: $22500 - $40000 PER YEAR FOR UP TO 5 YEARS

DEADLINE(S): OCT 1

FIELD(S): LEUKEMIA AND ALLIED DISEASES RESEARCH

POST-DOCTORAL AWARDS OPEN TO APPLICANTS WITH PH.D; MD OR EQUIVALENT DEGREES. AMOUNT; TYPE AND LENGTH OF AWARD IS BASED ON EXPERIENCE AND TRAINING.

WRITE FOR COMPLETE INFORMATION.

1057

LIFE AND HEALTH INSURANCE MEDICAL RESEARCH FUND (YOUNG SCIENTIST SCHOLARSHIP PROGRAM)

1001 PENNSYLVANIA AVE N.W.
WASHINGTON DC 20004
202/624-2312

AMOUNT: $16000

DEADLINE(S): MAR 1

FIELD(S): BIOMEDICAL RESEARCH

OPEN TO GRADUATE STUDENTS WHO ARE IN THEIR SECOND YEAR OF A JOINT MD/PH.D PROGRAM AT A USA MEDICAL SCHOOL. FUND'S PURPOSE IS TO PROVIDE TRAINING FOR YOUNG SCIENTISTS IN BIOMEDICAL RESEARCH.

USA CITIZEN. WRITE FOR COMPLETE INFORMATION.

1058

LUPUS FOUNDATION OF AMERICA (STUDENT SUMMER FELLOWSHIP PROGRAM)

4 RESEARCH PLACE - SUITE 180
ROCKVILLE MD 20850
301/670-9292

AMOUNT: $2000

DEADLINE(S): FEB 1

FIELD(S): LUPUS ERYTHEMATOSUS RESEARCH

SUMMER FELLOWSHIPS OPEN TO UNDERGRADS; GRADS & POST-GRADS BUT APPLICANTS ALREADY HAVING COLLEGE DEGREE ARE PREFERRED. APPLICATIONS ARE EVALUATED NIH-STYLE. PURPOSE IS TO ENCOURAGE STUDENTS TO PURSUE RESEARCH CAREERS IN ABOVE AREAS.

RESEARCH MAY BE CONDUCTED AT ANY RECOGNIZED INSTITUTION IN THE USA. APPLICATION MATERIALS AVAILABLE IN DECEMBER. 10 AWARDS PER YEAR. WRITE FOR COMPLETE INFORMATION.

1059

MARCH OF DIMES BIRTH DEFECTS FOUNDATION (PREDOCTORAL GRADUATE RESEARCH TRAINING FELLOWSHIPS)

1275 MAMARONECK AVE
WHITE PLAINS NY 10605
914/428-7100

AMOUNT: $12000

DEADLINE(S): MAR 1

FIELD(S): BIRTH DEFECTS RESEARCH

MEDICAL RESEARCH

FELLOWSHIPS ARE TO SUPPORT FULL TIME GRADUATE TRAINING LEADING TO THE PH.D DEGREE AND STIMULATE TRAINING AND THESIS RESEARCH FOCUSING ON BIRTH DEFECTS. FOREIGN STUDENTS MUST PLAN TO REMAIN IN USA AFTER COMPLETION OF DEGREE.

DEANS OF MEDICAL SCHOOL SHOULD SUBMIT APPLICATIONS FROM NO MORE THAN TWO OF THEIR BEST STUDENTS. WRITE FOR COMPLETE INFORMATION.

1060

MILHEIM FOUNDATION FOR CANCER RESEARCH (CANCER RESEARCH GRANTS)

COLORADO NAT'L BANK; PO BOX 5168
DENVER CO 80217
303/892-4051

AMOUNT: $1125 TO $23485

DEADLINE(S): MAR 15

FIELD(S): CANCER RESEARCH

GRANTS FOR RESEARCH INTO THE PREVENTION; TREATMENT AND CURE OF CANCER. FUNDS MUST BE EXPENDED IN USA. GRANTS MAY NOT BE USED TO PAY SALARIES OF ACADEMIC PERSONNEL; INCLUDING MD'S; PH.D'S AND THOSE STUDING FOR THOSE DEGREES.

WRITE TO TRUST ADMINISTRATOR MARGARET ARMSTRONG AT ABOVE ADDRESS FOR COMPLETE INFORMATION.

1061

MONTREAL NEUROLOGICAL INSTITUTE (IZAAK WALTON KILLAM FELLOWSHIPS; JEANNE TIMMINS FELLOWSHIPS)

3801 UNIVERSITY
MONTREAL QUEBEC H3A 2B4 CANADA
514/398-1903

AMOUNT: CANADIAN $25000

DEADLINE(S): DEC 15; JUN 15

FIELD(S): NEUROSCIENCES

FELLOWSHIPS AT THE INSTITUTE FOR RESEARCH AND STUDY IN CLINICAL AND BASIC NEUROSCIENCES. OPEN TO NEUROLOGISTS; NEUROSURGEONS AND PH.D'S OF ALL NATIONALITIES.

WRITE TO THE INSTITUTE DIRECTOR FOR COMPLETE INFORMATION.

1062

MULTIPLE SCLEROSIS SOCIETY (FELLOWSHIPS & GRANTS)

733 THIRD AVE
NEW YORK NY 10017
212/986-3240

AMOUNT: VARIES

DEADLINE(S): VARIOUS

FIELD(S): MULTIPLE SCLEROSIS & ALLIED DISEASES

PROGRAMS TO STIMULATE; COORDINATE & SUPPORT RESEARCH INTO CAUSE; PREVENTION; ALLEVIATION & CURE OF MS. OPEN TO ADVANCED DOCTORATES (MD/PH.D) RECENT MD/PH.D'S & SENIOR INVESTIGATORS. NO SCHOLARSHIP OR PRE-DOCTORAL SUPPORT IS AVAILABLE.

WRITE FOR COMPLETE INFORMATION.

1063

MUSCULAR DYSTROPHY ASSOCIATION (POST-DOCTORAL FELLOWSHIP PROGRAM)

3561 E SUNRISE BLVD
TUCSON AZ 85718
602/529-2000

AMOUNT: $25000 AND $28000

DEADLINE(S): JUL 10; JAN 10

FIELD(S): MEDICINE; BIOLOGICAL SCIENCES; LIFE SCIENCES

GRANTS & FELLOWSHIPS FOR POST-DOCTORAL RESEARCH INTO CAUSES; DIAGNOSIS & TREATMENT OF NEUROMUSCULAR DISEASES. PREFERENCE TO THOSE WHO RECEIVED M.D.; PH.D.; D.SC. OR EQUIVALENT DEGREE WITHIN 3 YEARS OF STARTING DATE OF SUPPORT PERIOD.

100 RESEARCH FELLOWSHIPS PER YEAR. WRITE FOR COMPLETE INFORMATION.

1064

MYASTHENIA GRAVIS FOUNDATION INC (DR. KERMIT E. OSSERMAN POST-DOCTORAL RESEARCH FELLOWSHIP; BLANCHE MC CLURE POST-DOCTORAL RESEARCH FELLOWSHIPS)

53 W. JACKSON #660
CHICAGO IL 60604
312/427-8437

AMOUNT: $28000 SUPPORT SERVICES GRANT

DEADLINE(S): NOV 1

FIELD(S): MYASTHENIA GRAVIS

POST-DOCTORAL FELLOWSHIPS FOR FULL-TIME RESEARCH ON MYASTHENIA GRAVIS OR RELATED CONDITIONS UNDER SUPERVISION OF A SPECIFIED PRECEPTOR.

WRITE FOR COMPLETE INFORMATION.

1065

MYASTHENIA GRAVIS FOUNDATION INC (HENRY R.VIETS FELLOWSHIP)

53 W. JACKSON #660
CHICAGO IL 60604
312/427-6252

AMOUNT: $2000

DEADLINE(S): MAR 15

FIELD(S): MYASTHENIA GRAVIS

OPEN TO MEDICAL OR PRE-MEDICAL STUDENTS PURSUING EITHER BASIC OR CLINICAL RESEARCH RELATED TO PROBLEMS OF MYASTHENIA GRAVIS UNDER THE SUPERVISION OF SPECIFIED PRECEPTOR; EITHER IN OWN MEDICAL SCHOOL OR IN ANOTHER NEAR PLACE OF RESIDENCE.

4 TO 8 FELLOWSHIPS PER YEAR. RENEWABLE. WRITE FOR COMPLETE INFORMATION.

1066

NATIONAL HEMOPHILIA FOUNDATION (JUDITH GRAHAM POOLE POST-DOCTORAL RESEARCH FELLOWSHIPS)

110 GREENE ST - STE 303
NEW YORK NY 10012
212/219-8180; FAX 212/966-9247

AMOUNT: $35000

DEADLINE(S): DEC 15

FIELD(S): HEMOPHILIA RESEARCH

POST-DOCTORAL (MD OR PH.D) FELLOWSHIPS AWARDED THROUGH PROFESSIONAL AND GRADUATE SCHOOLS OR RESEARCH INSTITUTIONS FOR HEMOPHILIA-RELATED RESEARCH. NOT OPEN TO ESTABLISHED INVESTIGATORS OR FACULTY MEMBERS.

AWARDS FOR ONE YEAR. RENEWABLE DEPENDING ON DEMONSTRATED PROGRESS. WRITE TO GILLIAM EARNEST; MS; AT ADDRESS ABOVE FOR COMPLETE INFORMATION.

1067

NATIONAL INSTITUTE OF ARTHRITIS/ MUSCULO-SKELETAL & SKIN DISEASES (ARTHRITIS/BONE & SKIN DISEASES RESEARCH GRANTS)

NATIONAL INSTITUTES OF HEALTH; BLDG 31
ROOM 4C-32
BETHESDA MD 20892
301/496-0802

AMOUNT: VARIES

DEADLINE(S): VARIES

FIELD(S): ARTHRITIS/OSTEOPATHIC/ DERMATOLOGY RESEARCH

DOCTORAL AND POST-DOCTORAL RESEARCH GRANTS FOR LABORATORY AND CLINICAL RESEARCH ON ARTHRITIS AND RHEUMATIC DISEASES; BONE AND MUSCULO-SKELETAL DISEASES; AND CUTANEOUS DISEASES. US CITIZEN.

40 FELLOWS AND 185 INSTITUTIONAL TRAINEES PER YEAR. WRITE FOR COMPLETE INFORMATION.

1068

NATIONAL RESEARCH COUNCIL (NRC POSTDOCTORAL & SENIOR RESEARCH ASSOCIATESHIP AWARDS)

ASSOCIATESHIP PROGRAMS GR430/D3; 2101
CONSTITUTION AVE. NW
WASHINGTON DC 20418
202/334-2760

AMOUNT: ANNUAL STIPEND FROM 27750 TO 44000 + BENEFITS

DEADLINE(S): JAN 15; APR 15; AUG 15

FIELD(S): CHEMISTRY; EARTH & ATMOSPHERIC SCIENCES; ENGINEERING & APPLIED SCIENCES; COMPUTER SCIENCE; MATHEMATICS; BIOLOGICAL & MEDICAL SCIENCES SPACE & PLANETARY SCIENCES; PHYSICS

POSTDOCTORAL & SENIOR ASSOCIATESHIP AWARDS FOR RESEARCH AT ONE OF 38 PARTICIPATING SPONSOR FEDERAL LABORATORIES. USA CITIZENSHIP REQUIRED FOR SOME OF THE SPONSOR LABORATORIES; MANY ARE OPEN TO FOREIGN NATIONALS.

WRITE FOR COMPLETE INFORMATION AND APPLICATION MATERIALS.

1069

NATIONAL SOCIETY TO PREVENT BLINDNESS (GRANT IN AID)

500 EAST REMINGTON RD
SCHAUMBURG IL 60173
708/843-2020

AMOUNT: $12000

DEADLINE(S): MAR 1

FIELD(S): OPHTHALMOLOGY AND VISUAL SCIENCES

POSTDOCTORAL GRANTS FOR RESEARCH THAT MAY LEAD TO ADVANCES IN PREVENTING BLINDNESS; TREATMENT AND CURE OF VISUAL DISORDERS; RESTORING VISION AND PRESERVING SIGHT.

AWARDS RENEWABLE FOR 1 YEAR. WRITE ADMINISTRATOR FOR BROCHURE AND APPLICATION.

1070

NATIONAL SOCIETY TO PREVENT BLINDNESS (POST-DOCTORAL RESEARCH FELLOWSHIP)

500 EAST REMINGTON RD
SCHAUMBURG IL 60173
708/843-2020

AMOUNT: $14000

DEADLINE(S): MAR 1

FIELD(S): OPTHALMOLOGY AND VISUAL SCIENCES

OPEN TO INDIVIDUALS WHO HOLD A DOCTORATE DEGREE WHO ARE INTERESTED IN ACADEMIC CAREERS INVOLVING BASIC OR CLINICAL RESEARCH IN OPTHALMOLOGY OR VISUAL SCIENCES.

AWARDS RENEWABLE FOR 1 YEAR. WRITE ADMINSTRATOR FOR BROCHURE AND APPLICATION.

1071

NATIONAL SOCIETY TO PREVENT BLINDNESS (STUDENT RESEARCH FELLOWSHIP)

500 EAST REMINGTON RD
SCHAUMBURG IL 60173
708/843-2020

AMOUNT: $1500 MAXIMUM ($500/MONTH)

DEADLINE(S): MAR 1

FIELD(S): OPTHALMOLOGY AND VISUAL SCIENCES

STIPEND OPEN TO UNDERGRADUATES; MEDICAL STUDENTS OR GRADUATE STUDENTS FOR FULL TIME EXTRACURRICULAR EYE-RELATED RESEARCH DURING THE SUMMER MONTHS.

WRITE ADMINISTRATOR FOR BROCHURE AND APPLICATION.

1072

ORENTREICH FOUNDATION FOR THE ADVANCEMENT OF SCIENCE (OFAS RESEARCH GRANTS)

910 FIFTH AVE
NEW YORK NY 10021
212/606-0836

AMOUNT: VARIES

DEADLINE(S): NONE SPECIFIED

FIELD(S): BIOMEDICAL RESEARCH

GRANTS OPEN TO APPLICANTS AT OR ABOVE POST-GRADUATE LEVEL IN SCIENCE OR MEDICINE AT ACCREDITED UNIVERSITIES & INSTITUTIONS IN THE USA. PREFERENCE TO RESEARCH FOCUSED IN DERMATOLOGY; AGING; ENDOCRINOLOGY & SERUM MARKERS FOR HUMAN DISEASE.

WRITE FOR COMPLETE INFORMATION.

1073

PFIZER PHARMACEUTICALS GROUP (PFIZER/ AGS POST-DOCTORAL FELLOWSHIP PROGRAM)

MEDICAL AFFAIRS PROGRAMS;
235 E.42ND ST
NEW YORK NY 10017
212/573-2880

AMOUNT: $40000 PER YEAR FOR 2 YEARS

DEADLINE(S): DEC 2

FIELD(S): GERIATRIC MEDICINE

POST-DOCTORAL RESEARCH FELLOWSHIPS IN GERIATRIC MEDICINE OPEN TO RECENT MD'S & DO'S WHO WILL COMPLETE THEIR RESIDENCY TRAINING BY JULY 1 OF YEAR FOLLOWING DEADLINE DATE.

WRITE FOR COMPLETE INFORMATION.

1074

PHARMACEUTICAL MANUFACTURERS ASSOCIATION FOUNDATION (FELLOWSHIPS FOR ADVANCED PRE-DOCTORAL TRAINING IN PHARMACOLOGY OR TOXICOLOGY)

1100 15TH STREET NW
WASHINGTON DC 20005
202/835-3400

AMOUNT: $6552 STIPEND + TUITION

DEADLINE(S): SEP 15

FIELD(S): PHARMACOLOGY/TOXICOLOGY

OPEN TO FULL-TIME IN-RESIDENCE PH.D CANDIDATES IN FIELDS OF PHARMACOLOGY OR TOXICOLOGY WHO HAVE COMPLETED AT LEAST 2 YEARS OF MEDICAL; PHARMACY; DENTAL OR VETERINARY SCHOOL IN USA.

APPROX 14 AWARDS PER YEAR. RENEWABLE. WRITE FOR COMPLETE INFORMATION.

1075

PHARMACEUTICAL MANUFACTURERS ASSOCIATION FOUNDATION (RESEARCH STARTER GRANTS)

1100 15TH STREET NW
WASHINGTON DC 20005
202/835-3400

AMOUNT: $10000 PER YEAR FOR 2 YEARS

DEADLINE(S): SEP 1

FIELD(S): PHARMACOLOGY; TOXICOLOGY; MORPHOLOGY; PHARMACEUTICS

RESEARCH STARTER GRANTS OPEN TO POST-DOCTORAL INSTRUCTORS; ASSISTANT PROFESSORS & INVESTIGATORS. PROGRAM INTENDED TO ASSIST THEM IN ESTABLISHING CAREERS AS INDEPENDENT INVESTIGATORS IN THE FIELDS ABOVE.

20 GRANTS PER YEAR. TENABLE AT USA INSTITUTIONS. WRITE FOR COMPLETE INFORMATION.

1076

SANDEE THOMPSON MEMORIAL SCHOLARSHIP FOUNDATION (SCHOLARSHIPS)

1211 NAPOLEON MANOR NE
LAWRENCEVILLE GA 30243
WRITTEN INQUIRY ONLY

AMOUNT: $500

DEADLINE(S): MAR 15

FIELD(S): MEDICINE; NURSING; PHYSICAL THERAPY; RELIGION

OPEN TO UNDERGRADUATE AND GRADUATE STUDENTS HAVING AN INTEREST IN SERVING HUMANINTY AND RELIEVING HUMAN SUFFERING. MUST HAVE MEDICAL OR RELIGIOUS ORIENTED CAREER GOAL WITH PHYSICAL THERAPY A HIGH PREFERENCE.

STUDENTS SHOULD BE ENTERING AT LEAST JUNIOR YEAR AT AN ACCREDITED COLEGE OR UNIVERSITY. FINANCIAL INFORMATION REQUIRED. SEND STAMPED; SELF ADDRESSED ENVELOPE FOR COMPLETE INFORMATION.

1077 ─────────────────────────

SUDDEN INFANT DEATH SYNDROME ALLIANCE (STUDENT RESEARCH FELLOWSHIP PROGRAM)

10500 LITTLE PATUXENT PKWY; STE 420
COLUMBIA MD 21044
301/964-8000

AMOUNT: $2000

DEADLINE(S): MAR 15

FIELD(S): SUDDEN INFANT DEATH SYNDROME RESEARCH

THE PROGRAM IS DESIGNED FOR STUDENTS IN MEDICINE AND RELATED PROFESSIONAL FIELDS. SHOULD HAVE COMPLETED AT LEAST SECOND YEAR OF STUDY AND BE ABLE TO SPEND AT LEAST EIGHT TO TWELVE WEEKS CONDUCTING RESEARCH AS IT RELATES TO SIDS.

WRITE FOR COMPLETE INFORMATION.

1078 ─────────────────────────

U.S. DEPT. OF HEALTH & HUMAN SERVICES (NATIONAL INSTITUTES OF HEALTH SUMMER GRADUATE PROGRAM)

BUILDING 31 ROOM B3C15
BETHESDA MD 20892
301/496-2403

AMOUNT: $8.13 - $17.87 PER HOUR (ESTIMATE - SALARY SCALE NOT AVAILABLE)

DEADLINE(S): MAR 16

FIELD(S): HEALTH SCIENCES RESEARCH

GRADUATE STUDENTS RECEIVE ON-THE-JOB TRAINING AT THE NIH IN SPECIALIZED AREAS RELATED TO THEIR INTEREST AND EXPERIENCE IN POSITIONS OF A PROFESSIONAL; SCIENTIFIC OR ANALYTIC NATURE. USA LEGAL RESIDENT.

WRITE FOR COMPLETE INFORMATION.

1079 ─────────────────────────

UNIVERSITY OF CAMBRIDGE (BURSARIES FOR MEDICAL RESEARCH)

BARTON ROAD
CAMBRIDGE CAMS CB3 9BB ENGLAND
0223-64811

AMOUNT: UP TO 300 POUNDS STERLING

DEADLINE(S): APR 30

FIELD(S): MEDICAL RESEARCH

OPEN TO PH.D CANDIDATES FOR BIOMEDICAL AND BIOCHEMICAL RESEARCH IN HUMAN OR ANIMAL MEDICINE AND RELATED AREAS AT WOLFSON COLLEGE. BURSARIES AWARDED ON MERIT OR NEED.

RENEWABLE. WRITE TO DR. E. CRUWYS; ADDRESS ABOVE; FOR COMPLETE INFORMATION.

1080 ─────────────────────────

WHITEHALL FOUNDATION INC (RESEARCH GRANTS-IN-AID)

249 ROYAL PALM WAY; SUITE 202
PALM BEACH FL 33480
407/655-4474; FAX 407/659-4978

AMOUNT: $15000 MAXIMUM

DEADLINE(S): ASSIGNED WHEN APPLICATION IS ISSUED

FIELD(S): INVERTEBRATE & VERTEBRATE NEUROBIOLOGY (EXCEPT HUMANS)

GRANTS-IN-AID OPEN TO ASSISTANT PROFESSORS & SENIOR SCIENTISTS FOR INVESTIGATIONS OF NEURAL MECHNAMISMS INVOLVED IN SENSORY; MOTOR OR OTHER COMPLEX FUNCTIONS OF THE WHOLE ORGANISM.

INITIAL APPROACH SHOULD BE A ONE PAGE LETTER SUMMARIZING THE PROJECT. WRITE FOR COMPLETE INFORMATION.

1081 ─────────────────────────

WHITEHALL FOUNDATION INC. (RESEARCH GRANTS)

249 ROYAL PALM WAY; SUITE 202
PALM BEACH FL 33480
407-655-4474 OR FAX 407-659-4978

AMOUNT: $40000 PER YEAR (AVERAGE)

DEADLINE(S): MAR 1; SEP 1; DEC 1

FIELD(S): INVERTEBRATE & VERTEBRATE NEUROBIOLOGY (EXCEPT HUMAN BEINGS)

OPEN TO ESTABLISHED SCIENTISTS OF ALL AGES WORKING AT ACCREDITED INSTITUTIONS. FOR INVESTIGATIONS OF NEURAL MECHANISMS INVOLVED IN SENSORY; MOTOR OR OTHER COMPLEX FUNCTIONS OF THE WHOLE ORGANISM AS THEY RELATE TO BEHAVIOR.

APPLICANTS MAY NOT BE SEEKING SALARY. WRITE FOR COMPLETE INFORMATION.

MEDICAL TECHNOLOGIES

1082

AMERICAN ART THERAPY ASSOCIATION (GLADYS AGELL AWARD FOR EXCELLENCE IN RESEARCH)

1202 ALLANSON ROAD
MUNDELEIN IL 60060
708/949-6064

AMOUNT: NOT SPECIFIED

DEADLINE(S): SEP 15

FIELD(S): ART THERAPY

OPEN TO AATA STUDENT MEMBERS. AWARD IS DESIGNED TO ENCOURAGE STUDENT RESEARCH AND GOES TO THE MOST OUTSTANDING PROJECT COMPLETED WITHIN THE PAST YEAR IN THE AREA OF APPLIED ART THERAPY.

US CITIZEN. WRITE FOR COMPLETE INFORMATION.

1083

AMERICAN DENTAL HYGIENISTS ASSN (GRADUATE FELLOWSHIP PROGRAM)

444 NORTH MICHIGAN AVE; SUITE 3400
CHICAGO IL 60611
312/440-8900

AMOUNT: $1500 MAXIMUM

DEADLINE(S): JAN 1 - MAY 1

FIELD(S): DENTAL HYGIENE EDUCATION

OPEN TO STUDENTS WHO WILL BE ENROLLED IN A FULL TIME GRADUATE PROGRAM IN THE YEAR THAT AWARD IS MADE. MINIMUM 3.0 GPA REQUIRED. MUST SUBMIT TRANSCRIPTS AND SHOW FINANCIAL NEED.

WRITE FOR COMPLETE INFORMATION.

1084

AMERICAN FOUNDATION FOR THE BLIND (RUDOLPH DILLMAN MEMORIAL SCHOLARSHIP)

15 WEST 16TH ST
NEW YORK NY 10011
212/620-2000; TDD 212/620-2158

AMOUNT: $2500

DEADLINE(S): APR 1

FIELD(S): REHABILITATION; EDUCATION OF BLIND & VISUALLY IMPAIRED

OPEN TO LEGALLY BLIND UNDERGRADUATE OR GRADUATE STUDENTS ACCEPTED TO OR ENROLLED IN AN ACCREDITED PROGRAM WITHIN THE BROAD AREAS OF REHABILITATION AND/OR EDUCATION OF THE BLIND AND VISUALLY IMPAIRED. USA CITIZEN.

THREE AWARDS PER YEAR. WRITE FOR COMPLETE INFORMATION.

1085

AMERICAN FOUNDATION FOR THE BLIND (TELESENSORY SCHOLARSHIP)

15 WEST 16TH ST
NEW YORK NY 10011
212/620-2000; TDD 212/620-2158

AMOUNT: $1000

DEADLINE(S): APR 1

FIELD(S): REHABILITATION; EDUCATION OF BLIND & VISUALLY IMPAIRED

OPEN TO LEGALLY BLIND UNDERGRADUATE & GRADUATE STUDENTS ACCEPTED TO OR ENROLLED IN AN ACCREDITED PROGRAM WITHIN THE BROAD AREAS OF REHABILITATION AND/OR EDUCATION OF THE BLIND AND VISUALLY IMPAIRED. USA CITIZEN.

WRITE FOR COMPLETE INFORMATION.

1086

AMERICAN KINESIOTHERAPY ASSOCIATION (SCHOLARSHIP PROGRAM)

PO BOX 611; WRIGHT BROS. STATION
DAYTON OH 45409
WRITTEN INQUIRY

AMOUNT: $500

DEADLINE(S): MAY 1

FIELD(S): KINESIOTHERAPY

OPEN TO STUDENTS WHO HOLD OR ARE IN THE PROCESS OF OBTAINING A DEGREE IN KINESIOTHERAPY; PLAN A CAREER IN KINESIOTHERAPY & ARE SPONSORED BY A CERTIFIED KINESIOTHERAPIST.

WRITE FOR COMPLETE INFORMATION.

1087

AMERICAN MEDICAL RECORD ASSOCIATION (FOUNDATION OF RECORD EDUCATION SCHOLARSHIP PROGRAM)

919 NORTH MICHIGAN AVENUE;
SUITE 1400
CHICAGO IL 60611
312/787-2672

AMOUNT: $3000

DEADLINE(S): AUG 1

FIELD(S): MEDICAL RECORDS

OPEN TO MASTER'S OR DOCTORAL CANDIDATES WHO ARE ACTIVE AMRA MEMBERS; CREDENTIALED MEDICAL RECORD PROFESSIONALS & HOLD A BACCALAUREATE DEGREE. AWARDS TENABLE AT ACCREDITED INSTITUTIONS IN THE USA. USA CITIZEN OR LEGAL RESIDENT.

WRITE FOR COMPLETE INFORMATION.

1088

AMERICAN MEDICAL RECORD ASSOCIATION (GRACE WHITING MYERS - MALCOLM T. MACEACHERN STUDENT LOAN FUND)

875 NORTH MICHIGAN AVENUE;
SUITE 1850
CHICAGO IL 60611
312/787-2672

AMOUNT: $1000 - $2400

DEADLINE(S): JUN 15; OCT 15

FIELD(S): MEDICAL RECORDS

OPEN TO UNDERGRADUATE STUDENTS BEGINNING THEIR FINAL YEAR OF AN ACCREDITED MEDICAL RECORD ADMINISTRATION OR MEDICAL RECORD TECHNOLOGY PROGRAM AND TO GRADUATE STUDENTS WORKING TOWARD A MASTERS OR PH.D IN THE MEDICAL RECORD FIELD.

APPLICANTS SHOULD BE FULL TIME STUDENTS AND USA CITIZENS.

1089

AMERICAN OCCUPATIONAL THERAPY ASSOCIATION (E.K. WISE LOAN PROGRAM)

1383 PICCARD DR; SUITE 203
ROCKVILLE MD 20849
301/948-9626

AMOUNT: UP TO $2000

DEADLINE(S): NONE

FIELD(S): OCCUPATIONAL THERAPY

OPEN TO FEMALES WHO ARE AOTA MEMBERS; HAVE A BA DEGREE & ARE ACCEPTED TO OR ENROLLED IN AN ADVANCED STANDING CURRICULUM OR A GRADUATE CURRICULUM FOR BASIC-PROFESSIONAL OCCUPATIONAL THERAPY EDUCATION. USA CITIZEN.

WRITE FOR COMPLETE INFORMATION.

1090

AMERICAN SOCIETY FOR MEDICAL TECHNOLOGY (EDUCATION & RESEARCH FUND-GRADUATE & ADVANCED STUDY SCHOLARSHIP PROGRAM)

2021 'L' STREET NW; SUITE 400
WASHINGTON DC 20036
202/785-3311

AMOUNT: $1000

DEADLINE(S): FEB 1

FIELD(S): MEDICAL TECHNOLOGY

PURPOSE IS TO ASSIST CLINICAL LABORATORY PRACTITIONERS AND EDUCATORS IN PURSUING GRADUATE OR ADVANCED STUDIES IN CLINICAL LAB SCIENCE OR RELATED SCIENCES. MUST HAVE PERFORMED CLINICAL LAB FUNCTIONS FOR AT LEAST 1 YEAR.

WRITE TO EXECUTIVE DIRECTOR AT ABOVE ADDRESS FOR COMPLETE INFORMATION. ENCLOSE STAMPED SELF ADDRESSED BUSINESS SIZE ENVELOPE.

1091

AMERICAN SOCIETY FOR MEDICAL TECHNOLOGY (EDUCATION & RESEARCH FUND-BAXTER HEALTH CARE HEMATOLOGY SCHOLARSHIPS)

2021 'L' STREET NW; SUITE 400
WASHINGTON DC 20036
202-785-3311

AMOUNT: $1000

DEADLINE(S): FEB 1

FIELD(S): HEMATOLOGY

SCHOLARSHIP FOR GRADUATE STUDY OR ADVANCED SPECIALTY STUDY. OPEN TO CLINICAL LABORATORY PRACTITIONERS & EDUCATORS WHO HAVE PERFORMED CLINICAL LABORATORY FUNCTIONS FOR AT LEAST ONE YEAR.

WRITE TO THE EXECUTIVE DIRECTOR AT ADDRESS ABOVE FOR COMPLETE INFORMATION. ENCLOSE STAMPED SELF ADDRESSED BUSINESS SIZE ENVELOPE.

1092

AMERICAN SOCIETY FOR MEDICAL TECHNOLOGY (EDUCATION & RESEARCH FUND-BAXTER HEALTH CARE DADE DIVISION IMMUNOHEMATOLOGY SCHOLARSHIP)

2021 'L' STREET NW; SUITE 400
WASHINGTON DC 20036
202-785-3311

AMOUNT: $1000

DEADLINE(S): FEB 1

FIELD(S): IMMUNOHEMATOLOGY

SCHOLARSHIP FOR GRADUATE STUDY OR ADVANCED SPECIALTY STUDY IN IMMUNOHEMATOLOGY. OPEN TO CLINICAL LABORATORY PRACTITIONERS & EDUCATORS WHO HAVE PERFORMED CLINICAL LABORATORY FUNCTIONS FOR AT LEAST ONE YEAR.

WRITE TO THE EXECUTIVE DIRECTOR AT ADDRESS ABOVE FOR COMPLETE INFORMATION. ENCLOSE STAMPED SELF ADDRESSED BUSINESS SIZE ENVELOPE.

MEDICAL TECHNOLOGIES

1093

AMERICAN SOCIETY FOR MEDICAL TECHNOLOGY (EDUCATION & RESEARCH FUND-ORTHO DIAGNOSTIC SYSTEMS IMMUNOHEMATOLOGY SCHOLARSHIPS)

2021 'L' STREET NW; SUITE 400
WASHINGTON DC 20036
202-785-3311

AMOUNT: $1000

DEADLINE(S): FEB 1

FIELD(S): IMMUNOHEMATOLOGY

SCHOLARSHIP FOR GRADUATE STUDY OR ADVANCED SPECIALTY STUDY. OPEN TO CLINICAL LABORATORY PRACTITIONERS & EDUCATORS WHO HAVE PERFORMED CLINICAL LABORATORY FUNCTIONS FOR AT LEAST ONE YEAR.

WRITE TO THE EXECUTIVE DIRECTOR AT ADDRESS ABOVE FOR COMPLETE INFORMATION. ENCLOSE STAMPED SELF ADDRESSED BUSINESS SIZE ENVELOPE.

1094

AMERICAN SPEECH-LANGUAGE-HEARING FOUNDATION (GRADUATE STUDENT SCHOLARSHIPS)

10801 ROCKVILLE PIKE
ROCKVILLE MD 20852
301/897-5700; FAX 301/571-0457

AMOUNT: $2000 - $4000

DEADLINE(S): JUN 15

FIELD(S): COMMUNICATION DISORDERS

OPEN TO FULL TIME GRADUATE STUDENTS IN COMMUNICATION SCIENCES AND DISORDERS PROGRAMS. $2000 AWARDS GO TO FOREIGN OR MINORITY STUDENT STUDYING IN THE USA AND TO A DISABLED STUDENT PURSUING GRADUATE STUDIES IN THE FIELD.

THERE ARE UP TO FOUR $4000 GENERAL GRADUATE STUDENT SCHOLARSHIPS. WRITE FOR COMPLETE INFORMATION.

1095

DAUGHTERS OF THE AMERICAN REVOLUTION (NSDAR OCCUPATIONAL THERAPY SCHOLARSHIPS)

1776 'D' ST NW
WASHINGTON DC 20006
202/879-3292

AMOUNT: $500 - $1000 (ONE TIME AWARD)

DEADLINE(S): FEB 15; AUG 15

FIELD(S): OCCUPATIONAL THERAPY; PHYSICAL THERAPY

OPEN TO GRADUATE AND UNDERGRAD STUDENTS ENROLLED IN AN ACCREDITED THERAPY PROGRAM IN THE USA. CANDIDATE MUST BE SPONSORED BY LOCAL DAR CHAPTER AND A USA CITIZEN. AWARDED BIANNUALLY BASED ON ACADEMIC EXCELLENCE; RECOMMENDATIONS; NEED.

SEND SELF ADDRESSED -STAMPED- ENVELOPE FOR COMPLETE INFORMATION.

1096

DELAWARE ACADEMY OF MEDICINE (STUDENT FINANCIAL AID-LOANS)

1925 LOVERING AVE
WILMINGTON DE 19806
302/656-1629

AMOUNT: $1000 - $5000

DEADLINE(S): MAY 15

FIELD(S): MEDICINE; DENTISTRY; ALLIED HEALTH FIELDS

DELAWARE RESIDENT. FOR FULL-TIME GRADUATE STUDY IN THE ABOVE AREAS AT ACCREDITED COLLEGES & UNIVERSITIES. USA CITIZEN OR LEGAL RESIDENT.

WRITE FOR COMPLETE INFORMATION.

1097

EASTER SEAL SOCIETY OF IOWA (SCHOLARSHIPS & AWARDS)

PO BOX 4002
DES MOINES IA 50333
515/289-1933

AMOUNT: $400 - $600

DEADLINE(S): APR 15

FIELD(S): PHYSICAL REHABILITATION; MENTAL REHABILITATION; & RELATED AREAS

OPEN TO IOWA RESIDENTS WHO ARE FULL-TIME UNDERGRADUATE SOPHOMORES; JUNIORS; SENIORS OR GRADUATE STUDENTS AT ACCREDITED INSTITUTIONS; PLANNING A CAREER IN THE BROAD FIELD OF REHABILITATION; FINANCIALLY NEEDY & IN TOP 40% OF THEIR CLASS.

6 SCHOLARSHIPS PER YEAR. RENEWABLE. WRITE FOR COMPLETE INFORMATION.

1098

EDWARD BANGS AND ELZA KELLEY FOUNDATION (SCHOLARSHIP PROGRAM)

243 SOUTH ST
HYANNIS MA 02601
508/775-3117

AMOUNT: UP TO $4000

DEADLINE(S): APR 30

FIELD(S): MEDICINE; NURSING; HEALTH
SCIENCES; RELATED FIELDS

OPEN TO RESIDENTS OF BARNSTABLE COUNTY
MASS. SCHOLARSHIPS ARE INTENDED TO
BENEFIT HEALTH AND WELFARE OF
BARNSTABLE COUNTY RESIDENTS. AWARDS
SUPPORT STUDY AT RECOGNIZED
UNDERGRADUATE; GRADUATE AND
PROFESSIONAL INSTITUTIONS.

FINANCIAL NEED IS A CONSIDERATION. WRITE
FOR COMPLETE INFORMATION.

1099

FAIRFAX COUNTY MEDICAL SOCIETY
FOUNDATION (SCHOLARSHIPS)

8100 OAK STREET
DUNN LORING VA 22027
703/560-4855

AMOUNT: $1500

DEADLINE(S): MAY 25

FIELD(S): MEDICAL DOCTOR; MEDICAL RELATED
DISCIPLINES; MEDICAL TECHNOLGOIES;
NURSING

OPEN TO UNDERGRADUATE AND GRADUATE
STUDENTS WHO ARE USA CITIZENS AND ARE
RESIDENTS OF FAIRFAX COUNTY; VA. FOR
STUDIES RELATED TO HUMAN HEALTH.
MUST DEMONSTRATE FINANCIAL NEED.

11 AWARDS PER YEAR; RENEWABLE. WRITE FOR
COMPLETE INFORMATION.

1100

FLORIDA DENTAL ASSOCIATION (DENTAL
HYGIENE SCHOLARSHIP PROGRAM)

3021 SWANN AVE
TAMPA FL 33609
813/877-7597

AMOUNT: VARIES

DEADLINE(S): JUL 1; DEC 1; APR 1

FIELD(S): DENTAL HYGIENE

OPEN TO RESIDENTS OF FLORIDA WHO HAVE
BEEN ACCEPTED FOR ENROLLMENT IN AN
ACCREDITED DENTAL HYGIENE SCHOOL IN
FLORIDA. PREFERENCE TO APPLICANTS
FROM AREAS IN FLORIDA WITH DENTAL
HYGIENIST SHORTAGES.

WRITE FOR COMPLETE INFORMATION.

1101

GENERAL FEDERATION OF WOMAN'S CLUBS
OF MASS. (COMMUNICATIONS DISORDER
SCHOLARSHIP)

PO BOX 679; 245 DUTTON RD
SUDBURY MA 01776
508/443-4569

AMOUNT: $500

DEADLINE(S): MAR 15

FIELD(S): SPEECH THERAPY

OPEN TO MASSACHUSETTS RESIDENT WHO HAS
APPLIED TO OR BEEN ACCEPTED AT SCHOOL
OF GRADUATE STUDY. US CITIZEN OR LEGAL
RESIDENT.

WRITE FOR COMPLETE INFORMATION. ENCLOSE
SELF ADDRESSED STAMPED ENVELOPE.

1102

INTERNATIONAL ORDER OF THE KING'S
DAUGHTERS AND SONS (HEALTH CAREERS
SCHOLARSHIPS)

PO BOX 1017
CHAUTAUQUA NY 14722
716/357-4951

AMOUNT: UP TO $1000

DEADLINE(S): APR 1

FIELD(S): MEDICINE; DENTISTRY; NURSING;
PHYSICAL THERAPY; OCCUPATIONAL
THERAPY; MEDICAL TECHNOLOGIES;
PHARMACY

OPEN TO STUDENTS ACCEPTED TO/ENROLLED IN
AN ACCREDITED USA OR CANADIAN 4-YR OR
GRADUATE SCHOOL. RN CANDIDATES MUST
HAVE COMPLETED 1ST YEAR; BA
CANDIDATES IN AT LEAST 3RD YEAR. PRE
MED STUDENTS -NOT- ELIGIBLE.

USA OR CANADIAN CITIZEN. THOSE SEEKING MD
OR DDS DEGREES MUST BE IN 2ND YR OF
MED OR DENTAL SCHOOL. FOR APPLICATION
SEND SASE TO MRS. MERLE RABER; 6024 E.
CHICAGO RD; JONESVILLE MI 49250.

1103

JEWISH VOCATIONAL SERVICE (MARCUS &
THERESA LEVIE EDUCATIONAL FUND
SCHOLARSHIPS)

1 SOUTH FRANKLIN STREET
CHICAGO IL 60606
312/346-6700 EXT 2214

AMOUNT: $5000

DEADLINE(S): MAR 1

FIELD(S): SOCIAL WORK; MEDICINE; DENTISTRY;
NURSING & OTHER RELATED PROFESSIONS &
VOCATIONS

OPEN TO COOK COUNTY RESIDENTS OF THE
JEWISH FAITH WHO PLAN CAREERS IN THE
HELPING PROFESSIONS. MUST SHOW
FINANCIAL NEED. FOR UNDERGRADUATE;
GRADUATE OR VOCATIONAL STUDY.
APPLICATIONS AVAILABLE BEGINNING DEC
1 FROM SCHOLARSHIP SECRETARY.

85-100 AWARDS PER YEAR. RENEWAL POSSIBLE
WITH REAPPLICATION. WRITE FOR
COMPLETE INFORMATION.

1104

LABAN/BARTENIEFF INSTITUTE OF MOVEMENT STUDIES (WORKSTUDY PROGRAMS)

11 E. 4TH ST.; 3RD FLOOR
NEW YORK NY 10003
212/477-4299

AMOUNT: $500 - $2500

DEADLINE(S): MAY 1

FIELD(S): HUMAN MOVEMENT STUDIES

OPEN TO GRADUATE STUDENTS & PROFESSIONALS IN DANCE; EDUCATION; HEALTH FIELDS; BEHAVIORAL SCIENCES; FITNESS; ATHLETIC TRAINING; ETC. FOR WORK STUDY -ONLY- AT THE LABAN/BARTENIEFF INSTITUTE IN THE LABAN MOVEMENT STUDIES CERTIFICATE PROGRAM.

WRITE FOR COMPLETE INFORMATION.

1105

MARYLAND HIGHER EDUCATION COMMISSION (REIMBURSEMENT OF FIREFIGHTER & RESCUE SQUAD MEMBERS)

STATE SCHOLARSHIP ADMINISTRATION; 16 FRANCIS ST.
ANNAPOLIS MD 21401
410/974-5370

AMOUNT: TUITION REIMBURSEMENT UP TO $2300

DEADLINE(S): JUL 1

FIELD(S): FIRE SERVICE OR EMERGENCY MEDICAL TECHNOLOGY

OPEN TO MARYLAND RESIDENTS AFFILIATED WITH AN ORGANIZED FIRE DEPARTMENT OR RESCUE SQUAD IN MARYLAND. FOR FULL OR PART TIME STUDY AT A MARYLAND INSTITUTION. REIMBURSEMENT MADE ONE YEAR AFTER SUCCESSFUL COMPLETION OF COURSE(S).

FOR UNDERGRADUATE OR GRADUATE STUDY IN MARYLAND. RENEWABLE. WRITE FOR COMPLETE INFORMATION.

1106

NATIONAL ASSOCIATION OF AMERICAN BUSINESS CLUBS (SCHOLARSHIPS)

PO BOX 5127
HIGH POINT NC 27262
919/869-2166

AMOUNT: $500 - $1500

DEADLINE(S): APR 15

FIELD(S): PHYSICAL THERAPY; MUSIC THERAPY; OCCUPATIONAL THERAPY; SPEECH-LANGUAGE PATHOLOGY; HEARING-AUDIOLOGY; THERAPEUTIC RECREATION.

OPEN TO UNDERGRADUATE JUNIORS; SENIORS & GRADUATE STUDENTS WHO HAVE GOOD SCHOLASTIC STANDING & PLAN TO ENTER PRACTICE IN HIS OR HER FIELD IN THE USA. GPA OF 3.0 OR BETTER (4.0 SCALE) AND USA CITIZENSHIP REQUIRED.

400-500 SCHOLARSHIPS PER YEAR. RENEWABLE WITH REAPPLICATION. WRITE FOR COMPLETE INFORMATION.

1107

NATIONAL ATHLETIC TRAINERS ASSOCIATION (NATA UNDERGRADUATE & GRADUATE SCHOLARSHIP PROGRAM)

2952 STEMMONS
DALLAS TX 75247
214/637-6282

AMOUNT: $1500

DEADLINE(S): FEB 1

FIELD(S): ATHLETIC TRAINER

SCHOLARSHIP PROGRAM OPEN TO STUDENT MEMBERS OF NATA WHO HAVE EXCELLENT ACADEMIC RECORD; HAVE EXCELLED AS STUDENT ATHLETIC TRAINER & HAVE COMPLETED AT LEAST THEIR FRESHMAN YEAR OF STUDY AT AN ACCREDITED COLLEGE OR UNIVERSITY IN THE USA.

30 AWARDS PER YEAR. WRITE TO NATA GRANTS & SCHOLARSHIPS COMMITTEE (ADDRESS ABOVE) FOR COMPLETE INFORMATION.

1108

NATIONAL STRENGTH & CONDITIONING ASSN (CHALLENGE SCHOLARSHIPS)

PO BOX 81410
LINCOLN NE 68501
402/472-3000

AMOUNT: $1000

DEADLINE(S): APR 17

FIELD(S): FIELDS RELATED TO STRENGTH & CONDITIONING

OPEN TO NATIONAL STRENGTH & CONDITIONING ASSN MEMBERS. AWARDS ARE FOR UNDERGRADUATE OR GRADUATE STUDY.

WRITE FOR COMPLETE INFORMATION.

1109

ORGANIZATION OF AMERICAN STATES DEPT OF FELLOWSHIPS & TRAINING (OAS PRA-FELLOWSHIPS)

TRAINEE SELECTION DIVISION
WASHINGTON DC 20006
202/789-3902

AMOUNT: TUITION + FEES; TRAVEL EXP & STIPEND

DEADLINE(S): APR 30; AUG 31

FIELD(S): ALL FIELDS EXCEPT MEDICINE & FOREIGN LANGUAGES

GRADUATE FELLOWSHIPS FOR USA CITIZENS OR PERMANENT RESIDENTS TO STUDY IN AN OAS MEMBER COUNTRY. MUST HAVE UNDERGRADUATE DEGREE AND HAVE DEMONSTRATED ABILITY TO PURSUE ADVANCED STUDIES IN CHOSEN FIELD.

APPLICANTS SHOULD BE FLUENT IN LANGUAGE OF COUNTRY OF INTENDED STUDY. PRIORITY IS GIVEN TO RESEARCH PROJECTS. WRITE FOR COMPLETE INFORMATION.

1110 ————————————————

SANDEE THOMPSON MEMORIAL SCHOLARSHIP FOUNDATION (SCHOLARSHIPS)

1211 NAPOLEON MANOR NE
LAWRENCEVILLE GA 30243
WRITTEN INQUIRY ONLY

AMOUNT: $500

DEADLINE(S): MAR 15

FIELD(S): MEDICINE; NURSING; PHYSICAL THERAPY; RELIGION

OPEN TO UNDERGRADUATE AND GRADUATE STUDENTS HAVING AN INTEREST IN SERVING HUMANINTY AND RELIEVING HUMAN SUFFERING. MUST HAVE MEDICAL OR RELIGIOUS ORIENTED CAREER GOAL WITH PHYSICAL THERAPY A HIGH PREFERENCE.

STUDENTS SHOULD BE ENTERING AT LEAST JUNIOR YEAR AT AN ACCREDITED COLEGE OR UNIVERSITY. FINANCIAL INFORMATION REQUIRED. SEND STAMPED; SELF ADDRESSED ENVELOPE FOR COMPLETE INFORMATION.

1111 ————————————————

U.S. DEPT. OF HEALTH AND HUMAN SERVICES (NATIONAL HEALTH SERVICE CORPS SCHOLARSHIPS - PHYSICIAN ASSISTANTS)

US PUBLIC HEALTH RECRUITMENT;
8201 GREENSBORO DR SUITE 600
MCLEAN VA 22102
703/734-6855 OR 800/221-9393

AMOUNT: TUITION; FEES; EXPENSES PLUS MONTHLY STIPEND

DEADLINE(S): NONE SPECIFIED

FIELD(S): PHYSICIAN ASSISTANT

OPEN TO USA CITIZENS ENROLLED OR ACCEPTED FOR ENROLLMENT IN A BACCALAUREATE OR POST BACCALAUREATE PROGRAM LEADING TO CERTIFICATION AS A PRIMARY CARE PHYSICAN ASSISTANT.

RECIPIENTS ARE OBLIGATED TO SERVE IN A HEALTH PROFESSIONAL SHORTAGE AREA FOR ONE YEAR FOR EACH YEAR OF SUPPORT (MINIMUM OF TWO YEARS). WRITE OR CALL FOR INFORMATION ONE YEAR PRIOR TO APPLYING.

NURSING

1112 ————————————————

ACADEMY OF MEDICINE OF CLEVELAND AUXILIARY (HEALTH CAREERS COMMITTEE-SCHOLARSHIPS)

11001 CEDAR AVE
CLEVELAND OH 44106
216-229-2200

AMOUNT: $400 TO $600

DEADLINE(S): APR 1

FIELD(S): NURSING

MUST BE RESIDENT OF CUYAHOGA COUNTY OH; ACCEPTED TO AN ACCREDITED UNDERGRAD PROGRAM FOR A SPECIFIC HEALTH CAREER IN A CUYAHOGA COUNTY SCHOOL OR HEALTH CARE FACILITY; DEMONSTRATE FINANCIAL NEED AND HAVE A GPA OF 2.0 OR BETTER (4.0 SCALE).

CONTACT MAURINE M. RUGGLES ADDRESS ABOVE FOR COMPLETE INFORMATION.

1113 ————————————————

AMERICAN ASSOCIATION OF CRITICAL CARE NURSES (EDUCATIONAL ADVANCEMENT SCHOLARSHIP PROGRAM)

101 COLUMBIA
ALISO VIEJO CA 92656
714/362-2000 OR 800/899-2226 EXT 376

AMOUNT: $1500

DEADLINE(S): JAN 15 POSTMARK

FIELD(S): CRITICAL CARE NURSING

OPEN TO AACN MEMBERS WHO ARE RN'S AND ARE WORKING OR HAVE WORKED IN A CRITICAL CARE UNIT. FOR UNDERGRADUATE (JUNIOR OR SENIOR STATUS) OR GRADUATE STUDY. SHOULD HAVE WORKED CRITICAL CARE FOR 1 YR OF THE LAST 3 AND HAVE 3.0 OR BETTER GPA.

37 AWARDS FOR BACCALAURETE STUDY AND 17 FOR GRADUATE STUDY PER YEAR. AT LEAST 20% OF THE AWARDS WILL GO TO ETHNIC MINORITIES. WRITE FOR COMPLETE INFORMATION.

NURSING

1114

AMERICAN ASSOCIATION OF NURSE ANESTHETISTS (EDUCATIONAL LOANS)

216 HIGGINS ROAD
PARK RIDGE IL 60068
708/692-7050

AMOUNT: $500 - $2500

DEADLINE(S): NONE

FIELD(S): NURSE ANESTHETIST

LOANS AVAILABLE TO AANA MEMBERS & ASSOCIATE MEMBERS ENROLLED IN A SCHOOL OF ANESTHESIA APPROVED BY THE COUNCIL ON ACCREDITATION OF NURSE ANESTHESIA EDUCATIONAL PROGRAMS. LOANS ARE INTENDED TO COVER UNEXPECTED EVENTS OF AN EMERGENCY NATURE.

CONTACT THE FINANCE DIRECTOR ADDRESS ABOVE FOR COMPLETE INFORMATION.

1115

AMERICAN CANCER SOCIETY (SCHOLARSHIPS IN CANCER NURSING)

1599 CLIFTON ROAD NE
ATLANTA GA 30329
404/329-7617

AMOUNT: $8000 PER YEAR

DEADLINE(S): FEB 15

FIELD(S): CANCER NURSING

OPEN TO GRADUATE NURSING STUDENTS PURSUING A MASTER'S OR DOCTORAL DEGREE IN CANCER NURSING AT AN ACCREDITED INSTITUTION. USA CITIZEN OR LEGAL RESIDENT.

MASTER'S CANDIDATES RECEIVE 2-YEAR AWARDS; DOCTORAL CANDIDATES RECEIVE 4-YEAR AWARDS. WRITE FOR COMPLETE INFORMATION.

1116

AMERICAN COLLEGE OF LEGAL MEDICINE (STUDENT WRITING COMPETITION)

JAY A. GOLD; EXECUTIVE DIRECTOR;
611 E. WELLS ST.
MILWAUKEE WI 53202
414/276-1881

AMOUNT: $1000

DEADLINE(S): FEB 1

FIELD(S): LEGAL MEDICINE

AWARD FOR THE BEST PAPER ON ANY ASPECT OF LEGAL MEDICINE OPEN TO STUDENTS ENROLLED IN AN ACCREDITED SCHOOL OF LAW; MEDICINE; DENTISTRY; PODIATRY; NURSING; PHARMACY; HEALTH SCIENCE OR HEALTH CARE ADMINISTRATION IN THE USA OR CANADA.

AWARDS ARE GIVEN TO FIRST PLACE WINNER IN EACH OF THREE CATEGORIES. WRITE FOR COMPLETE INFORMATION.

1117

AMERICAN COLLEGE OF NURSE-MIDWIVES FOUNDATION (SCHOLARSHIPS PROGRAM)

1522 'K' STREET NW #1000
WASHINGTON DC 20005
202/289-0171

AMOUNT: $1000

DEADLINE(S): MAR 1

FIELD(S): NURSE-MIDWIFERY

SCHOLARSHIPS OPEN TO STUDENTS ENROLLED IN ACNM ACCREDITED CERTIFICATE OR GRADUATE NURSE-MIDWIFERY PROGRAMS. STUDENT MEMBERSHIP IN ACNM & COMPLETION OF ONE CLINICAL MODULE OR SEMESTER ALSO REQUIRED.

5-10 AWARDS PER YEAR. APPLICATIONS & INFORMATION AVAILABLE FROM VIOLET BARKAUSKAS CNM; UNIV OF MICHIGAN SCHOOL OF OB NURSING; 400 N. INGALLS; ANN ARBOR MI 48109-0604.

1118

AMERICAN LEGION AUXILIARY (PAST PRESIDENTS PARLEY NURSING SCHOLARSHIP)

STATE VETERANS SERVICE BUILDING
ST PAUL MN 55155
612/224-7634

AMOUNT: $500

DEADLINE(S): MAR 15

FIELD(S): NURSING

MINNESOTA RESIDENT WHO IS A MEMBER OF THE DEPT OF MINNESOTA AMERICAN LEGION AUXILIARY AND HAS A 2.0 OR BETTER GPA. TO HELP NEEDY & DESERVING STUDENTS OR ADULTS COMMENCE OR FURTHER THEIR EDUCATION IN NURSING AT A MINNESOTA SCHOOL.

WRITE FOR COMPLETE INFORMATION.

1119

AMERICAN NURSES' ASSN (ICN/3M NURSING FELLOWSHIP PROGRAM)

600 MARYLAND AVE SW SUITE 100W
WASHINGTON DC 20024
202/554-4444

AMOUNT: $7500

DEADLINE(S): AUG 30

FIELD(S): NURSING

DOCTORAL FELLOWSHIPS OPEN TO NURSES WHO ARE ENROLLED IN ACCREDITED NURSING PH.D PROGRAM. APPLICANT MUST BE MEMBER IN GOOD STANDING OF HER/HIS STATE NURSES' ASSN FOR AT LEAST 2 YEARS.

CONTACT ADDRESS ABOVE OR YOUR STATE ASSN FOR COMPLETE INFORMATION.

1120

AMERICAN NURSES' ASSN (MINORITY FELLOWSHIP PROGRAMS - CLINICAL/ RESEARCH TRAINING FOR RN'S)

600 MARYLAND AVE SW; SUITE 100W
WASHINGTON DC 20024
WRITTEN INQUIRY ONLY

AMOUNT: UP TO $7500 PER YEAR

DEADLINE(S): JAN 15

FIELD(S): BEHAVIORAL SCIENCES; CLINICAL MENTAL HEALTH

OPEN TO RN'S WHO ARE ENROLLED FULL TIME IN AN ANA-APPROVED ACADEMIC PROGRAM LEADING TO A DOCTORAL DEGREE IN BEHAVORIAL SCIENCES OR PSYCHIATRIC NURSING BY THE TIME A FELLOWSHIP IS AWARDED. MUST BE USA CITIZEN OR PERMANENT RESIDENT.

MUST BE MEMBER OF ETHNIC OR RACIAL MINORITY GROUP & COMMITTED TO A CAREER RELATED TO ETHNIC MINORITY HEALTH. APPLICATIONS ACCEPTED IN FALL AND MUST BE RECEIVED BY JAN 15. WRITE FOR COMPLETE INFORMATION.

1121

AMERICAN NURSES FOUNDATION (NURSING RESEARCH GRANTS PROGRAM)

600 MARYLAND AVE SW; SUITE 100W
WASHINGTON DC 20024
202/544-4444

AMOUNT: $2700

DEADLINE(S): MAY 1

FIELD(S): NURSING RESEARCH

GRANTS PROGRAM IS DESIGNED FOR BEGINNING NURSE RESEARCHERS. PRIORITY IS BASED ON THE SCIENTIFIC MERIT OF THE PROPOSAL WITH CONSIDERATION GIVEN TO THE INVESTIGATOR'S ABILITY TO CONDUCT THE STUDY.

APPLICANTS MUST BE USA REGISTERED NURSES WHO HOLD AT LEAST A BACHELOR'S DEGREE. APPROX 25 AWARDS PER YEAR. WRITE FOR COMPLETE INFORMATION.

1122

ASSOCIATION OF OPERATING ROOM NURSES (AORN SCHOLARSHIP PROGRAM)

SCHOLARSHIP BOARD;
2170 S. PARKER RD. SUITE 300
DENVER CO 80231
303/755-6300

AMOUNT: TUITION & FEES

DEADLINE(S): MAY 1

FIELD(S): NURSING

OPEN TO ACTIVE OR ASSOCIATE AORN MEMBERS FOR AT LEAST 1 CONSECUTIVE YEAR PRIOR TO DEADLINE DATE. AWARDS SUPPORT PRE-NURSING; BA DEGREE; MASTER'S DEGREE & DOCTORAL DEGREE PROGRAMS ACCREDITED BY THE NLN OR OTHER ACCEPTABLE ACCREDITING BODY.

FOR FULL OR PART-TIME STUDY IN THE USA. MINIMUM 3.0 GPA ON 4.0 SCALE. RENEWABLE. WRITE FOR COMPLETE INFORMATION.

1123

COMMANDER; NAVY RECRUITING COMMAND (ARMED FORCES HEALTH PROFESSIONS SCHOLARSHIPS)

4015 WILSON BLVD.
ARLINGTON VA 22203
WRITTEN INQURIY

AMOUNT: $749 PER MONTH STIPEND + TUITION; FEES; BOOKS; LAB FEES ETC.

DEADLINE(S): NONE SPECIFIED

FIELD(S): MEDICINE; DENTISTRY; OPTOMETRY AND NURSE ANESTHESIA (MASTER'S DEGREE)

OPEN TO USA CITIZENS ENROLLED OR ACCEPTED FOR ENROLLMENT IN ANY OF THE ABOVE FIELDS AT AN ACCREDITED INSTITUTION IN THE USA OR PUERTO RICO. MUST QUALIFY FOR APPOINTMENT AS A NAVY OFFICER AND SIGN A CONTRACTUAL AGREEMENT.

WRITE FOR COMPLETE INFORMATION.

1124

COMMONWEALTH FUND (EXECUTIVE NURSE FELLOWSHIP PROGRAM)

UNIV. OF ROCHESTER SCHOOL OF NURSING; 601 ELMWOOD AVE.
ROCHESTER NY 14642
716/275-2919

AMOUNT: $15000

DEADLINE(S): FEB 15

FIELD(S): NURSING/BUSINESS ADMINISTRATION

OPEN TO APPLICANTS WHO ARE ACCEPTED FOR FULL TIME STUDY IN A JOINT MSN-MBA PROGRAM OR WHO HOLD A MASTER'S OR DOCTORAL DEGREE IN NURSING AND ARE ACCEPTED FOR FULL TIME STUDY IN AN MBA PROGRAM.

WRITE FOR COMPLETE INFORMATION

1125 ————————————————

CUYAHOGA COUNTY MEDICAL FOUNDATION (SCHOLARSHIP GRANT PROGRAM)

11001 CEDAR AVE
CLEVELAND OH 44106
216/229-2200

AMOUNT: $500 - $1500

DEADLINE(S): JUN 1

FIELD(S): MEDICINE; DENTISTRY; PHARMACY; NURSING; OSTEOPATHY

GRANTS OPEN TO RESIDENTS OF CUYAHOGA COUNTY WHO ARE ACCEPTED TO OR ENROLLED IN AN ACCREDITED PROFESSIONAL SCHOOL IN ONE OF THE ABOVE AREAS. USA CITIZEN.

APPROX 40 AWARDS PER YEAR. WRITE FOR COMPLETE INFORMATION.

1126 ————————————————

DEKALB COUNTY PRODUCERS SUPPLY & FARM BUREAU (MEDICAL SCHOLARSHIP)

315 N. 6TH ST
DEKALB IL 60115
815/756-6361

AMOUNT: VARIES

DEADLINE(S): VARIES

FIELD(S): MEDICAL DOCTOR; NURSING

APPLICANTS OR THEIR PARENTS MUST HAVE BEEN VOTING OR ASSOCIATE MEMBERS OF DEKALB COUNTY FARM BUREAU FOR AT LEAST 2 YEARS PRIOR TO APPLICATION. MUST AGREE TO PRACTICE IN RURAL ILLINOIS COMMUNITY FOR 3 YEARS UPON COMPLETION OF TRAINING.

MUST HAVE BEEN ACCEPTED TO OR BE ATTENDING MEDICAL SCHOOL OR NURSING PROGRAM. WRITE TO VIRGINIA FLEETWOOD; ADDRESS ABOVE; FOR COMPLETE INFORMATION.

1127 ————————————————

DELAWARE ACADEMY OF MEDICINE (STUDENT FINANCIAL AID-LOANS)

1925 LOVERING AVE
WILMINGTON DE 19806
302/656-1629

AMOUNT: $1000 - $5000

DEADLINE(S): MAY 15

FIELD(S): MEDICINE; DENTISTRY; ALLIED HEALTH FIELDS

DELAWARE RESIDENT. FOR FULL-TIME GRADUATE STUDY IN THE ABOVE AREAS AT ACCREDITED COLLEGES & UNIVERSITIES. USA CITIZEN OR LEGAL RESIDENT.

WRITE FOR COMPLETE INFORMATION.

1128 ————————————————

EDWARD BANGS AND ELZA KELLEY FOUNDATION (SCHOLARSHIP PROGRAM)

243 SOUTH ST
HYANNIS MA 02601
508/775-3117

AMOUNT: UP TO $4000

DEADLINE(S): APR 30

FIELD(S): MEDICINE; NURSING; HEALTH SCIENCES; RELATED FIELDS

OPEN TO RESIDENTS OF BARNSTABLE COUNTY MASS. SCHOLARSHIPS ARE INTENDED TO BENEFIT HEALTH AND WELFARE OF BARNSTABLE COUNTY RESIDENTS. AWARDS SUPPORT STUDY AT RECOGNIZED UNDERGRADUATE; GRADUATE AND PROFESSIONAL INSTITUTIONS.

FINANCIAL NEED IS A CONSIDERATION. WRITE FOR COMPLETE INFORMATION.

1129 ————————————————

EPILEPSY FOUNDATION OF AMERICA (BEHAVORIAL SCIENCES STUDENT FELLOWSHIPS)

4351 GARDEN CITY DR. SUITE 406
LANDOVER MD 20785
301/459-3700

AMOUNT: $1500

DEADLINE(S): MAR 2

FIELD(S): EPILEPSY RELATED STUDY OR TRAINING PROJECTS.

OPEN TO UNDERGRAD AND GRAD STUDENTS IN NURSING; PSYCHOLOGY AND RELATED AREAS WHO PROPOSE A 3-MONTH EPILEPSY-RELATED PROJECT TO BE CARRIED OUT IN A USA INSTITUTION AT WHICH THERE ARE ONGOING EPILEPSY RESEARCH; SERVICE OR TRAINING PROGRAMS.

FELLOWSHIP MUST BE UNDERTAKEN DURING A FREE PERIOD IN THE STUDENT'S YEAR. WRITE FOR COMPLETE INFORMATION.

1130 ————————————————

FAIRFAX COUNTY MEDICAL SOCIETY FOUNDATION (SCHOLARSHIPS)

8100 OAK STREET
DUNN LORING VA 22027
703/560-4855

AMOUNT: $1500

DEADLINE(S): MAY 25

FIELD(S): MEDICAL DOCTOR; MEDICAL RELATED DISCIPLINES; MEDICAL TECHNOLGOIES; NURSING

OPEN TO UNDERGRADUATE AND GRADUATE STUDENTS WHO ARE USA CITIZENS AND ARE RESIDENTS OF FAIRFAX COUNTY; VA. FOR STUDIES RELATED TO HUMAN HEALTH. MUST DEMONSTRATE FINANCIAL NEED.

11 AWARDS PER YEAR; RENEWABLE. WRITE FOR COMPLETE INFORMATION.

1131

FLORIDA ENDOWMENT FUND FOR HIGHER EDUCATION (MCKNIGHT DOCTORAL FELLOWSHIP PROGRAM)

201 E.KENNEDY BLVD; SUITE 1525
TAMPA FL 33602
813/272-2772

AMOUNT: $11000 STIPEND + $5000 TUITION & FEES (PER YEAR)

DEADLINE(S): JAN 15

FIELD(S): ALL FIELDS (EXCEPT LAW; MEDICINE & EDUCATION)

OPEN TO ALL AFRICAN-AMERICANS WITH AT LEAST A BACHELOR'S DEGREE FROM AN ACCREDITED INSTITUTION WHO WISH TO PURSUE A DOCTORAL DEGREE. PROGRAM RECRUITS NATIONWIDE; HOWEVER FELLOWS MUST ENROLL IN A FLORIDA INSTITUTION. USA CITIZEN.

25 AWARDS PER YEAR. RENEWABLE FOR UP TO 5 YEARS. WRITE FOR COMPLETE INFORMATION.

1132

HARVEY AND BERNICE JONES FOUNDATION

PO BOX 233
SPRINGDALE AR 72765
501/756-0611

AMOUNT: VARIES

DEADLINE(S): NONE SPECIFIED

FIELD(S): NURSING

SCHOLARSHIPS AVAILABLE TO RESIDENTS OF SPRINGDALE AR WHO WANT TO PURSUE A CAREER IN NURSING. MUST BE USA CITIZEN AND DEMONSTRATE FINANCIAL NEED.

NUMBER OF AWARDS PER YEAR VARIES. CONTACT ADDRESS ABOVE FOR COMPLETE INFORMATION.

1133

HEADQUARTERS; DEPT. OF THE ARMY (ARMED FORCES HEALTH PROFESSIONS SCHOLARSHIPS)

ATTN; SGPS-PDE; 5109 LEESBURG PIKE
FALLS CHURCH VA 22041
WRITTEN INQURIY

AMOUNT: $749 PER MONTH STIPEND + TUITION; FEES; BOOKS; LAB FEES ETC.

DEADLINE(S): NONE SPECIFIED

FIELD(S): MEDICINE; DENTISTRY; OPTOMETRY AND NURSE ANESTHESIA (MASTER'S DEGREE); CLINICAL PSYCHOLOGY (PH.D)

OPEN TO USA CITIZENS ENROLLED OR ACCEPTED FOR ENROLLMENT IN ANY OF THE ABOVE FIELDS AT AN ACCREDITED INSTITUTION IN THE USA OR PUERTO RICO. MUST QUALIFY FOR APPOINTMENT AS AN ARMY OFFICER AND SIGN A CONTRACTUAL AGREEMENT.

WRITE FOR COMPLETE INFORMATION.

1134

HEADQUARTERS; USAF RECRUITING SERVICE (ARMED FORCES HEALTH PROFESSIONS SCHOLARSHIPS)

MEDICAL RECRUITING DIVISION
RANDOLPH AFB TX 78150
WRITTEN INQURIY

AMOUNT: $749 PER MONTH STIPEND + TUITION; FEES; BOOKS; LAB FEES ETC.

DEADLINE(S): NONE SPECIFIED

FIELD(S): MEDICINE; DENTISTRY; OPTOMETRY AND NURSE ANESTHESIA (MASTER'S DEGREE); CLINICAL PSYCHOLOGY (PH.D)

OPEN TO USA CITIZENS ENROLLED OR ACCEPTED FOR ENROLLMENT IN ANY OF THE ABOVE FIELDS AT AN ACCREDITED INSTITUTION IN THE USA OR PUERTO RICO. MUST QUALIFY FOR APPOINTMENT AS AN AIR FORCE OFFICER AND SIGN A CONTRACTUAL AGREEMENT.

WRITE FOR COMPLETE INFORMATION.

1135

INDIANA STATE STUDENT ASSISTANCE COMMISSION (NURSING SCHOLARSHIP FUND)

150 W. MARKET ST - 5TH FLOOR
INDIANAPOLIS IN 46204
317/232-2350

AMOUNT: UP TO $5000

DEADLINE(S): VARIES WITH COLLEGE

FIELD(S): NURSING

NURSING

OPEN TO INDIANA RESIDENTS ENROLLED IN AN UNDERGRADUATE NURSING PROGRAM AT AN INDIANA COLLEGE OR UNIVERSITY. APPLICANTS MUST HAVE A GPA OF 2.0 OR BETTER (4.0 SCALE).

MUST DEMONSTRATE FINANCIAL NEED. WRITE FOR COMPLETE INFORMATION.

1136

INTERNATIONAL ORDER OF THE KING'S DAUGHTERS AND SONS (HEALTH CAREERS SCHOLARSHIPS)

PO BOX 1017
CHAUTAUQUA NY 14722
716/357-4951

AMOUNT: UP TO $1000

DEADLINE(S): APR 1

FIELD(S): MEDICINE; DENTISTRY; NURSING; PHYSICAL THERAPY; OCCUPATIONAL THERAPY; MEDICAL TECHNOLOGIES; PHARMACY

OPEN TO STUDENTS ACCEPTED TO/ENROLLED IN AN ACCREDITED USA OR CANADIAN 4-YR OR GRADUATE SCHOOL. RN CANDIDATES MUST HAVE COMPLETED 1ST YEAR; BA CANDIDATES IN AT LEAST 3RD YEAR. PRE MED STUDENTS -NOT- ELIGIBLE.

USA OR CANADIAN CITIZEN. THOSE SEEKING MD OR DDS DEGREES MUST BE IN 2ND YR OF MED OR DENTAL SCHOOL. FOR APPLICATION SEND SASE TO MRS. MERLE RABER; 6024 E. CHICAGO RD; JONESVILLE MI 49250.

1137

JEWISH VOCATIONAL SERVICE (MARCUS & THERESA LEVIE EDUCATIONAL FUND SCHOLARSHIPS)

1 SOUTH FRANKLIN STREET
CHICAGO IL 60606
312/346-6700 EXT 2214

AMOUNT: $5000

DEADLINE(S): MAR 1

FIELD(S): SOCIAL WORK; MEDICINE; DENTISTRY; NURSING & OTHER RELATED PROFESSIONS & VOCATIONS

OPEN TO COOK COUNTY RESIDENTS OF THE JEWISH FAITH WHO PLAN CAREERS IN THE HELPING PROFESSIONS. MUST SHOW FINANCIAL NEED. FOR UNDERGRADUATE; GRADUATE OR VOCATIONAL STUDY. APPLICATIONS AVAILABLE BEGINNING DEC 1 FROM SCHOLARSHIP SECRETARY.

85-100 AWARDS PER YEAR. RENEWAL POSSIBLE WITH REAPPLICATION. WRITE FOR COMPLETE INFORMATION.

1138

MARYLAND HIGHER EDUCATION COMMISSION (PROFESSIONAL SCHOOL SCHOLARSHIPS)

STATE SCHOLARSHIP ADMINISTRATION; 16 FRANCIS ST
ANNAPOLIS MD 21401
410/974-5370

AMOUNT: $200 - $1000

DEADLINE(S): MAR 1

FIELD(S): DENTISTRY; PHARMACY; MEDICINE; LAW; NURSING

OPEN TO MARYLAND RESIDENTS WHO HAVE BEEN ADMITTED AS FULL-TIME STUDENTS AT A PARTICIPATING GRADUATE INSTITUTION OF HIGHER LEARNING IN MARYLAND OR AN UNDERGRADUATE NURSING PROGRAM.

RENEWABLE UP TO 4 YEARS. WRITE FOR COMPLETE INFORMATION AND A LIST OF PARTICIPATING MARYLAND INSTITUTIONS.

1139

MARYLAND HIGHER EDUCATION COMMISSION (PROFESSIONAL SCHOOL SCHOLARSHIPS)

STATE SCHOLARSHIP ADMINISTRATION; 16 FRANCIS ST
ANNAPOLIS MD 21401
410/974-5370

AMOUNT: SCHOLARSHIP $2400/YEAR; GRANT $2400/YEAR

DEADLINE(S): SCHOLARSHIP JUN 15; GRANT MAR 1

FIELD(S): NURSING

MD RESIDENT. FOR FULL OR PART TIME GRAD OR UNDERGRAD STUDY IN MD. MUST AGREE TO SERVE AS FULL TIME NURSE IN MD AFTER GRADUATION AND HAVE 3.0 OR BETTER GPA. MUST HOLD NURSING SCHOLARSHIP AND SHOW FINANCIAL NEED FOR LIVING EXPENSES GRANT.

RENEWABLE, WRITE FOR COMPLETE INFORMATION.

1140

MATERNITY CENTER ASSOCIATION (HAZEL CORBIN ASSISTANCE FUND-STIPEND AWARDS)

48 EAST 92ND ST
NEW YORK NY 10128
212/369-7300

AMOUNT: MONTHLY STIPEND-AMOUNT VARIES

DEADLINE(S): VARIES

FIELD(S): NURSE-MIDWIFERY

MONTHLY STIPEND FOR NURSE-MIDWIFERY STUDENTS (THEY MUST BE NURSES ALREADY) WHO ARE ENROLLED IN AN ACCREDITED SCHOOL OF MIDWIFERY AND WHO PLAN TO PRACTICE NURSE-MIDWIFERY IN THE USA FOR AT LEAST 1 YEAR UPON CERTIFICATION.

WRITE FOR COMPLETE INFORMATION.

1141

MISSISSIPPI BOARD OF TRUSTEES OF STATE INSTITUTIONS OF HIGHER LEARNING (NURSING EDUCATION SCHOLARSHIP GRANTS)

3825 RIDGEWOOD ROAD
JACKSON MS 39211
601/982-6570

AMOUNT: $3000

DEADLINE(S): NONE SPECIFIED

FIELD(S): NURSING

OPEN TO REGISTERED NURSES WHO HAVE LIVED IN MISSISSIPPI AT LEAST ONE YEAR AND ARE ENROLLED IN A NURSING PROGRAM AT AN ACCREDITED MISSISSIPPI INSTITUTION IN PURSUIT OF A BACHELOR OF SCIENCE OR GRADUATE DEGREE.

SCHOLARSHIPS ARE RENEWABLE. WRITE FOR COMPLETE INFORMATION.

1142

MISSOURI LEAGUE FOR NURSING (SCHOLARSHIPS)

PO BOX 104476
JEFFERSON CITY MO 65110
314/635-5355

AMOUNT: $100 - $5000

DEADLINE(S): SEP 30

FIELD(S): NURSING

OPEN TO STUDENTS WHO RESIDE IN MISSOURI AND ARE ATTENDING AN NLN ACCREDITED SCHOOL IN MISSOURI. FOR COURSE WORK LEADING TO LICENSING AS AN LPN OR RN OR TO A BSN OR MSN DEGREE. MUST DEMONSTRATE FINANCIAL NEED.

APPLICATION MUST BE MADE THROUGH THE DIRECTOR OF NURSING AT THE STUDENT'S SCHOOL.

1143

NAACOG - THE ORGANIZATION FOR OBSTETRIC; GYNECOLOGIC & NEONATAL NURSES (NAACOG FELLOWSHIPS)

409 12TH ST SW
WASHINGTON DC 20024
202-863-2434; 800-673-8499 EXT 2434

AMOUNT: $2000

DEADLINE(S): APR 1

FIELD(S): NURSING OBSTETRICS; GYNECOLOGY; NEONATOLOGY

OPEN TO MEMBERS AND ASSOCIATE MEMBERS OF NAACOG WHO ARE PURSUING OR ALREADY HAVE A NURSING DEGREE AT ANY LEVEL. SHOULD HAVE 2 YEARS EXPERIENCE IN THE ABOVE AREAS.

THREE AWARDS ANNUALLY. WRITE TO THE EDUCATION AND RESEARCH DEPARTMENT AT THE ADDRESS ABOVE FOR COMPLETE INFORMATION.

1144

NATIONAL ASSOCIATION OF PEDIATRIC NURSE ASSOCIATES & PRACTITIONERS (NAPNAP-MCNEIL SCHOLARSHIPS)

1101 KINGS HIGHWAY NORTH; SUITE 206
CHERRY HILL NJ 08034
609/667-1773

AMOUNT: $2000

DEADLINE(S): MAY 30 AND SEP 30 (POSTMARK)

FIELD(S): PEDIATRIC NURSING

SCHOLARSHIPS OPEN TO STUDENTS ENROLLED IN A GRADUATE PEDIATRIC NURSE PRACTITIONER PROGRAM. FINANCIAL NEED IS A MAJOR CONSIDERATION. MUST BE USA CITIZEN.

WRITE FOR COMPLETE INFORMATION.

1145

NATIONAL BLACK NURSES' ASSOCIATION INC. (DR. LAURANNE SAMS SCHOLARSHIP)

PO BOX 1823
WASHINGTON DC 20013
202/393-6870

AMOUNT: $1000

DEADLINE(S): APR 15

FIELD(S): NURSING

SCHOLARSHIPS FOR STUDENTS ENROLLED IN A NURSING PROGRAM (A.D.; DIPLOMA; BSN; LPN/LVN) WHO ARE IN GOOD SCHOLASTIC STANDING AND ARE MEMBERS OF THE ASSOCIATION.

WRITE FOR COMPLETE INFORMATION.

1146

NATIONAL CENTER FOR NURSING RESEARCH (NRSA RESEARCH FELLOWSHIPS)

NATIONAL INSTITUTES OF HEALTH; WESTWOOD BLDG; ROOM 754
BETHESDA MD 20892
WRITTEN INQUIRY

AMOUNT: $8800 PREDOCTORAL; $18600 - $32300 POSTDOCTORAL

DEADLINE(S): DEC 5; APR 5; AUG 5

NURSING

FIELD(S): NURSING RESEARCH

NURSING RESEARCH GRANTS OPEN TO PROFESSIONAL REGISTERED NURSES HOLDING A B.A. OR M.A. DEGREE IN NURSING OR A PH.D. USA CITIZEN OR LEGAL RESIDENT.

PREDOCTORAL FELLOWSHIPS ARE RENEWABLE UP TO 5 YEARS AND POSTDOCTORAL UP TO 3 YEARS. WRITE FOR COMPLETE INFORMATION.

1147 ───────────────────

NATIONAL FOUNDATION FOR LONG TERM HEALTH CARE (REGISTERED NURSE EDUCATION AWARD)

AMERICAN HEALTH CARE ASSOCIATION; 1201 L ST NW
WASHINGTON DC 20005
202/842-4444

AMOUNT: $1000

DEADLINE(S): JUL 31

FIELD(S): NURSING

AWARDS FOR INITIAL OR CONTINUING TRAINING IN A REGISTERED NURSE PROGRAM FOR PEOPLE WORKING IN LONG-TERM CARE FACILITIES ASSOCIATED WITH AMERICAN HEALTH CARE ASSOCIATION. FOR STUDY IN USA ONLY.

15-20 AWARDS PER YEAR. WRITE FOR COMPLETE INFORMATION.

1148 ───────────────────

NATIONAL STUDENT NURSES ASSN FOUNDATION (SCHOLARSHIP PROGRAM)

555 WEST 57TH STREET
NEW YORK NY 10019
212/581-2215

AMOUNT: $1000 TO $2500

DEADLINE(S): FEB 1

FIELD(S): NURSING

OPEN TO STUDENTS ENROLLED IN STATE APPROVED SCHOOLS OF NURSING OR PRE-NURSING IN ASSOCIATE DEGREE; BACCALAUREATE; DIPLOMA; GENERIC DOCTORATE OR GENERIC MASTER'S PROGRAMS. FINANCIAL NEED; GRADES; COMMUNITY ACTIVITES ARE CONSIDERATIONS.

APPLICATIONS AVAILABLE SEPTEMBER THROUGH JAN 15. SEND SELF ADDRESSED STAMPED (52 CENTS) LEGAL SIZE ENVELOPE FOR APPLICATION. APPLICATION MUST BE ACCOMPANIED BY $5 PROCESSING FEE.

1149 ───────────────────

NEW HAMPSHIRE POST-SECONDARY EDUCATION COMMISSION (NURSING EDUCATION ASSISTANCE GRANTS)

TWO INDUSTRIAL PARK DR
CONCORD NH 03301
603/271-2555

AMOUNT: $600 - $2000

DEADLINE(S): JUN 1; DEC 15

FIELD(S): NURSING

OPEN TO NEW HAMPSHIRE RESIDENTS WHO ARE ACCEPTED TO OR ENROLLED IN AN APPROVED NURSING PROGRAM IN THE STATE OF NEW HAMPSHIRE. USA CITIZEN OR LEGAL RESIDENT. MUST DEMONSTRATE FINANCIAL NEED.

APPROX 110 GRANTS PER YEAR. WRITE FOR COMPLETE INFORMATION.

1150 ───────────────────

NURSES' EDUCATIONAL FUNDS INC (ANA SCHOLARSHIPS)

555 WEST 57TH ST
NEW YORK NY 10019
212/582-8820

AMOUNT: $2500 - $10000

DEADLINE(S): MAR 1

FIELD(S): NURSING

OPEN TO RN'S WHO ARE USA CITIZENS OR WHO INTEND TO BECOME CITIZENS & HAVE BEEN ACCEPTED INTO A GRADUATE NURSING DEGREE PROGRAM ACCREDITED BY THE NLN. MUST BE A MEMBER OF A NATIONAL PROFESSIONAL NURSES' ASSOCIATION.

16 AWARDS PER YEAR. FOR FULL-TIME STUDY AT THE MASTER'S DEGREE LEVEL. STUDY AT DOCTORAL LEVEL CAN BE PART TIME. WRITE FOR COMPLETE INFORMATION.

1151 ───────────────────

NURSES' EDUCATIONAL FUNDS INC (ESTELLE M OSBORNE SCHOLARSHIP FUND)

555 WEST 57TH ST
NEW YORK NY 10019
212/582-8820

AMOUNT: $2500 - $4500

DEADLINE(S): MAR 1

FIELD(S): NURSING

OPEN TO BLACK RN'S WHO ARE WHO ARE ENROLLED IN AN ACCREDITED MASTER'S PROGRAM IN NURSING. USA CITIZEN.

FOR FULL-TIME STUDY. WRITE FOR COMPLETE INFORMATION.

1152

NURSES' EDUCATIONAL FUNDS INC (M ELIZABETH CARNEGIE SCHOLARSHIP)

555 WEST 57TH ST
NEW YORK NY 10019
212/582-8820

AMOUNT: $2500 - $10000

DEADLINE(S): MAR 1

FIELD(S): NURSING

OPEN TO BLACK RN'S WHO ARE WHO ARE ENROLLED IN AN ACCREDITED DOCTORAL PROGRAM IN NURSING. USA CITIZEN.

FOR FULL TIME OR PART TIME STUDY. WRITE FOR COMPLETE INFORMATION.

1153

OHIO LEAGUE FOR NURSING (GRANTS AND LOANS)

STUDENT AID COMMITTEE;
2800 EUCLID AVE - SUITE 235
CLEVELAND OH 44115
216/781-7222

AMOUNT: VARIES

DEADLINE(S): FEB 1 - MAY 1

FIELD(S): NURSING

OPEN TO NURSING STUDENTS WHO ARE RESIDENTS OF GREATER CLEVELAND AREA (CUYAHOGA; GEAUGA; LAKE; LORAIN COUNTIES) & WILL AGREE TO WORK IN A HEALTH-CARE FACILITY IN THIS AREA FOR AT LEAST A YEAR AFTER GRADUATION. USA CITIZEN OR LEGAL RESIDENT.

40-45 AWARDS PER YEAR. WRITE FOR COMPLETE INFORMATION.

1154

ONCOLOGY NURSING FOUNDATION (SCHOLARSHIPS)

501 HOLIDAY DRIVE
PITTSBURGH PA 15220
412/921-7373

AMOUNT: $1000 UNDERGRAD (10); $2500 GRADUATE (8); $2500 DOCTORAL (5)

DEADLINE(S): JAN 15

FIELD(S): NURSING

OPEN TO REGISTERED NURSES WHO ARE SEEKING A BACHELOR'S; MASTER'S OR DOCTORAL DEGREE IN AN NLN ACCREDITED NURSING PROGRAM & HAVE AN INTEREST IN ONCOLOGY NURSING.

WRITE FOR COMPLETE INFORMATION.

1155

ORGANIZATION OF AMERICAN STATES DEPT OF FELLOWSHIPS & TRAINING (OAS PRA-FELLOWSHIPS)

TRAINEE SELECTION DIVISION
WASHINGTON DC 20006
202/789-3902

AMOUNT: TUITION + FEES; TRAVEL EXP & STIPEND

DEADLINE(S): APR 30; AUG 31

FIELD(S): ALL FIELDS EXCEPT MEDICINE & FOREIGN LANGUAGES

GRADUATE FELLOWSHIPS FOR USA CITIZENS OR PERMANENT RESIDENTS TO STUDY IN AN OAS MEMBER COUNTRY. MUST HAVE UNDERGRADUATE DEGREE AND HAVE DEMONSTRATED ABILITY TO PURSUE ADVANCED STUDIES IN CHOSEN FIELD.

APPLICANTS SHOULD BE FLUENT IN LANGUAGE OF COUNTRY OF INTENDED STUDY. PRIORITY IS GIVEN TO RESEARCH PROJECTS. WRITE FOR COMPLETE INFORMATION.

1156

SANDEE THOMPSON MEMORIAL SCHOLARSHIP FOUNDATION (SCHOLARSHIPS)

1211 NAPOLEON MANOR NE
LAWRENCEVILLE GA 30243
WRITTEN INQUIRY ONLY

AMOUNT: $500

DEADLINE(S): MAR 15

FIELD(S): MEDICINE; NURSING; PHYSICAL THERAPY; RELIGION

OPEN TO UNDERGRADUATE AND GRADUATE STUDENTS HAVING AN INTEREST IN SERVING HUMANINTY AND RELIEVING HUMAN SUFFERING. MUST HAVE MEDICAL OR RELIGIOUS ORIENTED CAREER GOAL WITH PHYSICAL THERAPY A HIGH PREFERENCE.

STUDENTS SHOULD BE ENTERING AT LEAST JUNIOR YEAR AT AN ACCREDITED COLEGE OR UNIVERSITY. FINANCIAL INFORMATION REQUIRED. SEND STAMPED; SELF ADDRESSED ENVELOPE FOR COMPLETE INFORMATION.

1157

SIGMA THETA TAU INTERNATIONAL (RESEARCH GRANTS)

550 WEST NORTH STREET
INDIANAPOLIS IN 46202
317/634-8171

AMOUNT: $3000

DEADLINE(S): MAR 1

FIELD(S): NURSING RESEARCH

NURSING

RESEARCH GRANTS TO SUPPORT WELL-DEFINED RESEARCH PROJECT PERTINENT TO NURSING. PREFERENCE WILL BE GIVEN TO SIGMA THETA TAU MEMBERS. OPEN TO REGISTERED NURSES WHO HAVE THEIR MASTERS DEGREE IN NURSING.

ALTHOUGH FUNDS MAY BE USED TO SUPPORT DISSERTAION RESEARCH THE DISSERTATION IS NOT ACCEPTABLE AS THE FINAL REPORT. WRITE FOR COMPLETE INFORMATION.

1158

U.S. DEPT. OF EDUCATION (INDIAN GRADUATE PROFESSIONAL FELLOWSHIPS)

400 MARYLAND AVENUE SW; RM 2177; MAIL STOP 6335
WASHINGTON DC 20202
202/401-1902

AMOUNT: $1000 - $34000 (AVERAGE $13000)

DEADLINE(S): FEB 7

FIELD(S): MEDICINE; PSYCHOLOGY; LAW; EDUCATION; RELATED FIELDS

FELLOWSHIPS FOR AMERICAN INDIANS OR ALASKAN NATIVES WHO ARE US CITZENS AND SEEKING GRADUATE DEREEES IN THE ABOVE FIELDS AT ACCREDITED INSTITUTIONS IN USA.

APPROXIMATELY 90 CONTINUATION AND 35 NEW AWARDS. WRITE FOR COMPLETE INFORMATION.

1159

U.S. DEPT. OF HEALTH AND HUMAN SERVICES-DIVISION OF NURSING (NURSE PRACTIONER; NURSE MIDWIFE SCHOLARSHIPS)

MCLEAN VA 22102
ROCKVILLE MD 20857
703/734-6855 OR 800/221-9393

AMOUNT: TUITION; FEES; EDUCATIONAL EXPENSES; MONTHLY STIPEND

DEADLINE(S): NONE SPECIFIED

FIELD(S): NURSE MIDWIFERY; NURSE PRACTITIONER

OPEN TO REGISTERED NURSES (THROUGH THEIR EDUCATIONAL INSTITUTIONS) FOR FULL-TIME GRADUATE STUDY IN PURSUIT OF A MASTER'S OR POST BACCALAUREATE PROGRAMS FOR NURSE PRACTITIONERS OR NURSE MIDWIVES.

RECIPIENTS ARE OBLIGATED TO SERVE IN A HEALTH PROFESSIONAL SHORTAGE AREA FOR AT LEAST TWO YEARS. WRITE FOR COMPLETE INFORMATION ONE YEAR PRIOR TO APPLYING.

1160

VIRGIN ISLANDS BOARD OF EDUCATION (NURSING & OTHER HEALTH SCHOLARSHIPS)

PO BOX 11900
ST THOMAS VI 00801
809/774-4546

AMOUNT: UP TO $1800

DEADLINE(S): MAR 31

FIELD(S): NURSING; MEDICINE; HEALTH RELATED AREAS

OPEN TO BONAFIDE RESIDENTS OF THE VIRGIN ISLANDS WHO ARE ACCEPTED BY AN ACCREDITED SCHOOL OF NURSING OR AN ACCREDITED INSTITUTION OFFERING COURSES IN ONE OF THE HEALTH RELATED FIELDS.

THIS SCHOLARSHIP IS GRANTED FOR ONE ACADEMIC YEAR. RECIPIENTS MAY REAPPLY WITH AT LEAST A 'C' AVERAGE. WRITE FOR COMPLETE INFORMATION.

1161

VIRGINIA BAPTIST GENERAL BOARD (JULIAN A HUDGENS TRUST FUND)

PO BOX 8568
RICHMOND VA 23226
WRITTEN INQUIRY

AMOUNT: VARIES

DEADLINE(S): AUG

FIELD(S): NURSING

OPEN TO RESIDENTS OF VIRGINIA WHO ARE PURSUING A CAREER AS A NURSING MISSIONARY & ARE A MEMBER OF A CHURCH ASSOCIATED WITH THE BAPTIST GENERAL ASSN OF VIRGINIA.

LOANS ARE NON-REPAYABLE IF RECIPIENT WORKS AS A MISSIONARY FOR 2 YEARS. WRITE FOR COMPLETE INFORMATION.

1162

VIRGINIA DEPARTMENT OF HEALTH - PUBLIC HEALTH NURSING (VIRGINIA STATE NURSING SCHOLARSHIPS)

1500 E. MAIN ST.; PO BOX 2448
RICHMOND VA 23218
WRITTEN INQUIRY

AMOUNT: $150 - $2000

DEADLINE(S): APR 30 FOR ENROLLED STUDENTS; JUN 30 FOR ENTERING STUDENTS.

FIELD(S): NURSING

OPEN TO VIRGINIA RESIDENTS ENROLLED OR ACCEPTED IN A VIRGINIA SCHOOL OF NURSING. FOR FULL TIME STUDY LEADING TO AN UNDERGRADUATE OR GRADUATE NURSING DEGREE. MUST AGREE TO ENGAGE IN FULL TIME NURSING PRACTICE IN VIRGINIA UPON GRADUATION.

SCHOLARSHIPS ARE RENEWABLE. MUST DEMONSTRATE FINANCIAL NEED AND HAVE AT LEAST A 2.5 CUMULATIVE GRADE POINT AVERAGE. WRITE FOR COMPLETE INFORMATION.

1163

WISCONSIN LEAGUE FOR NURSING INC (SCHOLARSHIP)

2121 EAST NEWPORT AVE
MILWAUKEE WI 53211
414/332-6271

AMOUNT: $500

DEADLINE(S): FEB 28

FIELD(S): NURSING

WISC RESIDENT ENROLLED IN NATIONAL LEAGUE FOR NURSING ACCREDITED PROGRAM IN WISC. CATEGORIES- RN SEEKING BSN/STUDENT SEEKING RN (ADN DIPLOMA OR BSN)/BSN-RN'S SEEKING MSN. GPA 3.0 OR BETTER. HALFWAY THROUGH ACADEMIC PROGRAM. US

MUST DEMONSTRATE FINANCIAL NEED AND BE RECOMMENDED BY DEAN OR DIRECTOR. WRITE FOR COMPLETE INFORMATION.

NUTRITION

1164

ABBIE SARGENT MEMORIAL SCHOLARSHIP INC (SCHOLARSHIPS)

295 SHEEP DAVIS ROAD
CONCORD NH 03301
603/224-1934

AMOUNT: $200

DEADLINE(S): MAR 15

FIELD(S): AGRICULTURE; VETERINARY MEDICINE; HOME ECONOMICS

OPEN TO NEW HAMPSHIRE RESIDENT WHO IS HIGH SCHOOL GRADUATE WITH GOOD GRADES AND CHARACTER. FOR UNDERGRADUATE OR GRADUATE STUDY. USA LEGAL RESIDENT. DEMONSTRATE FINANCIAL NEED.

RENEWABLE WITH REAPPLICATION. WRITE FOR COMPLETE INFORMATION.

1165

AMERICAN ASSOCIATION OF CEREAL CHEMISTS (UNDERGRADUATE SCHOLARSHIPS AND GRADUATE FELLOWSHIPS)

SCHOLARSHIP DEPT.;
3340 PILOT KNOB RD.
ST PAUL MN 55121
612/454-7250

AMOUNT: $1000 - $2000 UNDERGRAD; $2000 - $3000 GRAD

DEADLINE(S): APR 1

FIELD(S): FOOD SCIENCE

SCHOLARSHIPS AND FELLOWSHIPS OPEN TO STUDENTS MAJORING IN OR INTERESTED IN A CAREER IN CEREAL SCIENCE OR TECHNOLOGY; INCLUDING BAKING OR RELATED AREA. STRONG ACADEMIC RECORD AND CAREER INTEREST ARE THE IMPORTANT CRITERIA.

AACC MEMBERSHIP IS HELPFUL BUT NOT NECESSARY. WRITE FOR COMPLETE INFORMATION.

1166

AMERICAN DIETETIC ASSOCIATION FOUNDATION (DIETETIC INTERNSHIPS)

216 WEST JACKSON BLVD - SUITE 800
CHICAGO IL 60606
800/877-1600 EXT 4876

AMOUNT: $250 - $2500

DEADLINE(S): FEB 13 - REQUEST APPLICATION BY JAN 15

FIELD(S): DIETETIC INTERNSHIPS

OPEN TO STUDENTS WHO HAVE APPLIED TO AN ADA-ACCREDITED DIETETIC INTERNSHIP AND WHO SHOW PROMISE OF BEING A VALUABLE CONTRIBUTING MEMBER TO THE PROFESSION. USA CITIZENSHIP REQUIRED.

FINANCIAL NEED; PROFESSIONAL POTENTIAL & SCHOLARSHIP ARE CONSIDERATIONS. WRITE FOR COMPLETE INFORMATION.

1167

AMERICAN DIETETIC ASSOCIATION FOUNDATION (GRADUATE SCHOLARSHIPS)

216 WEST JACKSON - SUITE 800
CHICAGO IL 60606
800/877-1600 EXT 4877

AMOUNT: $250 - $2500

DEADLINE(S): FEB 13

FIELD(S): DIETETICS; NUTRITION

OPEN TO GRADUATE STUDENTS WHO INTEND TO PRACTICE IN THE FIELD OF DIETETICS. SOME SCHOLARSHIPS REQUIRE SPECIFIC AREAS OF STUDY AND STATUS AS A REGISTERED DIETICIAN. USA CITIZENSHIP REQUIRED.

REQUEST APPLICATIONS BETWEEN SEP 15 & JAN 15. COMPLETED APPLICATIONS MUST BE POSTMARKED BY FEB 15. FINANCIAL NEED IS A CONSIDERATION. WRITE FOR COMPLETE INFORMATION.

1168 ─────────────────

AMERICAN DIETETIC ASSOCIATION FOUNDATION (KRAFT GENERAL FOODS FELLOWSHIP PROGRAM)

216 WEST JACKSON - SUITE 800
CHICAGO IL 60606
312/899-0040

AMOUNT: $10000 PER YEAR

DEADLINE(S): JUN 1

FIELD(S): NUTRITION

OPEN TO SENIOR UNDERGRADUATE & GRADUATE STUDENTS WHO PROPOSE TO PURSUE GRADUATE WORK RELATED TO NUTRITION RESEARCH OR NUTRITION EDUCATION & CONSUMER AWARENESS AT RECOGNIZED INSTITUTIONS IN THE USA. FOR CITIZENS OF USA; MEXICO & CANADA.

FELLOWSHIPS RENEWABLE FOR UP TO 3 YEARS. WRITE FOR COMPLETE INFORMATION.

1169 ─────────────────

AMERICAN DIETETIC ASSOCIATION FOUNDATION (PREPROFESSIONAL PRACTICE PROGRAM - AP4)

216 W JACKSON BLVD - SUITE 800
CHICAGO IL 60606
800/877-1600 EXT 4876

AMOUNT: $250 - $2500

DEADLINE(S): FEB 13 (REQUEST APPLICATION BY JAN 15)

FIELD(S): DIETETICS

OPEN TO UNDERGRADUATE AND GRADUATE STUDENTS WHO ARE ENROLLED OR PLAN TO ENROL IN AN ADA-APPROVED PREPROFESSIONAL PRACTICE PROGRAM AND WHO SHOW PROMISE OF BEING A VALUABLE CONTRIBUTING MEMBER OF THE PROFESSION. USA CITIZENSHIP REQUIRED.

FINANCIAL NEED; PROFESSIONAL POTENTIAL & SCHOLARSHIP ARE CONSIDERATIONS. WRITE FOR COMPLETE INFORMATION.

1170 ─────────────────

AMERICAN HOME ECONOMICS ASSOCIATION FOUNDATION (NATIONAL FELLOWSHIPS)

1555 KING ST
ALEXANDRIA VA 22314
703/706-4600

AMOUNT: $3000

DEADLINE(S): JAN 15

FIELD(S): HOME ECONOMICS

ANNUAL FELLOWSHIPS OPEN TO GRADUATE STUDENTS WHO HAVE AT LEAST ONE YEAR OF PROFESSIONAL HOME ECONOMICS EXPERIENCE OR TRAINEESHIP. STUDY IN AREAS OF ADMINISTRATION; AGING; CLOTHING; TEXTILES; OR HOME ECONOMICS COMMUNICATION IS ENCOURAGED.

FOR USA CITIZENS OR PERMANENT RESIDENTS. APPLICATION FEE OF $15 FOR AHEA MEMBERS; $30 FOR OTHERS; MUST ACCOMPANY EACH REQUEST FOR APPLICATION FORMS. WRITE FOR COMPLETE INFORMATION.

1171 ─────────────────

DELAWARE ACADEMY OF MEDICINE (STUDENT FINANCIAL AID-LOANS)

1925 LOVERING AVE
WILMINGTON DE 19806
302/656-1629

AMOUNT: $1000 - $5000

DEADLINE(S): MAY 15

FIELD(S): MEDICINE; DENTISTRY; ALLIED HEALTH FIELDS

DELAWARE RESIDENT. FOR FULL-TIME GRADUATE STUDY IN THE ABOVE AREAS AT ACCREDITED COLLEGES & UNIVERSITIES. USA CITIZEN OR LEGAL RESIDENT.

WRITE FOR COMPLETE INFORMATION.

1172 ─────────────────

EDUCATIONAL FOUNDATION OF NATIONAL RESTAURANT ASSOC (TEACHER WORK-STUDY GRANT)

250 S.WACKER DR; SUITE 1400
CHICAGO IL 60606
312/715-1010

AMOUNT: $2000

DEADLINE(S): FEB 15

FIELD(S): FOOD MANAGEMENT/SCIENCE

GRADUATE FELLOWSHIPS FOR TEACHERS AND ADMINISTRATORS ENROLLED IN MASTERS OR DOCTORAL PROGRAM TO IMPROVE THEIR SKILLS IN TEACHING FOOD SERVICE COURSES OR ADMINISTERING FOOD SERVICE CAREER EDUCATION.

UP TO 25 GRANTS PER YEAR. WRITE FOR COMPLETE INFORMATION.

1173 ——————————————

EDUCATIONAL FOUNDATION OF NATIONAL RESTAURANT ASSOC (GRADUATE FELLOWSHIP)

250 S.WACKER DR; SUITE 1400
CHICAGO IL 60606
312/715-1010

AMOUNT: $1000 TO $2000

DEADLINE(S): FEB 15

FIELD(S): FOOD MANAGEMENT/SCIENCE

OPEN TO FULL TIME TEACHER OR ADMINISTRATOR OF A FOODSERVICE/ HOSPITALITY PROGRAM WHO IS ACCEPTED IN A GRADUATE DEGREE PROGRAM FOR THE FALL TERM. FOR THOSE WHO WANT TO IMPROVE SKILLS IN TEACHING OR ADMINISTRATION.

7 FELLOWSHIPS PER YEAR. WRITE FOR COMPLETE INFORMATION.

1174 ——————————————

FLORIDA ENDOWMENT FUND FOR HIGHER EDUCATION (MCKNIGHT DOCTORAL FELLOWSHIP PROGRAM)

201 E.KENNEDY BLVD; SUITE 1525
TAMPA FL 33602
813/272-2772

AMOUNT: $11000 STIPEND + $5000 TUITION & FEES (PER YEAR)

DEADLINE(S): JAN 15

FIELD(S): ALL FIELDS (EXCEPT LAW; MEDICINE & EDUCATION)

OPEN TO ALL AFRICAN-AMERICANS WITH AT LEAST A BACHELOR'S DEGREE FROM AN ACCREDITED INSTITUTION WHO WISH TO PURSUE A DOCTORAL DEGREE. PROGRAM RECRUITS NATIONWIDE; HOWEVER FELLOWS MUST ENROLL IN A FLORIDA INSTITUTION. USA CITIZEN.

25 AWARDS PER YEAR. RENEWABLE FOR UP TO 5 YEARS. WRITE FOR COMPLETE INFORMATION.

1175 ——————————————

HOTEL EMPLOYEES & RESTAURANT EMPLOYEES INTERNATIONAL UNION (EDWARD T. HANLEY SCHOLARSHIP)

1219 28TH STREET NW
WASHINGTON DC 20007
202/393-4373

AMOUNT: TUITION; FEES; ROOM & BOARD; VALUE OVER $6500 PER YEAR

DEADLINE(S): APR 1

FIELD(S): CULINARY ARTS

2 YR SCHOLARSHIP TO CULINARY INSTITUTE OF AMERICA IN NY. OPEN TO H.E.R.E. UNION MEMBERS (MINIMUM 1 YEAR) AND CANDIDATES RECOMMENDED BY UNION MEMBERS. APPLICATIONS ARE BY THE VICE PRESIDENTIAL DISTRICT IN WHICH THE MEMBER LIVES.

RESIDENTS OF ODD NUMBERED DISTRICTS APPLY IN ODD NUMBERED YEARS; EVEN NUMBERED DISTRICTS IN EVEN YEARS. APPLICATIONS ARE PUBLISHED IN JAN FEB & MAR EDITIONS OF "CATERING INDUSTRY EMPLOYEE." WRITE FOR COMPLETE INFORMATION.

1176 ——————————————

INSTITUTE OF FOOD TECHNOLOGISTS (GRADUATE FELLOWSHIPS)

221 NORTH LA SALLE STREET #300
CHICAGO IL 60601
312/782-8424

AMOUNT: $1000 - $10000

DEADLINE(S): FEB 1

FIELD(S): FOOD SCIENCE & TECHNOLOGY

OPEN TO SENIOR UNDERGRADS WHO WILL BE ENROLLED IN GRADUATE STUDIES WHEN FELLOWSHIP BECOMES EFFECTIVE; OR GRAD STUDENT WORKING TOWARD AN M.S. AND/ OR PH.D. APPLICANTS MUST BE SCHOLASTICALLY OUTSTANDING AND HAVE WELL ROUNDED PERSONALITY.

28 AWARDS PER YEAR. SOME RENEWABLE UPON REAPPLICATION. WRITE FOR COMPLETE INFORMATION.

1177 ——————————————

KAPPA OMICRON NU (ADVISER'S FELLOWSHIPS)

4990 NORTHWIND DR. SUITE 140
HASLETT MI 48840
517/351-8335

AMOUNT: $2000

DEADLINE(S): JAN 15

FIELD(S): HOME ECONOMICS

FELLOWSHIPS OPEN TO MEMBERS OF KAPPA OMICRON NU - NATIONAL HOME ECONOMICS HONOR SOCIETY. AWARDS SUPPORT FULL TIME STUDY IN HOME ECONOMICS AT THE GRADUATE OR POST-GRADUATE LEVEL.

WRITE FOR COMPLETE INFORMATION.

NUTRITION

KAPPA OMICRON NU (DOCTORAL FELLOWSHIPS)

4990 NORTHWIND DR. SUITE 140
EAST LANSING MI 48823
517/339-3324

AMOUNT: $2000

DEADLINE(S): JAN 15

FIELD(S): HOME ECONOMICS AND RELATED FIELDS

FELLOWSHIPS FOR DOCTORAL CANDIDATES OPEN TO KAPPA OMICRON NU MEMBERS WITH DEMONSTRATED SCHOLARSHIP; RESEARCH AND LEADERSHIP POTENTIAL. STUDY SHOULD BE AT A COLLEGE OR UNIVERSITY HAVING STRONG RESEARCH PROGRAMS AND SUPPORTING DISCIPLINES.

WRITE FOR COMPLETE INFORMATION.

1179

KAPPA OMICRON NU (MASTER'S FELLOWSHIPS)

4990 NORTHWIND DR. SUITE 140
EAST LANSING MI 48823
517/351-8335

AMOUNT: $1000 - $2000

DEADLINE(S): APR 1

FIELD(S): HOME ECONOMICS AND RELATED FIELDS

OPEN TO KAPPA OMICRON NU MEMBERS WHO HAVE DEMONSTRATED SCHOLARSHIP; RESEARCH AND LEADERSHIP POTENTIAL. FOR GRADUATE STUDY AT INSTITUTIONS WITH STRONG RESEARCH PROGRAMS AND SUPPORTING DISCIPLINES FOR THE CHOSEN MAJOR.

$2000 EILEEN C. MADDOX FELLOWSHIP IS AWARDED ANNUALLY; $1000 NATIONAL ALUMNI FELLOWSHIP IS AWARDED BIENNIALLY IN UNEVEN YEARS. WRITE FOR COMPLETE INFORMATION.

1180

KAPPA OMICRON NU (RESEARCH/PROJECT GRANTS)

4990 NORTHWIND DR. SUITE 140
EAST LANSING MI 48823
517/351-8335

AMOUNT: $3500

DEADLINE(S): DEC 15

FIELD(S): HOME ECONOMICS AND RELATED FIELDS

OPEN TO KAPPA OMICRON NU MEMBERS WHO HAVE DEMONSTRATED SCHOLARSHIP; RESEARCH; AND LEADERSHIP POTENTIAL. AWARDS ARE FOR HOME ECONOMICS RESEARCH AT INSTITUTIONS HAVING STRONG RESEARCH PROGRAMS.

WRITE FOR COMPLETE INFORMATION.

1181

ORGANIZATION OF AMERICAN STATES DEPT OF FELLOWSHIPS & TRAINING (OAS PRA-FELLOWSHIPS)

TRAINEE SELECTION DIVISION
WASHINGTON DC 20006
202/789-3902

AMOUNT: TUITION + FEES; TRAVEL EXP & STIPEND

DEADLINE(S): APR 30; AUG 31

FIELD(S): ALL FIELDS EXCEPT MEDICINE & FOREIGN LANGUAGES

GRADUATE FELLOWSHIPS FOR USA CITIZENS OR PERMANENT RESIDENTS TO STUDY IN AN OAS MEMBER COUNTRY. MUST HAVE UNDERGRADUATE DEGREE AND HAVE DEMONSTRATED ABILITY TO PURSUE ADVANCED STUDIES IN CHOSEN FIELD.

APPLICANTS SHOULD BE FLUENT IN LANGUAGE OF COUNTRY OF INTENDED STUDY. PRIORITY IS GIVEN TO RESEARCH PROJECTS. WRITE FOR COMPLETE INFORMATION.

1182

PHI UPSILON OMICRON NATIONAL OFFICE (FOUNDERS; CANDLE; DIAMOND ANNIVERSARY & PRESIDENTS FELLOWSHIPS)

208 MOUNT HALL; 1050 CARMACK ROAD
COLUMBUS OH 43210
614/421-7860

AMOUNT: UP TO $1500

DEADLINE(S): MAR 1

FIELD(S): HOME ECONOMICS

OPEN TO PHI U MEMBERS ENROLLED IN A DOCTORAL OR MASTER'S DEGREE PROGRAM IN HOME ECONOMICS. SELECTION FOR AWARDS IS BASED ON SCHOLASTIC RECORD; PARTICIPATION IN PHI U; AHEA AND OTHER ACTIVITIES.

WRITE FOR COMPLETE INFORMATION.

1183

PHI UPSILON OMICRON NATIONAL OFFICE (JANICE CORY BULLOCK SCHOLARSHIP)

208 MOUNT HALL; 1050 CARMACK ROAD
COLUMBUS OH 43210
614/421-7860

AMOUNT: $500

SCHOOL OF SOCIAL SCIENCE

DEADLINE(S): MAR 1

FIELD(S): HOME ECONOMICS

OPEN TO PHI U HOMEMAKERS WHO DESIRE TO CONTINUE AN EDUCATION FOR EITHER UNDERGRADUATE OR GRADUATE WORK IN HOME ECONOMICS WHICH WILL ENABLE HER TO BE GAINFULLY EMPLOYED.

WRITE FOR COMPLETE INFORMATION.

1184

SCHOOL FOOD SERVICE FOUNDATION (SCHOLARSHIPS AND LOANS)

1600 DUKE ST - 7TH FLOOR
ALEXANDRIA VA 22314
703-739-3900 OR 800-877-8822

AMOUNT: $150 - $1000

DEADLINE(S): APR 15

FIELD(S): FOOD SCIENCE & NUTRITION; FOOD SERVICE MANAGEMENT

OPEN TO ASFSA MEMBERS FOR GRADUATE OR UNDERGRADUATE STUDY IN THE ABOVE FIELDS. 3 SCHOLARSHIP PROGRAMS ARE OFFERED TO THOSE MEMBERS PLANNING A CAREER IN SCHOOL FOOD SERVICE. ONE OF THE SCHOLARSHIPS IS AVAILABLE TO CHILDREN OF ASFSA MEMBERS.

MUST DEMONSTRATE FINANCIAL NEED AND HAVE A GPA OF 2.7 OR BETTER. WRITE FOR COMPLETE INFORMATION.

1185

STATLER FOUNDATION (SCHOLARSHIPS)

107 DELAWARE AVE; SUITE 508
BUFFALO NY 14202
716/852-1104

AMOUNT: $500 PER YEAR

DEADLINE(S): APR 15

FIELD(S): FOOD MANAGEMENT; CULINARY ARTS; HOTEL-MOTEL MANAGEMENT

OPEN TO UNDERGRADUATE OR GRADUATE STUDENTS WHO ARE ACCEPTED TO OR ENROLLED FULL TIME AT A USA INSTITUTION IN AN ACCREDITED PROGRAM OF STUDY IN ANY OF THE ABOVE AREAS.

APPROX 900 AWARDS PER YEAR. RENEWABLE. WRITE FOR COMPLETE INFORMATION.

1186

TUSKEGEE INSTITUTE (GRADUATE RESEARCH FELLOWSHIPS AND ASSISTANTSHIPS)

ADMISSIONS OFFICE
TUSKEGEE INSTITUTE AL 36088
205/727-8500

AMOUNT: TUITION

DEADLINE(S): MAR 15

FIELD(S): CHEMISTRY; ENGINEERING; ENVIRONMENTAL SCIENCE; LIFE SCIENCES; NUTRITION; EDUCATION

GRADUATE RESEARCH FELLOWSHIPS AND GRADUATE ASSISTANTSHIPS ARE AVAILABLE TO QUALIFIED INDIVIDUALS WHO WISH TO ENTER TUSKEGEE INSTITUTE'S GRADUATE PROGRAM IN PURSUIT OF A MASTER'S DEGREE.

WRITE FOR COMPLETE INFORMATION.

1187

WOMEN GROCERS OF AMERICA (MARY MACEY SCHOLARSHIP PROGRAM)

1825 SAMUEL MORSE DR
RESTON VA 22090
703/437-5300

AMOUNT: $500

DEADLINE(S): JUN 1

FIELD(S): FOOD MANAGEMENT/SCIENCE

OPEN TO UNDERGRADUATE & GRADUATE STUDENTS PURSUING A COURSE OF STUDY LEADING TO A FOOD INDUSTRY RELATED CAREER. AWARDS ARE TENABLE AT RECOGNIZED COLLEGES & UNIVERSITIES.

WRITE FOR COMPLETE INFORMATION.

SCHOOL OF SOCIAL SCIENCE

1188

AMERICAN INSTITUTE OF PAKISTAN STUDIES (GRANT PROGRAM)

WAKE FOREST UNIV; PO BOX 7568
WINSTON-SALEM NC 27109
919/759-5453; FAX 919/759-6104

AMOUNT: VARIES

DEADLINE(S): JAN 1

FIELD(S): HUMANITIES; SOCIAL SCIENCES

FELLOWSHIPS TO SUPPORT STUDY & RESEARCH IN THE COUNTRY OF PAKISTAN. OPEN TO POST-DOCTORAL RESEARCHERS & PH.D CANDIDATES AT USA INSTITUTIONS WHO HAVE COMPLETED ALL COURSEWORK EXCEPT FOR THE DISSERTATION. USA OR CANADIAN CITIZEN.

7-10 AWARDS PER YEAR. WRITE FOR COMPLETE INFORMATION.

1189

AMERICAN RESEARCH INSTITUTE IN TURKEY (DOCTORAL DISSERTATION RESEARCH FELLOWSHIPS)

C/O UNIVERSITY MUSEUM;
33RD & SPRUCE STREETS
PHILADELPHIA PA 19104
215/898-3474

SCHOOL OF SOCIAL SCIENCE

AMOUNT: $1000 - $4000

DEADLINE(S): NOV 15

FIELD(S): HUMANITIES; SOCIAL SCIENCES

FELLOWSHIPS TO SUPPORT DOCTORAL DISSERTATION RESEARCH IN THE COUNTRY OF TURKEY. OPEN TO PH.D CANDIDATES AT USA & CANADIAN INSTITUTIONS WHO HAVE COMPLETED ALL COURSEWORK EXCEPT FOR THE DISSERTATION.

8-10 AWARDS PER YEAR. WRITE FOR COMPLETE INFORMATION.

1190 ────────────────

ASSOCIATION FOR WOMEN IN SCIENCE EDUCATIONAL FOUNDATION (AWIS PRE-DOCTORAL AWARDS)

1522 K STREET NW SUITE 820
WASHINGTON DC 20005
202/408-0742

AMOUNT: $500

DEADLINE(S): JAN 15

FIELD(S): ENGINEERING; LIFE SCIENCES; MATHEMATICS; PHYSICAL SCIENCES; BEHAVIORAL SCIENCES; SOCIAL SCIENCES

SCHOLARSHIP AID & INCENTIVE AWARDS OPEN TO WOMEN WHO ARE WORKING ACTIVELY TOWARDS A DOCTORAL DEGREE IN THE ABOVE AREAS. USA CITIZENS MAY STUDY IN USA OR ABROAD; NON-CITIZENS MUST BE ENROLLED IN USA INSTITUTION.

APPLICATIONS ARE AVAILABLE OCT 1 - DEC 15. WRITE FOR COMPLETE INFORMATION.

1191 ────────────────

COMMITTEE ON SCHOLARLY COMMUNICATION WITH CHINA (CHINESE FELLOWSHIPS FOR SCHOLARLY DEVELOPMENT)

1055 THOMAS JEFFERSON ST NW;
SUITE 2013
WASHINGTON DC 20007
202/337-1250; FAX 202/337-3109

AMOUNT: VARIES

DEADLINE(S): LIVING AND TRAVEL EXPENSES FOR 1 SEMESTER (AUG - DEC)

FIELD(S): SOCIAL SCIENCES; HUMANITIES; CHINESE STUDIES

OPEN TO CHINESE SCHOLARS IN THE SOCIAL SCIENCES AND HUMANITIES WITH THE MA OR PH.D (OR EQUIVALENT) FROM A CHINESE INSTITUTION TO CONDUCT POSTGRADUATE RESEARCH AT A USA INSTITUTION. AN AMERICAN SCHOLAR MUST NOMINATE THE CHINESE CANDIDATE.

SCHOLARS ENROLLED IN USA DEGREE PROGRAMS ARE NOT ELIGIBLE. WRITE FOR COMPLETE INFORMATION.

1192 ────────────────

COMMITTEE ON SCHOLARLY COMMUNICATION WITH CHINA (POSTDOCTORAL RESEARCH PROGRAM)

1055 THOMAS JEFFERSON ST NW;
SUITE 2013
WASHINGTON DC 20007
202/337-1250; FAX 202/337-3109

AMOUNT: VARIES

DEADLINE(S): OCT 16

FIELD(S): SOCIAL SCIENCES; HUMANITIES; CHINESE STUDIES

POST DOCTORAL GRANTS TO SUPPORT IN DEPTH RESEARCH ON THE PEOPLES REPUBLIC OF CHINA; THE CHINESE PORTION OF A COMPARATIVE STUDY OR EXPLORATORY RESEARCH ON AN ASPECT OF CONTEMPORARY CHINA. USA CITIZEN OR PERMANENT RESIDENT.

APPROX 15 AWARDS PER YEAR. WRITE FOR COMPLETE INFORMATION.

1193 ────────────────

COMMITTEE ON SCHOLARLY COMMUNICATION WITH CHINA (GRADUATE PROGRAM)

1055 THOMAS JEFFERSON ST NW;
SUITE 2013
WASHINGTON DC 20007
202/337-1250; FAX 202/337-3109

AMOUNT: $15000 (APPROX)

DEADLINE(S): OCT 16

FIELD(S): SOCIAL SCIENCES; HUMANITIES; CHINESE STUDIES

GRANTS FOR INDIVIDUALS ENROLLED IN A GRADUATE PROGRAM IN THE SOCIAL SCIENCES OR HUMANITIES TO DO COURSEWORK IN AN ACADEMIC DISCIPLINE AT A CHINESE UNIVERSITY. ALSO SUPPORTS DISSERTATION RESEARCH. USA CITIZEN OR PERMANENT RESIDENT.

MUST HAVE CHINESE LANGUAGE PROFICIENCY. 15 AWARDS PER YEAR; RENEWABLE. WRITE FOR COMPLETE INFORMATION.

1194 ────────────────

CONGRESSIONAL FELLOWSHIP PROGRAM (MORRIS K. UDALL FELLOWSHIPS)

CONGRESS OF THE UNITED STATES; OFFICE OF TECHNOLOGY ASSESSMENT
WASHINGTON DC 20510
202/224-8713

AMOUNT: $35000 - $70000

DEADLINE(S): JAN 31

FIELD(S): PHYSICAL OR BIOLOGICAL SCIENCES; ENGINEERING; LAW; ECONOMICS; ENVIRONMENTAL OR SOCIAL SCIENCES; PUBLIC POLICY

ONE YEAR FELLOWSHIP PROGRAM HELD -ONLY- IN WASHINGTO DC. CANDIDATES MUST HAVE EXTENSIVE EXPERIENCE IN SCIENCE OR TECHNOLOGY ISSUES OR HAVE COMPLETED DOCTORAL LEVEL RESEARCH. EXCEPTIONAL COMPETENCY IN ABOVE AREAS REQUIRED.

CONSIDERATIONS INCLUDE ACHIEVEMENT RECORDS AND CANDIDATE'S POTENTIAL IN ONE OR MORE OF OTA'S ASSESSMENT STUDIES. WRITE FOR COMPLETE INFORMATION.

1195

GETTY CENTER FOR THE HISTORY OF ART & THE HUMANITIES (PREDOCTORAL & POSTDOCTORAL FELLOWSHIPS)

DR H.H.HYMANS;
401 WILSHIRE BLVD; #400
SANTA MONICA CA 90401
310/458-9811

AMOUNT: $15000 PREDOCTORAL; $20000 POSTDOCTORAL

DEADLINE(S): DEC 1

FIELD(S): HUMANITIES; SOCIAL SCIENCES; ANTHROPOLOGY; ART/SCIENCE HISTORY; LITERATURE; PHILOSOPHY ETC.

OPEN TO PRE & POSTDOCTORAL SCHOLARS WHOSE AREAS OF RESEARCH COMPLEMENT THE CENTER'S PROGRAMS & RESOURCES. PREDOCTORAL CANDIDATES SHOULD EXPECT TO COMPLETE DISSERTATIONS DURING THE FELLOWSHIP YEAR.

POSTDOCTORALS SHOULD HAVE RECEIVED DOCTORATE IN HUMANITIES OR SOCIAL SCIENCES WITHIN LAST 3 YEARS & BE REWRITING DISSERTATIONS FOR PUBLICATION. WRITE FOR COMPLETE INFORMATION.

1196

HARRY FRANK GUGGENHEIM FOUNDATION (DISSERTATION FELLOWSHIPS)

527 MADISON AVE
NEW YORK NY 10022
212/644-4907

AMOUNT: $10000

DEADLINE(S): FEB 1

FIELD(S): BEHAVORIAL SCIENCE; SOCIAL SCIENCE

AWARDS ARE INTENDED FOR SUPPORT DURING THE WRITING OF THE PH.D THESIS IN DISCIPLINES ADDRESSING THE CAUSES; MANIFESTATIONS AND CONTROL OF VIOLENCE; AGGRESSION AND DOMINANCE. APPLICANTS MUST HAVE COMPLETED RESEARCH AND BE READY TO WRITE.

OPEN TO CITIZENS OF ANY COUNTY WHO ARE STUDYING AT COLLEGES OR UNIVERSITIES IN ANY COUNTRY. WRITE FOR COMPLETE INFORMATION.

1197

HARRY FRANK GUGGENHEIM FOUNDATION (POST-DOCTORAL RESEARCH GRANTS)

527 MADISON AVE
NEW YORK NY 10022
212/644-4907

AMOUNT: $15000 - $35000

DEADLINE(S): FEB 1; AUG 1

FIELD(S): BEHAVORIAL SCIENCES; SOCIAL SCIENCES

POST-DOCTORAL GRANTS FOR RESEARCHERS IN THE ABOVE FIELDS WHOSE WORK LEADS TO A BETTER UNDERSTANDING OF THE CAUSES; MANIFESTATIONS & CONTROL OF VIOLENCE; AGGRESSION; AND DOMINANCE IN THE MODERN WORLD.

35-40 GRANTS PER YEAR. AVERAGE 2 YEAR DURATION. WRITE FOR COMPLETE INFORMATION.

1198

INSTITUTE FOR ADVANCED STUDY (POST-DOCTORAL FELLOWSHIP AWARDS)

OLDEN LANE
PRINCETON NJ 08540
609-734-8000

AMOUNT: VARIES ACCORDING TO SCHOOL

DEADLINE(S): CHECK WITH SCHOOL

FIELD(S): HISTORICAL STUDIES; SOCIAL SCIENCES; NATURAL SCIENCES; MATHEMATICS

POST-DOCTORAL FELLOWSHIPS AT THE INSTITUTE FOR ADVANCED STUDY FOR THOSE WHOSE TERM CAN BE EXPECTED TO RESULT IN A WORK OF SIGNIFICANCE AND INDIVIDUALITY.

150-160 FELLOWSHIPS PER ACADEMIC YEAR ALTHOUGH SOME CAN BE EXTENDED. REQUEST APPLICATION MATERIALS FROM SCHOOL'S ADMINISTRATIVE OFFICER.

1199

NATIONAL ASSN OF THE DEAF (STOKOE SCHOLARSHIP FUND)

814 THAYER AVE
SILVER SPRING MD 20910
301/587-1788 VOICE; 301/587-1789 TDD

AMOUNT: $1000

DEADLINE(S): MAR 15

FIELD(S): SOCIAL SCIENCES

OPEN TO ANY DEAF GRADUATE STUDENT. AWARD IS FOR RESEARCH PROJECT ON SIGN LANGUAGE OR SOME ASPECT OF THE DEAF COMMUNITY. GOAL IS TO INCREASE THE INVOLVEMENT OF DEAF SOCIAL SCIENTISTS IN THESE AREAS.

WRITE FOR COMPLETE INFORMATION.

1200

NATIONAL FEDERATION OF THE BLIND (ELLEN SETTERFIELD MEMORIAL SCHOLARSHIP)

814 4TH AVE #200
GRINNELL IA 50112
515/236-3366

AMOUNT: $2000

DEADLINE(S): MAR 31

FIELD(S): SOCIAL SCIENCES

SCHOLARSHIPS OPEN TO LEGALLY BLIND STUDENTS PURSUING A GRADUATE DEGREE IN THE SOCIAL SCIENCES. AWARDS BASED ON ACADEMIC EXCELLENCE; SERVICE TO THE COMMUNITY; FINANCIAL NEED.

WRITE FOR COMPLETE INFORMATION.

1201

NATIONAL HUMANITIES CENTER (POST-DOCTORAL FELLOWSHIPS)

PO BOX 12256; 7 ALEXANDER DR
RESEARCH TRIANGLE PARK NC 27709
919/549-0661

AMOUNT: STIPEND + TRAVEL EXPENSES

DEADLINE(S): OCT 15

FIELD(S): HISTORY; LANGUAGES & LITERATURE; PHILOSOPHY; OTHER FIELDS IN THE LIBERAL ARTS

POST-DOCTORAL RESEARCH FELLOWSHIPS OPEN TO YOUNG & SENIOR SCHOLARS FROM ANY NATION. AWARDS SUPPORT RESEARCH & WRITING AT THE CENTER. SCHOLARS FROM OTHER AREAS SUCH AS NATURAL SCIENCES; ARTS; PROFESSIONS & PUBLIC LIFE ALSO MAY APPLY.

30-35 FELLOWSHIPS PER YEAR. WRITE FOR COMPLETE INFORMATION.

1202

NATIONAL RESEARCH COUNCIL (NATIONAL SCIENCE FOUNDATION MINORITY GRADUATE FELLOWSHIPS)

2101 CONSTITUTION AVE.
WASHINGTON DC 20418
202/334-2872

AMOUNT: $14000 STIPEND (12 MONTHS) + UP TO $7500 FOR TUITION AND FEES

DEADLINE(S): NOV 6

FIELD(S): ENGINEERING; MATHEMATICS; COMPUTER SCIENCE; CHEMISTRY; EARTH SCIENCES; LIFE SCIENCES; PSYCHOLOGY; SOCIAL SCIENCES

OPEN MINORITY GRADUATE STUDENTS (MASTERS OR PH.D) WHO ARE USA CITIZENS OR LEGAL RESIDENTS & ARE AT OR NEAR THE BEGINNING OF THEIR GRADUATE STUDY. FELLOWSHIPS TENABLE AT ACCREDITED INSTITUTION OFFERING ADVANCED DEGREES IN THE FIELDS ABOVE.

APPROX 150 NEW 3-YEAR FELLOWSHIPS AWARDED EACH YEAR. WRITE FOR COMPLETE INFORMATION.

1203

OMEGA PSI PHI FRATERNITY (GEORGE E. MEARES MEMORIAL SCHOLARSHIP)

C/O MINNIE MEARES DRAUGHN;
1004 SPENCER AVE.
GASTONIA NC 28052
WRITTEN INQUIRY

AMOUNT: $1000

DEADLINE(S): APR 1

FIELD(S): SOCIAL SCIENCES

SCHOLARSHIPS ARE GRANTED FOR THE SUPPORT OF GRADUATE STUDY IN SOCIAL WORK; SOCIAL SCIENCES AND CRIMINAL JUSTICE. THE PRESENT EMPHASIS IS ON PROBATION/PAROLE BUT IT MAY INCLUDE RELATED CORRECTIONAL SERVICES. USA CITIZEN.

WRITE FOR COMPLETE INFORMATION.

1204

ORGANIZATION OF AMERICAN STATES DEPT OF FELLOWSHIPS & TRAINING (OAS PRA-FELLOWSHIPS)

TRAINEE SELECTION DIVISION
WASHINGTON DC 20006
202/789-3902

AMOUNT: TUITION + FEES; TRAVEL EXP & STIPEND

DEADLINE(S): APR 30; AUG 31

FIELD(S): ALL FIELDS EXCEPT MEDICINE & FOREIGN LANGUAGES

GRADUATE FELLOWSHIPS FOR USA CITIZENS OR PERMANENT RESIDENTS TO STUDY IN AN OAS MEMBER COUNTRY. MUST HAVE UNDERGRADUATE DEGREE AND HAVE DEMONSTRATED ABILITY TO PURSUE ADVANCED STUDIES IN CHOSEN FIELD.

APPLICANTS SHOULD BE FLUENT IN LANGUAGE OF COUNTRY OF INTENDED STUDY. PRIORITY IS GIVEN TO RESEARCH PROJECTS. WRITE FOR COMPLETE INFORMATION.

1205 ─────────────────────

PI GAMMA MU INTERNATIONAL HONOR SOCIETY IN SOCIAL SCIENCE (SCHOLARSHIPS)

1717 AMES
WINFIELD KS 67156
316/221-3128

AMOUNT: $1000

DEADLINE(S): JAN 30

FIELD(S): SOCIAL SCIENCES; ECONOMICS; HISTORY; POLITICAL SCIENCE; SOCIOLOGY; ANTHROPOLOGY; INTERNATIONAL RELATIONS

APPLICANTS MUST BE MEMBERS OF PI GAMMA MU. CRITERIA FOR SELECTION ARE GPA; LETTERS OF RECOMMENDATION; EXTRA-CURRICULAR ACTIVITIES AND FINANCIAL NEED. FOR GRADUATE STUDY ONLY. MUST STUDY FULL TIME.

10 SCHOLARSHIPS PER YEAR. CONTACT EXECUTIVE DIRECTOR INA TURNER GRAY AT ADDRESS ABOVE FOR COMPLETE INFORMATION.

1206 ─────────────────────

RESOURCES FOR THE FUTURE (GILBERT F. WHITE FELLOWSHIP PROGRAM)

1616 'P' STREET NW
WASHINGTON DC 20036
202/328-5067

AMOUNT: $35000 STIPEND + $1000 MOVING/ LIVING EXPENSES

DEADLINE(S): MAR 1

FIELD(S): SOCIAL SCIENCES; NATURAL RESOURCES; ENERGY; ENVIRONMENT

POST-DOCTORAL RESIDENT FELLOWSHIPS FOR YOUNG PROFESSIONALS WHO WISH TO DEVOTE A YEAR TO SCHOLARLY WORK ON A SOCIAL OR POLICY PROBLEM IN AREAS OF NATURAL RESOURCES; ENERGY OR ENVIRONMENT. FACULTY MEMBERS ON SABBATICAL ENCOURAGED TO APPLY.

FELLOWSHIPS AWARDED FOR A MINIMUM OF 9 MOS.; MAXIMUM OF 12 MOS. ADDRESS INQUIRIES TO FELLOWSHIP DIRECTOR.

1207 ─────────────────────

RESOURCES FOR THE FUTURE (SMALL GRANTS PROGRAM)

1616 'P' STREET NW
WASHINGTON DC 20036
202/328-5067

AMOUNT: $30000 MAXIMUM

DEADLINE(S): MAR 1

FIELD(S): NATURAL RESOURCES; ENERGY; ENVIRONMENTAL ISSUES

POST-DOCTORAL RESEARCH GRANTS OPEN TO RESEARCHERS OF ALL NATIONALITIES. PROPOSALS MAY ORIGINATE IN THE HUMANITIES; SOCIAL OR NATURAL SCIENCES & MAY BE THEORETICAL OR APPLIED RESEARCH. 2 MONTHS - 2 YEARS. ONGOING PROJECTS ALSO CONSIDERED.

GRANTS CAN ONLY BE MADE THROUGH TAX-EXEMPT INSTITUTIONS. WRITE FOR COMPLETE INFORMATION.

1208 ─────────────────────

SOCIAL SCIENCE RESEARCH COUNCIL (POST-DOCTORAL GRANTS FOR ADVANCED AREA RESEARCH)

605 THIRD AVENUE
NEW YORK NY 10158
212/661-0280

AMOUNT: VARIES

DEADLINE(S): DEC 1

FIELD(S): HUMANITIES; SOCIAL SCIENCES

OPEN TO SCHOLARS WHOSE PREVIOUS WORK HAS DEMONSTRATED THEIR COMPETENCE FOR RESEARCH IN THE SOCIAL SCIENCE OR HUMANITIES AND WHO HOLD THE PH.D DEGREE OR HAVE EQUIVALENT RESEARCH EXPERIENCE.

PROGRAMS ARE TO SUPPORT RESEARCH IN ONE COUNTRY; COMPARATIVE RESEARCH BETWEEN COUNTRIES IN AN AREA; AND COMPARATIVE RESEARCH BETWEEN AREAS. WRITE FOR COMPLETE INFORMATION.

1209 ─────────────────────

WILLIAM T. GRANT FOUNDATION (FACULTY SCHOLARS PROGRAM - RESEARCH ON CHILDREN; ADOLESCENTS AND YOUTH)

515 MADISON AVE.
NEW YORK NY 10022
WRITTEN INQUIRY

AMOUNT: UP TO $35000 PER YEAR FOR 5 YEARS

DEADLINE(S): JUL 1

FIELD(S): CHILD DEVELOPMENT AND MENTAL HEALTH

COMMUNICATION

OPEN TO FACULTY MEMBERS AT UNIVERSITIES & NON-PROFIT INSTITUTIONS; NATIONAL & INTERNATIONAL. AWARD IS FOR BEGINNING INVESTIGATORS INTERESTED IN THE CAUSES & CONSEQUENCES OF FACTORS WHICH COMPROMISE THE HEALTHY DEVELOPMENT OF CHILDREN.

WRITE FOR COMPLETE INFORMATION.

1210 ────────────────────

WOODROW WILSON INTERNATIONAL CENTER FOR SCHOLARS (FELLOWSHIPS IN THE HUMANITIES AND SOCIAL SCIENCES)

FELLOWSHIPS OFFICE;
WOODROW WILSON CENTER
WASHINGTON DC 20560
202/357-2841

AMOUNT: UP TO $52000

DEADLINE(S): OCT 1

FIELD(S): HUMANITIES; SOCIAL SCIENCES

OPEN TO INDIVIDUALS FROM ANY COUNTRY WHO HAVE OUTSTANDING CAPABILITIES AND EXPERIENCE FROM A WIDE VARIETY OF BACKGROUNDS. ACADEMIC PARTICIPANTS LIMITED TO POSTDOCTORAL LEVEL AND SHOULD HAVE PUBLISHED A MAJOR WORK BEYOND PH.D DISSERTATION.

APPROXIMATELY 30 FELLOWSHIPS ANNUALLY TO SCHOLARS WITH OUTSTANDING PROJECT PROPOSALS; ESPECIALLY THOSE TRANSCENDING NARROW SPECIALITIES. WRITE FOR COMPLETE INFORMATION.

1211 ────────────────────

WOODROW WILSON NATIONAL FELLOWSHIP FOUNDATION (NEWCOMBE DISSERTATION FELLOWSHIPS)

BOX 642
PRINCETON NJ 08542
609/924-4666

AMOUNT: $12000 STIPEND

DEADLINE(S): DEC 13

FIELD(S): SOCIAL SCIENCES; HUMANITIES; EDUCATION

OPEN TO PH.D; TH.D & ED.D CANDIDATES IN THE USA WHO WILL COMPLETE ALL DOCTORAL REQUIREMENTS EXCEPT THE DISSERTATION BY NOV 29. THESE AWARDS ARE NOT DESIGNED TO FINANCE FIELD WORK BUT RATHER THE COMPLETION OF DISSERTATION WRITING.

ELIGIBLE PROPOSALS WILL HAVE ETHICAL OR RELIGIOUS VALUES AS A CENTRAL CONCERN. REQUEST APPLICATION BY NOV. 29. WRITE FOR COMPLETE INFORMATION.

COMMUNICATIONS

1212 ────────────────────

AMERICAN ANTIQUARIAN SOCIETY (VISITING RESEARCH FELLOWSHIPS)

185 SALISBURY ST
WORCESTER MA 01609
508/755-5221

AMOUNT: $850 PER MONTH

DEADLINE(S): JAN 15

FIELD(S): AMERICAN HISTORY; BIBLIOGRAPHY; PRINTING & PUBLISHING (THROUGH 1876)

FELLOWSHIPS OF ONE TO THREE MONTHS DURATION AT THE SOCIETY LIBRARY. FOR DOCTORAL DISSERTATION RESEARCH AND POST-DOCTORAL RESEARCH IN THE ABOVE FIELDS.

RECIPIENTS ARE EXPECTED TO BE IN REGULAR AND CONTINUOUS RESIDENCE AT THE SOCIETY LIBRARY DURING THE PERIOD OF THE GRANT. WRITE FOR COMPLETE INFORMATION.

1213 ────────────────────

AMERICAN INSTITUTE OF POLISH CULTURE INC. (SCHOLARSHIPS)

1440 79TH STREET CAUSEWAY SUITE 117
MIAMI FL 33141
305/864-2349

AMOUNT: $2500

DEADLINE(S): JAN 15

FIELD(S): JOURNALISM/PUBLIC RELATIONS

SCHOLARSHIPS TO ENCOURAGE YOUNG AMERICANS OF POLISH DESCENT TO PURSUE THE ABOVE PROFESSIONS. AWARD CAN BE USED AT ANY ACCREDITED AMERICAN COLLEGE. THE RULING CRITERIA FOR SELECTION ARE ACHIEVEMENT/TALENT & INVOLVEMENT IN PUBLIC LIFE.

AWARDS RENEWABLE. FOR FULL-TIME STUDY ONLY. CONTACT PROF. ZDZISLAW WESOLOWSKI AT ADDRESS ABOVE FOR COMPLETE INFORMATION.

1214 ────────────────────

AMERICAN POLITICAL SCIENCE ASSN (CONGRESSIONAL FELLOWSHIPS FOR PRINT & BROADCAST JOURNALISTS)

1527 NEW HAMPSHIRE AVE NW
WASHINGTON DC 20036
202/483-2512

AMOUNT: $20000 STIPEND + TRAVEL ALLOWANCE

DEADLINE(S): DEC 1

FIELD(S): JOURNALISM

PROGRAM GIVES JOURNALISTS AN OPPORTUNITY TO WORK AS CONGRESSIONAL AIDES FOR 9 MONTHS AND TO STRENGTHEN THEIR UNDERSTANDING OF CONGRESS AND NATIONAL POLITICS. MUST BE USA CITIZEN; HAVE BACHELOR'S DEGREE & 2-10 YEARS FULL TIME EXPERIENCE.

CONTACT ADDRESS ABOVE FOR COMPLETE INFORMATION AND APPLICATION PROCEDURES.

1215 ————————————————

AMERICAN WOMEN IN RADIO & TELEVISION (HOUSTON INTERNSHIP PROGRAM)

APRILLE MEEK; AWRT-HOUSTON;
PO BOX 980908
HOUSTON TX 77098
WRITTEN INQUIRY

AMOUNT: $500 PER YEAR

DEADLINE(S): MAR 1

FIELD(S): RADIO; TELEVISION; FILM & VIDEO; ADVERTISING; MARKETING

INTERNSHIPS OPEN TO STUDENTS WHO ARE JUNIORS; SENIORS OR GRADUATE STUDENTS AT GREATER HOUSTON AREA COLLEGES & UNIVERSITIES.

WRITE FOR COMPLETE INFORMATION.

1216 ————————————————

ASIAN AMERICAN JOURNALISTS ASSOCIATION (SCHOLARSHIP AWARDS)

1765 SUTTER ST - ROOM 1000
SAN FRANCISCO CA 94115
415/346-2051

AMOUNT: UP TO $2000

DEADLINE(S): APR 15

FIELD(S): JOURNALISM; MASS COMMUNICATIONS

OPEN TO STUDENTS WITH A DEMONSTRATED ABILITY & SERIOUS CAREER INTEREST IN PRINT; PHOTO OR BROADCAST JOURNALISM. AWARDS BASED ON SCHOLASTIC ACHIEVEMENT; COMMITMENT TO JOURNALISM & TO THE ASIAN PACIFIC AMERICAN COMMUNITY; & FINANCIAL NEED.

FOR UNDERGRADUATE OR GRADUATE STUDY. WRITE FOR COMPLETE INFORMATION.

1217 ————————————————

ASSOCIATED PRESS TELEVISION-RADIO ASSOCIATION OF CALIFORNIA/NEVADA (APTRA-CLETE ROBERTS MEMORIAL JOURNALISM SCHOLARSHIP AWARDS)

RACHEL AMBROSE; ASSOCIATED PRESS; 221 S. FIGUEROA ST. #300
LOS ANGELES CA 90012
213/626-1200

AMOUNT: $1500

DEADLINE(S): DEC 18

FIELD(S): BROADCAST JOURNALISM

OPEN TO STUDENTS WITH A BROADCAST JOURNALISM CAREER OBJECTIVE WHO ARE STUDYING IN CALIFORNIA OR NEVADA. FOR UNDERGRADUATE OR GRADUATE STUDY.

WRITE FOR COMPLETE INFORMATION.

1218 ————————————————

ASSOCIATION FOR EDUCATION IN JOURNALISM & MASS COMMUNICATION (CORRESPONDENTS FUND SCHOLARSHIPS)

UNIV OF SOUTH CAROLINA
COLLEGE OF JOURNALISM
COLUMBIA SC 29208
803/777-2005

AMOUNT: UP TO $2000

DEADLINE(S): APR 30

FIELD(S): JOURNALISM; MASS COMMUNICATIONS; LIBERAL ARTS

OPEN TO CHILDREN OF PRINT OR BROADCAST JOURNALISTS WHO ARE FOREIGN CORRESPONDENTS FOR A USA NEWS MEDIUM. FOR UNDERGRADUATE; GRADUATE OR POST-GRADUATE STUDY AT ANY ACCREDITED COLLEGE OR UNIVERSITY IN THE USA.

PREFERENCE TO JOURNALISM OR COMMUNICATIONS MAJORS. 8-15 RENEWABLE AWARDS PER YEAR. WRITE FOR COMPLETE INFORMATION.

1219 ————————————————

ASSOCIATION FOR EDUCATION IN JOURNALISM AND MASS COMMUNICATIONS (SUMMER JOURNALISM INTERNSHIP FOR MINORITIES)

NYU INST OF AFRO-AMERICAN AFFAIRS; 269 MERCER - SUITE 601
NEW YORK NY 10003
212/998-2130

AMOUNT: SALARY OF AT LEAST $200 PER WEEK

DEADLINE(S): NOV 3 TO REQUEST APPLICATION; DEC 15 TO SUBMIT APPLICATION.

FIELD(S): JOURNALISM; MASS COMMUNICATIONS; ADVERTISING; PUBLIC RELATIONS; PHOTO JOURNALISM; BROADCASTING

OPEN TO MEMBERS OF ETHNIC MINORITIES WHOSE CREDENTIALS REFLECT AN INTEREST IN AND COMMITMENT TO JOURNALISM. INTERNS WILL BE PLACED FOR 10 WEEKS IN AN ENTRY LEVEL POSITION WITH PARTICIPATING COMPANIES; PRIMARILY IN THE NY/NJ AREA.

WRITE FOR COMPLETE INFORMATION.

COMMUNICATIONS

1220

BROADCAST EDUCATION ASSOCIATION (SCHOLARSHIPS IN BROADCASTING)

1771 N STREET NW
WASHINGTON DC 20036
202/429-5354

AMOUNT: $1250 - $3000

DEADLINE(S): JAN 15

FIELD(S): BROADCASTING

SCHOLARSHIPS ARE AWARDED FOR ONE SCHOLASTIC YEAR FOR DEGREE WORK AT THE JUNIOR; SENIOR OR GRADUATE LEVEL. APPLICANTS MUST SHOW EVIDENCE OF SUPERIOR ACADEMIC PERFORMANCE AND POTENTIAL. APPLICATIONS WILL NOT BE SENT OUT AFTER DEC 15.

SCHOLARSHIP WINNERS MUST STUDY AT A CAMPUS WHERE AT LEAST ONE DEPARTMENT IS A BEA INSTITUTIONAL MEMBER. WRITE FOR COMPLETE INFORMATION.

1221

CDS INTERNATIONAL INC (ROBERT BOSCH FOUNDATION FELLOWSHIPS)

330 SEVENTH AVE
NEW YORK NY 10001
212/760-1400

AMOUNT: 3500 DEUTSCH MARKS PER MONTH + TRAVEL EXPENSES

DEADLINE(S): OCT 15

FIELD(S): BUSINESS ADMIN; ECONOMICS; JOURNALISM; MASS COMMUNICATIONS; LAW; POLITICAL SCIENCE; PUBLIC AFFAIRS

9-MONTH FELLOWSHIP PROGRAM IN GERMANY INVOLVING WORK INTERNSHIPS IN FEDERAL GOVERNMENT & THEN IN REGIONAL GOVERNMENT OR PRIVATE INDUSTRY; SUPPLEMENTED BY SPECIAL SEMINARS IN BERLIN; PARIS & BRUSSELS. USA CITIZEN.

OPEN TO YOUNG PROFESSIONALS & STUDENTS WHO HOLD A GRADUATE DEGREE IN ANY OF THE ABOVE AREAS OR HAVE EQUIVALENT PROFESSIONAL EXPERIENCE. 15 AWARDS PER YEAR. WRITE FOR COMPLETE INFORMATION.

1222

CHARLES PRICE SCHOOL OF ADVERTISING AND JOURNALISM INC. (SCHOLARSHIP PROGRAM)

1700 WALNUT ST
PHILADELPHIA PA 19103
215/546-2747

AMOUNT: $500 - $1000

DEADLINE(S): VARIES

FIELD(S): ADVERTISING/JOURNALISM/PUBLIC RELATIONS

SCHOLARSHIPS FOR STUDY IN ABOVE FIELDS - AT- CHARLES PRICE SCHOOL OF ADVERTISING & JOURNALISM. UNDERGRADUATE JUNIORS AND SENIORS AND GRADUATE STUDENTS MAY APPLY. USA CITIZEN.

6 SCHOLARSHIPS PER YEAR. WRITE FOR COMPLETE INFORMATION.

1223

COUNCIL FOR THE ADVANCEMENT OF SCIENCE WRITING INC (FELLOWSHIPS)

PO BOX 404
GREENLAWN NY 11740
WRITTEN INQUIRY

AMOUNT: $1000 - $2000

DEADLINE(S): JUN 1

FIELD(S): SCIENCE WRITING

GRADUATE FELLOWSHIPS FOR STUDENTS & JOURNALISTS WHO WISH TO PURSUE A CAREER IN SCIENCE WRITING. FOR STUDY IN USA. USA CITIZEN.

WRITE FOR COMPLETE INFORMATION.

1224

DOG WRITERS' EDUCATIONAL TRUST (SCHOLARSHIPS)

BERTA I PICKETT; PO BOX 2220
PAYSON AZ 85547
602/474-8867

AMOUNT: $1000

DEADLINE(S): DEC 31

FIELD(S): VETERINARY MEDICINE; ANIMAL BEHAVIOR; JOURNALISM

OPEN TO APPLICANTS WHOSE PARENTS; GRANDPARENTS OR OTHER CLOSE RELATIVES (OR THE APPLICANT) ARE OR HAVE BEEN INVOLVED IN THE WORLD OF DOGS AS EXHIBITORS; BREEDERS; HANDLERS; JUDGES; CLUB OFFICERS OR OTHER ACTIVITIES.

SCHOLARSHIPS SUPPORT UNDERGRADUATE OR GRADUATE STUDY. 10 AWARDS PER YEAR. SEND SELF ADDRESSED STAMPED ENVELOPE FOR COMPLETE INFORMATION AND APPLICATION.

1225

DOW JONES NEWSPAPER FUND INC (EDITING INTERN PROGRAM FOR COLLEGE JUNIORS SENIORS AND GRADUATE STUDENTS)

PO BOX 300
PRINCETON NJ 08543
609/452-2820

AMOUNT: $1000

DEADLINE(S): NOV 15

FIELD(S): JOURNALISM

OPEN TO COLLEGE JUNIORS SENIORS &
    GRADUATE STUDENTS WITH A SINCERE
    DESIRE FOR CAREER IN JOURNALISM.
    RECIPIENTS RECIEIVE $1000 SCHOLARSHIP;
    FREE 2-WEEK PRE-INTERNSHIP RESIDENCY &
    SUMMER COPY EDITOR JOB ON DAILY PAPER
    AT REGULAR WAGES.

JOURNALISM MAJOR NOT REQUIRED. UP TO 45
    AWARDS PER YEAR. APPLICATIONS
    AVAILABLE FROM SEP 1 TO NOV 1. WRITE
    FOR COMPLETE INFORMATION.

1226

**FLORIDA ENDOWMENT FUND FOR HIGHER
EDUCATION (MCKNIGHT DOCTORAL
FELLOWSHIP PROGRAM)**

201 E.KENNEDY BLVD; SUITE 1525
TAMPA FL 33602
813/272-2772

AMOUNT: $11000 STIPEND + $5000 TUITION &
    FEES (PER YEAR)

DEADLINE(S): JAN 15

FIELD(S): ALL FIELDS (EXCEPT LAW; MEDICINE
    & EDUCATION)

OPEN TO ALL AFRICAN-AMERICANS WITH AT
    LEAST A BACHELOR'S DEGREE FROM AN
    ACCREDITED INSTITUTION WHO WISH TO
    PURSUE A DOCTORAL DEGREE. PROGRAM
    RECRUITS NATIONWIDE; HOWEVER
    FELLOWS MUST ENROLL IN A FLORIDA
    INSTITUTION. USA CITIZEN.

25 AWARDS PER YEAR. RENEWABLE FOR UP TO 5
    YEARS. WRITE FOR COMPLETE
    INFORMATION.

1227

FREEDOM FORUM (SCHOLARSHIPS)

1101 WILSON BLVD
ARLINGTON VA 22209
703/528-0850

AMOUNT: $2500 UNDERGRADS; $4000
    GRADUATES

DEADLINE(S): JAN 31

FIELD(S): JOURNALISM

OPEN TO HIGH SCHOOL SENIORS AND
    UNDERGRADUATE OR GRADUATE COLLEGE
    STUDENTS WITH CAREER GOALS AND
    MAJORS IN PRINT OR BROADCAST
    JOURNALISM OR ADVERTISING.
    APPLICATIONS MUST BE REQUESTED BEFORE
    JAN 22.

WRITE FOR COMPLETE INFORMATION STATING
    WHAT YEAR OF COLLEGE YOU WILL BE IN
    AS OF SEPTEMBER.

1228

**INTER AMERICAN PRESS ASSN (SCHOLARSHIPS
FOR LATIN AMERICANS & WEST INDIANS)**

2911 NW 39TH ST
MIAMI FL 33142
305/634-2465

AMOUNT: $10000

DEADLINE(S): AUG 1

FIELD(S): JOURNALISM

OPEN TO GRADUATE STUDENTS & YOUNG
    JOURNALISTS (AGED 21-35) WHO ARE
    CITIZENS OF LATIN AMERICA OR WEST
    INDIES. AWARDS FOR 1 ACADEMIC YEAR OF
    GRADUATE STUDY AT A USA OR CANADIAN
    ACCREDITED SCHOOL OF JOURNALISM.
    FLUENCY IN ENGLISH REQUIRED.

WRITE FOR COMPLETE INFORMATION.

1229

**INTER AMERICAN PRESS ASSN (SCHOLARSHIPS
FOR STUDY IN LATIN AMERICA & WEST
INDIES)**

2911 NW 39TH ST
MIAMI FL 33142
305/634-2465

AMOUNT: $10000

DEADLINE(S): AUG 1

FIELD(S): JOURNALISM

OPEN TO GRADUATE STUDENTS & YOUNG
    JOURNALISTS (AGED 21-35) WHO ARE
    CITIZENS OF USA OR CANADA. AWARDS FOR
    1 ACADEMIC YEAR OF STUDY; RESEARCH;
    WORK EXPERIENCE IN LATIN AMERICAN OR
    W. INDIAN COUNTRY. FLUENCY IN
    COUNTRY'S LANGUAGE REQUIRED.

WRITE FOR COMPLETE INFORMATION.

1230

**JOHN BAYLISS BROADCAST FOUNDATION
(SCHOLARSHIP)**

PO BOX 221070
CARMEL CA 93922
408/624-1536

AMOUNT: $2000

DEADLINE(S): APR 30

FIELD(S): RADIO BROADCASTING

OPEN TO UNDERGRADS IN THEIR JUNIOR OR
    SENIOR YEAR AND TO GRADUATE STUDENTS
    WHO ASPIRE TO A CAREER IN RADIO.
    APPLICANTS SHOULD HAVE A 3.0 OR BETTER
    GPA. FINANCIAL NEED IS A CONSIDERATION.
    USA CITIZEN OR LEGAL RESIDENT.

WRITE FOR COMPLETE INFORMATION.

1231

JOURNALISM FOUNDATION OF METROPOLITAN ST. LOUIS (SCHOLARSHIPS)

C/O PATRICK GAVEN;
900 N TUCKER BLVD
ST. LOUIS MO 63101
314/340-8000

AMOUNT: $750-2500

DEADLINE(S): FEB 28

FIELD(S): JOURNALISM/COMMUNICATIONS

OPEN TO ST LOUIS METRO RESIDENTS ENTERING THEIR JUNIOR/SENIOR YEAR OF COLLEGE OR GRADUATE SCHOOL. MUST HAVE A DESIRE TO PURSUE A CAREER IN JOURNALISM & WRITING TALENT (SAMPLES).

17 OR MORE SCHOLARSHIPS PER YEAR. CONTACT PATRICIA RICE (CHAIRMAN) ADDRESS ABOVE FOR COMPLETE INFORMATION.

1232

NATIONAL ASSN OF HISPANIC JOURNALISTS (MARK ZAMBRANO SCHOLARSHIP FUND)

NATIONAL PRESS BUILDING; SUITE 1193
WASHINGTON DC 20045
202/622-7145

AMOUNT: $1000

DEADLINE(S): DEC 31

FIELD(S): PRINT OR BROADCAST JOURNALISM; PHOTOJOURNALISM

OPEN TO UNDERGRAD JUNIORS & SENIORS AND GRAD STUDENTS WHO ARE COMMITTED TO PURSUING A CAREER IN PRINT OR BROADCAST JOURNALISM OR PHOTOJOURNALISM. IT IS NOT NECESSARY TO BE A JOURNALISM OR BROADCAST MAJOR NOR IS HISPANIC ANCESTRY REQUIRED.

AWARDS TENABLE AT ACCREDITED INSTITUTIONS IN THE USA & ITS TERRITORIES. WRITE FOR COMPLETE INFORMATION.

1233

NATIONAL ASSN OF HISPANIC JOURNALISTS (NAHJ SCHOLARSHIP PROGRAM)

NATIONAL PRESS BUILDING; SUITE 1193
WASHINGTON DC 20045
202/622-7145

AMOUNT: VARIES

DEADLINE(S): MAR 11

FIELD(S): PRINT OR BROADCAST JOURNALISM; PHOTOJOURNALISM

OPEN TO HIGH SCHOOL SENIORS; UNDERGRADUATE & GRADUATE STUDENTS WHO ARE COMMITTED TO A CAREER IN PRINT OR BROADCAST JOURNALISM OR PHOTOJOURNALISM. IT IS NOT NECESSARY TO MAJOR IN THESE AREAS NOR IS IT REQUIRED TO BE OF HISPANIC ANCESTRY.

AWARDS TENABLE AT ACCREDITED 2-YEAR OR 4-YEAR SCHOOLS IN THE USA & ITS TERRITORIES. WRITE FOR COMPLETE INFORMATION.

1234

NATIONAL ASSOCIATION OF BLACK JOURNALISTS (NABJ SCHOLARSHIP PROGRAM)

BOX 17212
WASHINGTON DC 20041
703/648-1270

AMOUNT: $2500

DEADLINE(S): MAR 31

FIELD(S): JOURNALISM

OPEN TO AFRIAN AMERICAN UNDERGRADUATE OR GRADUATE STUDENTS WHO ARE ACCEPTED TO OR ENROLLED IN AN ACCREDITED JOURNALISM PROGRAM MAJORING IN PRINT; PHOTO; RADIO; OR TELEVISION. GPA OF 2.5 OR BETTER (4.0 SCALE) IS REQUIRED.

12 AWARDS PER YEAR. WRITE FOR COMPLETE INFORMATION.

1235

NATIONAL BROADCASTING COMPANY INC (MINORITY FELLOWSHIPS PROGRAM)

30 ROCKEFELLER PLAZA
NEW YORK NY 10112
212/664-5016

AMOUNT: VARIES

DEADLINE(S): VARIES

FIELD(S): BROADCASTING; JOURNALISM; BUSINESS ADMINISTRATION

OPEN TO MINORITY GRADUATE STUDENTS WHO ATTEND DESIGNATED COLLEGES OR UNIVERSITIES. THE SCHOOLS ARE CHANGED EACH YEAR. APPLICANTS MUST BE USA CITIZENS OR LEGAL RESIDENTS.

APPLICATION MUST BE MADE THROUGH STUDENT'S COLLEGE. INQUIRE AT FINANCIAL AID OFFICE OR WRITE FOR COMPLETE INFORMATION.

1236

NATIONAL FEDERATION OF PRESS WOMEN INC (HELEN M MALLOCH SCHOLARSHIP)

PO BOX 99
BLUE SPRINGS MO 64013
816/229-1666

AMOUNT: $500 - $1000

DEADLINE(S): MAY 1

FIELD(S): JOURNALISM

WOMEN. UNDERGRADUATE JUNIOR/SENIOR OR GRADUATE STUDENT MAJORING IN JOURNALISM AT A COLLEGE OR UNIVERSITY OF THE STUDENT'S CHOICE.

WRITE FOR COMPLETE INFORMATION.

1237

NATIONAL FEDERATION OF PRESS WOMEN INC (PROFESSIONAL EDUCATION SCHOLARSHIP)

PO BOX 99
BLUE SPRINGS MO 64013
816/229-1666

AMOUNT: $1000

DEADLINE(S): MAY 1

FIELD(S): JOURNALISM

FOR MEMBERS OF THE NATIONAL FEDERATION OF PRESS WOMEN WHO WANT TO CONTINUE OR RETURN TO COLLEGE AS A JOURNALISM MAJOR. FINANCIAL NEED IS A CONSIDERATION BUT IS NOT PARAMOUNT.

WRITE FOR COMPLETE INFORMATION.

1238

NATIONAL RIGHT TO WORK COMMITTEE (WILLIAM B. RUGGLES JOURNALISM SCHOLARSHIP)

8001 BRADDOCK RD; SUITE 500
SPRINGFIELD VA 22160
703/321-9820

AMOUNT: $2000

DEADLINE(S): MAR 31

FIELD(S): JOURNALISM

SCHOLARSHIPS ARE OPEN TO UNDERGRADUATE AND GRADUATE STUDENTS MAJORING IN JOURNALISM AT ACCREDITED USA INSTITUTIONS OF HIGHER LEARNING WHO EXEMPLIFY THE DEDICATION TO PRINCIPLE & HIGH JOURNALISTIC STANDARDS OF THE LATE WILLIAM B. RUGGLES.

WRITE FOR COMPLETE INFORMATION.

1239

NEW YORK FINANCIAL WRITERS' ASSOCIATION (SCHOLARSHIP PROGRAM)

PO BOX 21
SYOSSET NY 11791
516/921-7766

AMOUNT: $2000

DEADLINE(S): LATE DEC

FIELD(S): FINANCIAL JOURNALISM

OPEN TO UNDERGRADUATE & GRADUATE STUDENTS WHO ARE ENROLLED IN AN ACCREDITED COLLEGE OR UNIVERSITY IN METROPOLITAN NEW YORK CITY & ARE PURSUING A COURSE OF STUDY LEADING TO A FINANCIAL OR BUSINESS JOURNALISM CAREER.

WRITE FOR COMPLETE INFORMATION.

1240

NEW YORK STATE SENATE (LEGISLATIVE FELLOWS PROGRAM; R.J.ROTH JOURNALISM FELLOWSHIP; R.A.WIEBE PUBLIC SERVICE FELLOWSHIP)

STATE CAPITOL ROOM 500A
ALBANY NY 12247
518/455-2611

AMOUNT: $22575

DEADLINE(S): SPRING

FIELD(S): POLITICAL SCIENCE; GOVERNMENT; PUBLIC SERVICE; JOURNALISM; PUBLIC RELATIONS

NY STATE RESIDENT. OPEN TO GRADUATE STUDENTS ENROLLED IN ACCREDITED PROGRAMS IN THE ABOVE AREAS. FELLOWS WORK AS REGULAR LEGISLATIVE STAFF MEMBERS OF THE OFFICES TO WHICH THEY ARE ASSIGNED. USA CITIZEN.

14 FELLOWSHIPS PER YEAR. WRITE FOR COMPLETE INFORMATION.

1241

NEW YORK UNIVERSITY (GALLATIN DIVISION SPECIAL AWARDS & SCHOLARSHIPS)

715 BROADWAY 6TH FLOOR
NEW YORK NY 10003
212/598-7077

AMOUNT: VARIES WITH AWARD

DEADLINE(S): NONE SPECIFIED

FIELD(S): PUBLISHING

VARIOUS SPECIAL AWARDS AND SCHOLARSHIPS ARE AVAILABLE TO UNDERGRADUATE AND GRADUATE STUDENTS ENROLLED IN THE GALLATIN DIVISION OF NEW YORK UNIVERSITY.

COMMUNICATIONS

104 SPECIAL AWARDS AND SCHOLARSHIPS PER YEAR. CONTACT ADDRESS ABOVE FOR COMPLETE INFORMATION.

1242

RADIO AND TELEVISION NEWS DIRECTORS FOUNDATION (BROADCAST JOURNALISM SCHOLARSHIP AWARDS)

1000 CONNECTICUT AVE NW; SUITE 615
WASHINGTON DC 20036
202/659-6510

AMOUNT: $1000 - $2000

DEADLINE(S): MAR 15

FIELD(S): RADIO & TELEVISION JOURNALISM

OPEN TO UNDERGRADUATE SOPHOMORES AND ABOVE AND MASTERS DEGREE CANDIDATES WHOSE CAREER OBJECTIVE IS RADIO AND TELEVISION NEWS. AWARDS ARE FOR 1 YEAR OF UNDERGRADUATE OR GRADUATE STUDY.

12 SCHOLARSHIPS AND 3 FELLOWSHIPS PER YEAR. NOT RENEWABLE. WRITE FOR COMPLETE INFORMATION.

1243

RADIO FREE EUROPE/RADIO LIBERTY (MEDIA & OPINION RESEARCH ON EASTERN EUROPE & THE FORMER SOVIET UNION)

PERSONNEL DIVISION;
1201 CONNECTICUT AVE NW
WASHINGTON DC 20036
WRITTEN INQUIRY

AMOUNT: DAILY STIPEND OF 48 GERMAN MARKS PLUS ACCOMMODATIONS

DEADLINE(S): FEB 22

FIELD(S): COMMUNICATIONS; MARKET RESEARCH; STATISTICS; SOCIOLOGY; SOCIAL PSYCHOLOGY; EAST EUROPEAN STUDIES

INTERNSHIP OPEN TO GRADUATE STUDENT OR EXCEPTIONALLY QUALIFIED UNDERGRADUATE IN THE ABOVE AREAS WHO CAN DEMONSTRATE KNOWLEDGE OF QUANTITIVE RESEARCH METHODS; COMPUTER APPLICATIONS AND PUBLIC OPINION SURVEY TECHNIQUES.

EAST EUROPEAN LANGUAGE SKILLS WOULD BE AN ADVANTAGE. WRITE FOR COMPLETE INFORMATION.

1244

SCRIPPS HOWARD FOUNDATION (SCRIPPS HOWARD FOUNDATION SCHOLARSHIPS)

312 WALNUT ST - 28TH FLOOR;
PO BOX 5380
CINCINNATI OH 45201
513/977-3035

AMOUNT: $500 TO $3000

DEADLINE(S): DEC 20 FOR AN APPLICATION; FEB 25 FOR MAILING IN APPLICATION

FIELD(S): JOURNALISM; COMMUNICATIONS

PREFERENCE TO (BUT NO LIMITED TO) FULL-TIME UNDERGRAD JUNIORS; SENIORS; GRAD STUDENTS OR PREVIOUS RECIPIENTS WHO ARE PREPARING TO WORK IN ANY PRINT OR BROADCAST MEDIA. USA CITIZEN OR LEGAL RESIDENT.

RENEWABLE WITH REAPPLICATION. SUBMIT LETTER WITH REQUEST FOR SCHOLARSHIP APPLICATION BEFORE DEC 20 STATING COLLEGE MAJOR AND CAREER GOAL.

1245

SOCIETY FOR TECHNICAL COMMUNICATION (GRADUATE SCHOLARSHIPS)

901 N. STUART ST. SUITE 304
ARLINGTON VA 22203
703/522-4114

AMOUNT: $1500

DEADLINE(S): FEB 15

FIELD(S): TECHNICAL COMMUNICATION

OPEN TO FULL-TIME GRADUATE STUDENTS WHO ARE ENROLLED IN AN ACCREDITED MASTER'S OR DOCTORAL DEGREE PROGRAM FOR CAREER IN ANY AREA OF TECHNICAL COMMUNICATION.

AWARDS TENABLE AT RECOGNIZED COLLEGES & UNIVERSITIES IN USA & CANADA. 6 AWARDS PER YEAR. WRITE FOR COMPLETE INFORMATION.

1246

SWEDISH INFORMATION SERVICE (BICENTENNIAL FUND GRANTS)

ONE DAG HAMMARSKJOLD PLAZA;
45TH FLOOR
NEW YORK NY 10017
212/751-5900

AMOUNT: 20000 SWEDISH KRONA

DEADLINE(S): FEB 1

FIELD(S): POLITICAL SCIENCE; BUSINESS ADMIN; EDUCATION; COMMUNICATION; CULTURE; ENVIRONMENTAL STUDIES

GRANTS TO PROVIDE THE OPPORTUNITY FOR THOSE IN A POSITION TO INFLUENCE PUBLIC OPINION AND CONTRIBUTE TO THE DEVELOPMENT OF THEIR SOCIETY. 3-6 WEEK INTENSIVE STUDY VISITS IN SWEDEN IN ANY OF THE ABOVE AREAS OR THEIR RELATED FIELDS.

US CITIZEN OR LEGAL RESIDENT. APPROXIMATELY 10 GRANTS PER YEAR. WRITE FOR COMPLETE INFORMATION.

1247

U.S. DEPT. OF EDUCATION (JACOB K JAVITS FELLOWSHIP PROGRAM)

PO BOX 84
WASHINGTON DC 20044
800/4FED-AID

AMOUNT: $15000 PER YEAR ON AVERAGE

DEADLINE(S): MAR 15

FIELD(S): ARTS; HUMANITIES; SOCIAL SCIENCES

FELLOWSHIPS TO ASSIST STUDENTS OF SUPERIOR ABILITIES IN STUDIES FOR DOCTORAL-LEVEL DEGREES IN SPECIFIED SUBFIELDS OF THE ABOVE AREAS. USA CITIZEN OR LEGAL RESIDENT.

APPLICATION PACKAGE AVAILABLE LATE OCT OR EARLY NOV. APPROX 100 AWARDS PER YEAR; RENEWABLE UP TO 48 MONTHS. WRITE FOR COMPLETE INFORMATION.

1248

UNITED METHODIST COMMUNICATIONS (STOODY-WEST FELLOWSHIP FOR GRADUATE STUDY IN JOURNALISM)

475 RIVERSIDE DR; SUITE 1901
NEW YORK NY 10115
212/663-8900

AMOUNT: $6000

DEADLINE(S): MAR 1

FIELD(S): RELIGIOUS JOURNALISM

CHRISTIAN FAITH. FELLOWSHIP OPEN TO STUDENTS ENROLLED IN ACCREDITED GRADUATE SCHOOLS OF COMMUNICATION OR JOURNALISM (PRINT; ELECTRONIC OR AUDIOVISUAL) AND PLANNING TO ENGAGE IN RELIGIOUS JOURNALISM.

PURPOSE OF THE FELLOWSHIP IS TO ENHANCE THE RECIPIENT'S POTENTIAL PROFESSIONAL COMPETENCE & THEREBY HELP TO PERPETUATE THE STANDARDS EXEMPLIFIED BY RALPH STOODY & ARTHUR WEST. WRITE FOR COMPLETE INFORMATION.

1249

UNIVERSITY OF MARYLAND (FELLOWSHIPS AND ASSISTANTSHIPS)

COLLEGE OF JOURNALISM -
GRADUATE OFFICE
COLLEGE PARK MD 20742
301/405-2380

AMOUNT: $10000 + REMISSION OF 10 CREDITS OF TUITION

DEADLINE(S): FEB 1

FIELD(S): ADVERTISING; PUBLIC RELATIONS; PUBLIC AFFAIRS REPORTING; BROADCAST JOURNALISM

OPEN TO GRADUATE STUDENTS FOR STUDY AT THE UNIVERSITY OF MARYLAND'S COLLEGE OF JOURNALISM. ELIGIBILITY IS BASED ON MERIT.

WRITE FOR COMPLETE INFORMATION.

1250

WOMEN IN COMMUNICATIONS - DETROIT CHAPTER (LUCY CORBETT; LENORE UPTON & MARY BUTLER SCHOLARSHIPS FOR MICHIGAN RESIDENTS)

PO BOX 688
HAMBURG MI 48139
313/791-1277

AMOUNT: $1000; $500; $500

DEADLINE(S): APR 2

FIELD(S): COMMUNICATIONS

OPEN TO MICHIGAN RESIDENTS. SCHOLARSHIPS TO BE USED FOR TUITION BY UNDERGRADUATE JUNIOR OR SENIOR OR GRADUATE STUDENT WHO IS MAJORING IN COMMUNICATIONS OR JOURNALISM AT A COLLEGE OR UNIVERSITY IN THE STATE OF MICHIGAN.

WRITE FOR COMPLETE INFORMATION.

HISTORY

1251

AMERICAN ANTIQUARIAN SOCIETY (VISITING RESEARCH FELLOWSHIPS)

185 SALISBURY ST
WORCESTER MA 01609
508/755-5221

AMOUNT: $850 PER MONTH

DEADLINE(S): JAN 15

FIELD(S): AMERICAN HISTORY; BIBLIOGRAPHY; PRINTING & PUBLISHING (THROUGH 1876)

FELLOWSHIPS OF ONE TO THREE MONTHS DURATION AT THE SOCIETY LIBRARY. FOR DOCTORAL DISSERTATION RESEARCH AND POST-DOCTORAL RESEARCH IN THE ABOVE FIELDS.

RECIPIENTS ARE EXPECTED TO BE IN REGULAR AND CONTINUOUS RESIDENCE AT THE SOCIETY LIBRARY DURING THE PERIOD OF THE GRANT. WRITE FOR COMPLETE INFORMATION.

1252

AMERICAN COUNCIL OF LEARNED SOCIETIES (ACLS FELLOWSHIPS)

OFFICE OF FELLOWSHIPS & GRANTS;
228 E. 45TH ST.
NEW YORK NY 10017
WRITTEN INQUIRY

HISTORY

AMOUNT: UP TO $20000

DEADLINE(S): SEP 30

FIELD(S): HUMANITIES; SOCIAL SCIENCES; OTHER AREAS HAVING PREDOMINATELY HUMANISTIC EMPHASIS

OPEN TO USA CITIZENS OR LEGAL RESIDENTS WHO HOLD THE PH.D OR ITS EQUIVALENT. FELLOWSHIPS ARE DESIGNED TO HELP SCHOLARS DEVOTE 2 TO 12 CONTINUOUS MONTHS TO FULL TIME RESEARCH.

WRITE FOR COMPLETE INFORMATION.

1253

AMERICAN HISTORICAL ASSN (ALBERT BEVERIDGE GRANTS)

400 A STREET SE
WASHINGTON DC 20003
202/544-2422

AMOUNT: UP TO $1000

DEADLINE(S): FEB 1

FIELD(S): WESTERN HEMISPHERE HISTORY (AMERICAS)

OPEN TO ANY GRADUATE OR POST-GRADUATE TO SUPPORT RESEARCH ON THE HISTORY OF THE AMERICAS HEMISPHERE. SHOULD JOIN AHA BEFORE APPLYING SINCE ONLY AHA MEMBERS ARE ELIGIBLE.

20-25 AWARDS PER YEAR. WRITE FOR COMPLETE INFORMATION.

1254

AMERICAN HISTORICAL ASSN (FELLOWSHIPS IN AEROSPACE HISTORY)

400 A STREET SE
WASHINGTON DC 20003
202/544-2422

AMOUNT: $25000 PH.D'S; $16000 PH.D CANDIDATES + TRAVEL EXPENSES

DEADLINE(S): FEB 1

FIELD(S): AMERICAN HISTORY-AEROSPACE

SUPPORTED BY NASA. FELLOWSHIP TO SPEND 6 MONTHS TO 1 YEAR AS PART OF THE HISTORY OFFICE AT NASA IN PURSUIT OF A PROPOSED RESEARCH PROJECT. OPEN TO PH.D'S & ADVANCED PH.D CANDIDATES WHO HAVE COMPLETED ALL CLASS WORK EXCEPT DISSERTATION.

US CITIZEN. MONEY CANNOT BE USED TO PAY TUITION. WRITE FOR COMPLETE INFORMATION.

1255

AMERICAN HISTORICAL ASSN (J FRANKLIN JAMESON FELLOWSHIP)

400 A STREET SE
WASHINGTON DC 20003
202/544-2422

AMOUNT: $10000

DEADLINE(S): MAR 15

FIELD(S): AMERICAN HISTORY

OPEN TO SCHOLARS WHO HAVE RECEIVED THE PH.D WITHIN THE PAST 5 YEARS. FELLOWSHIP IS TO SUPPORT SIGNIFICANT SCHOLARLY RESEARCH IN AMERICAN HISTORY IN THE LIBRARY OF CONGRESS COLLECTIONS. AWARD IS FOR ONE SEMESTER; CAN BE EXTENDED.

WRITE FOR COMPLETE INFORMATION.

1256

AMERICAN HISTORICAL ASSN (LITTLETON-GRISWOLD GRANTS)

400 A STREET SE
WASHINGTON DC 20003
202/544-2422

AMOUNT: $1000

DEADLINE(S): FEB 1

FIELD(S): AMERICAN LEGAL HISTORY

OPEN TO ANY GRADUATE STUDENT OR POST-GRADUATE TO SUPPORT A RESEARCH PROJECT ON AMERICAN LEGAL HISTORY AND THE FIELD OF LAW AND SOCIETY. SHOULD JOIN THE AHA PRIOR TO APPLYING SINCE ONLY AHA MEMBERS ARE ELIGIBLE.

5-7 AWARDS PER YEAR. WRITE FOR COMPLETE INFORMATION.

1257

AMERICAN HISTORICAL ASSN (MICHAEL KRAUS RESEARCH AWARD GRANT)

400 A STREET SE
WASHINGTON DC 20003
202/544-2422

AMOUNT: $800

DEADLINE(S): FEB 1

FIELD(S): AMERICAN HISTORY

OPEN TO GRAD STUDENTS & POST-GRADS. CASH AWARD FOR MOST DESERVING PROPOSAL RELATING TO WORK IN PROGRESS ON AMERICAN COLONIAL HISTORY WITH PARTICULAR REFERENCE TO INTERCULTURAL ASPECTS OF AMERICAN AND EUROPEAN RELATIONS.

SHOULD JOIN AHA PRIOR TO APPLYING SINCE ONLY MEMBERS ARE ELIGIBLE. WRITE FOR COMPLETE INFORMATION.

1258

AMERICAN HISTORIAL ASSOCIATION (PUBLISHED BOOK AWARDS)

400 A STREET SE
WASHINGTON DC 20003
202/544-2422

AMOUNT: $500 - $2000

DEADLINE(S): MAY 15

FIELD(S): HISTORICAL WRITING (ALREADY PUBLISHED BOOKS ONLY)

AWARDS OFFERED FOR ALREADY PUBLISHED BOOKS ON HISTORICAL SUBJECTS RANGING FROM 17TH CENTURY EUROPEAN HISTORY TO THE HISTORY OF THE FEMINIST MOVEMENT.

NOT A CONTESTAND -NOT- FOR HIGH SCHOOL. FOR ALREADY PUBLISHED WORKS ONLY. WRITE FOR DETAILS.

1259 ───────────────

AMERICAN PHILOSOPHICAL SOCIETY (JOHN CLARKE SLATER FELLOWSHIP)

LIBRARY; 105 S. FIFTH ST.
PHILADELPHIA PA 19106
WRITTEN INQUIRY ONLY

AMOUNT: $12000

DEADLINE(S): DEC 1

FIELD(S): HISTORY OF PHYSICAL SCIENCE

OPEN TO DOCTORAL CANDIDATES WHO HAVE PASSED THEIR PRELIMINARY EXAMINATIONS AND ARE WRITING DISSERTATIONS ON THE HISTORY OF 20TH CENTURY PHYSICAL SCIENCES.

WRITE FOR COMPLETE INFORMATION.

1260 ───────────────

AMERICAN PHILOSOPHICAL SOCIETY (PHILLIPS GRANTS ON NORTH AMERICAN INDIANS)

LIBRARY; 105 S. FIFTH ST.
PHILADELPHIA PA 19106
WRITTEN INQUIRY

AMOUNT: $1300 (AVERAGE)

DEADLINE(S): MAR 15

FIELD(S): AMERICAN INDIAN HISTORY

FOR RESEARCH INTO THE LINGUISTICS AND ETHNOHISTORY OF NORTH AMERICAN INDIANS. OPEN TO GRADUATE STUDENTS AS WELL AS POSTDOCTORAL CANDIDATES.

WRITE FOR COMPLETE INFORMATION.

1261 ───────────────

ARCHAEOLOGICAL INSTITUTE OF AMERICA (OLIVIA JAMES TRAVELING FELLOWSHIP)

675 COMMONWEALTH AVE
BOSTON MA 02215
617/353-9361; FAX 617/353-6550

AMOUNT: $11500 STIPEND

DEADLINE(S): NOV 15

FIELD(S): ARCHAEOLOGY; CLASSICS; SCULPTURE; HISTORY; ARCHITECTURE

FOR GRADUATE OR POST-GRADUATE STUDY IN GREECE; AEGEAN ISLANDS; SICILY; SOUTHERN ITALY; ASIA MINOR OR MESOPOTAMIA. PREFERENCE IS FOR DISSERTATION OR RECENT PH.D RESEARCH. WILL NOT SUPPORT FIELD EXCAVATION. USA CITIZEN OR LEGAL RESIDENT.

WRITE FOR COMPLETE INFORMATION.

1262 ───────────────

BRANDEIS UNIVERSITY (IRVING & ROSE CROWN PH.D FELLOWSHIPS & TUITION SCHOLARSHIPS)

DEPARTMENT OF HISTORY
WALTHAM MA 02254
617/736-2270

AMOUNT: UP TO $8500; TUITION SCHOLARSHIPS

DEADLINE(S): MAR 1

FIELD(S): AMERICAN HISTORY

ALL PERSONS ACCEPTED TO PH.D PROGRAM ARE ELIGIBLE FOR FELLOWSHIPS & TUITION SCHOLARSHIPS. BOTH PROGRAMS ARE BASED ON MERIT.

AWARDS ARE RENEWABLE. WRITE FOR COMPLETE INFORMATION.

1263 ───────────────

CENTER FOR MEDIEVAL AND RENAISSANCE STUDIES (RESEARCH ASSISTANTSHIP)

C/O UCLA; 212 ROYCE HALL
LOS ANGELES CA 90024
213/825-1880

AMOUNT: $1115 - $1425

DEADLINE(S): MID MAR

FIELD(S): MEDIEVAL & RENAISSANCE STUDIES.

RESEARCH ASSISTANTSHIPS ARE OFFERED ON A COMPETITIVE BASIS TO GRADUATE STUDENTS AT UCLA. EACH ASSISTANT IS ASSIGNED TO FACULTY MEMBERS IN HIS OWN OR RELATED FIELD FOR APPROX 20 HOURS A WEEK. MUST BE REGISTERED UCLA STUDENT.

4 ASSISTANTSHIPS PER YEAR. THE AWARD IS FOR ONE YEAR; IT IS NOT AUTOMATICALLY RENEWABLE NOR CAN IT BE HELD CONCURRENTLY WITH A SECOND MAJOR AWARD. PREFERENCE IS GIVEN TO CONTINUING STUDENTS.

1264 ───────────────

COMMITTEE ON INSTITUTIONAL COOPERATION (CIC PREDOCTORAL FELLOWSHIPS)

KIRKWOOD HALL RM 111; INDIANA UNIV.
BLOOMINGTON IN 47405
812/855-0822

AMOUNT: $9500 + TUITION (5 YEARS)

HISTORY

DEADLINE(S): JAN 2

FIELD(S): HUMANITIES; SOCIAL SCIENCES; NATURAL SCIENCES; MATHEMATICS; ENGINEERING

PREDOCTORAL FELLOWSHIPS FOR USA CITIZENS OF AFRICAN AMERICAN; AMERICAN INDIAN; MEXICAN AMERICAN OR PUERTO RICAN HERITAGE. MUST HOLD OR EXPECT TO RECEIVE BACHELOR'S DEGREE BY LATE SUMMER FROM A REGIONALLY ACCREDITED COLLEGE OR UNIVERSITY.

AWARDS FOR SPECIFIED UNIVERSITIES IN IL; IN; IA; MI; MN; OH; WI; PA. WRITE FOR DETAILS.

1265 ─────────────

CONFERENCE ON LATIN AMERICAN HISTORY (JAMES R. SCOBIE MEMORIAL AWARD FOR PRELIMINARY PH.D. RESEARCH)

LATIN AMERICAN AREA CTR; U OF ARIZ; 1522 E. DRACHMAN
TUCSON AZ 85721
602/622-4002; FAX 602/622-0177

AMOUNT: $900

DEADLINE(S): MAR 15

FIELD(S): LATIN AMERICAN HISTORY

TRAVEL GRANT WILL BE AWARDED EACH YEAR FOR USE DURING THE FOLLOWING SUMMER FOR PRELIMINARY PH.D RESEARCH (NOT DISSERTATION RESEARCH).

WRITE FOR COMPLETE INFORMATION.

1266 ─────────────

COUNCIL FOR EUROPEAN STUDIES (PRE-DISSERTATION FELLOWSHIP PROGRAM)

C/O COLUMBIA UNIV; BOX 44 SCHERMERHORN HALL
NEW YORK NY 10027
212/854-4172

AMOUNT: $3000

DEADLINE(S): FEB 1

FIELD(S): EUROPEAN HISTORY; SOCIOLOGY; POLITICAL SCIENCE; ANTHROPOLOGY; ECONOMICS

GRANTS FOR EXPLORATORY RESEARCH IN EUROPE FOR GRAD STUDENTS WHO HAVE COMPLETED AT LEAST TWO YEARS GRADUATE STUDY AND INTEND TO PURSUE A PH.D. USA OR CANADIAN CITIZEN OR LEGAL RESIDENT.

APPLICANTS SHOULD HAVE AT LEAST ONE YEAR OF STUDY IN AN APPROPRIATE FOREIGN LANGUAGE OR MUST SHOW WHY THE REQUIREMENT IS INAPPROPRIATE. WRITE FOR COMPLETE INFORMATION.

1267 ─────────────

DIRKSEN CONGRESSIONAL CENTER (CONGRESSIONAL RESEARCH GRANTS PROGRAM)

301 S 4TH ST - SUITE A
PEKIN IL 61554
309/347-7113; FAX 309/347-6432

AMOUNT: UP TO $3500; POSSIBLY SALARY TO $1500/MO

DEADLINE(S): MAR 31 (POSTMARK)

FIELD(S): POLITICAL SCIENCE; AMERICAN HISTORY (WITH EMPHASIS ON US CONGRESS OR CONGRESSIONAL LEADERSHIP)

OPEN TO ANYONE WITH A SERIOUS INTEREST IN STUDYING THE US CONGRESS. RESEARCH MUST BE ORIGINAL CULMINATING IN NEW KNOWLEDGE OR NEW INTERPRETATION OR BOTH. POLITICAL SCIENTISTS; HISTORIANS; BIOGRAPHERS; JOURNALISTS AND OTHERS MAY APPLY.

WRITE FOR COMPLETE INFORMATION.

1268 ─────────────

EARLY AMERICAN INDUSTRIES ASSN INC (GRANTS-IN-AID)

GRANTS IN AID COORDINATOR;
1324 SHALLCROSS AVE.
WILMINGTON DE 19806
302/652-7297

AMOUNT: $500 - $1000

DEADLINE(S): MAR 15

FIELD(S): AMERICAN INDUSTRIAL HISTORY

OPEN TO GRAD OR POST-GRAD RESEARCHERS HAVING PROJECTS RELATED TO THE ASSOCIATION'S PURPOSES. GRANTS ARE TO ENCOURAGE STUDY & BETTER UNDERSTANDING OF EARLY AMERICAN INDUSTRY. PROJECTS MAY HAVE INSTITUTIONAL SPONSOR OR BE SELF DIRECTED.

PROJECTS SHOULD RELATE TO THE DISCOVERY; IDENTIFICATION; CLASSIFICATION & EXHIBITION OF OBSOLETE TOOLS; IMPLEMENTS & MECHANICAL DEVICES USED IN EARLY AMERICA. USA CITIZENS. WRITE FOR COMPLETE INFORMATION.

1269 ─────────────

FLORIDA ENDOWMENT FUND FOR HIGHER EDUCATION (MCKNIGHT DOCTORAL FELLOWSHIP PROGRAM)

201 E.KENNEDY BLVD; SUITE 1525
TAMPA FL 33602
813/272-2772

AMOUNT: $11000 STIPEND + $5000 TUITION & FEES (PER YEAR)

DEADLINE(S): JAN 15

FIELD(S): ALL FIELDS (EXCEPT LAW; MEDICINE & EDUCATION)

OPEN TO ALL AFRICAN-AMERICANS WITH AT LEAST A BACHELOR'S DEGREE FROM AN ACCREDITED INSTITUTION WHO WISH TO PURSUE A DOCTORAL DEGREE. PROGRAM RECRUITS NATIONWIDE; HOWEVER FELLOWS MUST ENROLL IN A FLORIDA INSTITUTION. USA CITIZEN.

25 AWARDS PER YEAR. RENEWABLE FOR UP TO 5 YEARS. WRITE FOR COMPLETE INFORMATION.

1270 ————————————————

FOLGER SHAKESPEARE LIBRARY (SENIOR SCHOLAR FELLOWSHIPS)

C/O SHARON CARROLL;
201 E. CAPITOL ST. SE
WASHINGTON DC 20003
202/544-4600

AMOUNT: $9600; $14400; $27500 STIPENDS

DEADLINE(S): NOV 1

FIELD(S): RENAISSANCE STUDIES

FOLGER LONG-TERM FELLOWSHIPS AVAILABLE TO SENIOR SCHOLARS WHO HAVE MADE SUBSTANTIAL CONTRIBUTIONS IN THEIR FIELDS OF RESEARCH & ARE PURSUING PROJECTS APPROPRIATE TO THE FOLGER COLLECTIONS.

FELLOWSHIPS ARE FOR 6-9 MONTHS. WRITE ADDRESS ABOVE FOR COMPLETE INFORMATION.

1271 ————————————————

FOLGER SHAKESPEARE LIBRARY (SHORT-TERM RESEARCH FELLOWSHIPS)

C/O SHARON CARROLL;
201 E. CAPITOL ST. SE
WASHINGTON DC 20003
202/544-4600

AMOUNT: $1600 PER MONTH STIPEND

DEADLINE(S): MAR 1

FIELD(S): RENAISSANCE STUDIES

SHORT-TERM (1-3 MONTHS) POST-DOCTORAL FELLOWSHIPS FOR RESEARCH AT THE FOLGER LIBRARY WHICH HOUSES AN EXTENSIVE COLLECTION OF RENAISSANCE BOOKS AND MANUSCRIPTS.

WRITE FOR COMPLETE INFORMATION.

1272 ————————————————

GERMANISTIC SOCIETY OF AMERICA (FOREIGN STUDY SCHOLARSHIPS)

809 UNITED NATIONS PLAZA
NEW YORK NY 10017
212/984-5330

AMOUNT: $8500

DEADLINE(S): OCT 31

FIELD(S): HISTORY; POLITICAL SCIENCE; INT'L RELATIONS; PUBLIC AFFAIRS; LANGUAGE; PHILOSOPHY; LITERATURE

APPLICANTS MUST BE US CITIZENS WITH A BACHELORS DEGREE. AWARDS ARE FOR GRADUATE STUDY AT A WEST GERMAN UNIVERSITY.

SELECTION IS BASED UPON PROPOSED PROJECT; LANGUAGE FLUENCY; ACADEMIC ACHIEVEMENT; & REFERENCES. WRITE FOR COMPLETE INFORMATION.

1273 ————————————————

GETTY CENTER FOR THE HISTORY OF ART & THE HUMANITIES (PREDOCTORAL & POSTDOCTORAL FELLOWSHIPS)

DR H.H.HYMANS;
401 WILSHIRE BLVD; #400
SANTA MONICA CA 90401
310/458-9811

AMOUNT: $15000 PREDOCTORAL; $20000 POSTDOCTORAL

DEADLINE(S): DEC 1

FIELD(S): HUMANITIES; SOCIAL SCIENCES; ANTHROPOLOGY; ART/SCIENCE HISTORY; LITERATURE; PHILOSOPHY ETC.

OPEN TO PRE & POSTDOCTORAL SCHOLARS WHOSE AREAS OF RESEARCH COMPLEMENT THE CENTER'S PROGRAMS & RESOURCES. PREDOCTORAL CANDIDATES SHOULD EXPECT TO COMPLETE DISSERTATIONS DURING THE FELLOWSHIP YEAR.

POSTDOCTORALS SHOULD HAVE RECEIVED DOCTORATE IN HUMANITIES OR SOCIAL SCIENCES WITHIN LAST 3 YEARS & BE REWRITING DISSERTATIONS FOR PUBLICATION. WRITE FOR COMPLETE INFORMATION.

1274 ————————————————

HAGLEY PROGRAM (GRADUATE FELLOWSHIPS)

C/O DEPT. OF HISTORY;
UNIV. OF DELAWARE
NEWARK DE 19716
302/451-8226

AMOUNT: FULL TUITION + STIPEND OF $9100 MASTERS; $10080 PH.D

DEADLINE(S): FEB 1

FIELD(S): AMERICAN HISTORY

HISTORY

GRADUATE FELLOWSHIPS FOR STUDY OF THE HISTORY OF INDUSTRIALIZATION IN AMERICA. APPLICANTS MUST HAVE STRONG AMERICAN HISTORY BACKGROUND AND TAKE APTITUDE PORTION OF THE GRE NO LATER THAN DECEMBER TO ASSURE FULL CONSIDERATION OF APPLICATION.

3 TO 4 FELLOWSHIPS PER CALENDAR YEAR. AWARD PROVIDES TUITION PLUS TRAVEL ALLOWANCE. WRITE FOR COMPLETE INFORMATION.

1275

HARRY S TRUMAN LIBRARY INSTITUTE (GRANTS-IN-AID PROGRAM)

SECRETARY
INDEPENDENCE MO 64050
816-833-1400

AMOUNT: VARIES

DEADLINE(S): VARIES

FIELD(S): AMERICAN HISTORY

OPEN TO SCHOLARS INVESTIGATING SOME ASPECT OF THE POLITICAL ECONOMIC AND SOCIAL DEVELOPMENT OF THE USA BETWEEN APR 12 1945 AND JAN 20 1953 OR THE PUBLIC CAREER OF PRESIDENT HARRY S TRUMAN.

WRITE TO THE SECRETARY OF THE HARRY S TRUMAN LIBRARY INSTITUTE; INDEPENDENCE MO; FOR APPLICATION FORMS AND COMPLETE INFORMATION.

1276

HISTORICAL COMMISSION OF THE SOUTHERN BAPTIST CONVENTION (STUDY GRANTS)

901 COMMERCE STREET SUITE 400
NASHVILLE TN 37203-3630
615/244-0344

AMOUNT: $100 - $500

DEADLINE(S): APR 1

FIELD(S): HISTORY OF BAPTISTS

OPEN TO GRADUATE STUDENTS; COLLEGE & SEMINARY PROFESSORS; HISTORIANS & OTHER WRITERS. FOR RESEARCH PROJECTS INVOLVING STUDY OF SOME MAJOR FACET OF HISTORY OF BAPTISTS.

MAJOR SOURCES OF INFORMATION FOR STUDY ARE IN THE SOUTHERN BAPTIST HISTORICAL LIBRARY & ARCHIVES OPERATED BY THE COMMISSION. WRITE FOR COMPLETE INFORMATION.

1277

HOOVER INSTITUTION ON WAR; REVOLUTION AND PEACE (NATIONAL FELLOWS PROGRAM)

STANFORD UNIVERSITY
STANFORD CA 94305
415/723-0163

AMOUNT: $32000

DEADLINE(S): JAN 13

FIELD(S): SOCIOLOGY; MODERN HISTORY; POLITICAL SCIENCE; ECONOMICS; INT'L RELATIONS; EDUCATION; LAW

POST-DOCTORAL FELLOWSHIPS THAT PROVIDE PARTICULARLY GIFTED JUNIOR SCHOLARS THE OPPORTUNITY TO SPEND ONE FULL YEAR ON UNRESTRICTED CREATIVE RESEARCH AND WRITING AT THE HOOVER INSTITUTION. USA OR CANADIAN CITIZEN.

12 TO 14 FELLOWSHIPS PER YEAR. RECIPIENTS ARE EXPECTED TO STAY IN RESIDENCY AT THE HOOVER INSTITUTION. WRITE FOR COMPLETE INFORMATION.

1278

INSTITUT FUR EUROPAISCHE GESCHICHTE (FELLOWSHIP PROGRAM)

ALTE UNIVERSITATSSTRASSE 19
D-6500 MAINZ; GERMANY
06131/39 93 60; FAX 23 79 88

AMOUNT: DM1220 - DM1490

DEADLINE(S): NONE SPECIFIED

FIELD(S): EUROPEAN HISTORY

OPEN TO ADVANCED PH.D CANDIDATES & POST-DOCTORAL APPLICANTS. COMPLETION OF DISSERTATION IS NOT ESSENTIAL; BUT IS PREFERABLE. FELLOWSHIPS ALSO GRANTED TO APPLICANTS WHOSE RESEARCH REQUIRES INVESTIGATIONS IN GERMAN ARCHIVES.

APPROX 30 6-12 MONTH FELLOWSHIPS PER YEAR. RENEWABLE. WRITE FOR COMPLETE INFORMATION.

1279

INSTITUTE FOR ADVANCED STUDY (POST-DOCTORAL FELLOWSHIP AWARDS)

OLDEN LANE
PRINCETON NJ 08540
609-734-8000

AMOUNT: VARIES ACCORDING TO SCHOOL

DEADLINE(S): CHECK WITH SCHOOL

FIELD(S): HISTORICAL STUDIES; SOCIAL SCIENCES; NATURAL SCIENCES; MATHEMATICS

POST-DOCTORAL FELLOWSHIPS AT THE
INSTITUTE FOR ADVANCED STUDY FOR
THOSE WHOSE TERM CAN BE EXPECTED TO
RESULT IN A WORK OF SIGNIFICANCE AND
INDIVIDUALITY.

150-160 FELLOWSHIPS PER ACADEMIC YEAR
ALTHOUGH SOME CAN BE EXTENDED.
REQUEST APPLICATION MATERIALS FROM
SCHOOL'S ADMINISTRATIVE OFFICER.

1280

INSTITUTE OF EARLY AMERICAN HISTORY AND CULTURE (POST-DOCTORAL FELLOWSHIP PROGRAM)

BOX 220
WILLIAMSBURG VA 23187
804/221-1110

AMOUNT: $27000 STIPEND + SOME RESEARCH TRAVEL FUNDS

DEADLINE(S): NOV 15

FIELD(S): EARLY AMERICAN HISTORY AND CULTURE (PRIOR TO 1820)

POSTDOCTORAL RESEARCH FELLOWSHIPS AT
THE INSTITUTE OPEN TO PROMISING JUNIOR
SCHOLARS IN ANY AREA OF EARLY
AMERICAN STUDIES. APPOINTMENTS ARE
FOR 2 YEARS. RESIDENT OF USA FOR AT
LEAST 3 YEARS.

WRITE FOR COMPLETE INFORMATION.

1281

MARY MCEWEN SCHIMKE SCHOLARSHIP (SUPPORT SCHOLARSHIPS)

C/O WELLESLEY COLLEGE;
SECRETARY GRADUATE FELLOWSHIPS; CAREER CENTER
WELLESLEY MA 02181
617/283-3525

AMOUNT: UP TO $1000 STIPEND

DEADLINE(S): DEC 1

FIELD(S): LITERATURE; AMERICAN HISTORY; PREFERENCE GIVEN TO AMERICAN STUDIES

SUPPLEMENTAL AWARD FOR THE PURPOSE OF
AFFORDING RELIEF FROM HOUSEHOLD AND
CHILD CARE WHILE PURSUING GRADUATE
STUDY. AWARD IS BASED ON SCHOLARLY
EXPECTATION AND IDENTIFIED NEED.

CANDIDATE MUST BE OVER 30 AND CURRENTLY
ENGAGED IN GRADUATE STUDY IN
GRADUATE STUDY IN LITERATURE AND/OR
HISTORY WITH PREFERENCE GIVEN TO
AMERICAN STUDIES. WRITE FOR COMPLETE
INFORMATION.

1282

NATIONAL HISTORICAL PUBLICATIONS AND RECORDS COMMISSION (POST-DOCTORAL FELLOWSHIPS)

NATIONAL ARCHIVES BUILDING
WASHINGTON DC 20408
202/501-5605

AMOUNT: $25000

DEADLINE(S): MAR 1

FIELD(S): AMERICAN HISTORY-HISTORICAL EDITING

POST DOCTORAL FELLOWSHIPS FOR STUDENTS
OF AMERICAN HISTORY OR AMERICAN
CIVILIZATION WHO DEMONSTRATE A
SPECIAL NEED FOR OR AN INTEREST IN
SPECIALIZED TRAINING IN HISTORICAL
EDITING. USA CITIZEN OR LEGAL RESIDENT.

WRITE FOR COMPLETE INFORMATION.

1283

NATIONAL HUMANITIES CENTER (POST-DOCTORAL FELLOWSHIPS)

PO BOX 12256; 7 ALEXANDER DR
RESEARCH TRIANGLE PARK NC 27709
919/549-0661

AMOUNT: STIPEND + TRAVEL EXPENSES

DEADLINE(S): OCT 15

FIELD(S): HISTORY; LANGUAGES & LITERATURE; PHILOSOPHY; OTHER FIELDS IN THE LIBERAL ARTS

POST-DOCTORAL RESEARCH FELLOWSHIPS OPEN
TO YOUNG & SENIOR SCHOLARS FROM ANY
NATION. AWARDS SUPPORT RESEARCH &
WRITING AT THE CENTER. SCHOLARS FROM
OTHER AREAS SUCH AS NATURAL SCIENCES;
ARTS; PROFESSIONS & PUBLIC LIFE ALSO
MAY APPLY.

30-35 FELLOWSHIPS PER YEAR. WRITE FOR COMPLETE INFORMATION.

1284

NATIONAL RESEARCH COUNCIL (NATIONAL SCIENCE FOUNDATION GRADUATE FELLOWSHIPS)

2101 CONSTITUTION AVE
WASHINGTON DC 20418
202/334-2872

AMOUNT: $14000 STIPEND + $7000 TUITION ALLOWANCE

DEADLINE(S): NOV 10

FIELD(S): SOCIAL SCIENCES; PHYSICAL SCIENCES; MATHEMATICS; BIOLOGY; ENGINEERING

DOCTORAL) WHO HAVE NOT COMPLETED MORE THAN 1 YEAR OF GRAD STUDY. FELLOWSHIPS TENABLE AT ANY ACCREDITED INSTITUTION OFFERING ADVANCED DEGREES IN THE AREAS ABOVE. USA CITIZEN OR PERMANENT RESIDENT.

OPEN TO HISTORY & PHILOSOPHY OF SCIENCE STUDENTS ALSO. 950 NEW 3-YEAR FELLOWSHIPS AWARDED EACH YEAR. WRITE FOR COMPLETE INFORMATION.

1285

NATIONAL SPACE CLUB (DR. ROBERT H. GODDARD HISTORICAL ESSAY AWARD)

655 15TH ST NW #300
WASHINGTON DC 20005
202/639-4210

AMOUNT: $1000

DEADLINE(S): DEC 1

FIELD(S): AEROSPACE HISTORY

ESSAY COMPETITION OPEN TO ANY USA CITIZEN ON A TOPIC DEALING WITH ANY SIGNIFICANT ASPECT OF THE HISTORICAL DEVELOPMENT OF ROCKETRY AND ASTRONAUTICS. ESSAYS SHOULD NOT EXCEED 5000 WORDS AND SHOULD BE FULLY DOCUMENTED.

WRITE FOR COMPLETE INFORMATION.

1286

NEWCOMEN SOCIETY OF THE UNITED STATES (NEWCOMEN-HARVARD ANNUAL POST-DOCTORAL FELLOWSHIP IN BUSINESS HISTORY)

412 NEWCOMEN ROAD
EXTON PA 19341
215/363-6600

AMOUNT: $40000

DEADLINE(S): MAR 15

FIELD(S): HISTORY - BUSINESS

INDIVIDUALS HAVING A DOCTORATE IN HISTORY WHO ARE ACTIVE IN EDUCATION MAY APPLY FOR FELLOWSHIPS IN BUSINESS HISTORY AT HARVARD GRADUATE SCHOOL OF BUSINESS ADMINISTRATION.

FOR COMPLETE INFORMATION WRITE TO PROF. THOMAS K. MCCRAW; GRADUATE SCHOOL OF BUSINESS ADMINISTRATION; HARVARD UNIVERSITY; SOLDIERS FIELD ROAD; BOSTON MA 02163.

1287

PHI ALPHA THETA-INTERNATIONAL HONOR SOCIETY IN HISTORY (PAT SCHOLARSHIP GRANTS)

2333 LIBERTY STREET
ALLENTOWN PA 18104
215/433-4140

AMOUNT: $750; $1000; $1250

DEADLINE(S): MAR 15

FIELD(S): HISTORY/PAT MEMBERS

GRADUATE FELLOWSHIPS FOR MEMBERS OF PHI ALPHA THETA FOR WORK LEADING TO THE MASTER'S DEGREE IN HISTORY OR FOR ADVANCED GRADUATE STUDY.

6 AWARDS PER YEAR. WRITE FOR COMPLETE INFORMATION.

1288

PHI ALPHA THETA-INTERNATIONAL HONOR SOCIETY IN HISTORY (ADVANCED GRADUATE STUDENT MEMBER AWARD)

2333 LIBERTY STREET
ALLENTOWN PA 18104
215/433-4140

AMOUNT: $1000

DEADLINE(S): JUN 1

FIELD(S): HISTORY/PAT MEMBERS

DOCTORAL FELLOWSHIP FOR ADVANCED PH.D STUDENTS WHO ARE MEMBERS OF PHI ALPHA THETA. THE AWARD IS INTENDED FOR PROJECTS CONNECTED WITH COMPLETION OF PH.D DEGREE SUCH AS RESEARCH TRAVEL; RESEARCH MATERIALS; DISSERTATION EXPENSES ETC.

WRITE FOR COMPLETE INFORMATION.

1289

PRINCETON UNIVERSITY-SHELBY CULLOM DAVIS CENTER FOR HISTORICAL STUDIES (POST-DOCTORAL FELLOWSHIPS)

C/O 129 DICKINSON HALL; HISTORY DEPT
PRINCETON NJ 08544
609/258-4997

AMOUNT: UP TO $56000 PER YEAR

DEADLINE(S): DEC 1

FIELD(S): HISTORY

POST-DOCTORAL FELLOWSHIPS AT PRINCETON FOR HIGHLY RECOMMENDED YOUNG SCHOLARS AND SENIOR SCHOLARS WITH ESTABLISHED REPUTATIONS. THEME FOR 1991-94 IS 'PROOF AND PERSUASION.'

CANDIDATES SHOULD HAVE COMPLETED THEIR DISSERTATION AND HAVE A FULL-TIME PAID POSITION TO RETURN TO. WRITE FOR COMPLETE INFORMATION.

1290

SMITHSONIAN INSTITUTION (NATIONAL AIR & SPACE MUSEUM GUGGENHEIM FELLOWSHIPS)

INTERPRETIVE PROGRAMS; ROOM 3341; MRC-313;
6TH & INDEPENDENCE AVE SW
WASHINGTON DC 20560
WRITTEN INQUIRY

AMOUNT: $13000 - $21000 STIPEND + TRAVEL ALLOWANCE

DEADLINE(S): JAN 15

FIELD(S): AVIATION; AERONAUTICS; SPACE SCIENCE & EXPLORATION; EARTH & PLANETARY SCIENCES; LIFE SCIENCES

PRE-DOCTORAL APPLICANTS SHOULD HAVE COMPLETED PRELIMINARY COURSE WORK & EXAMS AND BE ENGAGED IN DISSERTATION RESEARCH. POST-DOCTORAL APPLICANTS SHOULD HAVE RECEIVED THEIR PH.D WITHIN THE PAST SEVEN YEARS.

OPEN TO ALL NATIONALITIES. FLUENCY IN ENGLISH REQUIRED. DURATION IS 6-12 MONTHS. WRITE FOR COMPLETE INFORMATION.

1291

SOCIAL SCIENCE RESEARCH COUNCIL (INTERNATIONAL PREDISSERTATION FELLOWSHIP PROGRAM)

ELLEN PERECMAN; 605 THIRD AVE.
NEW YORK NY 10158
212-661-0280

AMOUNT: VARIES

DEADLINE(S): TO BE ANNOUNCED BY PARTICIPATING UNIVERSITIES

FIELD(S): ECONOMICS; POLITICAL SCIENCE; PSYCHOLOGY SOCIOLOGY; OTHER SOCIAL SCIENCE DISCIPLINES

OPEN TO PH.D CANDIDATES ENROLLED IN SOCIAL SCIENCES PROGRAMS AT SELECTED UNIVERSITIES. STUDENTS SHOULD BE INTERESTED IN SUPPLEMENTING THEIR DISCIPLINARY SKILLS WITH AREA AND LANGUAGE STUDIES.

FELLOWS UNDERTAKE A PROGRAM OF STUDY IN OR ON AFRICA; CHINA; LATIN AMERICA; THE CARIBBEAN; THE NEAR & MIDDLE EAST; SOUTH ASIA OR SOUTHEAST ASIA. WRITE FOR COMPLETE INFORMATION.

1292

SOCIETY FOR HISTORIANS OF AMERICAN FOREIGN RELATIONS (W. STULL HOLT DISSERTATION FELLOWSHIP)

C/O PROF. WILLIAM STUECK; DEPT OF HISTORY;
UNIVERSITY OF GEORGIA
ATHENS GA 30602
404/542-2053

AMOUNT: $1500

DEADLINE(S): APR 1

FIELD(S): AMERICAN FOREIGN RELATIONS HISTORY

PH.D DISSERTATION FELLOWSHIPS TO HELP DEFRAY TRAVEL AND LIVING EXPENSES CONNECTED WITH RESEARCH AND/OR WRITING OF DISSERTATION.

WRITE FOR COMPLETE INFORMATION.

1293

SOCIETY OF AMERICAN HISTORIANS (ALLAN NEVINS PRIZE)

603 FAYERWEATHER HALL;
COLUMBIA UNIV.
NEW YORK NY 10027
212/854-2221 OR 212/854-5943

AMOUNT: $1000

DEADLINE(S): DEC 31

FIELD(S): AMERICAN HISTORY

AWARD FOR BEST DISSERTATION OF THE PRECEDING YEAR. QUALIFIED INDIVIDUALS WHO HAVE WRITTEN APPROPRIATE DOCTORAL DISSERTATIONS MAY BE RECOMMENDED BY THEIR DEPARTMENTS.

IN ADDITION TO THE AWARD THE MANUSCRIPT IS SUBMITTED FOR PUBLICATION WHICH USUALLY RESULTS IN A PUBLISHING CONTRACT. WRITE FOR COMPLETE INFORMATION.

1294

SOURISSEAU ACADEMY FOR STATE AND LOCAL HISTORY (RESEARCH GRANT)

C/O SAN JOSE STATE UNIVERSITY
SAN JOSE CA. 95192
408/924-6510 OR 408/227-2657

AMOUNT: $500

DEADLINE(S): APR 1; NOV 1

FIELD(S): CALIFORNIA HISTORY

GRANTS ARE AVAILABLE TO SUPPORT UNDERGRADUATE AND GRADUATE RESEARCH ON CALIFORNIA HISTORY. PREFERENCE TO RESEARCH ON SANTA CLARA COUNTY HISTORY.

5-10 AWARDS PER YEAR ARE GRANTED FOR PROJECT EXPENSES. WRITE FOR COMPLETE INFORMATION.

1295

STATE HISTORICAL SOCIETY OF WISCONSIN (ALICE E. SMITH FELLOWSHIP)

816 STATE ST
MADISON WI 53706
608/264-6464

AMOUNT: $2000

DEADLINE(S): JUL 15

FIELD(S): AMERICAN HISTORY

OUTRIGHT GRANT OPEN TO ANY WOMAN DOING RESEARCH IN AMERICAN HISTORY. PREFERENCE WILL BE GIVEN TO GRADUATE RESEARCH ON HISTORY OF MID-WEST OR STATE OF WISCONSIN. TRANSCRIPTS; WORK SAMPLES & REFERENCES ARE NEITHER REQUIRED NOR SOUGHT.

LETTERS OF APPLICATION SHOULD DESCRIBE IN DETAIL THE APPLICANT'S CURRENT RESEARCH. SEND TO STATE HISTORIAN AT ADDRESS ABOVE.

1296

U.S. AIR FORCE (DISSERTATION YEAR FELLOWSHIPS IN US MILITARY/AEROSPACE HISTORY)

OFFICE OF AIR FORCE HISTORY;
HQ USAF; CHO - BLDG 5681
BOLLING AFB DC 20332
202-767-5764

AMOUNT: $10000

DEADLINE(S): MAR 15

FIELD(S): US MILITARY AEROSPACE HISTORY/US MILITARY HISTORY

DOCTORAL DISSERTATION FELLOWSHIPS OPEN TO USA CITIZENS WHO ARE CIVILIANS AND ARE ENROLLED IN A RECOGNIZED GRADUATE SCHOOL. MUST HAVE AN APPROVED DISSERTATION TOPIC AND HAVE ALL COURSE WORK COMPLETED EXCEPT FOR DISSERTATION.

WRITE FOR COMPLETE INFORMATION.

1297

U.S. AIR FORCE HISTORICAL FOUNDATION (AFHF FELLOWSHIP)

BUILDING 1535 - STOP 44
ANDREWS AFB MD 20331
301/736-1959

AMOUNT: $1000

DEADLINE(S): DEC 1

FIELD(S): AVIATION HISTORY

DOCTORAL DISSERTATION POST-DOCTORAL GRANTS TO INCREASE OUTPUT OF SOUNDLY RESEARCHED HISTORY OF AVIATION. MUST SHOW EVIDENCE OF ABILITY TO WRITE PUBLISHABLE MATERIAL. USA CITIZEN OR LEGAL RESIDENT.

FELLOWSHIPS OCCASIONALLY RENEWABLE. WRITE FOR COMPLETE INFORMATION.

1298

U.S. ARMY CENTER OF MILITARY HISTORY (DISSERTATION FELLOWSHIPS)

DISSERTATION FELOWSHIP COMMITTEE; 1099 14TH ST NW
WASHINGTON DC 20005
202/504-5402

AMOUNT: $8000 STIPEND

DEADLINE(S): FEB 1

FIELD(S): USA MILITARY HISTORY

DOCTORAL DISSERTATION FELLOWSHIPS FOR CIVILIAN PH.D CANDIDATES AT RECOGNIZED GRAD SCHOOLS. ALL REQUIREMENTS FOR PH.D (EXCEPT DISSERTATION) SHOULD BE COMPLETED BY SEPT OF AWARD YEAR. USA CITIZEN OR LEGAL RESIDENT.

WRITE FOR COMPLETE INFORMATION.

1299

U.S. ARMY MILITARY HISTORY INSTITUTE (ADVANCED RESEARCH GRANT PROGRAM)

GRANTS PROGRAM
CARLISLE BARRACKS PA 17013
717/245-4227

AMOUNT: $750

DEADLINE(S): JAN 1

FIELD(S): MILITARY HISTORY

APPLICANTS MUST HOLD GRADUATE DEGREE OR HAVE EQUIVALENT PROFESSIONAL EXPERIENCE IN PURSUING RESEARCH TOPICS IN THE DISCIPLINE OF MILITARY HISTORY; THE US ARMY AND USAMHI. RESEARCH IS DONE AT THE INSTITUTE.

WRITE FOR COMPLETE INFORMATION.

1300

U.S. DEPT. OF EDUCATION (JACOB K JAVITS FELLOWSHIP PROGRAM)

PO BOX 84
WASHINGTON DC 20044
800/4FED-AID

AMOUNT: $15000 PER YEAR ON AVERAGE

DEADLINE(S): MAR 15

FIELD(S): ARTS; HUMANITIES; SOCIAL SCIENCES

FELLOWSHIPS TO ASSIST STUDENTS OF SUPERIOR ABILITIES IN STUDIES FOR DOCTORAL-LEVEL DEGREES IN SPECIFIED SUBFIELDS OF THE ABOVE AREAS. USA CITIZEN OR LEGAL RESIDENT.

APPLICATION PACKAGE AVAILABLE LATE OCT OR EARLY NOV. APPROX 100 AWARDS PER YEAR; RENEWABLE UP TO 48 MONTHS. WRITE FOR COMPLETE INFORMATION.

1301

U.S. MARINE CORPS HISTORICAL CENTER (DISSERTATION FELLOWSHIPS)

BUILDING 58; WASHINGTON NAVY YARD
WASHINGTON DC 20374
202/433-3840

AMOUNT: $7500

DEADLINE(S): MAY 1

FIELD(S): U.S. MILITARY HISTORY & RELATED AREAS

FOR PH.D CANDIDATES IN A RECOGNIZED
GRADUATE SCHOOL WHO HAVE AN
APPROVED PERTINENT DISSERTATION TOPIC
AND HAVE COMPLETED ALL PH.D
REQUIREMENTS EXCEPT FOR THE
DISSERTATION. USA CITIZEN.

WRITE FOR COMPLETE INFORMATION.

1302

**U.S. MARINE CORPS HISTORICAL CENTER
(MASTER'S THESIS FELLOWSHIPS)**

BUILDING 58; WASHINGTON NAVY YARD
WASHINGTON DC 20374
202/433-3840

AMOUNT: $2500

DEADLINE(S): MAY 1

FIELD(S): U.S. MILITARY HISTORY & RELATED
AREAS

THESIS FELLOWSHIPS FOR MASTER'S
CANDIDATES ENROLLED IN A RECOGNIZED
GRADUATE SCHOOL. US CITIZEN OR LEGAL
RESIDENT.

WRITE FOR COMPLETE INFORMATION.

1303

**U.S. MARINE CORPS HISTORICAL CENTER
(RESEARCH GRANTS)**

BUILDING 58; WASHINGTON NAVY YARD
WASHINGTON DC 20374
202/433-3839; 202/433-3837

AMOUNT: $400 - $2000

DEADLINE(S): NONE SPECIFIED

FIELD(S): U.S. MILITARY HISTORY & RELATED
AREAS

GRADUATE-LEVEL AND ADVANCED STUDY
RESEARCH GRANTS FOR INDIVIDUALS WHO
HAVE DEMONSTRATED ABILITY AND
SPECIAL APTITUDE FOR ADVANCED STUDY
IN AMERICAN MILITARY HISTORY AND
RELATED FIELDS.

5 AWARDS PER YEAR. WRITE FOR COMPLETE
INFORMATION.

1304

**UNIVERSITY OF LONDON-WARBURG INSTITUTE
(FRANCES A. YATES FELLOWSHIPS)**

WOBURN SQUARE
LONDON WC1H 0AB ENGLAND
071/580-9663

AMOUNT: SHORT-TERM 700-1650 POUNDS
STERLING; LONG-TERM 6000-9000 POUNDS
STERLING

DEADLINE(S): EARLY DEC

FIELD(S): CULTURAL & INTELLECTUAL HISTORY

POST-GRADUATE FELLOWSHIPS TO STUDY ANY
ASPECT OF THE ABOVE BUT PREFERENCE
GIVEN TO THOSE WITH SPECIAL INTEREST IN
MEDIEVAL & RENAISSANCE ENCYCLOPEDIA
OF KNOWLEDGE TO WHICH DAME FRANCES
YATES CONTRIBUTED.

AWARDS TENABLE AT WARBURG INSTITUTE.
WRITE FOR COMPLETE INFORMATION.

1305

**WESTERN HISTORY ASSN (RUNDELL
GRADUATE STUDENT AWARD)**

UNIVERSITY OF NEW MEXICO
ALBUQUERQUE NM 87131
WRITTEN INQUIRY

AMOUNT: $1000

DEADLINE(S): MAY 1

FIELD(S): WESTERN HISTORY

OPEN TO DOCTORAL CANDIDATES WHO HAVE
COMPLETED THE COMPREHENSIVE
EXAMINATIONS FOR THE PH.D AND ARE
RESEARCHING THEIR DISSERTATION
SUBJECT. APPLICANTS MUST BE NOMINATED
BY THEIR GRADUATE ADVISOR.

WRITE FOR COMPLETE INFORMATION.

LAW

1306

**AMERICAN ASSOCIATION OF LAW LIBRARIES
(SCHOLARSHIPS FOR LIBRARY SCHOOL
GRADUATES ATTENDING LAW SCHOOL)**

53 W. JACKSON BLVD. SUITE 940
CHICAGO IL 60604
312/939-4764

AMOUNT: VARIES

DEADLINE(S): APR 1

FIELD(S): LAW LIBRARIANSHIP

OPEN TO A LIBRARY SCHOOL GRADUATE WHO IS
WORKING TOWARD A LAW DEGREE IN AN
ACCREDITED LAW SCHOOL AND HAS NO
MORE THAN 36 SEMESTER (54 QUARTER)
CREDIT HOURS OF STUDY REMAINING
BEFORE QUALIFYING FOR A LAW DEGREE.

APPLICANTS SHOULD HAVE MEANINGFUL LAW
LIBRARY EXPERIENCE. WRITE FOR
COMPLETE INFORMATION.

1307

**AMERICAN COLLEGE OF LEGAL MEDICINE
(STUDENT WRITING COMPETITION)**

JAY A. GOLD; EXECUTIVE DIRECTOR;
611 E. WELLS ST.
MILWAUKEE WI 53202
414/276-1881

AMOUNT: $1000

DEADLINE(S): FEB 1

FIELD(S): LEGAL MEDICINE

AWARD FOR THE BEST PAPER ON ANY ASPECT OF
LEGAL MEDICINE OPEN TO STUDENTS
ENROLLED IN AN ACCREDITED SCHOOL OF
LAW; MEDICINE; DENTISTRY; PODIATRY;
NURSING; PHARMACY; HEALTH SCIENCE OR
HEALTH CARE ADMINISTRATION IN THE USA
OR CANADA.

AWARDS ARE GIVEN TO FIRST PLACE WINNER IN
EACH OF THREE CATEGORIES. WRITE FOR
COMPLETE INFORMATION.

1308

**AMERICAN FOUNDATION FOR THE BLIND
(LOUIS H. RIVES JR. SCHOLARSHIP FUND)**

15 WEST 16TH ST
NEW YORK NY 10011
212/620-2000; TDD 212/620-2158

AMOUNT: UP TO $2500

DEADLINE(S): APR 1

FIELD(S): LAW

OPEN TO LEGALLY BLIND STUDENTS WHO HAVE
BEEN ACCEPTED AT AN ACCREDITED LAW
SCHOOL. USA CITIZEN.

-SCHOLARSHIP NOT AVAILABLE FOR 1992- WRITE
FOR COMPLETE INFORMATION.

1309

**AMERICAN PHILOSOPHICAL SOCIETY (HENRY
M. PHILLIPS GRANTS IN JURISPRUDENCE)**

104 S. 5TH ST.
PHILADELPHIA PA 19106
WRITTEN INQUIRY

AMOUNT: $4000 MAXIMUM

DEADLINE(S): DEC 1

FIELD(S): JURISPRUDENCE RESEARCH

GRANTS FOR POST-DOCTORAL RESEARCH IN
JURISPRUDENCE.

WRITE FOR COMPLETE INFORMATION.

1310

**AMERICAN SOCIETY OF COMPOSERS AUTHORS
AND PUBLISHERS (NATHAN BURKAN
MEMORIAL COMPETITION)**

ONE LINCOLN PLAZA
NEW YORK NY 10023
212/595-3050

AMOUNT: $200 $500 (LOCAL AWARDS); $500
$1000 $1500 $2000 $3000 (NATIONAL
AWARDS)

DEADLINE(S): JUN 15

FIELD(S): COPYRIGHT LAW

PRIZES FOR 3RD-YEAR LAW STUDENTS AT USA
SCHOOLS FOR BEST PAPER ON COPYRIGHT
LAW. TOP ENTRIES ARE ENTERED IN
NATIONAL COMPETITION.

APPROX 100 AWARDS PER YEAR. WRITE FOR
COMPLETE INFORMATION.

1311

**ARMENIAN GENERAL BENEVOLENT UNION
(GRADUATE SCHOLARSHIP PROGRAM)**

585 SADDLE RIVER RD
SADDLE BROOK NJ 07662
201/797-7600

AMOUNT: $1000

DEADLINE(S): APR 30

FIELD(S): LAW; MEDICINE; INTERNATIONAL
RELATIONS; ARMENIAN STUDIES

GRANTS AND LOANS OPEN TO FULLY
MATRICULATED STUDENTS OF ARMENIAN
DESCENT IN ACCREDITED COLLEGES AND
UNIVERSITIES IN THE USA. REQUEST
APPLICATIONS BETWEEN JAN 1 AND MAR 15.
-WRITTEN REQUESTS ONLY-.

LOANS ARE WITHOUT INTEREST. REPAYMENT IS
TO BEGIN 1 YEAR AFTER LEAVING SCHOOL
AND MUST BE COMPLETED WITHIN 3 YEARS.
WRITE FOR COMPLETE INFORMATION.

1312

**ASSOCIATION OF FORMER AGENTS OF THE U.S.
SECRET SERVICE - AFAUSS - (DIETRICH/
CROSS/HANLY SCHOLARSHIPS)**

PO BOX 11681
ALEXANDRIA VA 22312
WRITTEN INQUIRY

AMOUNT: $500 - $1500

DEADLINE(S): MAY 1

FIELD(S): LAW ENFORCEMENT; POLICE
ADMINISTRATION

OPEN TO UNDERGRADUATE STUDENTS WHO
HAVE COMPLETED AT LEAST ONE YEAR OF
STUDY AND GRADUATE STUDENTS
WORKING TOWARDS AN ADVANCED DEGREE
IN THE ABOVE AREAS. USA CITIZEN.

WRITE FOR COMPLETE INFORMATION.

1313

**CDS INTERNATIONAL INC (ROBERT BOSCH
FOUNDATION FELLOWSHIPS)**

330 SEVENTH AVE
NEW YORK NY 10001
212/760-1400

AMOUNT: 3500 DEUTSCH MARKS PER MONTH +
TRAVEL EXPENSES

DEADLINE(S): OCT 15

FIELD(S): BUSINESS ADMIN; ECONOMICS; JOURNALISM; MASS COMMUNICATIONS; LAW; POLITICAL SCIENCE; PUBLIC AFFAIRS

9-MONTH FELLOWSHIP PROGRAM IN GERMANY INVOLVING WORK INTERNSHIPS IN FEDERAL GOVERNMENT & THEN IN REGIONAL GOVERNMENT OR PRIVATE INDUSTRY; SUPPLEMENTED BY SPECIAL SEMINARS IN BERLIN; PARIS & BRUSSELS. USA CITIZEN.

OPEN TO YOUNG PROFESSIONALS & STUDENTS WHO HOLD A GRADUATE DEGREE IN ANY OF THE ABOVE AREAS OR HAVE EQUIVALENT PROFESSIONAL EXPERIENCE. 15 AWARDS PER YEAR. WRITE FOR COMPLETE INFORMATION.

1314

CONGRESSIONAL FELLOWSHIP PROGRAM (MORRIS K. UDALL FELLOWSHIPS)

CONGRESS OF THE UNITED STATES; OFFICE OF TECHNOLOGY ASSESSMENT
WASHINGTON DC 20510
202/224-8713

AMOUNT: $35000 - $70000

DEADLINE(S): JAN 31

FIELD(S): PHYSICAL OR BIOLOGICAL SCIENCES; ENGINEERING; LAW; ECONOMICS; ENVIRONMENTAL OR SOCIAL SCIENCES; PUBLIC POLICY

ONE YEAR FELLOWSHIP PROGRAM HELD -ONLY- IN WASHINGTO DC. CANDIDATES MUST HAVE EXTENSIVE EXPERIENCE IN SCIENCE OR TECHNOLOGY ISSUES OR HAVE COMPLETED DOCTORAL LEVEL RESEARCH. EXCEPTIONAL COMPETENCY IN ABOVE AREAS REQUIRED.

CONSIDERATIONS INCLUDE ACHIEVEMENT RECORDS AND CANDIDATE'S POTENTIAL IN ONE OR MORE OF OTA'S ASSESSMENT STUDIES. WRITE FOR COMPLETE INFORMATION.

1315

COUNCIL ON LEGAL EDUCATION OPPORTUNITY (CLEO STIPENDS)

1800 M STREET NW SUITE 290
NORTH LOBBY
WASHINGTON DC 20036
202/785-4840

AMOUNT: $3650 PER YEAR MAXIMUM

DEADLINE(S): SEP 1 - MAR 1

FIELD(S): LAW

OPEN TO PRE-LAW STUDENTS. RECIPIENTS MUST ATTEND A SUMMER INSTITUTE. GRADUATES OF THE INSTITUTE USUALLY RECEIVE STIPEND FOR THREE YEARS OF LAW SCHOOL. 200 AWARDS ANNUALLY. MUST BE USA CITIZEN OR LEGAL RESIDENT.

THE INSTITUTE HELPS STUDENTS EVALUATE THEIR POTENTIAL FOR LAW STUDY BY EXPOSING THEM TO AN INTENSIVE SIX-WEEK COURSE OF LEGAL WRITING ANALYSIS AND RESEARCH.

1316

EARL WARREN LEGAL TRAINING PROGRAM (SCHOLARSHIPS)

99 HUDSON ST. 16TH FLOOR
NEW YORK NY 10013
212/219-1900

AMOUNT: VARIES

DEADLINE(S): MAR 15

FIELD(S): LAW

SCHOLARSHIPS FOR ENTERING BLACK LAW STUDENTS. EMPHASIS ON APPLICANTS WHO WISH TO ENTER LAW SCHOOLS IN THE SOUTH. MUST SUBMIT PROOF OF ACCEPTANCE TO AN ACCREDITED LAW SCHOOL. US CITIZEN OR LEGAL RESIDENT.

US CITIZENS UNDER 35 YEARS OF AGE PREFERRED. WRITE FOR COMPLETE INFORMATION.

1317

FLORIDA DEPT. OF EDUCATION (VIRGIL HAWKINS FELLOWSHIP)

OFFICE OF STUDENT FINANCIAL ASSISTANCE; 1344 FLORIDA EDUCATION CENTER
TALLAHASSEE FL 32399
WRITTEN INQUIRY ONLY

AMOUNT: $5000 PER YEAR

DEADLINE(S): SET BY PARTICIPATING INSTITUTIONS

FIELD(S): LAW/MINORITY STUDENTS

OPEN TO FIRST YEAR MINORITY LAW STUDENTS WHO HAVE BEEN ADMITTED TO THE LAW SCHOOL AT FLA STATE UNIVERSITY OR THE UNIVERSITY OF FLA. MUST BE MEMBER OF ETHNIC GROUP PREVIOUSLY DENIED ACCESS TO PREDOMINATELY WHITE FLORIDA INSTITUTIONS.

AWARD IS $5000 PER YEAR FOR UP TO A MAXIMUM OF SIX SEMESTERS. WRITE FOR COMPLETE INFORMATION.

1318

H. FLETCHER BROWN FUND (SCHOLARSHIPS)

C/O BANK OF DELAWARE; TRUST DEPT; PO BOX 791
WILMINGTON DE 19899
302/429-2827

AMOUNT: VARIES

DEADLINE(S): APR 15

LAW

FIELD(S): MEDICINE; DENTISTRY; LAW; ENGINEERING; CHEMISTRY

OPEN TO STUDENTS BORN IN DELAWARE; GRADUATED FROM A DELAWARE HIGH SCHOOL & STILL RESIDING IN DELAWARE. FOR FOUR YEARS OF STUDY (UNDERGRAD OR GRAD) LEADING TO A DEGREE THAT ENABLES APPLICANT TO PRACTICE IN CHOSEN FIELD.

SCHOLARSHIPS ARE BASED ON NEED; SCHOLASTIC ACHIEVEMENT; GOOD MORAL CHARACTER. RENEWABLE. WRITE FOR COMPLETE INFORMATION.

1319

HOOVER INSTITUTION ON WAR; REVOLUTION AND PEACE (NATIONAL FELLOWS PROGRAM)

STANFORD UNIVERSITY
STANFORD CA 94305
415/723-0163

AMOUNT: $32000

DEADLINE(S): JAN 13

FIELD(S): SOCIOLOGY; MODERN HISTORY; POLITICAL SCIENCE; ECONOMICS; INT'L RELATIONS; EDUCATION; LAW

POST-DOCTORAL FELLOWSHIPS THAT PROVIDE PARTICULARLY GIFTED JUNIOR SCHOLARS THE OPPORTUNITY TO SPEND ONE FULL YEAR ON UNRESTRICTED CREATIVE RESEARCH AND WRITING AT THE HOOVER INSTITUTION. USA OR CANADIAN CITIZEN.

12 TO 14 FELLOWSHIPS PER YEAR. RECIPIENTS ARE EXPECTED TO STAY IN RESIDENCY AT THE HOOVER INSTITUTION. WRITE FOR COMPLETE INFORMATION.

1320

MARYLAND HIGHER EDUCATION COMMISSION (PROFESSIONAL SCHOOL SCHOLARSHIPS)

STATE SCHOLARSHIP ADMINISTRATION; 16 FRANCIS ST
ANNAPOLIS MD 21401
410/974-5370

AMOUNT: $200 - $1000

DEADLINE(S): MAR 1

FIELD(S): DENTISTRY; PHARMACY; MEDICINE; LAW; NURSING

OPEN TO MARYLAND RESIDENTS WHO HAVE BEEN ADMITTED AS FULL-TIME STUDENTS AT A PARTICIPATING GRADUATE INSTITUTION OF HIGHER LEARNING IN MARYLAND OR AN UNDERGRADUATE NURSING PROGRAM.

RENEWABLE UP TO 4 YEARS. WRITE FOR COMPLETE INFORMATION AND A LIST OF PARTICIPATING MARYLAND INSTITUTIONS.

1321

MCROBERTS MEMORIAL LAW SCHOLARSHIP FUND (HATTIE FEGER MCROBERTS SCHOLARSHIP)

FIRST OF AMERICA TRUST COMPANY;
301 SW ADAMS ST.
PEORIA IL 61631
309/655-5573

AMOUNT: VARIES

DEADLINE(S): JUN 1

FIELD(S): LAW

OPEN TO UNMARRIED MALES WHO HAVE BEEN RESIDENTS OF THE COUNTY OF PEORIA (ILLINOIS) FOR AT LEAST 5 YEARS. AWARD SUPPORTS GRADUATE STUDY IN AN ACCREDITED LL.B OR J.D. DEGREE PROGRAM. USA CITIZEN.

20 SCHOLARSHIPS PER YEAR. WRITE FOR COMPLETE INFORMATION.

1322

MEXICAN AMERICAN LEGAL DEFENSE AND EDUCATIONAL FUND (LAW SCHOOL SCHOLARSHIP PROGRAM)

634 SOUTH SPRING ST; 11TH FLOOR
LOS ANGELES CA 90014
213/629-2512

AMOUNT: $1000

DEADLINE(S): MAY 30

FIELD(S): LAW

OPEN TO FULL-TIME LAW STUDENTS OF HISPANIC DESCENT ACCEPTED TO/ENROLLED IN AN ACCREDITED LAW SCHOOL. US CITIZEN OR LEGAL RESIDENT.

21 SCHOLARSHIPS PER YEAR. WRITE FOR COMPLETE INFORMATION.

1323

MUTUAL ASSOCIATION FOR PROFESSIONAL SERVICES (MAPS SCHOLARSHIP FUND)

11828 RANCHO BERNARDO RD #209
SAN DIEGO CA 92128
619/451-7618

AMOUNT: VARIABLE

DEADLINE(S): MAR 31

FIELD(S): LAW; MEDICINE; DENTISTRY; PODIATRY; VETERINARY MEDICINE; OPTOMETRY

PROGRAM IS FOR GRADUATE STUDENTS IN THE ABOVE AREAS. NOMINATION BY A MEMBER OF MAPS HELPFUL BUT NOT REQUIRED. CONSIDERATIONS ARE FINANCIAL NEED; CHARACTER AND ACHIEVEMENT. APPLICATIONS ARE ACCEPTED BEGINNING JAN 1.

ONLY THE FIRST 50 APPLICATIONS RECEIVED
WILL BE CONSIDERED. IF FEWER THAN 50
APPLICATIONS ARE RECEIVED MAR 31
DEADLINE APPLIES. WRITE FOR COMPLETE
INFORMATION.

1324

NATION INSTITUTE (ROBERT MASUR FELLOWSHIP IN CIVIL LIBERTIES)

72 FIFTH AVE
NEW YORK NY 10011
212/242-8400

AMOUNT: $1000 STIPEND

DEADLINE(S): FEB 1

FIELD(S): LAW

ANNUAL FELLOWSHIP OPEN TO STUDENTS WHO
ARE ENROLLED AT ACCREDITED LAW
SCHOOLS IN THE NEW YORK CITY AREA &
DISPLAY COMMITMENT TO PUBLIC INTEREST
WORK. FELLOWS WORK AT THE INSTITUTE'S
JUSTICE PROGRAM IN NEW YORK CITY.

WRITE FOR COMPLETE INFORMATION.

1325

NATIONAL ASSOCIATION OF BLACK WOMEN ATTORNEYS INC (ANNUAL SCHOLARSHIP AWARDS)

3711 MACOMB ST N.W.
WASHINGTON DC 20016
202/966-9693

AMOUNT: $1000 MINIMUM

DEADLINE(S): VARIES

FIELD(S): LAW (WRITING COMPETITION)

WRITING COMPETITION OPEN TO FEMALE LAW
STUDENTS WHO ARE MEMBERS OF AN
ETHNIC MINORITY GROUP. OPEN TO
GRADUATE STUDENTS ENROLLED IN A
RECOGNIZED LAW SCHOOL.

WRITE FOR COMPLETE INFORMATION.

1326

NATIONAL FEDERATION OF THE BLIND (HOWARD BROWN RICKARD SCHOLARSHIP)

814 4TH AVE #200
GRINNELL IA 50112
515/236-3366

AMOUNT: $2500

DEADLINE(S): MAR 31

FIELD(S): NATURAL SCIENCES; ARCHITECTURE;
ENGINEERING; MEDICINE; LAW

SCHOLARSHIPS FOR UNDERGRADUATE OR
GRADUATE STUDY IN THE ABOVE AREAS.
OPEN TO LEGALLY BLIND STUDENTS
ENROLLED FULL TIME AT ACCREDITED POST
SECONDARY INSTITUTIONS.

AWARDS BASED ON ACADEMIC EXCELLENCE;
SERVICE TO THE COMMUNITY AND
FINANCIAL NEED. WRITE FOR COMPLETE
INFORMATION.

1327

PRESIDENT'S COMMISSION ON WHITE HOUSE FELLOWSHIPS (FELLOWSHIP PROGRAM)

712 JACKSON PLACE NW
WASHINGTON DC 20503
202/395-4522

AMOUNT: WAGE (UP TO GS-15 STEP 3)

DEADLINE(S): DEC 1

FIELD(S): PUBLIC SERVICE; GOVERNMENT;
COMMUNITY INVOLVEMENT; LEADERSHIP

OPEN TO COLLEGE GRADUATES BETWEEN THE
AGES OF 30 AND 39 WHO DESIRE ONE YEAR
OF FIRST HAND EXPERIENCE IN
GOVERNMENT. FELLOWSHIPS OPEN TO A
WIDE VARIETY OF EDUCATIONAL
BACKGROUNDS AND CAREER INTERESTS.

WRITE FOR COMPLETE INFORMATION.

1328

PUERTO RICAN LEGAL DEFENSE & EDUCATION FUND INC. (SCHOLARSHIP PROGRAMS)

99 HUDSON STREET
NEW YORK NY 10013
212-219-3360

AMOUNT: VARIES WITH NEED

DEADLINE(S): VARIES YEAR TO YEAR

FIELD(S): LAW / LATINO-HISPANIC STUDENT

OPEN TO ANY LAW STUDENT IN ANY COUNTRY
WHO IS OF LATINO OR HISPANIC ANCESTRY
OR CITIZENSHIP; IS ENROLLED IN AN
ACCREDITED LAW SCHOOL AND CAN
DEMONSTRATE FINANCIAL NEED.

FUND ALSO OFFERS A SUMMER LAW INTERNSHIP
PROGRAM. WRITE FOR COMPLETE
INFORMATION.

1329

SPACE FOUNDATION (SPACE INDUSTRIALIZATION FELLOWSHIP)

4800 RESEARCH FOREST DR
THE WOODLANDS TX 77381
713/363-7944; FAX 713/363-7914

AMOUNT: $4000

DEADLINE(S): OCT 1

FIELD(S): SCIENCES & ENGINEERING; BUSINESS;
LAW; ECONOMICS; SOCIAL SCIENCES;
ENVIRONMENTAL STUDIES; HUMANITIES

POLITICAL SCIENCE

OPEN TO SUPERIOR GRADUATE STUDENTS IN THE ABOVE DISCIPLINES WHO INTEND TO DEVOTE THEIR CAREERS TO THE FURTHERANCE OF PRACTICAL SPACE RESEARCH; ENGINEERING; BUSINESS OR OTHER APPLICATION VENTURES.

CONTACT DR. DAVID J. NORTON; EDUCATIONAL GRANT PROGRAM CHAIRMAN; ADDRESS ABOVE; FOR COMPLETE INFORMATION.

1330

SUPREME COURT OF THE UNITED STATES (JUDICIAL FELLOWS PROGRAM)

ATTN - JUDICIAL FELLOWS PROGRAM DIRECTOR
WASHINGTON DC 20543
202/479-3400

AMOUNT: $65753 SALARY (GS-15)

DEADLINE(S): NOV 15

FIELD(S): LAW (JUDICIAL ADMINISTRATION)

OPEN TO EXCEPTIONALLY TALENTED PEOPLE CAPABLE OF MAKING SIGNIFICANT CONTRIBUTIONS TO THE IMPROVEMENT OF THE USA JUDICIAL SYSTEM. SHOULD HAVE 1 OR MORE GRADUATE DEGREES IN ANY AREA & 2-5 YEARS OF EXEMPLARY PROFESSIONAL EXPERIENCE.

NORMAL DURATION IS 1 YEAR. WRITE FOR COMPLETE INFORMATION.

1331

TY COBB EDUCATIONAL FOUNDATION (GRADUATE SCHOLARSHIP PROGRAM)

P.O. BOX 725
FOREST PARK GA 30051
WRITTEN INQUIRY

AMOUNT: $3000

DEADLINE(S): JUN 15

FIELD(S): MEDICINE; DENTISTRY; VETERINARY MEDICINE; LAW

OPEN TO GRADUATE STUDENTS IN THE ABOVE FIELDS WHO ARE RESIDENTS OF GEORGIA; HAVE SATISFACTORY GRADES AND ARE ABLE TO DEMONSTRATE FINANCIAL NEED.

WRITE FOR COMPLETE INFORMATION.

1332

U.S. DEPT. OF EDUCATION (INDIAN GRADUATE PROFESSIONAL FELLOWSHIPS)

400 MARYLAND AVENUE SW; RM 2177; MAIL STOP 6335
WASHINGTON DC 20202
202/401-1902

AMOUNT: $1000 - $34000 (AVERAGE $13000)

DEADLINE(S): FEB 7

FIELD(S): MEDICINE; PSYCHOLOGY; LAW; EDUCATION; RELATED FIELDS

FELLOWSHIPS FOR AMERICAN INDIANS OR ALASKAN NATIVES WHO ARE US CITZENS AND SEEKING GRADUATE DEREEES IN THE ABOVE FIELDS AT ACCREDITED INSTITUTIONS IN USA.

APPROXIMATELY 90 CONTINUATION AND 35 NEW AWARDS. WRITE FOR COMPLETE INFORMATION.

POLITICAL SCIENCE

1333

AMERICAN JEWISH COMMITTEE (HAROLD W ROSENTHAL FELLOWSHIP)

2027 MASSACHUSETTS AVE NW
WASHINGTON DC 20036
202/265-2000

AMOUNT: $1650 STIPEND

DEADLINE(S): APR

FIELD(S): POLITICAL SCIENCE; GOVERNMENT SERVICE; FOREIGN AFFAIRS

OPEN TO COLLEGE SENIORS & GRAD STUDENTS. FELLOWSHIP PROVIDES OPPORTUNITY FOR A STUDENT TO SPEND A SUMMER WORKING IN THE OFFICE OF A MEMBER OF CONGRESS OR EXECUTIVE BRANCH ON FOREIGN AFFAIRS AND GOVERNMENT SERVICE ISSUES. US CITIZEN.

APPLICATIONS ARE AVAILABLE FROM THE ADDRESS ABOVE HOWEVER THEY MUST BE SUBMITTED WITH A RECOMMENDATION FROM YOUR DEAN. SELECTED FELLOWS WILL ALSO RECEIVE PREFERENTIAL TREATMENT FOR A EUROPEAN COMMUNITY 3-5 WEEK TRAVEL STUDY.

1334

AMERICAN POLITICAL SCIENCE ASSN (APSA GRADUATE FELLOWSHIPS FOR AFRICAN AMERICAN STUDENTS)

1527 NEW HAMPSHIRE AVENUE NW
WASHINGTON DC 20036
202/483-2512

AMOUNT: $6000

DEADLINE(S): DEC 1

FIELD(S): POLITICAL SCIENCE

OPEN TO AFRICAN AMERICAN GRADUATE STUDENTS WHO QUALIFY TO ENROLL IN DOCTORAL PROGRAMS IN POLITICAL SCIENCE. POTENTIAL FOR SUCCESS IN GRAD STUDIES AND FINANCIAL NEED WILL BE GIVEN MAJOR CONSIDERATION. FOR DOCTORAL STUDY ONLY.

MUST BE USA CITIZEN. THREE AWARDS PER YEAR. WRITE FOR COMPLETE INFORMATION.

1335

AMERICAN POLITICAL SCIENCE ASSN (CONGRESSIONAL FELLOWSHIPS FOR POLITICAL SCIENTISTS)

1527 NEW HAMPSHIRE AVE NW
WASHINGTON DC 20036
202/483-2512

AMOUNT: UP TO $20000 STIPEND + TRAVEL ALLOWANCE

DEADLINE(S): DEC 1

FIELD(S): POLITICAL SCIENCE

POST-DOCTORATE FELLOWSHIPS FOR PEOPLE WITH A SCHOLARLY INTEREST IN CONGRESS AND THE POLICY-MAKING PROCESS WHO HAVE COMPLETED A PH.D WITHIN LAST 15 YRS (OR NEAR COMPLETION).

FELLOWSHIP STIPEND MAY BE SUPPLEMENTED AT FELLOW'S INITIATIVE WITH UNIVERSITY SUPPORT. WRITE FOR APPLICATION FORMS AND COMPLETE INFORMATION.

1336

AMERICAN POLITICAL SCIENCE ASSN (GRADUATE FELLOWSHIPS FOR LATINO STUDENTS)

1527 NEW HAMPSHIRE AVE NW
WASHINGTON DC 20036
202/483-2512

AMOUNT: $6000

DEADLINE(S): DEC 1

FIELD(S): POLITICAL SCIENCE

OPEN TO LATINO STUDENTS WHO PLAN TO ENROLL IN DOCTORAL PROGRAMS IN POLITICAL SCIENCE. POTENTIAL FOR SUCCESS IN GRADUATE STUDIES AND FINANCIAL NEED WILL BE GIVEN MAJOR CONSIDERATION. MUST BE USA CITIZEN.

FUNDS ARE FOR DOCTORAL STUDY -ONLY-. WRITE FOR COMPLETE INFORMATION.

1337

ARMENIAN GENERAL BENEVOLENT UNION (GRADUATE SCHOLARSHIP PROGRAM)

585 SADDLE RIVER RD
SADDLE BROOK NJ 07662
201/797-7600

AMOUNT: $1000

DEADLINE(S): APR 30

FIELD(S): LAW; MEDICINE; INTERNATIONAL RELATIONS; ARMENIAN STUDIES

GRANTS AND LOANS OPEN TO FULLY MATRICULATED STUDENTS OF ARMENIAN DESCENT IN ACCREDITED COLLEGES AND UNIVERSITIES IN THE USA. REQUEST APPLICATIONS BETWEEN JAN 1 AND MAR 15. -WRITTEN REQUESTS ONLY-.

LOANS ARE WITHOUT INTEREST. REPAYMENT IS TO BEGIN 1 YEAR AFTER LEAVING SCHOOL AND MUST BE COMPLETED WITHIN 3 YEARS. WRITE FOR COMPLETE INFORMATION.

1338

BROOKING INSTITUTION (RESEARCH FELLOWSHIPS)

1775 MASSACHUSETTS AVE NW
WASHINGTON DC 20036
202/797-6000

AMOUNT: $13500

DEADLINE(S): DEC 15

FIELD(S): FOREIGN POLICY; GOVERNMENT; ECONOMICS

OPEN TO PH.D CANDIDATES NOMINATED BY THEIR GRADUATE DEPARTMENTS. APPLICATIONS FROM INDIVIDUALS NOT SO NOMINATED CANNOT BE ACCEPTED. AWARDS SUPPORT RESEARCH BY PH.D CANDIDATES WHO HAVE COMPLETED ALL COURSEWORK EXCEPT FOR THE DISSERTATION.

APPROX 10 AWARDS PER YEAR. NOMINATION FORMS MAY BE OBTAINED BY YOUR DEPARTMENT HEAD FROM THE ADDRESS ABOVE.

1339

CDS INTERNATIONAL INC (ROBERT BOSCH FOUNDATION FELLOWSHIPS)

330 SEVENTH AVE
NEW YORK NY 10001
212/760-1400

AMOUNT: 3500 DEUTSCH MARKS PER MONTH + TRAVEL EXPENSES

DEADLINE(S): OCT 15

FIELD(S): BUSINESS ADMIN; ECONOMICS; JOURNALISM; MASS COMMUNICATIONS; LAW; POLITICAL SCIENCE; PUBLIC AFFAIRS

9-MONTH FELLOWSHIP PROGRAM IN GERMANY INVOLVING WORK INTERNSHIPS IN FEDERAL GOVERNMENT & THEN IN REGIONAL GOVERNMENT OR PRIVATE INDUSTRY; SUPPLEMENTED BY SPECIAL SEMINARS IN BERLIN; PARIS & BRUSSELS. USA CITIZEN.

OPEN TO YOUNG PROFESSIONALS & STUDENTS WHO HOLD A GRADUATE DEGREE IN ANY OF THE ABOVE AREAS OR HAVE EQUIVALENT PROFESSIONAL EXPERIENCE. 15 AWARDS PER YEAR. WRITE FOR COMPLETE INFORMATION.

POLITICAL SCIENCE

1340

COMMITTEE ON INSTITUTIONAL COOPERATION (CIC PREDOCTORAL FELLOWSHIPS)

KIRKWOOD HALL RM 111; INDIANA UNIV.
BLOOMINGTON IN 47405
812/855-0822

AMOUNT: $9500 + TUITION (5 YEARS)

DEADLINE(S): JAN 2

FIELD(S): HUMANITIES; SOCIAL SCIENCES; NATURAL SCIENCES; MATHEMATICS; ENGINEERING

PREDOCTORAL FELLOWSHIPS FOR USA CITIZENS OF AFRICAN AMERICAN; AMERICAN INDIAN; MEXICAN AMERICAN OR PUERTO RICAN HERITAGE. MUST HOLD OR EXPECT TO RECEIVE BACHELOR'S DEGREE BY LATE SUMMER FROM A REGIONALLY ACCREDITED COLLEGE OR UNIVERSITY.

AWARDS FOR SPECIFIED UNIVERSITIES IN IL; IN; IA; MI; MN; OH; WI; PA. WRITE FOR DETAILS.

1341

CONGRESSIONAL FELLOWSHIP PROGRAM (MORRIS K. UDALL FELLOWSHIPS)

CONGRESS OF THE UNITED STATES; OFFICE OF TECHNOLOGY ASSESSMENT
WASHINGTON DC 20510
202/224-8713

AMOUNT: $35000 - $70000

DEADLINE(S): JAN 31

FIELD(S): PHYSICAL OR BIOLOGICAL SCIENCES; ENGINEERING; LAW; ECONOMICS; ENVIRONMENTAL OR SOCIAL SCIENCES; PUBLIC POLICY

ONE YEAR FELLOWSHIP PROGRAM HELD -ONLY- IN WASHINGTO DC. CANDIDATES MUST HAVE EXTENSIVE EXPERIENCE IN SCIENCE OR TECHNOLOGY ISSUES OR HAVE COMPLETED DOCTORAL LEVEL RESEARCH. EXCEPTIONAL COMPETENCY IN ABOVE AREAS REQUIRED.

CONSIDERATIONS INCLUDE ACHIEVEMENT RECORDS AND CANDIDATE'S POTENTIAL IN ONE OR MORE OF OTA'S ASSESSMENT STUDIES. WRITE FOR COMPLETE INFORMATION.

1342

CORO FOUNDATION (FELLOWS PROGRAM)

1 ECKER ST #330
SAN FRANCISCO CA 94105
415/546-9690

AMOUNT: UP TO $10000

DEADLINE(S): JAN 30

FIELD(S): PUBLIC AFFAIRS

THE FELLOWS PROGRAM IN PUBLIC AFFAIRS IS DESIGNED FOR INDIVIDUALS WHO HAVE COMPLETED THEIR UNDERGRADUATE EDUCATION; HAVE DEMONSTRATED LEADERSHIP ABILITIES AND ARE COMMITTED TO CAREERS IN PUBLIC AFFAIRS.

THIS IS A NINE MONTH FULL-TIME GRADUATE LEVEL PROGRAM OFFERED ANNUALLY IN FOUR CITIES - SAN FRANCISCO; LOS ANGELES; ST. LOUIS AND NEW YORK. CONTACT ADDRESS ABOVE FOR COMPLETE INFORMATION.

1343

COUNCIL FOR EUROPEAN STUDIES (PRE-DISSERTATION FELLOWSHIP PROGRAM)

C/O COLUMBIA UNIV; BOX 44 SCHERMERHORN HALL
NEW YORK NY 10027
212/854-4172

AMOUNT: $3000

DEADLINE(S): FEB 1

FIELD(S): EUROPEAN HISTORY; SOCIOLOGY; POLITICAL SCIENCE; ANTHROPOLOGY; ECONOMICS

GRANTS FOR EXPLORATORY RESEARCH IN EUROPE FOR GRAD STUDENTS WHO HAVE COMPLETED AT LEAST TWO YEARS GRADUATE STUDY AND INTEND TO PURSUE A PH.D. USA OR CANADIAN CITIZEN OR LEGAL RESIDENT.

APPLICANTS SHOULD HAVE AT LEAST ONE YEAR OF STUDY IN AN APPROPRIATE FOREIGN LANGUAGE OR MUST SHOW WHY THE REQUIREMENT IS INAPPROPRIATE. WRITE FOR COMPLETE INFORMATION.

1344

DIRKSEN CONGRESSIONAL CENTER (CONGRESSIONAL RESEARCH GRANTS PROGRAM)

301 S 4TH ST - SUITE A
PEKIN IL 61554
309/347-7113; FAX 309/347-6432

AMOUNT: UP TO $3500; POSSIBLY SALARY TO $1500/MO

DEADLINE(S): MAR 31 (POSTMARK)

FIELD(S): POLITICAL SCIENCE; AMERICAN HISTORY (WITH EMPHASIS ON US CONGRESS OR CONGRESSIONAL LEADERSHIP)

OPEN TO ANYONE WITH A SERIOUS INTEREST IN STUDYING THE US CONGRESS. RESEARCH MUST BE ORIGINAL CULMINATING IN NEW KNOWLEDGE OR NEW INTERPRETATION OR BOTH. POLITICAL SCIENTISTS; HISTORIANS; BIOGRAPHERS; JOURNALISTS AND OTHERS MAY APPLY.

WRITE FOR COMPLETE INFORMATION.

1345

EAST-WEST CENTER (GRADUATE FELLOWSHIPS)

1777 EAST-WEST RD; ROOM 2066
HONOLULU HI 96848
808/944-7736

AMOUNT: VARIES

DEADLINE(S): DEC 1

FIELD(S): INTERNATIONAL RELATIONS

OPEN TO CITIZENS OR LEGAL PERMANENT RESIDENTS OF AN ASIAN OR PACIFIC COUNTRY OR THE USA WHO WISH TO PARTICIPATE IN EWC EDUCATIONAL & RESEARCH PROGRAMS WHILE PURSUING A MASTER'S OR DOCTORATE DEGREE AT THE UNIVERSITY OF HAWAII.

WRITE FOR COMPLETE INFORMATION.

1346

FERIS FOUNDATION OF AMERICA (ALBERT GALLATIN FELLOWSHIPS)

ALLEN LYNCH; 2016 MINOR RD
CHARLOTTESVILLE VA 22903
804/296-8215

AMOUNT: 1700 SWISS FRANCS PER MONTH + TRAVEL; OTHER ALLOWANCES

DEADLINE(S): MAR 13

FIELD(S): INTERNATIONAL RELATIONS

ONE YEAR GRANTS OPEN TO DOCTORAL CANDIDATES IN INTERNATIONAL RELATIONS FROM USA ACADEMIC INSTITUTIONS FOR STUDY IN SWITZERLAND AND FROM SWISS INSTITUTIONS FOR STUDY IN THE USA.

FLUENCY IN FRENCH IS REQUIRED SINCE STUDIES ARE CONDUCTED IN ENGLISH AND FRENCH. WRITE FOR COMPLETE INFORMATION.

1347

FLETCHER SCHOOL OF LAW AND DIPLOMACY (FELLOWSHIPS)

TUFTS UNIVERSITY
MEDFORD MA 02155
617/381-3040

AMOUNT: $2000 - $25000

DEADLINE(S): JAN 15

FIELD(S): INTERNATIONAL RELATIONS

FELLOWSHIPS OPEN TO APPLICANTS WHO ARE ACCEPTED/ENROLLED AS FULL-TIME GRADUATE STUDENT AT THE FLETCHER SCHOOL OF LAW AND DIPLOMACY.

120 FELLOWSHIPS PER YEAR. RENEWABLE. WRITE FOR COMPLETE INFORMATION.

1348

FLORIDA ENDOWMENT FUND FOR HIGHER EDUCATION (MCKNIGHT DOCTORAL FELLOWSHIP PROGRAM)

201 E.KENNEDY BLVD; SUITE 1525
TAMPA FL 33602
813/272-2772

AMOUNT: $11000 STIPEND + $5000 TUITION & FEES (PER YEAR)

DEADLINE(S): JAN 15

FIELD(S): ALL FIELDS (EXCEPT LAW; MEDICINE & EDUCATION)

OPEN TO ALL AFRICAN-AMERICANS WITH AT LEAST A BACHELOR'S DEGREE FROM AN ACCREDITED INSTITUTION WHO WISH TO PURSUE A DOCTORAL DEGREE. PROGRAM RECRUITS NATIONWIDE; HOWEVER FELLOWS MUST ENROLL IN A FLORIDA INSTITUTION. USA CITIZEN.

25 AWARDS PER YEAR. RENEWABLE FOR UP TO 5 YEARS. WRITE FOR COMPLETE INFORMATION.

1349

GEORGE AND CAROL OLMSTED FOUNDATION (SCHOLARSHIPS)

1515 NORTH COURTHOUSE ROAD; SUITE 305
ARLINGTON VA 22201
703/527-9070

AMOUNT: $5500

DEADLINE(S): NONE SPECIFIED

FIELD(S): INTERNATIONAL RELATIONS; POLITICAL SCIENCE

OPEN TO CAREER OFFICER IN ONE OF THE ARMED SERVICES OF THE USA. MUST HAVE ATTENDED ONE OF THE 3 SERVICE ACADEMIES. MUST DEMONSTRATE SCHOLASTIC; LITERARY; AND LINGUISTIC ABILITIES; SUCCESS IN OUTDOOR SPORTS; QUALITIES OF LEADERSHIP.

FOR GRADUATE STUDY. THE OLMSTEAD FOUNDATION DOES -NOT- ACCEPT APPLICATIONS. APPLY THROUGH MILITARY SERVICE.

1350

GERMAN MARSHAL FUND OF THE UNITED STATES (POST-DOCTORAL FELLOWSHIP PROGRAM)

11 DUPONT CIRCLE N.W.
WASHINGTON D.C. 20036
202/745-3950

AMOUNT: $30000 STIPEND PLUS $2000 TRAVEL ALLOWANCE

DEADLINE(S): NOV 15

FIELD(S): USA - EUROPEAN ISSUES

POLITICAL SCIENCE

POST-DOCTORAL FELLOWSHIPS FOR OUTSTANDING SOCIAL SCIENTISTS TO RESEARCH USA - EUROPEAN ISSUES. MUST BE USA CITIZEN OR LEGAL RESIDENT.

11 AWARDS PER YEAR. WRITE FOR COMPLETE INFORMATION.

1351

GERMANISTIC SOCIETY OF AMERICA (FOREIGN STUDY SCHOLARSHIPS)

809 UNITED NATIONS PLAZA
NEW YORK NY 10017
212/984-5330

AMOUNT: $8500

DEADLINE(S): OCT 31

FIELD(S): HISTORY; POLITICAL SCIENCE; INT'L RELATIONS; PUBLIC AFFAIRS; LANGUAGE; PHILOSOPHY; LITERATURE

APPLICANTS MUST BE US CITIZENS WITH A BACHELORS DEGREE. AWARDS ARE FOR GRADUATE STUDY AT A WEST GERMAN UNIVERSITY.

SELECTION IS BASED UPON PROPOSED PROJECT; LANGUAGE FLUENCY; ACADEMIC ACHIEVEMENT; & REFERENCES. WRITE FOR COMPLETE INFORMATION.

1352

HOOVER INSTITUTION ON WAR; REVOLUTION AND PEACE (NATIONAL FELLOWS PROGRAM)

STANFORD UNIVERSITY
STANFORD CA 94305
415/723-0163

AMOUNT: $32000

DEADLINE(S): JAN 13

FIELD(S): SOCIOLOGY; MODERN HISTORY; POLITICAL SCIENCE; ECONOMICS; INT'L RELATIONS; EDUCATION; LAW

POST-DOCTORAL FELLOWSHIPS THAT PROVIDE PARTICULARLY GIFTED JUNIOR SCHOLARS THE OPPORTUNITY TO SPEND ONE FULL YEAR ON UNRESTRICTED CREATIVE RESEARCH AND WRITING AT THE HOOVER INSTITUTION. USA OR CANADIAN CITIZEN.

12 TO 14 FELLOWSHIPS PER YEAR. RECIPIENTS ARE EXPECTED TO STAY IN RESIDENCY AT THE HOOVER INSTITUTION. WRITE FOR COMPLETE INFORMATION.

1353

HUDSON INSTITUTE (HERMAN KAHN FELLOWSHIP)

PO BOX 26919; 5395 EMERSON WAY
INDIANAPOLIS IN 46226
317/545-1000

AMOUNT: $18000

DEADLINE(S): APR 15

FIELD(S): EDUCATION; ECONOMICS; NATIONAL SECURITY STUDIES

FELLOWSHIPS FOR PH.D CANDIDATES WHO HAVE COMPLETED ALL COURSEWORK & ARE DOING THEIR DISSERTATION ON A POLICY-RELEVANT ISSUE. DEMONSTRATE HIGH LEVEL OF ACADEMIC ACHIEVEMENT. US CITIZEN.

WRITE FOR COMPLETE INFORMATION.

1354

INSTITUTE FOR THE STUDY OF WORLD POLITICS (RESEARCH GRANTS)

1755 MASSACHUSETTS AVE NW -
SUITE 500
WASHINGTON DC 20036
WRITTEN INQUIRY ONLY

AMOUNT: VARIES

DEADLINE(S): FEB 15

FIELD(S): INTERNATIONAL RELATIONS; ENVIRONMENTAL ISSUES; POPULATION STUDIES (SOCIAL SCIENCE ASPECTS) HUMAN RIGHTS; ARMS CONTROL; THIRD WORLD DEVELOPMENT.

FOR DOCTORAL CANDIDATES CONDUCTING DISSERTATION RESEARCH IN ABOVE AREAS. FINANCIAL NEED IS A CONSIDERATION.

20-25 FELLOWSHIPS PER YEAR. WRITE FOR COMPLETE INFORMATION.

1355

INSTITUTE OF WORLD AFFAIRS (SCHOLARSHIPS FOR SUMMER SEMINARS)

375 TWIN LAKES ROAD
SALISBURY CT 06068
203/824-5135

AMOUNT: $250 - $400

DEADLINE(S): VARIOUS

FIELD(S): INTERNATIONAL RELATIONS; INTERNATIONAL FINANCE

SCHOLARSHIPS TO ATTEND INSTITUTE OF WORLD AFFAIRS SUMMER SEMINARS. OPEN TO GRADUATE STUDENTS; POST-GRADUATES & PROFESSIONALS OF ALL NATIONALITIES. SELECTION BASED ON APPLICANT'S BACKGROUND & RECOMMENDATIONS.

WRITE FOR COMPLETE INFORMATION.

1356

JESSE MARVIN UNRUH ASSEMBLY FELLOWSHIP PROGRAM

1020 N ST SUITE 402
SACRAMENTO CA 95814
916/324-1761 OR 800/776-1761

AMOUNT: $1560 MONTHLY STIPEND + HEALTH; VISION & DENTAL BENEFITS

DEADLINE(S): MAR 1 (POSTMARK)

FIELD(S): ALL FIELDS OF STUDY

GRADUATE FELLOWSHIPS WITH CALIF ASSEMBLY. MUST HAVE COMPLETED A B.A. OR B.S. DEGREE BY THE TIME THE FELLOWSHIP YEAR BEGINS IN OCTOBER. FELLOWSHIPS ARE FULL TIME EMPLOYMENT WITH THE CALIF. ASSEMBLY FOR 11 MONTHS.

FELLOWS EARN A MAXIMUM OF 12 UNITS OF GRADUATE COURSE CREDIT. -NO SCHOLARSHIPS- ARE AWARDED. WRITE FOR COMPLETE INFORMATION.

1357 ──────────────────────────────

NATIONAL RESEARCH COUNCIL (NATIONAL SCIENCE FOUNDATION GRADUATE FELLOWSHIPS)

2101 CONSTITUTION AVE
WASHINGTON DC 20418
202/334-2872

AMOUNT: $14000 STIPEND + $7000 TUITION ALLOWANCE

DEADLINE(S): NOV 10

FIELD(S): SOCIAL SCIENCES; PHYSICAL SCIENCES; MATHEMATICS; BIOLOGY; ENGINEERING

DOCTORAL) WHO HAVE NOT COMPLETED MORE THAN 1 YEAR OF GRAD STUDY. FELLOWSHIPS TENABLE AT ANY ACCREDITED INSTITUTION OFFERING ADVANCED DEGREES IN THE AREAS ABOVE. USA CITIZEN OR PERMANENT RESIDENT.

OPEN TO HISTORY & PHILOSOPHY OF SCIENCE STUDENTS ALSO. 950 NEW 3-YEAR FELLOWSHIPS AWARDED EACH YEAR. WRITE FOR COMPLETE INFORMATION.

1358 ──────────────────────────────

NEW YORK CITY DEPT. OF PERSONNEL (URBAN FELLOWS PROGRAM)

2 WASHINGTON ST.; 15TH FLOOR
NEW YORK NY 10004
212/487-5698

AMOUNT: $17000 STIPEND

DEADLINE(S): JAN 26

FIELD(S): PUBLIC ADMINISTRATION; URBAN PLANNING; GOVERNMENT; PUBLIC SERVICE; URBAN AFFAIRS

FELLOWSHIP PROGRAM PROVIDES ONE ACADEMIC YEAR (9 MONTHS) OF FULL-TIME WORK EXPERIENCE IN URBAN GOVERNMENT. OPEN TO GRADUATING COLLEGE SENIORS AND RECENT COLLEGE GRADUATES. USA CITIZEN.

WRITE FOR COMPLETE INFORMATION.

1359 ──────────────────────────────

NEW YORK STATE SENATE (LEGISLATIVE FELLOWS PROGRAM; R.J.ROTH JOURNALISM FELLOWSHIP; R.A.WIEBE PUBLIC SERVICE FELLOWSHIP)

STATE CAPITOL ROOM 500A
ALBANY NY 12247
518/455-2611

AMOUNT: $22575

DEADLINE(S): SPRING

FIELD(S): POLITICAL SCIENCE; GOVERNMENT; PUBLIC SERVICE; JOURNALISM; PUBLIC RELATIONS

NY STATE RESIDENT. OPEN TO GRADUATE STUDENTS ENROLLED IN ACCREDITED PROGRAMS IN THE ABOVE AREAS. FELLOWS WORK AS REGULAR LEGISLATIVE STAFF MEMBERS OF THE OFFICES TO WHICH THEY ARE ASSIGNED. USA CITIZEN.

14 FELLOWSHIPS PER YEAR. WRITE FOR COMPLETE INFORMATION.

1360 ──────────────────────────────

OLMSTED (GEORGE & CAROL) FOUNDATION (SCHOLARSHIPS)

1515 NORTH COURTHOUSE ROAD; SUITE 305
ARLINGTON VA 22201
703/527-9070

AMOUNT: $3000

DEADLINE(S): NONE SPECIFIED

FIELD(S): POLITICAL SCIENCE

OPEN TO CURRENT CAREER OFFICERS OF THE USA ARMED SERVICES WHO ATTENDED ONE OF THE THREE SERVICE ACADEMIES. MUST DEMONSTRATE SCHOLASTIC; LITERARY; AND LINGUISTIC ABILITIES; SUCCESS IN OUTDOOR SPORTS; LEADERSHIP QUALITIES.

FOR GRADUATE STUDY. MUST BE NOMINATED BY DEPT OF DEFENSE. WRITE FOR COMPLETE INFORMATION.

1361 ──────────────────────────────

PRESIDENT'S COMMISSION ON WHITE HOUSE FELLOWSHIPS (FELLOWSHIP PROGRAM)

712 JACKSON PLACE NW
WASHINGTON DC 20503
202/395-4522

AMOUNT: WAGE (UP TO GS-15 STEP 3)

DEADLINE(S): DEC 1

FIELD(S): PUBLIC SERVICE; GOVERNMENT; COMMUNITY INVOLVEMENT; LEADERSHIP

POLITICAL SCIENCE

OPEN TO COLLEGE GRADUATES BETWEEN THE AGES OF 30 AND 39 WHO DESIRE ONE YEAR OF FIRST HAND EXPERIENCE IN GOVERNMENT. FELLOWSHIPS OPEN TO A WIDE VARIETY OF EDUCATIONAL BACKGROUNDS AND CAREER INTERESTS.

WRITE FOR COMPLETE INFORMATION.

1362

SOCIAL SCIENCE RESEARCH COUNCIL (INTERNATIONAL PREDISSERTATION FELLOWSHIP PROGRAM)

ELLEN PERECMAN; 605 THIRD AVE.
NEW YORK NY 10158
212/661-0280

AMOUNT: VARIES

DEADLINE(S): TO BE ANNOUNCED BY PARTICIPATING UNIVERSITIES

FIELD(S): ECONOMICS; POLITICAL SCIENCE; PSYCHOLOGY SOCIOLOGY; OTHER SOCIAL SCIENCE DISCIPLINES

OPEN TO PH.D CANDIDATES ENROLLED IN SOCIAL SCIENCES PROGRAMS AT SELECTED UNIVERSITIES. STUDENTS SHOULD BE INTERESTED IN SUPPLEMENTING THEIR DISCIPLINARY SKILLS WITH AREA AND LANGUAGE STUDIES.

FELLOWS UNDERTAKE A PROGRAM OF STUDY IN OR ON AFRICA; CHINA; LATIN AMERICA; THE CARIBBEAN; THE NEAR & MIDDLE EAST; SOUTH ASIA OR SOUTH EAST ASIA. WRITE FOR COMPLETE INFORMATION.

1363

SOCIAL SCIENCE RESEARCH COUNCIL (MACARTHUR FOUNDATION FELLOWSHIPS)

605 THIRD AVE;
FELLOWSHIPS COORDINATOR
NEW YORK NY 10158
212/661-0280

AMOUNT: $12500-$17500 PRE-DOC; $25000-$30000 POST-DOC PER YEAR

DEADLINE(S): DEC 1

FIELD(S): DOCTORAL DISSERTATION & POST-DOCTORAL RESEARCH FELLOWSHIPS TO SUPPORT FULL-TIME RESEARCH ON THE IMPLICATIONS FOR SECURITY ISSUES OF WORLDWIDE CULTURAL; SOCIAL ECONOMIC & POLITICAL CHANGES.

FELLOWS ARE REQUIRED TO UNDERTAKE TRAINING THAT ADDS NEW COMPETENCE TO THE DISCIPLINARY SKILL THEY ALREADY POSSESS. WRITE FOR COMPLETE INFORMATION.

1364

SWEDISH INFORMATION SERVICE (BICENTENNIAL FUND GRANTS)

ONE DAG HAMMARSKJOLD PLAZA;
45TH FLOOR
NEW YORK NY 10017
212/751-9500

AMOUNT: 20000 SWEDISH KRONA

DEADLINE(S): FEB 1

FIELD(S): POLITICAL SCIENCE; BUSINESS ADMIN; EDUCATION; COMMUNICATION; CULTURE; ENVIRONMENTAL STUDIES

GRANTS TO PROVIDE THE OPPORTUNITY FOR THOSE IN A POSITION TO INFLUENCE PUBLIC OPINION AND CONTRIBUTE TO THE DEVELOPMENT OF THEIR SOCIETY. 3-6 WEEK INTENSIVE STUDY VISITS IN SWEDEN IN ANY OF THE ABOVE AREAS OR THEIR RELATED FIELDS.

US CITIZEN OR LEGAL RESIDENT. APPROXIMATELY 10 GRANTS PER YEAR. WRITE FOR COMPLETE INFORMATION.

1365

U.S. ARMS CONTROL AND DISARMAMENT AGENCY (HUBERT H HUMPHREY FELLOWSHIP PROGRAM)

OPERATIONS ANALYSIS ROOM 5726;
320 21ST ST. NW
WASHINGTON DC 20451
202/647-4695

AMOUNT: $5000 STIPEND + UP TO $3400 TUITION GRANT

DEADLINE(S): MAR 15

FIELD(S): ARMS CONTROL AND DISARMAMENT

DOCTORAL DISSERTATION RESEARCH FELLOWSHIPS FOR APPLICANTS WHO HAVE COMPLETED ALL PH.D COURSE WORK EXCEPT FOR THE DISSERTATION AT AN ACCREDITED USA INSTITUTION. USA CITIZEN OR LEGAL RESIDENT.

THIRD YEAR LAW STUDENTS ALSO MAY APPLY. FELLOWSHIPS NORMALLY AWARDED FOR A PERIOD OF 12 MONTHS. CONTACT ADDRESS ABOVE FOR COMPLETE INFORMATION.

1366

U.S. ARMS CONTROL AND DISARMAMENT AGENCY (WILLIAM C FOSTER VISITING SCHOLARS FELLOWSHIP PROGRAM)

PERSONNEL OFFICER; ROOM 5722
WASHINGTON DC 20451
202/632-8714

AMOUNT: SALARY + TRAVEL EXPENSES

DEADLINE(S): JAN 31

FIELD(S): ARMS CONTROL AND DISARMAMENT

PROGRAM OPEN TO FACULTY OF RECOGNIZED INSTITUTIONS OF HIGHER LEARNING WHO WISH TO LEND THEIR EXPERTISE IN AREAS RELEVANT TO THE ACDA FOR A PERIOD OF ONE YEAR. USA CITIZEN OR LEGAL RESIDENT.

WRITE FOR COMPLETE INFORMATION.

1367 ─────────────────────

U.S. DEPT. OF EDUCATION (FLAS FELLOWSHIPS)

CENTER FOR INTERNATIONAL EDUCTION; ATRB
WASHINGTON DC 20202
202/708-7283

AMOUNT: TUITION & FEES + $8000 STIPEND

DEADLINE(S): VARIES

FIELD(S): FOREIGN LANGUAGE & AREA OR INTERNATIONAL STUDIES

FELLOWSHIPS FOR GRADUATE STUDENTS AT ACCREDITED INSTITUTIONS IN USA WHO ARE PREPARING FOR CAREER AS SPECIALIST IN UNCOMMON FOREIGN LANGUAGE & AREA OR INTERNATIONAL STUDIES. USA CITIZEN OR LEGAL RESIDENT.

APPROX 1000 FELLOWSHIPS PER YEAR. RENEWABLE. CONTACT YOUR INSTITUTION'S FINANCIAL AID OFFICE FOR COMPLETE INFORMATION.

1368 ─────────────────────

U.S. DEPT. OF EDUCATION (JACOB K JAVITS FELLOWSHIP PROGRAM)

PO BOX 84
WASHINGTON DC 20044
800/4FED-AID

AMOUNT: $15000 PER YEAR ON AVERAGE

DEADLINE(S): MAR 15

FIELD(S): ARTS; HUMANITIES; SOCIAL SCIENCES

FELLOWSHIPS TO ASSIST STUDENTS OF SUPERIOR ABILITIES IN STUDIES FOR DOCTORAL-LEVEL DEGREES IN SPECIFIED SUBFIELDS OF THE ABOVE AREAS. USA CITIZEN OR LEGAL RESIDENT.

APPLICATION PACKAGE AVAILABLE LATE OCT OR EARLY NOV. APPROX 100 AWARDS PER YEAR; RENEWABLE UP TO 48 MONTHS. WRITE FOR COMPLETE INFORMATION.

1369 ─────────────────────

WOLCOTT FOUNDATION (FELLOWSHIP AWARD)

402 BEASLEY ST
MONROE LA 71203
318/343-1602

AMOUNT: TUITION + BOOKS; FEES & UP TO $150 PER MONTH STIPEND

DEADLINE(S): FEB 1

FIELD(S): BUSINESS ADMINISTRATION; PUBLIC SERVICE; INTERNATIONAL RELATIONS; GOVERNMENT; PUBLIC ADMINSTRATION

OPEN TO STUDENTS ENROLLED IN ACCREDITED PROGRAM LEADING TO MASTER'S DEGREE WITH GPA OF AT LEAST 3.0 ON 4.0 SCALE. PREFERENCE TO (BUT NOT LIMITED TO) APPLICANTS WITH MASONIC BACKGROUND. USA CITIZEN.

FELLOWSHIPS ARE FOR 36 SEMESTER HOURS AND TENABLE AT GEORGE WASHINGTON UNIVERSITY. WRITE FOR COMPLETE INFORMATION.

PSYCHOLOGY

1370 ─────────────────────

AMERICAN FOUNDATION FOR THE BLIND (DELTA GAMMA FOUNDATION FLORENCE HARVEY MEMORIAL SCHOLARSHIP)

15 WEST 16TH ST
NEW YORK NY 10011
212/620-2000; TDD 212/620-2158

AMOUNT: $1000

DEADLINE(S): APR 1

FIELD(S): REHABILITATION AND/OR EDUCATION OF THE VISUALLY IMPAIRED AND BLIND

OPEN TO LEGALLY BLIND UNDERGRADUATE AND GRADUATE COLLEGE STUDENTS OF GOOD CHARACTER WHO HAVE EXHIBITED ACADEMIC EXCELLENCE AND ARE STUDYING IN THE FIELD OF EDUCATION AND/OR REHABILITATION OF THE VISUALLY IMPAIRED AND BLIND.

MUST BE USA CITIZEN. WRITE FOR COMPLETE INFORMATION.

1371 ─────────────────────

AMERICAN FOUNDATION FOR THE BLIND (RUDOLPH DILLMAN MEMORIAL SCHOLARSHIP)

15 WEST 16TH ST
NEW YORK NY 10011
212/620-2000; TDD 212/620-2158

AMOUNT: $2500

DEADLINE(S): APR 1

FIELD(S): REHABILITATION; EDUCATION OF BLIND & VISUALLY IMPAIRED

OPEN TO LEGALLY BLIND UNDERGRADUATE OR GRADUATE STUDENTS ACCEPTED TO OR ENROLLED IN AN ACCREDITED PROGRAM WITHIN THE BROAD AREAS OF REHABILITATION AND/OR EDUCATION OF THE BLIND AND VISUALLY IMPAIRED. USA CITIZEN.

THREE AWARDS PER YEAR. WRITE FOR COMPLETE INFORMATION.

PSYCHOLOGY

1372

AMERICAN FOUNDATION FOR THE BLIND (TELESENSORY SCHOLARSHIP)

15 WEST 16TH ST
NEW YORK NY 10011
212/620-2000; TDD 212/620-2158

AMOUNT: $1000

DEADLINE(S): APR 1

FIELD(S): REHABILITATION; EDUCATION OF BLIND & VISUALLY IMPAIRED

OPEN TO LEGALLY BLIND UNDERGRADUATE & GRADUATE STUDENTS ACCEPTED TO OR ENROLLED IN AN ACCREDITED PROGRAM WITHIN THE BROAD AREAS OF REHABILITATION AND/OR EDUCATION OF THE BLIND AND VISUALLY IMPAIRED. USA CITIZEN.

WRITE FOR COMPLETE INFORMATION.

1373

AMERICAN PSYCHOLOGICAL ASSOCIATION (MINORITY FELLOWSHIP PROGRAM)

1200 17TH STREET NW
WASHINGTON DC 20036
202/955-7761

AMOUNT: UP TO $7333 STIPEND PER YEAR

DEADLINE(S): JAN 15

FIELD(S): PSYCHOLOGY; NEUROSCIENCE

FELLOWSHIPS FOR MINORITY STUDENTS PURSUING DOCTORAL DEGREES AT ACCREDITED INSTITUTIONS. THERE ARE 2 PROGRAMS; ONE TO SUPPORT TRAINING OF CLINICIANS & ONE TO SUPPORT TRAINING OF RESEARCHERS. US CITIZEN OR LEGAL RESIDENT.

30 AWARDS PER YEAR. FELLOWSHIPS ARE RENEWABLE. WRITE FOR COMPLETE INFORMATION.

1374

AMERICAN SOCIOLOGICAL ASSOCIATION (MINORITY FELLOWSHIP PROGRAM)

1722 'N' STREET NW
WASHINGTON DC 20036
202/833-3410

AMOUNT: $8800 STIPEND

DEADLINE(S): DEC 31

FIELD(S): SOCIOLOGY; MENTAL HEALTH

OPEN TO USA CITIZENS OR PERMANENT RESIDENTS (PARTICULARLY ETHNIC MINORITIES) WHO DOCUMENT AN INTEREST IN AND COMMITMENT TO TEACHING; RESEARCH; AND SERVICE CAREERS ON THE SOCIOLOGICAL ASPECTS OF MENTAL HEALTH ISSUES.

PROSPECTIVE AND CURRENT GRAD STUDENTS WILL BE CONSIDERED FOR THE DOCTORAL FELLOWSHIPS. APPROX 10 AWARDS PER YEAR. FELLOWS MUST AGREE TO A PERIOD OF RESEARCH UPON COMPLETION OF DEGREE. WRITE FOR COMPLETE INFORMATION.

1375

ASSOCIATION FOR WOMEN IN SCIENCE EDUCATIONAL FOUNDATION (AWIS PRE-DOCTORAL AWARDS)

1522 K STREET NW SUITE 820
WASHINGTON DC 20005
202/408-0742

AMOUNT: $500

DEADLINE(S): JAN 15

FIELD(S): ENGINEERING; LIFE SCIENCES; MATHEMATICS; PHYSICAL SCIENCES; BEHAVIORAL SCIENCES; SOCIAL SCIENCES

SCHOLARSHIP AID & INCENTIVE AWARDS OPEN TO WOMEN WHO ARE WORKING ACTIVELY TOWARDS A DOCTORAL DEGREE IN THE ABOVE AREAS. USA CITIZENS MAY STUDY IN USA OR ABROAD; NON-CITIZENS MUST BE ENROLLED IN USA INSTITUTION.

APPLICATIONS ARE AVAILABLE OCT 1 - DEC 15. WRITE FOR COMPLETE INFORMATION.

1376

CALIFORNIA ASSN OF MARRIAGE & FAMILY THERAPISTS (CAMFT EDUCATION FOUNDATION SCHOLARSHIPS)

3465 CAMINO DEL RIO SOUTH; SUITE 350
SAN DIEGO CA 92108
619/280-0505

AMOUNT: $1000

DEADLINE(S): FEB 28

FIELD(S): MARRIAGE & FAMILY THERAPY

OPEN TO GRADUATE STUDENTS AT RECOGNIZED INSTITUTIONS. AWARDS SUPPORT GRADUATE RESEARCH IN MARRIAGE & FAMILY THERAPY. PREFERENCE TO (BUT NOT LIMITED TO) CAMFT MEMBERS.

WRITE FOR COMPLETE INFORMATION.

1377

COMMITTEE ON INSTITUTIONAL COOPERATION (CIC PREDOCTORAL FELLOWSHIPS)

KIRKWOOD HALL RM 111; INDIANA UNIV.
BLOOMINGTON IN 47405
812/855-0822

AMOUNT: $9500 + TUITION (5 YEARS)

DEADLINE(S): JAN 2

FIELD(S): HUMANITIES; SOCIAL SCIENCES; NATURAL SCIENCES; MATHEMATICS; ENGINEERING

PREDOCTORAL FELLOWSHIPS FOR USA CITIZENS OF AFRICAN AMERICAN; AMERICAN INDIAN; MEXICAN AMERICAN OR PUERTO RICAN HERITAGE. MUST HOLD OR EXPECT TO RECEIVE BACHELOR'S DEGREE BY LATE SUMMER FROM A REGIONALLY ACCREDITED COLLEGE OR UNIVERSITY.

AWARDS FOR SPECIFIED UNIVERSITIES IN IL; IN; IA; MI; MN; OH; WI; PA. WRITE FOR DETAILS.

1378

EASTER SEAL SOCIETY OF IOWA (SCHOLARSHIPS & AWARDS)

PO BOX 4002
DES MOINES IA 50333
515/289-1933

AMOUNT: $400 - $600

DEADLINE(S): APR 15

FIELD(S): PHYSICAL REHABILITATION; MENTAL REHABILITATION; & RELATED AREAS

OPEN TO IOWA RESIDENTS WHO ARE FULL-TIME UNDERGRADUATE SOPHOMORES; JUNIORS; SENIORS OR GRADUATE STUDENTS AT ACCREDITED INSTITUTIONS; PLANNING A CAREER IN THE BROAD FIELD OF REHABILITATION; FINANCIALLY NEEDY & IN TOP 40% OF THEIR CLASS.

6 SCHOLARSHIPS PER YEAR. RENEWABLE. WRITE FOR COMPLETE INFORMATION.

1379

EPILEPSY FOUNDATION OF AMERICA (BEHAVORIAL SCIENCES STUDENT FELLOWSHIPS)

4351 GARDEN CITY DR. SUITE 406
LANDOVER MD 20785
301/459-3700

AMOUNT: $1500

DEADLINE(S): MAR 2

FIELD(S): EPILEPSY RELATED STUDY OR TRAINING PROJECTS.

OPEN TO UNDERGRAD AND GRAD STUDENTS IN NURSING; PSYCHOLOGY AND RELATED AREAS WHO PROPOSE A 3-MONTH EPILEPSY-RELATED PROJECT TO BE CARRIED OUT IN A USA INSTITUTION AT WHICH THERE ARE ONGOING EPILEPSY RESEARCH; SERVICE OR TRAINING PROGRAMS.

FELLOWSHIP MUST BE UNDERTAKEN DURING A FREE PERIOD IN THE STUDENT'S YEAR. WRITE FOR COMPLETE INFORMATION.

1380

FLORIDA ENDOWMENT FUND FOR HIGHER EDUCATION (MCKNIGHT DOCTORAL FELLOWSHIP PROGRAM)

201 E.KENNEDY BLVD; SUITE 1525
TAMPA FL 33602
813/272-2772

AMOUNT: $11000 STIPEND + $5000 TUITION & FEES (PER YEAR)

DEADLINE(S): JAN 15

FIELD(S): ALL FIELDS (EXCEPT LAW; MEDICINE & EDUCATION)

OPEN TO ALL AFRICAN-AMERICANS WITH AT LEAST A BACHELOR'S DEGREE FROM AN ACCREDITED INSTITUTION WHO WISH TO PURSUE A DOCTORAL DEGREE. PROGRAM RECRUITS NATIONWIDE; HOWEVER FELLOWS MUST ENROLL IN A FLORIDA INSTITUTION. USA CITIZEN.

25 AWARDS PER YEAR. RENEWABLE FOR UP TO 5 YEARS. WRITE FOR COMPLETE INFORMATION.

1381

FRAGRANCE RESEARCH FUND (RESEARCH GRANTS)

145 EAST 32ND ST - 14TH FLOOR
NEW YORK NY 10016
212/725-2755; FAX 212/779-9058

AMOUNT: UP TO $50000

DEADLINE(S): JAN 1

FIELD(S): OLFACTORY RESEARCH

POST-GRADUATE GRANTS TO SUPPORT RESEARCH IN OLFACTORY AROMA-CHOLOGY. OPEN TO CLINICAL PSYCHOLOGISTS AFFILIATED WITH RECOGNIZED COLLEGE OR UNIVERSITY PROGRAMS.

APPLICANTS MUST HAVE DOCTORAL DEGREE. GRANTS ARE RENEWABLE. WRITE FOR COMPLETE INFORMATION.

1382

HARRY FRANK GUGGENHEIM FOUNDATION (DISSERTATION FELLOWSHIPS)

527 MADISON AVE
NEW YORK NY 10022
212/644-4907

AMOUNT: $10000

DEADLINE(S): FEB 1

FIELD(S): BEHAVORIAL SCIENCE; SOCIAL SCIENCE

PSYCHOLOGY

AWARDS ARE INTENDED FOR SUPPORT DURING THE WRITING OF THE PH.D THESIS IN DISCIPLINES ADDRESSING THE CAUSES; MANIFESTATIONS AND CONTROL OF VIOLENCE; AGGRESSION AND DOMINANCE. APPLICANTS MUST HAVE COMPLETED RESEARCH AND BE READY TO WRITE.

OPEN TO CITIZENS OF ANY COUNTY WHO ARE STUDYING AT COLLEGES OR UNIVERSITIES IN ANY COUNTRY. WRITE FOR COMPLETE INFORMATION.

1383

HARRY FRANK GUGGENHEIM FOUNDATION (POST-DOCTORAL RESEARCH GRANTS)

527 MADISON AVE
NEW YORK NY 10022
212/644-4907

AMOUNT: $15000 - $35000

DEADLINE(S): FEB 1; AUG 1

FIELD(S): BEHAVORIAL SCIENCES; SOCIAL SCIENCES

POST-DOCTORAL GRANTS FOR RESEARCHERS IN THE ABOVE FIELDS WHOSE WORK LEADS TO A BETTER UNDERSTANDING OF THE CAUSES; MANIFESTATIONS & CONTROL OF VIOLENCE; AGGRESSION; AND DOMINANCE IN THE MODERN WORLD.

35-40 GRANTS PER YEAR. AVERAGE 2 YEAR DURATION. WRITE FOR COMPLETE INFORMATION.

1384

HEADQUARTERS; DEPT. OF THE ARMY (ARMED FORCES HEALTH PROFESSIONS SCHOLARSHIPS)

ATTN; SGPS-PDE; 5109 LEESBURG PIKE
FALLS CHURCH VA 22041
WRITTEN INQURIY

AMOUNT: $749 PER MONTH STIPEND + TUITION; FEES; BOOKS; LAB FEES ETC.

DEADLINE(S): NONE SPECIFIED

FIELD(S): MEDICINE; DENTISTRY; OPTOMETRY AND NURSE ANESTHESIA (MASTER'S DEGREE); CLINICAL PSYCHOLOGY (PH.D)

OPEN TO USA CITIZENS ENROLLED OR ACCEPTED FOR ENROLLMENT IN ANY OF THE ABOVE FIELDS AT AN ACCREDITED INSTITUTION IN THE USA OR PUERTO RICO. MUST QUALIFY FOR APPOINTMENT AS AN ARMY OFFICER AND SIGN A CONTRACTUAL AGREEMENT.

WRITE FOR COMPLETE INFORMATION.

1385

HEADQUARTERS; USAF RECRUITING SERVICE (ARMED FORCES HEALTH PROFESSIONS SCHOLARSHIPS)

MEDICAL RECRUITING DIVISION
RANDOLPH AFB TX 78150
WRITTEN INQURIY

AMOUNT: $749 PER MONTH STIPEND + TUITION; FEES; BOOKS; LAB FEES ETC.

DEADLINE(S): NONE SPECIFIED

FIELD(S): MEDICINE; DENTISTRY; OPTOMETRY AND NURSE ANESTHESIA (MASTER'S DEGREE); CLINICAL PSYCHOLOGY (PH.D)

OPEN TO USA CITIZENS ENROLLED OR ACCEPTED FOR ENROLLMENT IN ANY OF THE ABOVE FIELDS AT AN ACCREDITED INSTITUTION IN THE USA OR PUERTO RICO. MUST QUALIFY FOR APPOINTMENT AS AN AIR FORCE OFFICER AND SIGN A CONTRACTUAL AGREEMENT.

WRITE FOR COMPLETE INFORMATION.

1386

HENRY A.MURRAY RESEARCH CENTER AT RADCLIFFE COLLEGE (DISSERTATION AWARD PROGRAM)

10 GARDEN ST
CAMBRIDGE MA 02138
617/495-8140; FAX 617/495-8422

AMOUNT: $2500

DEADLINE(S): APR 1 (POSTMARK)

FIELD(S): SOCIAL & BEHAVORIAL SCIENCES

DOCTORAL DISSERTATION GRANTS OPEN TO GRADUATE STUDENTS DOING RESEARCH IN THE SOCIAL AND BEHAVORIAL SCIENCES. DISSERTATION TOPIC SHOULD FOCUS ON ISSUES IN HUMAN DEVELOPMENT OR PERSONALITY. USA CITIZEN OR LEGAL RESIDENT.

PRIORITY WILL BE GIVEN TO PROJECTS THAT DRAW ON MURRAY RESEARCH CENTER RESOURCES BUT THIS IS NOT REQUIRED TO APPLY. WRITE FOR COMPLETE INFORMATION.

1387

INSTITUTE FOR RATIONAL-EMOTIVE THERAPY (FELLOWSHIP TRAINING PROGRAM)

45 EAST 65TH ST.
NEW YORK NY 10021
212/535-0822

AMOUNT: $6000 PER YEAR (2 YEAR PROGRAM)

DEADLINE(S): VARIES

FIELD(S): PSYCHOLOGY

POST-DOCTORAL FELLOWSHIPS AND INTERNSHIPS IN COGNITIVE BEHAVIOR THERAPY. APPLICANTS MUST HAVE A PH.D. IN PSYCHOLOGY; OR AN M.D. OR AN M.S.W. AND BE ELIGIBLE FOR STATE CERTIFICATION.

12 AWARDS PER YEAR. WRITE FOR COMPLETE INFORMATION.

1388 ───────────────

JAMES MCKEEN CATTELL FUND (SUPPLEMENTAL SABBATICAL FELLOWSHIP AWARDS)

GREGORY KIMBLE; DUKE UNIV PSYCHOLOGY DEPT
DURHAM NC 27706
919/660-5739

AMOUNT: $2400

DEADLINE(S): DEC 1

FIELD(S): PSYCHOLOGY

POST-DOCTORATE RESEARCH FELLOWSHIPS. LIMITED TO TENURED FACULTY MEMBERS IN PSYCHOLOGY DEPARTMENTS IN USA OR CANADA WHO ARE ELIGIBLE FOR SABBATICAL LEAVE.

APPROXIMATELY 5 AWARDS PER YEAR. WRITE FOR COMPLETE INFORMATION.

1389 ───────────────

JOHN FREDERICK STEINMAN (PSYCHOLOGY FELLOWSHIP)

8 WEST KING STREET
LANCASTER PA 17603
WRITTEN INQUIRY

AMOUNT: $3500

DEADLINE(S): FEB 1

FIELD(S): PSYCHOLOGY

OPEN TO THOSE HOLDING A MASTER'S DEGREE OR BETTER; WHO MAJORED IN PSYCHOLOGY AND WHO WISH TO STUDY PSYCHOLOGY FOR TWO MORE YEARS TO BECOME A FULLY QUALIFIED CLINICAL OR SCHOOL PSYCHOLOGIST.

PREFERENCE TO THOSE WHO AGREE TO PRACTICE IN THE AREA SERVING LANCASTER COUNTY PA. WRITE FOR COMPLETE INFORMATION.

1390 ───────────────

LABAN/BARTENIEFF INSTITUTE OF MOVEMENT STUDIES (WORKSTUDY PROGRAMS)

11 E. 4TH ST.; 3RD FLOOR
NEW YORK NY 10003
212/477-4299

AMOUNT: $500 - $2500

DEADLINE(S): MAY 1

FIELD(S): HUMAN MOVEMENT STUDIES

OPEN TO GRADUATE STUDENTS & PROFESSIONALS IN DANCE; EDUCATION; HEALTH FIELDS; BEHAVIORAL SCIENCES; FITNESS; ATHLETIC TRAINING; ETC. FOR WORK STUDY -ONLY- AT THE LABAN/ BARTENIEFF INSTITUTE IN THE LABAN MOVEMENT STUDIES CERTIFICATE PROGRAM.

WRITE FOR COMPLETE INFORMATION.

1391 ───────────────

NATIONAL CHAMBER OF COMMERCE FOR WOMEN (SCHOLARSHIPS & RESEARCH GRANTS)

10 WATERSIDE PLAZA; SUITE 6H
NEW YORK NY 10010
212/685-3454

AMOUNT: VARIES

DEADLINE(S): NONE

FIELD(S): BEHAVIORAL SCIENCE

SCHOLARSHIPS & GRANTS OPEN TO POST-GRADUATES; GRADUATE STUDENTS & PROFESSIONALS IN THE BEHAVIORAL SCIENCES. AWARDS SUPPORT STUDY AND/OR RESEARCH PROJECTS. PREFERENCE TO (BUT NOT LIMITED TO) ORGANIZATIONAL BEHAVIOR & BUSINESS ETHICS.

WRITE FOR COMPLETE INFORMATION.

1392 ───────────────

NATIONAL RESEARCH COUNCIL (NATIONAL SCIENCE FOUNDATION MINORITY GRADUATE FELLOWSHIPS)

2101 CONSTITUTION AVE.
WASHINGTON DC 20418
202/334-2872

AMOUNT: $14000 STIPEND (12 MONTHS) + UP TO $7500 FOR TUITION AND FEES

DEADLINE(S): NOV 6

FIELD(S): ENGINEERING; MATHEMATICS; COMPUTER SCIENCE; CHEMISTRY; EARTH SCIENCES; LIFE SCIENCES; PSYCHOLOGY; SOCIAL SCIENCES

OPEN MINORITY GRADUATE STUDENTS (MASTERS OR PH.D) WHO ARE USA CITIZENS OR LEGAL RESIDENTS & ARE AT OR NEAR THE BEGINNING OF THEIR GRADUATE STUDY. FELLOWSHIPS TENABLE AT ACCREDITED INSTITUTION OFFERING ADVANCED DEGREES IN THE FIELDS ABOVE.

APPROX 150 NEW 3-YEAR FELLOWSHIPS AWARDED EACH YEAR. WRITE FOR COMPLETE INFORMATION.

PSYCHOLOGY

1393

NATIONAL RESEARCH COUNCIL (NATIONAL SCIENCE FOUNDATION GRADUATE FELLOWSHIPS)

2101 CONSTITUTION AVE
WASHINGTON DC 20418
202/334-2872

AMOUNT: $14000 STIPEND + $7000 TUITION ALLOWANCE

DEADLINE(S): NOV 10

FIELD(S): SOCIAL SCIENCES; PHYSICAL SCIENCES; MATHEMATICS; BIOLOGY; ENGINEERING

DOCTORAL) WHO HAVE NOT COMPLETED MORE THAN 1 YEAR OF GRAD STUDY. FELLOWSHIPS TENABLE AT ANY ACCREDITED INSTITUTION OFFERING ADVANCED DEGREES IN THE AREAS ABOVE. USA CITIZEN OR PERMANENT RESIDENT.

OPEN TO HISTORY & PHILOSOPHY OF SCIENCE STUDENTS ALSO. 950 NEW 3-YEAR FELLOWSHIPS AWARDED EACH YEAR. WRITE FOR COMPLETE INFORMATION.

1394

NORTH CAROLINA STUDENT LOAN PROGRAM FOR HEALTH; SCIENCE; & MATHEMATICS (LOANS)

3824 BARRETT DR.; SUITE 304
RALEIGH NC 27619
919/733-2164

AMOUNT: $2500 - $7500 PER YEAR

DEADLINE(S): JAN 8 - MAY 5

FIELD(S): HEALTH PROFESSIONS; SCIENCES; ENGINEERING

LOW-INTEREST SCHOLARSHIP LOANS OPEN TO NORTH CAROLINA RESIDENTS OF AT LEAST 1 YEAR WHO ARE PURSUING AN ASSOCIATES; UNDERGRADUATE OR GRADUATE DEGREE IN THE ABOVE FIELDS AT AN ACCREDITED INSTITUTION IN THE USA.

LOANS MAY BE RETIRED AFTER GRADUATION BY WORKING (1 YEAR FOR EACH YEAR FUNDED) AT DESIGNATED INSTITUTIONS. WRITE FOR COMPLETE DETAILS.

1395

PARAPSYCHOLOGY FOUNDATION (EILEEN J. GARRETT RESEARCH SCHOLARSHIP)

228 EAST 71ST STREET
NEW YORK NY 10021
212/628-1550; FAX 212/628-1559

AMOUNT: $3000

DEADLINE(S): JUL 15

FIELD(S): PARAPSYCHOLOGY

OPEN TO ANY UNDERGRAD OR GRAD STUDENT WISING TO PURSUE THE ACADEMIC STUDY OF THE SCIENCE OF PARAPSYCHOLOGY. FUNDING IS FOR STUDY; RESEARCH & EXPERIMENTATION ONLY. APPLICANTS MUST DEMONSTRATE PREVIOUS ACADEMIC INTEREST IN PARAPSYCHOLOGY.

APPROX 15 AWARDS PER YEAR. WRITE FOR COMPLETE INFORMATION.

1396

PARAPSYCHOLOGY FOUNDATION (GRANT PROGRAM)

228 EAST 71ST STREET
NEW YORK NY 10021
212/628-1550; FAX 628-1559

AMOUNT: UP TO $3000

DEADLINE(S): NONE

FIELD(S): PARAPSYCHOLOGY

GRANTS OPEN TO SCIENTISTS; UNIVERSITIES; LABORATORIES & OTHERS CONDUCTING RESEARCH IN TELEPATHY; PRECOGNITION; PSYCHOKINESIS & RELATED PHENOMENA. GRANTS WILL NOT COVER TRAVEL EXPENSES OR ACADEMIC DEGREE STUDY.

APPROX 15 AWARDS PER YEAR. WRITE FOR COMPLETE INFORMATION.

1397

RADIO FREE EUROPE/RADIO LIBERTY (MEDIA & OPINION RESEARCH ON EASTERN EUROPE & THE FORMER SOVIET UNION)

PERSONNEL DIVISION;
1201 CONNECTICUT AVE NW
WAHINGTON DC 20036
WRITTEN INQUIRY

AMOUNT: DAILY STIPEND OF 48 GERMAN MARKS PLUS ACCOMMODATIONS

DEADLINE(S): FEB 22

FIELD(S): COMMUNICATIONS; MARKET RESEARCH; STATISTICS; SOCIOLOGY; SOCIAL PSYCHOLOGY; EAST EUROPEAN STUDIES

INTERNSHIP OPEN TO GRADUATE STUDENT OR EXCEPTIONALLY QUALIFIED UNDERGRADUATE IN THE ABOVE AREAS WHO CAN DEMONSTRATE KNOWLEDGE OF QUANTITIVE RESEARCH METHODS; COMPUTER APPLICATIONS AND PUBLIC OPINION SURVEY TECHNIQUES.

EAST EUROPEAN LANGUAGE SKILLS WOULD BE AN ADVANTAGE. WRITE FOR COMPLETE INFORMATION.

1398

SAN BERNARDINO COUNTY MENTAL HEALTH DEPARTMENT (PSYCHOLOGY INTERN TRAINING)

700 EAST GILBERT ST
SAN BERNARDINO CA 92415
714/387-7000

AMOUNT: $12179 STIPEND

DEADLINE(S): JAN 6

FIELD(S): CLINICAL PSYCHOLOGY

STIPEND FOR PRE-DOCTORAL ON-SITE INTERN TRAINING FOR CLINICAL PSYCHOLOGISTS. DURATION IS ONE YEAR. OPEN TO PH.D CANDIDATES WITH A MASTERS DEGREE OR EQUIVALENT TRAINING.

8 AWARDS PER YEAR. WRITE FOR COMPLETE INFORMATION.

1399

SOCIAL SCIENCE RESEARCH COUNCIL (INTERNATIONAL PREDISSERTATION FELLOWSHIP PROGRAM)

ELLEN PERECMAN; 605 THIRD AVE.
NEW YORK NY 10158
212-661-0280

AMOUNT: VARIES

DEADLINE(S): TO BE ANNOUNCED BY PARTICIPATING UNIVERSITIES

FIELD(S): ECONOMICS; POLITICAL SCIENCE; PSYCHOLOGY SOCIOLOGY; OTHER SOCIAL SCIENCE DISCIPLINES

OPEN TO PH.D CANDIDATES ENROLLED IN SOCIAL SCIENCES PROGRAMS AT SELECTED UNIVERSITIES. STUDENTS SHOULD BE INTERESTED IN SUPPLEMENTING THEIR DISCIPLINARY SKILLS WITH AREA AND LANGUAGE STUDIES.

FELLOWS UNDERTAKE A PROGRAM OF STUDY IN OR ON AFRICA; CHINA; LATIN AMERICA; THE CARIBBEAN; THE NEAR & MIDDLE EAST; SOUTH ASIA OR SOUTHEAST ASIA. WRITE FOR COMPLETE INFORMATION.

1400

SOCIETY FOR THE SCIENTIFIC STUDY OF SEX (STUDENT RESEARCH GRANT)

PO BOX 208
MT VERNON IA 52314
319/895-8407

AMOUNT: $500

DEADLINE(S): FEB 1 & SEP 1

FIELD(S): HUMAN SEXUALITY

OPEN TO ANY STUDENT ENROLLED IN A DEGREE GRANTING PROGRAM AT AN ACCREDITED INSTITUTION. CAN BE MASTERS THESIS OR DOCTORAL DISSERTATION BUT THIS IS NOT A REQUIREMENT.

WRITE TO KATHRYN KELLEY PH.D AT ABOVE ADDRESS FOR APPLICATION AND COMPLETE INFORMATION.

1401

U.S. DEPT. OF EDUCATION (INDIAN GRADUATE PROFESSIONAL FELLOWSHIPS)

400 MARYLAND AVENUE SW; RM 2177; MAIL STOP 6335
WASHINGTON DC 20202
202/401-1902

AMOUNT: $1000 - $34000 (AVERAGE $13000)

DEADLINE(S): FEB 7

FIELD(S): MEDICINE; PSYCHOLOGY; LAW; EDUCATION; RELATED FIELDS

FELLOWSHIPS FOR AMERICAN INDIANS OR ALASKAN NATIVES WHO ARE US CITZENS AND SEEKING GRADUATE DEREEES IN THE ABOVE FIELDS AT ACCREDITED INSTITUTIONS IN USA.

APPROXIMATELY 90 CONTINUATION AND 35 NEW AWARDS. WRITE FOR COMPLETE INFORMATION.

1402

U.S. DEPT. OF EDUCATION (JACOB K JAVITS FELLOWSHIP PROGRAM)

PO BOX 84
WASHINGTON DC 20044
800/4FED-AID

AMOUNT: $15000 PER YEAR ON AVERAGE

DEADLINE(S): MAR 15

FIELD(S): ARTS; HUMANITIES; SOCIAL SCIENCES

FELLOWSHIPS TO ASSIST STUDENTS OF SUPERIOR ABILITIES IN STUDIES FOR DOCTORAL-LEVEL DEGREES IN SPECIFIED SUBFIELDS OF THE ABOVE AREAS. USA CITIZEN OR LEGAL RESIDENT.

APPLICATION PACKAGE AVAILABLE LATE OCT OR EARLY NOV. APPROX 100 AWARDS PER YEAR; RENEWABLE UP TO 48 MONTHS. WRITE FOR COMPLETE INFORMATION.

1403

VETERANS ADMINISTRATION (PSYCHOLOGY STIPEND TRAINING PROGRAM)

AFFILIATIONS & TUITION PROGRAMS DIV. 143C;
810 VERMONT AVE
WASHINGTON DC 20420
202/535-7525

AMOUNT: $12350 - $15700

DEADLINE(S): JAN 30

FIELD(S): CLINICAL PSYCHOLOGY; COUNSELING PSYCHOLOGY

PROGRAM OPEN TO PROSPECTIVE INTERNS WHO ARE ENROLLED IN AN APA ACCREDITED PROGRAM LEADING TO THE DOCTORAL DEGREE IN CLINICAL OR COUNSELING PSYCHOLOGY. 345 AWARDS AT 85 VA SITES PER YEAR. MUST BE USA CITIZEN.

FOR COMPLETE INFORMATION CONTACT ADDRESS ABOVE OR THE DIRECTOR OF CLINICAL TRAINING AT THE NEAREST VA SITE.

1404 ——————————————————

WILLIAM T. GRANT FOUNDATION (FACULTY SCHOLARS PROGRAM - RESEARCH ON CHILDREN; ADOLESCENTS AND YOUTH)

515 MADISON AVE.
NEW YORK NY 10022
WRITTEN INQUIRY

AMOUNT: UP TO $35000 PER YEAR FOR 5 YEARS

DEADLINE(S): JUL 1

FIELD(S): CHILD DEVELOPMENT AND MENTAL HEALTH

OPEN TO FACULTY MEMBERS AT UNIVERSITIES & NON-PROFIT INSTITUTIONS; NATIONAL & INTERNATIONAL. AWARD IS FOR BEGINNING INVESTIGATORS INTERESTED IN THE CAUSES & CONSEQUENCES OF FACTORS WHICH COMPROMISE THE HEALTHY DEVELOPMENT OF CHILDREN.

WRITE FOR COMPLETE INFORMATION.

SOCIOLOGY

1405 ——————————————————

AMERICAN SOCIOLOGICAL ASSOCIATION (MINORITY FELLOWSHIP PROGRAM)

1722 'N' STREET NW
WASHINGTON DC 20036
202/833-3410

AMOUNT: $8800 STIPEND

DEADLINE(S): DEC 31

FIELD(S): SOCIOLOGY; MENTAL HEALTH

OPEN TO USA CITIZENS OR PERMANENT RESIDENTS (PARTICULARLY ETHNIC MINORITIES) WHO DOCUMENT AN INTEREST IN AND COMMITMENT TO TEACHING; RESEARCH; AND SERVICE CAREERS ON THE SOCIOLOGICAL ASPECTS OF MENTAL HEALTH ISSUES.

PROSPECTIVE AND CURRENT GRAD STUDENTS WILL BE CONSIDERED FOR THE DOCTORAL FELLOWSHIPS. APPROX 10 AWARDS PER YEAR. FELLOWS MUST AGREE TO A PERIOD OF RESEARCH UPON COMPLETION OF DEGREE. WRITE FOR COMPLETE INFORMATION.

1406 ——————————————————

B'NAI B'RITH YOUTH ORGANIZATION (SCHOLARSHIP PROGRAM)

1640 RHODE ISLAND AVENUE NW
WASHINGTON DC 20036
202-857-6633

AMOUNT: $2500 PER YEAR

DEADLINE(S): EACH SPRING

FIELD(S): SOCIAL WORK

JEWISH FAITH. FIRST OR SECOND-YEAR GRADUATE STUDENTS ATTENDING ACCREDITED GRADUATE SCHOOLS OF SOCIAL WORK OR COLLEGE SENIORS PLANNING TO ATTEND A GRADUATE SCHOOL OF SOCIAL WORK.

SHOW EVIDENCE OF GOOD SCHOLARSHIP; INTEREST IN WORKING FOR JEWISH AGENCIES & HAVE KNOWLEDGE OF JEWISH COMMUNAL STRUCTURE & INSTITUTIONS. RENEWABLE. WRITE FOR COMPLETE INFORMATION.

1407 ——————————————————

COUNCIL FOR EUROPEAN STUDIES (PRE-DISSERTATION FELLOWSHIP PROGRAM)

C/O COLUMBIA UNIV; BOX 44 SCHERMERHORN HALL
NEW YORK NY 10027
212/854-4172

AMOUNT: $3000

DEADLINE(S): FEB 1

FIELD(S): EUROPEAN HISTORY; SOCIOLOGY; POLITICAL SCIENCE; ANTHROPOLOGY; ECONOMICS

GRANTS FOR EXPLORATORY RESEARCH IN EUROPE FOR GRAD STUDENTS WHO HAVE COMPLETED AT LEAST TWO YEARS GRADUATE STUDY AND INTEND TO PURSUE A PH.D. USA OR CANADIAN CITIZEN OR LEGAL RESIDENT.

APPLICANTS SHOULD HAVE AT LEAST ONE YEAR OF STUDY IN AN APPROPRIATE FOREIGN LANGUAGE OR MUST SHOW WHY THE REQUIREMENT IS INAPPROPRIATE. WRITE FOR COMPLETE INFORMATION.

1408 ——————————————————

COUNCIL ON SOCIAL WORK EDUCATION (MINORITY FELLOWSHIP PROGRAM)

1600 DUKE ST. - STE. 300
ALEXANDRIA VA 22314
703/683-8080

AMOUNT: $733 MONTHLY STIPEND

DEADLINE(S): FEB 28

FIELD(S): SOCIAL WORK

FELLOWSHIPS OPEN TO MINORITY STUDENTS WITH AN MSW WHO ARE PURSUING A DOCTORAL PROGRAM IN SOCIAL WORK AND ARE INTERESTED IN MENTAL HEALTH RESEARCH OR MENTAL HEALTH SERVICES TO MINORITIES. PRIORITY TO THOSE WHO CAN SHOW FINANCIAL NEED.

USA CITIZEN OR LEGAL RESIDENT. 10 AWARDS PER YEAR. WRITE FOR COMPLETE INFORMATION.

1409

EASTER SEAL SOCIETY OF IOWA (SCHOLARSHIPS & AWARDS)

PO BOX 4002
DES MOINES IA 50333
515/289-1933

AMOUNT: $400 - $600

DEADLINE(S): APR 15

FIELD(S): PHYSICAL REHABILITATION; MENTAL REHABILITATION; & RELATED AREAS

OPEN TO IOWA RESIDENTS WHO ARE FULL-TIME UNDERGRADUATE SOPHOMORES; JUNIORS; SENIORS OR GRADUATE STUDENTS AT ACCREDITED INSTITUTIONS; PLANNING A CAREER IN THE BROAD FIELD OF REHABILITATION; FINANCIALLY NEEDY & IN TOP 40% OF THEIR CLASS.

6 SCHOLARSHIPS PER YEAR. RENEWABLE. WRITE FOR COMPLETE INFORMATION.

1410

FLORIDA ENDOWMENT FUND FOR HIGHER EDUCATION (MCKNIGHT DOCTORAL FELLOWSHIP PROGRAM)

201 E.KENNEDY BLVD; SUITE 1525
TAMPA FL 33602
813/272-2772

AMOUNT: $11000 STIPEND + $5000 TUITION & FEES (PER YEAR)

DEADLINE(S): JAN 15

FIELD(S): ALL FIELDS (EXCEPT LAW; MEDICINE & EDUCATION)

OPEN TO ALL AFRICAN-AMERICANS WITH AT LEAST A BACHELOR'S DEGREE FROM AN ACCREDITED INSTITUTION WHO WISH TO PURSUE A DOCTORAL DEGREE. PROGRAM RECRUITS NATIONWIDE; HOWEVER FELLOWS MUST ENROLL IN A FLORIDA INSTITUTION. USA CITIZEN.

25 AWARDS PER YEAR. RENEWABLE FOR UP TO 5 YEARS. WRITE FOR COMPLETE INFORMATION.

1411

HENRY A.MURRAY RESEARCH CENTER AT RADCLIFFE COLLEGE (DISSERTATION AWARD PROGRAM)

10 GARDEN ST
CAMBRIDGE MA 02138
617/495-8140; FAX 617/495-8422

AMOUNT: $2500

DEADLINE(S): APR 1 (POSTMARK)

FIELD(S): SOCIAL & BEHAVIORIAL SCIENCES

DOCTORAL DISSERTATION GRANTS OPEN TO GRADUATE STUDENTS DOING RESEARCH IN THE SOCIAL AND BEHAVIORIAL SCIENCES. DISSERTATION TOPIC SHOULD FOCUS ON ISSUES IN HUMAN DEVELOPMENT OR PERSONALITY. USA CITIZEN OR LEGAL RESIDENT.

PRIORITY WILL BE GIVEN TO PROJECTS THAT DRAW ON MURRAY RESEARCH CENTER RESOURCES BUT THIS IS NOT REQUIRED TO APPLY. WRITE FOR COMPLETE INFORMATION.

1412

HOOVER INSTITUTION ON WAR; REVOLUTION AND PEACE (NATIONAL FELLOWS PROGRAM)

STANFORD UNIVERSITY
STANFORD CA 94305
415/723-0163

AMOUNT: $32000

DEADLINE(S): JAN 13

FIELD(S): SOCIOLOGY; MODERN HISTORY; POLITICAL SCIENCE; ECONOMICS; INT'L RELATIONS; EDUCATION; LAW

POST-DOCTORAL FELLOWSHIPS THAT PROVIDE PARTICULARLY GIFTED JUNIOR SCHOLARS THE OPPORTUNITY TO SPEND ONE FULL YEAR ON UNRESTRICTED CREATIVE RESEARCH AND WRITING AT THE HOOVER INSTITUTION. USA OR CANADIAN CITIZEN.

12 TO 14 FELLOWSHIPS PER YEAR. RECIPIENTS ARE EXPECTED TO STAY IN RESIDENCY AT THE HOOVER INSTITUTION. WRITE FOR COMPLETE INFORMATION.

1413

HUMAN RELATIONS AREA FILES INC (STUDENT RESEARCH PRIZE COMPETITION)

PO BOX 2054; YALE STATION
NEW HAVEN CT 06520
203/777-2334

AMOUNT: $250

DEADLINE(S): MAR 15

FIELD(S): SOCIOLOGY

SOCIOLOGY

THE HUMAN RELATIONS AREA FILES WILL PRESENT A CASH PRIZE FOR THE BEST SOCIAL SCIENCE PAPER IN CROSS CULTURAL RESEARCH. OPEN TO GRADUATE STUDENTS AT DEGREE GRANTING INSTITUTIONS.

WRITE FOR COMPLETE INFORMATION.

1414

JEWISH COMMUNITY CENTERS ASSOCIATION (JCCA SCHOLARSHIP PROGRAM)

SCHOLARSHIP COORDINATOR;
15 E. 26TH ST.
NEW YORK NY 10010
212/532-4949

AMOUNT: $7500

DEADLINE(S): FEB 1

FIELD(S): ADULT EDUCATION; EARLY CHILDHOOD EDUCATION; PHYSICAL EDUCATION; SOCIAL WORK; JEWISH STUDIES; BUSINESS ADMINISTRATION

OPEN TO INDIVIDUALS OF THE JEWISH FAITH WHO ARE ENROLLED IN A MASTERS DEGREE PROGRAM AND HAVE A STRONG DESIRE TO WORK IN THE JEWISH COMMUNITY CENTER FIELD. USA OR CANADIAN CITIZEN.

10 AWARDS PER YEAR. WRITE FOR COMPLETE INFORMATION.

1415

JEWISH VOCATIONAL SERVICE (MARCUS & THERESA LEVIE EDUCATIONAL FUND SCHOLARSHIPS)

1 SOUTH FRANKLIN STREET
CHICAGO IL 60606
312/346-6700 EXT 2214

AMOUNT: $5000

DEADLINE(S): MAR 1

FIELD(S): SOCIAL WORK; MEDICINE; DENTISTRY; NURSING & OTHER RELATED PROFESSIONS & VOCATIONS

OPEN TO COOK COUNTY RESIDENTS OF THE JEWISH FAITH WHO PLAN CAREERS IN THE HELPING PROFESSIONS. MUST SHOW FINANCIAL NEED. FOR UNDERGRADUATE; GRADUATE OR VOCATIONAL STUDY. APPLICATIONS AVAILABLE BEGINNING DEC 1 FROM SCHOLARSHIP SECRETARY.

85-100 AWARDS PER YEAR. RENEWAL POSSIBLE WITH REAPPLICATION. WRITE FOR COMPLETE INFORMATION.

1416

JOHN FREDERICK STEINMAN FUND (SOCIAL WORKER FELLOWSHIPS)

8 WEST KING STREET
LANCASTER PA 17603
WRITTEN INQUIRY

AMOUNT: $3500

DEADLINE(S): FEB 1

FIELD(S): SOCIAL WORK

OPEN TO APPLICANTS WHO HOLD AT LEAST A BACHELOR'S DEGREE FROM AN ACCREDITED COLLEGE OR UNIVERSITY. FOR ADVANCED STUDY TO BECOME TRAINED SOCIAL CASE WORKERS OR SPECIAL GRADUATE TRAINING IN MENTAL HEALTH PRACTICE.

PREFERENCE TO THOSE WHO AGREE TO PRACTICE IN A LOCATION SERVING RESIDENTS OF LANCASTER COUNTY PA. WRITE FOR COMPLETE INFORMATION.

1417

NEW YORK CITY DEPT. OF PERSONNEL (URBAN FELLOWS PROGRAM)

2 WASHINGTON ST.; 15TH FLOOR
NEW YORK NY 10004
212/487-5698

AMOUNT: $17000 STIPEND

DEADLINE(S): JAN 26

FIELD(S): PUBLIC ADMINISTRATION; URBAN PLANNING; GOVERNMENT; PUBLIC SERVICE; URBAN AFFAIRS

FELLOWSHIP PROGRAM PROVIDES ONE ACADEMIC YEAR (9 MONTHS) OF FULL-TIME WORK EXPERIENCE IN URBAN GOVERNMENT. OPEN TO GRADUATING COLLEGE SENIORS AND RECENT COLLEGE GRADUATES. USA CITIZEN.

WRITE FOR COMPLETE INFORMATION.

1418

PHOENIX BUDGET & RESEARCH DEPT (MANAGEMENT INTERN PROGRAM)

251 WEST WASHINGTON ST
PHOENIX AZ 85003
602/262-4800

AMOUNT: $1960 PER MONTH

DEADLINE(S): JAN 10

FIELD(S): PUBLIC ADMINISTRATION; URBAN STUDIES & RELATED FIELDS

ANNUAL MANAGEMENT INTERNSHIP PROGRAM OPEN TO CANDIDATES WHO HOLD A MASTER'S DEGREE OR HAVE COMPLETED ALL MASTER'S DEGREE COURSEWORK IN THE ABOVE FIELDS. THIS IS AN INTERNSHIP - NOT- A SCHOLARSHIP OR GRANT.

WRITE FOR COMPLETE INFORMATION.

1419

POPULATION COUNCIL (FELLOWSHIPS)

FELLOWSHIP OFFICE;
ONE DAG HAMMARSKJOLD PLAZA
NEW YORK NY 10017
212/644-1782

AMOUNT: TUITION; MONTHLY STIPEND; RESEARCH & TRAVEL EXPENSES

DEADLINE(S): NOV 15

FIELD(S): POPULATION STUDIES; DEMOGRAPHY; SOCIOLOGY

DOCTORAL; POST-DOCTORAL & MIDCAREER TRAINING FELLOWSHIPS IN THE ABOVE FIELDS. DOCTORAL CANDIDATES SHOULD HAVE MADE CONSIDERABLE PROGRESS TOWARD THEIR PH.D. OR AN EQUIVALENT DEGREE IN ONE OF THE SOCIAL SCIENCES.

20-25 AWARDS ARE MADE FOR UP TO ONE YEAR. SELECTION CRITERIA WILL STRESS ACADEMIC EXCELLENCE AND PROSPECTIVE CONTRIBUTION TO THE POPULATION FIELD. WRITE FOR COMPLETE INFORMATION.

1420

PRESIDENT'S COMMISSION ON WHITE HOUSE FELLOWSHIPS (FELLOWSHIP PROGRAM)

712 JACKSON PLACE NW
WASHINGTON DC 20503
202/395-4522

AMOUNT: WAGE (UP TO GS-15 STEP 3)

DEADLINE(S): DEC 1

FIELD(S): PUBLIC SERVICE; GOVERNMENT; COMMUNITY INVOLVEMENT; LEADERSHIP

OPEN TO COLLEGE GRADUATES BETWEEN THE AGES OF 30 AND 39 WHO DESIRE ONE YEAR OF FIRST HAND EXPERIENCE IN GOVERNMENT. FELLOWSHIPS OPEN TO A WIDE VARIETY OF EDUCATIONAL BACKGROUNDS AND CAREER INTERESTS.

WRITE FOR COMPLETE INFORMATION.

1421

RADIO FREE EUROPE/RADIO LIBERTY (MEDIA & OPINION RESEARCH ON EASTERN EUROPE & THE FORMER SOVIET UNION)

PERSONNEL DIVISION;
1201 CONNECTICUT AVE NW
WAHINGTON DC 20036
WRITTEN INQUIRY

AMOUNT: DAILY STIPEND OF 48 GERMAN MARKS PLUS ACCOMMODATIONS

DEADLINE(S): FEB 22

FIELD(S): COMMUNICATIONS; MARKET RESEARCH; STATISTICS; SOCIOLOGY; SOCIAL PSYCHOLOGY; EAST EUROPEAN STUDIES

INTERNSHIP OPEN TO GRADUATE STUDENT OR EXCEPTIONALLY QUALIFIED UNDERGRADUATE IN THE ABOVE AREAS WHO CAN DEMONSTRATE KNOWLEDGE OF QUANTITIVE RESEARCH METHODS; COMPUTER APPLICATIONS AND PUBLIC OPINION SURVEY TECHNIQUES.

EAST EUROPEAN LANGUAGE SKILLS WOULD BE AN ADVANTAGE. WRITE FOR COMPLETE INFORMATION.

1422

SOCIAL SCIENCE RESEARCH COUNCIL (INTERNATIONAL PREDISSERTATION FELLOWSHIP PROGRAM)

ELLEN PERECMAN; 605 THIRD AVE.
NEW YORK NY 10158
212-661-0280

AMOUNT: VARIES

DEADLINE(S): TO BE ANNOUNCED BY PARTICIPATING UNIVERSITIES

FIELD(S): ECONOMICS; POLITICAL SCIENCE; PSYCHOLOGY SOCIOLOGY; OTHER SOCIAL SCIENCE DISCIPLINES

OPEN TO PH.D CANDIDATES ENROLLED IN SOCIAL SCIENCES PROGRAMS AT SELECTED UNIVERSITIES. STUDENTS SHOULD BE INTERESTED IN SUPPLEMENTING THEIR DISCIPLINARY SKILLS WITH AREA AND LANGUAGE STUDIES.

FELLOWS UNDERTAKE A PROGRAM OF STUDY IN OR ON AFRICA; CHINA; LATIN AMERICA; THE CARIBBEAN; THE NEAR & MIDDLE EAST; SOUTH ASIA OR SOUTHEAST ASIA. WRITE FOR COMPLETE INFORMATION.

1423

SOCIETY FOR THE PSYCHOLOGICAL STUDY OF SOCIAL ISSUES (GRANTS-IN-AID PROGRAM)

PO BOX 1248
ANN ARBOR MI 48106
313/662-9130

AMOUNT: $1000

DEADLINE(S): FEB 1; MAY 1; NOV 15; APR 15

FIELD(S): SOCIAL ISSUES

GRANTS OF UP TO $1000 ARE AVAILABLE FOR SCIENTIFIC RESEARCH IN A SOCIAL PROBLEM AREA RELATED TO THE BASIC INTERESTS AND GOALS OF SPSSI. PROPOSALS ON SEXISM & RACISM ARE PARTICULARLY WELCOMED.

WRITE FOR COMPLETE INFORMATION.

1424

SPACE FOUNDATION (SPACE INDUSTRIALIZATION FELLOWSHIP)

4800 RESEARCH FOREST DR
THE WOODLANDS TX 77381
713/363-7944; FAX 713/363-7914

AMOUNT: $4000

DEADLINE(S): OCT 1

FIELD(S): SCIENCES & ENGINEERING; BUSINESS; LAW; ECONOMICS; SOCIAL SCIENCES; ENVIRONMENTAL STUDIES; HUMANITIES

OPEN TO SUPERIOR GRADUATE STUDENTS IN THE ABOVE DISCIPLINES WHO INTEND TO DEVOTE THEIR CAREERS TO THE FURTHERANCE OF PRACTICAL SPACE RESEARCH; ENGINEERING; BUSINESS OR OTHER APPLICATION VENTURES.

CONTACT DR. DAVID J. NORTON; EDUCATIONAL GRANT PROGRAM CHAIRMAN; ADDRESS ABOVE; FOR COMPLETE INFORMATION.

1425

U.S. DEPT. OF EDUCATION (JACOB K JAVITS FELLOWSHIP PROGRAM)

PO BOX 84
WASHINGTON DC 20044
800/4FED-AID

AMOUNT: $15000 PER YEAR ON AVERAGE

DEADLINE(S): MAR 15

FIELD(S): ARTS; HUMANITIES; SOCIAL SCIENCES

FELLOWSHIPS TO ASSIST STUDENTS OF SUPERIOR ABILITIES IN STUDIES FOR DOCTORAL-LEVEL DEGREES IN SPECIFIED SUBFIELDS OF THE ABOVE AREAS. USA CITIZEN OR LEGAL RESIDENT.

APPLICATION PACKAGE AVAILABLE LATE OCT OR EARLY NOV. APPROX 100 AWARDS PER YEAR; RENEWABLE UP TO 48 MONTHS. WRITE FOR COMPLETE INFORMATION.

1426

WILLIAM T. GRANT FOUNDATION (FACULTY SCHOLARS PROGRAM - RESEARCH ON CHILDREN; ADOLESCENTS AND YOUTH)

515 MADISON AVE.
NEW YORK NY 10022
WRITTEN INQUIRY

AMOUNT: UP TO $35000 PER YEAR FOR 5 YEARS

DEADLINE(S): JUL 1

FIELD(S): CHILD DEVELOPMENT AND MENTAL HEALTH

OPEN TO FACULTY MEMBERS AT UNIVERSITIES & NON-PROFIT INSTITUTIONS; NATIONAL & INTERNATIONAL. AWARD IS FOR BEGINNING INVESTIGATORS INTERESTED IN THE CAUSES & CONSEQUENCES OF FACTORS WHICH COMPROMISE THE HEALTHY DEVELOPMENT OF CHILDREN.

WRITE FOR COMPLETE INFORMATION.

GENERAL

1427

AIR FORCE AID SOCIETY (LOANS)

1745 JEFFERSON DAVIS HWY #202
ARLINGTON VA 22202
703/692-9313

AMOUNT: $100 - $7500

DEADLINE(S): NONE

FIELD(S): ALL FIELDS OF STUDY

OPEN TO ACTIVE OR RETIRED AIR FORCE/AIR NATIONAL GUARD OR AIR FORCE RESERVE MEMBERS AND THEIR SPOUSES; WIDOWS OR CHILDREN.

LOANS RENEWABLE. ALL LEVELS OF STUDY. US CITIZEN OR LEGAL RESIDENT. WRITE FOR COMPLETE INFORMATION.

1428

ALABAMA COMMISSION ON HIGHER EDUCATION (SCHOLARSHIPS; GRANTS; LOANS; WORK STUDY PROGRAMS)

SUITE 221/ONE COURT SQUARE
MONTGOMERY AL 36197
WRITTEN INQUIRY

AMOUNT: VARIES

DEADLINE(S): NONE SPECIFIED

FIELD(S): ALL FIELDS OF STUDY

THE COMMISSION ADMINISTERS A NUMBER OF FINANCIAL AID PROGRAMS TENABLE AT POST SECONDARY INSTITUTIONS IN ALABAMA. SOME AWARDS ARE NEED BASED.

WRITE FOR THE 'FINANCIAL AID SOURCES IN ALABAMA' BROCHURE OR CONTACT HIGH SCHOOL GUIDANCE COUNSELOR OR COLLEGE FINANCIAL AID OFFICER.

1429

ALABAMA DEPARTMENT OF VETERANS AFFAIRS (G.I. DEPENDENT CHILDREN SCHOLARSHIP PROGRAM)

PO BOX 1509
MONTGOMERY AL 36102
205/242-5077

AMOUNT: VARIES

DEADLINE(S): NONE

FIELD(S): ALL FIELDS OF STUDY

ALABAMA RESIDENT. OPEN TO DEPENDENT CHILDREN (UNDER 26 YEARS OLD) OF VETERANS WHO WERE ALABAMA RESIDENTS FOR AT LEAST 5 YEARS PRIOR TO ACTIVE DUTY & DIED AS RESULT OF MILITARY SERVICE; WAS/IS MIA OR POW OR BECAME 20% - 100% DISABLED.

AWARDS TENABLE AT STATE SUPPORTED
INSTITUTIONS IN ALABAMA. TOTALLY
DISABLED VETS NOT ORIGINAL ALABAMA
RESIDENTS MAY QUALIFY AFTER 5 YEARS OF
ALA. RESIDENCY. WRITE FOR COMPLETE
INFORMATION.

1430

ALABAMA DEPARTMENT OF VETERANS
AFFAIRS (G.I. UNREMARRIED WIFE/WIDOW
SCHOLARSHIP PROGRAM)

PO BOX 1509
MONTGOMERY AL 36102
205/242-5077

AMOUNT: VARIES

DEADLINE(S): NONE

FIELD(S): ALL FIELDS OF STUDY

OPEN TO UNREMARRIED WIFE OR WIDOW OF
VETERAN WHO WAS AN ALABAMA
RESIDENT FOR AT LEAST 5 YEARS PRIOR TO
ACTIVE DUTY & DIED AS RESULT OF
MILITARY SERVICE; WAS/IS MIA OR POW OR
BECAME 20% - 100% DISABLED.

VETS NOT ORIGINAL ALA. RESIDENTS BUT WITH
100% SERVICE CONNECTED DISABILITY MAY
QUALIFY AFTER 5 YEARS ALA. RESIDENCY.
AWARDS TENABLE AT STATE SUPPORTED
ALA. INSTITUIONS. WRITE FOR COMPLETE
INFORMATION.

1431

ALASKA COMMISSION ON POST-SECONDARY
EDUCATION (STUDENT LOAN PROGRAM;
FAMILY LOAN PROGRAM)

PO BOX 110505
JUNEAU AK 99811
907/465-2962

AMOUNT: $5500 - $6500

DEADLINE(S): MAY 15

FIELD(S): ALL AREAS OF STUDY

OPEN TO ALASKA RESIDENTS OF AT LEAST 2
YEARS. THESE LOW-INTEREST LOANS (8%
STUDENT; 5% FAMILY) SUPPORT FULL-TIME
STUDY AT ANY ACCREDITED VOCATIONAL;
UNDERGRADATE OR GRADUATE
INSTITUTION.

UP TO $5500 AVAILABLE FOR VOCATIONAL OR
UNDERGRADUATE STUDY AND UP TO $6500
FOR GRADUATE STUDY. RENEWABLE. WRITE
FOR COMPLETE INFORMATION.

1432

ALBERT BAKER FUND (STUDENT LOANS)

5 THIRD ST #717
SAN FRANCISCO CA 94103
415/543-7028

AMOUNT: $1200 - $2000

DEADLINE(S): JUL 1

FIELD(S): ALL AREAS OF STUDY

OPEN TO STUDENTS WHO ARE MEMBERS OF THE
MOTHER CHURCH - THE FIRST CHURCH OF
CHRIST SCIENTIST IN BOSTON - AND ARE
ACTIVE AS CHRISTIAN SCIENTISTS. STUDENT
MUST HAVE OTHER PRIMARY LENDER AND
BE ENROLLED IN AN ACCREDITED COLLEGE
OR UNIVERSITY.

FOREIGN STUDENTS MUST HAVE COSIGNER WHO
IS A USA CITIZEN. AVERAGE OF 160 AWARDS
PER YEAR. WRITE FOR COMPLETE
INFORMATION.

1433

ALEXANDER VON HUMBOLDT FOUNDATION
(RESEARCH FELLOWSHIPS FOR FOREIGN
SCHOLARS)

JEAN-PAUL-STRASSE 12
D-5300 BONN 2; GERMANY
0228-833-0

AMOUNT: DM3000 - DM3800 PER MONTH +
EXPENSES

DEADLINE(S): NONE SPECIFIED

FIELD(S): ALL FIELDS OF STUDY

OPEN TO ANY QUALIFIED SCHOLAR (UP TO AGE
40) FOR POST-DOCTORAL RESEARCH IN
GERMANY IN ANY FIELD. HUMANITIES AND
SOCIAL SCIENCES SCHOLARS MUST PROVE
(BY A LANGUAGE CERTIFICATE) THAT THEY
HAVE A GOOD COMMAND OF THE GERMAN
LANGUAGE.

APPROX 500 FELLOWSHIPS PER YEAR. DURATION
IS 6-24 MONTHS. WRITE TO THE ATTENTION
OF THE SELECTION DEPT FOR COMPLETE
INFORMATION.

1434

ALGONQUIN COUNCIL; BOY SCOUTS OF
AMERICA (COLLEGE LOAN PROGRAM)

PO BOX 149; 34 DELOSS ST
FRAMINGHAM MA 01781
617/872-6551

AMOUNT: $1000

DEADLINE(S): NONE

FIELD(S): ALL AREAS

OPEN TO EXPLORER SCOUT WITH A MINIMUM OF
3 YEARS AS A REGISTERED MEMBER OF THE
ALGONQUIN COUNCIL. MUST DEMONSTRATE
GOOD SCHOLARSHIP ABILITY AND
FINANCIAL NEED.

WRITE FOR COMPLETE INFORMATION.

1435

ALPHA LAMBDA DELTA (FELLOWSHIPS FOR MEMBERS)

PO BOX 1576
MUNCIE IN 47308
317/282-5620

AMOUNT: $3000

DEADLINE(S): DEC 31

FIELD(S): ALL FIELDS OF STUDY

GRADUATE FELLOWSHIPS OPEN TO ALPHA LAMBDA DELTA MEMBERS WHO HAVE A GPA OF AT LEAST 3.5 ON 4.0 SCALE. INITIAL INQUIRY SHOULD INCLUDE MEMBERSHIP DATE AND SCHOOL WHERE YOU ARE A MEMBER.

15 FELLOWSHIPS PER YEAR. WRITE FOR COMPLETE INFORMATION.

1436

AMERICAN ASSOCIATION OF UNIVERSITY WOMEN (AAUW EDUCATIONAL FOUNDATION INTERNATIONAL FELLOWSHIPS)

1111 16TH STREET NW
WASHINGTON DC 20036
202/728-7603

AMOUNT: $14000

DEADLINE(S): NOV 15 (TO REQUEST APPLICATION FORMS)

FIELD(S): ALL FIELDS OF STUDY

FELLOWSHIPS OPEN TO WOMEN FOR ONE YEAR OF GRADUATE STUDY OR RESEARCH. AWARDS ARE NOT RENEWABLE.

WRITE FOR COMPLETE INFORMATION.

1437

AMERICAN ASSOCIATION OF UNIVERSITY WOMEN (DISSERTATION FELLOWSHIPS)

1111 16TH STREET NW
WASHINGTON DC 20036
202/728-7602

AMOUNT: $13500

DEADLINE(S): NOV 16 (POSTMARK)

FIELD(S): ALL FIELDS OF STUDY EXCEPT ENGINEERING

FELLOWSHIPS ARE FOR WOMEN WHO WILL COMPLETE WRITING THEIR DOCTORAL DISSERTATIONS BETWEEN JUL 1 AND JUN 30 OF THE FOLLOWING YEAR. APPLICANTS MUST HAVE COMPLETED ALL COURSE WORK AND PASSED ALL PRELIMINARY EXAMS.

DEGREE SHOULD BE RECEIVED AT THE END OF THE AWARD YEAR. APPLICATIONS AVAILABLE AUG 1 - NOV 1. WRITE FOR COMPLETE INFORMATION.

1438

AMERICAN ASSOCIATION OF UNIVERSITY WOMEN (IFUW FELLOWSHIPS & GRANTS)

1111 16TH ST NW
WASHINGTON DC 20036
202/785-7700

AMOUNT: VARIES

DEADLINE(S): OCT 1 OF ODD NUMBERED YEARS

FIELD(S): ALL FIELDS OF STUDY

OPEN TO MEMBERS OF ANY NATIONAL FEDERATION OR ASSOCIATION OF UNIVERSITY WOMEN AFFILIATED WITH IFUW. FOR PH.D CANDIDATES WHO HAVE COMPLETED AT LEAST 1 YEAR OF STUDY. FOR WORK BEGINNING IN EVEN YEARS AS FELLOWSHIPS ARE AWARDED EVERY 2 YEARS.

WRITE FOR COMPLETE INFORMATION.

1439

AMERICAN ASSOCIATION OF UNIVERSITY WOMEN (POST-DOCTORAL FELLOWSHIPS)

1111 16TH STREET NW
WASHINGTON DC 20036
202/728-7602

AMOUNT: $20000 - $25000

DEADLINE(S): AUG 1 - NOV 1

FIELD(S): ALL FIELDS OF STUDY

POSTDOCTORAL FELLOWSHIPS FOR WOMEN IN ALL FIELDS OF STUDY WHO WILL HAVE ACHIEVED A DOCTORATE BY NOV 15. THERE ARE NINE FELLOWSHIPS IN THIS CATEGORY INCLUDING ONE DESIGNATED FOR A WOMAN FROM AN UNDERREPRESENTED MINORITY GROUP.

WRITE FOR COMPLETE INFORMATION.

1440

AMERICAN COUNCIL OF THE BLIND (FLOYD QUALLS MEMORIAL SCHOLARSHIPS)

1155 15TH ST NW; STE 720
WASHINGTON DC 20005
202/467-5081

AMOUNT: $1000 - $2000

DEADLINE(S): MAR 15

FIELD(S): ALL FIELDS OF STUDY

SCHOLARSHIPS OPEN TO LEGALLY BLIND APPLICANTS WHO HAVE BEEN ACCEPTED TO OR ARE ENROLLED IN AN ACCREDITED INSTITUTION FOR VOCATIONAL; TECHNICAL; UNDERGRADUATE; GRADUATE OR PROFESSIONAL STUDIES. USA CITIZEN OR LEGAL RESIDENT.

WRITE FOR COMPLETE INFORMATION.

1441

**AMERICAN FOUNDATION FOR THE BLIND
(HELEN KELLER SCHOLARSHIP FUND)**

15 WEST 16TH ST
NEW YORK NY 10011
212/620-2000; TDD 212/620-2158

AMOUNT: $1000 - $3000

DEADLINE(S): APR 1

FIELD(S): ALL AREAS OF STUDY

OPEN TO COLLEGE OR UNIVERSITY STUDENTS
WHO ARE LEGALLY BLIND AND DEAF FOR
HELP WITH THEIR READING; TUTORING OR
EQUIPMENT ACQUISITION
EXPENSES.STUDENT MUST BE USA CITIZEN
AND SUBMIT PROOF OF BOTH LEGAL
BLINDNESS AND DEAFNESS.

-THIS SCHOLARSHIP IS NOT AVAILABLE FOR 1992-
WRITE FOR COMPLETE INFORMATION.

1442

**AMERICAN FOUNDATION FOR THE BLIND
(KAREN D. CARSEL MEMORIAL
SCHOLARSHIP)**

15 WEST 16TH ST
NEW YORK NY 10011
212/620-2000; TDD 212/620-2158

AMOUNT: $500

DEADLINE(S): JUN 1

FIELD(S): ALL AREAS OF STUDY

OPEN TO LEGALLY BLIND GRADUATE STUDENTS
WHO ARE ENROLLED FULL TIME IN AN
ACCREDITED INSTITUTION & PRESENT
EVIDENCE OF ECONOMIC NEED. USA
CITIZEN.

WRITE FOR COMPLETE INFORMATION.

1443

**AMERICAN FRIENDS OF THE LONDON SCHOOL
OF ECONOMICS (AFLSE SCHOLARSHIP
PROGRAM)**

733 15TH ST NW; SUITE 700
WASHINGTON DC 20005
202/347-3232

AMOUNT: FULL TUITION - APPROX 6500 POUNDS
STERLING

DEADLINE(S): FEB 15

FIELD(S): SOCIAL SCIENCES; ECONOMICS

SCHOLARSHIPS AWARDED ANNUALLY TO USA
CITIZENS OR LEGAL RESIDENTS FOR ONE
YEAR OF GRADUATE STUDY AT THE LONDON
SCHOOL OF ECONOMICS. FOR NEWLY
ENROLLED STUDENTS ONLY.

APPROX 4 SCHOLARSHIPS PER YEAR. WRITE FOR
COMPLETE INFORMATION.

1444

**AMERICAN GEOPHYSICAL UNION
(CONGRESSIONAL SCIENCE FELLOWSHIP
PROGRAM)**

2000 FLORIDA AVE NW
WASHINGTON DC 20009
202/462-6900

AMOUNT: $35000 STIPEND + EXPENSES

DEADLINE(S): FEB 15

FIELD(S): ALL FIELDS OF STUDY

ONE YEAR FELLOWSHIP TO WORK ON THE STAFF
OF ONE OF THE MEMBERS OF THE UNITED
STATES CONGRESS OR CONGRESSIONAL
COMMITTEE. OPEN TO AGU MEMBERS ONLY.
US CITIZEN OR LEGAL RESIDENT.

WRITE FOR COMPLETE INFORMATION.

1445

**AMERICAN INDIAN GRADUATE CENTER
(GRADUATE FELLOWSHIPS)**

4520 MONTGOMERY BLVD NE #1B
ALBUQUERQUE NM 87109
505/881-4584

AMOUNT: UP TO $10000 PER YEAR

DEADLINE(S): JUN 1

FIELD(S): ALL AREAS OF STUDY

FELLOWSHIPS OPEN TO NATIVE AMERICANS WHO
ARE ENROLLED MEMBERS OF FEDERALLY
RECOGNIZED TRIBES OR ALASKA NATIVE
GROUPS & ARE ACCEPTED TO OR ENROLLED
IN AN ACCREDITED MASTERS; DOCTORAL OR
PROFESSIONAL DEGREE PROGRAM IN THE
USA. USA CITIZEN.

APPROX 400 AWARDS PER YEAR. RENEWABLE.
WRITE FOR COMPLETE INFORMATION.

1446

**AMERICAN INSTITUTE OF INDIAN STUDIES
(AIIS JUNIOR FELLOWSHIPS)**

1130 E. 59TH ST.
CHICAGO IL 60637
312/702-8638

AMOUNT: UP TO $7000

DEADLINE(S): JUL 1

FIELD(S): ALL FIELDS OF STUDY

OPEN TO GRADUATE STUDENTS FROM ALL
ACADEMIC DISCIPLINES WHOSE
DISSERTATION RESEARCH REQUIRES STUDY
IN INDIA. JUNIOR FELLOWS WILL HAVE
FORMAL AFFILIATION WITH INDIAN
UNIVERSITIES AND INDIAN RESEARCH
SUPERVISORS.

AWARDS ARE AVAILABLE FOR UP TO 11 MONTHS.
WRITE FOR COMPLETE INFORMATION.

1447

AMERICAN MENSA EDUCATION & RESEARCH FOUNDATION (SCHOLARSHIPS)

2626 E 14TH ST
BROOKLYN NY 11235
WRITTEN INQUIRY

AMOUNT: $200 TO $1000

DEADLINE(S): JAN 31

FIELD(S): ALL FIELDS OF STUDY

OPEN TO STUDENTS ENROLLED FOR THE ACADEMIC YEAR FOLLOWING THE AWARD IN A DEGREE PROGRAM IN AN ACCREDITED AMERICAN INSTITUTION OF POST SECONDARY EDUCATION. APPLICANTS MUST SUBMIT AN ESSAY DESCRIBING CAREER; VOCATIONAL AND ACADEMIC GOALS.

ESSAY SHOULD BE FEWER THAN 550 WORDS AND MUST BE SPECIFIC RATHER THAN GENERAL. IT -MUST- BE ON AN OFFICIAL APPLICATION. SEND SELF ADDRESSED STAMPED ENVELOPE FOR APPLICATION AND COMPLETE INFORMATION.

1448

AMERICAN PHILOSOPHICAL SOCIETY (MELLON RESIDENT RESEARCH FELLOWSHIPS)

LIBRARY; 105 S. FIFTH ST.
PHILADELPHIA PA 19106
WRITTEN INQUIRY

AMOUNT: $1800 PER MONTH STIPEND

DEADLINE(S): MAR 1

FIELD(S): ALL FIELDS OF STUDY

OPEN TO SCHOLARS WHO LIVE WITHIN A 50 MILE RADIUS OF PHILADELPHIA. FOR RESEARCH IN THE SOCIETY'S LIBRARY. APPLICANTS SHOULD HAVE PH.D DEGREE OR HAVE PASSED THE PRELIMINARY PH.D EXAMS. INDEPENDENT SCHOLARS ALSO MAY APPLY.

FELLOWSHIP IS FOR A MINIMUM OF ONE MONTH AND A MAXIMUM OF THREE. WRITE FOR COMPLETE INFORMATION.

1449

AMERICAN PHILOSOPHICAL SOCIETY (RESEARCH GRANT AWARD)

104 S. 5TH ST.
PHILADELPHIA PA 19106
WRITTEN INQUIRY

AMOUNT: $5000 ($4000 TO FULL PROFESSORS)

DEADLINE(S): JAN 15; MAR 1; JUL 1; NOV 1

FIELD(S): ALL FIELDS OF STUDY

POSTDOCTORAL GRANTS TOWARD THE COST OF SCHOLARLY RESEARCH IN ALL AREAS OF KNOWLEDGE EXCEPT THOSE IN WHICH SUPPORT BY GOVERNMENT OR CORPORATIONS IS MORE APPROPRIATE.

WRITE FOR COMPLETE INFORMATION.

1450

AMERICAN RADIO RELAY LEAGUE FOUNDATION (EDWARD D JAIKINS MEMORIAL SCHOLARSHIP FUND)

225 MAIN ST
NEWINGTON CT 06111
203/666-1541

AMOUNT: $500

DEADLINE(S): FEB 15

FIELD(S): ALL AREAS OF STUDY

OPEN TO STUDENTS WHO ARE RESIDENTS OF THE FCC EIGHTH CALL DISTRICT (MICHIGAN; OHIO; W.VIRGINIA); ATTEND AN ACCREDITED INSTITUTION WITHIN THAT CALL DISTRICT; HAVE 3.0 GPA OR BETTER & ARE AT LEAST GENERAL CLASS LICENSED RADIO AMATEURS.

WRITE FOR COMPLETE INFORMATION.

1451

AMERICAN RADIO RELAY LEAGUE FOUNDATION (NEW ENGLAND FEMARA SCHOLARSHIP)

225 MAIN ST
NEWINGTON CT 06111
203/666-1541

AMOUNT: $600

DEADLINE(S): FEB 15

FIELD(S): ALL FIELDS OF STUDY

OPEN TO RESIDENTS OF THE SIX NEW ENGLAND STATES WHO ARE RADIO AMATEURS HOLDING AT LEAST A TECHNICIAN'S LICENSE.

WRITE FOR COMPLETE INFORMATION.

1452

AMERICAN RADIO RELAY LEAGUE FOUNDATION (YOU'VE GOT A FRIEND IN PENNSYLVANIA SCHOLARSHIP FUND)

225 MAIN ST
NEWINGTON CT 06111
203/666-1541

AMOUNT: $1000

DEADLINE(S): FEB 15

FIELD(S): ALL FIELDS OF STUDY

PREFERENCE TO PENNSYLVANIA RESIDENTS WHO ARE ARRL MEMBERS; AT LEAST GENERAL CLASS LICENSED RADIO AMATEURS & HAVE AN 'A' GRADE POINT AVERAGE IN GRADED COURSES (SPORTS & PHYSICAL EDUCATION GRADES EXCLUDED).

WRITE FOR COMPLETE INFORMATION.

1453

AMERICAN SAMOA GOVERNMENT (FINANCIAL AID PROGRAM)

DEPT OF EDUCATION; OFFICE OF STUDENT FINANCIAL PROGRAM
PAGO PAGO AMERICAN SAMOA 96799
684/633-4255

AMOUNT: $5000

DEADLINE(S): APR 30

FIELD(S): ALL FIELDS OF STUDY

SCHOLARSHIPS OPEN TO RESIDENTS OF AMERICAN SAMOA. AWARDS SUPPORT UNDERGRADUATE & GRADUATE STUDY AT ALL ACCREDITED COLLEGES & UNIVERSITIES. APPLICANTS FROM OFF ISLANDS MAY BE ELIGIBLE IF THEIR PARENTS ARE CITIZENS OF AMERICAN SAMOA.

APPROX 50 AWARDS PER YEAR. RENEWABLE. WRITE FOR COMPLETE INFORMATION.

1454

AMERICAN SCANDINAVIAN FOUNDATION (AWARDS FOR STUDY IN SCANDINAVIA)

725 PARK AVE
NEW YORK NY 10021
212/879-9779

AMOUNT: $2500 - $15000

DEADLINE(S): NOV 1

FIELD(S): ALL FIELDS OF STUDY

FELLOWSHIPS & GRANTS FOR ADVANCED STUDY OR RESEARCH IN DENMARK; FINLAND; ICELAND; NORWAY OR SWEDEN. OPEN TO USA CITIZENS & PERMANENT RESIDENTS WHO WILL HAVE COMPLETED THEIR UNDERGRAD EDUCATION BY THE TIME OVERSEAS PROGRAM BEGINS.

APPLICANTS SHOULD HAVE SOME ABILITY IN THE LANGUAGE OF THE COUNTRY OF INTENDED STUDY. WRITE FOR COMPLETE INFORMATION.

1455

AMERICAN SOCIETY OF ARMS COLLECTORS ('ANTIQUE WEAPONS' RESEARCH FELLOWSHIP)

COL. DEAN S. HARTLEY JR.;
520 ERIN AVE.
MONROE LA 71201
318/325-3624

AMOUNT: $2500

DEADLINE(S): MAR 15

FIELD(S): ALL AREAS OF STUDY

OPEN TO GRADUATE STUDENTS FOR RESEARCH INTO THE ORIGIN; MANUFACTURE; USE AND HISTORY OF RARE OR HISTORICAL WEAPONS. APPLICANTS SHOULD BE SEEKING A MASTERS OR DOCTORAL DEGREE IN AN AREA CONSISTENT WITH THE SOCIETY'S AIMS AND PURPOSES.

THE STUDENT'S RESEARCH EVENTUALLY MUST RESULT IN A SCHOLARLY REPORT THAT CAN BE PUBLISHED IN THE SOCIETY'S BULLETIN. RENEWABLE. WRITE FOR COMPLETE INFORMATION.

1456

APPALOOSA YOUTH FOUNDATION (YOUTH EDUCATIONAL SCHOLARSHIPS)

PO BOX 8403
MOSCOW ID 83843
208/882-5578

AMOUNT: $1000

DEADLINE(S): JUN 10

FIELD(S): ALL FIELDS OF STUDY

OPEN TO MEMBERS OF THEB APPALOOSA YOUTH ASSN OR THE APPALOOSA HORSE CLUB; CHILDREN OF APPALOOSA HORSE CLUB MEMBERS AND TO INDIVIDUALS SPONSORED BY A REGIONAL CLUB OR RACING ASSOCIATION.

11 SCHOLARSHIPS PER YEAR. RENEWABLE. CONTACT THE YOUTH COORDINATOR AT ADDRESS ABOVE FOR COMPLETE INFORMATION.

1457

ARKANSAS STUDENT LOAN GUARANTEE FOUNDATION (LOAN PROGRAM)

219 SOUTH VICTORY
LITTLE ROCK AR 72201
501/371-2634

AMOUNT: $2625 1ST & 2ND YR UNDERGRADS; $4000 3RD & 4TH YR; $7500 GRADUATE (PER YEAR)

DEADLINE(S): APR 15

FIELD(S): ALL FIELDS OF STUDY LEADING TO A DEGREE OR CERTIFICATE

LOANS OPEN TO ARKANSAS RESIDENT OR NON-RESIDENT ENROLLED AT ELIGIBLE ARKANSAS POST-SECONDARY EDUCATIONAL INSTITUTION. DEMONSTRATE FINANCIAL NEED. USA CITIZEN OR LEGAL RESIDENT.

WRITE FOR COMPLETE INFORMATION.

1458

ARMENIAN ASSEMBLY OF AMERICA (SCHOLARSHIP INFORMATION)

122 'C' STREET NW; SUITE 350
WASHINGTON DC 20001
201/393-3434

AMOUNT: VARIES

DEADLINE(S): VARIOUS

FIELD(S): ALL AREAS OF STUDY

THE ARMENIAN ASSEMBLY PREPARES AN ANNUAL BOOKLET TITLED 'DIRECTORY OF FINANCIAL AID FOR STUDENTS OF ARMENIAN DESCENT'. IT DESCRIBES NUMEROUS SCHOLARSHIP; LOAN & GRANT PROGRAMS THAT ARE AVAILABLE FROM SOURCES IN THE ARMENIAN COMMUNITY.

THE DIRECTORY IS FREE & IS AVAILABLE FROM THE ADDRESS ABOVE.

1459

ARMENIAN GENERAL BENEVOLENT UNION (AGBU 'EXCELLENCE' GRANT)

585 SADDLE RIVER RD
SADDLE BROOK NJ 07662
201/797-7600

AMOUNT: $5000

DEADLINE(S): APR 30

FIELD(S): ARMENIAN STUDIES; EDUCATION; INTERNATIONAL RELATIONS; JOURNALISM; PUBLIC ADMINISTRATION

OPEN TO GRADUATE AND POST GRADUATE STUDENTS OF ARMENIAN DESCENT WHO HAVE IMPECCABLE ACADEMIC ACHIEVEMENT AND EXCEPTIONAL COMPETENCE IN THEIR SUBJECT AREA. REQUEST APPLICATION IN WRITING ONLY BETWEEN JAN 1 AND MAR 15.

ONLY FOR STUDENTS ENROLLED AT COLUMBIA; HARVARD; UNIVERSITY OF MICHIGAN OR UCLA. WRITE FOR COMPLETE INFORMATION.

1460

ARMENIAN STUDENTS' ASSOCIATION OF AMERICA INC (SCHOLARSHIPS; FELLOWSHIPS)

C. WILLIAMSON; SCHOLARSHIP ADM.; 395 CONCORD AVE.
BELMONT MA 02178
WRITTEN INQUIRY

AMOUNT: $500 - $1500

DEADLINE(S): APR 1 (REQUEST APPLICATION BY FEB 15)

FIELD(S): ALL FIELDS OF STUDY

FOR FULL TIME GRADUATE OR UNDERGRADUATE STUDY IN USA BY STUDENT OF ARMENIAN DESCENT. UNDERGRADS MUST HAVE COMPLETED AT LEAST 1 YEAR OF POST-SECONDARY SCHOOLING; DEMONSTRATE FINANCIAL NEED AND HAVE GOOD ACADEMIC RECORD.

60 AWARDS PER YEAR; RENEWABLE. THERE IS A $5 APPLICATION FEE. RENEWABLE. WRITE FOR COMPLETE INFORMATION.

1461

ARTHUR C & FLORENCE S BOEHMER FUND (SCHOLARSHIPS)

C/O RINN & ELLIOT; PO BOX 1827
LODI CA 95240
209/369-2781

AMOUNT: YEARLY INCOME

DEADLINE(S): JUN 1

FIELD(S): MEDICAL

OPEN TO STUDENTS WHO ARE GRADUATES OF A HIGH SCHOOL WITHIN THE LODI (SAN JOAQUIN COUNTY CA) UNIFIED SCHOOL DISTRICT. FOR UNDERGRADUATE; GRADUATE OR POST-GRADUATE STUDY IN THE FIELD OF MEDICINE AT AN ACCREDITED INSTITUTION IN CALIFORNIA.

GRADE POINT AVERAGE OF 2.9 OR BETTER REQUIRED. SCHOLARSHIPS ARE RENEWABLE. WRITE FOR COMPLETE INFORMATION.

1462

ARTHUR C. & LUCIA S. PALMER FOUNDATION INC (GRANTS)

471 PENNSYLVANIA AVE
WAVERLY NY 14892
607/565-4603

AMOUNT: $3000

DEADLINE(S): APR 1

FIELD(S): ALL FIELDS OF STUDY

GRANTS OPEN TO STUDENTS WHO ARE RESIDENTS OF TIOGA COUNTY NY OR BRADFORD COUNTY PA. FINANCIAL NEED IS DISCUSSED DURING A REQUIRED INTERVIEW. AWARDS BASED ON MOTIVATION & FINANCIAL NEED.

WRITE FOR COMPLETE INFORMATION.

1463

ASSOCIATION FOR EDUCATION & REHABILITATION OF THE BLIND & VISUALLY IMPAIRED (FERRELL SCHOLARSHIP FUND)

206 N. WASHINGTON ST. - SUITE 320
ALEXANDRIA VA 22314
703/548-1884

AMOUNT: VARIES

DEADLINE(S): APR 15 OF EVEN NUMBERED YEARS

FIELD(S): CAREER FIELD IN SERVICES TO THE BLIND

OPEN TO LEGALLY BLIND STUDENTS ENROLLED IN A COLLEGE OR UNIVERSITY PROGRAM RELATED TO BLIND SERVICES SUCH AS ORIENTATION AND MOBILITY; SPECIAL EDUCATION; REHABILITATION TEACHING; VISION REHABILITATION.

FOR UNDERGRADUATE; GRADUATE OR POSTGRADUATE STUDY. WRITE FOR COMPLETE INFORMATION.

1464

ASSOCIATION ON AMERICAN INDIAN AFFAIRS INC (SEQUOYAH FELLOWSHIP PROGRAM)

245 FIFTH AVENUE; SUITE 1801
NEW YORK NY 10016
212/689-8270

AMOUNT: $1500 STIPEND

DEADLINE(S): SEP 13

FIELD(S): ALL FIELDS OF STUDY

GRADUATE FELLOWSHIPS OPEN TO AMERICAN INDIAN OR ALASKA NATIVE. PROOF OF TRIBAL AFFILIATION IS NECESSARY. APPLICANTS ARE ASKED FOR BIOGRAPHICAL DATA; EDUCATIONAL AND CAREER GOALS; INTERESTS AND FINANCIAL SITUATION.

APPLICATIONS ARE ACCEPTED JUL 1 - SEP 13. 10 AWARDS PER YEAR. SEND SELF ADDRESSED STAMPED ENVELOPE FOR COMPLETE INFORMATION.

1465

ASSOCIATION ON AMERICAN INDIAN AFFAIRS INC (EMERGENCY AID & HEALTH PROFESSION SCHOLARSHIPS)

245 FIFTH AVENUE; SUITE 1801
NEW YORK NY 10016
212/689-8270

AMOUNT: UP TO $300

DEADLINE(S): NONE

FIELD(S): ALL FIELDS OF STUDY

AMERICAN INDIAN OR ALASKAN NATIVE. PROOF OF TRIBAL AFFILIATION REQUIRED. EMERGENCY AID IS OFFERED ON FIRST COME FIRST SERVED BASIS WHEN FUNDS ARE AVAILABLE. STUDENTS SHOULD INQUIRE ONLY AFTER BEGINNING CLASSES.

WRITE FOR COMPLETE INFORMATION. ENCLOSE SELF ADDRESSED STAMPED ENVELOPE.

1466

ASSOCIATION OF COMMONWEALTH UNIVERSITIES (BRITISH MARSHALL SCHOLARSHIPS)

36 GORDON SQUARE
LONDON WC1H OPF ENGLAND
071/387-8572

AMOUNT: APPROX 13000 POUNDS STERLING PER YEAR

DEADLINE(S): OCT 18

FIELD(S): ALL AREAS OF STUDY

OPEN TO USA CITIZENS (UNDER 26 YEARS OLD) WHO ARE GRADUATES OF A COLLEGE OR UNIVERSITY. FOR GRADUATE DEGREE STUDY OF 2-3 ACADEMIC YEARS AT A UNIVERSITY IN THE UNITED KINGDOM.

APPROX 40 AWARDS PER YEAR. CONTACT BRITISH CONSULATES AT EMBASSIES IN WASHINGTON DC; CHICAGO; BOSTON; SAN FRANCISCO; ATLANTA OR WRITE TO ADDRESS ABOVE FOR COMPLETE INFORMATION.

1467

BELGIAN AMERICAN EDUCATIONL FOUNDATION (GRADUATE FELLOWSHIPS)

195 CHURCH ST
HAVEN CT 06510
203/777-5765

AMOUNT: $11000 STIPEND

DEADLINE(S): DEC 31

FIELD(S): ALL FIELDS OF STUDY

FELLOWSHIPS FOR GRADUATE STUDY IN BELGIUM. SHOULD HAVE SPEAKING & READING KNOWLEDGE OF FRENCH GERMAN OR DUTCH; AND HAVE MASTERS DEGREE OR BE WORKING TOWARD A PH.D. PREFERENCE TO APPLICANTS UNDER 30 YEARS OLD. USA CITIZEN.

10 AWARDS PER YEAR. AWARD INCLUDES ROUND-TRIP TRAVEL TO BELGIUM; LODGING; LIVING EXPENSES; TUITION & FEES. WRITE FOR COMPLETE INFORMATION.

1468

BERYL BUCK INSTITUTE FOR EDUCATION (SCHOLARSHIPS)

CAROL HORAN; 18 COMMERCIAL BLVD.
NOVATO CA 94949
415/883-0122

AMOUNT: $500 - $2000

DEADLINE(S): MAR 31

FIELD(S): ALL FIELDS OF STUDY

OPEN TO MARIN COUNTY CALIF. RESIDENTS WHO HAVE LIVED IN THE COUNTY SINCE SEP 1 OF THE YEAR PRIOR TO SUBMITTING AN APPLICATION. SCHOLARSHIPS TENABLE AT ACCREDITED COLLEGES & UNIVERSITIES AND VOCATIONAL OR TRADE PROGRAMS.

CONTACT HIGH SCHOOL OR COLLEGE COUNSELOR OR ADDRESS ABOVE FOR COMPLETE INFORMATION.

1469

BETA THETA PI GENERAL FRATERNITY (SCHOLARSHIPS & FELLOWSHIPS)

ADMINISTRATIVE OFFICE;
208 EAST HIGH ST
OXFORD OH 45056
513/523-7591

AMOUNT: $750 - $1500

DEADLINE(S): APR

FIELD(S): ALL FIELDS OF STUDY

OPEN TO UNDERGRADUATE AND GRADUATE STUDENTS WHO ARE BETA THETA PI MEMBERS IN GOOD STANDING AND HAVE A COMPETITIVE GRADE POINT AVERAGE.

30 SCHOLARSHIPS AND 8 FELLOWSHIPS PER YEAR; NON-RENEWABLE. WRITE FOR COMPLETE INFORMATION.

1470

BLINDED VETERANS ASSOCIATION (KATHERN F GRUBER SCHOLARSHIP PROGRAM)

477 H STREET NW
WASHINGTON DC 20001-2694
202/371-8880

AMOUNT: $2000

DEADLINE(S): APR 15

FIELD(S): ALL AREAS OF STUDY

OPEN TO CHILDREN & SPOUSES OF BLINDED VETERANS. THE VET MUST BE LEGALLY BLIND; EITHER SERVICE OR NON-SERVICE CONNECTED. MUST BE ACCEPTED OR ALREADY ENROLLED FULL-TIME IN AN ACCREDITED UNDERGRAD OR GRAD PROGRAM AND USA CITIZEN.

12 AWARDS PER YEAR. WRITE FOR COMPLETE INFORMATION.

1471

BOCES GENESEO MIGRANT CENTER (G. & J.MATTERA NATIONAL SCHOLARSHIP FUND)

HOLCOMB BLDG; ROOM 210
GENESEO NY 14454
716/245-5681

AMOUNT: UP TO $250

DEADLINE(S): NONE

FIELD(S): ALL FIELDS OF STUDY

OPEN TO MIGRANT FARMWORKERS IN THE USA AND THEIR DEPENDENT CHILDREN. AWARDS USUALLY SUPPORT UNDERGRADUATE STUDY BUT SOME SUPPORT HIGH SCHOOL GRADUATION AND GRADUATE STUDY.

60 AWARDS PER YEAR. RENEWABLE. WRITE FOR COMPLETE INFORMATION.

1472

BRITISH EMBASSY (MARSHAL SCHOLARSHIP PROGRAM)

3100 MASS AVE NW; EDUCATION OFFICE
WASHINGTON DC 20008
201/462-1340

AMOUNT: TUITION; FEES; STIPEND; BOOK ALLOWANCE; TRANSPORTATION

DEADLINE(S): OCT 15

FIELD(S): ALL FIELDS OF STUDY

OPEN TO USA CITIZENS WHO ARE UNDER 26 YEARS OLD & HOLD A BACHELORS DEGREE FROM A USA UNIVERSITY. AWARDS ARE FOR AT LEAST 2 YEARS AT A UNITED KINGDOM UNIVERSITY. GRADE POINT AVERAGE OF 3.7 OR BETTER IS REQUIRED (4.0 SCALE).

36 NEW AWARDS PER YEAR. CONTACT NEAREST BRITISH CONSULATE OR WRITE TO ADDRESS ABOVE FOR COMPLETE INFORMATION.

1473

BUSINESS AND PROFESSIONAL WOMEN'S CLUBS-NEW YORK STATE (GRACE LEGENDRE FELLOWSHIPS & ENDOWMENT FUND)

239 GENESEE ST; MAYRO BLDG #212
UTICA NY 13501
315/735-3114

AMOUNT: $1000

DEADLINE(S): FEB 28

FIELD(S): ALL FIELDS OF STUDY

WOMEN RESIDENTS OF NY STATE. FELLOWSHIPS & SCHOLARSHIPS FOR GRADUATE STUDY (MASTERS OR DOCTORATE) AT AN ACCREDITED NY STATE COLLEGE OR UNIVERSITY. USA CITIZEN.

WRITE FOR COMPLETE INFORMATION.

1474

CALIFORNIA STUDENT AID COMMISSION (GRADUATE FELLOWSHIP PROGRAM)

PO BOX 510624
SACRAMENTO CA 94245
916/445-0880

AMOUNT: $171-$1455 (STATE SCHOOLS); $595-$5517 (INDEPENDENT SCHOOLS)

DEADLINE(S): MAR 2

FIELD(S): ALL FIELDS OF STUDY

OPEN TO CA RESIDENTS WHO PLAN TO PURSUE A GRAD DEGREE AT AN ELIGIBLE CA GRAD SCHOOL AND BECOME A COLLEGE/UNIVERSITY FACULTY MEMBER. USA CITIZEN; LEGAL RESIDENT OR IN THE PROCESS OF ESTABLISHING RESIDENCE.

APPROXIMATELY 300 FELLOWSHIPS PER YEAR. RENEWABLE. CONTACT YOUR COUNSELOR; FINANCIAL AID OFFICE OR ADDRESS ABOVE FOR COMPLETE INFORMATION.

1475

CALIFORNIA STUDENT AID COMMISSION (LAW ENFORCEMENT PERSONNEL DEPENDENTS GRANT PROGRAM)

PO BOX 510624
SACRAMENTO CA 94245
916/322-2294

AMOUNT: UP TO $1500 PER YEAR

DEADLINE(S): NONE

FIELD(S): ALL FIELDS OF STUDY

OPEN TO THE NATURAL OR ADOPTED CHILD OF A CALIF LAW ENFORCEMENT OFFICER KILLED OR TOTALLY DISABLED IN THE PERFORMANCE OF HIS/HER DUTY. FOR UNDERGRAD OR GRAD STUDY AT ELIGIBLE CALIFORNIA SCHOOLS. MUST BE CALIFORNIA RESIDENT AND USA CITIZEN.

AWARDS LIMITED TO A MAXIMUM OF $6000 OVER SIX YEARS. MAY BE USED FOR TUITION; FEES; BOOKS; SUPPLIES; LIVING EXPENSES. WRITE FOR COMPLETE INFORMATION.

1476

CALIFORNIA TEACHERS ASSN (CTA SCHOLARSHIPS)

PO BOX 921; 1705 MURCHISON DRIVE
BURLINGAME CA 94011
415/697-1400

AMOUNT: $2000

DEADLINE(S): FEB 15

FIELD(S): ALL AREAS OF STUDY

OPEN TO ACTIVE CTA MEMBERS OR THEIR DEPENDENT CHILDREN FOR UNDERGRADUATE OR GRADUATE STUDY. APPLICATIONS AVAILABLE IN OCTOBER OF EACH YEAR FROM CTA HUMAN RIGHTS DEPARTMENT AT ADDRESS ABOVE.

TWENTY SCHOLARSHIPS PER YEAR. WRITE FOR COMPLETE INFORMATION.

1477

CALIFORNIA YOUNG WOMAN OF THE YEAR INC (SCHOLARSHIPS)

PO BOX 1863
SANTA ROSA CA 95402
707/576-7505

AMOUNT: $10000

DEADLINE(S): MAR 1

FIELD(S): ALL FIELDS OF STUDY

COMPETITION OPEN TO GIRLS IN THEIR JUNIOR YEAR OF HIGH SCHOOL WHO ARE USA CITIZENS AND CALIFORNIA RESIDENTS. WINNER RECEIVES $10000 COLLEGE SCHOLARSHIP; RUNNERS UP SHARE UP TO $30000 IN AWARDS. FOR UNDERGRADUATE OR GRADUATE STUDY.

AWARD CAN BE USED FOR BOOKS; FEES & TUITION AT ANY COLLEGE IN THE WORLD. WRITE TO C. (TING) GUGGIANA; ADDRESS ABOVE; FOR COMPLETE INFORMATION.

1478

CENTRAL SCHOLARSHIP BUREAU (INTEREST-FREE LOANS)

4001 CLARKS LANE
BALTIMORE MD 21215
301/358-8668

AMOUNT: $500 - $8000 (MAX THRU GRAD SCHOOL)

DEADLINE(S): JUN 1; DEC 1

FIELD(S): ALL FIELDS OF STUDY

INTEREST-FREE LOANS FOR RESIDENTS OF METROPOLITAN BALTIMORE AREA WHO HAVE EXHAUSTED ALL OTHER AVAILABLE AVENUES OF FUNDING. AID IS OFFERED FOR STUDY AT ANY ACCREDITED UNDERGRAD OR GRADUATE INSTITUTION.

AWARDS ARE MADE ON A NON-COMPETITIVE BASIS TO ANYONE WITH A SOUND EDUCATIONAL PLAN. 100 LOANS PER YEAR. MUST APPLY FIRST THROUGH GOVERNMENT AND SCHOOL. WRITE FOR COMPLETE INFORMATION.

1479

CHARLES B.KEESEE EDUCATIONAL FUND INC (SCHOLARSHIPS)

PO BOX 431
MARTINSVILLE VA 24114
703/632-2229

AMOUNT: VARIES

DEADLINE(S): MAR 1

FIELD(S): ALL FIELDS OF STUDY

OPEN TO ELIGIBLE RESIDENTS OF VIRGINIA & NORTH CAROLINA WHO ATTEND SCHOOL OR COLLEGE IN VIRGINIA THAT IS AFFILIATED WITH VIRGINIA BAPTIST GENERAL ASSOCIATION OR A SEMINARY OF SOUTHERN BAPTIST CONVENTION. USA CITIZEN.

750 AWARDS PER YEAR. WRITE FOR COMPLETE INFORMATION.

1480 ———————————————

CHAUTAUQUA REGION COMMUNITY FOUNDATION INC. (SCHOLARSHIP GRANTS)

104 HOTEL JAMESTOWN BLDG.
JAMESTOWN NY 14701
716/661-3390

AMOUNT: VARIES

DEADLINE(S): APR 8

FIELD(S): ALL FIELDS OF STUDY

SCHOLARSHIPS ARE OPEN TO STUDENTS WHO LIVE IN THE VICINITY OF JAMESTOWN NY WITH PREFERENCE TO STUDENTS IN 12 SCHOOL DISTRICTS IN SOUTHERN CHAUTAUQUA COUNTY. FOR FULL TIME STUDY.

WRITE FOR COMPLETE INFORMATION.

1481 ———————————————

COLLEGE FOUNDATION INC (FEDERAL PLUS LOANS UNDER N.C. INSURED STUDENT LOAN PROGRAM)

2100 YONKERS RD; PO BOX 12100
RALEIGH NC 27605
919/821-4771

AMOUNT: DIFFERENCE BETWEEN COST OF ATTENDING AND OTHER FINANCIAL AID RECEIVED

DEADLINE(S): VARIES

FIELD(S): ALL FIELDS OF STUDY

FOR PARENT OF STUDENT WHO IS DEPENDENT (BY FEDERAL DEFINITION) AND ENROLLED IN ELIGIBLE USA COLLEGE. IF THE STUDENT IS AT A COLLEGE NOT IN N.C. BORROWER MUST BE LEGAL N.C. RESIDENT. MUST MEET NATIONWIDE FEDERAL PLUS LOANS REQUIREMENTS.

APPROXIMATELY 2600 LOANS PER YEAR. MUST REAPPLY EACH YEAR. WRITE FOR COMPLETE INFORMATION.

1482 ———————————————

COLLEGE FOUNDATION INC (FEDERAL SUPPLEMENTAL LOANS FOR STUDENTS UNDER THE N.C. INSURED STUDENT LOAN PROGRAM)

2100 YONKERS RD; PO BOX 12100
RALEIGH NC 27605
919/821-4771

AMOUNT: $4000 - $5000 PER YEAR UNDERGRADS; UP TO $10000 PER YEAR GRADS

DEADLINE(S): VARIES

FIELD(S): ALL AREAS OF STUDY

FOR LEGAL RESIDENTS OF N.C. ENROLLED IN ELIGIBLE COLLEGES IN OR OUT OF STATE OR FOR OUT-OF-STATE STUDENTS ATTENDING ELIGIBLE COLLEGES IN N.C. MUST MEET ELIGIBILITY REQUIREMENTS OF THE NATIONWIDE FEDERAL SUPPLEMENTAL LOANS FOR STUDENTS.

APPROXIMATELY 3500 LOANS PER YEAR. MUST REAPPLY ANNUALLY. WRITE FOR COMPLETE INFORMATION.

1483 ———————————————

COLLEGE FOUNDATION INC. (NORTH CAROLINA INSURED STUDENT LOAN PROGRAM - STAFFORD LOANS)

PO BOX 12100; 2100 YONKERS ROAD
RALEIGH NC 27605
919/821-4771

AMOUNT: MAX OF $2625; $4000 OR $7500 PER YEAR DEPENDING ON LEVEL OF STUDY

DEADLINE(S): VARIES

FIELD(S): ALL FIELDS OF STUDY

OPEN TO LEGAL RESIDENTS OF N.C. ENROLLED IN AN ELIGIBLE IN-STATE OR OUT-OF-STATE COLLEGE OR AN OUT-OF-STATE STUDENT ATTENDING AN ELIGIBLE N.C. COLLEGE. MUST MEET NATIONWIDE ELIGIBILITY REQUIREMENTS OF STAFFORD LOANS.

APPROXIMATELY 36000 LOANS PER YEAR. FINANCIAL NEED MUST BE ESTABLISHED AND NEW LOAN APPLICATION REQUIRED YEARLY. WRITE FOR COMPLETE INFORMATION.

1484 ———————————————

COMMISSION FRANCO-AMERICAINE D'ECHANGES UNIVERSITAIRES ET CULTURELS (GRADUATE FELLOWSHIPS)

9 RUE CHARDIN
75016 PARIS FRANCE
33 (1) 45 20 46 54; FAX 33 (1) 42 88 04 79

AMOUNT: VARIES ACCORDING TO CATEGORY

DEADLINE(S): AUG 1 & OCT 31 FOR US RESEARCH SCHOLARS AND STUDENTS; DEC 1 & DEC 15 FOR FRENCH RESEARCH SCHOLARS & STUDENTS; OCT 15 FOR US EXCHANGE TEACHERS; JAN 15 FOR FRENCH EXCHANGE TEACHERS

FIELD(S): ALL FIELDS OF STUDY

FELLOWSHIPS FOR USA CITIZENS FOR STUDY AND RESEARCH IN FRANCE AND FOR FRENCH CITIZENS FOR STUDY IN THE USA UNDER FULBRIGHT SCHOLARSHIP PROGRAM.

20 POST FOR POST EXCHANGES FOR FRENCH SECONDARY SCHOOL TEACHERS OF ENGLISH AND USA SECONDARY SCHOOL TEACHERS OF FRENCH. WRITE FOR COMPLETE INFORMATION.

1485

COUNCIL FOR INTERNATIONAL EXCHANGE OF SCHOLARS (FULBRIGHT SCHOLAR GRANT PROGRAM)

3007 TILDEN ST NW - SUITE 5M
WASHINGTON DC 20008
202/686-7866

AMOUNT: VARIES WITH COUNTRY

DEADLINE(S): AUG 1

FIELD(S): ALL FIELDS OF STUDY

GRANT PROGRAM DESIGNED TO INCREASE MUTUAL UNDERSTANDING BETWEEN PEOPLE OF USA & PEOPLE OF OTHER COUNTRIES. FOR USA CITIZENS TO LECTURE AND/OR CONDUCT RESEARCH ABROAD. OPEN TO PH.D'S OR EQUIV; FACULTY; SCHOLARS/RESEARCHERS & PROFESSIONALS.

ANNUALLY OVER 1000 AWARDS OF 2-12 MONTHS IN MORE THAN 100 COUNTRIES. WRITE FOR COMPLETE INFORMATION.

1486

DANISH SISTERHOOD IN AMERICA (SCHOLARSHIP PROGRAM)

2916 NORTH 121ST ST
MILWAUKEE WI 53222
WRITTEN INQUIRY ONLY

AMOUNT: VARIES

DEADLINE(S): VARIES

FIELD(S): ALL AREAS OF STUDY

OPEN TO MEMBERS OF THE DANISH SISTERHOOD OF AMERICA. VARIOUS AWARD PROGRAMS FOR VOCATIONAL; UNDERGRADUATE AND GRADUATE STUDY.

WRITE TO THE ATTN OF LORRAINE MATTSEN ZEMBINSKI (NATIONAL TRUSTEE) FOR COMPLETE INFORMATION.

1487

DESCENDANTS OF THE SIGNERS OF THE DECLARATION OF INDEPENDENCE (SCHOLARSHIP GRANT)

12 RED FOX COURT
GREENVILLE SC 29615
803/297-9770

AMOUNT: $1200 - $2000

DEADLINE(S): MAR 15

FIELD(S): ALL AREAS OF STUDY

UNDERGRAD & GRAD AWARDS FOR STUDENTS WHO ARE DSDI MEMBERS AND CAN PROVE THEY ARE A DIRECT DESCENDANT OF A SIGNER OF THE DECLARATION OF INDEPENDENCE. MUST BE FULL TIME STUDENT ENROLLED IN A RECOGNIZED USA 4-YEAR COLLEGE OR UNIVERSITY.

APPLICANTS SHOULD NAME THEIR ANCESTOR-SIGNER WHEN REQUESTING APPLICATION OR THEY -WILL NOT- RECEIVE A RESPONSE. 6 TO 9 AWARDS PER YEAR RENEWABLE WITH REAPPLICATION. WRITE FOR COMPLETE INFORMATION.

1488

DISABLED AMERICAN VETERANS AUXILIARY (DAVA STUDENT LOANS)

3725 ALEXANDRIA PIKE
COLD SPRING KY 41076
606/441-7300

AMOUNT: UP TO MAXIMUM OF $1000 FOR 4 YEARS

DEADLINE(S): APR 25

FIELD(S): ALL FIELDS OF STUDY

CITIZEN OF U.S. WHO HAS BEEN ACCEPTED BY AN INSTITUTION OF HIGHER EDUCATION. CHILDREN WHOSE LIVING MOTHER IS A LIFE MEMBER OF DAV AUXILIARY OR IF MOTHER DECEASED; FATHER MUST BE A LIFE MEMBER FOR AT LEAST 1 YEAR.

40-42 LOANS PER YEAR. RENEWABLE. WRITE FOR COMPLETE INFORMATION.

1489

EDWARD ARTHUR MELLINGER EDUCATIONAL FOUNDATION INC (SCHOLARSHIPS AND LOANS)

PO BOX 278; 1025 EAST BROADWAY
MONMOUTH IL 61462
309/734-2419

AMOUNT: $750 MAXIMUM

DEADLINE(S): MAY 1

FIELD(S): ALL AREAS OF STUDY

SCHOLARSHIPS ARE AVAILABLE TO STUDENTS WHO RESIDE IN WESTERN ILLINOIS AND EASTERN IOWA WHO ARE ENROLLED IN UNDERGRADUATE PROGRAMS. LOANS ARE AVAILABLE FOR GRADUATE STUDY.

250 AWARDS PER YEAR. RENEWABLE. WRITE FOR COMPLETE INFORMATION.

1490

EDWARDS SCHOLARSHIP FUND (UNDERGRADUATE AND GRADUATE SCHOLARSHIPS)

10 POST OFFICE SQUARE SO.; SUITE 1230
BOSTON MA 02109
617/426-4434

AMOUNT: $250 TO $2500

DEADLINE(S): MAR 1

FIELD(S): ALL FIELDS OF STUDY

OPEN -ONLY- TO BOSTON RESIDENTS UNDER AGE 25 WHO CAN DEMONSTRATE FINANCIAL NEED; SCHOLASTIC ABILITY AND GOOD CHARACTER. FOR UNDERGRADUATE OR GRADUATE STUDY BUT UNDERGRADS RECEIVE PREFERENCE. FAMILY HOME MUST BE WITHIN BOSTON CITY LIMIT.

APPLICANTS MUST HAVE LIVED IN BOSTON FROM AT LEAST THE BEGINNING OF THEIR JUNIOR YEAR IN HIGH SCHOOL. WRITE FOR COMPLETE INFORMATION.

1491

EMANUEL STERNBERGER EDUCATIONAL FUND (LOAN PROGRAM)

PO BOX 1735
GREENSBORO NC 27401
919/275-6316

AMOUNT: $1000 FIRST YEAR; $2000 SUBSEQUENT YEARS; MAXIMUM $5000

DEADLINE(S): APR 30

FIELD(S): ALL FIELDS OF STUDY

OPEN TO RESIDENTS OF NORTH CAROLINA WHO ARE ENTERING THEIR JUNIOR OR SENIOR YEAR OF COLLEGE OR ARE A GRADUATE STUDENT. CONSIDERATIONS INCLUDE GRADES; ECONOMIC SITUTATION; REFERENCES; CREDIT RATING.

PERSONAL INTERVIEW IS REQUIRED. CAN BE USED AT ANY COLLEGE OR UNIVERSITY. WRITE FOR COMPLETE INFORMATION.

1492

EMBASSY OF MEXICO (MEXICAN GOVERNMENT SCHOLARSHIP)

OFFICE OF CULTURAL AFFAIRS; 1911 PENNSYLVANIA AVE N.W.
WASHINGTON DC 20006
202/728-1642

AMOUNT: VARIES

DEADLINE(S): NONE SPECIFIED

FIELD(S): ALL AREAS OF STUDY

OPEN TO MASTER'S OR DOCTOR'S CANDIDATES FROM NORTH AMERICA OR LATIN AMERICA. FOR GRADUATE STUDY AT MEXICAN UNIVERSITIES OR FOR RESEARCH IN MEXICO WHEN REQUIRED TO RECIEVE A DEGREE IN THE STUDENT'S HOME COUNTRY. FLUENCY IN SPANISH REQUIRED.

FOR STUDENTS BETWEEN 20 & 35 YEARS OLD. WRITE FOR COMPLETE INFORMATION.

1493

ETHEL N. BOWEN FOUNDATION (SCHOLARSHIPS)

P.O. BOX 1559
BLUEFIELD WV 24701
304/325-8181

AMOUNT: VARIES

DEADLINE(S): APR 30

FIELD(S): ALL AREAS OF STUDY

UNDERGRADUATE AND OCCASIONAL GRADUATE SCHOLARSHIPS OPEN TO RESIDENTS OF SOUTHWEST VIRGINIA.

20-25 AWARDS PER YEAR. WRITE FOR COMPLETE INFORMATION.

1494

FEDERAL EMPLOYEE EDUCATION & ASSISTANCE FUND (FEEA SCHOLARSHIP PROGRAM)

8441 W BOWLES AVE; SUITE 200
LITTLETON CO 80123
303/933-7580; 800/323-4140; FAX 303/933-7587

AMOUNT: $250 - $1000

DEADLINE(S): JUN 1 (APPLICATIONS AVAILABLE MAR THRU MAY)

FIELD(S): ALL FIELDS OF STUDY

OPEN TO CIVILIAN FEDERAL AND POSTAL EMPLOYEES (WITH AT LEAT 3 YEARS SERVICE) AND THEIR DEPENDENT FAMILY MEMBERS. MUST BE ENROLLED OR PLAN TO ENROLL IN A COURSE THAT WILL LEAD TO A 2-YEAR; 4-YEAR OR GRADUATE DEGREE. GPA OF 3.0 OR BETTER.

AWARDS ARE MERIT BASED. WINNERS MAY REAPPLY AND RECOMPETE EACH YEAR. SEND SELF ADDRESSED STAMPED ENVELOPE (BUSINESS SIZE) FOR COMPLETE INFORMATION.

1495

FEDERAL EMPLOYEE EDUCATION & ASSISTANCE FUND (FEEA TERI LOAN PROGRAM)

8441 W. BOWLES AVE; SUITE 200
LITTLETON CO 80123
303/933-7850; 800/323-4140; FAX 303/933-7587

AMOUNT: $2000 - $20000 PER YEAR

DEADLINE(S): NONE

FIELD(S): ALL FIELDS OF STUDY

LOANS OPEN TO ANY FEDERAL EMPLOYEE (INCLUDING POSTAL AND MILITARY) & THEIR DEPENDENTS OR SURVIVORS. FOR UNDERGRADUATE; GRADUATE OR POST-GRADUATE STUDY AT ANY ACCREDITED 2-YEAR OR 4-YEAR INSTITUTION. USA CITIZEN OR LEGAL RESIDENT.

SEND SELF-ADDRESSED STAMPED ENVELOPE FOR COMPLETE INFORMATION.

1496

FEILD CO-OPERATIVE ASSOCIATION (MISSISSIPPI RESIDENT LOANS)

PO BOX 5054
JACKSON MS 39216
601/939-9295

AMOUNT: $2000

DEADLINE(S): 2 MONTHS PRIOR TO REGISTRATION

FIELD(S): ALL FIELDS OF STUDY

OPEN -ONLY- TO MISSISSIPPI RESIDENTS WHO ARE UNDERGRADUATE JUNIORS & GRADUATE STUDENTS WITH SATISFACTORY ACADEMIC STANDING. DEMONSTRATE EVIDENCE OF NEED & PROMISE OF FINANCIAL RESPONSIBILITY. USA CITIZEN OR LEGAL RESIDENT.

THESE ARE LOANS -NOT- SCHOLARSHIPS. LOANS ARE RENWABLE. WRITE FOR COMPLETE INFORMATION.

1497

FIRST CAVALRY DIVISION ASSOCIATION (SCHOLARSHIPS)

302 N. MAIN
COPPERAS COVE TX 76522
WRITTEN INQUIRY

AMOUNT: $600 PER YEAR UP TO 4 YEARS MAX

DEADLINE(S): NONE SPECIFIED

FIELD(S): ALL FIELDS OF STUDY

AWARDS TO CHILDREN OF SOLDIERS WHO DIED OR WERE DECLARED 100% DISABLED FROM INJURIES WHILE SERVING WITH THE 1ST CALVARY DIVISION DURING & SINCE THE VIETNAM WAR OR DURING DESERT STORM.

IF DEATH OCCURRED AFTER 3/1/80 DECEASED PARENT MUST HAVE BEEN AN ASSOCIATION MEMBER AND SERVING WITH THE DIVISION AT THE TIME OF DEATH. WRITE FOR COMPLETE INFORMATION.

1498

FLORIDA DEPT. OF EDUCATION (FLORIDA STUDENTS REGENTS SCHOLARSHIP)

OFFICE OF STUDENT FINANCIAL ASSISTANCE;
1344 FLORIDA EDUCATION CENTER
TALLAHASSEE FL 32399
904/488-4234

AMOUNT: $5000

DEADLINE(S): NONE

FIELD(S): ALL FIELDS OF STUDY

SCHOLARSHIP AWARDED TO STUDENTS WHO SERVE/OR HAVE SERVED AS STUDENT MEMBERS OF THE FLORIDA BOARD OF REGENTS.

WRITE FOR COMPLETE INFORMATION.

1499

FLORIDA DEPT. OF EDUCATION (GUARANTEED STUDENT LOAN PROGRAM & PARENTS' PLUS LOANS)

OFFICE OF STUDENT FINANCIAL ASSISTANCE;
FLORIDA EDUCATION CENTER; SUITE 1344
TALLAHASSEE FL 32399
904/488-4095

AMOUNT: $2625 PER ACADEMIC YEAR; MAX $12500 UNDERGRAD & $25000 UNDERGRADUATE/GRADUATE COMBINED

DEADLINE(S): NONE SPECIFIED

FIELD(S): ALL FIELDS OF STUDY

US CITIZEN OR LEGAL RESIDENT. RESIDENT OF FLORIDA FOR AT LEAST 12 MONTHS. ENROLLED OR HAVE BEEN ACCEPTED AT LEAST 1/2 TIME IN ELIGIBLE FLORIDA INSTITUTION.

PARENTS WHO ARE RESIDENTS OF FLORIDA AND BORROWING FOR AN ELIGIBLE STUDENT ATTENDING A FLORIDA SCHOOL MAY BORROW UP TO $4000 PER ACADEMIC YEAR.

1500

FLORIDA DEPT. OF EDUCATION (JOSE MARTI SCHOLARSHIP CHALLENGE GRANT FUND)

OFFICE OF STUDENT FINANCIAL ASSISTANCE;
KNOTT BLDG
TALLAHASSEE FL 32399
904/487-0049

AMOUNT: $2000 PER YEAR

DEADLINE(S): APR 1

FIELD(S): ALL FIELDS OF STUDY

US CITIZEN OR LEGAL RESIDENT. HISPANIC-AMERICAN & FLORIDA RESIDENT FOR AT LEAST 1 YEAR. ENROLLED AS FULL-TIME UNDERGRADUATE OR GRADUATE STUDENT AT ELIGIBLE FLORIDA INSTITUTION.

NEED BASED AWARD IS $2000 PER YEAR FOR A MAX OF 8 SEMESTERS (12 QUARTERS) FOR UNDERGRADS OR A MAX OF 4 SEMESTERS (6 QUARTERS) FOR GRADUATE STUDY. WRITE FOR COMPLETE INFORMATION.

1501

FLORIDA DEPT. OF EDUCATION (SCHOLARSHIPS FOR CHILDREN OF DECEASED OR DISABLED VETERANS)

OFFICE OF STUDENT FINANCIAL ASSISTANCE;
1344 FLORIDA EDUCATION CENTER
TALLAHASSEE FL 32399
904/487-0049

GENERAL

AMOUNT: THE AMOUNT OF TUITION & FEES PER ACADEMIC YEAR

DEADLINE(S): APR 1 POSTMARK

FIELD(S): ALL FIELDS OF STUDY

US CITIZEN. 5-YEAR FLORIDA RESIDENT. ENROLLED FULL-TIME IN FLORIDA PUBLIC INSTITUTION. CHILDREN OF DECEASED OR 100% DISABLED WAR VETERANS/POW'S/OR MIA'S.

SCHOLARSHIPS ARE RENEWABLE. WRITE FOR COMPLETE INFORMATION.

1502

FLORIDA DEPT. OF EDUCATION (SEMINOLE/ MICCOSUKEE INDIAN SCHOLARSHIPS)

OFFICE OF STUDENT FINANCIAL ASSISTANCE; KNOTT BLDG
TALLAHASSEE FL 32399
904/487-0049

AMOUNT: VARIES

DEADLINE(S): NONE

FIELD(S): ALL FIELDS OF STUDY

USA CITIZEN AND FLORIDA RESIDENT WHO IS A MEMBER OF SEMINOLE OR MICCOSUKEE INDIAN TRIBE AND IS ENROLLED AS FULL OR PART TIME UNDERGRADUATE OR GRADUATE STUDENT AT AN ELIGIBLE FLORIDA INSTITUTION. MUST DEMONSTRATE FINANCIAL NEED.

SCHOLARSHIPS ARE RENEWABLE. WRITE FOR COMPLETE INFORMATION.

1503

FLORIDA HOUSE OF REPRESENTATIVES (LEGISLATIVE STAFF INTERNSHIP PROGRAM)

18 HOUSE OFFICE BLDG
TALLAHASSEE FL 32399
904/487-2390

AMOUNT: 36 HRS OF TUITION + 10800 STIPEND

DEADLINE(S): NOV 1

FIELD(S): ALL AREAS OF STUDY

INTERNSHIPS OPEN TO GRADUATE STUDENTS WHO ARE FLORIDA RESIDENTS OR NON-RESIDENTS ATTENDING FLORIDA UNIVERSITIES. INTERNSHIPS BEGIN IN MAY OF EACH YEAR AND RUN THROUGH THE FOLLOWING MAY.

40 INTERNSHIPS PER YEAR. WRITE FOR COMPLETE INFORMATION.

1504

GABRIEL J.BROWN TRUST (LOW-INTEREST LOAN FUND)

112 AVENUE 'E' WEST
BISMARCK ND 58501
701/223-5916

AMOUNT: VARIES

DEADLINE(S): JUN 15

FIELD(S): ALL FIELDS OF STUDY

SPECIAL LOW-INTEREST LOANS (6%) OPEN TO RESIDENTS OF NORTH DAKOTA WHO HAVE COMPLETED AT LEAST 2 YEARS OF UNDERGRADUATE STUDY AT A RECOGNIZED COLLEGE OR UNIVERSITY & HAVE A GPA OF 2.5 OR BETTER. USA CITIZEN.

APPROX 75 LOANS PER YEAR. RENEWABLE. CONTACT ADDRESS ABOVE FOR COMPLETE INFORMATION.

1505

GENERAL FEDERATION OF WOMAN'S CLUBS OF MASS. (GRADUATE SCHOLARSHIP)

245 DUTTON RD
SUDBURY MA 01776
508/443-4569

AMOUNT: $2000

DEADLINE(S): MAR 15

FIELD(S): MANY AREAS OF STUDY

OPEN TO WOMEN WHO HAVE RESIDED IN MASSACHUSETTS FOR AT LEAST FIVE YEARS. FOR GRADUATE STUDY IN SPECIFIC FIELDS WHICH CHANGE EACH YEAR. LETTER OF ENDORSEMENT FROM PRESIDENT OF WOMEN'S CLUB IN APPLICANT'S COMMUNITY OF RESIDENCE IS REQUIRED.

CONTACT LOCAL CLUB OR ADDRESS ABOVE FOR COMPLETE INFORMATION.

1506

GEORGE ABRAHAMIAN FOUNDATION (SCHOLARSHIPS FOR LOCAL ARMENIANS)

945 ADMIRAL STREET
PROVIDENCE RI 02904
401/831-2887

AMOUNT: VARIES

DEADLINE(S): SEP 1

FIELD(S): ALL AREAS OF STUDY

OPEN TO UNDERGRADUATE AND GRADUATE STUDENTS WHO ARE USA CITIZENS OF ARMENIAN ANCESTRY WHO LIVE IN PROVIDENCE RI; ARE OF GOOD CHARACTER; HAVE THE ABILITY TO LEARN AND CAN DEMONSTRATE FINANCIAL NEED.

RENEWABLE. WRITE FOR COMPLETE INFORMATION.

1507

GEORGE GROTEFEND SCHOLARSHIP FUND (GROTEFEND SCHOLARSHIP)

1644 MAGNOLIA AVE
REDDING CA 96001
916/225-0227

AMOUNT: $150 - $400

DEADLINE(S): APR 20 (APPLICATION SUBMISSION)

FIELD(S): ALL FIELDS OF STUDY

SCHOLARSHIPS OPEN TO APPLICANTS WHO COMPLETED ALL 4 YEARS OF HIGH SCHOOL IN SHASTA COUNTY CALIFORNIA. AWARDS SUPPORT ALL LEVELS OF STUDY AT RECOGNIZED COLLEGES & UNIVERSITIES. USA CITIZEN OR LEGAL RESIDENT.

300 AWARDS PER YEAR. WRITE FOR COMPLETE INFORMATION.

1508 —————————————————

H&R BLOCK FOUNDATION (SCHOLARSHIP FOUNDATION)

4410 MAIN STREET
KANSAS CITY MO 64111
816/753-6900

AMOUNT: $2000

DEADLINE(S): APR 10

FIELD(S): ALL AREAS OF STUDY

FOR CHILDREN OF ELIGIBLE EMPLOYEES OF H&R BLOCK INC/OR ONE OF ITS OWNED SUBSIDIARIES. BASED ON ACADEMIC CAPABILITY AND FINANCIAL NEED. MUST BE ENROLLED FULL TIME.

35 AWARDS PER YEAR. CONTACT ADDRESS ABOVE FOR COMPLETE INFORMATION.

1509 —————————————————

HARNESS TRACKS OF AMERICA (HARRY M. STEVENS-LADBROKE RACING & PENNSYLVANIA-ROSECROFT RACEWAY SCHOLARSHIPS)

35 AIRPORT RD #420
MORRISTOWN NJ 07960
201/285-9090

AMOUNT: $2500 - $3000

DEADLINE(S): MAY 30

FIELD(S): ALL FIELDS OF STUDY

OPEN TO YOUNG PERSONS ACTIVELY ENGAGED IN THE SPORT OF HARNESS RACING & CHILDREN OF PERSONS WHO ARE LICENSED AS A GROOM; TRAINER; DRIVER; ETC. AWARDS SUPPORT UNDERGRADUATE OR GRADUATE STUDY.

5 TO 6 SCHOLARSHIPS PER YEAR. RENEWABLE. WRITE FOR COMPLETE INFORMATION.

1510 —————————————————

HARRY E. & FLORENCE W. SNAYBERGER MEMORIAL FOUNDATION (GRANT AWARD)

C/O PENNSYLVANIA NATIONAL BANK & TRUST COMPANY; TRUST DEPT; CENTER & NORWEGIAN POTTSVILLE PA 17901
717/622-4200

AMOUNT: VARIES

DEADLINE(S): LAST WORKING DAY IN FEBURARY

FIELD(S): ALL AREAS OF STUDY

APPLICANTS MUST BE RESIDENTS OF SCHUYLKILL COUNTY PA AND APPLY FOR PHEAA AND PELL GRANTS. FAILURE TO QUALIFY FOR THESE GRANTS DOES NOT HARM CHANCES OF RECEIVING TRHE SNAYBERGER GRANT HOWEVER.

CONTACT MRS. CAROLYN B. BERNATONIS TRUST SECRETARY ADDRESS ABOVE.

1511 —————————————————

HARVARD/RADCLIFFE OFFICE OF ADMISSIONS AND FINANCIAL AID (SCHOLARSHIPS; GRANTS; LOANS & WORK STUDY PROGRAMS)

3RD FLOOR - BYERLY HALL; 8 GARDEN ST.
CAMBRIDGE MA 02138
617/495-1581

AMOUNT: VARIES

DEADLINE(S): NONE

FIELD(S): ALL FIELDS OF STUDY

ALL FINANCIAL AID IS NEED BASED EXCEPT FOR STUDENTS DESCENDED FROM ORIGINAL DONORS NAMED DOWNER; PENNOYER; MACHSONDALE & ELLIS WHO MAY BE ELIGIBLE FOR ASSISTANCE. NEED BASED FUNDS AVAILABLE TO ALL WHO ARE ADMITTED AND CAN SHOW NEED.

APPLICANTS MUST BE ACCEPTED FOR ADMISSION TO HARVARD BEFORE THEY WILL BE CONSIDERED FOR FUNDING. MANY FACTORS OTHER THAN FAMILY INCOME ARE CONSIDERED. WRITE FOR COMPLETE INFORMATION.

1512 —————————————————

HATTIE M. STRONG FOUNDATION (NO-INTEREST LOANS)

1735 EYE ST NW; RM 705
WASHINGTON DC 20006
202/331-1619

AMOUNT: UP TO $2500

DEADLINE(S): APPLY JAN 1 - MAR 31

FIELD(S): ALL FIELDS OF STUDY

OPEN TO USA UNDERGRADUATE & GRADUATE STUDENTS IN THEIR LAST YEAR OF STUDY IN THE USA OR ABROAD. LOANS ARE MADE SOLELY ON THE BASIS OF INDIVIDUAL MERIT. THERE IS NO INTEREST & NO COLLATERAL REQUIREMENT. USA CITIZEN.

APPROX 240 AWARDS PER YEAR. FINANCIAL NEED IS A CONSIDERATION. WRITE GIVING PERSONAL HISTORY; SCHOOL ATTENDED; SUBJECT STUDIED; DATE EXPECTED TO COMPLETE STUDIES & AMOUNT OF FUNDS NEEDED. SEND SELF ADDRESSED STAMPED ENVELOPE.

1513 ————————————

HAWAII EDUCATIONAL LOAN PROGRAM (PLUS/SLS)

1314 S. KING ST. #961
HONOLULU HI 96814
808/536-3731

AMOUNT: $4000

DEADLINE(S): NONE

FIELD(S): ALL AREAS OF STUDY

THIS IS A PARENTAL LOAN FOR EITHER PARENTS OF (DEPENDENT) UNDERGRADUATES; INDEPENDENT UNDERGRADUATES OR GRADUATE STUDENTS. THE LOAN MUST BE REPAID. VARIABLE INTEREST RATE CHANGES ANNUALLY.

WRITE FOR COMPLETE INFORMATION.

1514 ————————————

HONOR SOCIETY OF PHI KAPPA PHI (FIRST YEAR GRADUATE FELLOWSHIP)

C/O LSU; BOX 16000
BATON ROUGE LA 70893
504/388-4917

AMOUNT: $7000; $500

DEADLINE(S): FEB 1 (TO CHAPTER SECRETARY)

FIELD(S): ALL FIELDS OF STUDY/P.K.P. MEMBERS

FELLOWSHIPS FOR THE FIRST YEAR OF GRADUATE OR PROFESSIONAL STUDY REQUIRE MAINTAINING A HIGH SCHOLASTIC STANDING AND NOMINATION BY A CHAPTER OF PKP. STUDENT MUST BE OR ABOUT TO BECOME A MEMBER OF THE NOMINATING CHAPTER.

50 FELLOWSHIPS & 30 $500 AWARDS PER YEAR. STUDENTS SHOULD OBTAIN APPLICATION FROM THEIR LOCAL CHAPTER OFFICERS.

1515 ————————————

HORACE SMITH FUND (WALTER S BARR SCHOLARSHIP FELLOWSHIP & LOAN FUND)

PO BOX 3034; 1441 MAIN ST
SPRINGFIELD MA 01101
413/739-4222

AMOUNT: VARIES

DEADLINE(S): DEC 31 (SCHOLARSHIPS); FEB 1 (FELLOWSHIPS); JUL 1 (LOANS)

FIELD(S): ALL AREAS OF STUDY

OPEN TO GRADUATES OF HAMPDEN COUNTY MASS SECONDARY SCHOOLS FOR UNDERGRADUATE OR GRADUATE STUDY. FINANCIAL NEED IS OF PRIMARY IMPORTANCE. SCHOLARSHIP/FELLOWSHIP APPLICATIONS AVAILABLE AFTER SEP 1; LOAN APPLICATIONS AFTER APR 1.

SCHOLARSHIPS ARE FOR SENIORS FROM AGAWAM; CHICOPEE; E LONGMEADOW; LONGMEADOW; LUDLOW; SPRINGFIELD; W SPRINGFIELD & WILBRAHAM HIGH SCHOOLS. RENEWABLE. WRITE FOR COMPLETE INFORMATION.

1516 ————————————

HOWARD AND MAMIE NICHOLS SCHOLARSHIP TRUST (SCHOLARSHIPS)

WELLS FARGO BANK TRUST DEPT.; 2222 W. SHAW AVE.; SUITE 11
FRESNO CA 93711
209/442-6232 OR 805/395-0920

AMOUNT: VARIES

DEADLINE(S): FEB 28

FIELD(S): ALL FIELDS OF STUDY

OPEN TO GRADUATES OF KERN COUNTY CALIF HIGH SCHOOLS FOR FULL-TIME UNDERGRADUATE OR GRADUATE STUDY AT A POST-SECONDARY INSTITUTION. MUST DEMONSTRATE FINANCIAL NEED AND HAVE A 2.0 OR BETTER GPA.

APPROXIMATELY 100 AWARDS PER YEAR. RENEWABLE WITH REAPPLICATION. WRITE FOR COMPLETE INFORMATION.

1517 ————————————

HUALAPAI TRIBAL COUNCIL (SCHOLARSHIP PROGRAM)

PO BOX 179
PEACH SPRINGS AZ 86434
602/769-2216

AMOUNT: $700

DEADLINE(S): 2 WEEKS BEFORE EACH SEMESTER

FIELD(S): ALL AREAS OF STUDY

SCHOLARSHIPS ARE OFFERED TO STUDENTS WHO ARE ENROLLED FULL TIME AND MAINTAIN PASSING GRADES. APPLICANTS MUST BE A MEMBER OF THE HUALAPAI TRIBE.

CONTACT LINDA E. HAVATONE ADDRESS ABOVE.

1518 ————————————

ILLINOIS STUDENT ASSISTANCE COMMISSION (STATE & FEDERAL SCHOLARSHIPS; FELLOWSHIPS; GRANTS; LOANS)

106 WILMONT ROAD
DEERFIELD IL 60015

708/948-8550

AMOUNT: VARIES WITH PROGRAM
DEADLINE(S): VARIES

FIELD(S): ALL AREAS OF STUDY

COMMISSION ADMINISTERS A NUMBER OF STATE AND FEDERAL SCHOLARSHIP; FELLOWSHIP; GRANT AND LOAN PROGRAMS FOR ILLINOIS RESIDENTS.

WRITE FOR COMPLETE INFORMATION.

1519 ————————————

INDEPENDENCE FEDERAL SAVINGS BANK (GUARANTEED STUDENT LOAN PROGRAM)

1835 K STREET NW SUITE 300
WASHINGTON DC 20006
202/626-0473 OR 800/733-0473

AMOUNT: $2625 - $4000 UNDERGRADS; UP TO $7500 GRADUATES

DEADLINE(S): NONE

FIELD(S): ALL FIELDS OF STUDY

LOANS OPEN TO US CITIZENS WHO ARE ACCEPTED FOR ENROLLMENT OR ENROLLED IN A SCHOOL APPROVED BY THE US DEPT OF EDUCATION; HAVE A SATISFACTORY ACADEMIC RECORD AND CAN DEMONSTRATE FINANCIAL NEED.

WRITE FOR COMPLETE INFORMATION.

1520 ————————————

INSTITUTE OF INTERNATIONAL EDUCATION (FULBRIGHT AND INTERNATIONAL FELLOWSHIPS FOR USA CITIZENS)

809 UNITED NATIONS PLAZA
NEW YORK NY 10017
212/984-5330

AMOUNT: VARIES WITH COUNTRY

DEADLINE(S): OCT 31

FIELD(S): ALL FIELDS OF STUDY

GRADUATE FELLOWSHIPS FOR USA RESIDENTS TO STUDY/DO RESEARCH IN A FOREIGN COUNTRY. CRITERIA INCLUDE ACADEMIC RECORD AND PROFICIENCY IN THE LANGUATE OF COUNTRY STUDENT IS VISITING.

CONTACT YOUR GRADUATE INSTITUTION OR WRITE TO "US STUDENT PROGRAMS DIVISION"; ADDRESS ABOVE; FOR COMPLETE INFORMATION.

1521 ————————————

INSTITUTE OF INTERNATIONAL EDUCATION (FULBRIGHT GRANTS FOR FOREIGN NATIONS)

809 UNITED NATIONS PLAZA
NEW YORK NY 10017
212/984-5330

AMOUNT: VARIES WITH COUNTRY

DEADLINE(S): MAY 1; OCT 31

FIELD(S): ALL FIELDS OF STUDY

GRADUATE FELLOWSHIPS FOR STUDY AND/OR RESEARCH IN A COUNTRY OTHER THAN STUDENT'S OWN. PROFICIENCY IN LANGUAGE OF COUNTRY OF STUDY IS REQUIRED. FELLOWSHIPS MUST BE APPLIED FOR IN THE HOME COUNTRY.

INSTITUTE IS AN ADMINISTRATIVE AGENCY FOR A VARIETY OF SPONSORS. WRITE FOR COMPLETE INFORMATION.

1522 ————————————

INSTITUTE OF INTERNATIONAL EDUCATION (SCHOLARSHIPS FOR STUDY IN SWITZERLAND)

809 UNITED NATIONS PLAZA
NEW YORK NY 10017
212/883-8200; 212/984-5330 (US CITIZENS)

AMOUNT: BETWEEN 1300 AND 1500 SWISS FRANCS PER MONTH

DEADLINE(S): MAY 1 - OCT 31

FIELD(S): ALL AREAS OF STUDY

THE SWISS GOVERNMENT OFFERS SCHOLARSHIPS TO FOREIGN STUDENTS FOR POST-GRADUATE STUDY AT A SWISS UNIVERSITY. AWARDS ARE INTENDED TO ENABLE HOLDERS TO FURTHER THEIR STUDIES & BEGIN RESEARCH WORK.

NON-USA CITIZENS CONTACT ADDRESS ABOVE. USA CITIZENS SHOULD INQUIRE OF THEIR GRADUATE INSTITUTION OR WRITE TO ADDRESS AVOVE; ATTN 'US STUDENT PROGRAMS DIV'.

1523 ————————————

INTERNATIONAL ONEXIOCA (FOUNDERS MEMORIAL AWARD)

911 BARTLETT PLACE
WINDSOR CA 95492
WRITTEN INQUIRY ONLY

AMOUNT: $250

DEADLINE(S): JAN 7

FIELD(S): ALL FIELDS OF STUDY

ANNUAL AWARD IN MEMORY OF HERNESTO K ONEXIOCA/FOUNDER. ANYONE WITH THE NAME OF ONEXIOCA (WHO IS NOT A BLOOD/ OR MARRIAGE RELATIVE) & BORN ON JAN 1 IS ELIGIBLE TO APPLY.

ALL INQURIES -MUST- INCLUDE PROOF OF NAME AND BIRTH DATE. THOSE WITHOUT SUCH PROOF WILL -NOT- BE ACKNOWLEDGED.

1524

INTERNATIONAL SOCIETY FOR CLINICAL LABORATORY TECHNOLOGY (SCHOLARSHIP)

818 OLIVE ST #918
ST LOUIS MO 63101
314/241-1445

AMOUNT: VARIES

DEADLINE(S): JUL 31

FIELD(S): ALL FIELDS OF STUDY

OPEN TO ISCLT MEMBERS AND THEIR DEPENDENT CHILDREN. REQUIRES GRADUATION FROM AN ACCREDITED HIGH SCHOOL OR EQUIVALENT.

WRITE FOR COMPLETE INFORMATION.

1525

IOWA COLLEGE STUDENT AID COMMISSION (IOWA STAFFORD LOAN PROGRAM; IOWA PLUS/SLS LOANS)

201 JEWETT BLDG; 9TH & GRAND AVE
DES MOINES IA 50309
515/281-3501

AMOUNT: $2625 - $4000 UNDERGRAD; $7500 GRAD

DEADLINE(S): NONE

FIELD(S): ALL FIELDS OF STUDY

LOANS OPEN TO IOWA RESIDENT ENROLLED IN OR ATTENDING AN APPROVED INSTITUTION. MUST BE USA CITIZEN OR LEGAL RESIDENT AND DEMONSTRATE NEED.

WRITE FOR COMPLETE INFORMATION.

1526

JACKSONVILLE UNIVERSITY (SCHOLARSHIPS & GRANTS PROGRAMS)

DIRECTOR OF STUDENT FINANCIAL ASSISTANCE
JACKSONVILLE FL 32211
904/744-3950

AMOUNT: VARIES

DEADLINE(S): JAN 1 TO MAR 15

FIELD(S): ALL AREAS OF STUDY

JACKSONVILLE UNIVERSITY OFFERS NUMEROUS SCHOLARSHIPS; GRANTS-IN-AID; SERVICE AWARDS AND CAMPUS EMPLOYMENT. FINANCIAL NEED IS NOT NECESSARILY A CONSIDERATION. EARLY APPLICATIONS ARE ADVISED.

200 AWARDS PER YEAR FOR STUDY -ONLY- AT JACKSONVILLE UNIVERSITY. WRITE FOR COMPLETE INFORMATION.

1527

JAMES Z. NAURISON SCHOLARSHIP FUND (SCHOLARSHIPS)

P.O. BOX 9006
SPRINGFIELD MA 01101
413/787-8570

AMOUNT: $400 - $2000

DEADLINE(S): APR 15

FIELD(S): ALL FIELDS OF STUDY

OPEN TO UNDERGRADUATE AND GRADUATE STUDENTS WHO ARE RESIDENTS OF THE MASSACHUSETTS COUNTIES OF BERKSHIRE; FRANKLIN; HAMPDEN OR HAMPSHIRE OR OF THE CITY OF SUFFIELD OR ENFIELD CONNECTICUT. AWARDS BASED ON FINANCIAL NEED & ACADEMIC RECORD.

APPROXIMATELY 300 AWARDS PER YEAR. SELF ADDRESSED STAMPED ENVELOPE MUST ACCOMPANY REQUESTS FOR APPLICATION.

1528

JAPANESE AMERICAN CITIZENS LEAGUE (ABE & ESTER HAGIWARA STUDENT AID AWARD)

1765 SUTTER ST
SAN FRANCISCO CA 94115
415/921-5225

AMOUNT: VARIES

DEADLINE(S): APR 1

FIELD(S): ALL FIELDS OF STUDY

OPEN TO JACL MEMBERS OR THEIR CHILDREN OR ANY AMERICAN OF JAPANESE ANCESTRY. SCHOLARSHIP MAY BE USED FOR ANY LEVEL OF STUDY. USA CITIZEN OR LEGAL RESIDENT. MUST SUBMIT FAF FORM AS PROOF OF FINANCIAL NEED.

SEND STAMPED SELF ADDRESSED ENVELOPE FOR COMPLETE INFORMATION.

1529

JAPANESE AMERICAN CITIZENS LEAGUE (GRADUATE SCHOLARSHIPS)

1765 SUTTER STREET
SAN FRANCISCO CA 94115
415/921-5225

AMOUNT: VARIES

DEADLINE(S): APR 1

FIELD(S): ALL FIELDS OF STUDY

OPEN TO JACL MEMBERS OR THEIR CHILDREN OR ANY AMERICAN OF JAPANESE ANCESTRY. FOR GRADUATE STUDENTS CURRENTLY ENROLLED OR PLANNING TO ENROLL IN AN ACCREDITED GRADUATE SCHOOL. USA CITIZEN OR LEGAL RESIDENT.

7 SCHOLARSHIPS PER YEAR. SEND STAMPED SELF ADDRESSED ENVELOPE FOR COMPLETE INFORMATION.

1530

JEWISH FAMILY AND CHILDREN'S SERVICES (COLLEGE LOAN FUND)

1600 SCOTT ST
SAN FRANCISCO CA 94115
415/561-1226

AMOUNT: $5000 MAXIMUM (STUDENT LOAN)

DEADLINE(S): NONE

FIELD(S): ALL FIELDS OF STUDY

OPEN TO WORTHY COLLEGE STUDENTS OF THE JEWISH FAITH WITH LIMITED RESOURCES BUT WITH A DEMONSTRATED ABILITY TO REPAY. MUST RESIDE IN SAN FRANCISCO; SAN MATEO; SANTA CLARA; MARIN OR SONOMA COUNTY.

GUARANTORS OR CO-MAKERS ARE REQUIRED BUT NOT COLLATERAL. REPAYMENT TERMS FLEXIBLE; INTEREST USUALLY SET AT 80% OF CURRENT PRIME RATE. CONTACT LOCAL JFCS OFFICE FOR FORMS AND COMPLETE INFORMATION.

1531

JEWISH FAMILY AND CHILDREN'S SERVICES (FOGEL LOAN FUND)

1600 SCOTT STREET
SAN FRANCISCO CA 94115
415/561-1226

AMOUNT: VARIES

DEADLINE(S): NONE

FIELD(S): ALL FIELDS OF STUDY

LOANS TO HELP INDIVIDUALS OF ALL AGES FOR COLLEGE OR VOCATIONAL STUDIES AND FOR PERSONAL; BUSINESS OR PROFESSIONAL PURPOSES. APPLICANT MUST BE OF THE JEWISH FAITH AND HAVE SOUND PLAN FOR REPAYMENT.

SHOULD BE RESIDENT OF SAN FRANCISCO; SAN MATEO; SANTA CLARA; MARIN OR SONOMA COUNTY. GUARANTOR OR CO-MAKERS REQUIRED BUT NO COLLATERAL IS NEEDED. CONTACT JFCS OFFICE FOR COMPLETE INFORMATION.

1532

JEWISH FAMILY AND CHILDREN'S SERVICES (JACOB RASSEN MEMORIAL SCHOLARSHIP FUND)

1600 SCOTT STREET
SAN FRANCISCO CA 94115
415/561-1226

AMOUNT: UP TO $2000

DEADLINE(S): NONE

FIELD(S): STUDY TRIP TO ISRAEL

OPEN TO JEWISH STUDENT UNDER AGE 22 WITH DEMONSTRATED ACADEMIC ACHIEVEMENT AND FINANCIAL NEED WITH A DESIRE TO ENHANCE JEWISH IDENTITY AND INCREASE KNOWLEDGE OF AND CONNECTION TO ISRAEL.

MUST RESIDE IN SAN FRANCISCO; SAN MATEO; SANTA CLARA; MARIN OR SONOMA COUNTY. CONTACT LOCAL JFCS OFFICE FOR FORMS AND COMPLETE INFORMATION.

1533

JEWISH FAMILY AND CHILDREN'S SERVICES (STANLEY OLSON YOUTH SCHOLARSHIP FUND)

1600 SCOTT STREET
SAN FRANCISCO CA 94115
415/561-1226

AMOUNT: UP TO $2500

DEADLINE(S): NONE

FIELD(S): ALL AREAS OF STUDY (PREFERENCE TO ENGLISH MAJORS)

OPEN TO UNDERGRADUATE OR GRADUATE STUDENTS OF JEWISH FAITH WHO ARE 25 OR YOUNGER; HAVE DEMONSTRATED ACADEMIC ACHIEVEMENT AND FINANCIAL NEED AND HAVE BEEN ACCEPTED FOR ENROLLMENT IN A COLLEGE OR UNIVERSITY.

MUST RESIDE IN SAN FRANCISCO; SAN MATEO; SANTA CLARA; MARIN OR SONOMA COUNTY. CONTACT LOCAL JFCS OFFICE FOR APPLICATIONS AND COMPLETE INFORMATION.

1534

JEWISH SOCIAL SERVICE AGENCY OF METROPOLITAN WASHINGTON (LOAN FUND)

6123 MONTROSE ROAD
ROCKVILLE MD 20852
301/881-3700

AMOUNT: UP TO $2000

DEADLINE(S): JUN 1

FIELD(S): ALL FIELDS OF STUDY

OPEN TO JEWISH APPLICANTS 18 OR OLDER WHO ARE WITHIN TWO YEARS OF COMPLETING AN UNDERGRADUATE OR GRADUATE DEGREE OR A VOCATIONAL TRAINING PROGRAM AND ARE RESIDENTS OF THE WASHINGTON METROPOLITAN AREA. NO INTEREST LOAN; ONE TIME AWARD.

USA CITZEN OR PERMANENT RESIDENT WHO WILL SEEK CITIZENSHIP. WRITE FOR COMPLETE INFORMATION.

1535

JEWISH SOCIAL SERVICE AGENCY OF METROPOLITAN WASHINGTON (IRENE STAMBLER VOCATIONAL OPPORTUNITIES GRANT PROGRAM)

6123 MONTROSE ROAD
ROCKVILLE MD 20852
301/881-3700

AMOUNT: UP TO $2500

DEADLINE(S): NONE

FIELD(S): ALL FIELDS OF STUDY

OPEN TO JEWISH WOMEN WHO ARE RESIDENTS OF THE WASHINGTON METROPOLITAN AREA AND NEED TO IMPROVE THEIR EARNING POWER BECAUSE OF DIVORCE; SEPARATION OR DEATH OF THEIR SPOUSES.

GRANTS MAY BE USED TO COMPLETE AND EDUCATIONAL OR VOCATIONAL PROGRAM OR START OR EXPAND A SMALL BUSINESS. WRITE FOR COMPLETE INFORMATION.

1536

JUNIOR LEAGUE OF NORTHERN VIRGINIA (SCHOLARSHIPS)

7921 JONES BRANCH DR #320
MCLEAN VA 22102
703/893-0258

AMOUNT: $500 TO $2000

DEADLINE(S): DEC 15

FIELD(S): ALL FIELDS OF STUDY

OPEN TO WOMEN WHO ARE 28 YEARS OLD OR OLDER & ACCEPTED TO OR ENROLLED IN AN ACCREDITED COLLEGE OR UNIVERSITY AS AN UNDERGRADUATE OR GRADUATE STUDENT. MUST BE USA CITIZEN; NORTHERN VIRGINA RESIDENT; AND DEMONSTRATE FINANCIAL NEED.

8-10 AWARDS PER YEAR. WRITE FOR COMPLETE INFORMATION.

1537

KANSAS COMMISSION ON VETERANS' AFFAIRS (SCHOLARSHIPS)

700 SW JACKSON ST #701
TOPEKA KS 66603
913/296-3976

AMOUNT: FREE TUITION AND FEES IN STATE SUPPORTED INSTITUTIONS

DEADLINE(S): PRIOR TO ENROLLMENT

FIELD(S): ALL AREAS OF STUDY

OPEN TO DEPENDENT CHILD OF PERSON WHO ENTERED USA MILITARY SERVICE AS A RESIDENT OF KANSAS & WAS PRISONER OF WAR; MISSING OR KILLED IN ACTION OR DIED AS A RESULT OF SERVICE CONNECTED DISABILITIES INCURRED DURING SERVICE IN VIETNAM.

RENEWABLE TO MAXIMUM OF 12 SEMESTERS. WRITE FOR COMPLETE INFORMATION.

1538

KENTUCKY CENTER FOR VETERANS AFFAIRS (BENEFITS FOR VETERANS & THEIR DEPENDENTS)

545 S 3RD ST ROOM 123
LOUISVILLE KY 40202
501/595-4447

AMOUNT: VARIES

DEADLINE(S): NONE

FIELD(S): ALL FIELDS OF STUDY

KENTUCKY RESIDENTS. OPEN TO VETERANS & DEPENDENT CHILDREN; NAT'L GUARDSMEN; SPOUSES & NON-REMARRIED WIDOWS OF PERMANENTLY & TOTALLY DISABLED WAR VETERANS WHO SERVED DURING PERIODS OF FEDERALLY RECOGNIZED HOSTILITIES OR WAS POW OR MIA.

WRITE FOR COMPLETE INFORMATION.

1539

KNIGHTS OF COLUMBUS (GRADUATE FELLOWSHIPS)

CATHOLIC UNIVERSITY OF AMERICA ROOM 300
MCMAHON HALL NE
WASHINGTON DC 20064
203/772-2130

AMOUNT: $5000 STIPEND + FULL TUITION

DEADLINE(S): FEB 1 FOR FOLLOWING YEAR

FIELD(S): ALL FIELDS OF STUDY

-MUST- QUALIFY FOR ADMISSION TO CATHOLIC UNIVERSITY OF AMERICA GRADUATE SCHOOL AND BECOME A GRADUATE DEGREE CANDIDATE THERE. MUST SATISIFY ALL UNIVERSITY REGULATIONS.

UNSPECIFIED NUMBER OF FELLOWSHIPS. RENEWABLE. WRITE FOR COMPLETE INFORMATION.

1540

KNIGHTS TEMPLAR EDUCATIONAL FOUNDATION (SPECIAL LOW-INTEREST LOANS)

507 N ELSTON SUITE 101
CHICAGO IL 60630
312/777-3300

AMOUNT: $6000 PER STUDENT MAXIMUM

DEADLINE(S): VARIES

FIELD(S): ALL FIELDS OF STUDY

SPECIAL LOW-INTEREST LOANS (5% FIXED RATE).
NO PAYMENTS WHILE IN SCHOOL.
REPAYMENTS START AFTER GRADUATION
OR WHEN YOU LEAVE SCHOOL. OPEN TO
VOC-TECH STUDENTS OR JUNIOR/SENIOR
UNDERGRADUATE STUDENTS OR GRADUATE
STUDENTS.

USA CITIZEN OR LEGAL RESIDENT. REQUEST
INFORMATION FROM CHARLES R. NEUMANN;
GRAND RECORDER-SECRETARY.

1541

KOSCIUSZKO FOUNDATION (GRANTS TO
POLISH CITIZENS FOR STUDY IN USA)

15 EAST 65TH STREET
NEW YORK NY 10021
212/734-2130

AMOUNT: STIPEND (AMOUNT VARIES)

DEADLINE(S): OCT 15

FIELD(S): ALL FIELDS OF STUDY

OPEN TO POLISH CITIZENS LIVING IN POLAND
WHO HOLD THE MASTER'S DEGREE & WISH
TO STUDY IN THE USA. MUST HAVE
EXCELLENT COMMAND OF ENGLISH.
STIPEND COVERS HOUSING; LIVING COSTS;
ACCIDENT INSURANCE & (IF NECESSARY)
ROUND-TRIP TRANSPORTATION.

GRANTS ARE FOR 1 ACADEMIC YEAR (10
MONTHS); ARE NOT RENEWABLE AND DON'T
COVER TUITION. WRITE FOR COMPLETE
INFORMATION TO NEW YORK OR WARSAW
OFFICE. WARSAW ADDRESS IS UL. NOWY
SWIAT 4; ROOM 118; 0-3-921 WARSZAWA.

1542

KOSCIUSZKO FOUNDATION (TUITION
SCHOLARSHIPS)

15 EAST 65TH STREET
NEW YORK NY 10021
212/734-2130; FAX 212/628-4552

AMOUNT: NOT SPECIFIED

DEADLINE(S): JAN 15

FIELD(S): ALL FIELDS OF STUDY

OPEN TO FULL TIME GRADUATE STUDENTS OF
POLISH DESCENT WHO ARE USA CITIZENS OR
PERMANENT USA RESIDENTS AND TO
AMERICANS OF NON-POLISH DESCENT WHO
ARE PURSUING STUDIES/RESEARCH
RELATING TO POLISH SUBJECTS.

THERE IS A NON-REFUNDABLE $25 APPLICATION
FEE. CANDIDATES WHO ARE AT LEAST
ASSOCIATE MEMBERS OF THE FOUNDATION
ARE EXEMPT FROM THE APPLICATION FEE.
WRITE FOR COMPLETE INFORMATION.

1543

LEMBERG SCHOLARSHIP LOAN FUND
(SCHOLARSHIP-LOANS)

60 EAST 42ND ST; SUITE 1814
NEW YORK NY 10165
WRITTEN INQUIRY

AMOUNT: VARIES WITH NEED

DEADLINE(S): APR 1

FIELD(S): ALL AREAS OF STUDY

SPECIAL NO-INTEREST SCHOLARSHIP-LOANS
OPEN TO JEWISH MEN & WOMEN PURSUING
ANY UNDERGRADUATE; GRADUATE OR
PROFESSIONAL DEGREE. RECIPIENTS
ASSUME AN OBLIGATION TO REPAY THEIR
LOANS WITHIN 10 YEARS AFTER THE
COMPLETION OF THEIR STUDIES.

WRITE FOR COMPLETE INFORMATION.

1544

LEOPOLD SCHEPP FOUNDATION (GRADUATE
AWARDS)

551 FIFTH AVE - SUITE 2525
NEW YORK NY 10176
212/986-3078

AMOUNT: VARIES

DEADLINE(S): JUN 1 - DEC 31

FIELD(S): ALL AREAS OF STUDY (EXCEPT
MEDICINE)

OPEN TO GRADUATE STUDENTS AGE 40 OR
YOUNGER. FOR FULL-TIME STUDY AT
ACCREDITED COLLEGES OR UNIVERSITIES.
CRITERIA ARE CHARACTER; ACADEMIC
ABILITY; FINANCIAL NEED & AN INTERVIEW
IN NEW YORK. USA CITIZEN OR LEGAL
RESIDENT.

NO APPLICANT WILL BE CONSIDERED WHO HAS
ONLY THE DISSERTATION TO COMPLETE. 150
AWARDS PER YEAR. RENEWABLE WITH
REAPPLICATION. WRITE FOR COMPLETE
INFORMATION.

1545

LEOPOLD SCHEPP FOUNDATION (POST-
DOCTORAL AWARDS)

551 FIFTH AVE - SUITE 2525
NEW YORK NY 10176
212/986-3078

AMOUNT: VARIES

DEADLINE(S): JUN 1 - DEC 31

FIELD(S): ALL FIELDS OF STUDY

POST-DOCTORAL AWARDS. FOR INDEPENDENT
STUDY AND RESEARCH IN SPECIFIED FIELDS
WHICH WILL IMPROVE THE GENERAL
WELFARE OF MANKIND. USA CITIZEN OR
LEGAL RESIDENT.

INTERESTED PERSONS SHOULD INQUIRE AS TO THE AVAILABILITY OF GRANTS IN THEIR CHOSEN FIELD OF STUDY.

1546

LLOYD D. SWEET SCHOLARSHIP FOUNDATION (SCHOLARSHIPS)

BOX 217 (C/O MRS BETTY SPRINKLE)
CHINOOK MT 59523
406/357-3374

AMOUNT: VARIES

DEADLINE(S): MAR 2

FIELD(S): ALL AREAS OF STUDY

SCHOLARSHIPS OPEN TO MONTANA RESIDENTS WHO ARE GRADUATES OF CHINOOK HIGH SCHOOL. AWARDS ARE FOR FULL-TIME UNDERGRADUATE OR GRADUATE STUDY AT ACCREDITED COLLEGES & UNIVERSITIES IN THE USA.

APPROX 100 AWARDS PER YEAR. WRITE FOR COMPLETE INFORMATION.

1547

LOUISIANA REHABILITATION SERVICES (VOCATIONAL AID FOR THE HANDICAPPED)

1755 FLORIDA ST.
BATON ROUGE LA 70804
504/342-2285

AMOUNT: SEE BELOW

DEADLINE(S): NONE

FIELD(S): ALL AREAS OF STUDY

SEVERELY DISABLED PERSONS IN LOUISANA FOUND ELIGIBLE FOR VOCATIONAL REHABILITATION SERVICES CAN RECEIVE FULL TUITION IF THEY ALSO MEET THE AGENCY'S CRITERIA FOR COLLEGE TRAINING.

PROGRAM IS INTENDED TO INCREASE THE EMPLOYABILITY OF THE DISABLED. THEREFORE ONLY PROGRAMS RESULTING IN INCREASED EMPLOYABILITY WILL BE APPROVED. WRITE FOR COMPLETE INFORMATION.

1548

LOUISIANA STUDENT FINANCIAL ASSISTANCE COMISSION (SCHOLARSHIP; GRANT; LOAN PROGRAMS)

PO BOX 91202
BATON ROUGE LA 70821
504/922-1011; FAX 504/922-1089

AMOUNT: VARIED

DEADLINE(S): APR 1

FIELD(S): ALL AREAS OF STUDY

VARIOUS PROGRAMS FOR UNDERGRADUATE AND GRADUATE STUDY ADMINISTERED BY THE OSFA. OPEN TO LOUISIANA RESIDENTS. SOME PROGRAMS BASED ON FINANCIAL NEED; OTHERS ON ACADEMIC STANDING AND/OR SPECIFIC PROGRAMS OF STUDY.

CHECK WITH HIGH SCHOOL COUNSELOR OR WRITE FOR COMPLETE INFORMATION.

1549

MAINE EDUCATION ASSISTANCE DIVISION (HIGHER EDUCATION INTEREST-FREE LOANS)

STATE HOUSE STATION #119
AUGUSTA ME 04333
207/289-2183 (IN STATE 800/228-3734)

AMOUNT: $1500 PER YEAR

DEADLINE(S): APR 1

FIELD(S): ALL FIELDS OF STUDY; PREFERENCE TO EDUCATION MAJORS

MAINE RESIDENTS. HIGH SCHOOL SENIORS; COLLEGE STUDENTS & TEACHERS ARE ELIGIBLE TO APPLY FOR INTEREST FREE LOANS. LOANS ARE COMPETITIVE & BASED ON ACADEMIC MERIT; RELEVANCE OF FIELD OF STUDY ETC.

400 NEW AWARDS PER YEAR. RENEWABLE. WRITE FOR COMPLETE INFORMATION.

1550

MAKARIOS SCHOLARSHIP FUND INC (SCHOLARSHIPS)

13 EAST 40TH STREET
NEW YORK NY 10016
212/696-4590

AMOUNT: $1000

DEADLINE(S): MAY 1

FIELD(S): ALL AREAS OF STUDY

OPEN TO STUDENTS OF CYPRIOT OR GREEK ORIGIN. AWARDS SUPPORT FULL-TIME UNDERGRADUATE OR GRADUATE STUDY AT AN ACCREDITED COLLEGE OR UNIVERSITY IN THE USA. MUST DEMONSTRATE FINANCIAL NEED.

6 AWARDS PER YEAR. WRITE FOR COMPLETE INFORMATION.

1551

MARTIN LUTHER KING JR SCHOLARSHIP FOUNDATION (SCHOLARSHIPS)

PO BOX 751
PORTLAND OR 97207
503-229-3000

AMOUNT: FULL TUITION

DEADLINE(S): JUL 31 - FALL; DEC 2 - WINTER; MAR 3 - SPRING

FIELD(S): ALL AREAS OF STUDY

OPEN TO STUDENTS AT ALL LEVELS OF STUDY WHO RESIDE IN OREGON AND PLAN TO ATTEND OR ALREADY ATTEND AN OREGON SCHOOL. A GPA OF 3.0 OR BETTER AND PROOF OF ADMISSION TO A POST-SECONDARY INSTITUTION REQUIRED.

WRITE FOR COMPLETE INFORMATION.

1552

MARYLAND HIGHER EDUCATION COMMISSION (EDWARD T. CONROY MEMORIAL SCHOLARSHIPS)

STATE SCHOLARSHIP ADMINISTRATION; 16 FRANCIS ST
ANNAPOLIS MD 21401
410/974-5370

AMOUNT: UP TO $2400 FOR TUITION & MANDATORY FEES

DEADLINE(S): JUL 15

FIELD(S): ALL FIELDS OF STUDY

OPEN TO DEPENDENT CHILDREN OF 100% DISABLED OR KILLED IN THE LINE OF MILIARY DUTY WHO WERE MARYLAND RESIDENTS AT THE TIME OF DISABILITY OR DEATH AND TO DEPENDENT CHILDREN OF MIA'S OR POW'S OF THE VIETNAM CONFLICT. USA CITIZEN.

FOR UNDERGRADUATE OR GRADUATE STUDY; FULL OR PART TIME. WRITE FOR COMPLETE INFORMATION.

1553

MARYLAND HIGHER EDUCATION COMMISSION (HOUSE OF DELEGATE SCHOLARSHIPS)

STATE SCHOLARSHIP ADMINISTRATION; 16 FRANCIS ST.
ANNAPOLIS MD 21401
410/974-5370

AMOUNT: VARIABLE - MINIMUM $200

DEADLINE(S): ESTABLISHED BY INDIVIDUAL DELEGATES

FIELD(S): ALL FIELDS OF STUDY

MARYLAND RESIDENT. FOR STUDENTS LIVING IN DISTRICT OF MEMBER OF HOUSE OF DELEGATES. UNDERGRADUATE OR GRADUATE STUDY IN MARYLAND OR OUT-OF-STATE WITH UNIQUE MAJOR. US CITIZEN OR LEGAL RESIDENT.

DURATION UP TO 4 YEARS; 2-4 SCHOLARSHIPS PER DISTRICT. ALSO FOR FULL OR PART TIME STUDY AT CERTAIN PRIVATE CAREER SCHOOLS AND DIPLOMA SCHOOLS OF NURSING. WRITE TO YOUR DELEGATE FOR COMPLETE INFORMATION.

1554

MARYLAND HIGHER EDUCATION COMMISSION (LOAN ASSISTANCE REPAYMENT PROGRAM)

STATE SCHOLARSHIP ADMINISTRATION; 16 FRANCIS ST.
ANNAPOLIS MD 21401
410/974-5370

AMOUNT: UP TO $7500

DEADLINE(S): JUL 31

FIELD(S): STUDENT LOAN REPAYMENT ASSISTANCE

OPEN TO EMPLOYEES OF MARYLAND STATE OR LOCAL GOVERNMENT OR NON-PROFIT ORGANIZATIONS WHO HAVE COMPLETED A DEGREE AT A MARYLAND INSTITUTION. PRIORITY GIVEN TO THOSE WORKING IN CRITICAL SHORTAGE EMPLOYMENT FIELDS.

WRITE FOR COMPLETE INFORMATION.

1555

MARYLAND HIGHER EDUCATION COMMISSION (SENATORIAL SCHOLARSHIP PROGRAM)

STATE SCHOLARSHIP ADMINISTRATION; 16 FRANCIS ST
ANNAPOLIS MD 21401
410/974-5370

AMOUNT: $400 - $2000

DEADLINE(S): MAR 1

FIELD(S): ALL FIELDS OF STUDY

OPEN TO MARYLAND RESIDENTS FOR UNDERGRAD STUDY AT MD DEGREE GRANTING INSTITUTIONS; CERTAIN PRIVATE CAREER SCHOOLS & NURSING DIPLOMA SCHOOLS IN MARYLAND. FOR FULL OR PART TIME STUDY. SAT OR ACT REQUIRED.

STUDENTS WITH UNIQUE MAJORS OR WITH IMPAIRED HEARING MAY ATTEND OUT OF STATE. DURATION IS 1-4 YEARS WITH AUTOMATIC RENEWAL UNTIL DEGREE IS GRANTED. WRITE FOR COMPLETE INFORMATION.

1556

MASSACHUSETTS SCHOLARSHIP OFFICE (VETERANS TUITION EXEMPTION PROGRAM)

330 STUART STREET - 3RD FLOOR
BOSTON MA 02116
617/727-9420

AMOUNT: TUITION EXEMPTION

DEADLINE(S): NONE

FIELD(S): ALL AREAS OF STUDY

OPEN TO MILITARY VETERANS WHO ARE PERMANENT REESIDENTS OF MASSACHUSETTS. AWARDS ARE TENABLE AT MASSACHUSETTS POST-SECONDARY INSTITUTIONS.

CONTACT VETERANS AGENT AT COLLEGE OR ADDRESS ABOVE FOR COMPLETE INFORMATION.

1557

MICHIGAN COMMISSION ON INDIAN AFFAIRS; MICHIGAN DEPT OF CIVIL RIGHTS (TUITION WAIVER PROGRAM)

PO BOX 30026
LANSING MI 48909
517/373-0654

AMOUNT: TUITION (ONLY) WAIVER

DEADLINE(S): 8 WEEKS PRIOR TO CLASS REGISTRATION

FIELD(S): ALL AREAS

OPEN TO ANY MICHIGAN RESIDENT WHO IS AT LEAST 1/4 NORTH AMERICAN INDIAN (CERTIFIED BY THEIR TRIBAL NATION) & WILLING TO ATTEND ANY PUBLIC MICHIGAN COMMUNITY COLLEGE; COLLEGE OR UNIVERSITY.

AWARD IS FOR ALL LEVELS OF STUDY AND IS RENEWABLE. MUST BE MICHIGAN RESIDENTS FOR AT LEAST 12 MONTHS BEFORE CLASS REGISTRATION. WRITE FOR COMPLETE INFORMATION.

1558

MICHIGAN DEPARTMENT OF EDUCATION (MICHIGAN TUITION GRANTS)

STUDENT FINANCIAL ASSISTANCE SERVICES; PO BOX 30008
LANSING MI 48909
517/373-3394

AMOUNT: $100 - $2100

DEADLINE(S): VARIES

FIELD(S): ALL FIELDS OF STUDY

OPEN TO MICHIGAN RESIDENTS WHO ENROLLED AT LEAST HALF TIME AT INDEPENDENT NON-PROFIT MICHIGAN INSTITUTIONS (LIST AVAILABLE FROM ABOVE ADDRESS). BOTH UNDERGRADUATE AND GRADUATE STUDENTS WHO CAN DEMONSTRATE FINANCIAL NEED ARE ELIGIBLE.

GRANTS RENEWABLE. WRITE FOR COMPLETE INFORMATION.

1559

MICHIGAN GUARANTY AGENCY (STAFFORD; SLS; PLUS LOANS)

PO BOX 30047
LANSING MI 48909
517/373-0760

AMOUNT: UP TO $7500

DEADLINE(S): NONE SPECIFIED

FIELD(S): ALL AREAS OF STUDY

GUARANTEED STUDENT LOANS AVAILABLE TO STUDENTS OR PARENTS OF STUDENTS WHO ARE ENROLLED IN AN ELIGIBLE INSTITUTION.

WRITE FOR COMPLETE INFORMATION.

1560

MILITARY ORDER OF THE PURPLE HEART (SONS; DAUGHTERS & GRANDCHILDREN SCHOLARSHIP PROGRAM)

NATIONAL HEADQUARTERS 5413-B BACKLICK ROAD
SPRINGFIELD VA 22151
703/642-5360

AMOUNT: $1000 PER YEAR

DEADLINE(S): JUL 15

FIELD(S): ALL AREAS OF STUDY

OPEN TO CHILDREN & GRANDCHILDREN OF MILITARY ORDER OF PURPLE HEART MEMBERS. APPLICANTS MUST DEMONSTRATE ACADEMIC ACHIEVEMENT & ENROLL IN A FULL-TIME PROGRAM OF STUDY AT ANY LEVEL. USA CITIZEN OR LEGAL RESIDENT.

FINANCIAL NEED IS A CONSIDERATION. SCHOLARSHIPS RENEWABLE UP TO 4 YEARS PROVIDED 2.5 GPA IS MAINTAINED. WRITE FOR COMPLETE INFORMATION.

1561

MINNESOTA CHIPPEWA TRIBE (SCHOLARSHIP FUND)

PO BOX 217
CASS LAKE MN 56633
218/335-8584

AMOUNT: UP TO $3000

DEADLINE(S): JUN 1

FIELD(S): ALL FIELDS OF STUDY

OPEN TO ENROLLED MEMBERS OF THE MINNESOTA CHIPPEWA TRIBE AND THOSE ELIGIBLE FOR ENROLLMENT. AWARDS ARE TENABLE AT RECOGNIZED UNDERGRADUATE AND GRADUATE INSTITUTIONS. USA CITIZEN.

APPROX 850 AWARDS PER YEAR. WRITE FOR COMPLETE INFORMATION.

1562

MINNESOTA HIGHER EDUCATION COORDINATING BOARD (GRANTS)

CAPITOL SQUARE BLDG. - SUITE 400; 550 CEDAR ST.
ST PAUL MN 55101
612/296-3974

AMOUNT: $100 - $5848

DEADLINE(S): MAY 31

FIELD(S): ALL FIELDS OF STUDY

OPEN TO MINNESOTA RESIDENTS TO ATTEND ELIGIBLE MN COLLEGES & UNIVERSITIES. CANDIDATES MAY NOT HOLD 4 YEAR DEGREE OR HAVE ATTENDED COLLEGE FOR 4 YEARS; MAY NOT BE IN DEFAULT ON A STUDENT LOAN OR DELINQUENT IN CHILD SUPPORT PAYMENTS.

65000 AWARDS PER YEAR. WRITE FOR COMPLETE INFORMATION.

1563

MINNESOTA STATE DEPARTMENT OF VETERANS AFFAIRS (VETERANS GRANTS)

VETERANS SERVICE BLDG; BENEFITS DIV
ST PAUL MN 55155
612/296-2562

AMOUNT: $350

DEADLINE(S): NONE

FIELD(S): ALL AREAS OF STUDY

OPEN TO VETERANS WHO WERE RESIDENTS OF MINNESOTA AT THE TIME OF THEIR ENTRY INTO THE ARMED FORCES OF THE USA & WERE HONORABLY DISCHARGED AFTER HAVING SERVED ON ACTIVE DUTY FOR AT LEAST 181 CONSECUTIVE DAYS. USA CITIZEN OR LEGAL RESIDENT.

GRANTS MAY BE USED FOR TUITION AT ANY POST SECONDARY INSTITUTION WITHIN MINNESOTA. NOT RENEWABLE. WRITE FOR COMPLETE INFORMATION.

1564

MIRAMAR OFFICERS WIVES CLUB (SCHOLARSHIPS)

PO BOX 45241 N.A.S. MIRAMAR
SAN DIEGO CA 92145
WRITTEN INQUIRY

AMOUNT: $700 AVE

DEADLINE(S): APR 15

FIELD(S): ALL AREAS OF STUDY

OPEN TO SPOUSES AND CHILDREN OF OFFICER OR ENLISTED NAVY; MARINE CORPS OR COAST GUARD MEMBERS ON ACTIVE DUTY; RETIRED WITH PAY OR DECEASED. RECIPIENTS MUST RESIDE IN THE SAN DIEGO AREA.

WRITE FOR COMPLETE INFORMATION.

1565

MISSOURI COORDINATING BOARD FOR HIGHER EDUCATION (MISSOURI GUARANTEED STUDENT LOAN PROGRAM)

PO BOX 1438; 101 ADAMS ST
JEFFERSON CITY MO 65102
314/751-3940

AMOUNT: UP TO $23000 (TOTAL) FOR UNDERGRADUATE STUDY; $8500 PER YEAR FOR GRADUATE STUDENTS TO A MAXIMUM OF $65000 (BOTH UNDERGRAD & GRAD)

DEADLINE(S): BY END OF ACADEMIC PERIOD

FIELD(S): ALL FIELDS OF STUDY

OPEN TO MISSOURI RESIDENTS OR STUDENTS ATTENDING SCHOOL IN MISSOURI. US CITIZEN OR LEGAL RESIDENT.

WRITE FOR COMPLETE INFORMATION.

1566

MONTANA UNIVERSITY SYSTEM (INDIAN FEES WAIVER PROGRAM)

2500 BROADWAY
HELENA MT 59620
WRITTEN INQUIRY

AMOUNT: WAIVER OF REGISTRATION & INCIDENTAL FEES

DEADLINE(S): NONE

FIELD(S): ALL FIELDS OF STUDY

ONE-FOURTH OR MORE INDIAN BLOOD & MONTANA RESIDENT FOR AT LEAST A YEAR BEFORE ENROLLING IN THE MONTANA UNIVERSITY SYSTEM. MUST DEMONSTRATE FINANCIAL NEED. EACH UNIT OF THE MONTANA UNIVERSITY SYSTEM MAKES ITS OWN RULES GOVERNING SELECTION.

500 WAIVERS PER YEAR. WRITE FOR COMPLETE INFORMATION.

1567

MONTANA UNIVERSITY SYSTEM (MONTANA GUARANTEED STUDENT LOAN PROGRAM)

35 SOUTH LAST CHANCE GULCH
HELENA MT 59620
406/444-6594

AMOUNT: $2625 - $4000 PER YEAR UNDERGRADS; $7500 PER YEAR GRADS

DEADLINE(S): NONE

FIELD(S): ALL FIELDS OF STUDY

THE MGSLP IS NOT A LENDER; IT DOES NOT MAKE LOANS TO STUDENTS. RATHER IT GUARANTEES THEIR LOANS WHICH ARE MADE BY REGULAR LENDING INSTITUTIONS SUCH AS BANKS; SAVINGS AND LOAN ASSNS; MUST DEMONSTRATE FINANCIAL NEED.

MUST BE A RESIDENT OF MONTANA ATTENDING AN ELIGIBLE MONTANA SCHOOL. WRITE FOR COMPLETE INFORMATION.

1568

MORTAR BOARD NATIONAL FOUNDATION (FELLOWSHIPS)

1250 CHAMBERS ROAD #170
COLUMBUS OH 43212
614/488-4094

AMOUNT: $1000

DEADLINE(S): JAN 15

FIELD(S): ALL FIELDS OF STUDY

FELLOWSHIPS ARE AWARDED ONLY TO MORTAR BOARD MEMBERS IN GOOD STANDING PURSUING GRADUATE OR PROFESSIONAL STUDY.

12 AWARDS PER YEAR. WRITE FOR COMPLETE INFORMATION.

1569

MOTHER JOSEPH ROGAN MARYMOUNT FOUNDATION (GRANT PROGRAM & LOAN PROGRAM)

C/O JOSEPH E. LYNCH;
2217 CLAYVILLE CT.
CHESTERFIELD MO 63017
314/391-6248

AMOUNT: $400 TO $750

DEADLINE(S): MAY 1

FIELD(S): ALL AREAS OF STUDY

GRANTS AND LOANS FOR STUDENTS WHO ARE USA CITIZENS; LIVE IN THE METROPOLITAN ST LOUIS AREA AND ARE ENTERING OR ENROLLED IN A HIGH SCHOOL; VOCATIONAL/TECHNICAL SCHOOL; COLLEGE OR UNIVERSITY.

WRITE FOR COMPLETE INFORMATION.

1570

MUSKEGON COUNTY COMMUNITY FOUNDATION (SCHOLARSHIP PROGRAM)

425 WEST WESTERN AVE; SUITE 304
MUSKEGON MI 49440
616/722-4538

AMOUNT: $500+

DEADLINE(S): APR 16

FIELD(S): ALL FIELDS OF STUDY

OPEN TO MUSKEGON COUNTY MICHIGAN RESIDENTS ONLY. SCHOLARSHIPS FOR 2-YEAR OR 4-YEAR UNDERGRADUATE STUDY OR GRADUATE SCHOOL. USA CITIZEN OR LEGAL RESIDENT. FINANCIAL NEED AND ACADEMIC STANDING ARE CONSIDERATIONS.

284 AWARDS PER YEAR (130 ARE RENEWALS). WRITE FOR COMPLETE INFORMATION.

1571

NAACP NATIONAL HEADQUARTERS (AGNES JONES JACKSON SCHOLARSHIP)

4805 MT HOPE DR
BALTIMORE MD 21215
301/358-8900

AMOUNT: $1500 - $2500

DEADLINE(S): APR 30

FIELD(S): ALL AREAS OF STUDY

UNDERGRADUAT ($1500) & GRADUATE ($2500) SCHOLARSHIPS OPEN TO APPLICATNS WHO HAVE BEEN NAACP MEMBERS FOR AT LEAST 1 YEAR & WILL BE UNDER AGE OF 25 ON APR 30. MINIMUM GPA OF 2.5-HIGH SCHOOL; 2.0-UNDERGRADUATE & 3.0-GRADUATE STUDENT.

SEND LEGAL SIZE SELF-ADDRESSED STAMPED ENVELOPE TO ADDRESS ABOVE FOR APPLICATON AND COMPLETE INFORMATION.

1572

NATIONAL 4-H COUNCIL (NATIONAL 4-H AWARD PROGRAMS)

7100 CONNECTICUT AVE
CHEVY CHASE MD 20815
301/961-2904

AMOUNT: $750 - $1500

DEADLINE(S): NONE SPECIFIED

FIELD(S): ALL FIELDS OF STUDY

PRESENT OR FORMER 4-H MEMBERS ARE ELIGIBLE FOR MUTITUDE OF SCHOLARSHIP & AWARD PROGRAMS FOR POST-SECONDARY EDUCATION. CONTACT YOUR LOCAL 4-H AGENT OR STATE LEADER FOR INFORMATION & APPLICATIONS.

THE 4-H DIGEST (A SUMMARY OF SCHOLARSHIP PROGRAMS) & NATIONAL 4-H COLLEGE SCHOLARSHIP PROGRAMS CHECKLIST SHOULD BE AVAILABLE FROM YOUR LOCAL OR STATE AGENT. IF NOT SEND SELF-ADDRESSED STAMPED ENVELOPE TO ADDRESS ABOVE FOR DETAILS.

1573

NATIONAL ART MATERIALS TRADE ASSN (NAMTA SCHOLARSHIPS)

178 LAKEVIEW AVE
CLIFTON NJ 07011
201/546-6400

AMOUNT: VARIES

DEADLINE(S): MAR 15

FIELD(S): ALL AREAS OF STUDY

OPEN TO NAMTA EMPLOYEES; MEMBERS AND THEIR RELATIVES OR TO INDIVIDUALS IN AN ORGANIZATION RELATED TO ART OR THE ART MATERIALS INDUSTRY. FOR UNDERGRADUATE OR GRADUATE STUDY.

SELECTION BASED ON FINANCIAL NEED; GRADES; ACTIVITIES; INTERESTS AND CAREER CHOICE. WRITE FOR COMPLETE INFORMATION.

1574

NATIONAL ASSOCIATION OF UNIVERSITY WOMEN (FELLOWSHIP AWARD)

PO BOX 1452
LAURINBURG NC 28353
215/248-3387

AMOUNT: $2500

DEADLINE(S): APR 30

FIELD(S): ALL AREAS OF STUDY

FELLOWSHIP IS OFFERED BY ASSOCIATION IN SUPPORT OF A WOMAN WHO HOLDS A MASTERS DEGREE AND IS ENROLLED IN A PROGRAM LEADING TO A DOCTORAL DEGREE.

PRIORITY IS GIVEN TO BLACK WOMEN. WRITE FOR COMPLETE INFORMATION.

1575

NATIONAL COLLEGIATE ATHLETIC ASSOCIATION (GRADUATE SCHOLARSHIP PROGRAM)

6201 COLLEGE BLVD
OVERLAND PARK KS 66211
913-339-1906

AMOUNT: NOT SPECIFIED

DEADLINE(S): VARIES ACCORDING TO SPORT

FIELD(S): ALL AREAS OF STUDY

GRANTS TO SUPPORT GRADUATE STUDY BY STUDENT-ATHLETES ATTENDING NCAA MEMBER INSTITUTIONS WHO ARE NOMINATED BY THEIR FACULTY ATHLETIC REPRESENTATIVE OR DIRECTOR OF ATHLETICS. GPA OF 3.0 OR BETTER IS REQUIRED.

SELECTIONS ARE MADE IN THE ACADEMIC YEAR IN WHICH THE STUDENT COMPLETES HIS OR HER FINAL SEASON OF ELIGIBILITY FOR INTERCOLLEGIATE ATHLETICS UNDER NCAA LEGISLATION. CONTACT YOUR AD OR ADDRESS ABOVE FOR COMPLETE INFORMATION.

1576

NATIONAL FEDERATION OF THE BLIND (EZRA DAVIS-AMERICAN BROTHERHOOD FOR THE BLIND SCHOLARSHIP)

814 4TH AVE #200
GRINNELL IA 50112
515/236-3366

AMOUNT: $6000

DEADLINE(S): MAR 31

FIELD(S): ALL FIELDS OF STUDY

OPEN TO LEGALLY BLIND STUDENTS PURSUING OR PLANNING TO PURSUE A FULL TIME POST-SECONDARY COURSE OF STUDY. AWARDS ARE BASED ON ACADEMIC EXCELLENCE; COMMUNITY SERVICE AND FINANCIAL NEED.

WRITE FOR COMPLETE INFORMATION.

1577

NATIONAL FEDERATION OF THE BLIND (FRANK WALTON HORN MEMORIAL SCHOLARSHIP)

814 4TH AVE #200
GRINNELL IA 50112
515/236-3366

AMOUNT: $2500

DEADLINE(S): MAR 31

FIELD(S): ALL FIELDS OF STUDY

SCHOLARSHIP FOR LEGALLY BLIND STUDENTS STUDYING (OR PLANNING TO STUDY) AT ANY POST-SECONDARY LEVEL. FOR ALL FIELDS OF STUDY BUT PREFERENCE WILL BE GIVEN TO ARCHITECTURE AND ENGINEERING MAJORS.

AWARDS BASED ON ACADEMIC EXELLENCE; SERVICE TO THE COMMUNITY; FINANCIAL NEED. WRITE FOR COMPLETE INFORMATION.

1578

NATIONAL FEDERATION OF THE BLIND (HERMIONE GRANT CALHOUN SCHOLARSHIPS)

814 4TH AVE #200
GRINNELL IA 50112
515/236-3366

AMOUNT: $2000

DEADLINE(S): MAR 31

FIELD(S): ALL FIELDS OF STUDY

SCHOLARSHIPS OPEN TO LEGALLY BLIND FEMALE UNDERGRADUATE AND GRADUATE STUDENTS. AWARDS BASED ON ACADEMIC EXCELLENCE; SERVICE TO THE COMMUNITY; FINANCIAL NEED.

WRITE FOR COMPLETE INFORMATION.

1579

NATIONAL FEDERATION OF THE BLIND (MELVA T. OWEN MEMORIAL SCHOLARSHIP)

814 4TH AVE #200
GRINNELL IA 50112
515/236-3366

AMOUNT: $2500

DEADLINE(S): MAR 31

FIELD(S): ALL FIELDS OF STUDY

OPEN TO LEGALLY BLIND STUDENTS FOR ALL POST-SECONDARY AREAS OF STUDY DIRECTED TOWARDS ATTAINING FINANCIAL INDEPENDENCE. EXCLUDES RELIGION AND THOSE SEEKING ONLY TO FURTHER THEIR GENERAL AND CULTURAL EDUCATION.

AWARDS BASED ON ACADEMIC EXCELLENCE; SERVICE TO THE COMMUNITY AND FINANCIAL NEED. WRITE FOR COMPLETE INFORMATION.

1580

NATIONAL FEDERATION OF THE BLIND (SCHOLARSHIPS)

814 4TH AVE #200
GRINNELL IA 50112
515/236-3366

AMOUNT: $2000 - $4000

DEADLINE(S): MAR 31

FIELD(S): ALL FIELDS OF STUDY

16 SCHOLARSHIPS (2 FOR $4000 EA; 5 FOR $2500 EA; 9 FOR $2000 EA) WILL BE GIVEN. APPLICANTS MUST BE LEGALLY BLIND AND STUDYING (OR PLANNING TO STUDY) FULL TIME AT THE POST SECONDARY LEVEL.

AWARDS ARE ON THE BASIS OF ACADEMIC EXCELLENCE; COMMUNITY SERVICE AND FINANCIAL NEED. WRITE FOR COMPLETE INFORMATION.

1581

NATIONAL HISPANIC SCHOLARSHIP FUND (SCHOLARSHIPS)

PO BOX 728
NOVATO CA 94948
WRITTEN INQUIRY

AMOUNT: VARIES

DEADLINE(S): APR 1 - JUN 15

FIELD(S): ALL FIELDS OF STUDY

OPEN TO US CITIZENS OR PERMANENT RESIDENTS OF HISPANIC PARENTAGE ENROLLED FULL TIME AS UNDERGRADUATE OR GRADUATE STUDENT IN USA COLLEGE OR UNIVERSITY. APPLICANTS MUST HAVE COMPLETED AT LEAST 15 UNITS/CREDITS PRIOR TO FALL REGISTRATION.

COMMUNITY COLLEGE UNITS MUST BE TRANSFERABLE TO A 4-YEAR INSTITUTION. FINANCIAL NEED IS A CONSIDERATION. SEND BUSINESS SIZE SELF ADDRESSED STAMPED ENVELOPE FOR COMPLETE INFORMATION.

1582

NATIONAL PHYSICAL SCIENCE CONSORTIUM (GRADUATE FELLOWSHIPS FOR MINORITIES AND WOMEN IN THE PHYSICAL SCIENCES)

C/O NEW MEXICO STATE UNIVERSITY; BOX 30001; DEPT. 3 NPS
LAS CRUCES NM 88003
800/952-4118

AMOUNT: $10000 TO $15000 PER YEAR

DEADLINE(S): NOV 15

FIELD(S): ASTRONOMY; CHEMISTRY; COMPUTER SCIENCE; GEOLOGY; MATERIAL SCIENCE; MATHEMATICS; PHYSICS

OPEN TO USA CITIZENS WHO ARE BLACK; HISPANIC; NATIVE AMERICAN AND/OR FEMALE WHO HAVE AN UNDERGRADUATE GPA OF AT LEAST 3.0 AND ARE ELIGIBLE TO PURSUE GRADUATE STUDY IN THE ABOVE AREAS AT A PARTICIPATING NPSC MEMBER UNIVERSITY.

RENEWABLE FOR UP TO SIX YEARS. TOTAL VALUE OF AWARD UP TO $180000. WRITE FOR COMPLETE INFORMATION.

1583

NATIONAL TWENTY AND FOUR (MEMORIAL SCHOLARSHIPS)

C/O ETHEL M MATUSCHKA; 6000 LUCERNE CT #2
MEQUON WI 53092
WRITTEN INQUIRY

AMOUNT: MAXIMUM OF $500

DEADLINE(S): MAY 1

FIELD(S): ALL AREAS OF STUDY

OPEN TO MEMBERS & DEPENDENTS OF MEMBERS BETWEEN THE AGES OF 16 AND 25. SELECTION IS BASED ON FINANCIAL NEED; SCHOLASTIC STANDING & SCHOOL ACTIVITIES.

WRITE FOR COMPLETE INFORMATION -ONLY- IF ABOVE QUALIFICATIONS ARE MET.

1584

NEGRO EDUCATIONAL EMERGENCY DRIVE (NEED SCHOLARSHIP PROGRAM)

643 LIBERTY AVE; 17TH FL
PITTSBURGH PA 15222
412/566-2760

AMOUNT: $100 - $1000

DEADLINE(S): APR 30

FIELD(S): ALL AREAS OF STUDY

PENNSYLVANIA RESIDENT. OPEN TO BLACK RESIDENTS WITH A HIGH SCHOOL DIPLOMA OR GED WHO RESIDE IN ALLEGHENY; ARMSTRONG; BEAVER; BUTLER; WASHINGTON OR WESTMORELAND COUNTIES. USA CITIZEN.

400 SCHOLARSHIPS PER YEAR. RENEWABLE. WRITE FOR COMPLETE INFORMATION.

1585

NEVADA DEPT OF EDUCATION (STUDENT INCENTIVE GRANT PROGRAM)

CAPITOL COMPLEX; 400 W.KING ST
CARSON CITY NV 89701
702/687-5915

AMOUNT: UP TO $2500

DEADLINE(S): NONE SPECIFIED

FIELD(S): ALL FIELDS OF STUDY

STUDENT INCENTIVE GRANTS AVAILABLE TO NEVADA RESIDENTS ENROLLED IN ELIGIBLE NEVADA INSTITUTIONS.

APPLICATION MUST BE MADE THROUGH THE FINANCIAL AID OFFICE OF ELIGIBLE PARTICIPATING INSTITUTIONS.

1586

NEW ENGLAND BOARD OF HIGHER EDUCATION (NEW ENGLAND REGIONAL STUDENT PROGRAM)

45 TEMPLE PL
BOSTON MA 02111
617/357-9620

AMOUNT: TUITION REDUCTION (AVG VALUE $2900)

DEADLINE(S): VARIES

FIELD(S): ALL FIELDS OF STUDY

UNDER THIS PROGRAM NEW ENGLAND RESIDENTS MAY ATTEND PUBLIC COLLEGES & UNIVERSITIES IN OTHER NEW ENGLAND STATES AT A REDUCED TUITION RATE FOR CERTAIN DEGREE PROGRAMS WHICH ARE NOT AVAILABLE IN THEIR OWN STATE'S PUBLIC INSTITUTIONS.

5883 AWARDS LAST YEAR. WRITE FOR COMPLETE INFORMATION.

1587

NEW ENGLAND EDUCATION LOAN MARKETING CORPORATION (NELLIE MAE - EXCEL & SHARE LOANS)

50 BRAINTREE HILL PARK - SUITE 300
BRAINTREE MA 02184-1763
617/849-1325

AMOUNT: $2000 - $20000

DEADLINE(S): NONE SPECIFIED

FIELD(S): ALL FIELDS OF STUDY

VARIETY OF LOANS AVAILABLE FOR UNDERGRADUATE AND GRADUATE STUDY AT ACCREDITED DEGREE GRANTING COLLEGES OR UNIVERSITIES. VARIED REPAYMENT AND INTEREST RATE OPTIONS. CUMULATIVE MAXIMUM LOAN OF $80000 PER STUDENT.

WRITE FOR COMPLETE INFORMATION.

1588

NEW HAMPSHIRE HIGHER EDUCATION ASSISTANCE FOUNDATION (FEDERAL FAMILY EDUCATION LOAN PROGRAM)

PO BOX 877; 143 N MAIN ST
CONCORD NH 03301
603/225-6612 OR 800/525-2577

AMOUNT: VARIES WITH PROGRAM

DEADLINE(S): NONE

FIELD(S): ALL FIELDS OF STUDY

OPEN TO NEW HAMPSHIRE RESIDENTS PURSUING A COLLEGE EDUCATION IN OR OUT OF STATE AND TO NON-RESIDENTS WHO ATTEND A NEW HAMPSHIRE COLLEGE OR UNIVERSITY. THE FOUNDATION ADMINISTERS A VARIETY OF STUDENT AND PARENT LOAN PROGRAMS.

USA CITIZEN. WRITE FOR COMPLETE INFORMATION.

1589

NEW JERSEY DEPT OF HIGHER EDUCATION (EDUCATIONAL OPPORTUNITY FUND GRANTS)

OFFICE OF STUDENT ASSISTANCE; CN 540
TRENTON NJ 08625
609/588-3230; 800/792-8670 IN NJ

AMOUNT: $200-$1950 UNDERGRAD; $200-$4000 GRADUATE STUDENT

DEADLINE(S): OCT 1; MAR 1

FIELD(S): ALL AREAS OF STUDY

NEW JERSEY RESIDENT FOR AT LEAST 12 MONTHS PRIOR TO APPLICATION. GRANTS FOR ECONOMICALLY AND EDUCATIONALLY DISADVANTAGED STUDENTS. FOR UNDERGRADUATE OR GRADUATE STUDY IN NEW JERSEY. MUST DEMONSTRATE NEED. US CITIZEN OR LEGAL RESIDENT.

GRANTS RENEWABLE. WRITE FOR COMPLETE INFORMATION.

1590

NEW JERSEY DEPT OF HIGHER EDUCATION (HIGHER EDUCATION LOAN PROGRAM)

OFFICE OF STUDENT ASSISTANCE; CN 540
TRENTON NJ 08625
609/588-3200; 800/792-8670 IN NJ

GENERAL

AMOUNT: $2625 UNDERGRAD; $7500 GRADUATE STUDENT

DEADLINE(S): 2 MONTHS PRIOR TO DATE OF NEED

FIELD(S): ALL AREAS OF STUDY

US CITIZENS OR LEGAL RESIDENTS. RESIDENTS OF NEW JERSEY FOR 6 MONTHS PRIOR TO FILING APPLICATION OR OUT-OF-STATE STUDENT ATTENDING SCHOOL IN NJ. APPLIES TO ALL LEVELS OF STUDY.

WRITE FOR COMPLETE INFORMATION.

1591

NEW JERSEY DEPT OF HIGHER EDUCATION (VETERANS TUITION CREDIT PROGRAM)

OFFICE OF STUDENT ASSISTANCE; CN 540
TRENTON NJ 08625
609-588-3200; 800-792-8670 IN NJ

AMOUNT: $400 FULL TIME; $200 HALF TIME

DEADLINE(S): OCT 1; MAR 1

FIELD(S): ALL AREAS OF STUDY

OPEN TO USA VETERANS WHO SERVED BETWEEN DEC 31 1960 - AUG 1 1974 & WERE RESIDENTS OF NJ AT TIME OF INDUCTION OR DISCHARGE. APPLIES TO ALL LEVELS OF STUDY.

WRITE FOR COMPLETE INFORMATION.

1592

NEW YORK STATE EDUCATION DEPARTMENT (AWARDS; SCHOLARSHIPS & FELLOWSHIPS)

STATE & FEDERAL SCHOLARSHIP & FELLOWSHIP UNIT; CULTURAL EDUCATION CENTER
ALBANY NY 12230
WRITTEN INQUIRY

AMOUNT: VARIES

DEADLINE(S): VARIES

FIELD(S): ALL FIELDS OF STUDY

VARIOUS STATE AND FEDERAL PROGRAMS ADMINISTERED BY THE NY STATE EDUCATION DEPARTMENT OPEN TO RESIDENTS OF NEW YORK STATE. ONE YEAR'S NY RESIDENCY IMMEDIATELY PRECEDING EFFECTIVE DATE OF AWARD IS REQUIRED.

WRITE FOR COMPLETE INFORMATION.

1593

NEW YORK STATE HIGHER EDUCATION SERVICES CORPORATION (STATE & FEDERAL SCHOLARSHIPS; FELLOWSHIPS; GRANTS; LOANS)

STUDENT INFORMATION; 99 WASHINGTON AVE
ALBANY NY 12255
518/473-7087

AMOUNT: VARIES WITH PROGRAM

DEADLINE(S): VARIES

FIELD(S): ALL FIELDS OF STUDY

THE CORPORATION ADMINISTERS A VARIETY OF FEDERAL AND STATE SCHOLARSHIPS; FELLOWSHIPS; GRANTS AND LOANS. OPEN TO NEW YORK STATE RESIDENTS. SOME PROGRAMS CARRY A SERVICE OBLIGATION FOR EACH YEAR SUPPORT IS RECEIVED.

WRITE FOR COMPLETE INFORMATION.

1594

NORTH CAROLINA DIVISION OF SERVICES FOR THE BLIND (REHABILITATION ASSISTANCE FOR VISUALLY HANDICAPPED)

309 ASHE AVE.
RALEIGH NC 27606
919-733-9700

AMOUNT: TUITION; FEES; BOOKS AND SUPPLIES

DEADLINE(S): NONE

FIELD(S): ALL AREAS OF STUDY

NORTH CAROLINA RESIDENT. LEGALLY BLIND OR HAVE A PROGRESSIVE EYE CONDITION WHICH MAY RESULT IN BLINDNESS THEREBY CREATING AN EMPLOYMENT HANDICAP FOR THE INDIVIDUAL. UNDERGRAD OR GRAD STUDENT AT NC SCHOOL.

WRITE FOR COMPLETE INFORMATION.

1595

NORTH CAROLINA STATE EDUCATION ASSISTANCE AUTHORITY (STUDENT FINANCIAL AID FOR NORTH CAROLINIANS)

PO BOX 2688
CHAPEL HILL NC 27515
919/549-8614

AMOUNT: VARIES

DEADLINE(S): VARIOUS

FIELD(S): ALL FIELDS OF STUDY

THE STATE OF NC; PRIVATE NC ORGANIZATIONS & THE FEDERAL GOVERNMENT FUND NUMEROUS SCHOLARSHIP; GRANT; WORK-STUDY & LOAN PROGRAMS FOR NORTH CAROLINA RESIDENTS AT ALL LEVELS OF STUDY.

THE NC STATE EDUCATION ASSISTANCE AUTHORITY ANNUALLY PUBLISHES A FINANCIAL AID BOOKLET DESCRIBING IN DETAIL VARIOUS PROGRAMS FOR NORTH CAROLINA RESIDENTS. A COPY IS AVAILABLE FREE TO NC RESIDENT UNDERGRADUATES FROM THE ADDRESS ABOVE.

1596

OHIO BOARD OF REGENTS (STUDENT GRANT PROGRAM)

30 E. BROAD ST. 36TH FLOOR
COLUMBUS OH 43266
614/466-7420

AMOUNT: VARIES

DEADLINE(S): VARIES

FIELD(S): ALL APPROVED DEGREE PROGRAMS (NOT LEADING TO THEOLOGY)

OPEN TO OHIO RESIDENTS ATTENDING ELIGIBLE OHIO PRIVATE INDSTITUTIONS. MUST BE A FULL TIME STUDENT IN A BACHELOR'S DEGREE PROGRAM & HAVE -NOT- ATTENDED COLLEGE ON A FULL TIME BASIS PRIOR TO JUL 1 1984.

UNSPECIFIED NUMBER OF GRANTS PER YEAR. RENEWABLE. WRITE FOR COMPLETE INFORMATION.

1597

OHIO WAR ORPHANS SCHOLARSHIP BOARD (SCHOLARSHIPS)

3600 STATE OFFICE TOWER 30 BROAD ST.
COLUMBUS OH 43266
614/466-1190

AMOUNT: FULL TUITION AT PUBLIC SCHOOLS; EQUIVALENT AMOUNT AT PRIVATE SCHOOLS

DEADLINE(S): JUL 1

FIELD(S): ALL AREAS OF STUDY

OHIO RESIDENT & DEPENDENT OF VETERAN WHO SERVED FOR AT LEAST 90 DAYS DURING WAR & AS A RESULT IS NOW 60% OR MORE DISABLED OR 100% DISABLED FOR ANY REASON OR IS DECEASED.

350 AWARDS PER YEAR. WRITE FOR COMPLETE INFORMATION.

1598

OREGON DEPARTMENT OF VETERANS' AFFAIRS (EDUCATIONAL SCHOLARSHIP AID FOR OREGON VETERANS)

700 SUMMER ST NE; SUITE 150
SALEM OR 97310
800/692-9666

AMOUNT: $35 - $50 PER MONTH

DEADLINE(S): NONE

FIELD(S): ALL FIELDS OF STUDY

RESIDENT OF OREGON FOR TWO YEARS PRIOR TO MILITARY SERVICE AND AT TIME OF ENROLLMENT. MUST BE A USA CITIZEN WITH A QUALIFYING MILITARY SERVICE RECORD. FOR STUDY IN AN ACCREDITED OREGON SCHOOL.

APPLICANTS MUST HAVE ARMED FORCES EXPEDITIONARY MEDAL OR THE VIETNAM SERVICE MEDAL OR BE A VETERAN OF THE KOREAN CONFLICT (ACTIVE DUTY). 30 AWARDS PER YEAR. WRITE FOR COMPLETE INFORMATION.

1599

OREGON STATE SCHOLARSHIP COMMISSION (OREGON GUARANTEED STUDENT LOANS)

1445 WILLAMETTE ST
EUGENE OR 97401
503/346-3200

AMOUNT: $2625 - $4000 UNDERGRAD; $7500 GRADUATE (ANNUAL MAXIMUM)

DEADLINE(S): NONE SPECIFIED

FIELD(S): ALL FIELDS OF STUDY

OPEN TO USA CITIZENS OR PERMANENT RESIDENTS WHO ARE ATTENDING AN ELIGIBLE OREGON INSTITUTION AND TO OREGON RESIDENTS ATTENDING ANY ELIGIBLE INSTITUTION OUTSIDE OF OREGON AT LEAST HALF TIME.

WRITE FOR COMPLETE INFORMATION.

1600

OREGON STATE SCHOLARSHIP COMMISSION (PRIVATE SCHOLARSHIP PROGRAMS ADMINISTERED BY THE COMMISSION)

1445 WILLAMETTE ST
EUGENE OR 97401
503/346-1240 OR 800/452-8807

AMOUNT: $250 - $3000

DEADLINE(S): VARIES

FIELD(S): ALL FIELDS OF STUDY

70 DIFFERENT PRIVATE SCHOLARSHIP PROGRAMS ARE ADMINISTERED BY THE COMMISSION AND ARE OPEN TO OREGON RESIDENTS. SOME ARE TIED TO A SPECIFIC FIELD AND/OR LEVEL OF STUDY BUT IN GENERAL THEY ARE AVAILABLE TO ALL LEVELS AND FIELDS OF STUDY.

WRITE FOR COMPLETE INFORMATION.

1601

PHI ETA SIGMA (SCHOLARSHIP PROGRAM)

228 FOY UNION BLDG.
AUBURN UNIVERSITY AL 36849
205-826-5856

AMOUNT: 10 $2000 SCHOLARSHIPS; 22 $1000 SCHOLARSHIPS

DEADLINE(S): MAR 1

FIELD(S): ALL AREAS OF STUDY

MUST BE MEMBER OF PHI ETA SIGMA. CONTACT LOCAL CHAPTER ADVISER FOR APPLICATION AND REQUIREMENTS. -DO NOT- CALL OR WRITE ADDRESS ABOVE; ALL INFORMATION TO COME FROM LOCAL CHAPTER.

32 SCHOLARSHIPS PER YEAR. NOT RENEWABLE.

1602 ――――――――――――――

PORTUGUESE CONTINENTAL UNION (SCHOLARSHIPS)

899 BOYLSTON STREET
BOSTON MA 02115
617/536-2916

AMOUNT: VARIES

DEADLINE(S): FEB 15 TO MAR 31

FIELD(S): ALL AREAS OF STUDY

OPEN TO PORTUGUESE CONTINENTAL UNION MEMBERS WHO ARE ENROLLED IN AN UNDERGRADUATE OR GRADUATE PROGRAM AT AN ACCREDITED COLLEGE OR UNIVERSITY. ONE YEAR MEMBERSHIP REQUIRED.

FINANCIAL NEED IS A CONSIDERATION. WRITE FOR COMPLETE INFORMATION.

1603 ――――――――――――――

PRESBYTERIAN CHURCH-USA (NATIVE AMERICAN EDUCATION GRANTS)

FINANCIAL AID FOR STUDIES; CHURCH VOCATION UNIT; 100 WITHERSPOON ST.
LOUISVILLE KY 40202
502/569-5760

AMOUNT: $200 - $1500

DEADLINE(S): JUN 1

FIELD(S): ALL FIELDS OF STUDY

OPEN TO NATIVE AMERICAN INDIANS; ALEUTS & ESKIMOS WHO HAVE COMPLETED AT LEAST ONE SEMESTER OF WORK AT AN ACCREDITED INSTITUTION OF HIGHER EDUCATION. PREFERENCE TO PRESBYTERIAN STUDENTS AT THE UNDERGRADUATE LEVEL. MUST BE USA CITIZEN.

RENEWAL IS BASED ON CONTINUED FINANCIAL NEED AND SATISFACTORY ACADEMIC PROGRESS. WRITE FOR COMPLETE INFORMATION.

1604 ――――――――――――――

PRESBYTERIAN CHURCH-USA (STUDENT LOAN FUND)

CHURCH VOCATIONS UNIT; 100 WITHERSPOON ST
LOUISVILLE KY 40202
502/569-5735

AMOUNT: UP TO $1000 PER YEAR

DEADLINE(S): NONE SPECIFIED

FIELD(S): ALL FIELDS OF STUDY

LOANS OPEN TO COMMUNICANT MEMBERS OF THE PRESBYTERIAN CHURCH (USA) WHO ARE USA CITIZENS OR PERMANENT RESIDENTS. FOR FULL TIME UNDERGRADUATE OR GRADUATE STUDY. NO INTEREST WHILE IN SCHOOL; REPAYABLE AT 8% APR THEREAFTER.

GPA OF 2.0 OR BETTER REQUIRED. THOSE PREPARING FOR PROFESSIONAL CHURCH OCCUPATIONS CAN BORROW UP TO $2000 PER ACADEMIC YEAR. WRITE FOR COMPLETE INFORMATION.

1605 ――――――――――――――

PROFESSIONAL HORSEMEN'S ASSOCIATION OF AMERICA INC. (FINANCIAL ASSISTANCE)

PO BOX 572; LONG HILL RD
NEW VERNON NJ 07976
201/538-3797

AMOUNT: $500

DEADLINE(S): MAY 1

FIELD(S): ALL AREAS OF STUDY

MEMBERS OR DEPENDENTS OF MEMBERS OF THE PROFESSIONAL HORSEMEN'S ASSOCIATION RECEIVE FIRST CONSIDERATION FOR FINANCIAL ASSISTANCE. AWARDS CAN BE USED FOR COLLEGE OR TRADE SCHOOL.

WRITE TO MR. ALEX FORMAN; SCHOLARSHIP COMMITTEE CHAIRMAN; ADDRESS ABOVE FOR COMPLETE INFORMATION.

1606 ――――――――――――――

PUBLIC EMPLOYEES ROUNDTABLE (PUBLIC SERVICE SCHOLARSHIPS)

PO BOX 14270
WASHINGTON DC 20044
202/927-5000; FAX 202/927-5001

AMOUNT: $500 - $1000

DEADLINE(S): MAY 15

FIELD(S): ALL FIELDS OF STUDY

OPEN TO GRADUATE STUDENTS & UNDERGRADUATE SOPHOMORES; JUNIORS; SENIORS WHO ARE PLANNING A CAREER IN GOVERNMENT. MINIMUM OF 3.5 CUMULATIVE GPA. PREFERENCE TO APPLICANTS WITH SOME PUBLIC SERVICE WORK EXPERIENCE (PAID OR UNPAID).

10 TO 15 AWARDS PER YEAR. APPLICATIONS AVAILABLE AS OF FEB 1. SEND SELF ADDRESSED -STAMPED- ENVELOPE FOR APPLICATION.

1607 —————————————————

RHODE ISLAND HIGHER EDUCATION ASSISTANCE AUTHORITY (LOAN PROGRAM; PLUS LOANS)

560 JEFFERSON BLVD
WARWICK RI 02886
401-277-2050

AMOUNT: UP TO $4000-UNDERGRADUATE; UP TO $7500 GRADUATE

DEADLINE(S): NONE SPECIFIED

FIELD(S): ALL FIELDS OF STUDY

OPEN TO RHODE ISLAND RESIDENTS OR NON-RESIDENTS ATTENDING AN ELIGIBLE RHODE ISLAND SCHOOL. MUST BE USA CITIZENS OR LEGAL RESIDENTS AND BE ENROLLED AT LEAST HALF TIME. RHODE ISLAND RESIDENTS MAY ATTEND SCHOOLS OUTSIDE THE STATE.

MUST DEMONSTRATE FINANCIAL NEED. WRITE FOR CURRENT INTEREST RATES AND COMPLETE INFORMATION.

1608 —————————————————

SACHS FOUNDATION (SCHOLARSHIP PROGRAM)

90 S. CASCADE AVE.; SUITE 1410
COLORADO SPRINGS CO 80903
719/633-2353

AMOUNT: $3000

DEADLINE(S): MAR 1

FIELD(S): ALL AREAS OF STUDY

OPEN TO BLACK RESIDENTS OF COLORADO WHO ARE HIGH SCHOOL GRADUATES; USA CITIZENS; HAVE A 3.4 OR BETTER GPA AND CAN DEMONSTRATE FINANCIAL NEED. AWARDS ARE FOR UNDERGRADUATE OR GRADUATE STUDY AT ANY ACCREDITED COLLEGE OR UNIVERSITY.

50 SCHOLARSHIPS PER YEAR. RENEWABLE IF STUDENT MAINTAINS A 2.5 OR BETTER GPA. GRANTS ARE FOR UP TO 4 YEARS IN DURATION. WRITE FOR COMPLETE INFORMATION.

1609 —————————————————

SAINT ANDREW'S SOCIETY OF THE STATE OF NEW YORK (GRADUATE SCHOLARSHIP PROGRAM)

71 W 23RD ST 10TH FL
NEW YORK NY 10010
212/807-1730

AMOUNT: UP TO $12000

DEADLINE(S): NOV 30

FIELD(S): ALL FIELDS OF STUDY

OPEN TO UNDERGRADUATE SENIORS AT ACCREDITED USA INSTITUTIONS WHO ARE OF SCOTTISH ANCESTRY. SCHOLARSHIPS ARE FOR A YEAR OF GRADUATE STUDY AT A SCOTTISH UNIVERSITY.

PREFERENCE TO APPLICANTS WHO HAVE NOT STUDIED IN GREAT BRITAIN. FINANCAL NEED IS A CONSIDERATION. WRITE FOR COMPLETE INFORMATION.

1610 —————————————————

SAN FRANCISCO STATE UNIVERSITY (OVER-60 PROGRAM)

ADMISSIONS OFFICE; 1600 HOLLOWAY AVE
SAN FRANCISCO CA 94132
415/338-2037

AMOUNT: ADMISSIONS AND REGISTRATION FEES WAIVER

DEADLINE(S): NONE

FIELD(S): ALL FIELDS

OPEN TO CALIFORNIA RESIDENTS OVER 60 YEARS OF AGE WHO HAVE LIVED IN THE STATE FOR AT LEAST ONE YEAR BY SEPTEMBER 20TH. MUST MEET THE UNIVERSITY'S REGULAR ADMISSIONS STANDARDS. TOTAL COST IS $3 PER SEMESTER.

WRITE ADMISSIONS OFFICE FOR COMPLETE INFORMATION.

1611 —————————————————

SAN JOSE STATE UNIVERSITY (SCHOLARSHIPS)

FINANCIAL AID OFFICE SJSU-ONE WASHINGTON SQUARE
SAN JOSE CA 95192
408/924-6063

AMOUNT: $50 - $1000

DEADLINE(S): JAN 1 - MAR 1

FIELD(S): ALL FIELDS OF STUDY

SCHOLARSHIPS ARE AWARDED COMPETITIVELY TO STUDENTS ENROLLED AT SAN JOSE STATE ON THE BASIS OF GRADE POINT AVERAGE. MOST REQUIRE A DEMONSTRATION OF FINANCIAL NEED.

STUDENTS INTERESTED IN GRADUATE FELLOWSHIPS AND ASSISTANTSHIPS SHOULD APPLY DIRECTLY TO THEIR DEPARTMENT DEAN'S OFFICE. 450 SCHOLARSHIPS PER YEAR. WRITE FOR COMPLETE INFORMATION.

1612 —————————————————

SAN RAFAEL INDOOR SPORTS CLUB INC. (SCHOLARSHIPS FOR DISABLED STUDENTS)

C/O COLLEGE OF MARIN; FINANCIAL AID OFFICE
KENTFIELD CA 94904
415/924-3549

AMOUNT: $300 PER YEAR

GENERAL

DEADLINE(S): MAY 1

FIELD(S): ALL AREAS OF STUDY

OPEN TO STUDENTS ENROLLED IN OR PLANNING
TO ENROLL IN THE DISABLED STUDENTS
PROGRAM AT THE COLLEGE OF MARIN.
MUST HAVE A COURSE LOAD OF SIX UNITS
OR MORE AND MAINTAIN A 3.0 OR BETTER
GPA.

WRITE FOR COMPLETE INFORMATION.

1613

SCREEN ACTORS GUILD FOUNDATION (JOHN L
DALES SCHOLARSHIP FUND)

7065 HOLLYWOOD BLVD
HOLLYWOOD CA 90028
213/856-6670

AMOUNT: VARIES

DEADLINE(S): MAR 1

FIELD(S): ALL AREAS OF STUDY

SCHOLARSHIPS OPEN TO SAG MEMBERS WITH AT
LEAST 5 YEARS MEMBERSHIP OR
DEPENDENT CHILDREN OF MEMBERS WITH
AT LEAST 8 YEARS MEMBERSHIP. AWARDS
ARE FOR ANY LEVEL OF UNDERGRADUATE;
GRADUATE OR POST-GRADUATE STUDY.

FINANCIAL NEED IS A CONSIDERATION.
RENEWABLE YEARLY WITH REAPPLICATION.
WRITE FOR COMPLETE INFORMATION.

1614

SCRIPPS HOWARD FOUNDATION (ELLEN B.
SCRIPPS FELLOWSHIPS)

312 WALNUT ST - 28TH FLOOR; PO BOX 5380
CINCINNATI OH 45201
513/977-3035

AMOUNT: UP TO $3000

DEADLINE(S): DEC 20 FOR AN APPLICATION; FEB
25 FOR MAILING IN APPLICATION

FIELD(S): ALL FIELDS OF STUDY

FELLOWSHIPS FOR WORKING JOURNALISTS WHO
WANT TO PURSUE FURTHER EDUCATION AT
AN ACCREDITED UNIVERSITY IN ANY FIELD
OF GRADUATE STUDIES. PURPOSE IS TO HELP
JOURNALISTS BECOME MORE PROFICIENT IN
THEIR SPECIALTY. USA CITIZEN OR LEGAL
RESIDENT.

QUALIFIED APPLICANTS SHOULD SUBMIT SELF-
ADDRESSED TYPEWRITTEN MAILING LABEL
WITH REQUEST FOR AN APPLICATION
PREFERABLY DURING NOVEMBER BUT
BEFORE DEC. 20.

1615

SEMINOLE TRIBE OF FLORIDA (HIGHER
EDUCATION AWARDS)

6073 STIRLING ROAD
HOLLYWOOD FL 33024
305/321-1047

AMOUNT: VARIES

DEADLINE(S): APR 15; JUL 15; NOV 15

FIELD(S): ALL AREAS OF STUDY

OPEN TO ENROLLED MEMBERS OF THE SEMINOLE
TRIBE OF FLORIDA OR TO THOSE ELIIBIBLE
TO BECOME A MEMBER. FOR
UNDERGRADUATE OR GRADUATE STUDY AT
AN ACCREDITED COLLEGE OR UNIVERSITY.

AWARDS RENEWABLE. WRITE FOR COMPLETE
INFORMATION.

1616

SENECA NATION HIGHER EDUCATION
(EDUCATION GRANTS)

BOX 231
SALAMANCA NY 14779
716/945-1790

AMOUNT: UP TO $5000

DEADLINE(S): JUL 15; DEC 31; MAY 20

FIELD(S): ALL AREAS OF STUDY

ENROLLED MEMBERS OF THE SENECA NATION OF
INDIANS WHO ARE IN NEED OF FUNDING FOR
POST-SECONDARY EDUCATION AND ARE
ACCEPTED IN AN ACCREDITED PROGRAM OF
STUDY. FUNDS MAY BE USED TOWARD
ASSOCIATES; BACHELORS; MASTERS OR
DOCTORS DEGREE.

AWARD IS BASED ON FINANCIAL NEED. WRITE
FOR COMPLETE INFORMATION.

1617

SMITHSONIAN INSTITUTION (GRADUATE; PRE-
DOCTORAL; POST-DOCTORAL & SENIOR
POSTDOCTORAL FELLOWSHIPS)

OFFICE OF FELLOWSHIPS AND GRANTS; 955
L'ENFANT PLAZA; ROOM 7300
WASHINGTON DC 20560
908/287-2371

AMOUNT: VARIES

DEADLINE(S): JAN 15

FIELD(S): ALL FIELDS OF STUDY

FELLOWSHIPS FOR RESEARCH IN RESIDENCE
USING THE SMITHSONIAN'S COLLECTIONS &
FACILITES. OPEN TO GRADUATE STUDENTS;
PH.D CANDIDATES WORKING ON THEIR
DISSERTATION; POST-DOCTORAL
RESEARCHERS & PROFESSIONAL SCHOLARS.

WRITE FOR COMPLETE INFORMATION.

1618

SONS OF ITALY FOUNDATION (NATIONAL LEADERSHIP GRANTS)

219 'E' STREET NE
WASHINGTON DC 20002
202/547-2900

AMOUNT: $2000

DEADLINE(S): MAR 15

FIELD(S): ALL FIELDS OF STUDY

NATIONAL LEADERSHIP GRANT COMPETITION IS OPEN TO ANY FULL-TIME STUDENT OF ITALIAN HERITAGE STUDYING AT AN ACCREDITED COLLEGE OR UNIVERSITY. FOR UNDERGRADUATE OR GRADUATE STUDY.

WRITE FOR COMPLETE INFORMATION. ALSO CONTACT LOCAL AND STATE LODGES WHICH ALSO OFFER SCHOLARSHIPS TO MEMBERS AND THEIR CHILDREN.

1619

SOUTH CAROLINA STUDENT LOAN CORPORATION

P.O. BOX 21487
COLUMBIA SC 29221
803/798-0916

AMOUNT: $2625 PER YEAR FROSH/SOPH; $4000 PER YEAR JR/SR; $7500 PER YEAR GRAD

DEADLINE(S): 30 DAYS BEFORE END OF LOAN PERIOD

FIELD(S): ALL AREAS OF STUDY

OPEN TO USA CITIZENS OR ELIGIBLE NON-CITIZENS. MUST BE ENROLLED OR ACCEPTED FOR ENROLLMENT AT AN ELIGIBLE POST-SECONDARY SCHOOL. AMOUNT OF LOAN DETERMINED BY COST OF SCHOOL AND FINANCIAL NEED.

INTEREST BEGINS AT 8% AND INCREASES TO 10% AT FIFTH YEAR OF REPAYMENT. LOAN MUST BE RENEWED ANNUALLY. WRITE FOR COMPLETE INFORMATION.

1620

SOUTH DAKOTA EDUCATION ASSISTANCE CORPORATION (GUARANTEED STUDENT LOAN PROGRAM - STAFFORD; PLUS AND SLS LOANS)

115 FIRST AVE. SW
ABERDEEN SD 57401
605/225-6423

AMOUNT: VARIES

DEADLINE(S): NONE

FIELD(S): ALL AREAS OF STUDY

SOUTH DAKOTA RESIDENT ENROLLED IN AN ELIGIBLE SCHOOL ON AT LEAST A HALF-TIME BASIS. US CITIZEN OR LEGAL RESIDENT.

LOANS ARE RENEWABLE. WRITE FOR COMPLETE INFORMATION.

1621

STEVEN KNEZEVICH TRUST (GRANTS)

100 E. WISCONSIN AVE. SUITE 1020
MILWAUKEE WI 53202
414-271-6364

AMOUNT: $100 TO $800

DEADLINE(S): NOV 1

FIELD(S): ALL AREAS OF STUDY

UNDERGRADUATE & GRADUATE GRANTS FOR STUDENTS OF SERBIAN DESCENT. MUST ESTABLISH EVIDENCE OF ANCESTRAL HERITAGE. IT IS COMMON PRACTICE FOR STUDENTS TO BE INTERVIEWED IN MILWAUKEE PRIOR TO GRANTING THE AWARD.

ADDRESS INQUIRIES TO STANLEY HACK. INCLUDE SELF-ADDRESSED STAMPED ENVELOPE.

1622

STUDENT AID FOUNDATION (LOANS)

1393 SHEFFIELD PARKWAY
MARIETTA GA 30062
404/973-0256

AMOUNT: UNDERGRADUATES $2500 PER YEAR; GRADUATE STUDENTS $3000 PER YEAR

DEADLINE(S): APR 15

FIELD(S): ALL AREAS OF STUDY

LOANS AVAILABLE ONLY TO WOMEN WHO ARE RESIDENTS OF GEORGIA OR ARE ATTENDING SCHOOLS IN GEORGIA. GRADES; FINANCIAL NEED; PERSONAL INTEGRITY AND SENSE OF RESPONSIBILITY ARE CONSIDERATIONS.

35 LOANS PER YEAR. RENEWABLE WITH REAPPLICATION.

1623

SWEDISH INSTITUTE (SCHOLARSHIPS FOR STUDY OR RESEARCH IN SWEDEN)

PO BOX 7434
S-103 91 STOCKHOLM SWEDEN
WRITTEN INQUIRY

AMOUNT: SEK 6700 PER MONTH

DEADLINE(S): APPLICATIONS AVAILABLE - ONLY- BETWEEN SEP 1 AND DEC 1

FIELD(S): ALL FIELDS OF STUDY

OPEN TO STUDENTS & RESEARCHERS WHO ARE - NOT- SWEDISH CITIZENS. FOR STUDY OR RESEARCH IN SWEDEN WHEN IT CANNOT BE DONE EQUALLY AS WELL IN ANOTHER COUNTRY. DURATION IS NORMALLY 1 ACADEMIC YEAR. KNOWLEDGE OF SWEDISH OR ENGLISH REQUIRED.

GENERAL

AWARDS TENABLE AT ANY SWEDISH UNIVERSITY; EDUCATIONAL INSTITUTION OR FOR INDEPENDENT RESEARCH. WRITE FOR COMPLETE INFORMATION.

1624

TEXAS A & M UNIVERSITY (ACADEMIC EXCELLENCE AWARDS)

STUDENT FINANCIAL AID OFFICE
COLLEGE STATION TX 77843
409/845-5852

AMOUNT: $500 - $1500

DEADLINE(S): MAR 1

FIELD(S): ALL FIELDS OF STUDY

OPEN TO FULL-TIME UNDERGRADUATE & GRADUATE STUDENTS AT TEXAS A & M UNIVERSITY. AWARDS ARE INTENDED TO RECOGNIZE & ASSIST STUDENTS WHO ARE MAKING EXCELLENT SCHOLASTIC PROGRESS.

APPROX 500 AWARDS PER YEAR. AWARDS GRANTED FOR ONE YEAR. APPLICATIONS ARE AVAILABLE AT THE STUDENT FINANCIAL AID OFFICE DURING JANUARY & FEBRUARY.

1625

TEXAS COMMERCE BANK (FRANKLIN LINDSEY STUDENT LOAN FUND)

PO BOX 550
AUSTIN TX 78789
512/476-6611

AMOUNT: UP TO $3000 PER ACADEMIC YEAR

DEADLINE(S): MAY 1

FIELD(S): ALL FIELDS OF STUDY

LOANS AVAILABLE TO STUDENTS WHO HAVE COMPLETED AT LEAST 1 YEAR AT A TEXAS COLLEGE OR UNIVERSITY & HAVE MAINTAINED NO LESS THAN A 'C' AVERAGE FOR ALL COURSEWORK.

WRITE FOR COMPLETE INFORMATION.

1626

TEXAS HIGHER EDUCATION COORDINATING BOARD (SCHOLARSHIPS; GRANTS & LOANS)

PO BOX 12788; CAPITOL STATION
AUSTIN TX 78711
512/483-6340

AMOUNT: VARIES

DEADLINE(S): VARIES WITH PROGRAM

FIELD(S): ALL FIELDS OF STUDY

OPEN TO TEXAS RESIDENTS ATTENDING TEXAS INSTITUTIONS. NUMEROUS STATE-ADMINISTERED STUDENT FINANCIAL AID PROGRAMS INCLUDING SCHOLARSHIPS; GRANTS & LOANS.

CONTACT YOUR SCHOOL'S FINANCIAL AID OFFICE OR WRITE TO THE ADDRESS AVOVE FOR THE BOOKLET 'FINANCIAL AID FOR TEXAS STUDENTS' WHICH DESCRIBES ALL PROGRAMS IN DETAIL.

1627

TEXAS SWEDISH CULTURAL FOUNDATION (SCHOLARSHIPS FOR STUDY IN SWEDEN)

C/O MRS GUDRUN WALLGREN MERRILL; 2234 INWOOD DR
HOUSTON TX 77019
713/522-7154

AMOUNT: $2500

DEADLINE(S): FEB 1

FIELD(S): ALL FIELDS OF STUDY

OPEN TO YOUNG OUTSTANDING GRADUATES OF INSTITUTES OF HIGHER LEARNING FOR CONTINUED STUDIES IN SWEDEN FOR TEXAS STUDENTS AND IN TEXAS FOR SWEDISH STUDENTS. APPLICANTS MUST BE LEGAL RESIDENTS OF TEXAS OR OF SWEDEN.

WRITE FOR COMPLETE INFORMATION.

1628

THETA DELTA CHI EDUCATIONAL FOUNDATION (SCHOLARSHIP)

135 BAY STATE ROAD
BOSTON MA 02215
WRITTEN INQUIRY

AMOUNT: $1000

DEADLINE(S): APR 30

FIELD(S): ALL FIELDS OF STUDY

SCHOLARSHIPS OPEN TO ACTIVE MEMBERS OF THETA DELTA CHI. CONSIDERATIONS INCLUDE PAST SERVICE TO THE FRATERNITY; SCHOLASTIC ACHIEVEMENTS AND PROMISE AND FINANCIAL NEED. PREFERENCE TO UNDERGRADS BUT GRADUATE STUDENTS WILL BE CONSIDERED.

WRITE FOR COMPLETE INFORMATION.

1629

THOMAS J. WATSON FOUNDATION (FELLOWSHIP PROGRAM)

217 ANGELL ST
PROVIDENCE RI 02906
401/274-1952

AMOUNT: $15000 SINGLE; $21000 WITH ACCOMPANYING FINANCIAL AND LEGAL DEPENDENT

DEADLINE(S): NOV 1

FIELD(S): ALL FIELDS OF STUDY

OPEN TO GRADUATING SENIORS AT THE 52 USA COLLEGES ON THE FOUNDATION'S ROSTER. FELLOWSHIP PROVIDES FOR ONE YEAR OF INDEPENDENT STUDY AND TRAVEL ABROAD IMMEDIATELY FOLLOWING GRADUATION.

CANDIDATES MUST BE NOMINATED BY THEIR COLLEGE. UP TO 65 AWARDS PER YEAR. WRITE FOR LIST OF PARTICIPATING INSTITUTIONS AND COMPLETE INFORMATION.

1630

TOWSON STATE UNIVERSITY

SCHOLARSHIP OFFICE
TOWSON MD 21204
301/321-3702

AMOUNT: VARIES

DEADLINE(S): VARIOUS

FIELD(S): ALL FIELDS OF STUDY

NUMEROUS SCHOLARSHIP AND AWARD PROGRAMS AVAILABLE TO ENTERING FRESHMEN AND TO GRADUATE AND TRANSFER STUDENTS.

WRITE FOR SCHOLARSHIPS AND AWARDS BOOKLET WHICH DESCRIBES EACH PROGRAM IN DETAIL.

1631

TULANE UNIVERSITY (SCHOLARSHIPS & FELLOWSHIPS)

ADMISSIONS OFFICE
NEW ORLEANS LA 70118
504/865-5731

AMOUNT: VARIES

DEADLINE(S): VARIOUS

FIELD(S): ALL AREAS OF STUDY

NUMEROUS SCHOLARSHIP & FELLOWSHIP PROGRAMS FOR UNDERGRADUATE & GRADUATE STUDY AT TULANE UNIVERSITY. THERE ALSO IS AN HONORS PROGRAM FOR OUTSTANDING STUDENTS ACCEPTED FOR ENROLLMENT AT TULANE.

WRITE FOR COMPLETE INFORMATION.

1632

U.S. COAST GUARD MUTUAL ASSISTANCE (ADMIRAL ROLAND STUDENT LOAN PROGRAM)

COAST GUARD HEADQUARTERS (GZMA)
WASHINGTON DC 20593
202/267-1683

AMOUNT: UP TO $2700 PER YEAR (UNDERGRADUATES); $7500 (GRADUATES)

DEADLINE(S): NONE SPECIFIED

FIELD(S): ALL AREAS OF STUDY

FOR MEMBERS & DEPENDENTS OF COAST GUARD MUTUAL ASSISTANCE MEMBERS WHO ARE ENROLLED AT LEAST ONE-HALF TIME IN AN APPROVED POST-SECONDARY SCHOOL.

LOANS RENEWABLE FOR UP TO FOUR YEARS. MUST REAPPLY ANNUALLY. WRITE FOR COMPLETE INFORMATION.

1633

U.S. DEPT. OF INTERIOR; BUREAU OF INDIAN AFFAIRS (HIGHER EDUCATION GRANT PROGRAM)

MS 3530 - MIB 5422
WASHINGTON DC 20240
202/208-4871

AMOUNT: VARIES DEPENDING ON NEED

DEADLINE(S): VARIES

FIELD(S): ALL AREAS OF STUDY

OPEN TO ENROLLED MEMBERS OF INDIAN TRIBES OR ALASKA NATIVE DESCENDANTS ELIGIBLE TO RECEIVE SERVICES FROM THE SECRETARY OF THE INTERIOR. FOR STUDY LEADING TO ASSOCIATES; BACHELORS OR GRADUATE DEGREE.

MUST DEMONSTRATE FINANCIAL NEED. - CONTACT HOME AGENCY; TRIBE OR BIA AREA OFFICE - OR FINANCIAL AID OFFICE AT CHOSEN COLLEGE.

1634

UNITED DAUGHTERS OF THE CONFEDERACY (SCHOLARSHIPS)

BUSINESS OFFICE; MEMORIAL BLDG; 328 NORTH BLVD.
RICHMOND VA 23220
804/355-1636

AMOUNT: $400 - $1500

DEADLINE(S): FEB 15

FIELD(S): ALL AREAS OF STUDY

OPEN TO DESCENDANTS OF WORTHY CONFEDERATE VETERANS. APPLICANTS WHO ARE COLLATERAL DESCENDANTS MUST BE ACTIVE MEMBERS OF THE UNITED DAUGHTERS OF THE CONFEDERACY OR OF THE CHILDREN OF THE CONFEDERACY & MUST BE SPONSORED BY A UDC CHAPTER.

MOST AWARDS FOR UNDERGRADUATE STUDY. FOR COMPLETE INFORMATION SEND STAMPED SELF-ADDRESSED #10 ENVELOPE TO ADDRESS ABOVE OR CONTACT THE EDUCATION DIRECTOR IN THE DIVISION WHERE YOU RESIDE.

1635

UNITED FOOD & COMMERCIAL WORKERS UNION - LOCAL 555 (SCHOLARSHIP PROGRAM)

PO BOX 23555
TIGARD OR 97223
503/684-2822

AMOUNT: $900 - $1200

DEADLINE(S): MAR 15

FIELD(S): ALL FIELDS OF STUDY

PROGRAM OPEN -ONLY- TO LOCAL 555 MEMBERS (IN GOOD STANDING FOR AT LEAST 1 YEAR); THEIR CHILDREN & SPOUSES. SCHOLARSHIPS MAY BE USED AT ANY ACCREDITED UNIVERSITY; COLLEGE; TECHNICAL-VOCATIONAL SCHOOL; JUNIOR COLLEGE OR COMMUNITY COLLEGE.

WRITE FOR COMPLETE INFORMATION -ONLY- IF YOU ARE A UFCW LOCAL 555 MEMBER OR RELATIVE OF A MEMBER.

1636

UNITED NEGRO COLLEGE FUND (SCHOLARSHIPS)

EDUCATIONAL SERVICES DEPARTMENT; 500 E. 62ND ST.
NEW YORK NY 10021
212/326-1100

AMOUNT: $500 TO $7500 PER YEAR

DEADLINE(S): VARIES

FIELD(S): ALL AREAS OF STUDY

SCHOLARSHIPS AVAILABLE TO STUDENTS WHO ENROLL IN ONE OF THE 41 UNITED NEGRO COLLEGE FUND MEMBER INSTITUTIONS. FINANCIAL NEED MUST BE ESTABLISHED THROUGH THE FINANCIAL AID OFFICE AT A UNCF COLLEGE.

FOR INFORMATION AND A LIST OF THE UNCF CAMPUSES WRITE TO THE ADDRESS ABOVE.

1637

UNITED STUDENT AID FUNDS INC. (GUARANTEED STUDENT LOAN PROGRAM; PLUS LOANS)

1912 CAPITOL AVE #320
CHEYENNE WY 82001
307/635-3259

AMOUNT: $2645 - $4000 UNDERGRADUATES; $7500 GRADUATES

DEADLINE(S): NONE

FIELD(S): ALL FIELDS OF STUDY

LOW-INTEREST LOANS ARE AVAILABLE TO WYOMING RESIDENTS WHO ARE CITIZENS OR PERMANENT RESIDENTS OF THE USA & ENROLLED AT LEAST 1/2 TIME IN SCHOOL. MUST DEMONSTRATE FINANCIAL NEED.

WRITE FOR COMPLETE INFORMATION.

1638

UNIVERSITY OF CAMBRIDGE-CORPUS CHRISTI COLLEGE (RESEARCH SCHOLARSHIPS)

TUTOR FOR ADVANCED STUDIES
CAMBRIDGE CB2 1RH ENGLAND
022/333-8063

AMOUNT: TUITION + 4300 POUNDS STERLING (MAINTENANCE ALLOWANCE)

DEADLINE(S): MAR 30

FIELD(S): ALL AREAS OF STUDY

FOR POST-GRADUATE STUDY. OPEN TO STUDENTS WHO APPLY TO THE BOARD OF GRADUATE STUDIES AND WHO NAME CORPUS CHRISTI COLLEGE AS THEIR COLLEGE OF PREFERENCE.

AWARDS ARE RENEWABLE FOR UP TO 3 YEARS. WRITE FOR COMPLETE INFORMATION.

1639

UNIVERSITY OF CAMBRIDGE-WOLFSON COLLEGE (BURSARIES)

BARTON ROAD
CAMBRIDGE CAMS CB3 9BB ENGLAND
0223-335900

AMOUNT: VARIES

DEADLINE(S): APR 30

FIELD(S): ALL FIELDS OF STUDY

BURSARIES AWARDED TO POST-GRADUATE STUDENTS ADMITTED TO WOLFSON COLLEGE.

RENEWABLE. WRITE DR. E. CRUWYS; ADDRESS ABOVE; FOR COMPLETE INFORMATION.

1640

UNIVERSITY OF EDINBURGH (POST-GRADUATE STUDENTSHIP)

OLD COLLEGE SOUTH BRIDGE
EDINBURGH EH8 9YL SCOTLAND UK
031/650-2159

AMOUNT: APPROX 5% BELOW THE VALUE OF RESEARCH COUNCIL OR OTHER GOVERNMENT-FUNDED AWARDS FOR SUBJECT PLUS FEES AT THE HOME RATE.

DEADLINE(S): APR 30

FIELD(S): ALL FIELDS OF STUDY (RESEARCH DEGREES ONLY)

STUDENTSHIPS AWARDED TO BEST QUALIFIED APPLICANTS FOR POST-GRADUATE RESEARCH DEGREES AT THE UNIVERSITY. OPEN TO ALL NATIONALITIES.

AWARDS RENEWABLE FOR UP TO TWO YEARS. APPROXIMATELY 10 NEW AWARDS PER YEAR. WRITE FOR COMPLETE INFORMATION.

1641

UNIVERSITY OF EXETER (POST-GRADUATE SCHOLARSHIPS)

ASST. REGISTRAR; POSTGRADUATE ADMISSIONS; NORTHCOTE HOUSE; THE QUEEN'S DRIVE
EXETER EX4 4QJ DEVON ENGLAND
WRITTEN INQUIRY

AMOUNT: FEES AND MAINTENANCE ALLOWANCE

DEADLINE(S): MAY 30

FIELD(S): ALL AREAS OF STUDY

OPEN TO APPLICANTS WHO HAVE BEEN OFFERED A PLACE TO STUDY FOR A HIGHER DEGREE AT EXETER UNIVERSITY. NOMINATIONS ARE SUBMITTED BY DEPARTMENTS; NOT THE STUDENT.

APPROX 20 AWARDS PER YEAR. FOR STUDY AT THE UNIVERSITY OF EXETER ONLY. RENEWABLE FOR A MAXIMUM OF THREE YEARS. WRITE FOR COMPLETE INFORMATION.

1642

UNIVERSITY OF GUELPH (GRADUATE VISA STUDENT SCHOLARSHIP)

FACULTY OF GRADUATE STUDIES
GUELPH ONTARIO NIG 2W1 CANADA
519/824-4120 EXT 2441

AMOUNT: $5000 - $9500

DEADLINE(S): MAR 1; JUL 1; NOV 1

FIELD(S): ALL FIELDS OF STUDY

OPEN TO NON-CANADIANS ACCEPTED FOR GRADUATE STUDY AT THE UNIVERSITY WHO ARE OUTSTANDING STUDENTS WITH "FIRST CLASS" GRADE AVERAGE. STUDENTS MUST BE NOMINATED BY DEPARTMENT HEAD; THEY MAY NOT MAKE APPLICATION.

20 AWARDS PER YEAR. CONTINUATION OF AWARD IS CONTINGENT ON MAINTENANCE OF A HIGH ACADEMIC PERFORMANCE.

1643

UNIVERSITY OF IOWA (GRADUATE ASSISTANTSHIP)

LABOR CENTER M210 OH
IOWA CITY IA 52242
319/335-4144

AMOUNT: $3800 STIPEND

DEADLINE(S): APR 15

FIELD(S): ALL AREAS OF STUDY

OPEN TO MEMBER OR DEPENDENT OF A MEMBER IN THE IOWA FEDERATION OF LABOR AFL-CIO. MUST DEMONSTRATE FINANCIAL NEED & BE ACCEPTED INTO A GRADUATE OR PROFESSIONAL PROGRAM OF STUDY AT THE UNIVERSITY OF IOWA.

THE 9-MONTH APPOINTMENT REQUIRES THAT THE STUDENT ALLOCATE 10 HOURS OF PROFESSIONAL ACTIVITY PER WEEK.

1644

UNIVERSITY OF IOWA FOUNDATION (DAVID BRAVERMAN SCHOLARSHIP)

C/O UNIV OF IOWA; SERVICES FOR PERSONS WITH DISABILITIES; 3101 BURGE HALL
IOWA CITY IA 52242
319/335-1462

AMOUNT: $1500

DEADLINE(S): APR 15

FIELD(S): ALL AREAS OF STUDY

SCHOLARSHIPS AVAILABLE TO PHYSICALLY DISABLED STUDENTS WHO HAVE BEEN ACCEPTED IN A UNIVERSITY OF IOWA GRADUATE OR PROFESSIONAL PROGRAM. APPLICANTS MUST BE ABLE TO DEMONSTRATE ACADEMIC ABILITY AND SERVICE TO THE COMMUNITY.

WRITE FOR COMPLETE INFORMATION.

1645

UNIVERSITY OF LONDON (OVERSEAS RESEARCH STUDENTS FEE SUPPORT SCHEME)

SENATE HOUSE; ROOM 21A; MALET ST
LONDON WC1E 7HU ENGLAND
01-636-8000

AMOUNT: VARIES

DEADLINE(S): NONE

FIELD(S): ALL AREAS OF STUDY

PROGRAM TO SUPPORT FOREIGN STUDENTS WHO WISH TO DO POST-GRADUATE WORK AT THE UNIVERSITY OF LONDON. APPLICANTS MUST BE A GRADUATE OF A RECOGNIZED COLLEGE OR UNIVERSITY.

FOR APPLICATION WRITE TO THE COMMITTEE OF VICE-CHANCELLORS & PRINCIPALS; 29 TAVISTOCK SQUARE; LONDON WC1 9EZ ENGLAND.

1646

UNIVERSITY OF OXFORD-ST. CATHERINE'S COLLEGE (GRADUATE SCHOLARSHIPS)

MANOR ROAD; ATTN SENIOR TUTOR
OXFORD OX1 3UJ ENGLAND
0865-249541

AMOUNT: 1500 POUNDS STERLING

DEADLINE(S): APR 30

FIELD(S): ALL FIELDS OF STUDY

COMPETITIVE SCHOLARSHIPS ARE AVAILABLE TO NON-BRITISH CITIZENS FOR GRADUATE STUDY AT ST. CATHERINE'S COLLEGE AT OXFORD UNIVERSITY.

AWARDS ARE RENEWABLE. WRITE FOR COMPLETE INFORMATION.

1647

UNIVERSITY OF OXFORD-SOMERVILLE COLLEGE (JANET WATSON BURSARY)

COLLEGE SECRETARY; SOMERVILLE COLLEGE
OXFORD OX2 6HD ENGLAND
865-270600

AMOUNT: 2400 POUNDS STERLING

DEADLINE(S): APR 1

FIELD(S): ALL FIELDS OF STUDY

BURSARY IS OFFERED FOR A USA WOMAN GRADUATE WISHING TO READ FOR A FURTHER DEGREE AT OXFORD AS A MEMBER OF THE COLLEGE. SOMERVILLE ADMITS ONLY WOMEN. USA CITIZEN.

RENEWABLE FOR A SECOND YEAR. WRITE FOR COMPLETE INFORMATION.

1648

UNIVERSITY OF TENNESSEE (HILTON A SMITH FELLOWSHIP)

218 STUDENT SERVICES BLDG
KNOXVILLE TN 37996
615/974-3251

AMOUNT: TUITION & FEES + $5000 STIPEND

DEADLINE(S): FEB 15

FIELD(S): ALL AREAS OF STUDY

OPEN TO ANY FULL TIME GRADUATE STUDENT ADMITTED TO OR ALREADY ATTENDING THE UNIV OF TENN (KNOXVILLE). GPA OF 3.6 OR BETTER IS REQUIRED & APPLICANTS SHOULD HAVE SUPERIOR RANKINGS ON RATING FORMS. MUST REAPPLY EACH YEAR FOR RENEWAL.

15-25 AWARDS PER YEAR. WRITE TO THE OFFICE OF GRADUATE ADMISSIONS & RECORDS FOR COMPLETE INFORMATION.

1649

UNIVERSITY OF TENNESSEE KNOXVILLE (GRADUATE & PROFESSIONAL OPPORTUNITIES PROGRAM)

GRADUATE SCHOOL; 404 ANDY HOLT TOWER
KNOXVILLE TN 37996
615/974-2475

AMOUNT: TUITION & FEES + $10000 STIPEND (MAXIMUM)

DEADLINE(S): VARIES

FIELD(S): ALL FIELDS OF STUDY

GRADUATE FELLOWSHIPS OPEN TO BLACK AMERICANS WHO ARE ENTERING AN APPROVED PROGRAM AT THE UNIVERSITY OF TENNESSEE KNOXVILLE. AWARD IS RENEWABLE FOR 1-2 YEARS. USA CITIZEN.

WRITE FOR COMPLETE INFORMATION.

1650

VIRGINIA DEPT OF VETERANS' AFFAIRS (WAR ORPHANS EDUCATION PROGRAM)

PO BOX 809; 210 FRANKLIN RD SW #1012
ROANOKE VA 24004
703/857-7104

AMOUNT: FREE TUITION

DEADLINE(S): NONE

FIELD(S): ALL FIELDS OF STUDY

OPEN TO SURVIVING/DEPENDENT CHILDREN (AGED 16-25) OF USA MILITARY PERSONNEL WHO WERE/ARE VIRGINIA RESIDENTS & AS A RESULT OF WAR/ARMED CONFLICT ARE DECEASED; DISABLED; PRISONER OF WAR OR MISSING IN ACTION.

ELIGIBLE APPLICANTS ENTITLED TO UP TO 48 MONTHS OF FREE TUITION AT ANY STATE SUPPORTED VOCATIONAL; UNDERGRADUATE OR GRADUATE INSTITUTION. WRITE FOR COMPLETE INFORMATION.

1651

VIRGINIA STATE COUNCIL OF HIGHER EDUCATION (TUITION ASSISTANCE GRANT PROGRAM)

101 N.14TH ST; JAMES MONROE BLDG
RICHMOND VA 23219
804/225-2141

AMOUNT: $1275

DEADLINE(S): JUL 31; SEP 10

FIELD(S): ALL AREAS OF STUDY

OPEN TO VIRGINIA RESIDENTS WHO ARE FULL-TIME UNDERGRADUATE; GRADUATE OR PROFESSIONAL STUDENTS AT ELIGIBLE PRIVATE COLLEGES & UNIVERSITIES IN VIRGINIA.

GRANTS ARE RENEWABLE UP TO 4 YEARS FOR UNDERGRADUATE STUDENTS & UP TO 3 YEARS FOR GRADUATE STUDENTS. WRITE FOR COMPLETE INFORMATION.

1652

VIRGINIA STUDENT ASSISTANCE AUTHORITIES (GUARANTEED STUDENT LOAN PROGRAMS)

411 E FRANKLIN ST SUITE 300
RICHMOND VA 23219
804/755-4000 OR 800/792-LOAN

AMOUNT: VARIES

DEADLINE(S): NONE

FIELD(S): ALL FIELDS OF STUDY

VARIOUS LOAN PROGRAMS OPEN TO STUDENTS ENROLLED IN APPROVED INSTITUTIONS. ELIGIBILITY GOVERNED BY SEAA & FEDERAL REGULATIONS.

CONTACT COLLEGE FINANCIAL AID OFFICE OR WRITE TO ADDRESS ABOVE FOR COMPLETE INFORMATION.

1653

W.K. KELLOGG FOUNDATION (NATIONAL FELLOWSHIP PROGRAM)

1 MICHIGAN AVE E.
BATTLE CREEK MI 49017
800/367-0873

AMOUNT: $35000 OVER THREE YEARS

DEADLINE(S): DEC 15

FIELD(S): LEADERSHIP DEVELOPMENT

OPEN TO PROFESSIONALS IN THE EARLY YEARS OF THEIR CAREER (2 TO 12 YEARS AFTER COMPLETING EDUCATION) WHO ARE OF EXCEPTIONAL MERIT AND COMPETENCE. FELLOWS MAINTAIN THEIR PRESENT EMPLOYMENT WHILE PURSUING FELLOWSHIP ACTIVITIES.

THIS IS A LEADERSHIP DEVELOPMENT PROGRAM. NOT OPEN TO GOVERNMENT OFFICIALS; SPOUSES OR DEPENDENTS. USA CITIZENSHIP REQUIRED.

1654

WASHINGTON POST (THOMAS EWING MEMORIAL EDUCATIONAL GRANTS FOR NEWSPAPER CARRIERS)

1150 15TH ST NW
WASHINGTON DC 20079
202/334-5799

AMOUNT: $1000 - $2000

DEADLINE(S): LAST FRIDAY IN JANUARY

FIELD(S): ALL AREAS

OPEN TO CURRENT POST CARRIERS WHO HAVE BEEN ON-ROUTE THE PAST 18 MONTHS. AWARD IS INTENDED TO ASSIST & ENCOURAGE PURSUIT OF HIGHER EDUCATION AT ANY LEVEL.

25-35 AWARDS PER YEAR. WRITE FOR COMPLETE INFORMATION.

1655

WASHINGTON UNIVERSITY IN ST LOUIS (OLIN FELLOWSHIPS FOR WOMEN IN GRADUATE STUDY)

GRADUATE SCHOOL OF ARTS AND SCIENCES BOX 1187
ST LOUIS MO 63130
314/935-6848

AMOUNT: $16000 - $32000

DEADLINE(S): FEB 1

FIELD(S): ALL FIELDS OF STUDY

OPEN TO ANY FEMALE GRADUATE OF AN UNDERGRADUATE INSTITUTION IN THE USA WHO PLANS TO PREPARE FOR A CAREER IN HIGHER EDUCATION OR THE PROFESSIONS THROUGH ADVANCED STUDY AT WASHINGTON UNIVERSITY.

AWARDS ARE RENEWABLE FOR A PERIOD OF FOUR YEARS OR UNTIL THE COMPLETION OF THE PROGRAM WHICHEVER IS FIRST.

1656

WASIE FOUNDATION (SCHOLARSHIP PROGRAM)

909 FOSHAY TOWER
MINNEAPOLIS MN 55402
612/332-3883

AMOUNT: $1000 - $5000

DEADLINE(S): APR 15

FIELD(S): ALL FIELDS OF STUDY

UNDERGRADUATE & GRADUATE SCHOLARSHIPS OPEN TO QUALIFIED STUDENTS OF POLISH DESCENT WHO ARE OF THE CHRISTIAN FAITH. AWARDS TENABLE ONLY IN MINNESOTA AT 10 SPECIFIED INSTITUTIONS OF HIGHER EDUCATION.

50 AWARDS PER YEAR. WRITE FOR LIST OF MINNESOTA COLLEGES AT WHICH AWARD IS TENABLE. APPLICATIONS ARE SENT OUT IN JANUARY AND MUST BE RECEIVED BY APR 15.

1657

WEST VIRGINIA UNIVERSITY (W.E.B. DUBOIS FELLOWSHIP)

OFFICE OF ACADEMIC AFFAIRS & RESEARCH; PO BOX 6203
MORGANTOWN WV 26506
304/293-2021

AMOUNT: $8000 + TUITION AND MANDATORY FEES

DEADLINE(S): MAR 1

FIELD(S): ALL FIELDS OF STUDY

GRADUATE FELLOWSHIPS AT WEST VIRGINIA UNIV FOR BLACK US CITIZENS. APPLICANTS MUST HAVE BACHELORS DEGREE FROM AN ACCREDITED COLLEGE OR UNIVERSITY & BE ADMITTED TO A GRAD/OR PROFESSIONAL PROGRAM AT WEST VIRGINIA UNIV.

FELLOWSHIPS RENEWABLE. WRITE FOR COMPLETE INFORMATION.

1658

WILLIAM B. RICE AID FUND INC. (SCHOLARSHIP & LOAN PROGRAM)

C/O HUDSON SAVINGS BANK; PO BOX 868
HUDSON MA 01749
508/562-2664

AMOUNT: $1000

DEADLINE(S): APR; JUL & DEC

FIELD(S): ALL AREAS OF STUDY

APPLICANTS MUST BE RESIDENTS OF HUDSON
MASS AND DEMONSTRATE FINANCIAL NEED.
SCHOLARSHIPS ARE AVAILABLE ONLY TO
GRADUATE STUDENTS.

6 SCHOLARSHIPS AND 20 LOANS ARE AVAILABLE.
CONTACT ALEXANDER HARASKU
TREASURER ADDRESS ABOVE FOR
COMPLETE INFORMATION.

1659

WISCONSIN DEPARTMENT OF VETERANS AFFAIRS (DECEASED VETERANS' SURVIVORS ECONOMIC ASSISTANCE LOAN/ EDUCATION GRANTS)

PO BOX 7843
MADISON WI 53707
608/266-1311

AMOUNT: $4500 MAXIMUM

DEADLINE(S): NONE SPECIFIED

FIELD(S): ALL AREAS OF STUDY

OPEN TO SURVIVING SPOUSES (WHO HAVE NOT
REMARRIED) OF DECEASED ELIGIBLE
VETERANS AND TO THE MINOR DEPENDENT
CHILDREN OF THE DECEASED VETERANS.
MUST BE RESIDENTS OF WISCONSIN AT THE
TIME OF APPLICATION.

APPROX 5700 GRANTS AND LOANS PER YEAR.
CONTACT A WISCONSIN VETERANS SERVICE
OFFICER IN YOUR COUNTY OF RESIDENCE
FOR COMPLETE INFORMATION.

1660

WISCONSIN DEPARTMENT OF VETERANS AFFAIRS (VETERANS ECONOMIC ASSISTANCE LOAN/EDUCATION GRANTS)

PO BOX 7843
MADISON WI 53707
608/266-1311

AMOUNT: $4500 MAXIMUM

DEADLINE(S): NONE SPECIFIED

FIELD(S): ALL AREAS OF STUDY

OPEN TO VETERANS (AS DEFINED IN WISCONSIN
STATUTE 45.35-5) WHO ARE LIVING IN
WISCONSIN AT THE TIME OF APPLICATION.
THERE ARE LIMITATIONS ON INCOME.

APPROX 5700 GRANTS AND LOANS PER YEAR.
WRITE FOR COMPLETE INFORMATION.

1661

WISCONSIN HIGHER EDUCATION AIDS BOARD (STUDENT FINANCIAL AID PROGRAM)

PO BOX 7885
MADISON WI 53707
608/267-2206; FAX 608/267-2808

AMOUNT: VARIES

DEADLINE(S): NONE SPECIFIED

FIELD(S): ALL AREAS OF STUDY

BOARD ADMINISTERS A VARIETY OF STATE AND
FEDERAL PROGRAMS THAT ARE AVAILABLE
TO WISCONSIN RESIDENTS WHO ARE
ENROLLED AT LEAST HALF TIME AND
MAINTAIN SATISFACTORY ACADEMIC
RECORD. MOST REQUIRE DEMONSTRATION
OF FINANCIAL NEED.

WRITE FOR COMPLETE INFORMATION.

1662

WOMEN'S RESEARCH AND EDUCATION INSTITUTE (CONGRESSIONAL FELLOWSHIPS FOR WOMEN AND PUBLIC POLICY)

1700 18TH ST NW; SUITE 400
WASHINGTON DC 20009
202/328-7070

AMOUNT: $9000 STIPEND FOR ACADEMIC YEAR +
$1500 FOR TUITION

DEADLINE(S): FEB 14

FIELD(S): GOVERNMENT; PUBLIC SERVICE;
WOMEN'S ISSUES

ANNUAL FELLOWSHIP PROGRAM THAT PLACES
WOMEN GRADUATE STUDENTS IN IN
WASHINGTON DC & ON STRATEGIC
COMMITTEE STAFFS; ENCOURAGING MORE
EFFECTIVE PARTICIPATION BY WOMEN IN
POLICY FORMATION AT ALL LEVELS. USA
CITIZEN OR LEGAL RESIDENT.

FELLOWS ALSO RECEIVE 6 CREDIT-HOURS. 10
FELLOWSHIPS PER YEAR. WRITE FOR
COMPLETE INFORMATION.

1663

WOMEN'S SPORTS FOUNDATION (TRAVEL & TRAINING GRANTS)

342 MADISON AVE #728
NEW YORK NY 10173
212/972-9170

AMOUNT: UP TO $1500 (INDIVIDUAL); UP TO
$3000 (TEAM)

DEADLINE(S): MAR 15; JULY 15; NOV 15

FIELD(S): ALL FIELDS OF STUDY

THIS FUND WAS ESTABLISHED TO PROVIDE ASSISTANCE TO ASPIRING FEMALE ATHLETES & FEMALE TEAMS TO ACHIEVE HIGHER PERFORMANCE LEVELS & RANKING WITHIN THEIR SPORT. USA CITIZEN.

GRANTS ARE AVAILABLE FOR TRAINING; COACHING; EQUIPMENT & TRAVEL TO SCHEDULED COMPETITIVE EVENTS. WRITE FOR COMPLETE INFORMATION.

1664 ─────────────

YAKIMA INDIAN NATION (SCHOLARSHIP PROGRAM)

PO BOX 151
TOPPENISH WA 98948
509/865-5121

AMOUNT: $1000 PER YEAR

DEADLINE(S): JUL 1

FIELD(S): ALL AREAS OF STUDY

PROGRAM OPEN TO ENROLLED MEMBERS OF THE YAKIMA INDIAN NATION. AWARDS TENABLE AT RECOGNIZED UNDERGRADUATE & GRADUATE INSTITUTIONS. USA CITIZEN.

APPROX 200 AWARDS PER YEAR. WRITE FOR COMPLETE INFORMATION.

Helpful Publications

1665

A JOURNALIST'S ROAD TO SUCCESS - A CAREER AND SCHOLARSHIP GUIDE

AUTHOR-DJNF

DOW JONES NEWSPAPER FUND INC
PO BOX 300
PRINCETON NJ 08543

COST-$3 PER COPY

HIGHLY RECOMMENDED FOR PRINT OR BROADCAST COMMUNICATIONS STUDENTS OR JOURNALISTS. COMPREHENSIVE BOOKLET DESCRIBING WHAT AND WHERE TO STUDY; HOW TO PAY FOR IT; WHERE THE JOBS ARE AND HOW TO FIND THEM. TO ORDER CALL 800/DOW-FUND.

1666

ABC'S OF FINANCIAL AID (MONTANA FINANCIAL AID HANDBOOK)

AUTHOR-MONTANA GUARANTEED STUDENT LOAN PROGRAM

MONTANA CAREER INFORMATION SYSTEM
2500 BROADWAY; PO BOX 203101
HELENA MT 59620

COST-FREE

DESCRIBES EDUCATIONAL COSTS AND FINANCIAL AID AVAILABLE IN MONTANA AS WELL AS APPLICATION AND AWARD PROCEDURES AND FINANCIAL AID PROGRAMS.

1667

ACADEMIC YEAR ABROAD

AUTHOR-SARA STEEN; EDITOR

INSTITUTE OF INTERNATIONAL EDUCATION
IIE BOOKS; 809 UNITED NATIONS PLAZA
NEW YORK NY 10017

COST-$39.95 + $3 HANDLING

PROVIDES INFORMATION ON MORE THAN 1900 POST-SECONDARY STUDY PROGRAMS OUTSIDE THE USA.

1668

AFL-CIO GUIDE TO UNION-SPONSORED SCHOLARSHIPS

AUTHOR-AFL-CIO DEPARTMENT OF EDUCATION

AFL-CIO
815 16TH STREET NW
WASHINGTON DC 20006

COST-FREE TO UNION MEMBERS; $3 NON-UNION

COMPREHENSIVE GUIDE FOR UNION MEMBERS & THEIR DEPENDENT CHILDREN. DESCRIBES LOCAL; NATIONAL & INTERNATIONL UNION-SPONSORED SCHOLARSHIP PROGRAMS. ALSO INCLUDES A BIBLIOGRAPHY OF OTHER FINANCIAL AID SOURCES.

1669

AMERICAN INSTITUTE OF ARCHITECTS INFORMATION POSTER & BOOKLET

AUTHOR-AIA

AMERICAN INSTITUTE OF ARCHITECTS
1735 NEW YORK AVENUE NW
WASHINGTON DC 20006

COST-FREE

PROVIDES LIST OF ACCREDITED PROFESSIONAL PROGRAMS AND CAREER INFORMATION.

1670

ANNUAL REGISTER OF GRANT SUPPORT

AUTHOR-REED REFERENCE PUBLISHING

NATIONAL REGISTER PUBLISHING CO
121 CHANLON RD
NEW PROVIDENCE NJ 07974

COST-$165.00 + $11.55 SHIPPING/HANDLING

COMPREHENSIVE ANNUAL REFERENCE BOOK WHICH CAN BE FOUND AT MOST MAJOR LIBRARIES. DETAILS THOUSANDS OF GRANTS FOR RESEARCH WHICH ARE OPEN TO INDIVIDUALS & ORGANIZATIONS.

1671

ART CALENDAR

AUTHOR-CAROLYN BLAKESLEE; EDITOR IN CHIEF

ART CALENDAR
PO BOX 199
UPPER FAIRMOUNT 21867

COST-$32/ONE YEAR

MONTHLY PUBLICATION CONTAINING ARTICLES OF INTEREST TO ARTISTS INCLUDING LISTINGS OF GRANTS & FELLOWSHIPS; EXHIBITS ETC. SAMPLE COPY IS AVAILABLE FOR $5.

1672

ASSISTANTSHIPS AND GRADUATE FELLOWSHIPS IN THE MATHEMATICAL SCIENCES

AUTHOR-AMS

AMERICAN MATHEMATICAL SOCIETY
PO BOX 1571; ANNEX STATION
PROVIDENCE RI 02901

COST-$17 ($10 FOR MEMBERS)

ANNUAL PUBLICATION WHICH DESCRIBES ASSISTANTSHIPS AND FELLOWSHIPS IN THE MATHEMATICAL SCIENCES OPEN TO GRADUATE STUDENTS AT ACCREDITED INSTITUTIONS. UPDATED EDITIONS PUBLISHED EVERY OCTOBER.

1673

BARRON'S GUIDE TO LAW SCHOOLS (10TH EDITION)

AUTHOR-GARY A. MUNNEKE J.D. ISBN 0-8120-4864-4

BARRON'S EDUCATIONAL SERIES INC.
250 WIRELESS BLVD
HAUPPAUGE NY 11788

COST-$14.95

COMPREHENSIVE GUIDE COVERING MORE THAN 200 ABA-APPROVED AMERICAN LAW SCHOOLS. ADVICE ON ATTENDING LAW SCHOOL.

1674

BASIC FACTS ON STUDY ABROAD

AUTHOR-IIE

INSTITUTE OF INTERNATIONAL EDUCATION
IIE BOOKS; 809 UNITED NATIONS PLAZA
NEW YORK NY 10017

COST-FREE

BROCHURE OFFERING ESSENTIAL INFORMATION ON PLANNING FOR UNDERGRADUATE AND GRADUATE STUDY OUTSIDE THE USA.

1675

CAREER GUIDE FOR SINGERS

AUTHOR-MARY MCDONALD; EDITOR

OPERA AMERICA
777 14TH ST NW; SUITE 520
WASHINGTON DC 20005

COST-$25 NON MEMBERS; $15 MEMBERS

DIRECTORY CONTAINING INFORMATION ON AUDITIONS; GRANTS AND COMPETITIONS FOR YOUNG SINGERS CONTEMPLATING A CAREER IN OPERA.

1676

CHRONICLE CAREER INDEX

AUTHOR-CGP; ISBN #1-55631-187-7

CHRONICLE GUIDANCE PUBLICATIONS
AURORA ST EXTENSION; PO BOX 1190
MORAVIA NY 13118

COST-$14.25

COMPREHENSIVE REFERENCE LISTING OF CAREER AND VOCATIONAL MATERIALS FOR STUDENTS AND COUNSELORS. DESCRIBES ABOUT 500 SOURCES OF PUBLICATIONS & AUDIOVISUAL MATERIALS. 90 PAGES.

1677

CHRONICLE FINANCIAL AID GUIDE

AUTHOR-CGP; ISBN #1-55631-186-9

CHRONICAL GUIDANCE PUBLICATIONS
AURORA ST EXTENSION; PO BOX 1190
MORAVIA NY 13118

COST-$19.97

ANNUAL GUIDE THAT CONTAINS INFORMATION ON FINANCIAL AID PROGRAMS OFFERED NATIONALLY & REGIONALLY BY PUBLIC & PRIVATE ORGANIZATIONS. PROGRAMS SUPPORT STUDY AND/OR RESEARCH AT THE UNDERGRADUATE; GRADUATE & POST-GRADUATE LEVELS. 534 PAGES.

1678

CHRONICLE FOUR-YEAR COLLEGE DATABOOK

AUTHOR-CGP; ISBN #1-55631-184-2

CHRONICLE GUIDANCE PUBLICATIONS
AURORA ST EXTENSION; PO BOX 1190
MORAVIA NY 13118

COST-$19.99

EXCELLENT REFERENCE BOOK IN 2 SECTIONS. 'MAJORS' SECTION LISTS 2111 INSTITUTIONS OFFERING 926 4-YEAR; GRADUATE & PROFESSIONAL MAJORS. 'CHARTS' SECTION CONTAINS COMPREHENSIVE INFORMATION & STATISTICS ON EACH OF THE SCHOOLS. 548 PAGES.

1679

COLLEGE DEGREES BY MAIL

AUTHOR-JOHN BEAR PH.D; ISBN 0-89815-379-4

TEN SPEED PRESS
BOX 7123
BERKELEY CA 94707

COST-$12.95 + $2.50 SHIPPING & HANDLING

LISTING OF 100 COLLEGES THAT OFFER BACHELORS; MASTERS; DOCTORATES AND LAW DEGREES BY HOME STUDY. BOOK IS THE SUCCESSOR TO BEAR'S GUIDE TO EARNING NONTRADITIONAL COLLEGE DEGREES. 214 PAGES.

HELPFUL PUBLICATIONS

1680

COLLEGE FINANCIAL AID EMERGENCY KIT

AUTHOR-JOYCE LAIN KENNEDY & DR. HERM
    DAVIS

SUN FEATURES INC
BOX 368-K
CARDIFF CA 92007

COST-$5.50 (INCLUDES POSTAGE AND HANDLING)

40-PAGE BOOKLET FILLED WITH TIPS ON HOW TO
    MEET THE COSTS OF TUITION; ROOM &
    BOARD. THIS 1993-94 EDITION TELLS WHAT
    IS AVAILABLE; WHOM TO ASK AND HOW TO
    ASK.

1681

CORPORATE TUITION AID PROGRAMS

AUTHOR-JOSEPH P O'NEILL; ISBN #0-87866-482-3

PETERSON'S GUIDES
DEPT 7707; PO BOX 2123
PRINCETON NJ 08543

COST-$14.95

BIENNIAL PUBLICATION WHICH DESCRIBES THE
    EMPLOYEE TUITION BENEFIT PROGRAMS OF
    730 OF AMERICA'S LARGEST BANKS;
    RETAILERS; UTILITIES; TRANSPORTATION;
    SERVICE & INDUSTRIAL FIRMS. 208 PAGES.

1682

DENTISTRY AS A CAREER

AUTHOR-AADS

AMERICAN ASSOCIATION OF DENTAL SCHOOLS
1625 MASS AVE NW
WASHINGTON DC 20036

COST-FREE

BROCHURE DISCUSSES DENTISTRY AS A CAREER
    AND OFFERS ADVICE ON PLANNING FOR A
    DENTAL EDUCATION.

1683

DIRECTORY OF ATHLETIC SCHOLARSHIPS

AUTHOR-ALAN GREEN; ISBN #0-8169-1549-X

FACTS ON FILE INC
460 PARK AVE SOUTH
NEW YORK NY 10016

COST-$29.95

CONTAINS THE INS & OUTS OF THE RECRUITING
    PROCESS; SCHOOL BY SCHOOL INDEX; SPORT
    BY SPORT INDEX & STATE BY STATE INDEX.

1684

DIRECTORY OF COLLEGE FACILITIES & SERVICES FOR PEOPLE WITH DISABILITIES

AUTHOR-CAROL H. THOMAS & JAMES L.
    THOMAS; ISBN 0-89774-604-X

ORYX PRESS
4041 NORTH CENTRAL AVE. #700
PHOENIX AZ 85012

COST-$115.00

COMPLETE BOOK ON COLLEGE FACILITIES &
    SERVICES FOR PEOPLE WITH DISABILITIES IN
    THE USA & CANADA. ALSO CONTAINS
    INFORMATION ON ASSOCIATIONS; CENTERS;
    ORGANIZATIONS; SOCIETIES;
    CLEARINGHOUSES & DATA BASES.

1685

DIRECTORY OF EDUCATIONAL INSTITUTIONS

AUTHOR-AICS

ASSOCIATION OF INDEPENDENT COLLEGES AND
SCHOOLS
1 DUPONT CIRCLE #350
WASHINGTON DC 20036

COST-$5.00

THIS DIRECTORY IS PUBLISHED ANNUALLY TO
    PROVIDE INFORMATION ON MORE THAN 650
    INSTITUTIONS ACCREDITED BY THE AICS.
    INFORMATION CAN BE OBTAINED ABOUT
    ANY OF THE LISTED SCHOOLS THROUGH
    AICS.

1686

DIRECTORY OF FINANCIAL AIDS FOR MINORITIES

AUTHOR-GAIL ANN SCHLACHTER

REFERENCE SERVICE PRESS
1100 INDUSTRIAL RD; SUITE 9
SAN CARLOS CA 94070

COST-$47.50 + $4 SHIPPING

DESCRIBES OVER 2000 SCHOLARSHIPS;
    FELLOWSHIPS; GRANTS; LOANS; AWARDS &
    INTERNSHIPS SET ASIDE FOR ETHNIC
    MINORITIES. COVERS ALL LEVELS OF STUDY.
    600 PAGES.

1687

DIRECTORY OF FINANCIAL AIDS FOR WOMEN

AUTHOR-GAIL ANN SCHLACHTER

REFERENCE SERVICE PRESS
1100 INDUSTRIAL RD; SUITE 9
SAN CARLOS CA 94070

COST-$45 + $4 SHIPPING

CONTAINS OVER 1700 DESCRIPTIONS OF

SCHOLARSHIPS; FELLOWSHIPS; GRANTS; LOANS; AWARDS & INTERNSHIPS SET ASIDE FOR WOMEN. COVERS ALL LEVELS OF STUDY. 478 PAGES.

1688

DIRECTORY OF NATIONAL INFORMATION SOURCES ON DISABILITIES

AUTHOR-DEPT. OF EDUCATION

U.S. DEPT. OF EDUCATION
CLEARINGHOUSE ON THE HANDICAPPED; OFFICE OF SPECIAL EDUCATION AND REHABILITATIVE SERVICES
WASHINGTON DC 20202

COST-FREE

DIRECTORY WHICH INVENTORIES RESOURCES AT THE NATIONAL LEVEL (PUBLIC & PRIVATE) WHICH HAVE INFORMATION AND/OR DIRECT SERVICES PERTINENT TO THE HANDICAPPED & PEOPLE INVOLVED IN EDUCATING; TRAINING OR HELPING THE HANDICAPPED.

1689

DIRECTORY OF POSTGRADUATE STUDY - COURSES & SCHOLARSHIPS

AUTHOR-MARY BROWN; EDITOR

GRADUATE CAREERS COUNCIL OF AUSTRALIA
PO BOX 28
PARKVILLE VICTORIA 3052 AUSTRALIA

COST-AUST $30

160-PAGE BOOKLET THAT DESCRIBES NUMEROUS SCHOLARSHIP; FELLOWSHIP & GRANT PROGRAMS OPEN TO STUDENTS WHO WISH TO DO GRADUATE & POST-GRADUATE STUDY IN AUSTRALIA.

1690

DIRECTORY OF RESEARCH GRANTS 1993

AUTHOR-ORYX

ORYX PRESS
4041 N.CENTRAL AVE.
PHOENIX AZ 85012

COST-$125

ANNUAL REFERENCE BOOK WHICH CAN BE FOUND IN MOST MAJOR LIBRARIES. EXCELLENT TOOL FOR ANY PERSON OR ORGANIZATION LOOKING FOR RESEARCH FUNDING. ORGANIZED BY GRANT TITLE WITH EXTENSIVE INDEXES.

1691

DIRECTORY OF SPECIAL PROGRAMS FOR MINORITY GROUP MEMBERS

AUTHOR-ISBN 0-912048-39-5

GARRETT PARK PRESS
PO BOX 190F
GARRETT PARK MD 20896

COST-$30

COMPREHENSIVE BOOK WHICH DESCRIBES CAREER INFORMATION SERVICES; EMPLOYMENT SKILLS BANKS & EDUCATIONAL FINANCIAL AID SOURCES FOR MINORITY GROUP MEMBERS. 348 PAGES.

1692

EDUCATIONAL OPPORTUNITIES IN THE NAVY

AUTHOR-USN

U.S. NAVY
BUREAU OF NAVAL PERSONNEL; PERSONAL EXCELLENCE & PARTNERSHIPS DIV (PERS-602)
WASHINGTON DC 20370

COST-FREE

VARIOUS NAVY-ORIENTED ORGANIZATIONS SPONSOR SCHOLARSHIPS OR OFFER AID FOR UNDERGRADUATE & GRADUATE STUDY. DEPENDENT CHILDREN OF CURRENT OR FORMER MEMBERS OF THE NAVY; MARINE CORPS OR COAST GUARD ARE ELIGIBLE TO APPLY.

1693

EEO BIMONTHLY

AUTHOR-CRS PUBLICATIONS

CAREER RESEARCH SYSTEMS INC
1800 SHERMAN PLACE
EVANSTON IL 60201

COST-$42.00/YEAR

BI-MONTHLY PUBLICATION CONTAINING DETAILED CAREER OPPORTUNITY PROFILES ON AMERICAN COMPANIES; GEOGRAPHIC EMPLOYER LISTINGS & OCCUPATIONAL INDEX.

1694

ENCYCLOPEDIA OF ASSOCIATIONS; VOL 1

AUTHOR-ISBN #0-8103-7945-7

GALE RESEARCH INC
835 PENOBSCOT BLDG
DETROIT MI 48226

COST-$320

AN OUTSTANDING RESEARCH TOOL! 3-PART SET OF REFERENCE BOOKS WHICH CAN BE FOUND IN MOST MAJOR LIBRARIES.

CONTAINS DETAILED INFORMATION ON OVER 22000 ASSOCIATIONS; ORGANIZATIONS; UNIONS; ETC. INCLUDES NAME & KEY WORD INDEX.

1695

EXPLORING CAREERS IN MUSIC

AUTHOR-PAUL BJORNEBERG; ISBN 0-940796-86-4

MUSIC EDUCATORS NATIONAL CONFERENCE
1902 ASSOCIATION DRIVE
RESTON VA 22091

COST-FREE

INFORMATIVE BOOKLET DISCUSSING CAREERS IN THE PERFORMING ARTS; MUSIC EDUCATION; THE MUSIC BUSINESS; RECORDING INDUSTRY AND ALLIED FIELDS.

1696

FACTFILE 12 - FILM AND TELEVISION GRANTS AND SCHOLARSHIPS

AUTHOR-ANDREA ALSBERG AND DAVID H. CHADDERDON

AMERICAN FILM INSTITUTE
PO BOX 27999
LOS ANGELES CA 90027

COST-$9.95 + $2 SHIPPING/HANDLING. CA RESIDENTS ADD SALES TAX

LISTS 57 SPECIFIC GRANT PROGRAMS GIVING DETAILS ON AMOUNTS GIVEN; DEADLINES; ELIGIBILITY. LISTS SCHOLARSHIP PROGRAMS SPECIFICALLY FOR FILM; TELEVISION AND VIDEO STUDENTS. 56 PAGES.

1697

FACTFILE 2 - CAREERS IN FILM AND TELEVISION

AUTHOR-DEBORAH A. DAVIDSON

AMERICAN FILM INSTITUTE
PO BOX 27999
LOS ANGELES CA 90027

COST-$9.95 + $2 SHIPPING/HANDLING. CA RESIDENTS ADD SALES TAX

LISTS UNIONS; GUILDS AND PROFESSIONAL ORGANIZATIONS AND GIVES INFORMATION IN INTERN AND APPRENTICESHIP PROGRAMS IN DIRECTING; DISTRIBUTION; FILM AND TELEVISION PRODUCTION AND WRITING. 46 PAGES.

1698

FEDERAL BENEFITS FOR VETERANS & DEPENDENTS (S/N 051-000-00198-2)

AUTHOR-VETERANS ADMINISTRATION

SUPERINTENDENT OF DOCUMENTS
U.S. GOVERNMENT PRINTING OFFICE
WASHINGTON DC 20402

COST-$2.75

94-PAGE BOOKLET CONTAINING DETAILS OF ALL FEDERAL BENEFIT PROGRAMS AVAILABLE TO VETERANS & THEIR DEPENDENTS.

1699

FELLOWSHIP GUIDE TO WESTERN EUROPE

AUTHOR-CAROLYN MORLEY; EDITOR

COUNCIL FOR EUROPEAN STUDIES
C/O COLUMBIA UNIV; BOX 44 SCHERMERHORN
NEW YORK NY 10027

COST-$8.00 (PREPAID CHECK TO COLUMBIA UNIV)

THIS BOOKLET IS INTENDED TO ASSIST USA & EUROPEAN STUDENTS IN FINDING FUNDS FOR TRAVEL & STUDY IN THE SOCIAL SCIENCES & HUMANITIES IN EUROPE.

1700

FINANCIAL AID FOR MINORITIES - AWARDS OPEN TO STUDENTS WITH ANY MAJOR

AUTHOR-ISBN 0-912048-93-1

GARRETT PARK PRESS
PO BOX 190F
GARRETT PARK MD 20896

COST-$4.95

THIS BOOKLET LISTS SOURCES OF FINANCIAL AID AND CLARIFIES APPLICATION PROCEDURES. INCLUDES A BIBLIOGRAPHY OF OTHER SOURCES OF FUNDING INFORMATION.

1701

FINANCIAL AID FOR MINORITIES IN BUSINESS & LAW

AUTHOR-ISBN 0-912048-88-3

GARRETT PARK PRESS
PO BOX 190F
GARRETT PARK MD 20896

COST-$4.95

THIS BOOKLET LISTS SOURCES OF FINANCIAL AID AND CLARIFIES APPLICATION PROCEDURES. INCLUDES A BIBLIOGRAPHY OF OTHER SOURCES OF FUNDING INFORMATION.

1702 ──────────────────────

FINANCIAL AID FOR MINORITIES IN EDUCATION

AUTHOR-ISBN 0-912048-99-9

GARRETT PARK PRESS
PO BOX 190F
GARRETT PARK MD 20896

COST-$4.95

THIS BOOKLET CONTAINS FINANCIAL AID OPPORTUNITIES FOR ELEMENTARY; SECONDARY & ADMINISTRATIVE PROGRAMS. ALSO FIELDS SUCH AS COUNSELING; SPECIAL ED. & SPEECH PATHOLOGY.

1703 ──────────────────────

FINANCIAL AID FOR MINORITIES IN ENGINEERING & SCIENCE

AUTHOR-ISBN 0-912048-98-0

GARRETT PARK PRESS
PO BOX 190F
GARRETT PARK MD 20896

COST-$4.95

INDIVIDUAL AWARDS AND GENERAL PROGRAMS OFFERED FOR GRADUATE AND PROFESSIONAL STUDY BY PRIVATE ORGANIZATIONS; FOUNDATIONS; FEDERAL AND STATE GOVERNMENTS; COLLEGES AND UNIVERSITIES.

1704 ──────────────────────

FINANCIAL AID FOR MINORITIES IN HEALTH FIELDS

AUTHOR-ISBN 0-912048-96-4

GARRETT PARK PRESS
PO BOX 190F
GARRETT PARK MD 20896

COST-$4.95

INCLUDES INDIVIDUAL AWARDS AND GENERAL PROGRAMS OFFERED FOR GRADUATE OR PROFESSIONAL STUDY BY PRIVATE ORGANIZATIONS; FOUNDATIONS; FEDERAL AND STATE GOVERNMENTS; COLLEGES AND UNIVERSITIES.

1705 ──────────────────────

FINANCIAL AID FOR MINORITIES IN JOURNALISM & MASS COMMUNICATIONS

AUTHOR-ISBN 0-912048-84-0

GARRETT PARK PRESS
PO BOX 190F
GARRETT PARK MD 20896

COST-$4.95

THIS BOOKLET LISTS SPECIFIC SOURCES OF FINANCIAL AID FOR MINORITY STUDENTS AND ALSO HELPS TO EXPLAIN HOW TO GO ABOUT APPLYING FOR THEM.

1706 ──────────────────────

FINANCIAL AID FOR THE DISABLED & THEIR FAMILIES

AUTHOR-GAIL ANN SCHLACHTER & R.DAVID WEBER

REFERENCE SERVICE PRESS
1100 INDUSTRIAL RD; SUITE 9
SAN CARLOS CA 94070

COST-$37.50 + $4 SHIPPING

CONTAINS OVER 800 REFERENCES & CROSS-REFERENCES TO SCHOLARSHIPS; FELLOWSHIPS; GRANTS; LOANS; AWARDS & INTERNSHIPS SET ASIDE FOR THE DISABLED & THEIR FAMILIES. COVERS ALL LEVELS OF STUDY. 310 PAGES.

1707 ──────────────────────

FINANCIAL AID FOR VETERANS; MILITARY PERSONNEL & THEIR FAMILIES

AUTHOR-GAIL ANN SCHLACHTER & R.DAVID WEBER

REFERENCE SERVICE PRESS
1100 INDUSTRIAL RD; SUITE 9
SAN CARLOS CA 94070

COST-$37.50 + $4 SHIPPING

CONTAINS OVER 900 DESCRIPTIONS OF SCHOLARSHIPS; FELLOWSHIPS; GRANTS; LOANS; AWARDS & INTERNSHIPS SET ASIDE FOR VETERANS; MILITARY PERSONNEL & THEIR FAMILIES. COVERS ALL LEVELS OF STUDY. 300 PAGES.

1708 ──────────────────────

FINANCIAL ASSISTANCE FOR LIBRARY EDUCATION

AUTHOR-ALA

AMERICAN LIBRARY ASSOCIATION
OFFICE FOR LIBRARY PERSONNEL RESOURCES; 50 EAST HURON ST
CHICAGO IL 60611

COST-$1.00 FOR POSTAGE/HANDLING

AN EXCELLENT SUMMARY OF FELLOWSHIPS; SCHOLARSHIPS; GRANTS-IN-AID; LOAN FUNDS & OTHER FINANCIAL ASSISTANCE FOR LIBRARY EDUCATION. PUBLISHED ANNUALLY EACH FALL FOR THE FOLLOWING YEAR.

1709 ──────────────────────

FINDING MONEY FOR COLLEGE

AUTHOR-JOHN BEAR; PH.D

TEN SPEED PRESS
PO BOX 7123
BERKELEY CA 94707

COST-$7.95

IN THIS BOOK DR. BEAR BUILDS ON THE EXTENSIVE RESEARCH HE HAS DONE IN

EDUCATION TO SEARCH OUT THE UNCONVENTIONAL; THE OVERLOOKED; THE ORDINARY BUT NOT WELL UNDERSTOOD SOURCES OF ASSISTANCE & HOW TO PURSUE THEM. 168 PAGES.

1710 ——————————————

FISKE GUIDE TO COLLEGES

AUTHOR-NEW YORK TIMES BOOKS; ISBN 812-92024-4

TIMES BOOKS
400 HAHN RD
WESTMINSTER MD 21157

COST-$16

DESCRIBES THE TOP-RATED 265 OUT OF 2000 POSSIBLE 4-YEAR SCHOOLS IN THE USA. THEY ARE RATED FOR ACADEMICS; SOCIAL LIFE & QUALITY OF LIFE.

1711 ——————————————

FLORIDA STUDENT FINANCIAL AID - FACT SHEETS

AUTHOR-DEPT OF EDUCATION

FLORIDA DEPARTMENT OF EDUCATION
1344 FLORIDA EDUCATION CENTER
TALLAHASSEE FL 32399

COST-FREE

BOOKLET CONTAINING INFORMATION ON ALL FLORIDA GRANTS; SCHOLARSHIPS AND TEACHER PROGRAMS.

1712 ——————————————

FOUNDATION DIRECTORY (THE)

AUTHOR-ISBN #0-87954-439-2 (SOFT COVER); 0-87954-438-4 (HARD COVER)

FOUNDATION CENTER
79 FIFTH AVE
NEW YORK NY 10003

COST-$150 SOFT COVER; $175 HARD COVER

AUTHORITATIVE ANNUAL REFERENCE BOOK FOUND IN MOST MAJOR LIBRARIES. CONTAINS DETAILED INFORMATION ON OVER 8700 OF AMERICA'S LARGEST FOUNDATIONS. INDEXES ALLOW GRANTSEEKERS; RESEARCHERS; ETC. TO QUICKLY LOCATE FOUNDATIONS OF INTEREST.

1713 ——————————————

GET SMART FAST

AUTHOR-SONDRA GEOFFRION

ACCESS SUCCESS ASSOCIATES
PO BOX 1686
GOLETA CA 93116

COST-$6.95 EACH (CA RESIDENTS ADD 7.75% SALES TAX); (POSTAGE $2.50 USA; $4 FOREIGN)

61 PAGE HANDBOOK FOR ACADEMIC SUCCESS WHICH EXPLAINS HOW TO MASTER THE ART OF STUDYING; WRITE ESSAYS; PREPARE FOR AND TAKE TESTS; ETC.

1714 ——————————————

GOVERNMENT ASSISTANCE ALMANAC (6TH EDITION)

AUTHOR-J.ROBERT DUMOUCHEL; ISBN 1-55888-789-5

OMNIGRAPHICS INC
2500 PENOBSCOT BLDG
DETROIT MI 48226

COST-$84

COMPREHENSIVE GUIDE TO MORE THAN 600 BILLION WORTH OF FEDERAL PROGRAMS AVAILABLE TO THE AMERICAN PUBLIC. CONTAINS 768 PAGES AND 1157 ENTRIES DETAILING PROGRAMS OF BENEFIT TO STUDENTS; EDUCATORS; RESEARCHERS AND CONSUMERS.

1715 ——————————————

GRADUATE ASSISTANTSHIP DIRECTORY IN THE COMPUTER SCIENCES

AUTHOR-ACM

ASSN FOR COMPUTING MACHINERY
11 W.42ND ST; 3RD FLOOR
NEW YORK NY 10036

COST-$22 + $3 SHIPPING/HANDLING

LISTS GRADUATE PROGRAMS IN COMPUTER SCIENCE & RELATED AREAS. DESCRIBES SIZE OF INSTITUTIONS' FACULTIES; EQUIPMENT AVAILABLE & FINANCIAL AID.

1716 ——————————————

GRADUATE FACULTY AND PROGRAMS IN POLITICAL SCIENCE

AUTHOR-COMPILED BY PATRICIA SPELLMAN

AMERICAN POLITICAL SCIENCE ASSN
1527 NEW HAMPSHIRE AVE NW
WASHINGTON DC 20036

COST-$25 (APSA MEMBERS); $45 (NON-MEMBERS) + $3.50 SHIPPING

THIS BOOK PROVIDES A CONCISE SUMMARY OF GRADUATE PROGRAMS IN POLITICAL SCIENCE AT MASTERS AND DOCTORS LEVELS IN THE USA AND CANADA. INCLUDES DEADLINES FOR APPLICATIONS AND A SECTION ON FINANCIAL AID FOR EACH CAMPUS.

1717

GRANTS IN THE HUMANITIES

AUTHOR-W.E. COLEMAN; ISBN #0-918212-80-4

NEAL SCHUMAN PUBLISHERS INC
100 VARICK ST
NEW YORK NY 10013

COST-$29.95

THIS BOOK IS INTENDED PRIMARILY FOR
SCHOLARS WHO ARE LOOKING FOR
FUNDING SOURCES THAT SUPPORT
RESEARCH IN THE HUMANITIES. 175 PAGES.

1718

GRANTS REGISTER (THE) 1991-1993

AUTHOR-REFERENCE; ISBN 0-312-05194-8; ISSN
0072-5471

ST. MARTIN'S PRESS INC
175 FIFTH AVE; CASH SALES
NEW YORK NY 10010

COST-$85

THIS REFERENCE BOOK CAN BE FOUND IN MOST
MAJOR LIBRARIES. IT IS PRIMARILY
INTENDED FOR STUDENTS & RESEARCHERS
AT OR ABOVE THE GRADUATE LEVEL OF
STUDY. MORE THAN 700 FUNDING SOURCES.

1719

GRANTS; FELLOWSHIPS & PRIZES OF INTEREST TO HISTORIANS

AUTHOR-AHA

AMERICAN HISTORICAL ASSOCIATION
400 'A' STREET SE
WASHINGTON DC 20003

COST-$8 AHA MEMBERS; $10 NON-MEMBERS

OVER 350 LISTINGS OF FUNDING PROGRAMS FOR
GRADUATE RESEARCH IN HISTORY. ALSO
INCLUDED ARE BOOK AWARDS & PRIZES.
ORGANIZED BY PRE- & POST-DOCTORAL
LEVELS. FEDERAL; STATE; LOCAL & FOREIGN
SOURCES.

1720

GUIDE TO GRANTS & FELLOWSHIPS IN LINGUISTICS

AUTHOR-LSA

LINGUISTIC SOCIETY OF AMERICA
1325 18TH ST NW
WASHINGTON DC 20036

COST-$6.50

COMPLETE GUIDE TO INSTITUTIONS THAT OFFER
GRANTS; FELLOWSHIPS AND SCHOLARSHIPS
IN LANGUAGES & LINGUISTICS. AWARDS
ARE FOR GRADUATE STUDENTS ONLY.

1721

GUIDE TO RESEARCH SUPPORT

AUTHOR-KENNETH LEE HERRING; EDITOR. ISBN
0-912704-83-7

AMERICAN PSYCHOLOGICAL ASSOCIATION
ORDER DEPARTMENT; 750 1ST ST. N.E.
WASHINGTON DC 20002

COST-$30 NON-MEMBERS; $22 MEMBERS; + $3.50
SHIPPING/HANDLING

A COMPREHENSIVE DIRECTORY OF FUNDING
SOURCES FOCUSING ON THE BEHAVORIAL
SCIENCES. IDENTIFIES FEDERAL PROGRAMS
AND PRIVATE SOURCES THAT PROVIDE
SUPPORT FOR RESEARCH TOPICS OF
INTEREST TO PSYCHOLOGISTS. 276 PAGES.

1722

GUIDE TO SOURCES OF INFORMATION ON PARAPSYCHOLOGY

AUTHOR-EILEEN J. GARRETT LIBRARY

PARAPSYCHOLOGY FOUNDATION
228 EAST 71ST STREET
NEW YORK NY 10021

COST-$2

AN ANNUAL LISTING OF SOURCES OF
INFORMATION ON MAJOR
PARAPSYCHOLOGY ORGANIZATIONS;
JOURNALS; BOOKS & RESEARCH.

1723

GUIDELINES FOR THE PREPARATION OF SCHOOL ADMINISTRATORS

AUTHOR-AASA

AMERICAN ASSN OF SCHOOL ADMINISTRATORS
1801 NORTH MOORE ST
ARLINGTON VA 22209

COST-$5.00 PREPAID

PEOPLE WHO ARE PLANNING A CAREER IN
SCHOOL ADMINISTRATION WILL FIND THIS
BOOK HELPFUL IN EXPLAINING THE
DEMANDS AND EXPECTATIONS OF SCHOOLS
AS WELL AS THOSE WHO PLAY KEY ROLES IN
RECOMMENDING OR ESTABLISHING
CERTIFICATION REQUIREMENTS.

1724

HANDICAPPED FUNDING DIRECTORY

AUTHOR-RICHARD M. ECKSTEIN; EDITOR

RESEARCH GRANT GUIDES
PO BOX 1214
LOXAHATCHEE FL 33470

COST-$39.50 + $4 HANDLING

COMPLETE GUIDE TO FUNDING SOURCES IN THE
USA FOR HANDICAPPED PROGRAMS AND
SERVICES.

HELPFUL PUBLICATIONS

1725

HAPPIER BY DEGREES

AUTHOR-PAM MENDELSOHN

TEN SPEED PRESS
PO BOX 7123
BERKELEY CA 94707

COST-$8.95 + $1.25 SHIPPING & HANDLING

EXCELLENT BOOK FOR WOMEN JUST STARTING
OUT OR RETURNING TO COLLEGE. THIS IS A
COMPREHENSIVE GUIDE TO THE ENTIRE
PROCESS OF ENTERING INTO A NEW
ACADEMIC FIELD INCLUDING FINANCIAL
AID; CHILD CARE; ETC. 266 PAGES.

1726

HOW TO FIND OUT ABOUT FINANCIAL AID

AUTHOR-GAIL ANN SCHLACHTER

REFERENCE SERVICE PRESS
1100 INDUSTRIAL RD; SUITE 9
SAN CARLOS CA 94070

COST-$35 + $4 SHIPPING

A COMPREHENSIVE GUIDE TO MORE THAN 700
PRINT & ONLINE DIRECTORIES THAT
IDENTIFY OVER $21 BILLION IN FINANCIAL
AID AVAILABLE TO UNDERGRADUATE
STUDENTS; GRADUATE STUDENTS &
RESEARCHERS.

1727

INDEX OF MAJORS

AUTHOR-CBP; ISBN #0-87447-410-8

COLLEGE BOARD PUBLICATIONS
PO BOX 886
NEW YORK NY 10101

COST-$15.95

DESCRIBES OVER 580 MAJOR PROGRAMS OF
STUDY AT 2900 UNDERGRADUATE &
GRADUATE SCHOOLS. ALSO LISTS SCHOOLS
THAT HAVE RELIGIOUS AFFILIATIONS;
SPECIAL ACADEMIC PROGRAMS & SPECIAL
ADMISSIONS PROCEDURES. 736 PAGES.

1728

INTERNATIONAL JOBS

AUTHOR-ERIC KOCHER

ADDISON-WESLEY PUBLISHING CO
1 JACOB WAY
READING MA 01867

COST-$12.95

A HANDBOOK LISTING MORE THAN 500 CAREER
OPPORTUNITIES AROUND THE WORLD.

1729

INTERNSHIPS

AUTHOR-PETERSON'S

PETERSON'S GUIDES
202 CARNEGIE CENTER - PO BOX 2123
PRINCETON NJ 08543

COST-$28.95 + $5.75 SHIPPING & HANDLING

LISTS ON THE JOB TRAINING OPPORTUNITIES FOR
TODAY'S JOB MARKET ARRANGED BY
CAREER FIELD & INDEXED
GEOGRAPHICALLY.

1730

JOURNALISM AND MASS COMMUNICATION DIRECTORY

AUTHOR-AEJMC

ASSOCIATION FOR EDUCATION IN JOURNALISM &
MASS COMMUNICATIONS
1621 COLLEGE ST; UNIV SOUTH CAROLINA
COLUMBIA SC 29208

COST-$20 USA; $30 FOREIGN

ANNUAL DIRECTORY LISTING OVER 350 SCHOOLS
AND DEPARTMENTS OF JOURNALISM AND
MASS COMMUNICATION; INFORMATION ON
NATIONAL FUNDS; FELLOWSHIPS AND
FOUNDATIONS; COLLEGIATE AND
SCHOLASTIC SERVICES. OVER 2500
INDIVIDUAL MEMBERS.

1731

JOURNALISM CAREER GUIDE FOR MINORITIES

AUTHOR-DJNF

DOW JONES NEWSPAPER FUND INC
PO BOX 300
PRINCETON NJ 08543-0300

COST-FREE

COMPREHENSIVE GUIDE WHICH LISTS
NEWSPAPER RECRUITERS FOR COLLEGE
STUDENTS WHO ARE LOOKING FOR WORK AS
REPORTERS & EDITORS. ALSO INCLUDES
CAREER INFORMATION; JOBS; SALARIES;
INTERN PROGRAMS & MUCH MORE. TO
ORDER CALL 1-800-DOW FUND.

1732

LEARNING DISABILITY INFORMATION

AUTHOR-ODS

ORTON DYSLEXIA SOCIETY
CHESTER BUILDING/SUITE 382; 8600 LASALLE RD
BALTIMORE MD 21204

COST-FREE

NATIONAL ORGANIZATION FORMED TO HELP
LEARNING DISABLED CHILDREN & THEIR
PARENTS. THERE ARE LOCAL CHAPTERS

THROUGHOUT THE USA. CONTACT ADDRESS ABOVE FOR DETAILS ON MEMBERSHIP; SERVICES OFFERED & LOCATION OF THE NEAREST CHAPTER.

1733

LEARNING DISABILITY INFORMATION

AUTHOR-ODS-CALIF

ORTON DYSLEXIA SOCIETY; NORTHERN CALIFORNIA BRANCH
1244 SIERRA AVE
SAN JOSE CA 95126

COST-FREE

OTYON DYSLEXIA SOCIETY (ODS) IS A NAT;L ORGANIZATION FORMED TO HELP LEARNING DISABLED CHILDREN & THEIR PARENTS. SEND SASE TO ADDRESS ABOVE FOR DETAILS ON MEMBERSHIP AND SERVICES OFFERED BY THE N. CALIFORNIA CHAPTER.

1734

MAKING IT THROUGH COLLEGE

AUTHOR-PSC

PROFESSIONAL STAFF CONGRESS
25 WEST 43RD STREET; 5TH FLOOR
NEW YORK NY 10036

COST-$1.00

HANDY BOOKLET DESCRIBING HOW TO MAKE IT THROUGH COLLEGE. INCLUDES INFORMATION ON HOW TO COPE WITH COMPETITION; GETTING ORGANIZED; STUDY TECHNIQUES; SOLVING WORK OVERLOADS AND MORE. 14 PAGES.

1735

MEDICAL SCHOOL ADMISSION REQUIREMENTS

AUTHOR-CYNTHIA T. BENNETT

ASSOCIATION OF AMERICAN MEDICAL COLLEGES
2450 N ST NW
WASHINGTON DC 20037

COST-$10 + SHIPPING

CONTAINS COMPLETE ADMISSION REQUIREMENTS OF ALL ACCREDITED MEDICAL SCHOOLS IN USA & CANADA.

1736

MEDICINE - A CHANCE TO MAKE A DIFFERENCE

AUTHOR-AMA

AMERICAN MEDICAL ASSOCIATION
ORDER PROCESSING; PO BOX 109050
CHICAGO IL 60610

COST-$5.00

FOR COLLEGE STUDENTS CONSIDERING A CAREER IN MEDICINE. ANSWERS QUESTIONS ABOUT THE PROFESSION AND MEDICAL EDUCATION INCLUDING PREREQUISITES; ADMISSION REQUIREMENTS AND CHOOSING A MEDICAL SCHOOL.

1737

NAEA SCHOLARSHIP BOOK

AUTHOR-NAEA

NATIONAL ART EDUCATION ASSOCIATION
1916 ASSOCIATION DRIVE
RESTON VA 22091

COST-$12

LISTS OVER $12.5 MILLION IN ART SCHOLARSHIPS; AWARDS; FELLOWSHIPS & GRADUATE ASSISTANT PROGRAMS IN THE USA & CANADA.

1738

NATIONAL DIRECTORY OF ARTS INTERNSHIPS

AUTHOR-NNAP

AMERICAN COUNCIL FOR THE ARTS (ACA BOOKS)
ONE E. 53RD ST.
NEW YORK NY 10022

COST-$35

DETAILED LISTINGS OF MORE THAN 2100 ON-THE-JOB OPPORTUNITIES NATIONWIDE IN THE FIELDS OF DANCE; THEATER; MUSIC; ART; DESIGN; FILM AND VIDEO. 360 PAGES.

1739

NATIONAL DIRECTORY OF CORPORATE GIVING

AUTHOR-TFC; ISBN 0-87954-400-7

FOUNDATION CENTER (THE)
79 FIFTH AVENUE/16TH STREET
NEW YORK NY 10003

COST-$199.50 (INCLUDING SHIPPING/HANDLING)

BOOK PROFILES 2000 PROGRAMS MAKING CONTRIBUTIONS TO NONPROFIT ORGANIZATIONS. A VALUABLE TOOL TO ASSIST GRANT SEEKERS IN FINDING POTENTIAL SUPPORT.

1740

NEED A LIFT?

AUTHOR-AMERICAN LEGION

AMERICAN LEGION EDUCATION PROGRAM
PO BOX 1050
INDIANAPOLIS IN 46206

COST-$2.00

OUTSTANDING GUIDE TO EDUCATION & EMPLOYMENT OPPORTUNITIES. CONTAINS COMPLETE INFO ON THE FINANCIAL AID PROCESS (HOW; WHEN & WHERE TO START); SCHOLARSHIPS; LOANS & CAREER INFORMATION ADDRESSES. 120 PAGES.

HELPFUL PUBLICATIONS

1741

NURSING EDUCATION; ENROLLING IN A COLLEGE OR UNIVERSITY

AUTHOR-AMERICAN NURSES ASSOCIATION

AMERICAN NURSES ASSOCIATION
2420 PERSHING ROAD
KANSAS CITY MO 64108

COST-$3.50 MEMBERS; $4.95 NON-MEMBERS

HOW-TO BOOKLET THAT ANSWERS THE MOST COMMON QUESTIONS ASKED BY PROSPECTIVE NURSING STUDENTS. HOW TO CHOOSE A SCHOOL; HOW TO GET INFORMATION FROM SCHOOLS; HOW TO APPLY; HOW TO OBTAIN FINANCIAL AID & THE TYPES AVAILABLE.

1742

OCCUPATIONAL OUTLOOK HANDBOOK

AUTHOR-U.S. BUREAU OF LABOR STATISTICS; STOCK #029-001-03090-8 (CLOTH); 029-001-03091-6 (PAPER)

SUPERINTENDENT OF DOCUMENTS
U.S. GOVERNMENT PRINTING OFFICE
WASHINGTON DC 20402

COST-$26 (CLOTH BOUND); $23 (PAPER)

ANNUAL PUBLICATION DESIGNED TO ASSIST INDIVIDUALS IN SELECTING APPROPRIATE CAREERS. DESCRIBES OVER 200 OCCUPATIONS IN GREAT DETAIL AND INCLUDES CURRENT & PROJECTED JOB PROSPECTS FOR EACH. 492 PAGES.

1743

OCEAN OPPORTUNITIES

AUTHOR-COMPILED BY THE INSTITUTE OF ELECTRICAL & ELECTRONIC ENGINEERS AND THE MARINE TECHNOLOGY SOCIETY.

MARINE TECHNOLOGY CENTER
1828 L ST NW SUITE 906
WASHINGTON DC 20006

COST-$3 FOR SHIPPING/HANDLING

BOOKLET WHICH EXPLORES CAREER OPPORTUNITIES IN THE MARINE SCIENCES.

1744

OFFICIAL HANDBOOK FOR THE CLEP EXAMINATIONS

AUTHOR-CBP; ISBN #0-87447-455-8

COLLEGE BOARD PUBLICATIONS
PO BOX 886
NEW YORK NY 10101

COST-$15

OFFICIAL GUIDE TO THE COLLEGE LEVEL EXAMINATION PROGRAM (CLEP) TESTS FROM THE ACTUAL SPONSORS OF THE TESTS. CONTAINS SAMPLE QUESTIONS & ANSWERS; ADVICE ON HOW TO PREPARE FOR TESTS; WHICH COLLEGES GRANT CREDIT FOR CLEP & MUCH MORE. 500 PGS.

1745

PHARMACY SCHOOL ADMISSION REQUIREMENTS

AUTHOR-AACP

AMERICAN ASSOCIATION OF COLLEGES OF PHARMACY
OFFICE OF STUDENT AFFAIRS; 1426 PRINCE ST
ALEXANDRIA VA 22314

COST-$20 PREPAID

114-PAGE BOOKLET THAT IS UPDATED ANNUALLY. IT CONTAINS COMPARATIVE INFORMATION CHARTS AND THE GENERAL HISTORY AND CURRENT ADMISSION REQUIREMENTS FOR ACCREDITED PHARMACY PROGRAMS.

1746

PILOT TRAINING GUIDE

AUTHOR-FAPA

FUTURE AVIATION PROFESSIONALS OF AMERICA (FAPA)
4959 MASSACHUSETTS BLVD
ATLANTA GA 30337

COST-$20.95

BOOKLET DESIGNED TO HELP BEGINNER AND ADVANCED PILOTS MAKE DECISIONS ABOUT THEIR TRAINING. INCLUDES LIST OF FAA APPROVED FLIGHT TRAINING SCHOOLS IN USA.

1747

POWER STUDY TO UP YOUR GRADES AND GPA

AUTHOR-SONDRA GEOFFRION

ACCESS SUCCESS ASSOCIATES
PO BOX 1686
GOLETA CA 93116

COST-$4.95 + $2.50 USA POSTAGE; $4 FOREIGN POSTAGE. CA RESIDENTS ADD 7.75% SALES TAX

ONE OF 5 EXCELLENT BOOKLETS EXPLAINING TECHNIQUES TO DISCOVER WHAT WILL BE TESTED; CUT STUDY TIME IN HALF; PREPARE THOROUGHLY; WRITE ESSAYS; TAKE TESTS. OTHER TITLES COVER MATH; ENGLISH; SOCIAL STUDIES; SCIENCE.

1748

POWER STUDY TO UP YOUR GRADES IN MATH

AUTHOR-SONDRA GEOFFRION

ACCESS SUCCESS ASSOCIATES
PO BOX 1686
GOLETA CA 93116

COST-$4.95 + $2.50 USA POSTAGE; $4 FOREIGN
POSTAGE. CA RESIDENTS ADD 7.75% SALES
TAX

ONE OF 5 EXCELLENT BOOKLETS EXPLAINING
TECHNIQUES TO DISCOVER WHAT WILL BE
TESTED; CUT STUDY TIME IN HALF; PREPARE
THOROUGHLY; WRITE ESSAYS; TAKE TESTS.
OTHER TITLES COVER ENGLISH; SOCIAL
STUDIES; SCIENCE AND IMPROVING GRADE
POINT AVERAGE.

1749

POWER STUDY TO UP YOUR GRADES IN ENGLISH

AUTHOR-SONDRA GEOFFRION

ACCESS SUCCESS ASSOCIATES
PO BOX 1686
GOLETA CA 93116

COST-$4.95 + $2.50 USA POSTAGE; $4 FOREIGN
POSTAGE. CA RESIDENTS ADD SALES TAX

ONE OF 5 EXCELLENT BOOKLETS EXPLAINING
TECHNIQUES TO DISCOVER WHAT WILL BE
TESTED; CUT STUDY TIME IN HALF; PREPARE
THOROUGHLY; WRITE ESSAYS; TAKE TESTS.
OTHER TITLES COVER MATH; SOCIAL
STUDIES; SCIENCE AND IMPROVING GRADE
POINT AVERAGE.

1750

POWER STUDY TO UP YOUR GRADES IN SOCIAL STUDIES

AUTHOR-SONDRA GEOFFRION

ACCESS SUCCESS ASSOCIATES
PO BOX 1686
GOLETA CA 93116

COST-$4.95 + $2.50 USA POSTAGE; $4 FOREIGN
POSTAGE. CA RESIDENTS ADD 7.75% SALES
TAX

ONE OF 5 EXCELLENT BOOKLETS EXPLAINING
TECHNIQUES TO DISCOVER WHAT WILL BE
TESTED; CUT STUDY TIME IN HALF; PREPARE
THOROUGHLY; WRITE ESSAYS; TAKE TESTS.
OTHER TITLES COVER MATH; ENGLISH;
SCIENCE; AND IMPROVING GRADE POINT
AVERAGE.

1751

POWER STUDY TO UP YOUR GRADES IN SCIENCE

AUTHOR-SONDRA GEOFFRION

ACCESS SUCCESS ASSOCIATES
PO BOX 1686
GOLETA CA 93116

COST-$4.95 + $2.50 USA POSTAGE; $4 FOREIGN
POSTAGE. CA RESIDENTS ADD 7.75% SALES
TAX

ONE OF 5 EXCELLENT BOOKLETS EXPLAINING
HOW TO DISCOVER WHAT WILL BE TESTED;
CUT STUDY TIME IN HALF; PREPARE
THOROUGHLY; WRITE ESSAYS; TAKE TESTS.
OTHER TITLES COVER MATH; ENGLISH;
SOCIAL STUDIES; AND IMPROVING GRADE
POINT AVERAGE.

1752

PROCEEDINGS AND ADDRESSES OF THE AMERICAN PHILOSOPHICAL ASSOCIATION

AUTHOR-APA

AMERICAN PHILOSOPHICAL ASSOCIATION (THE)
UNIVERSITY OF DELAWARE
NEWARK DE 19716

COST-$10

ANNUAL ISSUE CONTAINS LISTS OF GRANTS AND
FELLOWSHIPS OF INTEREST TO
PHILOSOPHERS.

1753

PUBLIC WORKS GRADUATE EDUCATION

AUTHOR-APWA

AMERICAN PUBLIC WORKS ASSOCIATION
1313 EAST 60TH STREET
CHICAGO IL 60637

COST-FREE

DESCRIBES THE BROAD RANGE OF TOPICS &
ISSUES COVERED IN GRADUATE PUBLIC
WORKS CURRICULA AT VARIOUS
UNIVERSITIES & SOME OF THE CAREER
OPPORTUNITIES IN PUBLIC WORKS
MANAGEMENT. 12 PAGES.

1754

SAVE A FORTUNE

AUTHOR-PHILLIP GODWIN; ISBN # 0-945332-05-X

AGORA BOOKS
842 E.BALTIMORE ST
BALTIMORE MD 21202

COST-$14.95

A COMMON SENSE PLAN TO BUILDING WEALTH
THROUGH SAVING RATHER THAN EARNING.
INCLUDES INFO ON HOW TO SAVE ON TAXES;
EDUCATION; HOUSING; TRAVEL; HEALTH;
ETC. 209 PAGES.

HELPFUL PUBLICATIONS

1755

SCHOLARSHIPS & LOANS FOR NURSING EDUCATION

AUTHOR-NLN; ISBN #0-88737-505-7

NATIONAL LEAGUE FOR NURSING
350 HUDSON ST
NEW YORK NY 10014

COST-$10.95 + $3.50 POSTAGE

COMPLETE GUIDE TO FINANCIAL AID FOR
NURSING AND HEALTH CARE PROFESSIONS.
LISTS SCHOLARSHIPS; FELLOWSHIPS;
GRANTS; TRAINEESHIPS; LOANS & SPECIAL
AWARDS. 82 PAGES.

1756

STUDENT FINANCIAL AID & SCHOLARSHIPS AT WYOMING COLLEGES

AUTHOR-

UNIVERSITY OF WYOMING; DIV. OF FINANCIAL
AID
PO BOX 3335
LARAMIE WY 82071

COST-FREE

DESCRIPTION OF POST-SECONDARY STUDENT AID
& SCHOLARSHIP PROGRAMS THAT ARE
AVAILABLE TO WYOMING STUDENTS.
BOOKLETS CAN BE OBTAINED AT ALL
WYOMING HIGH SCHOOLS AND COLLEGES.

1757

STUDENT GUIDE TO FINANCIAL AID

AUTHOR-U.S. DEPARTMENT OF EDUCATION

FEDERAL STUDENT AID INFORMATION CENTER
PO BOX 84
WASHINGTON DC 20044

COST-FREE

LISTS QUALIFICATIONS & SOURCES OF
INFORMATION FOR FEDERAL GRANTS;
LOANS AND WORK-STUDY PROGRAMS.

1758

STUDY ABROAD (VOL 27; 1992-94)

AUTHOR-UNESCO

UNITED NATIONS EDUCATIONAL; SCIENTIFIC
AND CULTURAL ORGANIZATION
UNIPUB; UNESCO AGENT U7154; 4611-F
ASSEMBLY DRIVE
LANHAM MD 20706

COST-$24.00 + POSTAGE & HANDLING

PRINTED IN ENGLISH; FRENCH & SPANISH THIS
VOLUME LISTS 3700 INTERNATIONAL STUDY
PROGRAMS IN ALL ACADEMIC &
PROFESSIONAL FIELDS IN MORE THAN 124
COUNTRIES.

1759

TAFT CORPORATE GIVING DIRECTORY

AUTHOR-ISBN #0-914756-79-6

TAFT GROUP
12300 TWINBROOK PKWY; SUITE 450
ROCKVILLE MD 20852

COST-$327.00

THIS REFERENCE BOOK CAN BE FOUND IN MOST
MAJOR LIBRARIES. CONTAINS
COMPREHENSIVE INFORMATION ON OVER
500 FOUNDATIONS WHICH ARE SPONSORED
BY TOP CORPORATIONS. 859 PAGES.

1760

THE A'S & B'S OF ACADEMIC SCHOLARSHIPS

AUTHOR-DEBBIE KLEIN; EDITOR

OCTAMERON ASSOCIATES
PO BOX 2748
ALEXANDRIA VA 22301

COST-$7.50 POSTPAID

PROVIDES INFORMATION ON ACADEMIC
SCHOLARSHIPS AT 1200 SCHOOLS. ALSO
INFORMATION ON PREREQUISITES.

1761

THE FACTS ABOUT ARMY ROTC

AUTHOR-U.S. ARMY

U.S. ARMY - COLLEGE ARMY ROTC
GOLD QUEST CENTER - PO BOX 3279
WARMINSTER PA 18974

COST-FREE

PROVIDES INFORMATION ON TYPES OF
SCHOLARSHIPS AVAILABLE; ELIGIBILITY;
DEADLINES; APPLICATION PROCEDURES AND
MONETARY VALUE.

1762

UNIVERSITY CURRICULA IN OCEANOGRAPHY AND RELATED FIELDS

AUTHOR-MARINE TECHNOLOGY SOCIETY

MARINE TECHNOLOGY SOCIETY
1828 L ST NW - SUITE 906
WASHINGTON DC 20036

COST-$5 SHIPPING/HANDLING

A GUIDE TO CURRENT MARINE DEGREE
PROGRAMS AND VOCATIONAL INSTRUCTION
AVAILABLE IN THE MARINE FIELD.
CONSOLIDATES AND HIGHLIGHTS DATA
NEEDED BY HIGH SCHOOL STUDENTS AS
WELL AS COLLEGE STUDENTS SEEKING
ADVANCED DEGREES.

1763 ─────────────────────

UNLOCKING POTENTIAL

AUTHOR-BARBARA SCHEIBER & JEANNE TALPERS; ISBN #0-917561-30-9

ADLER & ADLER PUBLISHERS INC
WOODBINE HOUSE; 5615 FISHERS LN
ROCKVILLE MD 20852

COST-$12.95

A STEP-BY-STEP GUIDE ON COLLEGE & OTHER CHOICES FOR LEARNING DISABLED PEOPLE. DISCUSSES CHOOSING THE RIGHT POST-SECONDARY SCHOOL; ADMISSIONS PROCESS; OVERCOMING ACADEMIC HURDLES & MUCH MORE. 195 PAGES.

1764 ─────────────────────

VACATION STUDY ABROAD

AUTHOR-SARA STEEN; EDITOR

INSTITUTE OF INTERNATIONAL EDUCATION
IIE BOOKS; 809 UNITED NATIONS PLAZA
NEW YORK NY 10017

COST-$31.95

GUIDE TO SOME 1450 SUMMER OR SHORT TERM STUDY-ABROAD PROGRAMS SPONSORED BY USA COLLEGES; UNIVERSITIES; PRIVATE INSTITUTIONS & FOREIGN INSTITUTIONS. 330 PAGES.

1765 ─────────────────────

WHAT COLOR IS YOUR PARACHUTE?

AUTHOR-RICHARD N. BOLLES; ISBN #0-89815-492-8

TEN SPEED PRESS
PO BOX 7123
BERKELEY CA 94707

COST-$14.95 PLUS $2 POSTAGE

STEP-BY-STEP CAREER PLANNING GUIDE. HIGHLY RECOMMENDED FOR ANYONE WHO IS JOB HUNTING OR CHANGING CAREERS. VALUABLE TIPS ON ASSESSING YOUR SKILLS; RESUME WRITING; HANDLING JOB INTERVIEWS. 464 PAGES.

1766 ─────────────────────

WORK-STUDY-TRAVEL ABROAD - THE WHOLE WORLD HANDBOOK

AUTHOR-ST. MARTINS PRESS

COUNCIL ON INTERNATIONAL EDUCATIONAL EXCHANGE
205 E.42ND ST; 16TH FLOOR
NEW YORK NY 10017

COST-$12.95

EXCELLENT BOOK ON THE BASICS OF TRAVELING; WORKING AND STUDYING ABROAD. HOW TO FIND OUT ABOUT STUDY-ABROAD OPPORTUNITIES; GRANTS; SCHOLARSHIPS; EXCHANGE PROGRAMS AND TEACHING OPPORTUNITIES. ALSO INFORMATION ON THE CHEAPEST WAYS TO TRAVEL.

1767 ─────────────────────

WORLD DIRECTORY OF MEDICAL SCHOOLS

AUTHOR-WHO

WORLD HEALTH ORGANIZATION
WHO PUBLICATION CENTER; 49 SHERIDAN AVE.
ALBANY NY 12210

COST-$35

COMPREHENSIVE BOOK WHICH DESCRIBES THE MEDICAL EDUCATION PROGRAMS & SCHOOLS IN EACH COUNTRY. ARRANGED IN ORDER BY COUNTRY OR AREA.

1768 ─────────────────────

YOU...THE DOCTOR

AUTHOR-AMA

AMERICAN MEDICAL ASSOCIATION
535 NORTH DEARBORN ST
CHICAGO IL 60610

COST-FREE

PAMPHLET THAT DESCRIBES OPPORTUNITIES IN THE MEDICAL PROFESSION AND DETAILS THE PREPARATIONS FOR THE PRACTICE OF MEDICINE.

Career Information

1769 'LAW AS A CAREER' BOOKLET
AMERICAN BAR ASSOCIATION
750 NORTH LAKE SHORE DR
CHICAGO IL 60611

1770 ACCOUNTING CAREER INFORMATION
NATIONAL SOCIETY OF PUBLIC ACCOUNTANTS
1010 NORTH FAIRFAX ST
ALEXANDRIA VA 22314

1771 ACCOUNTING CAREER INFORMATION
INSTITUTE OF MANAGEMENT ACCOUNTANTS
10 PARAGON DR
MONTVALE NJ 07645

1772 ACCOUNTING CAREER INFORMATION FOR WOMEN
AMERICAN SOCIETY OF WOMAN ACCOUNTANTS
NATIONAL HEADQUARTERS; 1755 LYNFIELD RD.
SUITE 222
MEMPHIS TN 38119

1773 ACTUARIAL SCIENCE CAREER INFORMATION
SOCIETY OF ACTUARIES
475 N. MARTINGALE RD. SUITE 800
SCHAUMBURG IL 60173

1774 ADVERTISING CAREER INFORMATION
AMERICAN ADVERTISING FEDERATION
EDUCATION SERVICES; SUITE 1000; 1400 K ST. NW
WASHINGTON DC 20005

1775 AERONAUTICS CAREER INFORMATION
AMERICAN INSTITUTE OF AERONAUTICS AND
ASTRONAUTICS - STUDENT PROGRAMS DEPT.
370 L'ENFANT PROMENADE SW
WASHINGTON DC 20024

1776 AEROSPACE EDUCATION CAREER INFORMATION
AEROSPACE EDUCATION FOUNDATION
1501 LEE HIGHWAY
ARLINGTON VA 22209

1777 AGRICULTURAL ENGINEERING (CAREER INFORMATION)
AMERICAN SOCIETY OF AGRICULTURAL
ENGINEERS
2950 NILES ROAD
ST JOSEPH MI 49085

1778 AGRICULTURE CAREER INFORMATION
AMERICAN FARM BUREAU FEDERATION
225 TOUHY AVE
PARK RIDGE IL 60068

1779 AGRONOMY CAREER INFORMATION
AMERICAN SOCIETY OF AGRONOMY
677 SOUTH SEGOE ROAD
MADISON WI 53711

1780 AIR FORCE (CAREER INFORMATION)
HEADQUARTERS; U.S. AIR FORCE
USAF RECRUITING SERVICE
RANDOLPH AFB TX 78148

1781 AIRLINE (CAREER INFORMATION)
AIR TRANSPORT ASSOCIATION OF AMERICA
1301 PENNSLVANIA AVE NW; SUITE 1100
WASHINGTON DC 20004

1782 ANIMAL BIOLOGY/ZOOLOGIST CAREER INFORMATION
AMERICAN SOCIETY OF ZOOLOGISTS
104 SIRIUS CIRCLE
THOUSAND OAKS CA 91360

1783 ANIMAL SCIENCE CAREER INFORMATION
NATIONAL ASSOCIATION OF ANIMAL BREEDERS
INC
401 BERNADETTE DRIVE; PO BOX 1033
COLUMBIA MO 65205

1784 ANIMAL SCIENCE CAREER INFORMATION
AMERICAN SOCIETY OF ANIMAL SCIENCE
BUSINESS OFFICE; 309 W. CLARK ST.
CHAMPAIGN IL 61820

1785 ANTHROPOLOGIST CAREER INFORMATION
AMERICAN ANTHROPOLOGICAL ASSOCIATION
1703 NEW HAMPSHIRE AVE NW
WASHINGTON DC 20009

1786 APPRAISER CAREER INFORMATION (REAL ESTATE; GEMOLOGY; MACHINERY & EQUIPMENT; PERSONAL PROPERTY; ETC.)
AMERICAN SOCIETY OF APPRAISERS
PO BOX 17265
WASHINGTON DC 20041

1787 APPRENTICESHIP (CAREER INFORMATION)
U.S. DEPT. OF LABOR BUREAU OF
APPRENTICESHIP AND TRAINING
200 CONSTITUTION AVE NW; RM N-4649
WASHINGTON DC 20210

1788 ARCHAEOLOGIST CAREER INFORMATION
ARCHAEOLOGICAL INSTITUTE OF AMERICA
675 COMMONWEALTH AVE
BOSTON MA 02215

1789 ARCHAEOLOGY CAREER INFORMATION
SOCIETY FOR AMERICAN ARCHAEOLOGY
808 17TH ST NW #200
WASHINGTON DC 20006

1790 ARCHITECTURE CAREER INFORMATION
AMERICAN INSTITUTE OF ARCHITECTS
1735 NEW YORK AVENUE NW
WASHINGTON DC 20006

1791 ASTRONOMY CAREER INFORMATION
AMERICAN ASTRONOMICAL SOCIETY
EDUCATION OFFICER; ASTRONOMY DEPT.;
UNIVERSITY OF TEXAS
AUSTIN TX 78712

1792 AUDIOLOGY CAREER INFORMATION
AMERICAN SPEECH-LANGUAGE-HEARING
ASSOCIATION
10801 ROCKVILLE PIKE
ROCKVILLE MD 20852

**1793 AUTHOR/WRITER (CAREER
INFORMATION)**
PEN AMERICAN CENTER
568 BROADWAY; SUITE 401
NEW YORK NY 10012

**1794 AUTOMOTIVE ENGINEERING (CAREER
INFORMATION)**
SOCIETY OF AUTOMOTIVE ENGINEERS INC
400 COMMONWEALTH DRIVE
WARRENDALE PA 15096

1795 BANKING (CAREER INFORMATION)
AMERICAN BANKERS ASSOCIATION
LIBRARY & INFORMATION SYSTEMS; 1120
CONNECTICUT AVE NW
WASHINGTON DC 20036

1796 BIOLOGIST CAREER INFORMATION
AMERICAN INSTITUTE OF BIOLOGICAL SCIENCES
730 11TH ST NW
WASHINGTON DC 20001

**1797 BIOTECHNOLOGY (CAREER
INFORMATION)**
INDUSTRIAL BIOTECHNOLOGY ASSOCIATION
1625 'K' STREET NW; SUITE 1100
WASHINGTON DC 20006

1798 BROADCAST NEWS CAREER INFORMATION
RADIO & TELEVISION NEWS DIRECTORS ASSN.
1000 CONNECTICUT AVE NW; SUITE 615
WASHINGTON DC 20036

1799 BROADCASTING CAREER INFORMATION
AMERICAN WOMEN IN RADIO & TELEVISION
1101 CONNECTICUT AVE NW; SUITE 700
WASHINGTON DC 20036

**1800 BUSINESS ADMINISTRATION CAREER
INFORMATION**
AMERICAN ASSEMBLY OF COLLEGIATE SCHOOLS
OF BUSINESS
605 OLD BALLAS RD #220
ST LOUIS MO 63141

**1801 BUSINESS EDUCATION (CAREER
INFORMATION)**
NATIONAL BUSINESS EDUCATION ASSOCIATION
1914 ASSOCIATION DR
RESTON VA 22091

1802 CAREERS IN THE DENTAL PROFESSION
AMERICAN DENTAL ASSOCIATION
211 E. CHICAGO AVE. SUITE 1804
CHICAGO IL 60611

1803 CARTOONING CAREER INFORMATION
NEWSPAPER FEATURES COUNCIL
37 ARCH ST
GREENWICH CT 06830

1804 CHIROPRACTIC (CAREER INFORMATION)
AMERICAN CHIROPRACTIC ASSOCIATION
1701 CLARENDON BLVD
ARLINGTON VA 22209

**1805 CHIROPRACTIC CAREER & SCHOOLS
INFORMATION**
INTERNATIONAL CHIROPRACTORS ASSOCIATION
1110 N. GLEBE ROAD SUITE 1000
ARLINGTON VA 22201

**1806 CIVIL ENGINEERING CAREER
INFORMATION**
AMERICAN SOCIETY OF CIVIL ENGINEERS
345 E. 47TH ST.
NEW YORK NY 10017

**1807 CLINICAL CHEMIST (CAREER
INFORMATION)**
AMERICAN ASSOCIATION FOR CLINICAL
CHEMISTRY
2029 K ST NW; SEVENTH FLOOR
WASHINGTON DC 20006

**1808 COMMUNICATIONS CAREER & SCHOOLS
INFORMATION**
ACCREDITING COUNCIL ON EDUCATION IN
JOURNALISM AND MASS COMMUNICATION
UNIVERSITY OF KANSAS SCHOOL OF
JOURNALISM
LAWRENCE KS 66045

**1809 COMPUTER SCIENCE CAREER
INFORMATION**
IEEE - USA
1828 L ST NW - SUITE 1202
WASHINGTON DC 20036

CAREER INFORMATION

1810 CONSTRUCTION CAREER INFORMATION
ASSOCIATED GENERAL CONTRACTORS OF
    AMERICA
1957 'E' ST NW
WASHINGTON DC 20006

1811 COSMETOLOGY CAREER INFORMATION
ASSOCIATION OF ACCREDITED COSMETOLOGY
    SCHOOLS
5201 LEESBURG PIKE; SUITE 205
FALLS CHURCH VA 22041

1812 CRAFTSMEN CAREER INFORMATION
AMERICAN CRAFT COUNCIL
72 SPRING ST
NEW YORK NY 10012

1813 CREATIVE WRITING (CAREER INFORMATION)
NATIONAL WRITERS CLUB
1450 S.HAVANA; SUITE 620
AURORA CO 80012

1814 DANCE CAREER INFORMATION
AMERICAN ALLIANCE FOR HEALTH; PHYSICAL
    EDUCATION; RECREATION & DANCE
1900 ASSOCIATION DR
RESTON VA 22091

1815 DATA PROCESSING MANAGEMENT (CAREER INFORMATION)
DATA PROCESSING MANAGEMENT ASSOCIATION
505 BUSSE HIGHWAY
PARK RIDGE IL 60068

1816 DEMOGRAPHY
POPULATION ASSOCIATION OF AMERICA
1722 N STREET NW
WASHINGTON DC 20036

1817 DENTAL ASSISTANT CAREER INFORMATION
AMERICAN DENTAL ASSISTANTS ASSN
919 N.MICHIGAN AVE; SUITE 3400
CHICAGO IL 60611

1818 DENTAL HYGIENIST (CAREER INFORMATION)
AMERICAN DENTAL HYGIENISTS ASSN INSTITUTE
    FOR ORAL HEALTH
444 NORTH MICHIGAN AVENUE; SUITE 3400
CHICAGO IL 60611

1819 DENTAL LAB TECHNOLOGY CAREER INFORMATION
NATIONAL ASSOCIATION OF DENTAL
    LABORATORIES
3801 MT VERNON AVE
ALEXANDRIA VA 22305

1820 DENTISTRY CAREER INFORMATION
AMERICAN ASSOCIATION OF DENTAL SCHOOLS
1625 MASSACHUSETTS AVE NW; SUITE 502
WASHINGTON DC 20036

1821 DIETETIC CAREER INFORMATION
AMERICAN DIETETIC ASSOCIATION
ATTN MEMBERSHIP DEPARTMENT; 216 W.
JACKSON BLVD - SUITE 800
CHICAGO IL 60606

1822 DRAMA/ACTING (CAREER INFORMATION)
SCREEN ACTORS GUILD
7065 HOLLYWOOD BLVD
HOLLYWOOD CA 90028

1823 EDUCATION CAREER INFORMATION
AMERICAN FEDERATION OF TEACHERS
PUBLIC AFFIARS DEPARTMENT - 555 NEW JERSEY
AVE NW
WASHINGTON DC 20001

1824 EDUCATION CAREERS INFORMATION
NATIONAL EDUCATION ASSOCIATION
1201 16TH STREET NW
WASHINGTON DC 20036

1825 ELECTRICAL ENGINEERING CAREER INFORMATION
INSTITUTE OF ELECTRICAL AND ELECTRONICS
    ENGINEERS - UNITED STATES ACTIVITIES
1828 L ST NW - SUITE 1202
WASHINGTON DC 20036

1826 ENERGY CAREERS INFORMATION
AMERICAN GAS ASSOC
1515 WILSON BLVD.
ARLINGTON VA 22209

1827 ENGINEERING (CONSULTING) CAREER INFORMATION
AMERICAN CONSULTING ENGINEERS COUNCIL
1015 15TH NW #802
WASHINGTON DC 20005

1828 ENGINEERING (CAREER INFORMATION)
NATIONAL SOCIETY OF PROFESSIONAL
    ENGINEERS
1420 KING STREET
ALEXANDRIA VA 22314

1829 ENGINEERING CAREER INFORMATION
JUNIOR ENGINEERING TECHNICAL SOCIETY INC
    (JETS)
1420 KING ST; SUITE 405
ALEXANDRIA VA 22314

1830 ENTOMOLOGY (CAREER INFORMATION)
ENTOMOLOGICAL SOCIETY OF AMERICA
9301 ANNAPOLIS ROAD
LANHAM MD 20706

1831 ENVIRONMENTAL STUDIES & CAREER INFORMATION
U.S. ENVIRONMENTAL PROTECTION AGENCY
401 M STREET SW; OFFICE OF PUBLIC AFFAIRS
WASHINGTON DC 20460

1832 F.B.I. CAREER INFORMATION
FEDERAL BUREAU OF INVESTIGATION
DEPARTMENT OF JUSTICE
WASHINGTON DC 20535

1833 FARM MANAGEMENT CAREER INFORMATION
U.S. DEPT. OF AGRICULTURE; FARMERS HOME ADMINISTRATION
HUMAN RESOURCES; 14TH & INDEPENDENCE AVE SW
WASHINGTON DC 20250

1834 FASHION DESIGN CAREER INFORMATION
FASHION INSTITUTE OF TECHNOLOGY
227 WEST 27TH STREET
NEW YORK NY 10001

1835 FIRE SERVICE (CAREER INFORMATION)
NATIONAL FIRE PROTECTION ASSOCIATION
1 BATTERYMARCH PARK; PO BOX 9101
QUINCY MA 02269

1836 FISHERIES (CAREER & UNIVERSITY INFORMATION)
AMERICAN FISHERIES SOCIETY
5410 GROSVENOR LANE - SUITE 110
BETHESDA MD 20814

1837 FLORISTRY CAREER INFORMATION
SOCIETY OF AMERICAN FLORISTS
1601 DUKE ST
ALEXANDRIA VA 22314

1838 FOOD AND NUTRITION SERVICE (CAREER INFORMATION)
U.S. DEPT. OF AGRICULTURE; FOOD AND NUTRITION SERVICE
PERSONNEL DIVISION; ROOM 620 - 1301 PARK CENTER DR
ALEXANDRIA VA 22302

1839 FOOD RETAILING (CAREER INFORMATION)
FOOD MARKETING INSTITUTE
800 CONNECTICUT AVE NW
WASHINGTON DC 20006

1840 FOOD TECHNOLOGY/SCIENCE CAREER INFORMATION
INSTITUTE OF FOOD TECHNOLOGISTS
221 NORTH LASALLE STREET
CHICAGO IL 60601

1841 FOODSERVICE (CAREER INFORMATION)
EDUCATIONAL FOUNDATION OF NATIONAL RESTAURANT ASSOC
250 S.WACKER DR; SUITE 1400
CHICAGO IL 60606

1842 FOREIGN LANGUAGES CAREER INFORMATION
MODERN LANGUAGE ASSOCIATION OF AMERICA
10 ASTOR PLACE
NEW YORK NY 10003

1843 FOREIGN SERVICE OFFICER CAREER INFORMATION
U.S. DEPT. OF STATE-RECRUITMENT DIVISION
PO BOX 9317-ROSSLYN STATION
ARLINGTON VA 22219

1844 FOREST SERVICE CAREER INFORMATION
U.S. DEPT. OF AGRICULTURE
14TH & INDEPENDENCE AVENUE; ROOM 801 RPE
WASHINGTON DC 20250

1845 FORESTRY CAREER INFORMATION
SOCIETY OF AMERICAN FORESTERS
5400 GROSVENOR LANE
BETHESDA MD 20814

1846 FUNERAL DIRECTOR (CAREER INFORMATION)
NATIONAL FUNERAL DIRECTORS ASSN
11121 WEST OKLAHOMA AVE
MILWAUKEE WI 53227

1847 GEOGRAPHY CAREER INFORMATION
ASSOCIATION OF AMERICAN GEOGRAPHERS
1710 SIXTEENTH ST NW
WASHINGTON DC 20009

1848 GEOLOGICAL SCIENCES CAREER INFORMATION
AMERICAN GEOLOGICAL INSTITUTE
4220 KING STREET
ALEXANDRIA VA 22302

1849 GEOPHYSICIST CAREER INFORMATION
SOCIETY OF EXPLORATION GEOPHYSICISTS
PO BOX 702740
TULSA OK 74170

1850 GEOPHYSICS CAREER INFORMATION
AMERICAN GEOPHYSICAL UNION
2000 FLORIDA AVENUE NW
WASHINGTON DC 20009

1851 GRAPHIC ARTS CAREER INFORMATION
EDUCATION COUNCIL ON GRAPHIC ARTS INC
1899 PRESTON WHITE DR.
RESTON VA 22091

CAREER INFORMATION

1852 GRAPHIC ARTS CAREER INFORMATION
AMERICAN INSTITUTE OF GRAPHIC ARTS
1059 THIRD AVE
NEW YORK NY 10021

1853 HEALTH FIELDS CAREER INFORMATION
NATIONAL HEALTH COUNCIL INC.
1730 M ST NW; SUITE 500
WASHINGTON DC 20036

1854 HEALTH PROFESSIONALS PRACTICE OPPORTUNITY (CAREER INFORMATION)
U.S. DEPT. OF HEALTH AND HUMAN SERVICES-NATIONAL HEALTH SERVICE CORPS
8201 GREENSBORO DR; SUITE 600
MCLEAN VA 22102

1855 HEATING & AIR CONDITIONING ENGINEER CAREER INFORMATION
REFRIGERATION SERVICE ENGINEERS SOCIETY
1666 RAND ROAD
DES PLAINES IL 60016

1856 HOME ECONOMIST CAREER INFORMATION
AMERICAN HOME ECONOMICS ASSOCIATION
1555 KING ST
ALEXANDRIA VA 22314

1857 HORTICULTURE CAREER INFORMATION
AMERICAN ASSOCIATION OF NURSERYMEN
1250 'I' STREET NW
WASHINGTON DC 20005

1858 HOSPITAL ADMINISTRATION CAREER INFORMATION
AMERICAN COLLEGE OF HEALTH CARE EXECUTIVES
840 NORTH LAKE SHORE DRIVE
CHICAGO IL 60611

1859 HOTEL MANAGEMENT CAREER INFORMATION
AMERICAN HOTEL AND MOTEL ASSOCIATION
1201 NEW YORK AVE NW; SUITE 600
WASHINGTON DC 20005

1860 ILLUMINATING ENGINEERING CAREER INFORMATION
ILLUMINATING ENGINEERING SOCIETY OF NORTH AMERICA
345 EAST 47TH STREET
NEW YORK NY 10017

1861 INSURANCE - CAREER INFORMATION
INSURANCE INFORMATION INSTITUTE
110 WILLIAM STREET
NEW YORK NY 10038

1862 INSURANCE CAREER INFORMATION
ALLIANCE OF AMERICAN INSURERS
1501 WOODFIELD RD; SUITE 400W
SCHAUMBURG IL 60173

1863 JOURNALISM CAREER INFORMATION FOR MINORITIES
AMERICAN SOCIETY OF NEWSPAPER EDITORS
PO BOX 17004; MINORITY AFFAIRS DIRECTOR
WASHINGTON DC 20041

1864 LANDSCAPE ARCHITECTURE CAREER INFORMATION
AMERICAN SOCIETY OF LANDSCAPE ARCHITECTS
4401 CONNECTICUT AVE NW; 5TH FL
WASHINGTON DC 20008

1865 LAW LIBRARIANSHIP
AMERICAN ASSOCIATION OF LAW LIBRARIES
53 WEST JACKSON BLVD; SUITE 940
CHICAGO IL 60604

1866 LEARNING DISABLED (EDUCATION & CAREER INFORMATION)
LEARNING DISABILITIES ASSOCIATION OF AMERICA
4156 LIBRARY RD
PITTSBURGH PA 15234

1867 LIBRARY SCIENCE CAREER INFORMATION
AMERICAN LIBRARY ASSN
OFFICE FOR LIBRARY PERSONNEL RESOURCES; 50 EAST HURON ST.
CHICAGO IL 60611

1868 MACHINE TECHNOLOGY (CAREER INFORMATION)
AMT - THE ASSOCIATION FOR MANUFACTURING TECHNOLOGY
7901 WESTPARK DR
MCLEAN VA 22102

1869 MACHINE TECHNOLOGY (CAREER INFORMATION)
NATIONAL TOOLING AND MACHINING ASSN
9300 LIVINGSTON ROAD
FT WASHINGTON MD 20744

1870 MANAGEMENT CAREER INFORMATION
CLUB FOUNDATION (THE)
1733 KING ST
ALEXANDRIA VA 22314

1871 MANAGEMENT CAREER INFORMATION
AMERICAN MANAGEMENT ASSOCIATION
135 WEST 50TH STREET
NEW YORK NY 10020

1872 MARINE TECHNOLOGY (CAREER INFORMATION)
U.S. DEPT. OF COMMERCE/NOAA (NATIONAL SEA GRANT COLLEGE PROGRAM; R/OR-1)
1335 EAST-WEST HWY
SILVER SPRING MD 20910

1873 MATHEMATICIAN CAREER INFORMATION
MATHEMATICAL ASSOCIATION OF AMERICA
1529 18TH STREET NW
WASHINGTON DC 20036

1874 MATHEMATICS TEACHER CAREER INFORMATION
NATIONAL COUNCIL OF TEACHERS OF MATHEMATICS
1906 ASSOCIATION DRIVE
RESTON VA 22091

1875 MECHANICAL ENGINEER CAREER INFORMATION
AMERICAN SOCIETY OF MECHANICAL ENGINEERS
UNITED ENGINEERING CENTER 345 EAST 47TH STREET
NEW YORK NY 10017

1876 MEDICAL LABORATORY CAREER INFORMATION
AMERICAN SOCIETY OF CLINICAL PATHOLOGISTS
CAREERS; 2100 W. HARRISON
CHICAGO IL 60612

1877 MEDICAL RECORDS CAREER INFORMATION
AMERICAN MEDICAL RECORD ASSOCIATION
919 NORTH MICHIGAN AVE; SUITE 1400
CHICAGO IL 60611

1878 MEDICAL TECHNOLOGIST CAREER INFORMATION
AMERICAN MEDICAL TECHNOLOGISTS
710 HIGGINS ROAD
PARK RIDGE IL 60068

1879 MEDICINE CAREER INFORMATION
AMERICAN MEDICAL ASSOCIATION
515 N STATE ST
CHICAGO IL 60610

1880 METALLURGY & MATERIALS SCIENCE CAREER INFORMATION
ASM INTERNATIONAL
STUDENT OUTREACH PROGRAM
MATERIALS PARK OH 44073

1881 MICROBIOLOGY CAREER INFORMATION
AMERICAN SOCIETY FOR MICROBIOLOGY
1325 MASSACHUSETTS AVE NW
WASHINGTON DC 20005

1882 MOTION PICTURE (CAREER INFORMATION)
SOCIETY OF MOTION PICTURE AND TELEVISION ENGINEERS
595 W.HARTSDALE AVE
WHITE PLAINS NY 10607

1883 MOTION PICTURE CAREER INFORMATION
ACADEMY OF MOTION PICTURE ARTS AND SCIENCES
8949 WILSHIRE BLVD
BEVERLY HILLS CA 90211

1884 MUSIC CAREER INFORMATION.
MUSIC EDUCATORS NATIONAL CONFERENCE
1902 ASSOCIATION DRIVE
RESTON VA 22091

1885 MUSIC PERFORMER & COMPOSER CAREER INFORMATION
AMERICAN MUSIC CENTER
DIRECTOR OF INFORMATION; 30 W. 26TH ST. SUITE 1001
NEW YORK NY 10010

1886 MUSIC THERAPY (CAREER INFORMATION)
NATIONAL ASSOCIATION FOR MUSIC THERAPY
8455 COLESVILLE ROAD; SUITE 930
SILVER SPRING MD 20910

1887 NAVAL ARCHITECTURE (CAREER INFORMATION)
SOCIETY OF NAVAL ARCHITECTS & MARINE ENGINEERS
601 PAVONIA AVE
JERSEY CITY NJ 07306

1888 NAVAL/MARINE ENGINEERING (CAREER INFORMATION)
SOCIETY OF NAVAL ARCHITECTS & MARINE ENGINEERS
601 PAVONIA AVE
JERSEY CITY NJ 07306

1889 NEWSPAPER INDUSTRY (CAREER INFORMATION)
NEWSPAPER ASSOCIATION OF AMERICA
THE NEWSPAPER CENTER; 11600 SUNRISE VALLEY DR
RESTON VA 22091

1890 NURSE ANESTHETIST CAREER INFORMATION
AMERICAN ASSOCIATION OF NURSE ANESTHETISTS
216 HIGGINS RD
PARKRIDGE IL 60068

1891 NURSING (CAREER INFORMATION)
NATIONAL LEAGUE FOR NURSING INC
350 HUDSON ST
NEW YORK NY 10014

CAREER INFORMATION

1892 NURSING CAREER INFORMATION
AMERICAN NURSES ASSN
600 MARYLAND AVE SW; SUITE 100 WEST
WASHINGTON DC 20024

1893 NUTRITIONIST CAREER INFORMATION
AMERICAN DIETETIC ASSOCIATION
ATTN MEMBERSHIP DEPARTMENT; 216 W
JACKSON BLVD - SUITE 800
CHICAGO IL 60606

**1894 OCEANOGRAPHY & MARINE SCIENCE
(CAREER INFORMATION)**
MARINE TECHNOLOGY SOCIETY
1828 L STREET NW; SUITE 906
WASHINGTON DC 20036

1895 OPTOMETRIC ASSISTANT/TECHNICIAN
AMERICAN OPTOMETRIC ASSN
243 NORTH LINDBERGH BLVD
ST LOUIS MO 63141

1896 OPTOMETRIST CAREER INFORMATION
NATIONAL OPTOMETRIC ASSOCIATION
2838 S INDIANA AVE
CHICAGO IL 60616

1897 OPTOMETRY CAREER INFORMATION
AMERICAN OPTOMETRIC ASSN
243 NORTH LINDBERGH BLVD
ST LOUIS MO 63141

1898 ORNITHOLOGIST CAREER INFORMATION
AMERICAN ORNITHOLOGISTS' UNION
SMITHSONIAN INSTITUTION; DIV OF BIRDS
WASHINGTON DC 20560

**1899 OSTEOPATHIC MEDICINE CAREER
INFORMATION**
AMERICAN OSTEOPATHIC ASSN.
142 E ONTARIO ST
CHICAGO IL 60611

1900 PALEONTOLOGY (CAREER INFORMATION)
PALEONTOLOGICAL SOCIETY
DR. DONALD L. WOLBERG; SECRETARY; PO BOX
1937
SOCORRO NM 87801

1901 PATHOLOGY (CAREER INFORMATION)
INTERSOCIETY COMMITTEE ON PATHOLOGY
INFORMATION
4733 BETHESDA AVE; SUITE 735
BETHESDA MD 20814

1902 PEDIATRICIAN CAREER INFORMATION
AMERICAN ACADEMY OF PEDIATRICS
141 NW POINT BLVD; PO BOX 927
ELK GROVE VILLAGE IL 60009

**1903 PETROLEUM ENGINEERING CAREER
INFORMATION**
SOCIETY OF PETROLEUM ENGINEERS
222 PALISADAS CREEK DR; PO BOX 833836
RICHARDSON TX 75080

1904 PHARMACOLOGY CAREER INFORMATION
AMERICAN SOCIETY FOR PHARMACOLOGY AND
EXPERIMENTAL THERAPEUTICS INC.
9650 ROCKVILLE PIKE
BETHESDA MD 20814

**1905 PHARMACY (BOOKLET ON ACCREDITED
SCHOOLS)**
AMERICAN COUNCIL ON PHARMACEUTICAL
EDUCATION
311 W. SUPERIOR #512
CHICAGO IL 60610

1906 PHARMACY CAREER INFORMATION
AMERICAN ASSOCIATION OF COLLEGES OF
PHARMACY
OFFICE OF STUDENT AFFAIRS; 1426 PRINCE ST
ALEXANDRIA VA 22314

1907 PHARMACY CAREER INFORMATION
AMERICAN FOUNDATION FOR PHARMACEUTICAL
EDUCATION
PO BOX 7126; 618 SOMERSET ST
NORTH PLAINFIELD NJ 07060

**1908 PHOTOJOURNALISM CAREER
INFORMATION**
NATIONAL PRESS PHOTOGRAPHERS ASSN
3200 CROASDAILE DR #306
DURHAM NC 27705

**1909 PHYSICAL THERAPY CAREER
INFORMATION**
AMERICAN PHYSICAL THERAPY ASSOCIATION
1111 NORTH FAIRFAX ST
ALEXANDRIA VA 22314

1910 PHYSICS CAREER INFORMATION
AMERICAN INSTITUTE OF PHYSICS
335 EAST 45TH STREET
NEW YORK NY 10017

1911 PODIATRY CAREER INFORMATION
AMERICAN PODIATRIC MEDICAL ASSN
9312 OLD GEORGETOWN RD
BETHESDA MD 20814

**1912 POLITICAL SCIENCE CAREER
INFORMATION**
AMERICAN POLITICAL SCIENCE ASSN
1527 NEW HAMPSHIRE AVE NW
WASHINGTON DC 20036

1913 PRINTING INDUSTRY CAREER INFORMATION
PRINTING INDUSTRIES OF AMERICA INC.
ATTENTION CAREERS- MEMBER PROGRAMS; 100 DAINGERFIELD RD
ALEXANDRIA VA 22314

1914 PSYCHIATRY CAREER INFORMATION
AMERICAN PSYCHIATRIC ASSOCIATION
1400 'K' STREET NW
WASHINGTON DC 20005

1915 PSYCHOLOGY CAREER INFORMATION
AMERICAN PSYCHOLOGICAL ASSOCIATION
750 FIRST ST NE
WASHINGTON DC 20002

1916 PUBLIC RELATIONS (CAREER INFORMATION)
PUBLIC RELATIONS SOCIETY OF AMERICA
33 IRVING PLACE
NEW YORK NY 10003

1917 RADIOLOGIC TECHNOLOGIST CAREER INFORMATION
AMERICAN SOCIETY OF RADIOLOGIC TECHNOLOGISTS
15000 CENTRAL AVE SE
ALBUQUERQUE NM 87123

1918 RANGE MANAGEMENT (CAREER INFORMATION)
SOCIETY FOR RANGE MANAGEMENT
1839 YORK ST
DENVER CO 80206

1919 REAL ESTATE (CAREER INFORMATION)
NATIONAL ASSOCIATION OF REALTORS
777 14TH ST NW
WASHINGTON DC 20005

1920 REHABILITATION COUNSELING (CAREER INFORMATION)
NATIONAL REHABILITATION COUNSELING ASSOCIATION
633 S. WASHINGTON ST.
ALEXANDRIA VA 22314

1921 RURAL ELECTRIFICATION (CAREER INFORMATION)
U.S. DEPT. OF AGRICULTURE; RURAL ELECTRIFICATION ADMINISTRATION
14TH AND INDEPENDENCE AVE SW; ROOM 4032
WASHINGTON DC 20250

1922 SAFETY ENGINEER CAREER INFORMATION
AMERICAN SOCIETY OF SAFETY ENGINEERS
1800 EAST OAKTON ST
DES PLAINES IL 60018

1923 SCHOOL ADMINISTRATION CAREER INFORMATION
AMERICAN ASSOCIATION OF SCHOOL ADMINISTRATORS
1801 NORTH MOORE STREET
ARLINGTON VA 22209

1924 SCIENCE TEACHER CAREER INFORMATION
NATIONAL SCIENCE TEACHERS ASSN
ATTN OFFICE OF PUBLIC INFORMATION; 1742 CONNECTICUT AVE NW
WASHINGTON DC 20009

1925 SECRETARY (CAREER INFORMATION)
PROFESSIONAL SECRETARIES INTERNATIONAL
PO BOX 20404
KANSAS CITY MO 64195

1926 SOCIAL WORK CAREER INFORMATION
NATIONAL ASSOCIATION OF SOCIAL WORKERS
7981 EASTERN AVE
SILVER SPRINGS MD 20910

1927 SOCIOLOGIST CAREER INFORMATION
AMERICAN SOCIOLOGICAL ASSOCIATION
1722 'N' STREET NW
WASHINGTON DC 20036

1928 SOIL CONSERVATIONIST CAREER INFORMATION
SOIL & WATER CONSERVATION SOCIETY
7515 NE ANKENY ROAD
ANKENY IA 50021

1929 SOIL CONSERVATION CAREER INFORMATION
U.S. DEPT. OF AGRICULTURE; SOIL CONSERVATION SERVICE
PO BOX 2890
WASHINGTON DC 20013

1930 SPECIAL EDUCATION TEACHER CAREER INFORMATION
NATIONAL CLEARINGHOUSE FOR PROFESSIONS IN SPECIAL EDUCATION
1920 ASSOCIATION DRIVE
RESTON VA 22091

1931 SPECIAL EDUCATION TEACHER CAREER INFORMATION
ASSOCIATION FOR RETARDED CITIZENS (THE ARC)
300 E. BORDER ST. SUITE 300
ARLINGTON TX 76006

1932 SPEECH & HEARING THERAPIST CAREER INFORMATION
ALEXANDER GRAHAM BELL ASSOCIATION FOR THE DEAF
3417 VOLTA PLACE NW
WASHINGTON DC 23007

CAREER INFORMATION

1933 SPEECH PATHOLOGY CAREER INFORMATION

AMERICAN SPEECH-LANGUAGE-HEARING ASSOCIATION
10801 ROCKVILLE PIKE
ROCKVILLE MD 20852

1934 TRANSLATOR CAREER INFORMATION

AMERICAN TRANSLATORS ASSN
109 CROTON AVENUE
OSSINING NY 10562

1935 URBAN PLANNER CAREER INFORMATION

AMERICAN PLANNING ASSOCIATION
1776 MASSACHUSETTS AVE NW
WASHINGTON DC 20036

1936 VETERINARIAN CAREER INFORMATION

AMERICAN VETERINARY MEDICAL ASSOCIATION
1931 N. MEACHAM RD. SUITE 100
SCHAUMBURG IL 60173

1937 WATER POLLUTION CONTROL CAREER INFORMATION

WATER POLLUTION CONTROL FEDERATION
EDUCATION DEPT; 601 WYTHE ST
ALEXANDRIA VA 22314

1938 WELDING TECHNOLOGY CAREER INFORMATION

HOBART SCHOOL OF WELDING TECHNOLOGY
TRADE SQUARE EAST
TROY OH 45373

1939 WOMEN AIRLINE PILOT CAREER INFORMATION

INTERNATIONAL SOCIETY OF WOMEN AIRLINE PILOTS
ISA+21; PO BOX 66268
CHICAGO IL 60666

1940 WOMEN PILOT CAREER INFORMATION

NINETY-NINES (INTERNATIONAL ORGANIZATION OF WOMEN PILOTS)
PO BOX 59965
OKLAHOMA CITY OK 73159

1941 YOUTH LEADERSHIP CAREER INFORMATION

BOYS & GIRLS CLUBS OF AMERICA
771 FIRST AVENUE
NEW YORK NY 10017

1942 YOUTH LEADERSHIP CAREER INFORMATION

BOY SCOUTS OF AMERICA
NATIONAL EAGLE SCOUT ASSOCIATION; 1325 W. WALNUT HILL LN. SUM 220
IRVING TX 75015

Alphabetical Index

ALPHABETICAL INDEX

ALPHABETICAL INDEX

ALPHABETICAL INDEX

ALPHABETICAL INDEX

ALPHABETICAL INDEX

ALPHABETICAL INDEX

ALPHABETICAL INDEX

ALPHABETICAL INDEX

ALPHABETICAL INDEX

ALPHABETICAL INDEX

ALPHABETICAL INDEX

ALPHABETICAL INDEX

ALPHABETICAL INDEX

ALPHABETICAL INDEX